ADVANCED
WINDOWS NT

D1572942

ADVANCED WINDOWS NT™

The Developer's Guide to the Win32 Application Programming Interface.

JEFFREY RICHTER

PUBLISHED BY
Microsoft Press
A Division of Microsoft Corporation
One Microsoft Way
Redmond, Washington 98052-6399

Library of Congress Cataloging-in-Publication Data
Richter, Jeffrey.
    Advanced windows NT : the developer's guide to the Win32
application programming interface / Jeffrey M. Richter.
        p.   cm.
    Includes index.
    ISBN 1-55615-567-0
    1. Operating systems (Computers)   2. Windows NT.   3. Microsoft
Win32.   I. Title.
QA76.76.O63R545 1993
005.4'469--dc20   93-4951
                                                            CIP

Printed and bound in the United States of America.

1 2 3 4 5 6 7 8 9   FFG   9 8 7 6 5 4

Distributed to the book trade in Canada by Macmillan of Canada, a division of Canada Publishing Corporation.

Distributed to the book trade outside the United States and Canada by Penguin Books Ltd.

Penguin Books Ltd., Harmondsworth, Middlesex, England
Penguin Books Australia Ltd., Ringwood, Victoria, Australia
Penguin Books N.Z. Ltd., 182-190 Wairau Road, Auckland 10, New Zealand

British Cataloging-in-Publication Data available.

Borland is a registered trademark of Borland International, Inc. DEC is a registered trademark and Alpha AXP is a trademark of Digital Equipment Corporation. Intel is a registered trademark and Intel386, Intel486, and Pentium are trademarks of Intel Corporation. Microsoft and MS-DOS are registered trademarks and Windows and Windows NT are trademarks of Microsoft Corporation. MIPS is a registered trademark of MIPS Computer Systems, Inc. NT is a registered trademark of Northern Telecom Limited. Sequent is a registered trademark of Sequent Computer Systems, Inc.

Acquisitions Editor: Dean Holmes
Manuscript Editors: Nancy Siadek and Erin O'Connor
Project Editors: Nancy Siadek and Laura Sackerman
Technical Reviewer: Wm. Jeff Carey

To Susan "Q-bert" Ramee, for showing me that
computers are not at the center of the Universe
with all of the planets circling around.

—J "BBB" R

CONTENTS SUMMARY

CHAPTER ONE

PROCESSES AND THREADS **1**

▶ The Windows NT equivalent of a 16-bit Windows task is a process. Processes are separated and secure in Windows NT—one process cannot adversely affect another process, which was not true in 16-bit Windows. This chapter describes the life cycle of a process and how Windows NT manages it. It also describes how the Windows NT object manager works and how applications can create and manipulate Windows NT objects. Unlike 16-bit Windows' tasks, processes are not scheduled for execution by the operating system; instead, processes create one or more threads of execution. This chapter discusses how threads are created and destroyed, how the operating system schedules threads, and how the priorities of threads can be changed. Threads are the basis of Windows NT's truly preemptive scheduling.

CHAPTER TWO

MEMORY MANAGEMENT WITH HEAPS **59**

▶ Under 16-bit Windows, applications manage memory by using the local and global heaps provided by 16-bit Windows. Under Windows NT, memory management is significantly different. This chapter describes how the 16-bit local and global heap APIs are emulated in Windows NT. This chapter will be especially important to readers who want to port their programs to 32-bit Windows quickly without taking advantage of the more powerful memory management techniques provided by Windows NT. Windows NT also lets applications create multiple heaps for their own use. These new heaps are also discussed.

CHAPTER THREE

VIRTUAL MEMORY MANAGEMENT **85**

▶ The virtual memory manager is the cornerstone of Windows NT memory management. The heap managers discussed in the previous chapter are implemented by using Windows NT's virtual memory manager. Using virtual memory, a developer can reserve regions of address space without actually committing physical storage to the space. This chapter describes how Windows NT manages memory and how applications can take advantage of virtual memory.

CHAPTER FOUR

MEMORY-MAPPED FILES........................... **141**

▶ Memory-mapped files are the cornerstone of applications and dynamic-link library management in Windows NT, and they provide another means for using virtual memory. Each application or DLL loaded into memory is actually a memory-mapped file. Applications can use memory-mapped files to access data files as though the data for the file is actually loaded into memory. The advantage in using memory-mapped files is that the operating system buffers and caches the file's data to and from the disk. Using memory-mapped files is the only method supported by Windows NT that allows two (or more) applications to share a common data block.

CHAPTER FIVE

THREAD SYNCHRONIZATION...................... **173**

▶ Whenever multiple threads are executing simultaneously or being preemptively interrupted, an application often needs to force certain threads to stop executing until certain criteria are met. For example, two threads cannot simultaneously alter the contents of a string without potentially corrupting its contents. Windows NT offers several objects for performing thread synchronization. This chapter discusses these objects and describes techniques for using them.

CHAPTER SIX

▶ Both 16-bit Windows and OS/2 still allow an application to hang all running applications. Windows NT has corrected this problem by giving each thread its very own local input state. Adding this feature to Windows NT means that some applications (typically shell replacements and debugging tools) that ran correctly under 16-bit Windows will not function correctly under Windows NT. This chapter discusses why Microsoft added local input states to Windows NT and how an application can best take advantage of them. This chapter also discusses how window messages are processed.

CHAPTER SEVEN

▶ This chapter describes how to create DLLs for Windows NT and discusses characteristics that are unique to Windows NT DLLs and some techniques for exploiting them.

CHAPTER EIGHT

▶ In an environment in which multiple threads are running concurrently, it's important to associate data objects and variables with the individual threads of a process. This chapter describes two methods for associating threads.

CHAPTER NINE

▶ This chapter discusses how an application can manipulate the four file systems supported by Windows NT: FAT, CDFS, HPFS, and NTFS. It also discusses how to manipulate directory structures (creating, removing, and renaming), files (creating, moving, and copying), and the data contained by the files (reading and writing). Also discussed are some additional techniques for manipulating the file system, such as directory tree walking and file system change notifications. Finally, this chapter presents methods for using asynchronous file I/O.

TABLE OF CONTENTS

CHAPTER ONE

PROCESSES AND THREADS **1**

CHAPTER TWO

MEMORY MANAGEMENT WITH HEAPS **59**

CHAPTER THREE

VIRTUAL MEMORY MANAGEMENT **85**

CHAPTER TEN

STRUCTURED EXCEPTION HANDLING **551**

ACKNOWLEDGMENTS

Although my name appears alone on the cover of this book, many people have contributed in some form or another to this book's creation. In many cases, these people are good friends of mine (i.e., we occasionally go to movies or out to dinner), and in some cases, I have never met the individuals and have conversed with them only on the phone or by electronic mail. Regardless of our personal or professional standing, I could not have completed this book without the assistance or support of each of the following—I thank you all.

Susan "Q" Ramee for giving me her love and support throughout the entire process. Sue also proofread chapters and helped me come up with some ideas for the sample programs. And, of course, it would not be right to thank Sue without also thanking her two cats, Natt and Cato. Often, late at night, when I could not sleep and decided to write, Natt and Cato would keep me company. They would frequently shed on my notes and walk across the keyboard as I typed. Any typos you sea in thid boot are duw too Natt amd Cato, knot me, I assure you.

Jim Harkins is one of my best friends. His direct contribution to this book can be found in the alertable file I/O and file change notification sample programs. But Jim also helped me think through many of the thread synchronization issues. Whenever I think of Jim, I can hear him saying, "When was the last time you put chlorine in the Jacuzzi?" And, although not publicly known, Jim is the creator of the very popular and hilariously outrageous game "Guess What The Plant Said?"

Paul Yao is also a good friend who showed me how to "live it up" in Peoria. As far as the book goes, Paul gave me my first introduction to Windows NT memory management as well as numerous comments about several chapters. It was Paul who said, "To see how many instructions get executed in a local unwind on the MIPS machine, just go in the debugger and keep pressing F8 until you get in the *finally* block!" And, of course, I want to thank Becky for letting me have some Pogacha rolls to take home—YUM, they're soooo good.

Scott Ludwig, a lead Windows NT developer at Microsoft, was extremely patient with me and answered all of my questions. Through the discussions we have had, Scott has earned my utmost respect and admiration. Now that Windows NT has shipped, he deserves that vacation in Yellowstone.

Lou Perazzoli, Steve Wood, and Marc Lucovsky of the Windows NT development team reviewed a number of chapters and answered many questions related to threads and memory management.

Chuck Mitchell, Steve Salisbury, and Jonathan Mark of the Visual C++ for Windows NT team answered my questions about structured exception handling, thread-local storage, the C Runtime Library, and linking.

I would also like to thank/mention several additional developers on the Visual C++ for Windows NT team. I had the opportunity to work with: Byron Dazey ("That's a pretty complicated synchronization problem you have there."), Eric Lang ("That icon is a little disturbing."), Dan Spalding ("Why can't I print from NT?"), Matthew Tebbs ("Happy landings."), Bruce Johnson ("Can I borrow the network cable again?"), Jon Jorstad ("We don't need all these samples, do we?"), Dave Henderson ("Brazil"), and T.K. Brackman ("Good luck with the new house.").

Bernie McIlroy helped me test the sample applications on a DEC Alpha machine. Bernie thinks that all introductions should begin with "In the beginning…" and is also well known for his philosphy on life: "Life is a heck of a thing."

Numerous developers at Microsoft helped fill in the gaps for me: Mark Cliggett, Cameron Ferroni, Eric Fogelin, Randy Kath, and Steve Sinofsky.

Nancy Siadek, my editor at Microsoft Press, deserves an award for the amount of effort and dedication she gave to this book. I'm sure she had no idea what she was getting into. Nancy taught me more about writing in the short time I spent with her than I learned in all my years.

Jeff Carey, my technical editor at Microsoft Press, was a big help in letting me off the hook by answering many of Nancy's questions, which allowed me to rewrite some of the material.

I also want to thank the rest of the Microsoft Press team. Many of them I have never met, but I do appreciate all their efforts: Erin O'Connor, Laura Sackerman, Peggy Herman, Lisa Iversen, and Barb Runyan.

Thanks also to:

Dan Horn at Borland International, for his suggestions and comments on several chapters and for giving an apple to the teacher.

Jim Lane, Tom Van Baak, and Rich Peterson, for stepping in at the last minute to fix bugs in the DEC Alpha compiler.

Dean Holmes, acquisitions director at Microsoft Press, for signing me and for putting up with delays while I purchased my new house.

Gretchen Bilson and everyone at Microsoft Systems Journal, for encouraging me to continue writing.

Charles Petzold, for introducing me to Microsoft Press and hot and sour soup.

Carlos Richardson, for helping me get TJ-Net (my home network) up and running in my new house.

Everyone at Premia Corporation, for supplying me with early versions of CodeWright for Windows NT so I could create the sample programs in this book using a great text editor.

Everyone at Shapeware, Inc., for supplying me with Visio so I could create the original technical figures.

John Socha, for motivating me to move all the way from Philadelphia, PA, to Bellevue, WA.

Michele Leialoha, who can even make something as mundane as ''bookshelves'' funny.

Donna Murray, for her love, support, and friendship over the years.

My brother, Ron, for trying to find me a copy of Patrick Moraz's ''Salamander.'' Even though you never found it, I know you tried. I'll ask Peter Gabriel to autograph your golf clubs the next time he's in town.

My mom and dad, Arlene and Sylvan, for their love and support over the years. Both of you are welcome to visit me anytime you want. I'll keep the Jacuzzi hot and a bag of popcorn by the TV, and I'll order another set of contour pillows.

INTRODUCTION

I have really enjoyed writing this book. There is nothing I like more than being on the forefront of technology and learning new things. Windows NT is definitely on the forefront of technology and, boy, is there a lot of new stuff to learn. But don't let the amount of new stuff scare you. If you are already a Windows programmer, you will find that you can start writing applications for Windows NT after learning just a few simple techniques for porting your existing code. But these ported programs will not be taking advantage of the new, powerful, and exciting features that Windows NT offers.

After you have started working with Windows NT, you can begin incorporating more and more of these features in your applications. Many of the Windows NT features make it much easier to write programs. And, as I soon discovered when porting some of my own code, I was able to delete large sections of code from my existing programs and replace them with calls to facilities offered by Windows NT.

The new features are such a pleasure to use and work with that I hope to concentrate my efforts solely on writing Windows NT applications in the future. In fact, I recently had the opportunity to help someone debug a 16-bit Windows application that was crashing the system. We stayed up all night and couldn't track down the problem. We couldn't even use a debugger because the problem wouldn't manifest itself when the debugger was used. I call this a "Heisenbug." After working on the bug, I said, "This bug couldn't exist in Windows NT. Windows NT is so much nicer." The person I was working with would have killed me if she hadn't been so tired.

But as much as I enjoyed writing this book, I did have trouble keeping up the pace with the Windows NT developers. All through Windows NT's development cycle, Microsoft was adding new functions and new flags. This meant that I was constantly having to learn and write about new features. But then a wonderful thing happened. On July 27, 1993, my birthday, the Windows NT team gave me the best present an author could ask for: they released Windows NT to manufacturing! This was it. They could no longer add features to the system, and I heaved a sigh of Rolaids.

This book is the result of my experiences in working with Windows NT. I have learned a lot since the July 1992 Windows NT Prerelease Developers' Conference in San Francisco. Over the past year, I have chosen to concentrate on the aspects of Windows NT that I think will be the most useful to the majority of Windows NT applications developers: process and thread management, memory management, dynamic-link libraries, file systems and file I/O, and a comparison of Windows NT features with those of 16-bit Windows.

There is no doubt in my mind that Windows NT will become a standard operating system. First it will replace mainframe computers and minicomputers, and then in a few years (maybe many years), when memory prices start to drop, Windows NT will become the standard operating system for the personal computer as well. This book should help you get ready for developing applications for an environment that is destined to be the industry standard.

Let's Define Some Terms

I am a frequent speaker at industry events, and one often-asked question is: What is the difference between Win32 and Windows NT? I have also asked this question, and it has taken me a while to figure out the true meaning of these terms. So, in an effort to stop all this confusion once and for all, I will attempt to explain.

The Win32 API and Platforms That Support It

Win32 is the name of an API, that's all—no more, no less. So the set of functions that are available to call from your source code are contained in the Win32 API. When you write code, you are writing a Win32 program because you are calling functions in the Win32 API.

The Win32 API is implemented on several platforms, one of which is Windows NT. Windows NT is an operating system that can run multiple types of applications. For example, Windows NT can run OS/2 1.*x* character applications, MS-DOS applications, and 16-bit Windows applications. In addition, Windows NT can run Win32 applications (programs that call functions in the Win32 API), which are expected to be the most common form of application to run on Windows NT.

Other existing platforms are also capable of running Win32 applications. In fact, one of these platforms actually shipped before Windows NT. This platform is called Win32s. It is unfortunate that Win32s has *Win32* in its name because that confuses the issue. When you write a Win32 program and compile it, the result is an application that is capable of running on both the Win32s and the Windows NT platforms.

Now we get to the issue of CPUs. Windows NT is capable of running on machines that have different CPUs. If you compile your Win32 source code using a compiler that targets an *x*86 CPU, you will be able to run that Win32 application on any Win32 platform that runs on an *x*86 machine. However, if you compile your Win32 application for a MIPS CPU, you will be able to run that application only on a Win32 platform that is available for a MIPS machine. Currently, the only Win32 platform that exists for MIPS machines is Windows NT. Microsoft makes the Win32s platform available on *x*86 machines only.

All of these platforms contain implementations of all the Win32 functions, which means that you can call any of the functions in the Win32 API regardless of which platform you are running on. However, some of the implementations are limited. For example, the Win32 API contains a function called CreateThread that allows an application to create a new thread of execution. In the Windows NT implementation of the Win32 API, this function does exactly that—it creates a new thread of execution. However, in the Win32s implementation of the Win32 API, this function simply returns NULL, indicating that a new thread of execution could not be created.

The reason for this limitation is that Win32s is really just an extension to 16-bit Windows. Win32s implements most of the Win32 API by thunking calls to 16-bit Windows functions. Because 16-bit Windows does not support the creation of new threads of execution, Win32s does not support this feature. But remember, Win32s implements all of the Win32 functions, although some of the implementations are limited.

You might think from the discussion above that you can compile all the sample programs contained in this book and run them on the Win32s platform. This is true; however, most of the features that I discuss in this book (for example, multithreaded programming, virtual memory, and memory-mapped files) have full implementations on the Windows NT platform and have limited implementations on the Win32s platform. Because many of the functions I call have limited implementations on the Win32s platform, you will not truly experience the sample programs. You must run the sample programs on a Windows NT platform to see them in all their glory.

Windows NT and Its Subcomponents

Windows NT is the name of a complete operating system. When you purchase the retail version of Windows NT, you are buying a complete system that is capable of running MS-DOS applications, OS/2 1.x character applications, POSIX applications, 16-bit Windows applications, and Win32 applications. This complete system is composed of several subcomponents. For example, POSIX applications actually call functions that are contained in the POSIX subsystem, OS/2 applications make calls to the OS/2 subsystem, and Win32 applications make calls to the Win32 subsystem.

The Windows NT Executive regulates memory allocations, threads, files, and other resources for all of these subsystems. The Windows NT Executive is the core of the Windows NT operating system. Without it, there is no operating system. However, if you were to take away the POSIX or OS/2 subsystems, you would still have an operating system capable of running Win32 applications.

Within the Windows NT operating system, the Win32 subsystem is responsible for the implementation of the Win32 API. The subsystem implements the API by using the facilities available to it from the Windows NT Executive. So throughout this book you might see phrases like this:

Win32 allocates memory and returns.
Windows NT allocates memory and returns.
The Win32 subsystem allocates memory and returns.
The Windows NT Executive allocates memory and returns.

When I use one phrase rather than another, I'm trying to give you more detail into which part of the operating system is responsible for performing the requested operation. In some cases, I am purposely vague. For example, allocating memory by calling the GlobalAlloc function probably requires cooperation from both the Win32 subsystem as well as the Windows NT Executive. But since I'm not sure which subcomponent is ultimately responsible, I might say that "Win32 allocates the memory" because the Win32 subsystem decides how to process a call to GlobalAlloc.

Remember that when I offer more detail in a description, I am by definition implementation dependent—I'm discussing the Windows NT implementation of the Win32 API. Other implementations of the Win32 API implement some of the Win32 functions differently.

What I Expect from You

This book is for the Windows developer who already has some experience writing programs for 16-bit Windows. However, an extensive knowledge of 16-bit Windows is not necessary—only the basics of Windows programming, including window procedures, window messages, dialog boxes, and memory management. This book covers new features that have been introduced in the Win32 API as it runs under the Windows NT operating system. No attempt will be made to teach introductory Windows programming. This book also covers the type of issues you should expect when porting 16-bit Windows applications to be 32-bit.

About the Sample Applications

The purpose of the sample applications is to demonstrate with real code how to use the advanced features of Windows NT. You could never read enough text to replace the knowledge and experience that you gain by writing your own applications. I know that this has certainly been true of my experience with Windows NT. Many of the sample applications presented throughout this book are direct descendants of experimental programs that I created myself in an effort to understand how Windows NT works.

Programs Written in C

When it came time to decide on a language for the sample applications, I was torn between C and C++. For large projects, I always use C++ but the fact of the matter is that most Windows programmers are not using C++ yet, and I didn't want to alienate my largest potential audience.

Message Cracker Macros

If you are not writing your Windows NT application using C++ and a Windows class library (like Microsoft's Foundation Classes), I highly recommend that you use the message cracker macros defined in the WINDOWSX.H header file. These macros make your programs easier to write, read, and maintain. I feel so strongly about the message cracker macros that I have included an appendix in this book that describes the reasons why the message crackers exist and how to use them effectively.

Knowledge of 16-Bit Windows Programming

None of the programs presented rely on extensive knowledge of 16-bit Windows programs, although experience with 16-bit Windows programming is definitely a plus. The sample programs do assume that you are familiar with the creation and manipulation of dialog boxes and their child controls. Very little knowledge of GDI and KERNEL functions is required at all.

When presenting various topics in the book, I do make behavior comparisons between 16-bit Windows and Windows NT. If you already understand how 16-bit Windows behaves, you should have an easier time understanding how behaviors have changed in Windows NT.

Unrelated Code

I wanted to remove any code from the sample programs that was not directly related to the techniques I wanted to demonstrate. Unfortunately, this is not possible when writing any Windows program. For example, most Windows programming books repeat the code for registering window classes in every application presented in the book. I have done my best to reduce this type of nonrelevant code.

One way that I reduce nonrelevant code is by using techniques that are not always obvious to Windows programmers. For example, the user interface for most of the sample programs is a dialog box. In fact, most of the sample programs have a single line of code in WinMain that simply calls the DialogBox function. As a result, none of the sample programs initialize a WNDCLASS structure or call the RegisterClass function. In addition, only one sample application—FileChng in Chapter 9—has a message loop in it.

Independent Sample Applications

I have tried to keep the sample applications independent from one another. For example, the memory-mapped files chapter is the only chapter containing memory-mapped file sample programs. Because I have structured the sample programs so that they are independent, feel free to skip earlier chapters and proceed to later chapters.

Occasionally, you'll find a sample program that uses techniques or information presented in earlier chapters. For example, the SEHExcpt sample application presented in Chapter 10, "Structured Exception Handling," demonstrates how to manipulate virtual memory. I decided to mix these two topics in a single sample program because SEH is a very useful mechanism for manipulating virtual memory. In order to fully understand this sample application, you should read Chapter 3 prior to examining the SEHExcpt sample application.

STRICT Compliance

All of the sample programs have been compiled with the STRICT identifier defined, which catches frequent coding errors. For example, the passing of an incorrect handle type to a function is caught during compilation instead of at runtime. For more information about using the STRICT identifier, refer to the *Programming Techniques* documentation included in the Windows NT SDK.

Error Checking

Error checking should be a big part of any software project. Unfortunately, proper error checking can make the size and complexity of a software project grow exponentially. In order to make the sample applications more understandable and less cluttered, I have not put very much error-checking code into them. If you use any of my code fragments and incorporate them into your own production code, I strongly encourage you to examine my code closely and add any appropriate error checking.

Bug Free

I would love to say that all of the sample programs are bug free. But, as with all software, it's only bug free until someone finds a bug. Of course, I have given my own code several walk-throughs in the hope of catching everything. If you do find a bug, I would appreciate your reporting it to me via my CompuServe address: 70444,24.

Tested Platforms and Environments

The bulk of my research and development for this book has been on a machine with only one Intel 486 CPU. I have also recompiled and tested all the sample programs on a MIPS machine and on a DEC Alpha machine, using the compilers and linkers that come with the Windows NT SDK for these platforms.

I have also compiled and linked the sample programs using Microsoft's Visual C++ for Windows NT (for *x*86 only) and have tested many of the programs using Borland's 32-bit C++ compiler for Win32 (again, for *x*86 only). Some of the programs require modification when using Borland's 32-bit C++ compiler for Win32.

For most of the sample programs, I use no vendor-specific compiler extensions. These programs should compile and link regardless of the machine on which you are running Windows NT and regardless of which tools you are using to compile and link the sample programs.

However, seven of the sample programs do take advantage of three compiler-specific features: named data sections, static thread-local storage, and structured exception handling. If you are using tools other than those included in the Windows NT SDK, you might need to discover how your vendor exposes these three features and modify the seven sample programs accordingly.

The *x*86, MIPS, and Alpha compilers in the Windows NT SDK make the named data sections feature available using this syntax:

```
#pragma dataseg (...)
```

I use this construct only in three sample programs: ModUse, MultInst, and PMRest. All three of these sample programs appear in Chapter 7, "Dynamic-Link Libraries."

Only one sample program—TLSStat in Chapter 8—uses the static thread-local storage feature of the compiler. Microsoft compilers make this feature available using the new _ _ *declspec(thread)* keyword, whereas Borland's compiler uses the _ _ *thread* keyword.

And finally, three sample programs—SEHTerm, SEHExcpt, and SEHSoft—use the structured exception handling features of the compiler. All three of these are presented in Chapter 10. They are compiler-specific because they all use the following new keywords: _ _ *try*, _ _ *finally*, _ _ *leave*, and _ _ *except*. Because most compiler vendors will modify their compilers so that they will recognize these four new keywords, it is unlikely that you will have to modify the SEHTerm, SEHExcpt, and SEHSoft sample programs at all.

Unicode

Originally, I wrote all the sample programs so that they could compile natively using the ANSI character set only. Then, when I started writing the Unicode chapter, I became a very strong believer in Unicode and tried desperately to come up with a sample program for the

Unicode chapter. Then the answer came to me: Convert all the sample applications in the book so that they demonstrate Unicode. This conversion effort took only four hours and allows you to compile all the sample applications natively for both ANSI and Unicode.

The disadvantage in doing this is that you might see calls to unfamiliar functions that manipulate characters and strings within the sample applications. For the most part, you should be able to guess what that function does if you are familiar with the standard C Runtime functions for manipulating characters and strings. However, if you get stuck, you should refer to Chapter 11. This chapter explains in much greater detail what I have done in the sample programs. It is my hope that you not be confused by the new character and string functions and that you will see how easy it is to write your application code using Unicode.

Installing the Sample Programs

The companion disk contains the source code for all the sample applications presented throughout the book. In addition, the EXE and DLL files for both the *x*86 and MIPS versions of the sample programs are included. To get all these files on a single disk, it was necessary to compress the files. In order to install the files, you will need to run the SETUP batch file contained in the root directory of the floppy disk or manually decompress the files using the EXPAND.EXE utility that ships with Windows NT.

To install the files using the accompanying Setup program, insert the disk into a 3.5-inch disk drive and execute the SETUP.BAT file. There are two different kinds of installation.

SETUP uses the first type of installation if you are running Windows NT on either an *x*86 or a MIPS machine. In this case, the SETUP.BAT file on the floppy disk simply spawns the GUI-based SETUP program (ISETUP.EXE for *x*86 and MSETUP.EXE for MIPS). You do not need to specify any command-line parameters when invoking SETUP.BAT. You will be prompted for all the necessary information by the GUI-based SETUP program.

SETUP uses the second type of installation if you are running Windows NT on a hardware platform other than an *x*86 or a MIPS machine. In this case, the SETUP.BAT file must perform the complete installation by itself. To accomplish this, you must run SETUP.BAT and specify a location where the files should be installed. For example, the following line assumes that the floppy disk is in drive A and that you want to install the source code files to the ADVWINNT directory on drive C (this directory will be created if it doesn't exist):

```
C:\>A:\SETUP C:\ADVWINNT
```

The main difference between the two types of installation is whether the compiled EXE and DLL files are included. When using the x86 or MIPS GUI-based SETUP, all the source files are decompressed and copied to your hard disk. The EXE and DLL files are also decompressed and copied. At the end of the GUI-based SETUP, a new Program Manager group is created and all the sample programs are added to this group. Each application is represented by an icon, which also appears before each program listing in text. For the batch-file–based SETUP, only the source files are decompressed and copied—no EXE or DLL files are installed and nothing is added to the Program Manager.

Regardless of how the files are installed, a batch file called MAKEALL.BAT is also installed on your hard disk. Executing this batch file causes all the sample programs to be recompiled. This batch file assumes that you are using a version of the Windows NT SDK that is compatible with your hardware platform.

The sample programs are installed so that each sample resides in its very own subdirectory. The eight-letter name of each subdirectory contains the name of the sample program, and the subdirectory's extension indicates the chapter in the book where the program is presented. For example, the subdirectory FILECHNG.09 identifies the File Change sample application that is presented in Chapter 9. A complete description of the files can be found in the ADVWINNT.TXT file that is installed along with the sample applications.

CHAPTER ONE

PROCESSES AND THREADS

A process is a running instance of an application. Every process consists of blocks of code and data (loaded from EXEs and DLLs) that are located in the process's very own 4-GB address space. A process also owns other resources, such as files, dynamic memory allocations, and threads. The various resources that are created during a process's life are destroyed when the process is terminated.

A thread is the unit of execution in a process. Each thread in a process is associated with a sequence of CPU instructions, a set of CPU registers, and a stack. A process does not execute code—it is simply the address space where the code resides. Code contained in the address space of a process is executed by threads. In fact, threads are often referred to as "threads of execution."

In Windows NT, a process can contain several threads. Each of these individual threads is scheduled CPU time by the Windows NT Kernel. On a single-processor machine, the operating system gives the illusion that all these threads are running concurrently by offering time slices (called *quantums*) to the threads in a round-robin fashion. (See Figure 1-1 on the following page.)

Windows NT is a giant step forward from 16-bit Windows because it not only offers preemptive multitasking but also runs on machines that contain several CPUs. For example, Sequent is designing a computer system that includes 30 Intel CPUs. Each CPU can be assigned a thread of execution, allowing 30 threads to execute simultaneously. The Windows NT Kernel handles all the management and scheduling of threads on this type of system.

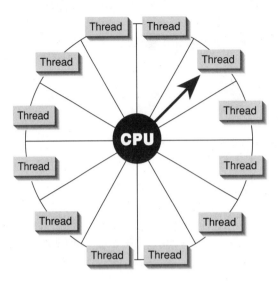

Figure 1-1.
Individual threads are scheduled time quantums by the Windows NT Kernel in a round-robin fashion.

When you design your software, you don't need to make any special provisions for multiprocessor systems. However, a process with multiple threads is more likely to malfunction on a multiprocessor system than on a single-processor system. Before shipping a multithreaded application, I strongly suggest that you thoroughly test it on a multiprocessor machine. Any synchronization problems waiting in your application might never show themselves on a single-processor machine.

When a Windows NT process is created, its first thread, called the primary thread, is automatically created by the system. This primary thread can then create additional threads. These additional threads can create even more threads. If you are familiar with OS/2, you know that the primary thread has a special attribute: When the primary thread ends, the whole process terminates even if other threads are still executing. This is not true for Windows NT. In Windows NT, if any thread contained in the process is still running, the process does not die; the process terminates only when all the threads contained in the process have ended.

Using the Win32 API, you can create two types of applications for Windows NT: GUI-based and console-based. A GUI-based application has a graphical front end. GUI applications create windows, have menus, interact with the user using dialog boxes, and use all the standard "Windowsy" stuff. The Program Manager and File Manager are typical examples of GUI-based applications.

Console-based applications more closely resemble MS-DOS text applications. Their output is text based, they don't create windows or process messages, and they don't require a graphical user interface. Although console-based applications are contained within a window on the screen, the window contains only text characters. The Microsoft C/C++ compiler and linker are typical examples of console-based applications.

Although there are two types of applications, the line between them is very fuzzy. It is possible to create console-based applications that display dialog boxes. For example, the compiler could have a special command-line switch that causes it to display a graphical dialog box, allowing you to select compilation switches instead of typing nonintuitive letter combinations on the command line. You could also create a GUI-based application that outputs character text strings to a console window for debugging. Of the two types, you are certainly encouraged to use a graphical user interface in your applications instead of using the old-fashioned character interface. It has been proven time and time again that GUI-based applications are much more user friendly.

In this chapter, I discuss the mechanics of creating processes and threads. The concepts apply to both GUI-based and console-based applications, but I emphasize GUI-based applications and don't discuss some of the finer details of creating console-based applications. If you want more information on creating console-based applications, please refer to the Win32 SDK documentation.

Windows NT Executive Objects

The system manages processes and threads as objects. So, before we get into the details of processes and threads, let's take a short side trip and discuss Windows NT objects. There are several different types of objects that are created and managed by the Windows NT Executive. These objects include:

Event objects	Pipe objects
File-mapping objects	Process objects
File objects	Semaphore objects
MailSlot objects	Thread objects
Mutex objects	

These objects are created by calling various Win32 functions. For example, the CreateFileMapping function causes the system to create a file-mapping object. When an object is created, the Windows NT Executive allocates a block of memory for the object, initializes the memory with some management information, and returns a handle to your application identifying this object. Your application can then pass this handle to other Win32 functions in order to manipulate the object.

Your application might also use other types of objects, such as menus, windows, mouse cursors, brushes, and fonts. These objects are created and maintained by the Win32 subsystem—not by the Windows NT Executive.

When you first start programming for Windows NT, you might be confused when differentiating a Win32 object from a Windows NT object. For example, is an icon a Win32 subsystem object or a Windows NT object? To determine the answer, I always ask myself, ''What does this object mean to the POSIX or OS/2 subsystems?'' Because the POSIX and OS/2 subsystems don't recognize the concept of an icon, an icon must be a Win32 subsystem object. On the other hand, POSIX, OS/2, and the Win32 subsystems all must work with processes, threads, and files—therefore, these must be Windows NT Executive objects.

If a Windows NT Executive object already exists, any application can open it (subject to security checks). For example, one application might create a file-mapping object, which is then available for another application to open. This capability allows the two applications to manipulate the same file-mapping object. When an application opens a Windows NT Executive object, the system does not create another block of memory for the object. Instead, the system increments a usage count associated with the already existing object and returns a handle, identifying the existing object, to the thread opening the object.

When a thread no longer needs to manipulate an object, it calls the CloseHandle function:

```
BOOL CloseHandle(HANDLE hObject);
```

This function causes the Windows NT Executive to decrement the usage count for the object, and if the usage count reaches 0 (zero), the system frees the memory allocated to manage the object.

To help make the system more robust and secure, a handle to a Windows NT Executive object is process-relative—that is, it is meaningful only to the process that called the Create or Open function. If a thread calls CreateFileMapping, the system might return the handle value 0x22222222. If a thread in another process opens the same file-mapping object, the system might return the handle value 0x12345678. Both handles identify the same file-mapping object although the values are different.

Because handles for objects are process-relative, a thread cannot successfully get a handle to an object and give that handle to a thread in another process through some form of interprocess communication (like sending a window message). When the thread in the receiving process attempts to use the handle, one of two things happens: The handle becomes invalid for that process, or the handle identifies a different object (created or opened by a thread in the receiving process). In either case, an error will most likely result when the handle is used.

Contrast this to the Win32 subsystem, in which objects use the same handle value among processes. For example, if a window is identified with a handle value of 0x34343434, all processes use this same value to refer to the window.

Creating a Process: The CreateProcess Function

A process is created when a thread in another process (such as the Program Manager) calls the CreateProcess function:

```
BOOL CreateProcess(
    LPCTSTR lpszImageName,
    LPCTSTR lpszCommandLine,
    LPSECURITY_ATTRIBUTES lpsaProcess,
    LPSECURITY_ATTRIBUTES lpsaThread,
    BOOL fInheritHandles,
    DWORD fdwCreate,
    LPVOID lpvEnvironment,
    LPTSTR lpszCurDir,
    LPSTARTUPINFO lpsiStartInfo,
    LPPROCESS_INFORMATION lppiProcInfo);
```

If you are familiar with the two 16-bit Windows functions for creating a process,

```
UINT WinExec(LPCSTR lpszCmdLine, UINT fuCmdShow);
```

and

```
DWORD LoadModule(LPCSTR lpszModule, LPVOID lpvParamBlock);
```

you can see from examining the number of parameters for these three functions that the new CreateProcess function offers you much more control over process creation. Both the WinExec and LoadModule functions are implemented internally as calls to the CreateProcess function. And because these functions are supplied only for backward compatibility with 16-bit Windows, Unicode versions of these functions do not exist—you can call these functions only by passing ANSI strings.

When you call CreateProcess, the system creates a 4-GB virtual address space for the new process and loads the specified process into this address space. The system then creates the primary thread for this process. This primary thread will begin by executing the C Runtime startup code, which will eventually call your WinMain function. If the system successfully creates the new process, CreateProcess returns TRUE.

OK, that's the broad overview. Now it's time to dissect each of the parameters for CreateProcess one by one.

lpszImageName

The *lpszImageName* parameter identifies the name of the executable file you want to run. CreateProcess assumes that the file is in the current directory unless a path is specified preceding the filename. If the file can't be found in the current directory, CreateProcess checks the system directory, the windows directory, and directories specified in the PATH environment variable (in this order) to locate the file.

You can pass NULL as the *lpszImageName* parameter. In this case, CreateProcess assumes that the name of the executable file is the first token (up to the first white-space character) of the *lpszCommandLine* parameter. CreateProcess also assumes that everything following the first white-space character identifies the command-line parameters to be passed to the newly created process.

lpszCommandLine

The *lpszCommandLine* parameter usually specifies any command-line arguments to be passed to the process. When the process begins, its WinMain function receives the address of the command-line arguments in its *lpszCmdLine* parameter. A process can also obtain the address of the command-line arguments that passed as the *lpszCommandLine* parameter of CreateProcess by calling the GetCommandLine function:

```
LPTSTR GetCommandLine(VOID);
```

This function returns a pointer to a buffer containing the full command line, including the full pathname of the executed file. Probably the most compelling reason to use the GetCommandLine function instead

ONE: Processes and Threads

of the *lpszCommandLine* parameter is that GetCommandLine exists in both Unicode and ANSI versions in the Win32 API, whereas the *lpszCommandLine* parameter always points to a buffer containing an ANSI character string.

lpsaProcess, *lpsaThread*, and *fInheritHandles*

The *lpsaProcess* and *lpsaThread* parameters identify security attributes to be given to the new process object and its primary thread object. You can pass NULL for these parameters, in which case the system gives these objects default security descriptors. Or you can allocate and initialize SECURITY_ATTRIBUTES structures to create and assign your own security privileges to the process and thread objects:

```
typedef struct _SECURITY_ATTRIBUTES {
    DWORD  nLength;
    LPVOID lpSecurityDescriptor;
    BOOL   bInheritHandle;
} SECURITY_ATTRIBUTES;
```

When you initialize this structure, the *nLength* member must be set to the size of the structure (that is, sizeof(SECURITY_ATTRIBUTES)). The *lpSecurityDescriptor* member is either NULL or a value provided by a call to functions such as InitializeSecurityDescriptor or SetSecurityDescriptorOwner. If *lpSecurityDescriptor* is NULL, the object will be assigned the default security descriptor of the calling process.

The last member, *bInheritHandle*, indicates whether the handle of the process/thread object is inheritable. Earlier in this chapter I said that object handles are process-specific, meaning that a single object has different handle values when used in different processes. This is mostly true, but Windows NT also allows the handles of Windows NT Executive objects to be inherited. This means that if one process has a handle to an inheritable file-mapping object and if this process creates another process, the system gives this new process a handle to the same file-mapping object. In addition, this handle value will be the same handle value used by the parent process.

If you initialize the *bInheritHandle* member to TRUE before calling CreateProcess, you are telling Windows NT that the handles it creates for the process object and the thread object are allowed to be inherited by any future processes that the parent process creates. An example is in order here.

Let's say that Process A creates Process B by calling CreateProcess and passing the address of a SECURITY_ATTRIBUTES structure for the *lpsaProcess* parameter in which the *bInheritHandle* member is set to TRUE. In this same call, the *lpsaThread* parameter points to another SECURITY_ATTRIBUTES structure in which its *bInheritHandles* member is set to FALSE.

When the system creates Process B, it allocates both a process object and a thread object and returns handles back to Process A in the structure pointed to by the *lppiProcInfo* parameter (discussed shortly). Process A can now manipulate the newly created process object and thread object by using these handles.

Now let's say that Process A is going to call CreateProcess a second time to create Process C. Process A can decide whether to grant Process C inheritance privileges. The *fInheritHandles* parameter is used for this purpose. If *fInheritHandles* is set to TRUE, the system lets Process C inherit any inheritable handles. In this case, the handle to Process B's process object is inheritable. The handle to Process B's primary thread object is not inheritable no matter what the value of the *fInheritHandles* parameter to CreateProcess is. Also, if Process A calls CreateProcess, passing FALSE for the *fInheritHandles* parameter, Process C cannot inherit any of the handles currently in use by Process A.

When a new process inherits the handles of its parent process, it's as if the child process created the objects itself. The child process has the same access rights to the object as the parent does, and if the child decides to create a child process itself, it can allow the new child to inherit the handles or not. Whenever a child process is allowed to inherit its parent's handles, the Windows NT Executive increments the usage count for the inherited objects. It is not until the usage count drops to 0 (zero) that the system actually destroys the object. This allows a child process to call CloseHandle for an object without affecting the parent's ability to continue to manipulate the object.

fdwCreate

The *fdwCreate* parameter identifies flags that affect how the new process is created. Multiple flags can be specified when combined with the boolean *OR* operator.

The DEBUG_PROCESS flag tells the system that the calling process wants to debug the new process and any processes created by the new process in the future. This flag instructs the system to notify the parent process (now the debugger) when certain events occur in any of the child processes (debuggees).

The DEBUG_ONLY_THIS_PROCESS flag is similar to the DEBUG-
_PROCESS flag except that the debugger is notified of special events oc-
curring only in that debuggee. If the debuggee creates any additional
processes, the debugger is not notified.

The CREATE_SUSPENDED flag causes the new process to be
created, but its primary thread is suspended. A debugger provides a
good example for using this flag. When a debugger is told to load a
debuggee, it must have Windows NT initialize the process, but the
debugger does not want to allow the process to begin execution yet.
Using this flag, the user debugging the application can set various
breakpoints throughout the program in case there are special events
that need trapping. Once all the breakpoints have been set, the user can
tell the debugger that the primary thread can resume execution.

The DETACHED_PROCESS flag blocks a console-based process's
access to its parent's console window and tells Windows NT to send its
output to a new console window. If a console-based process is created by
another console-based process, the new process will, by default, use the
parent's console window. (When you run the C compiler from the command shell, a new console window isn't created; the output is simply appended to the bottom of the window.) By specifying this flag, the new
process will send its output to a new console window.

The CREATE_NEW_CONSOLE flag tells Windows NT to create a
new console window for the new process. It is an error to specify both the
CREATE_NEW_CONSOLE and the DETACHED_PROCESS flags.

The CREATE_NO_WINDOW flag is used internally by the system
for virtual MS-DOS machines. It causes the process to have a console
without a window. You should not use this flag.

The CREATE_NEW_PROCESS_GROUP flag is used to modify
the list of processes that get notified when the user presses the Ctrl+C or
Ctrl+Break keys. If you have several console-based processes running
when the user presses one of these keys, the system notifies all the processes in a process group that the user wants to break out of the current
operation. By specifying this flag when creating a new console-based
process, you are creating a new process group. If the user presses Ctrl+C
or Ctrl+Break while a process in this new process group is active, the
system notifies only processes in this group of the user's request.

In addition to the flags listed above, you can also specify a priority
class when you're creating a new process. You don't have to specify a priority class, and for most applications, it is recommended that you don't.
The table on the following page shows the possible priority classes.

Priority Class	Flag Identifier
Idle	IDLE_PRIORITY_CLASS
Normal	NORMAL_PRIORITY_CLASS
High	HIGH_PRIORITY_CLASS
Realtime	REALTIME_PRIORITY_CLASS

These priority classes affect how the threads contained within the process are scheduled with respect to other processes' threads. See the section "How Windows NT Schedules Threads" for more information.

lpvEnvironment

The *lpvEnvironment* parameter points to a block of memory containing environment strings that are to be used by the new process. Most of the time, NULL is passed for this parameter, causing the child process to use the same set of environment strings that its parent is using. Or you can use the GetEnvironmentStrings function:

```
LPVOID GetEnvironmentStrings(VOID);
```

This function gets the address of the environment string data block that the calling process is using. You can use the address returned by this function as the *lpvEnvironment* parameter of CreateProcess. This is exactly what CreateProcess does if you pass NULL for the *lpvEnvironment* parameter.

You can alter the set of environment strings used by the child process in two ways. In the first method, you fill a memory block with a set of environment variable strings before calling CreateProcess. Each variable string in the memory block must have the following appearance:

```
name1=value1\0
name2=value2\0
name3=value3\0
 .
 .
 .
nameX=valueX\0
\0
```

The first part of each line is a name that identifies the variable. This name is followed by an equal sign, which is followed by the value you want to assign to the name. All the names on the left must be sorted in alphabetic order.

Because the equal sign is used to separate the name from the value, an equal sign cannot be part of the name. Also, spaces are significant. For example, if you declare these two variables,

```
XYZ= Windows NT          (Notice the space after the equal sign.)
ABC=Windows NT
```

and then compare the value of *XYZ* with the value of *ABC*, the system will report that the two variables are different. Any white space that appears following the name and preceding the equal sign is also significant. So, if you were to execute these two lines,

```
XYZ =Home                (Notice the space before the equal sign.)
XYZ=Work
```

the result would be that "*XYZ* " would contain "*Home*" and another variable "*XYZ*" would contain "*Work*". Finally, an additional zero byte must be placed at the end of all of the environment variables to notify Windows where the end of the block is.

The second way to alter the environment variables for the child process is by using the SetEnvironmentVariable function:

```
BOOL SetEnvironmentVariable(LPTSTR lpszName, LPTSTR lpszValue);
```

This function sets the variable identified by the *lpszName* parameter to the string value identified by the *lpszValue* parameter. Actually, calling this function adds an environment variable (if *lpszName* doesn't currently exist) or changes an environment variable (if *lpszName* currently exists) of the calling process. Then, if the calling process calls CreateProcess, passing NULL as the *lpvEnvironment* parameter, the new environment, including any additions or changes, is inherited by the child process.

Once the child process is initialized and executing, it can call the GetEnvironmentVariable function to retrieve individual environment variables from its own environment:

```
DWORD GetEnvironmentVariable(LPTSTR lpszName, LPTSTR lpszValue,
    DWORD cchValue);
```

When calling GetEnvironmentVariable, *lpszName* points to the desired variable name, *lpszValue* points to the buffer that will get the variable's string value, and *cchValue* indicates the maximum size of this buffer in characters. The function returns either the number of characters copied into the buffer or 0 (zero) if the variable name cannot be found in the environment. Using this function for retrieving variables is easier for the child process than using the GetEnvironmentStrings function and parsing the information.

lpszCurDir

The *lpszCurDir* parameter allows the process calling CreateProcess to tell Windows NT the names of the working drive and directory for the new process. If this parameter is NULL, the new process's working directory will be the same as that of the application spawning the new process. If this parameter is not NULL, *lpszCurDir* must point to a zero-terminated string containing the desired working drive and directory. Notice that you must specify a drive letter in the path.

lpsiStartInfo

The *lpsiStartInfo* parameter points to a STARTUPINFO structure:

```
typedef struct _STARTUPINFO {
    DWORD    cb;
    LPSTR    lpReserved;
    LPSTR    lpDesktop;
    LPSTR    lpTitle;
    DWORD    dwX;
    DWORD    dwY;
    DWORD    dwXSize;
    DWORD    dwYSize;
    DWORD    dwXCountChars;
    DWORD    dwYCountChars;
    DWORD    dwFillAttribute;
    DWORD    dwFlags;
    WORD     wShowWindow;
    WORD     cbReserved2;
    LPBYTE   lpReserved2;
    HANDLE   hStdInput;
    HANDLE   hStdOutput;
    HANDLE   hStdError;
} STARTUPINFO, *LPSTARTUPINFO;
```

This structure contains additional members that are used by Win32 when it creates the new process. We'll discuss each of these members in turn. Remember that Windows NT supports two types of Win32 applications—GUI and console. Some of the members in this structure can be used only in GUI applications or in console applications whereas some of the members can be used in either. The table on the following page indicates in which type of application each member can be included.

Member	GUI / Console / Both
cb	Both
lpReserved	Both
lpDesktop	Both
lpTitle	Console
dwX	Both
dwY	Both
dwXSize	Both
dwYSize	Both
dwXCountChars	Console
dwYCountChars	Console
dwFillAttribute	Console
dwFlags	Both
wShowWindow	GUI
cbReserved2	Both
lpReserved2	Both
hStdInput	Console
hStdOutput	Console
hStdError	Console

The *cb* member simply contains the number of bytes in the START-UPINFO structure. It acts as a version control in case Microsoft expands this structure in a future version of Win32. Your application must initialize *cb* to *sizeof(STARTUPINFO)*:

```
STARTUPINFO si;
si.cb = sizeof(si);
 .
 .
 .
```

The *lpReserved* member is reserved and must be initialized to NULL.

The *lpDesktop* member identifies the name of the desktop in which to start the application. If the desktop exists, this process is associated with this desktop. If it does not exist, a desktop with default attributes will be created with this name for this process. If *lpDesktop* is NULL (which is most common), the process is associated with the current desktop. The first version of Windows NT does not support multiple desktops, but Microsoft plans to add this feature in future versions.

The *lpTitle* member specifies the window title for a console application. If *lpTitle* is NULL, the name of the executable file is used as the window title. This member is not used by GUI-based applications.

The *dwX* and *dwY* members specify the *x* and *y* coordinates (in pixels) of the location where the application's window should be placed on the screen. These coordinates are used only if the child process creates its first overlapped window with CW_USEDEFAULT as the *x* parameter of CreateWindow. Console applications do not use graphics but display their contents inside a window. A console application is similar to an MS-DOS application in a window under 16-bit Windows. In console applications, these members indicate the upper left corner of the window containing the application.

The *dwXSize* and *dwYSize* parameters specify the width and height (in pixels) of a GUI application's first overlapped window. These values are used only if the child process creates the overlapped window with CW_USEDEFAULT as the *nWidth* parameter of CreateWindow. In console applications, these members indicate the width and height of the window containing the application.

The *dwXCountChars* and *dwYCountChars* members specify the character width and height of a console application's window.

The *dwFillAttribute* member specifies the text and background colors used by a console application.

The *wShowWindow* member specifies how the application's first overlapped window should appear if the application's first call to ShowWindow passes SW_SHOWDEFAULT as the *nCmdShow* parameter. This member can be any of the SW_* identifiers that are normally used with the ShowWindow function. See the discussion about the WinMain function later in this chapter for some notes about this member.

Both the *cbReserved2* and *lpReserved2* members are reserved and must be initialized to 0 (zero) and NULL respectively.

The *hStdInput*, *hStdOutput*, and *hStdError* members identify handles to buffers that a console application uses for input and output. By default, a console application's *hStdInput* handle identifies a keyboard buffer, whereas the *hStdOutput* and *hStdError* handles identify a console window's buffer.

I purposely saved the *dwFlags* member for last. This member contains a set of flags that modify how the process is to be created. Most of the flags simply tell CreateProcess whether there is useful information in other members of this structure or whether some of the members should be ignored. The table on the following page shows the list of possible flags and their meanings.

Flag	Meaning
STARTF_USESIZE	Use the *dwXSize* and *dwYSize* members.
STARTF_USESHOWWINDOW	Use the *wShowWindow* member.
STARTF_USEPOSITION	Use the *dwX* and *dwY* members.
STARTF_USECOUNTCHARS	Use the *dwXCountChars* and *dwYCountChars* members.
STARTF_USEFILLATTRIBUTE	Use the *dwFillAttribute* member.
STARTF_USESTDHANDLES	Use the *hStdInput*, *hStdOutput*, and *hStdError* members.

Two additional flags—STARTF_FORCEONFEEDBACK and STARTF_-_FORCEOFFFEEDBACK—give you control over the mouse cursor when invoking a new process. Because Windows NT supports true preemptive multitasking, it is possible to invoke an application from the Program Manager and, while the process is initializing, use another program. To give visual feedback to the user, CreateProcess temporarily changes the system's mouse cursor to a new cursor called a start glass:

This cursor indicates that you can wait for something to happen or you can continue to use the system. In the very early beta releases of Windows NT, this cursor didn't exist, and CreateProcess did not change the appearance of the cursor at all. Often, when I ran a program from the Program Manager, the program's windows did not appear immediately and the cursor still appeared as the normal arrow. So I clicked on the program icon again in the Program Manager. I kept doing this because it seemed that the Program Manager wasn't acknowledging my request. Soon, the program I wanted popped up on the screen followed by another, and another, and another. Now, I had to close all the additional instances of the program. It is amazing how big a difference changing the cursor can make. The problem is compounded, of course, because 16-bit Windows does change the cursor to an hourglass when an application is being initialized. Because I was expecting this, I thought that Windows NT wasn't working properly. Old habits are hard to break.

The CreateProcess function gives you control over the cursor when invoking another process. By specifying the STARTF_FORCEOFF-FEEDBACK flag, CreateProcess does not change the cursor into the start glass, leaving it as the normal arrow.

Specifying STARTF_FORCEONFEEDBACK causes CreateProcess to monitor the new process's initialization and to alter the cursor based on the result. When CreateProcess is called with this flag, the cursor changes into the start glass. If, after two seconds, the new process does not make a GUI call, CreateProcess resets the cursor to an arrow.

If the process does make a GUI call within two seconds, Create-Process waits for the application to show a window. This must occur within five seconds after making the GUI call. If a window is not displayed, CreateProcess resets the cursor. If a window is displayed, CreateProcess keeps the feedback cursor on for another five seconds. If, at any time, the application calls the GetMessage function, indicating that it is finished initializing, CreateProcess immediately resets the cursor and stops monitoring the new process.

The final flag to discuss is STARTF_SCREENSAVER. It tells the system that it's starting a screen-saver application, which causes the system to initialize the application in a very special way. When the process begins executing, the system allows the process to initialize at the foreground priority of the class that was specified in the call to Create-Process. As soon as the process makes a call to either GetMessage or PeekMessage, the system automatically changes the process's priority to the idle priority class.

If the screen-saver application is active and the user presses a key or moves the mouse, the system automatically boosts the priority class of the screen-saver application back to the foreground priority of the class flag passed to CreateProcess.

To start a screen-saver application, you should call CreateProcess using the NORMAL_PRIORITY_CLASS flag. Doing so has the following two effects:

1. The system allows the screen-saver application to initialize before making it run idle. If the screen-saver application ran 100 percent of its time at idle priority, normal and realtime processes would preempt it, and the screen-saver application would never get a chance to initialize.

2. The system allows the screen-saver application to terminate. Usually a screen saver terminates because the user starts using

an application. This application is probably running at normal priority, which would cause the threads in the screen-saver application to be preempted again, and the screen saver would never be able to terminate.

lppiProcInfo

The *lppiProcInfo* parameter points to a PROCESS_INFORMATION structure that CreateProcess will fill before it returns. The structure appears as follows:

```
typedef struct _PROCESS_INFORMATION {
   HANDLE hProcess;
   HANDLE hThread;
   DWORD  dwProcessId;
   DWORD  dwThreadId;
} PROCESS_INFORMATION;
```

As already mentioned, creating a new process causes the system to create an internal process object and an internal thread object. At creation time, the system gives each object an initial usage count of 1. Then, just before CreateProcess returns, the function opens the process object and the thread object and places the process-relative handles for each in the *hProcess* and *hThread* members of the PROCESS_INFORMATION structure. When CreateProcess opens these objects, the usage count for each increments to 2.

This means that before the Windows NT Executive can free the process object, the process must terminate (decrementing the usage count to 1) and the parent process must call CloseHandle (decrementing the usage count to 0). To free the thread object, the thread must terminate and the parent process must close the handle to the thread object.

Don't forget to close these handles. Failure to close handles is one of the most common mistakes developers make and results in a system memory leak because some Windows NT Executive objects are never destroyed.

When a process is created, the system assigns the process a unique identifier; no other process running in the system will have the same ID number. The same is true for threads. When a thread is created, the thread is also assigned a unique, systemwide ID number. Before CreateProcess returns, it fills the *dwProcessId* and *dwThreadId* members of the PROCESS_INFORMATION structure with these IDs. The parent process can use these two IDs to communicate with the child process.

17

It is extremely important to note that the Windows NT Executive reuses process and thread IDs. For example, let's say that when a process is created, Windows NT allocates a process object and assigns it the ID value 0x22222222. If a new process object is created, Windows NT doesn't assign the same ID number; however, if the first process object is freed, Windows NT might assign 0x22222222 to the next process object created.

This is important to know so that you avoid writing code that references an incorrect process object (or thread). It's easy to acquire a process ID and save the ID, but the next thing you know, the process identified by the ID is freed and a new process is created and given the same ID. When you use the saved process ID, you end up manipulating the new process, not the process that you originally acquired the handle to.

You can easily guarantee that this doesn't happen by making sure that you have an outstanding lock on the handle. In other words, make sure that you have incremented the usage count for the process object. Windows NT will never free the process object while it has a usage count greater than 0 (zero). In most situations, you will already have incremented the usage count. For example, the call to CreateProcess returns after incrementing the usage count for the process object. If you haven't already incremented the usage count, you can use the DuplicateHandle function to do so.

With the usage count incremented, you can feel free to use the process ID to your heart's content. When you no longer need the process ID, call CloseHandle to decrement the process object's usage count. Simply make sure that you don't use that process ID after you have called CloseHandle.

Terminating a Process

A process can be terminated in two ways: by calling the ExitProcess function, which is the most common method, or by calling the TerminateProcess function, which is a method that should be reserved as a last resort. This section discusses both methods for terminating a process and describes what actually happens when a process ends.

The ExitProcess Function

A process terminates when one of the threads in the process calls Exit-Process:

```
VOID ExitProcess(UINT fuExitCode);
```

This function terminates the process and sets the exit code of the process to *fuExitCode*. ExitProcess doesn't return a value because the process has terminated. If you include any code following the call to the Exit-Process function, that code will never execute.

This method is the most common because ExitProcess is called when WinMain returns to the C Runtime's startup code. The startup code calls ExitProcess, passing it the value returned from WinMain. Any other threads that are running in the process terminate along with the process.

Note that this example does not describe how Windows NT works but what happens when you write a C/C++ program for Windows NT. Windows NT doesn't terminate a process until all the threads running in the process have terminated.

So, if WinMain calls ExitThread instead of returning, the primary thread for your application stops executing, but the process continues to run as long as at least one other thread is running.

The TerminateProcess Function

A call to TerminateProcess also ends a process:

```
BOOL TerminateProcess(HANDLE hProcess, UINT fuExitCode);
```

This function is different from ExitProcess in one major way: A process can call TerminateProcess to terminate another process or itself. The *hProcess* parameter identifies the handle of the process to be terminated. When the process terminates, its exit code becomes the value you passed as the *fuExitCode* parameter.

Note that using TerminateProcess is discouraged; it should be used only if you can't force a process to exit by using another method. Normally when a process ends, Windows NT notifies any DLLs attached to the process that the process is ending. If you call TerminateProcess, however, Windows NT doesn't notify any DLLs attached to the process, which can mean that the process won't close down correctly. For example, a DLL might be written to flush data to a disk file when the process detaches from the DLL. Detachment usually occurs when an application unloads the DLL by calling FreeLibrary. Because the DLL isn't notified about the detachment when you use TerminateProcess, the DLL can't perform its normal cleanup. Windows NT does notify the DLL when a process ends normally or when ExitProcess is called. (See Chapter 7 for more information about DLLs.) Although it's possible that the DLL won't have a chance to clean up its data, Windows NT guarantees that any system resources used by the process are returned to the system regardless of how the process terminates.

A Process Ending

When a process ends, the following actions are set in motion:

1. All the threads in the process terminate their execution.

2. All the Win32 subsystem object handles and Windows NT object handles opened by the process are closed.

3. The process object status becomes signaled. (See Chapter 5 for more information about signaling.) Other threads in the system can suspend themselves until the process is terminated.

4. The termination status of the process changes from STILL_ACTIVE to the appropriate exit code.

When a process terminates, its associated Windows NT process object doesn't automatically become freed until all the outstanding references to the object are closed. Also, terminating a process does not cause any child processes that it spawned to terminate.

When a process terminates, the code for the process and any resources that the process allocated are removed from memory. However, the private memory that the system allocated for the process object is not freed until the process object's usage count reaches 0 (zero). This can happen only if all other processes that have created or opened handles to the now defunct process notify the system that they no longer need to reference the process. These processes notify the system by calling CloseHandle.

Once a process is no longer running, the parent process can't do much with the process handle. However, it can call GetExitCodeProcess to check whether the process identified by *hProcess* has terminated and, if so, determine its exit code.

```
BOOL GetExitCodeProcess(HANDLE hProcess, LPDWORD lpdwExitCode);
```

The exit code value is returned in the DWORD pointed to by *lpdwExitCode*. If the process hasn't terminated when GetExitCode-Process is called, the function fills the DWORD with the STILL_AC-TIVE identifier (defined as 0x103). If the function is successful, TRUE is returned. Using the child process's handle to determine when the child process has terminated is discussed further in Chapter 5.

When to Create a Thread

Every time a process is initialized, Windows NT creates a primary thread. This thread starts at the WinMain function and continues executing until the WinMain function returns. For many applications, this primary thread may be the only thread that the application requires. However, processes can create additional threads to help them do their work. The whole idea behind creating additional threads is to utilize the CPU's time as much as possible. For example, a spreadsheet program needs to perform recalculations as the data entries in the cells are changed by the user. Because recalculations of a complex spreadsheet might require several seconds to complete, a well-designed application should not recalculate the spreadsheet after each change made by the user. Instead, the spreadsheet's recalculation function should be executed as a separate thread, and this thread should have a lower priority than that of the primary thread. Then, if the user is typing, the primary thread is running, which means that Windows NT won't schedule any time to the recalculation thread. When the user stops typing, the primary thread is suspended waiting for input, and the recalculation thread is scheduled time. As soon as the user starts typing again, the primary thread, having a higher priority, preempts the recalculation thread. Creating an additional thread makes the program very responsive to the user. It is also rather easy to implement this type of design.

In a similar example, you can create an additional thread for a repagination function in a word processor that needs to repaginate the document as the user enters text into the document. Microsoft's Word for Windows, for example, must simulate multithreaded behavior in 16-bit Windows but could easily spawn a thread dedicated to repaginating the document for the Win32 version. The primary thread would be responsible for processing the user's input, and a background thread would be responsible for locating the page breaks.

It's also useful to create a separate thread to handle any printing tasks in an application. In this way the user can continue to use the application while it's printing. Many applications perform a long task and display a dialog box that allows the user to abort the task. For example, when the File Manager copies files, it displays a dialog box that lists the names of the source file and the destination file and also contains a Cancel button. If you click on the Cancel button while the files are being copied, you abort the operation.

In 16-bit Windows, implementing this type of functionality requires periodic calls to PeekMessage inside the File Copy loop. And calls to PeekMessage can be made only between file reading and writing. If a large data block is being read, the response to the button click doesn't occur until after the block has been read. If the file is being read from a floppy disk, this can take several seconds. Because the response is so sluggish, I have frequently clicked the button several times thinking that the system didn't know that I'd canceled the operation.

By putting the File Copy code in a different thread, you don't need to sprinkle calls to the PeekMessage function throughout your code—your user-interface thread operates independently. This means that a click on the Cancel button results in an immediate response.

Threads can also be used for creating applications that simulate real-world events. In Chapter 5, I show a simulation of a supermarket. Because each shopper is represented by his or her own thread, theoretically each shopper is independent of any other shopper and can enter, shop, check-out, and exit as he or she sees fit. The simulation can monitor this to determine how well the supermarket functions.

Although simulations can be performed under Windows NT, potential problems lurk. First, you would ideally want each shopper thread to be executed by its very own CPU. Because it is not practical to expect a CPU for every shopper thread, the solution is to incur a time overhead when the operating system preempts 1 thread and schedules another. For example, if your simulation has 2 threads and your machine has eight CPUs, the system can assign 1 thread to each CPU. However, if your simulation has 1,000 threads, the system will have to assign and reassign the 1,000 threads among the eight CPUs over and over again. And some overhead results when the operating system schedules a large number of threads among a few CPUs. If your simulation lasts a long time, this overhead has a relatively small impact on the simulation. However, if the simulation is short, the overhead of the operating system can take a larger percentage of the simulation's total execution time.

Second, the system itself requires threads to run while other processes might be executing. All these processes' threads need to be scheduled for CPU time as well, which almost certainly affects the outcome of the simulation.

And third, the simulation is useful only if you keep track of its progress. For example, the supermarket simulation, in Chapter 5, adds entries to a list box as the shoppers progress through the store; adding entries to the list box takes time away from the simulation. The principle known as the Heisenberg Uncertainty Principle states that "A more accurate determination of one quantity results in a less precise measurement of the other."[1] This is most definitely true here.

When Not to Create a Thread

Given access to an environment that supports multiple threads, many programmers feel that this is what they've been waiting for. If only they had had threads sooner, their applications would have been so simple to write. And, for some unknown reason, these programmers start dividing their application into pieces that can each execute as its own thread. This is not the way to go about developing an application.

Threads are incredibly useful and have a place, but when you use threads, you potentially create new problems while trying to solve the old ones. For example, let's say that you're developing a word processing application and want to allow the printing function to run as its own thread. This sounds like a good idea because the user can immediately go back and start editing the document while it is printing. But wait—this means that the data in the document might be changed *while* the document is printing. This is a whole new type of problem that needs to be addressed. Maybe it would be best not to have the printing take place in its own thread, but this seems a bit drastic. How about if you let the user edit another document but lock the printing document so that it can't be modified until the printing has completed? Or, here's a third idea: Copy the document to a temporary file, print the contents of the temporary file, and let the user modify the original. When the temporary file containing the document has finished printing, delete the temporary file.

As you can see, threads help solve some problems at the risk of creating new ones. Another common misuse of threads can arise in the development of an application's user interface. In most applications, all the user-interface components (windows) should be sharing the same thread. If you're producing a dialog box, for example, it wouldn't make much sense for a list box to be created by one thread and a button to be created by another.

---

1. Werner Heisenberg actually developed the theory with respect to quantum mechanics, not computer science.

Let's take this a step further and say that you have your own list-box control that sorts data every time an element is added or deleted. The sorting operation might take several seconds, so you decide to assign this control to its very own thread. In this way, the user can continue to work with other controls while the list-box control's thread continues sorting.

Doing this wouldn't be a very good idea. First, every thread that creates a window must also contain a GetMessage loop. Second, the Win32 subsystem is like a parallel universe in that it creates a complementary thread for itself for every thread you create that creates a window. This adds unnecessary overhead in your application. Third, because the list-box thread contains its own GetMessage loop, you also potentially open yourself up to some synchronization problems among the threads. You can solve this problem by assigning to the list box control a dedicated thread whose sole purpose is to sort elements in the background.

Now, having said all this, let me take some of it back. In rare situations, assigning individual threads to user-interface objects is useful. In the whole system each process has its own separate thread controlling its own user interface. For example, the Program Manager has one thread that creates and manipulates all its windows, and the File Manager has its own thread that creates and manipulates its own windows. These separate threads were assigned for protection and robustness. If the File Manager's thread enters an infinite loop, the resulting problem has no effect on the Program Manager's thread. This is quite different from the behavior we see in 16-bit Windows. In 16-bit Windows, if one application hangs, the entire system hangs. Windows NT allows you to switch away from the File Manager (even though it is hung) and start using the Program Manager. See Chapter 6 for more detail.

Another use for multiple threads in GUI components is MDI (multiple document interface) applications in which each MDI child window is running on its own thread. If one of the MDI child threads enters an infinite loop or starts a time-consuming procedure, the user could switch to another MDI child window and begin working with it while the other MDI child thread continues to chug along. This can be so useful, in fact, that Win32 offers a special function, shown below, whose result is similar to creating an MDI child window by sending the WM_MDICRE-ATE message to an MDIClient window.

```
HWND CreateMDIWindow(LPTSTR lpszClassName, LPTSTR lpszWindowName,
    DWORD dwStyle, int x, int y, int nWidth, int nHeight,
    HWND hwndParent, HINSTANCE hinst, LONG lParam);
```

The only difference is that the CreateMDIWindow function allows the MDI child to be created with its own thread.

The moral of the story is that multiple threads should be used judiciously. Don't use them only because you can. You can still write many useful and powerful applications using nothing more than the primary thread Windows NT assigns to the process. If after reading all this, you're convinced you have a valid need for threads, then read on.

The Life Cycle of a Thread

Conceiving a Thread: The CreateThread Function

We've already discussed how a process's primary thread comes into being when CreateProcess is called. However, if this primary thread wants to create additional threads, it does so by calling CreateThread:

```
HANDLE CreateThread(
    LPSECURITY_ATTRIBUTES lpsa,
    DWORD cbStack,
    LPTHREAD_START_ROUTINE lpStartAddr,
    LPVOID lpvThreadParm,
    DWORD fdwCreate,
    LPDWORD lpIDThread);
```

Like many of the functions that create Windows NT Executive objects, CreateThread also takes a pointer to a SECURITY_ATTRIBUTES structure as the *lpsa* parameter. You can also pass NULL if you want the default security attributes for the object.

When calling CreateThread, the *cbStack* parameter tells the thread how much address space it is allowed to use for its own stack. Every thread owns its very own stack. When CreateProcess starts an application, it calls CreateThread to initialize the process's primary thread. For the *cbStack* parameter, CreateProcess uses the value stored inside the executable file with the linker's /STACK switch:

```
/STACK:[reserve] [,commit]
```

The *reserve* argument sets the amount of memory the system should reserve in the address space for the thread's stack. The default is 1 MB. The *commit* argument specifies the amount of reserved address space that should initially be committed to the stack. The default is 1 page. (See Chapter 3 for a discussion of reserving and committing memory.) As the code in your thread executes, it is quite possible that you'll require more than 1 page of memory. When your thread overflows its stack, an exception is generated. (See Chapter 10 for more-detailed information about handling exceptions.) Windows NT catches the exception and commits another page (or whatever you specified for the commit argument) to the reserved space, which allows your thread's stacks to grow dynamically as needed.

When calling CreateThread, you can pass 0 (zero) to the *cbStack* parameter. In this case, CreateThread creates a stack for the new thread using the *commit* argument embedded in the EXE file by the linker. The amount of reserved space is always 1 MB. Windows NT sets a limit of 1 MB to stop applications that recurse endlessly.

Let's say that you are writing a function that calls itself recursively. This function also has a bug that causes endless recursion. Every time the function calls itself, a new stack frame is created on the stack. If Windows NT didn't set a maximum limit on the stack size, the recursive function would never stop calling itself. All of the process's address space would be allocated, and enormous amounts of virtual memory would become committed to the stack. By setting a stack limit, you prevent your application from using up enormous amounts of system resources, and you'll also know much sooner when a bug exists in your program.

The *lpStartAddr* parameter indicates the address of the function containing the code where the new thread should start executing. It is perfectly legal and actually quite useful to create multiple threads that all have the same function address as their starting point. For example, you might create an MDI application in which all the child windows behave similarly but each operates on its own thread. The thread function you write must have the same function prototype as this function:

```
DWORD WINAPI ThreadFunc(LPVOID lpvThreadParm) {
   DWORD dwResult = 0;
   .
   .
   .
   return(dwResult);
}
```

The thread function's *lpvThreadParm* parameter is the same as the *lpvThreadParm* parameter that you originally passed to CreateThread. CreateThread does nothing with this parameter except pass it on to the thread function when the thread starts executing. This parameter provides a way to pass an initialization value to the thread function. This initialization data can be either a 32-bit value or a 32-bit pointer to a data structure that contains additional information. If you pass the address to a structure, you must make sure that the memory containing the structure remains valid until the thread function no longer needs to access the members of the structure.

For example, you don't want one thread to create a local data structure on its stack, call CreateThread, pass the address to the structure, and then terminate. In this case, it's possible that the first thread will terminate before the new thread gets an opportunity to access the structure. However, because the structure is allocated on the first thread's stack, the data in this structure disappears when the thread's stack is freed. When the new thread attempts to access the memory address where the structure was, a memory access violation occurs.

CreateThread's *fdwCreate* parameter can take one of two values. If the value is 0 (zero), the thread starts executing immediately. If the value is CREATE_SUSPENDED, the system creates the thread and gets ready to execute the first instruction of the thread function but suspends the thread so that it doesn't start executing.

The last parameter of CreateThread, *lpIDThread*, must be a valid address to a DWORD that CreateThread will fill in with the ID that Windows NT assigns to the new thread. This parameter value cannot be NULL even if you are not interested in the thread's ID; passing NULL causes an access violation.

Immediately before CreateThread returns and the thread that called it continues to execute, the new thread is also executing—that is, as long as the CREATE_SUSPENDED flag wasn't specified.[2] Because the new thread is running simultaneously, the possibility of problems exists. Watch out for code like this:

```
DWORD WINAPI FirstThread (LPVOID lpvThreadParm) {
    int x = 0;
    DWORD dwResult = 0, dwThreadId;

    CreateThread(NULL, 0, SecondThread, (LPVOID) &x,
        0, &dwThreadId);

    return(dwResult);
}
```

(continued)

---

2. Actually, on a single CPU machine threads execute one at a time, but it's best to think of them all executing simultaneously. Also, the new thread's execution is subject to the priority levels of all other threads.

```
DWORD WINAPI SecondThread (LPVOID lpvThreadParm) {
    DWORD dwResult = 0;

    // Do some lengthy processing here.
    .
    .
    .
    * ((int *) lpvThreadParm) = 5;
    .
    .
    .
    return(dwResult);
}
```

In the code above, it is very likely that FirstThread will finish its work prior to SecondThread assigning 5 to FirstThread's *x*. If this happens, SecondThread won't know and will attempt to change the contents of what is now an invalid address. This is certain to cause the application to crash in a fiery ball of molten lava.[3] One way to solve the problem is to declare *x* as a static variable. In this way, the compiler will create a storage area for *x* in the application's data section rather than on the stack. However, this makes the function not reentrant. In other words, you couldn't create two threads that execute the same function because the static variable would be shared between the two threads.

Another way to solve this problem and more complex variations on this problem is to use synchronization objects, which are discussed in Chapter 5.

It's Alive: The WinMain Function

When a Win32 GUI-based process is invoked, the primary thread begins by executing the C Runtime startup code. This code initializes any variables needed by the startup code and calls the familiar WinMain function:

```
int WinMain(HINSTANCE hInstance, HINSTANCE hPrevInstance,
    LPSTR lpszCmdLine, int nCmdShow);
```

There are some important differences between the meanings of the parameters here and their meanings in the 16-bit Windows world. First, in 16-bit Windows, the *hModule* parameter for a task indicates the module database for an EXE or a DLL. Even if 200 instances of Notepad are running, there is only one module database for Notepad and, therefore, only one *hModule* value shared by all the instances. There can be

---

3. By fiery ball of molten lava I mean an access violation.

only one instance of a DLL loaded in 16-bit Windows, so only one *hModule* value exists for each loaded DLL.

In 16-bit Windows, each running instance of a task receives its very own *hInstance* value. This value identifies the task's default data segment. If 200 instances of Notepad are running, there are 200 *hInstance* values—one for each running instance. Because DLLs also have a default data segment, each loaded DLL also receives its very own *hInstance* value. You might think that because a DLL can be loaded only once, 16-bit Windows could use the same value for a DLL's *hModule* and its *hInstance*. However, this is not the case because *hModule* identifies the DLL's module database, and *hInstance* identifies its default data segment.

Windows NT makes no distinction between a process's *hModule* and *hInstance* values—they are one and the same. Wherever the Win32 documentation for a function states that *hModule* is required, you can pass *hInstance*, and vice versa. The actual value passed for the *hInstance* parameter to WinMain is the base address where the EXE file was mapped into the process's address space.

The base address where an application loads is determined by the linker. Different linkers can use different default base addresses. The lowest possible base address is 0x00010000 (64 KB). This is because the bottommost 64 KB of a process's address space is reserved by the system. You can change the base address where your application loads by using the */BASE: address* linker switch for Microsoft's linker.

If your application loads at a base address of 0x00010000, your application's *hInstance* value will also be 0x00010000. In fact, all the running instances of your application will load at the same base address but in their own address spaces. This means that all the instances of your application will have an *hInstance* value 0x00010000.

In 16-bit Windows, it is possible to call the DialogBox function and pass in an *hInstance* value that belongs to an application other than your own:

```
int DialogBox(HINSTANCE hInstance, LPCTSTR lpszTemplate,
   HWND hwndOwner, DLGPROC dlgprc);
```

This causes 16-bit Windows to load the dialog box template from the other application's resources. Of course, this is a questionable action to take anyway, but in Windows NT it's no longer possible to do this at all. When you make a call to a function that expects an *hInstance* value, Windows NT interprets the call to mean that you are requesting information from the EXE or DLL that is mapped into your own process's address space at the address indicated by the *hInstance* parameter.

Let's look at the next parameter to WinMain, *hPrevInstance*. In a 16-bit Windows application, this parameter specifies the instance handle of another instance of the same task. If no other instances of the task are running, *hPrevInstance* is passed as NULL. 16-bit Windows applications frequently examine this value for two reasons:

1. To determine whether another instance of the same task is already running and, if so, to terminate the newly invoked instance. This termination occurs if a program such as the File Manager wishes to allow only a single instance of itself to run at a time.

2. To determine whether window classes need to be registered. In 16-bit Windows, window classes need to be registered only once by a module. These classes are then shared among all instances of the same application. If a second instance attempts to register the same window classes a second time, the call to Register-Class fails. In Win32, each instance of an application must register its own window classes because window classes are no longer shared among all instances of the same application.

To ease the porting of a 16-bit Windows application to use the Win32 API, Microsoft decided to always pass NULL in the *hPrevInstance* parameter of WinMain. Because many 16-bit Windows applications examine this parameter when registering window classes, all instances see that *hPrevInstance* is NULL and automatically reregister their window classes.

While this decision eases the job of porting your applications, it also means that applications cannot use the value of *hPrevInstance* to prevent a second instance from running. An application must use alternative methods to determine whether other instances of itself are already running. In one method, the application calls FindWindow, looking for a particular window class and/or caption that uniquely identifies it. If FindWindow returns NULL, the application knows that it's the only instance of itself running. Another method for determining whether multiple instances of an application are running is presented in Chapter 7.

The third parameter to WinMain, *lpszCmdLine*, is the one parameter that retains its 16-bit Windows meaning. This parameter points to a zero-terminated string that contains the command-line passed to the application. This string is always in ANSI format and never in Unicode format. You can use the GetCommandLine function if you need to parse a Unicode version of the command line.

WinMain's last parameter is *nCmdShow*. When WinMain is called, the value of *nCmdShow* is always SW_SHOWDEFAULT. This value is new for Win32 and does not exist in 16-bit Windows. In 16-bit Windows, the *nCmdShow* parameter is usually either SW_SHOWNORMAL or SW-_SHOWMINNOACTIVE.

In 16-bit Windows, when you invoke an application from the Program Manager by double-clicking, the application's WinMain function is called with SW_SHOWNORMAL passed as the *nCmdShow* parameter. If you hold down the Shift key while double-clicking, the Program Manager invokes your application, passing SW_SHOWMINNOACTIVE as the *nCmdShow* parameter. In this way, the user can easily start an application normally or minimized.

Things work very differently in Windows NT. When your application attempts to show a window using SW_SHOWDEFAULT, Windows NT examines the *wCmdShow* member of the STARTUPINFO structure for the process and uses this value to determine how the window should be displayed. In addition, the first time your application makes a call to CreateWindow or to CreateWindowEx, passing CW_USEDEFAULT for the *x* parameter, Windows NT examines the *dwX* and *dwY* members of the STARTUPINFO structure and uses these values to determine the upper left corner of the window. Windows NT also uses the *dwXSize* and *dwYSize* members of this structure to determine the window's width and height if CW_USEDEFAULT was passed as the *nWidth* parameter to CreateWindow(Ex).

As previously discussed, Windows NT uses several of the members in the STARTUPINFO structure when a new process is created. Most of the time, your application will never have to examine the contents of the STARTUPINFO structure. However, if you want to examine this information for yourself, you can call GetStartupInfo to fill a START-UPINFO structure that you must first allocate:

```
VOID GetStartupInfo(LPSTARTUPINFO lpsi);
```

All Good Threads (and Processes) Must Come to an End

A thread can die in three ways. I refer to them as natural causes, suicide, and murder. In Windows NT, most objects that can be created are owned by the process that creates them. However, there are a few objects (windows, accelerators, and hooks) that can be owned by a thread. When the threads that create these objects die, Windows NT destroys these objects too.

A thread dies from natural causes when it returns from its function. The return value from the function indicates the thread's exit code. This exit code is similar to the exit code associated with a process. A thread can query the exit code of another thread by calling:

```
BOOL GetExitCodeThread(HANDLE hThread, LPDWORD lpdwExitCode);
```

If the thread has not ended, the DWORD that is pointed to by *lpdwExitCode* contains the STILL_ACTIVE identifier (which is defined as 0x103). Because STILL_ACTIVE is defined as 0x103, you might not want to have one of your own threads return a value of 0x103 if you expect to be calling GetExitCodeThread for that thread.

In OS/2, the primary thread in a process has a very special attribute: When the primary thread dies, the process and any other threads running in the process die. In Windows NT, on the other hand, all threads are created equal. That is, as long as the process has any threads at all running in it, the process continues to live. This is true even if the primary thread dies. However, when WinMain returns to the C Runtime startup code, the startup code makes an explicit call to Exit-Process, passing it the value returned from WinMain. ExitProcess forces the process (and any running threads in it) to terminate immediately.

A thread commits suicide if it calls ExitThread:

```
VOID ExitThread(DWORD fdwExitCode);
```

This function sets the exit code for the thread that calls the function and ends the thread. The function returns VOID because it doesn't return at all. Any code following the call to ExitThread will never be executed.

The third way a thread can die is by being murdered. This happens when a thread in the system calls TerminateThread:

```
BOOL TerminateThread(HANDLE hThread, DWORD dwExitCode);
```

The function ends the thread identified by the *hThread* parameter and sets its exit code to *dwExitCode*. The TerminateThread function exists so you can terminate a thread when it no longer responds. You should use it only as a last resort.

When a thread dies by natural causes or by committing suicide, the stack for the thread is destroyed. However, if the thread is murdered, Windows NT does not destroy the stack until the process that owns the thread exits because other threads might still be using pointers that reference data contained on the terminated thread's stack. If these other threads attempted to access the stack, an access violation would occur.

Also, when a thread ends, Windows NT notifies any DLLs attached to the process owning the thread that the thread is ending. If you call TerminateThread, however, Windows NT doesn't notify any DLLs attached to the process, which can mean that the process won't be closed down correctly. For example, a DLL might be written to flush data to a disk file when the thread detaches from the DLL. Because the DLL isn't notified about the detachment when you use TerminateThread, the DLL cannot perform its normal cleanup.

The ExitProcess and TerminateProcess functions discussed earlier also murder threads. The difference is that these functions murder all the threads contained in the process being terminated.

The following actions occur when a thread dies:

1. All Win32 object handles owned by the thread are closed.

2. The state of the thread object becomes signaled.

3. The termination status of the thread changes from STILL-_ACTIVE to the appropriate exit code.

4. If the thread is the last active thread in the process, the process ends.

When a thread terminates, its associated Windows NT thread object doesn't automatically become freed until all the outstanding references to the object are closed.

Gaining a Sense of One's Own Identity

Several Win32 functions require a process handle as a parameter. A thread can get the handle of the process that it is running in by calling GetCurrentProcess:

```
HANDLE GetCurrentProcess(VOID);
```

This function returns a pseudo-handle to the process; it doesn't create a new handle, and it doesn't increment the process object's usage count.

If you call CloseHandle and pass this pseudo-handle as the parameter, CloseHandle simply ignores the call and does nothing but return.

You can use pseudo-handles in calls to functions that require a process handle. For example, the line below changes the priority class of the calling process to HIGH_PRIORITY_CLASS:

```
SetPriorityClass(GetCurrentProcess(), HIGH_PRIORITY_CLASS);
```

The Win32 API also includes a few functions that require a process ID. A thread can acquire the ID of a running process by calling GetCurrentProcessID:

```
DWORD GetCurrentProcessId(VOID);
```

This function returns the systemwide ID that identifies the process.

When you call CreateThread, the handle of the newly created thread is returned to the thread making the call, but the new thread does not know what its own handle is. For a thread to acquire a handle to itself, it must call:

```
HANDLE GetCurrentThread(VOID);
```

A thread acquires its ID by calling:

```
DWORD GetCurrentThreadId(VOID);
```

Like GetCurrentProcess, GetCurrentThread returns a pseudo-handle that can be used only in the context of the current thread. The thread object's usage count is not incremented, and calls to CloseHandle passing the pseudo-handle have no effect.

Sometimes you might need to acquire a "real" handle to a thread instead of a pseudo-handle. By "real," I mean a handle that unambiguously identifies a unique thread. Examine the following code:

```
DWORD WINAPI ParentThread (LPVOID lpvThreadParm) {
    DWORD IDThread;
    HANDLE hThread = GetCurrentThread();
    CreateThread(NULL, 0, ChildThread, hThread, 0, &IDThread);
    // Function continues...
}

DWORD WINAPI ChildThread (LPVOID lpvThreadParm) {
    HANDLE hParentThread = (HANDLE) lpvThreadParm;
    SetThreadPriority(hParentThread, THREAD_PRIORITY_NORMAL);
    // Function continues...
}
```

Can you see the problem with this code fragment? The idea is to have the parent thread pass to the child thread a thread handle that identifies the parent thread. However, the parent thread is passing a pseudo-handle, not a "real" handle. When the child thread begins execution, it passes the pseudo-handle to the SetThreadPriority function, which causes the child thread—not the parent thread—to change priority. This happens because a thread pseudo-handle is a handle to the current thread—that is, a handle to whichever thread is making the function call.

To fix this code, we must turn the pseudo-handle into a "real" handle. This can be done by using the DuplicateHandle function:

```
BOOL DuplicateHandle(
    HANDLE hSourceProcess,
    HANDLE hSource,
    HANDLE hTargetProcess,
    LPHANDLE lphTarget,
    DWORD fdwAccess,
    BOOL fInherit,
    DWORD fdwOptions);
```

Usually this function is used to create a new process-relative handle from an object handle that is relative to another process. You pass the handle of the existing object in the *hSource* parameter, and you pass the handle of the process that this object is relative to in the *hSourceProcess* parameter. You pass the handle that identifies the process that should get the new handle in the *hTargetProcess* parameter. In the fourth parameter, *lphTarget*, you must pass the address of a HANDLE variable. DuplicateHandle fills this variable with the new handle. This new handle identifies the same object that the *hSource* parameter identifies, but the new handle is relative to the process identified by the *hTargetProcess* parameter. In other words, only the process identified by the *hProcess* parameter can use the object identified by the *hSourceProcess* parameter, and only the process identified by the *hTarget* parameter can use the object identified by the *lphTarget* parameter. The remaining three parameters allow you to specify how the new handle can be accessed, whether the new handle is inheritable by child processes of the target process, and whether the original object should be closed automatically. (See the *Win32 Programmer's Reference* for more information about the DuplicateHandle function.)

We can use the DuplicateHandle function in an unusual way to correct the code fragment discussed earlier. The corrected code fragment is on the following page.

```
DWORD WINAPI ParentThread (LPVOID lpvThreadParm) {
    DWORD IDThread;
    HANDLE hThread;

    DuplicateHandle(
    GetCurrentProcess(),      // Handle of process that thread
                              // pseudo-handle is relative to.
    GetCurrentThread(),       // Parent thread's pseudo-handle.

    GetCurrentProcess(),      // Handle of process that new,
                              // "real" thread handle is relative to.
    &hThread,                 // Will receive the new,
                              // "real" handle identifying
                              // the parent's thread.
    0,                        // Ignored because of
                              // DUPLICATE_SAME_ACCESS.
    FALSE,                    // New thread handle is not
                              // inheritable.
    DUPLICATE_SAME_ACCESS);   // New thread handle has same
                              // access as pseudo-handle.

    CreateThread(NULL, 0, ChildThread, hThread, 0, &IDThread);
    // Function continues...
}

DWORD WINAPI ChildThread (LPVOID lpvThreadParm) {
    HANDLE hParentThread = (HANDLE) lpvThreadParm;
    SetThreadPriority(hParentThread, THREAD_PRIORITY_NORMAL);
    CloseHandle(hParentThread);
    // Function continues...
}
```

Now when the parent thread executes, it converts the ambiguous pseudo-handle identifying the parent thread to a new, "real" handle that unambiguously identifies the parent thread, and it passes this "real" handle to CreateThread. When the child thread starts executing, its *lpvThreadParm* parameter contains the "real" thread handle. Any calls to functions, passing this handle, will now affect the parent thread, not the child thread.

It is very important to note that handles created by calling the DuplicateHandle function must be closed by calling CloseHandle. This is demonstrated in the code fragment above. Immediately after the call to SetThreadPriority, the child thread calls CloseHandle to decrement the parent thread object's usage count. In the code fragment above, I assumed that the child thread would not call any other functions using this handle. If other functions are to be called passing the parent thread's handle, the call to CloseHandle should not be made until the handle is no longer required by the child thread.

I should also point out that the DuplicateHandle function can be used to convert a pseudo-handle for a process to a "real" process handle as follows:

```
HANDLE hProcess;
DuplicateHandle(
    GetCurrentProcess(),       // Handle of process that process
                               // pseudo-handle is relative to.
    GetCurrentProcess(),       // Process's pseudo-handle.
    GetCurrentProcess(),       // Handle of process that new,
                               // "real" process handle is
                               // relative to.
    &hProcess,                 // Will receive the new, "real"
                               // handle identifying the process.
    0,                         // Ignored because of
                               // DUPLICATE_SAME_ACCESS.
    FALSE,                     // New thread handle is not
                               // inheritable.
    DUPLICATE_SAME_ACCESS);    // New process handle has same
                               // access as pseudo-handle.
    .
    .
    .
```

How Windows NT Schedules Threads

As Windows NT runs, it schedules time slices to all the active threads. If the machine has more than one CPU, Windows NT assigns one waiting thread to one CPU and another waiting thread to another CPU until all the CPUs are executing threads. Earlier I said that only active threads are allowed to run. But frequently threads are *suspended*, or not active. A thread can become suspended in a number of ways. For example, the primary thread of a process is suspended if the process was created using the CREATE_SUSPENDED flag mentioned earlier. Threads are also suspended when they call GetMessage and no messages are available in the thread's queue. Windows NT never assigns a suspended thread to a CPU until that thread is somehow *resumed*.

A thread that is suspended because no window messages are available is resumed by the system as soon as a message appears in that thread's queue. Later in this chapter, we'll discuss other ways that threads can be suspended and resumed.

Threads are assigned priorities. Priorities range from 1 to 31, with 31 representing the highest priority. When the Windows NT Kernel assigns a thread to a CPU, it treats all threads of the same priority as equal. That is, it simply assigns the first thread of priority 31 to a CPU, and after the thread's time slice is finished, it assigns the next priority 31 thread to the CPU. When all the priority 31 threads have had a time slice, the Windows NT Kernel assigns the first priority 31 thread back to the CPU. Note that if you always have at least one priority 31 thread for each CPU, other threads having priorities less than 31 are never assigned to a CPU and therefore never execute. This is called *starvation*. Starvation occurs when some threads are using so much of the CPU's time that other threads never execute.

So how do lower-priority threads get a chance to execute? Most threads in the system do get suspended from time to time. For example, if your application calls GetMessage and if GetMessage determines that there are no messages for you to process, it puts the thread to sleep. When a message does need processing, Windows NT wakes up the thread, allowing GetMessage to return, which causes the message to be processed.

When all the priority 31 threads are sleeping, the Kernel assigns any priority 30 threads to the available CPUs in the system. Naturally, it follows that priority 29 threads can execute only when both priority 31 and 30 threads are sleeping. You're probably thinking that threads with the priority of 1 will almost never get a chance to execute. But, in fact, most of the threads spend their time sleeping, allowing threads at all priority levels to run; some threads simply get to run more frequently than others.

Let me point out another issue here. If a priority 5 thread is running, and it creates a priority 6 thread, the system immediately halts the priority 5 thread, stealing from the thread any time remaining in its time slice. (This assumes that the new priority 6 thread is not created in the suspended state.) The system then assigns a full-time slice to the new priority 6 thread. This happens only when a thread creates a new thread that has a higher priority than its own. If the priority 5 thread creates another priority 5 (or lower) thread, the system allows the currently running priority 5 thread to complete its time slice.

When you create threads, you don't assign them priorities using numbers. Instead, the system determines the thread's priority number by using a two-step process. The first step is to assign a priority class to a process. A process's priority class tells Windows NT the priority required by the process compared to other running processes. The second step is to assign relative priority levels to threads owned by the process. The following sections discuss both steps.

Process Priority Classes

Windows NT supports four different priority classes: idle, normal, high and realtime. You assign a priority class to a process by *OR*ing one of the CreateProcess flags listed in the table below with the other *fdwCreate* flags when calling CreateProcess. The table below shows the priority number associated with each priority class:

Class	CreateProcess Flag	Level
Idle	IDLE_PRIORITY_CLASS	4
Normal	NORMAL_PRIORITY_CLASS	9 / 7
High	HIGH_PRIORITY_CLASS	13
Realtime	REALTIME_PRIORITY_CLASS	24

This means that any thread created by a process whose priority class is idle has the priority number 4.

I can't stress enough how important it is to select a priority class for your process carefully. When calling CreateProcess, most applications should either not specify a priority class or use the NORMAL_PRIORITY_CLASS flag. When you don't specify a priority class, the system assumes normal priority class unless the parent process has an idle priority class. In this case, the child process also has the idle priority class.

As you can see from the table above, a process running at normal priority can have two different levels—9 or 7. When the process is running in the foreground, its level is 9. When the process is running in the background, its level is 7.

39

When Windows NT combines the process's priority class with the individual thread's relative priority level, the result is the base priority number for the thread. Windows NT can dynamically alter a thread's priority number depending on whether the process runs in the foreground or in the background. When the user switches from using one process to using another, the newly active process becomes the foreground process, and the process that was exited becomes a background process. If the process that's becoming the foreground process has normal priority, Windows NT gives the process a boost by raising its priority class number from 7 to 9, which causes the process to behave more responsively to the user than the background processes do. Raising and lowering the priority for foreground or background processes is done only to processes running at normal priority.

Idle priority is perfect for system-monitoring applications. For example, you might write an application that periodically displays the amount of free physical memory on the system. Because you would not want this application to interfere with the performance of other applications in the system, you would set this process's priority class to IDLE_PRIORITY_CLASS.

Another good example of an application that can use idle priority is a screen saver. Most of the time, a screen saver simply monitors actions from the user. When the user is idle for a specified period of time, the screen saver activates itself. There is no reason to have the screen saver monitoring the user's actions at a very high priority, so the perfect priority for this process is idle priority.

High priority class should be used only when absolutely necessary. You probably wouldn't guess this, but the Task Manager (TASKMAN.EXE) runs at high priority. Most of the time, the Task Manager's thread is suspended, waiting to be awakened by the user pressing Ctrl+Esc. While the Task Manager's thread is suspended, Windows NT doesn't assign it to any CPU for processing, which allows lower-priority threads to execute. However, once the user does press Ctrl+Esc, Windows NT wakes up the Task Manager's thread. If any threads that have a lower priority level are executing, Windows NT preempts those threads immediately and allows the Task Manager to run. The Task Manager responds by displaying a dialog box that lists all the running applications.

Microsoft designed the Task Manager in this way because users expect the Task Manager to be extremely responsive, regardless of what else is going on in the system.

The Task Manager is very well-behaved. Most of the time it simply sits idle, not requiring any CPU time at all. If this were not the case, the whole system would perform much more slowly, and many applications would not respond.

The REALTIME_PRIORITY_CLASS flag should almost never be used. In fact, earlier betas of the Win32 API did not expose this priority class to applications even though it was part of the Windows NT Kernel. Realtime priority is extremely high, and because most threads execute at a lower priority, they will be affected by a process with this class. In fact, the threads in the system that control the mouse and the keyboard, background disk flushing, and Ctrl+Alt+Del trapping all operate at a lower priority class than realtime priority. If the user is moving the mouse, the thread responding to the mouse's movement will be pre-empted by a realtime thread. This affects the movement of the mouse, causing it to move jerkily rather than smoothly. Even more serious consequences can occur, such as loss of data.

Altering a Process's Priority Class

It might seem odd to you that the process that creates a child process chooses the priority class at which the child process runs. Let's consider the Program Manager as an example. When you run an application from the Program Manager, the Program Manager runs the process at normal priority. The Program Manager has no idea what the process does or how quickly it needs to operate. However, once the child process is running, it can change its own priority class by calling SetPriorityClass:

```
BOOL SetPriorityClass(HANDLE hProcess, DWORD fdwPriority);
```

This function changes the priority class identified by *hProcess* to the value specified in the *fdwPriority* parameter. The *fdwPriority* parameter can be only one of the following: IDLE_PRIORITY_CLASS, NORMAL-_PRIORITY_CLASS, HIGH_PRIORITY_CLASS, or REALTIME-_PRIORITY_CLASS. If the function succeeds, the return value is TRUE; otherwise, it's FALSE. Because this function takes a process handle, you can alter the priority class of any process running in the system as long as you have a handle to it and ample security rights.

The complementary function used to retrieve the priority class of a process is:

```
DWORD GetPriorityClass(HANDLE hProcess);
```

As you might expect, this function returns one of the flags listed on the previous page.

You can invoke a program using the command shell instead of using the Program Manager. Doing so causes the program to start using normal priority. However, if you invoke the program using the START command, you can use a switch to specify the starting priority of the application. For example, the following command entered at the command shell causes the system to invoke the Calculator and initially run it at low priority:

```
C:\> START /LOW CALC.EXE
```

The START command also recognizes the /NORMAL, /HIGH, and /REALTIME switches to start executing an application at normal priority (also the default), high priority, and realtime priority, respectively. Of course, once an application starts executing, it can call Set-PriorityClass to alter its own priority to whatever it chooses.

Setting a Thread's Relative Priority

Once a thread has been created, it runs at the priority-class level of the process that owns it. However, it is possible to raise or lower the priority of an individual thread. A thread's priority is always relative to the priority class of the process that owns it. So it is impossible to have one thread running at idle priority and another thread running at normal priority if both threads are part of the same process. If your application requires this, you'll need to break the application into two processes and use interprocess communication techniques to allow the two processes to converse.

You can change a thread's relative priority within a single process by calling SetThreadPriority:

```
BOOL SetThreadPriority(HANDLE hThread, int nPriority);
```

The first parameter is the handle to the thread whose priority class you're changing. The *nPriority* parameter can be one of the following values:

Identifier	Meaning
THREAD_PRIORITY_LOWEST	The thread's priority should be 2 less than the process's priority class.
THREAD_PRIORITY_BELOW_NORMAL	The thread's priority should be 1 less than the process's priority class.
THREAD_PRIORITY_NORMAL	The thread's priority should be the same as the process's priority class.
THREAD_PRIORITY_ABOVE_NORMAL	The thread's priority should be 1 more than the process's priority class.
THREAD_PRIORITY_HIGHEST	The thread's priority should be 2 more than the process's priority class.

When a thread is first created, its initial value is THREAD-_PRIORITY_NORMAL. The rules for threads within a process are similar to the rules for threads across processes. You should set a thread's priority to THREAD_PRIORITY_HIGHEST only when it is absolutely necessary in order for the thread to execute correctly. The scheduler will starve lower-priority threads if higher-priority threads require execution.

In addition to the above flags, two special flags can be passed to SetThreadPriority: THREAD_PRIORITY_IDLE and THREAD_PRI-ORITY_TIME_CRITICAL. Specifying THREAD_PRIORITY_IDLE causes the thread's priority level to be set to 1 regardless of whether the priority class for the process is idle, normal, or high. However, if the priority class for the process is realtime, THREAD_PRIORITY_IDLE sets the thread's priority level to 16. Specifying THREAD_PRIORITY-_TIME_CRITICAL causes the thread's priority level to be set to 15 regardless of whether the priority class for the process is idle, normal, or high. However, if the priority class for the process is realtime, THREAD_PRIORITY_TIME_CRITICAL sets the thread's priority level to 31. Figure 1-2 on the following page shows how the system combines a process's priority class with a thread's relative priority to determine a thread's base priority level.

Process Priority Class

Relative Thread Priority	Idle	Normal, in Background	Normal, in Foreground	High	Realtime
Time critical	15	15	15	15	31
Highest	6	9	11	15	26
Above normal	5	8	10	14	25
Normal	4	7	9	13	24
Below normal	3	6	8	12	23
Lowest	2	5	7	11	22
Idle	1	1	1	1	16

Figure 1-2.
How the system determines a thread's base priority level.

The complementary function to SetThreadPriority—GetThreadPriority—can be used to query a thread's relative priority:

```
int GetThreadPriority(HANDLE hThread);
```

The return value is one of the identifiers listed above or THREAD-_PRIORITY_ERROR_RETURN if an error occurs.

Changing a process's priority class has no effect on any of its thread's relative priorities. A thread's priority can change as it executes. The system can bump or boost a thread's priority to a higher level and slowly decrease the thread's priority as time goes on. Windows NT never decreases a thread's priority lower than its base priority.

A thread's priority is boosted when a user interacts directly with that thread. For example, when a user presses a key on the keyboard, the system determines which thread is to receive this hardware event. After the event is placed in that thread's queue, Windows NT boosts the dynamic priority of every thread in the owning process, which gives much livelier feedback to the user. When a message is sent or posted, the priority of the thread that needs to process the message is also boosted. Windows NT also raises the priority level of the process in the foreground. The new priority stays in effect until the user puts another process in the foreground.

Suspending and Resuming Threads

Earlier I mentioned that a thread can be created in a suspended state. The Windows NT Executive's thread object exists, and the thread's stack has been created; the thread simply doesn't execute any code. To allow the thread to begin execution, another thread must call ResumeThread and pass it the thread handle returned by the call to CreateThread (or the thread handle from the structure pointed to by the *lppiProcInfo* parameter passed to CreateProcess):

```
DWORD ResumeThread(HANDLE hThread);
```

If ResumeThread is successful, it returns the thread's previous suspend count.

A single thread can be suspended several times. If a thread is suspended three times, the thread must be resumed three times before it is eligible for assignment to a CPU. Aside from using the CREATE_SUSPENDED flag when creating a thread, you can suspend a thread by calling SuspendThread:

```
DWORD SuspendThread(HANDLE hThread);
```

This function can be called by any thread to suspend another thread. It goes without saying (but I'll say it anyway) that a thread can suspend itself but it cannot resume itself. Like ResumeThread, SuspendThread returns the thread's previous suspend count. A thread can be suspended as many as MAXIMUM_SUSPEND_COUNT times (defined as 127 in WINNT.H).

Child Processes

When you design an application, situations might arise in which you want another block of code to perform work. You assign work like this all the time by calling functions in threads. When you call a function, your code cannot continue processing until the function has returned. And in many situations, this synchronization is needed.

Another way to have another block of code perform work is to create a new thread within your process and have it help with the processing. This allows your code to continue processing while the other thread performs the work you requested. This technique is useful, but it creates synchronization problems when your thread needs to see the results of the new thread.

Another approach is to spawn off a new process—a child process—to help with the work. Let's say that the work you need to do is pretty complex. To process the work, you decide to simply create a new thread within the same process. You write some code, test it, and get some incorrect results. You might have an error in your algorithm, or maybe you dereferenced something incorrectly and accidentally over-wrote something important in your address space. One way to protect your address space while having the work processed is to have a new process perform the work. You could then wait for the new process to terminate before continuing on with your own work, or you could continue working while the new process works.

Unfortunately, the new process probably needs to perform operations on data contained in your address space. In this case, it might be a good idea to have the process run in its own address space and simply give it access to the relevant data contained in the parent process's address space, thus protecting all the data not relevant to the job. Windows NT gives you several different methods for transferring data between different processes: DDE, OLE, Pipes, Mailslots, etc. One of the most convenient ways to share the data is to use memory-mapped files, which is discussed in detail in Chapter 4.

If you want to create a new process, have it do some work, and wait for the result, you can use code similar to the following:

```
PROCESS_INFORMATION ProcessInformation;
DWORD dwExitCode;

BOOL fSuccess = CreateProcess(..., &ProcessInformation);
if (fSuccess) {
   HANDLE hProcess = ProcessInformation.hProcess;

   // Close the thread handle as soon as it is no longer needed!
   CloseHandle(ProcessInformation.hThread);

   if (WaitForSingleObject(hProcess, INFINITE) != WAIT_FAILED) {
      // The process terminated.
      fExist = GetExitCodeProcess(hProcess, &dwExitCode);
   }

   // Close the process handle as soon as it is no longer needed.
   CloseHandle(hProcess);
}
```

In the code fragment above, you create the new process and, if successful, call the WaitForSingleObject function:

```
DWORD WaitForSingleObject(HANDLE hObject, DWORD dwTimeout);
```

The WaitForSingleObject function is a function that we'll discuss exhaustively in Chapter 5. But, for now, all you need to know is that it waits until the object identified by the *hObject* parameter becomes *signaled*. Process objects become signaled when they terminate. So the call to WaitForSingleObject suspends the parent's thread until the child process terminates. After WaitForSingleObject returns, you can get the exit code of the child process by calling GetExitCodeProcess.

The calls to CloseHandle in the code fragment above cause Windows NT to decrement the usage count for the thread and process objects to 0 (zero), allowing the objects' memory to be freed.

You'll notice that in the code fragment, I close the handle to the child process's primary thread immediately after CreateProcess returns. Here's why this is a good practice: Suppose that the child process's primary thread spawns off another thread and then the primary thread terminates. In this case, if the parent process didn't have an outstanding handle to this object, Windows NT could free the child's primary thread object from its memory. But because the parent process does, Windows NT can't free the object until the parent process closes the handle.

Running Detached Child Processes

Most of the time, an application starts another process as a *detached process*. This means that after the process is created and executing, the parent process doesn't need to communicate with the new process or doesn't require that the child process complete its work before the parent process continues. This is how the Program Manager works. After the Program Manager creates a new process for the user, it doesn't care whether that process continues to live or whether the user terminates it.

To give up all ties to the child process, the Program Manager must release its handles to the new process and its primary thread by calling CloseHandle. The code sample below shows how to create a new process and how to let it run detached:

```
PROCESS_INFORMATION ProcessInformation;
BOOL fSuccess = CreateProcess(..., &ProcessInformation);
if (fSuccess) {
   CloseHandle(ProcessInformation.hThread);
   CloseHandle(ProcessInformation.hProcess);
}
```

What's Going On in the System

Two utilities that ship with the Win32 SDK for Windows NT—PSTAT.EXE and PVIEW.EXE—tell you which processes are loaded in the system and which threads exist in each process. Figure 1-3 shows a dump from the PSTAT.EXE application. It lists all the processes and threads currently running in the system. The *pid* field shows the process ID for each process. For example, the process ID for the Program Manager (PROGMAN.EXE) is 0xA0. The *pri* field to the right of the process ID shows the priority class value for the process. The Program Manager's priority value is 13, indicating that it has high priority.

Under each process is a list of threads owned by that process. The Event Log (EVENTLOG.EXE) has four threads. For each thread, the *tid* field shows the ID of the thread. The *pri* field indicates the priority number of the thread. The *cs* field shows the number of context switches for the thread. The status of the thread is shown at the end of the line. The word *Wait* indicates that the thread is suspended and is waiting for an event to occur before it can resume execution. The reason for the wait is also included.

```
Pstat version 0.2:  memory: 20032 kb  uptime:  0  2:30:10.575

PageFile: \DosDevices\F:\pagefile.sys
   Current Size:  32768 kb  Total Used:   8764 kb
   Peak Used  9680 kb

pid:  0 pri: 0 (null)
    tid:  0 pri:16 cs: 188262 Running

pid:  7 pri: 8 (null)
    tid:  8 pri: 0 cs:       433 Wait:FreePage
    tid:  6 pri:16 cs:       579 Wait:Executive
    tid:  5 pri:12 cs:       656 Wait:Executive
    tid:  4 pri:16 cs:       624 Wait:Executive
    tid:  3 pri:12 cs:       531 Wait:Executive
    tid:  2 pri:16 cs:       613 Wait:Executive
    tid:  1 pri:12 cs:       488 Wait:Executive
    tid: 28 pri:16 cs:       598 Wait:Executive
    tid: 27 pri:12 cs:       540 Wait:Executive
    tid: 26 pri:16 cs:       556 Wait:Executive
```

Figure 1-3.   *(continued)*
Output from the PSTAT.EXE application.

Figure 1-3. *continued*

```
    tid: 25 pri:12 cs:      546 Wait:Executive
    tid: 24 pri:18 cs:      260 Wait:VirtualMemory
    tid: 23 pri:17 cs:      212 Wait:FreePage
    tid: 22 pri:16 cs:     8992 Wait:Executive
    tid: 21 pri:16 cs:    16814 Wait:Executive
    tid: 20 pri:16 cs:        1 Wait:Executive
    tid: 1f pri:16 cs:        1 Wait:UserRequest
    tid: 1e pri:16 cs:        1 Wait:UserRequest
    tid: 1d pri:11 cs:        5 Wait:LpcReceive
    tid: 17 pri:17 cs:        1 Wait:VirtualMemory
    tid: 7c pri:16 cs:       20 Wait:Executive

pid: 1b pri:11 SMSS.EXE
    tid: 1c pri:13 cs:      344 Wait:UserRequest
    tid: 1a pri:13 cs:        7 Wait:LpcReceive
    tid: 19 pri:12 cs:        5 Wait:LpcReceive
    tid: 18 pri:13 cs:       13 Wait:Executive
    tid: 16 pri:12 cs:        5 Wait:LpcReceive
    tid: 15 pri:12 cs:        5 Wait:Executive
    tid: 14 pri:12 cs:        5 Wait:LpcReceive
    tid: 13 pri:13 cs:        6 Wait:Executive
    tid: 12 pri:12 cs:        5 Wait:LpcReceive

pid: 10 pri:11 CSRSS.EXE
    tid:  f pri:20 cs:     5765 Wait:UserRequest
    tid:  e pri:12 cs:       22 Wait:UserRequest
    tid:  d pri:11 cs:       34 Wait:Executive
    tid:  c pri:12 cs:      300 Wait:LpcReceive
    tid:  b pri:12 cs:      325 Wait:LpcReceive
    tid:  a pri:12 cs:      314 Wait:LpcReceive
    tid:  9 pri:12 cs:      292 Wait:LpcReceive
    tid: 48 pri:12 cs:        5 Wait:LpcReceive
    tid: 47 pri:12 cs:        7 Wait:LpcReceive
    tid: 38 pri:13 cs:      946 Wait:UserRequest
    tid: 37 pri:19 cs:   168639 Wait:UserRequest
    tid: 36 pri:12 cs:        9 Wait:UserRequest
    tid: 35 pri:31 cs:      903 Wait:UserRequest
    tid: 31 pri:12 cs:       12 Wait:EventPairLow
    tid: 53 pri:13 cs:       48 Wait:UserRequest
    tid: 4c pri:12 cs:       52 Wait:UserRequest
    tid: a6 pri:13 cs:       44 Wait:UserRequest
    tid: 6e pri:12 cs:       65 Wait:UserRequest
    tid: 6d pri:11 cs:      474 Wait:UserRequest
```

(continued)

Figure 1-3. *continued*

```
    tid: 9d pri:14 cs:   13863 Wait:UserRequest
    tid: 9c pri:12 cs:      98 Wait:UserRequest
    tid: a5 pri:12 cs:       6 Wait:EventPairLow
    tid: 69 pri:12 cs:       7 Wait:EventPairLow
    tid: a4 pri:12 cs:4574710 Wait:UserRequest
    tid: 97 pri:13 cs:   46430 Wait:UserRequest

pid: 45 pri: 8 OS2SS.EXE
    tid: 44 pri: 9 cs:       5 Wait:LpcReceive

pid: 42 pri: 8 PSXSS.EXE
    tid: 41 pri:10 cs:       6 Wait:LpcReceive
    tid: 40 pri:10 cs:       6 Wait:Executive
    tid: 3f pri:10 cs:       6 Wait:LpcReceive
    tid: 3e pri:10 cs:       6 Wait:Executive
    tid: 3d pri: 9 cs:       5 Wait:LpcReceive
    tid: 3c pri: 9 cs:       7 Wait:UserRequest

pid: 3a pri:13 WINLOGON.EXE
    tid: 3b pri:15 cs:     907 Wait:EventPairHigh
    tid: 39 pri:15 cs:       6 Wait:UserRequest

pid: 33 pri: 7 SCREG.EXE
    tid: 34 pri: 8 cs:     313 Wait:UserRequest
    tid: 32 pri: 8 cs:      17 Wait:DelayExecution
    tid: 30 pri: 8 cs:       8 Wait:UserRequest
    tid: 5d pri: 8 cs:     213 Wait:UserRequest

pid: 2e pri: 8 LSASS.EXE
    tid: 29 pri:10 cs:       6 Wait:LpcReceive
    tid: 2d pri:10 cs:     120 Wait:UserRequest
    tid: 68 pri:10 cs:      15 Wait:Executive
    tid: 67 pri: 9 cs:      18 Wait:LpcReceive
    tid: 66 pri: 9 cs:      34 Wait:LpcReceive
    tid: 65 pri:10 cs:      14 Wait:Executive
    tid: 63 pri:10 cs:      22 Wait:UserRequest

pid: 2c pri: 8 SPOOLSS.EXE
    tid: 2a pri: 7 cs:      58 Wait:DelayExecution
    tid: 71 pri: 8 cs:      12 Wait:UserRequest
    tid: 70 pri: 8 cs:      11 Wait:UserRequest
    tid: 99 pri:10 cs:      66 Wait:UserRequest

pid: 60 pri: 8 EVENTLOG.EXE
    tid: 61 pri:10 cs:      21 Wait:Executive
```

(continued)

Figure 1-3. *continued*

```
    tid: 5c pri:11 cs:     94 Wait:UserRequest
    tid: 5b pri:10 cs:      7 Wait:Executive
    tid: 5a pri:10 cs:     15 Wait:UserRequest

pid: 58 pri: 8 NETDDE.EXE
    tid: 59 pri:10 cs:     34 Wait:Executive
    tid: 5e pri: 9 cs:     18 Wait:UserRequest
    tid: 57 pri: 9 cs:      7 Wait:UserRequest
    tid: 56 pri:10 cs:     17 Wait:UserRequest
    tid: 55 pri:10 cs:     14 Wait:UserRequest
    tid: 54 pri: 9 cs:     79 Wait:EventPairHigh
    tid: 5f pri:11 cs:      7 Wait:UserRequest

pid: 51 pri: 8 (null)
    tid: 52 pri:15 cs:     49 Wait:UserRequest
    tid: 86 pri: 9 cs:      1 Wait:UserRequest
    tid: 85 pri: 9 cs:      1 Wait:UserRequest
    tid: 84 pri: 9 cs:      1 Wait:UserRequest
    tid: 83 pri: 9 cs:      1 Wait:UserRequest
    tid: 82 pri: 9 cs:      1 Wait:UserRequest
    tid: 81 pri: 9 cs:    300 Wait:UserRequest
    tid: 80 pri:11 cs:     31 Wait:FreePage

pid: 4f pri: 8 CLIPSRV.EXE
    tid: 50 pri:10 cs:     23 Wait:Executive
    tid: 4e pri: 9 cs:     77 Wait:EventPairHigh

pid: 4a pri: 8 LMSVCS.EXE
    tid: 4b pri:10 cs:     27 Wait:Executive
    tid: 49 pri:11 cs:    154 Wait:UserRequest
    tid: 88 pri:10 cs:     60 Wait:UserRequest
    tid: 7f pri:10 cs:      6 Wait:LpcReceive
    tid: 7e pri:10 cs:      6 Wait:LpcReceive
    tid: 7d pri:10 cs:      6 Wait:LpcReceive
    tid: 7b pri:10 cs:     22 Wait:UserRequest
    tid: 7a pri:10 cs:     57 Wait:UserRequest
    tid: 79 pri:10 cs:     83 Wait:UserRequest
    tid: 87 pri: 9 cs:      5 Wait:UserRequest
    tid: 6f pri:10 cs:      7 Wait:UserRequest

pid: 77 pri: 8 MSGSVC.EXE
    tid: 78 pri:10 cs:     22 Wait:Executive
```

(continued)

Figure 1-3. *continued*

```
     tid: 76 pri:10 cs:      51 Wait:UserRequest
     tid: 75 pri:10 cs:       7 Wait:UserRequest
     tid: 74 pri:10 cs:       6 Wait:UserRequest
     tid: 73 pri:10 cs:      11 Wait:UserRequest
     tid: 72 pri:11 cs:      11 Wait:UserRequest

pid: a7 pri: 8 NDDEAGNT.EXE
     tid: a8 pri:10 cs:      60 Wait:EventPairHigh

pid: a2 pri:13 TASKMAN.EXE
     tid: a3 pri:15 cs:      77 Wait:EventPairHigh

pid: a0 pri:13 PROGMAN.EXE
     tid: a1 pri:14 cs:   16233 Wait:EventPairHigh

pid: 9e pri: 7 NTVDM.EXE
     tid: 9f pri: 7 cs:     450 Wait:EventPairHigh
     tid: 9b pri: 7 cs:      21 Wait:UserRequest
     tid: 9a pri: 7 cs: 248664 Ready
     tid: 4d pri: 9 cs:      13 Wait:UserRequest
     tid: 64 pri:12 cs:4587766 Wait:EventPairHigh

pid: 2b pri: 7 WINHLP32.EXE
     tid: 98 pri: 8 cs:   45151 Wait:EventPairHigh

pid: 90 pri: 9 CMD.EXE
     tid: 8e pri:11 cs:     282 Wait:UserRequest

pid: 8d pri: 9 PSTAT.EXE
     tid: 8f pri:12 cs:       6 Running
```

Figure 1-4 shows how the PVIEW utility appears when you first execute it.

The *Process* list box lists all the processes running in the system. Listed to the right of each process is the amount of CPU time the process has used since it was started and the percentage of that time spent in privileged mode (the Windows NT Executive's code) versus user mode (the application's code). When you select a process, PVIEW updates the *Priority* group's radio buttons and fills the *Thread(s)* list box with a list of all the threads owned by the selected process, the amount of CPU time used by the thread, and the percentage of its time spent in privileged mode versus user mode. When you select a thread, PVIEW updates the *Thread Priority* group's radio buttons.

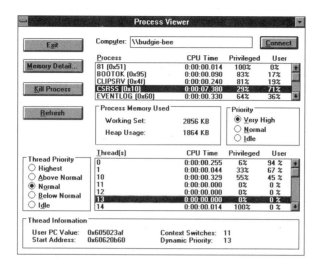

Figure 1-4.
The PVIEW utility.

Processes, Threads, and the C Runtime Library

Microsoft ships three C Runtime libraries in the Windows NT SDK. The table below lists the names of the libraries and their descriptions:

Library Name	Description
LIBC.LIB	Statically linked library for single-threaded applications.
LIBCMT.LIB	Statically linked library for multithreaded applications.
CRTDLL.LIB	Import library for dynamically linking the CRTDLL.DLL library. This library supports both single-threaded and multithreaded applications.

The first question you're probably asking yourself is "Why do I need one library for single-threaded applications and an additional library for multithreaded applications?" The reason is that the Standard

C Runtime Library was invented around 1970, long before threads became available. The inventors of the Library didn't consider the problems of using the C Runtime Library with multithreaded applications.

Consider, for example, the standard C Runtime global variable *errno*. Some functions set this variable when an error occurs. Let's say you have the following code fragment:

```
BOOL fFailure = (system("NOTEPAD.EXE README.TXT") == -1);

if (fFailure) {
   switch (errno) {
   case E2BIG:     // Argument list or environment too big.
      break;

   case ENOENT:    // Command interpreter cannot be found.
      break;

   case ENOEXEC:   // Command interpreter has bad format.
      break;

   case ENOMEM:    // Insufficient memory to run command.
      break;
   }
}
```

Now let's imagine that the thread executing the code above is interrupted after the call to the system and before the *if* statement. Let's further imagine that the thread is being interrupted to allow a second thread in the same process to execute and that this new thread will execute another C Runtime function that sets the global variable *errno*. When the CPU is later assigned back to the first thread, the value of *errno* no longer reflects the proper error code for the call to system above. To solve this problem, you need to assign each thread its very own *errno* variable.

This is only one example of how the Standard C Runtime Library was not designed for multithreaded applications—many other examples exist. Somehow you need to inform the Standard C Runtime Library that you're executing a multithreaded application so that a set of C Runtime instance data can be assigned to each thread. Here's how you can do this.

Whenever you call a C Runtime function that needs access to thread instance data, an internal C Runtime function is called. The internal function gets the current thread ID and maps it to the thread instance data. If the instance data hasn't been created yet, the internal function initializes it at this time. You might be wondering how this works for a global variable like *errno*. Well, *errno* is defined in the standard C headers like this:

```
#ifdef _MT
extern int * _errno(void);
#define errno          (*_errno())
#else
extern int errno;
#endif
```

If you're creating a multithreaded application, you need to specify the /MT switch on the compiler's command line. This causes the compiler to define the _MT identifier. Then, whenever you reference *errno*, you are actually making a call to the internal C Runtime Library function *_errno*. This function maps the current thread ID to the instance data and returns the value of the thread's very own *errno*. You'll also notice that the internal function *_errno* actually returns the address of the *errno* variable rather than the variable itself. This is necessary because it's possible to write code like this:

```
int *p = &errno;
if (*p == ENOMEM) {
  .
  .
  .
}
```

If the internal *_errno* function simply returned the value of *errno*, the above code wouldn't compile.

The multithreaded version of the C Runtime Library also places synchronization primitives around certain functions. For example, if two threads simultaneously call *malloc*, the heap could possibly become corrupted. The multithreaded version of the C Runtime Library prevents two threads from allocating memory from the heap at the same time. It does this by making the second thread wait until the first has returned from *malloc*. Then the second thread is allowed to enter. Synchronization is discussed in more detail in Chapter 5.

Obviously, the performance of the multithreaded version of the C Runtime Library is impacted by all this additional work. This is why Microsoft supplies the single-threaded version of the statically linked C Runtime Library in addition to the multithreaded version.

The dynamically linked version of the C Runtime Library was written to be generic so that it can be shared by any and all running applications that use the C Runtime Library functions. For this reason, the library exists only in a multithreaded version. Because the C Runtime Library is supplied in a DLL, applications (EXE files) don't need to include the code for the C Runtime Library function and are smaller as a result. Also, if Microsoft fixes a bug in the C Runtime Library DLL, applications will automatically gain the fix as well.

The C Runtime Library can create and associate its thread instance data with a thread at runtime, but there is one thing that the C Runtime Library cannot do after the thread has been created. If your thread is going to call the C Runtime's *signal* function, you must call the C Runtime function *_beginthread* to create a thread instead of the Win32 CreateThread function:

```
unsigned long _beginthread(void (*start_address)(void *),
    unsigned stack_size, void *arglist);
```

The *start_address* parameter indicates the address of the thread function. The *stack_size* parameter indicates the size of the stack. A value of 0 (zero) tells *_beginthread* to create the stack at the size indicated in the application's EXE file. The last parameter, *arglist*, can be any value. This value is passed to the thread function as its parameter. *_beginthread* returns the handle of the thread it just created. This handle can be used in any other Win32 functions that require thread handles. The C Runtime startup code for your application prepares your application's primary thread so you can call *signal*.

Normally, a thread uses the Win32 function ExitThread to terminate itself. But you should not use ExitThread for threads created with *_beginthread*. Instead, the C Runtime Library offers this function:

```
void _endthread(void);
```

If the thread function simply returns, the *_endthread* function is called implicitly. If *_endthread* is not called to terminate a thread created with *_beginthread*, the C Runtime data for the thread isn't freed and a memory leak will occur.

If you are making C Runtime calls in your thread, I strongly suggest that you use the _beginthread function instead of CreateThread. However, you should be aware that there are four disadvantages in using _beginthread/_endthread versus CreateThread/ExitThread:

- You can't assign security attributes to the new thread.

- You can't specify the CREATE_SUSPENDED flag to create the thread in a suspended state.

- You allocate C Runtime instance data for the thread whether or not you make C Runtime function calls. This is not a great disadvantage because the C Runtime instance data is very small, weighing in at under 70 bytes.

- The _endthread function doesn't let you specify an exit code as ExitThread does.

MEMORY MANAGEMENT WITH HEAPS

The memory management scheme used by an operating system is perhaps the most important key to understanding how the operating system does what it does. When you start working with a new operating system, many questions come to mind, such as "How do I share data between two applications?" "Where does the system store the information I'm looking for?" and "How can I make my program run more efficiently?" just to name a few.

I have found that, more often then not, a good understanding of how the system manages memory can help determine the answers to these questions quickly and accurately. So this chapter explores how Windows NT manages memory for itself and for applications. It starts by introducing heap management techniques. Heaps are not implemented deep in the bowels of Windows NT; instead, they are implemented using the lower-level memory management mechanisms that exist at the core of the operating system. Rather than beginning at the lower levels of memory management and building up to the more abstract levels, this chapter and the next present the information in the opposite order.

Readers coming from a 16-bit Windows programming background will be able to draw on their previous Windows programming knowledge to understand these new concepts. The area of heap management has changed significantly from 16-bit Windows to Windows NT, and one of the main objectives in this chapter is to present information to help you port your existing heap-related 16-bit Windows source code to use the new Win32 heap functions.

CPUs I Have Known

It's both interesting and exciting to watch advances in microcomputer architecture. The first microcomputer I ever owned was Tandy/Radio Shack's TRS-80 Model I. This computer was designed around the Z-80 microprocessor and came standard with 4 KB of RAM, although the machine could actually address up to 64 KB of memory. I can still remember how happy I was when I had earned enough money duplicating diskettes so that I could upgrade my machine to 16 KB of RAM.

When IBM introduced the IBM-PC, it had no idea of the impact it would have on the microcomputer industry. In fact, IBM was so skeptical of how well its PC would be received that the company decided to minimize its risk by utilizing hardware that was readily available instead of designing and manufacturing custom hardware. Because of this decision, IBM has been plagued almost from the beginning by many competitors making PC clones. If IBM could easily get the parts for the machines, anyone could.

Well, the PC was a big step forward because it used Intel's 8088 CPU. This 16-bit CPU allowed the processor to access as much as 1 MB of memory. But, as progress would have it, applications soon required even more than 1 MB of memory. This need to access more memory became so great a problem that several companies responded by offering various solutions.

Most of these solutions shared a common theme: to make different memory objects available in the same memory location at different times. The first of these solutions, which became known as the Expanded Memory Specification (EMS), was developed by a Lotus, Intel, and Microsoft collaboration. EMS allowed you to place a hardware card with, say, 2 MB of memory on it in your computer. The card would then be given instructions to swap various sections of the EMS memory into and out of a fixed 64-KB section of the CPU's addressable address space.

Another solution added overlay technology to applications' code segments. If segments of code had not been executed in a while, an overlay manager could overlay the code segment with another code segment from the same application. Both Borland and Microsoft offer this support today in their respective C/C++ compilers. Borland calls it VROOMM (Virtual Runtime Object-Oriented Memory Manager), and Microsoft calls it MOVE (Microsoft Overlay Virtual Environment).

In 1982, Intel introduced a new microprocessor, the 80286, which was capable of addressing up to 16 MB of memory. Unfortunately, the upper 15 MB of memory could be accessed only when the processor was set to a special mode called *protected mode* (used by 16-bit Windows). Protected mode also enabled additional features, such as virtual memory and support for the separation of tasks in a multitasking environment. For backward compatibility, the 80286 also contained *real mode,* the default mode of the processor, which allowed applications written for the 8086 to run. For years following, the 80286 was considered to be not much more than a fast 8086 because no software was developed to take advantage of its advanced features.

But the need to access more memory continued, and Microsoft soon introduced a technology that allowed applications running in real mode to access the additional memory that could be installed on 80286 machines. This technology was called the Extended Memory Specification (XMS). Applications running in real mode on an 80286 could access up to 15 MB of extended memory by making calls to functions contained in a device driver. Microsoft's implementation of this device driver is called HIMEM.SYS and is still used by 16-bit Windows today.

Once we had reached the point where the hardware and software could gain access to 16 MB of memory, it became practical to run several applications at once. This, in turn, further drove up the demand for memory. 16 MB may have been plenty for one application but not for six or seven applications running simultaneously. For this we needed a more powerful CPU with a more sophisticated memory architecture than the 80286.

Enter the 32-bit 80386. The 80386 offered several advantages over the 80286. In addition to supporting the 8086 real mode and the 16-bit protected mode of the 80286, the 80386 also offered a 32-bit protected mode and a virtual 8086 mode. The virtual 8086 mode enabled the operating system to create the illusion that several 8086 CPUs were available on the system. When in 32-bit protected mode, the operating system could instruct the 80386 to create virtual 8086 machines. Each of these virtual machines could support MS-DOS running an MS-DOS application. In fact, these applications could be preemptively multitasked by the 80386. The virtual 8086 mode was extremely important because it allowed a migration path for users. They could use the added benefits of 32-bit protected mode without having to give up all their current MS-DOS applications. Plus, they had the advantage of being able to run multiple MS-DOS applications concurrently.

I have neglected to say how much memory can be addressed by the 80386 in 32-bit protected mode (the mode used by Windows NT). The answer is a whopping 4 GB. Not only is it 4 GB, but each application running in this mode has its own 4-GB address space, which should be more than enough memory for even the most demanding of applications. The only problem is that memory isn't free. To purchase 4 GB of memory would cost approximately $204,800 at the time I'm writing this.

Most of you probably can't afford to walk up to your nearest computer store, lay this kind of money down on the counter, and push a wheelbarrow full of RAM back to your house. Besides, even if you could buy all this RAM, where would you put it? It certainly wouldn't fit in any 80386-based computer I've ever seen!

Instead, the 80386 was designed to support a technique called *page swapping,* which Microsoft implemented in both 16-bit Windows and Windows NT. Page swapping allows portions of the hard disk to simulate RAM. Of course, the CPU needs to work on data that is actually in memory. But if some of the data hasn't been accessed in a while, the operating system can step in and copy some of that data to a location on the hard disk. After the information has been copied, the RAM that was occupied by that data can be freed and reallocated to data required for another application. When the CPU needs to access the old data, the operating system again steps in, copies another application's data to the hard disk, and pulls the earlier data back into memory. The CPU can then do its stuff.

In 1989, Intel introduced the 80486. Having satisfied the demand for addressable memory with the 80386, Intel made no major improvements to the 80486's memory architecture. Instead, the most notable feature of the 80486 was improved execution speed. As I am writing this, Intel is releasing its next-generation CPU—Pentium. Again, there are no major changes to the memory management capabilities of the chip, but execution speed is improved. The biggest difference between this processor and its predecessors is its name: Pentium instead of the 80586.

I should mention here that Microsoft has designed Windows NT to run on computers that are based on Intel's 80*x*86 chips, as well as on computers based on other CPUs. This versatility is commonly referred to as portability, which was one of the main design goals for Windows NT. As of this writing, Microsoft has implemented Windows NT on the Intel 80*x*86 CPU, the MIPS R/4000 CPU, and DEC's Alpha CPU. Because Windows NT is ported to other CPU platforms, it is possible to develop applications that run across all these platforms, expanding the potential market for Win32 applications. To port your own application from one

CPU environment to the other, you'll need only to recompile. Other issues to consider are:

- The language in which you write your application must have a compiler that you intend to target available on all platforms.

- Your application cannot use architecture-specific constructs, such as CONTEXT structures that are CPU specific. (CONTEXT structures are discussed in Chapter 10.)

- Your data must be aligned on natural boundaries. For example, DWORDS must be aligned on even 32-bit addresses and doubles must be aligned on even 64-bit addresses.

Portability is not something that just happens; you must be careful to design and implement your code to adhere to portable constructs.

The Global and Local Heap APIs

In this section, I'll discuss how 16-bit Windows manages memory with the global and local heap APIs and how the heap APIs are mapped into the Win32 world of memory management. I'll cover all the global and local heap memory management functions, but I won't offer techniques for using them because I'm assuming that you're already familiar with 16-bit Windows programming techniques. Win32 supports the 16-bit Windows memory management functions solely for easy porting from one environment to another. If you are developing a new application that you intend to be a 32-bit application and if you do not intend to compile the application natively for 16-bit Windows, I recommend that you don't use the global and local memory functions—they're slower and have more overhead than do the new Win32 heap functions discussed at the end of this chapter.

16-bit Windows manages memory with a global heap and with local heaps. The global heap includes all the available memory in the system. When an application or a dynamic-link library (DLL) is loaded into memory, space for its code segments are allocated from the global heap. Every application and DLL is also assigned a data segment from the global heap, which can be as large as 64 KB. (See Figure 2-1.) This data segment contains the local heap for the application or DLL. Since this data segment is limited to 64 KB, the types of allocations that can be made from the local heap are restricted. For example, because the

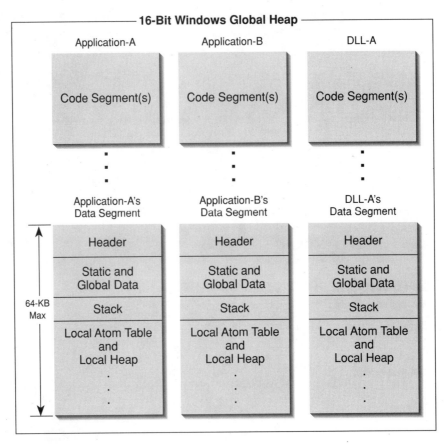

Figure 2-1.

The 16-bit Windows global heap contains applications' and DLLs' code segments, as well as a single data segment for each application and DLL.

local heap is allocated inside the data segment and the data segment cannot be larger than 64 KB, the local heap cannot be used to allocate objects that are larger than 64 KB. And the total size of all allocations made in the local heap must be less than 64 KB.

If this weren't bad enough, an application's stack is also located in the data segment. (This does not apply to DLLs, however, because they use the stack of the active task.) In 16-bit Windows, the stack must be at least 5 KB and is frequently larger. Also, any global or static variables for the application or DLL are located in the data segment.[1] And finally, any local

---

1. Some compilers allow static data to be stored in a code segment, which allows more room for data in the application's data segment.

atoms that an application or DLL might use are allocated from its data segment. So, as you can see, there isn't much memory left for the local heap.

Applications commonly make hundreds or even thousands of small allocations. It would be impossible for an application to satisfy all these allocations from the local heap. Using the global heap isn't a good solution either: Each global allocation requires several additional bytes for overhead, wasting precious memory; and 16-bit protected mode (enhanced mode) allows a maximum of only 8192 global allocations (4096 in standard mode) to be made. That's 8192 global allocations for all applications running in the system, not just for a single application.

To use memory more efficiently, many developers have been forced to implement their own memory suballocation schemes. These schemes usually allow applications to allocate a large block of memory from the global heap upon initialization and contain an algorithm for performing suballocations within this large block. This definitely seems to be a job for an operating system and not for application developers! As you might expect, none of these problems exist with Win32 under Windows NT.

In Win32, a default heap is created for each process when that process is started. (See Figure 2-2, on the following page.) This heap is accessible only to that process; no other process in the system can reference or change the contents of the heap in any way whatsoever. (This was another problem in 16-bit Windows: One application could accidentally overwrite the data maintained by another application.) The default heap is used by various Win32 functions when they need to allocate additional memory. For example, the C Runtime function *strdup* calls *malloc* to allocate a block of memory in order to make a copy of the string. This memory is allocated from the process's default heap.

In Windows NT, every process receives its very own handle table when initialized. This handle table is implemented as an array of structures. There is a major difference between 16-bit Windows global and local heap handles and Win32 global and local heap handles. In Win32, these heap handles are really pointers into a handle table that exists and is private to the process owning the heap. It's impossible to share the data in a memory block with another process. In 16-bit Windows, it is quite common for applications to send messages to other applications, passing the handle to a global block of memory. Doing this in Win32 means that you are passing the address of something that is private to your process to another process. When this other process attempts to use your handle, it will probably overwrite something in *its own* address

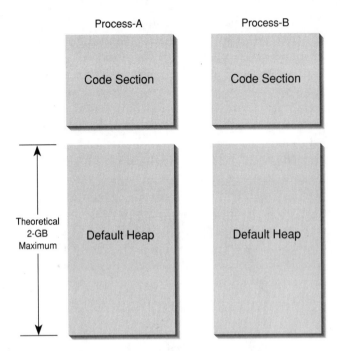

Process-A   Process-B

Code Section   Code Section

Theoretical 2-GB Maximum   Default Heap   Default Heap

Figure 2-2.
Each Win32 process has its own default heap.

space or it will cause an access violation. In either case, it most certainly will not access the data that you had intended to share. Win32 offers a different approach to sharing memory, called *memory-mapped files,* which will be discussed in Chapter 4.

Initially, Win32 allocates a small amount of memory to hold only a small number of handle table entries. As the application continues to make allocations from the handle table, additional handles may become necessary. When this happens, Win32 can increase the amount of memory used by the handle table, allowing additional handles to be allocated. The exact mechanism that Win32 uses to expand the handle table entry is called *virtual memory allocation* and is discussed in the next chapter.

Win32 makes no distinction between local heaps and global heaps. A process's local heap and global heap identify the same heap. This implies that a block of memory allocated by using the LocalAlloc function can be freed by making a call to the GlobalFree function and vice versa. In fact, this is exactly true in Windows NT. Examine the following code:

```
HGLOBAL hglb;
LPTSTR lp;
hGlb = GlobalAlloc(GMEM_ZEROINIT | GMEM_MOVEABLE, 10240);
lp = LocalLock(hGlb);
.
.
.
// Use the memory pointed to by 'lp'.
.
.
.
GlobalUnlock(hGlb);
LocalFree(hGlb);
```

Although this code does work, I certainly don't recommend that you write your own code this way. If you are developing an application that you intend to compile natively for both 16-bit Windows and Win32, use the API that makes the most sense for 16-bit Windows. If you are allocating large memory blocks, use the global API, and for small blocks use the local API. When compiling for only Win32, you shouldn't use the local and global functions at all. Instead, use the new heap functions presented later in this chapter.

16-Bit Windows Functions That Port to Win32

Figure 2-3, on the following page, shows what the 16-bit Windows memory management functions do in Win32. For each entry, the two functions listed perform the identical task on the heap. (Note that in Win32, both HGLOBAL and HLOCAL are typedefed as HANDLE.)

Of all the functions listed, only a few had semantic changes when they were ported to Win32. The following section covers these changes.

Functions with Semantic Changes

Whenever an application calls GlobalAlloc or LocalAlloc to allocate nonfixed memory, Windows NT must allocate a handle for the data, as well as memory space for the data. When GlobalAlloc or LocalAlloc returns, it returns a handle—the address of an entry in the handle table. For example, let's say that these lines of code are executed:

```
HGLOBAL hglb = GlobalAlloc(GMEM_MOVEABLE, 10);
LPVOID lpv = GlobalLock(hglb);
```

The variable *hglb* is an address to a structure in the handle table. When GlobalLock is called, the entry in the handle table is examined to determine the address of the memory block. GlobalLock then returns this address.

Both GlobalLock and LocalLock return the address to the memory block that was allocated. Immediately preceding this block in memory is an internal data structure consisting of 16 bytes. This data structure contains some internal management information, such as the size of the allocated block and the handle of the block. When allocating fixed memory blocks, Windows NT does not need to allocate a handle from the handle table. Instead, Windows NT simply allocates the memory block and returns the address to this block when GlobalAlloc or LocalAlloc returns.

16-Bit Windows Memory Function	Meaning in Win32

`HGLOBAL GlobalAlloc(UINT fuAlloc,`
`    DWORD cbAlloc);`
 	
`HLOCAL LocalAlloc(UINT fuAlloc,`
`    UINT cbAlloc);`
	Allocate a memory block.

`HGLOBAL GlobalDiscard`
`    (HGLOBAL hglb)`
`HLOCAL LocalDiscard(HLOCAL hlcl)`
	Discard a memory block. Actually macroed as:
	`GlobalReAlloc((hglb),`
	`    0, GMEM_MOVEABLE);`
	`LocalReAlloc((hglb),`
	`    0, LMEM_MOVEABLE);`

`UINT GlobalFlags(HGLOBAL hglb);` `UINT LocalFlags(HLOCAL hlcl);`	Return flag information about a memory block.
`HGLOBAL GlobalFree(HGLOBAL hglb);` `HLOCAL LocalFree(HLOCAL hlcl);`	Free a memory block.
`LPVOID GlobalLock(HGLOBAL hglb);` `LPVOID LocalLock(HLOCAL hlcl);`	Lock a memory block.
`BOOL GlobalUnlock(HGLOBAL hglb);` `BOOL LocalUnlock(HLOCAL hlcl);`	Unlock a memory block.

`HGLOBAL GlobalReAlloc`
`    (HGLOBAL hglb,`
`    DWORD cbNewSize,`
`    UINT fuAlloc);`
`HLOCAL LocalReAlloc(HLOCAL hlcl,`
`    UINT cbAlloc, UINT fuAlloc);`
	Change the size and/or flags of a memory block.

`DWORD GlobalSize(HGLOBAL hglb);` `UINT LocalSize(HLOCAL hlcl);`	Return the size of a memory block.
`HGLOBAL GlobalHandle(LPVOID lpvMem);` `HLOCAL LocalHandle(LPVOID lpvMem);`	Return the handle of the memory block containing the passed address.

Figure 2-3.
Memory functions ported from 16-bit Windows to Win32.

For GlobalAlloc and LocalAlloc, some of the flags' meanings have changed. Figure 2-4 shows all of the possible flags and what Windows NT does when it encounters each flag.

Flag	Meaning
GHND	Defined as (GMEM_MOVEABLE | GMEM_ZEROINIT)
LHND	Defined as (LMEM_MOVEABLE | LMEM_ZEROINIT)
GMEM_DDESHARE	Windows NT does not allow memory to be shared in this way. However, this flag may be used as a hint to Windows NT about how to share memory in the future.
GMEM_DISCARDABLE LMEM_DISCARDABLE	Allocate block as discardable. Windows NT ignores these flags.
GMEM_FIXED LMEM_FIXED	Allocate block as fixed.
GMEM_LOWER	Ignored by Windows NT.
GMEM_MOVEABLE LMEM_MOVEABLE	Allocate block as movable.
GMEM_NOCOMPACT LMEM_NOCOMPACT	Ignored by Windows NT.
GMEM_NODISCARD LMEM_NODISCARD	Ignored by Windows NT.
GMEM_NOT_BANKED	Ignored by Windows NT.
GMEM_NOTIFY LMEM_NOTIFY	Ignored by Windows NT.
GMEM_SHARE	Same as GMEM_DDESHARE.
GMEM_ZEROINIT LMEM_ZEROINIT	Zero contents of block after allocation.
GPTR	Defined as (GMEM_FIXED | GMEM_ZEROINIT)
LPTR	Defined as (LMEM_FIXED | LMEM_ZEROINIT)
NONZEROLHND	Defined as (LMEM_MOVEABLE)
NONZEROLPTR	Defined as (LMEM_FIXED)

Figure 2-4.

Memory flags and their meanings in Win32.

It is incorrect to call Global(Local)ReAlloc specifying the G(L)MEM-_DISCARDABLE flag without also including the G(L)MEM_MODIFY flag.[2]

Functions That Should Be Avoided

Figure 2-5 shows 16-bit Windows memory allocation functions that have been kept in Win32 to ease porting 16-bit Windows applications, but they are obsolete and should be avoided. Each of the functions existed for one or more of the following reasons:

- To allow applications to manipulate the shared global heap. In Win32, each application has its own address space, and this type of function is no longer necessary.

- To help manage discardable memory. In Win32, memory blocks are never discarded by the system. They can be discarded if an application explicitly calls GlobalDiscard or LocalDiscard. Both functions really resize their blocks to zero size anyway.

- To help manage movable memory. In Win32, memory blocks are never moved or compacted by the system.

Functions That Have Been Removed

The list that follows shows 16-bit Windows memory functions that have been totally removed from the Win32 API mainly because they were Intel processor-specific functions. Win32 is a portable API designed to offer all of its functions on any and all CPU platforms to which Win32 is ported. Calling the following functions results in a compiler error because no prototype or macro exists for them:

AllocDStoCSAlias	GlobalNotify
AllocSelector	GlobalPageLock
ChangeSelector	GlobalPageUnlock
FreeSelector	LocalInit
GetCodeInfo	SwitchStackBack
GlobalDOSAlloc	SwitchStackTo
GlobalDOSFree	

---

2. The G(L)MEM_MODIFY flag does not appear in Figure 2-4 because it is used only in conjunction with the GlobalReAlloc and LocalReAlloc functions.

16-Bit Windows Memory Function	Meaning in Windows NT
BOOL DefineHandleTable(WORD w)	Macro defined as ((w), TRUE)
DWORD GetFreeSpace(UINT u)	Macro defined as (0x100000L)
DWORD GlobalCompact(DWORD);	Always returns 0x100000
void GlobalFix(HGLOBAL);	Same as calling GlobalLock
HGLOBAL GlobalLRUNewest (HGLOBAL h)	Macro defined as (HANDLE)(h)
HGLOBAL GlobalLRUOldest (HGLOBAL h)	Macro defined as (HANDLE)(h)
void GlobalUnfix(HGLOBAL);	Same as calling GlobalUnlock
BOOL GlobalUnWire(HGLOBAL);	Same as calling GlobalUnlock
void *GlobalWire(HGLOBAL);	Same as calling GlobalLock
void LimitEmsPages(DWORD)	Macro defined as nothing
UINT LocalCompact(UINT);	Always returns 0x100000
UINT LocalShrink (HLOCAL, UINT);	Always returns 0x100000
HGLOBAL LockSegment(UINT w)	Macro defined as GlobalFix((HANDLE)(w))
LONG SetSwapAreaSize (UINT w)	Macro defined as (w)
void UnlockSegment(UINT w)	Macro defined as GlobalUnfix((HANDLE)(w))

Figure 2-5.
16-bit Windows memory functions that should be avoided in Win32.

Creating Your Own Win32 Heaps

So far, we've been discussing the functions that apply to the default heap that Win32 initializes for each process as soon as the process is initialized. For true 32-bit applications, these global and local heap functions should be completely avoided. They exist solely to make porting easier and to create applications that will be compiled natively for both Win32 and 16-bit Windows. They are much slower and less efficient than the new heap API functions that Win32 offers. These heap functions are very fast, do not use an internal handle table, have very little additional overhead, and allow an application to create and manage several different heaps. In fact, the Win32 implementation of the local and global heap functions is built on top of calls to the heap API discussed in this section. In 16-bit Windows, the ability of an application to create and manage multiple heaps was almost a necessity, as described earlier in this chapter. In Win32, the need for multiple heaps is not as important but can be useful in certain situations.

Basically, there are three main reasons why you would want to create special heaps in your own applications:

- Application protection

- More efficient memory management .

- Local access

Let's look at each one of these in detail.

Application Protection

For this discussion, imagine that your application needs to process a linked list of NODE structures and a binary tree of BRANCH structures. You have two C files: LNKLST.C, which contains the functions that process the linked list of NODEs; and BINTREE.C, which contains the functions that process the binary tree of BRANCHes.

Without storing the NODEs in one heap and the BRANCHes in a separate heap, your combined heap might look like Figure 2-6. Now let's say that there's a bug in the linked-list code that causes the 5 bytes after NODE 1 to be accidentally overwritten. This causes the data in BRANCH 3 to be corrupted. When the code in BINTREE.C later attempts to traverse the binary tree, it will probably fail because of this memory corruption. This will, of course, lead you to believe that there is a bug in your binary-tree code when, in fact, the bug exists in the linked-list code. Because the heap mixes the different types of objects, it becomes significantly more difficult to track down and isolate bugs.

By creating two separate heaps, one for NODEs and the other for BRANCHes, you localize your problems. A small bug in your linked-list code does not compromise the integrity of your binary tree and vice versa. It is still possible to have a bug in your code that causes a wild memory write to another heap, but this is far less likely to happen.

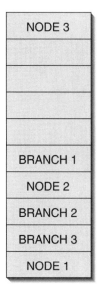

Figure 2-6.
*A combined heap that stores NODEs
and BRANCHes together.*

Efficient Memory Management

Heaps can be managed more efficiently by allocating objects of the
same size within them. For example, let's say that every NODE structure
requires 10 bytes and every BRANCH structure requires 15 bytes. All of
these objects are allocated from a single heap. Figure 2-7, on the following page, shows a fully occupied single heap containing several NODE
and BRANCH objects allocated within it. If NODE 2 and NODE 4 are
freed, memory in the heap becomes fragmented. If you now attempt to
allocate a BRANCH structure, the allocation will fail even though 20
bytes are available and a BRANCH needs only 15 bytes.

If each heap consisted only of objects that were the same size, freeing an object would guarantee that another object would fit perfectly
into the free object's space.

Local Access

The last reason to use separate heaps in your application is for local
access. Giving applications a 4-GB address space when you're using a
machine containing far less than 4 GB of physical memory requires that
Windows NT and the CPU work together. When Windows NT swaps a

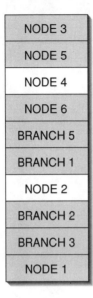

Figure 2-7.
*A single fragmented heap that contains
several NODE and BRANCH objects.*

page of physical memory out to its paging file, it takes a performance
hit. By the same token, another performance hit is taken when Windows
NT needs to swap a page of data back from the paging file into physical
memory. By keeping accesses to memory localized to a small range of addresses, it is less likely that Windows NT will need to swap pages between
physical memory and the paging file.

So, when designing an application, it's a good idea to allocate things
that will be accessed together close to each other. Returning to our
linked-list and binary-tree example, traversing the linked list is not related in any way to traversing the binary tree. By keeping all the NODEs
close together (in one heap), the NODEs will be in adjoining pages, and
most likely, several NODEs will fit within a single page of physical memory. Traversing through the linked list will not require that the CPU refer
to several different pages of memory for each NODE access.

If you were to allocate both NODEs and BRANCHes in a single
heap, the NODEs would not necessarily be close together. In the worst-
case situation, you might be able to have only one NODE per physical
page of memory (the remainder of each page occupied by BRANCHes).
In this case, traversing the linked list could cause page faults for each
NODE, which would make the process extremely slow.

The Win32 Heap API

Now that you have a good understanding of when and why to use multiple heaps, let's discuss how to use them. The Win32 heap API includes only seven functions.

HeapCreate

A Win32 application creates its own heap by calling HeapCreate:

```
HANDLE HeapCreate(DWORD flOptions, DWORD dwInitialSize,
    DWORD cbMaximumSize);
```

The first parameter, *flOptions*, identifies the flags that Win32 uses when creating the heap. You can specify 0 (zero), HEAP_NO_SERIAL-IZE, HEAP_GENERATE_EXCEPTIONS, or a combination of the two flags. If the HEAP_NO_SERIALIZE flag is specified, threads must exercise extreme caution when accessing the heap.

When an attempt is made to allocate a block of memory from the heap, the HeapAlloc function (discussed later) must do the following:

1. Traverse the linked list of allocated and freed memory blocks.

2. Find the address of a free block.

3. Allocate the new block by marking the free block as allocated.

4. Add a new entry into the linked list of memory blocks.

To illustrate how you might use the HEAP_NO_SERIALIZE flag, let's say that two threads are attempting to allocate blocks of memory from the same heap at the same time. The first thread might execute steps 1 and 2 above and get the address of a free memory block. However, before this thread can execute step 3, the second thread also executes steps 1 and 2. Because the first thread has not executed step 3 yet, the second thread finds the address to the same free memory block.

With both threads having found (what they believe to be) a free memory block in the heap, Thread 1 updates the linked list, marking the new block as allocated. Thread 2 then also updates the linked list, marking the same block as allocated. No one has detected a problem so far, but both threads return an address to the exact same block of memory.

This type of bug can be very difficult to track down because it usually doesn't manifest itself immediately. Instead, the bug waits in the background until the most inopportune moment. The potential problems are listed at the top of the next page.

- The linked list of memory blocks has been corrupted. This problem will not be discovered until an attempt to allocate or free a block is made.

- Both threads are sharing the same memory block. Thread 1 might write information to the block, and Thread 2 might write something to the same block. When Thread 1 examines the contents of the block, it will not recognize the data.

- One thread might proceed to use the block and free it, causing the other thread to overwrite unallocated memory. This will also corrupt the heap.

The solution to these problems is to allow a single thread exclusive access to the heap and its linked list until all the thread's operations have been performed. The absence of the HEAP_NO_SERIALIZE flag does exactly this. It is safe to use the HEAP_NO_SERIALIZE flag only if one or more of the following conditions are true for your process:

- Your process uses only a single thread.

- Your process uses multiple threads, but the heap is accessed by only a single thread.

- Your process uses multiple threads but manages access to the heap itself by using other forms of mutual exclusion, such as mutexes and semaphores, discussed in Chapter 5.

If you're not sure whether to use the HEAP_NO_SERIALIZE flag, don't use it. Not using it will make memory accesses perform more slowly, but you won't risk corrupting your hcap and its data. By thc way, all the global and local heap functions that access your default process heap are serialized. In this way, you don't need to worry about multiple threads in your application corrupting your default heap. In fact, as I mentioned earlier, the global and local APIs are built on top of the Win32 heap API.

The other flag, HEAP_GENERATE_EXCEPTIONS, causes the system to raise an exception whenever a heap function fails. An exception is just another way for the system to notify your application that an error has occurred. Sometimes, it's easier to design your application to look for exceptions rather than to check for return values. Exceptions are discussed in Chapter 10.

The second parameter of HeapCreate, *dwInitialSize*, indicates the number of bytes initially allocated to the heap. The final parameter, *dwMaximumSize*, indicates the maximum size that the heap can expand. If *dwMaximumSize* is 0 (zero), the heap can grow to fill all of available memory. If the heap is created successfully, HeapCreate returns a handle identifying the new heap. This handle is used by the functions discussed next.

GetProcessHeap

When your application starts, an automatic call to HeapCreate occurs. The heap created is used for all your allocations made by calls to GlobalAlloc and LocalAlloc. The GetProcessHeap function returns the handle to the automatically created heap:

```
HANDLE GetProcessHeap (VOID);
```

You can use this handle when calling any of the other heap functions discussed in the following sections except for HeapDestroy.

HeapAlloc

You allocate memory from a heap by calling HeapAlloc:

```
LPVOID HeapAlloc(HANDLE hHeap, DWORD dwFlags, DWORD dwBytes);
```

The first parameter, *hHeap*, identifies the handle of the heap from which an allocation should be made. This handle must be a handle that was returned by an earlier call to HeapCreate or GetProcessHeap. The *dwBytes* parameter specifies the number of bytes that are to be allocated from the heap. The middle parameter, *dwFlags*, allows you to specify flags that affect the allocation. Currently, only three flags are supported: HEAP_NO_SERIALIZE, HEAP_GENERATE_EXCEPTIONS, and HEAP_ZERO_MEMORY.

The purpose of the HEAP_ZERO_MEMORY flag should be pretty obvious. This flag causes Windows NT to zero the contents of the memory block before returning. The second flag, HEAP_GENERATE-_EXCEPTIONS, causes the HeapAlloc function to generate a software exception if insufficient memory is available in the heap to satisfy the request. When creating a heap with HeapCreate, you can specify the HEAP_GENERATE_EXCEPTIONS flag, which tells the heap that an exception should be raised when any heap function fails. If you specify this flag when calling HeapCreate, you don't need to specify it when calling HeapAlloc. On the other hand, you might want to create the heap without using this flag. In this case, specifying this flag to HeapAlloc affects the single call to HeapAlloc and not every heap function.

If HeapAlloc fails and then raises an exception, the exception raised will be one of the following:

Identifier	Meaning
STATUS_NO_MEMORY	The allocation attempt failed because of insufficient memory.
STATUS_ACCESS_VIOLATION	The allocation attempt failed because of heap corruption or improper function parameters.

A block allocated with HeapAlloc is fixed and nondiscardable, so it is quite possible for the heap to become fragmented as the application allocates and frees various memory blocks. If the block has been successfully allocated, HeapAlloc returns the address of the block. If the memory could not be allocated and HEAP_GENERATE_EXCEPTIONS was not specified, HeapAlloc returns NULL.

The last flag, HEAP_NO_SERIALIZE, allows you to force this individual call to HeapAlloc to not be serialized with other threads that are accessing the same heap. You should use this flag with caution since it is possible that the heap will become corrupted if other threads are manipulating the heap at the same time.

HeapSize

After a memory block has been allocated, the HeapSize function can be called to retrieve the actual size of the block:

```
DWORD HeapSize(HANDLE hHeap, DWORD dwFlags, LPCVOID lpMem);
```

The *hHeap* parameter (returned from an earlier call to either HeapCreate or GetProcessHeap) identifies the heap, and the *lpMem* parameter (returned from an earlier call to HeapAlloc) indicates the address of the block. The *dwFlags* parameter can be either 0 (zero) or HEAP_NO_SERIALIZE.

HeapReAlloc

Often it's necessary to alter the size of a memory block. Some applications initially allocate a larger-than-needed block to fill with data, and, then, after all the data has been placed into the block, the block is resized to a smaller size. Some applications begin by allocating a small block of memory and then attempt to enlarge the block when more data needs to be copied into it. Resizing a memory block is accomplished by calling the HeapReAlloc function as follows:

```
LPVOID HeapReAlloc(HANDLE hHeap, DWORD dwFlags, LPVOID lpMem,
   DWORD dwBytes);
```

As always, the *hHeap* parameter indicates the heap that contains the block you want to resize. The *dwFlags* parameter specifies the flags that HeapReAlloc should use when attempting to resize the block. Only these four flags are available: HEAP_GENERATE_EXCEPTIONS, HEAP_ZERO_MEMORY, HEAP_NO_SERIALIZE, and HEAP_RE-ALLOC_IN_PLACE_ONLY.

The first three flags have the same meaning as when they are used with HeapAlloc. The HEAP_REALLOC_IN_PLACE_ONLY flag tells HeapReAlloc that it is not allowed to move the memory block within the heap in order to satisfy the request. HeapReAlloc might attempt to do this if the memory block is growing. If HeapReAlloc is able to enlarge the memory block without moving it, it will do so and return the original address of the memory block. On the other hand, if HeapReAlloc must move the contents of the block, the address of the new, larger block is returned. If the block is made smaller, HeapReAlloc returns the original address of the memory block.

The remaining two parameters, *lpMem* and *dwBytes*, specify the current address of the block that you want to resize and the number of bytes that you want the block to become in size. HeapReAlloc returns the address of the new, resized block or NULL if the block cannot be resized.

HeapFree

When you no longer need the memory block, you can free it by calling HeapFree:

```
BOOL HeapFree(HANDLE hHeap, DWORD dwFlags, LPVOID lpMem);
```

HeapFree frees the memory block and returns TRUE if successful. The *dwFlags* parameter can be either 0 (zero) or HEAP_NO_SERIALIZE.

HeapDestroy

Finally, before your process or thread terminates, you'll want to destroy your heap by calling HeapDestroy:

```
BOOL HeapDestroy(HANDLE hHeap);
```

Calling HeapDestroy causes all the memory blocks contained within the heap to be freed and causes the memory occupied by the whole heap to be released back to the system. If the function is successful, HeapDestroy returns TRUE. If you don't explicitly destroy the heap before your process terminates, Windows NT will destroy it for you. However, a heap is destroyed only when a process terminates. If your thread creates a heap, the heap won't be destroyed when the thread terminates.

Using Heaps with C++

One of the best ways to take advantage of Win32's new heap API is by incorporating it into your existing C++ programs. In C++, class-object allocation is performed by calling the *new* operator instead of using the normal C Runtime routine *malloc*. Then, when we no longer need the class object, the *delete* operator is called instead of using the normal C Runtime routine *free*. For example, let's say that we have a class called CSomeClass and we want to allocate an instance of this class. To do this we would use syntax similar to the following:

```
CSomeClass *pCSomeClass = new CSomeClass;
```

When the C++ compiler examines this line, it first checks whether the CSomeClass class contains a function for the *new* operator; if it does, the compiler generates code to call this function. If the compiler doesn't find a function overloading the *new* operator, the compiler generates code to call the standard C++ *new* operator function.

After you're done using the allocated object, you can destroy it by calling the *delete* operator:

```
delete pCSomeClass;
```

By overloading the *new* and *delete* operators for our C++ class, we can easily take advantage of the new heap API. To do this, let's define our CSomeClass class in a header file like this:

```
class CSomeClass {
   private:

   static HHEAP hHeap;
   static unsigned int uNumAllocsInHeap;
```

```
// Other private data and member functions.
.
.
.

public:
void *operator new (size_t size);
void operator delete (void *p);
// Other public data and member functions.
.
.
.
};
```

In the code fragment above, I have declared two member variables, *hHeap* and *uNumAllocsInHeap*, as static variables. Because they are static, C++ will make all instances of CSomeClass share the same variables. That is, C++ will *not* allocate separate *hHeap* and *uNumAllocsInHeap* variables for each instance of the class that is created. This is very important to us because we want all of our instances of CSomeClass to be allocated within the same heap.

The *hHeap* variable will contain the handle to the heap within which CSomeClass objects should be allocated. The *uNumAllocsInHeap* variable is simply a counter of how many CSomeClass objects have been allocated within the heap. Every time a new CSomeClass object is allocated in the heap, *uNumAllocsInHeap* is incremented. Every time a CSomeClass object is destroyed, *uNumAllocsInHeap* is decremented. When *uNumAllocsInHeap* reaches 0 (zero), the heap is no longer necessary and is freed. The code to manipulate the heap should be included in a CPP file that looks like this:

```
HHEAP CSomeClass::hHeap = NULL;
unsigned int CSomeClass::uNumAllocsInHeap = 0;

void *CSomeClass::operator new (size_t size) {
    if (hHeap == NULL) {
        // Heap does not exist; create it.
        hHeap = HeapCreate(HEAP_NO_SERIALIZE, 0, 0);

        if (hHeap == NULL)
            return(NULL);
    }
```

(continued)

```
// The heap exists for CSomeClass objects.
void *p;
while ((p  = (void *) HeapAlloc(hHeap, 0, size)) == NULL) {
    // A CSomeClass object could not be allocated from the heap.
    if (_new_handler != NULL) {
        // Call the application-defined handler.
        (*_new_handler)();
    } else {
        // No application-defined handler exists; just return.
        break;
    }
}

if (p != NULL) {
    // Memory was allocated successfully; increment
    // the count of CSomeClass objects in the heap.
    uNumAllocsInHeap++;
}

// Return the address of the allocated CSomeClass object.
return(p);
}
```

You'll notice that I first defined the two static member variables, *hHeap* and *uNumAllocsInHeap*, at the top and initialized them as NULL and 0 (zero), respectively.

The C++ *new* operator receives one parameter—*size*. This parameter indicates the number of bytes required to hold a CSomeClass object. The first thing that our *new* operator function must do is create a heap if one hasn't previously been created. This is simply a matter of checking the *hHeap* variable to see if it is NULL. If it is, a new heap is created by calling HeapCreate, and the handle that HeapCreate returns is saved in *hHeap* so that the next call to the *new* operator will not create another heap—it will use the same heap we have just created.

When I called the HeapCreate function above, I used the HEAP-_NO_SERIALIZE flag because the remainder of the sample code is not multithread safe. In Chapter 5, I will discuss features of Win32 that can be incorporated into the above code to make it multithread safe. The other two parameters indicate the initial size and the maximum size of the heap, respectively. I chose 0 (zero) and 0 (zero) here. The first 0 (zero) means that the heap has no initial size, whereas the second 0 (zero) means that the heap can grow indefinitely. You may want to change either or both of these values depending on your needs.

You might think that it would be worthwhile to pass the *size* parameter to the *new* operator function as the second parameter to Heap-Create. In this way, you could initialize the heap so that it is large enough to contain one instance of the class. Then, the first time that HeapAlloc is called, it will execute faster because the heap won't have to resize itself to hold the class instance. Unfortunately, things don't always work the way that you want them to. Because each allocated memory block within the heap has an overhead associated with it, the call to HeapAlloc will still have to resize the heap so that it is large enough to contain the one class instance and its associated overhead.

Once the heap has been created, new CSomeClass objects can be allocated from it using HeapAlloc. The first parameter is the handle to the heap, and the second parameter is the size of the CSomeClass object. HeapAlloc returns the address to the allocated block.

Once the allocation was performed successfully, I incremented the *uNumAllocsInHeap* variable so that I knew there was one more allocation in the heap. The last thing that the *new* operator does is return the address of the newly allocated CSomeClass object.

Well, that's it for creating a new CSomeClass object. Let's turn our attention now to destroying one when our application no longer needs it. This is the responsibility of the *operator delete* function, coded as follows:

```
void CSomeClass::operator delete (void *p) {
   if (HeapFree(hHeap, 0, p)) {
      // Object was deleted successfully.
      uNumAllocsInHeap--;
   }

   if (uNumAllocsInHeap == 0) {
      // If there are no more objects in the heap,
      // destroy the heap.
      if (HeapDestroy(hHeap)) {
         // Set the heap handle to NULL so that the new operator
         // will know to create a new heap if a new CSomeClass
         // object is created.
         hHeap = NULL;
      }
   }
}
```

The *delete* operator function receives only one parameter: the address of the object being deleted. The first thing that the function does is call HeapFree, passing it the handle of the heap and the address of the object to be freed. If the object is freed successfully, *uNumAllocsInHeap* is decremented, indicating that one fewer CSomeClass object is in the heap. Next the function checks whether *uNumAllocsInHeap* is 0 (zero), and, if it is, calls HeapDestroy, passing it the heap handle. If the heap is destroyed successfully, *hHeap* is set to NULL. This is extremely important because our program might attempt to allocate another CSomeClass object sometime in the future. When it does, the *new* operator will be called and will examine the *hHeap* variable to determine whether it should use an existing heap or create a new one.

This example demonstrates a very convenient scheme for using multiple heaps. It is easy to set up and can be incorporated into several of your classes. You will probably want to give some thought to inheritance, however. If you derive a new class using CSomeClass as a base class, the new class will inherit CSomeClass's *new* and *delete* operators. The new class will also inherit CSomeClass's heap, which means that when the *new* operator is applied to the derived class, the memory for the derived class object will be allocated from the same heap that CSomeClass is using. Depending on your situation, this may or may not be what you want. If the objects are very different in size, you might be setting yourself up for a situation in which the heap may fragment badly. You might also be making it harder to track down bugs in your code, as mentioned in the Application Protection and Efficient Memory Management sections earlier in this chapter.

If you want to use a separate heap for derived classes, all you need to do is duplicate what I did in the CSomeClass class. More specifically, include another set of *hHeap* and *uNumAllocsInHeap* variables, and copy the code over for the *new* and *delete* operators. When you compile, the compiler will see that you have overloaded the *new* and *delete* operators for the derived class and will make calls to those functions instead of to the ones in the base class.

The only advantage you gain by not creating a heap for each class is the overhead and size of each heap that would otherwise be lost. This overhead is not great and is probably worth the potential gains. The compromise might be to have each class use its own heap and to let derived classes share the base class's heap when your application has been well tested and is close to shipping. But be aware that fragmentation may still be a problem.

CHAPTER THREE

VIRTUAL MEMORY MANAGEMENT

In the previous chapter, we saw how the 16-bit Windows memory functions map over to their Win32 equivalents and how Win32 adds more functions for creating and manipulating heaps. These memory management functions are straightforward and very easy to use, but they are best used for managing small objects. Many applications need to manage massive amounts of data—for example, a spreadsheet might allocate a structure for every possible cell. When it comes to large objects or, more likely, large arrays of small objects, the heap system can still be used but does not offer the efficiency that we might like. What we need is a memory allocation mechanism that offers more control over the memory allocation process.

Working with Virtual Memory

Windows NT offers a new approach to memory allocation using *virtual memory*. As mentioned in the previous chapter, Windows NT makes each process running in the system think it's executing in 4 GB of address space. The upper 2 GB of this space are reserved for system use (for the Windows NT Executive, Kernel, device drivers, etc.), so a process can't access it. But the bottom 2 GB *are* available to each process for making memory allocations by calling the Win32 virtual memory management functions. All the heap management functions discussed in the previous chapter are implemented internally using NT's virtual memory management functions.

You manipulate virtual memory in two stages. In the first stage you simply *reserve* an address space. For example, you might want to reserve a 5-MB address space out of your process's available 2 GB. When you do so, you're not allocating any physical memory at all; you're simply reserving an address space. Any attempts to access this address space in your program will cause an access violation to occur.

In the second stage, to actually use the reserved address space, you must tell Windows NT to allocate physical storage (a combination of physical memory and the paging file) and map that storage to the previously reserved address space. This action of allocating physical storage is called *committing* memory.

Proper use of virtual memory can make a programmer's life much easier. For example, say that your process uses an array of data structures, but you don't know how many entries in the array your application will need during the lifetime of your process. In 16-bit Windows, you allocate a memory block large enough to hold all the entries that you think the application will ever need, or you allocate a small amount of memory and expand it as more entries are needed in the array.

The problem with the first method is that memory is taken away from the system and any other applications that are running, even though this memory may never be used by the application. This is extremely wasteful. In the second method, you're not using memory until you need it. The problem is that when you do need it, it might not be available. And even if it is available, your application incurs a performance penalty if memory needs to be relocated and if pointers need to be adjusted. Using virtual memory is a compromise between these two methods.

Reserving an Address Space

You reserve an address space by calling VirtualAlloc:

```
LPVOID VirtualAlloc(LPVOID lpAddress, DWORD dwSize,
    DWORD flAllocationType, DWORD flProtect);
```

The *lpAddress* parameter contains a virtual address specifying where you would like Win32 to allocate the address space.

For most programmers, this is a rather new concept. Usually when you attempt to allocate memory, the operating system finds a block of memory large enough to satisfy the request, allocates the block, and returns its address. But, in Windows NT, a process can actually specify a base memory address where it would like the operating system to reserve the space.

Windows NT makes this possible because of the way it separates the reservation of virtual address space and the committing of physical storage. It is the CPU's responsibility (with some help from the operating system) to map an application's virtual address to the CPU's physical memory address. Because of this mapping, the CPU (with the operating system) has the ability to move and rearrange physical pages in memory while allowing the application to continue using its virtual addresses.

For example, say that you want Win32 to allocate an address space starting at 5 MB into your process's 2-GB area. In this case, you would pass 5,242,880 ($5 \times 1024 \times 1024$) as the *lpAddress* parameter.

When Windows NT allocates address space, it reserves the space in 64-KB chunks[1], as shown in Figure 3-1 on the next page. That is, an attempt to reserve an address space that spans 80 KB will actually result in an address space that spans 128 KB. Also, Windows NT can allocate address spaces starting only on an even 64-KB boundary. So, if you attempt to allocate an address space starting at byte 204,800 (3×64 KB $+ 8192$) in your process's address space, Windows NT will round that number down to an even multiple of 64 KB and will actually reserve the address space starting at address 196,608 (3×64 KB).

If you call the VirtualAlloc function requesting to reserve address space at an address that has already been reserved, VirtualAlloc cannot satisfy your request and fails, returning NULL. If VirtualAlloc can satisfy your request, it returns a value indicating the base address of the reserved address space. This is the same value that you passed to VirtualAlloc unless the address needed to be rounded down to an even 64-KB boundary.

Most of the time, when you call VirtualAlloc, you'll pass NULL as the *lpAddress* parameter. This tells VirtualAlloc to reserve the address space wherever it sees fit. The system keeps a record of free address ranges and allocates one of these. You have no guarantee that the system will reserve from the bottom of your address space up.

The *dwSize* parameter specifies the number of bytes to reserve in the address space. Because reserving space doesn't actually commit any memory, the action is quite fast. And the time required for Windows NT to reserve address space is not a function of how much space you are reserving. For example, reserving 10 MB is no faster than reserving 500

---

1. In beta versions of Windows NT, this 64-KB granularity was hard-coded. However, new CPU architectures may require different granularities. An application can determine the granularity at runtime by calling GetSystemInfo. A sample program demonstrating the GetSystemInfo function is shown later in this chapter.

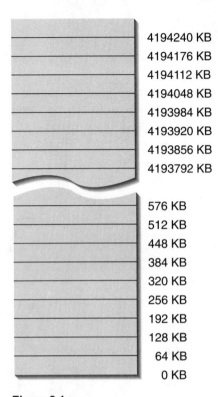

4194240 KB
4194176 KB
4194112 KB
4194048 KB
4193984 KB
4193920 KB
4193856 KB
4193792 KB

576 KB
512 KB
448 KB
384 KB
320 KB
256 KB
192 KB
128 KB
64 KB
0 KB

Figure 3-1.
Windows NT reserves address space in 64-KB chunks.

MB. To reserve the address space, you must pass MEM_RESERVE as the *flAllocationType* parameter.

The last parameter, *flProtect*, indicates the protection status of the memory *after* it has been committed. The table below shows the possible protection status attributes:

Attribute	Description
PAGE_NOACCESS	No access to the committed region of pages is allowed. Any attempt to read, write to, or execute the committed region results in an access violation (an exception).
PAGE_READONLY	Read-access to the committed region of pages is allowed. Any attempt to write to the committed region results in an access violation.
PAGE_READWRITE	Read/write access to the committed region of pages is allowed.

Additional PAGE_* identifiers are used internally by the system.

If you are reserving an address space that will eventually have pages of physical storage with the PAGE_READWRITE protection status committed to it, you should specify PAGE_READWRITE when the address space is reserved. The reason lies in the way the Windows NT memory manager keeps track of reserved address ranges.

When you reserve an address range, Windows NT creates an internal block of memory containing the starting address of the reserved address range, the number of bytes in the range, and the protection status of the entire range. If the pages in the range have different protection status attributes, the system must do additional record keeping to keep track of the different attributes. For this reason, it is more efficient to have all the pages in a particular range share the same protection status.

Regardless of the protection status given to a range of pages, if no physical storage is committed, any attempt to access the memory in the range will cause an access violation to be generated. This is identical to what happens if you reserve and commit storage to an address range using the PAGE_NOACCESS flag.

Now that you have reserved an address space, you must commit physical storage to the space before you can use it. Storage committed to an address space is either allocated from physical RAM or from Windows NT's paging file on your hard disk.

Committing Memory

To commit physical storage, call VirtualAlloc again, this time passing MEM_COMMIT as the *flAllocationType* parameters. You usually pass the same page protection attribute that was used when VirtualAlloc was called to reserve the address space. Although you can specify a different attribute from the table above, it's more efficient to use the same attribute.

From the reserved address space, you must tell VirtualAlloc where you want to commit physical storage. This is done by specifying the physical storage address in the *lpAddress* parameter. Note that you don't have to commit memory to the entire address space at one time—you can commit physical storage to only part of it.

Physical storage is committed in *pages*. Page size varies depending on the CPU. Intel and MIPS processors use 4-KB pages, and the DEC Alpha uses 8-KB pages. Your application can determine the page size being used on a machine at runtime by calling GetSystemInfo.

Let's look at an example of committing memory. Say you're running an Intel CPU and you reserved a 512-KB address space starting at address 5,242,880. Now you would like to commit a 6-KB portion of it starting at 2 KB into the reserved address space. To do this, call VirtualAlloc using the MEM_COMMIT flag (instead of the MEM_RESERVE flag):

```
VirtualAlloc(5242880 + (2 * 1024), 6 * 1024,
    MEM_COMMIT, PAGE_READWRITE);
```

In this case, Win32 must commit 8 KB of physical storage, covering the address range of 5,242,880 through 5,251,072 (5,242,880 + 8 KB). Both of these committed pages have a protection attribute of PAGE_READWRITE. Protection attributes are assigned on a whole-page basis. It is not possible to use different protection attributes for portions of the same page of storage. However, it is possible for one page in an address space to have one protection attribute (such as PAGE_READWRITE) and for another page in the same address space to have a different protection attribute (such as PAGE_READONLY).

Reserving an Address Space and Committing Memory Simultaneously

There will be times when you want to reserve an address space and commit storage to it simultaneously. You can do so by placing a single call to VirtualAlloc:

```
LPVOID lpv = VirtualAlloc(NULL, 100 * 1024,
    MEM_RESERVE | MEM_COMMIT, PAGE_READWRITE);
```

In this call, you are requesting 100 KB of memory. Win32 searches the address space to find a place for it because NULL was specified as the *lpAddress* parameter. VirtualAlloc then commits the physical pages of storage to the address space and marks them as being readable and writable. Finally, VirtualAlloc returns the virtual address of the 100-KB block, which is then saved in the *lpv* variable. If a large enough address space could not be found or if the 100 KB of physical storage could not be committed, VirtualAlloc returns NULL.

Using an Address Space

Once VirtualAlloc has returned an address to committed memory, you can start using that memory in your application. The tricky part comes in when you want to take an address space and commit physical memory to it in a sparse fashion. Perhaps you want to store an array of 10,000 structures, but, at any given time, only 100 structures contain any meaningful data. This is a perfect opportunity to use virtual memory.

Here is a better example. Let's say that you're designing a spreadsheet application. Each spreadsheet could contain 200 rows and 256 columns. For each cell in the spreadsheet, you need to store a structure (let's say struct CELLDATA) that describes the contents of the cell. It would be terribly inefficient for the application to allocate a two-dimensional matrix of CELLDATA structures:

```
CELLDATA CellData[200][256];
```

If the size of a CELLDATA structure were 128 bytes, it would require 6,553,600 ($200 \times 256 \times 128$) bytes of memory. That's a lot of memory to allocate right up front for a spreadsheet. But reserving an address space this large for the spreadsheet data doesn't require any memory at all. As the user enters data into the cells, memory is committed only as necessary. Because most of the cells in a spreadsheet are empty, no memory is committed to those regions. And because users tend to put data into cells that are near each other, the problem of committing several pages at a time isn't really a problem. The spreadsheet application can access its data as though it were actually a two-dimensional matrix. In spreadsheet programs written for operating systems that do not offer virtual memory allocation in this way, other methods must be implemented for storing the CELLDATA structures. Using linked lists is probably the most common method, but it has the disadvantage of being slower and requiring you to implement the linked-list management code. Based on this example, it's easy to see the advantages of virtual memory.

Unfortunately, there is a small problem with this virtual memory method. You must make sure that when the user is working with a cell of the spreadsheet, physical storage is committed to the address space before the CELLDATA structure is stored in memory. There are four different methods for doing this:

1. Call VirtualAlloc, passing the address of the CELLDATA you are about to store using the MEM_COMMIT flag. This causes Windows NT to commit memory to the page containing the structure. If memory has already been committed to this page, Windows NT does nothing. The disadvantage here is that you make an additional function call every time you alter a CELLDATA structure, which makes your program perform slower.

2. Determine (using the VirtualQuery function) whether physical memory has already been committed to the address space containing the CELLDATA structure. If it has, do nothing else; if it hasn't, call VirtualAlloc to commit the memory. This is actually worse than the first method; it increases the size of your code because of the calls to both VirtualQuery and VirtualAlloc. And it's slower because VirtualAlloc must determine for itself whether memory has already been committed before committing it again.

3. You could keep a record of which pages have been committed and which haven't. Doing so avoids the call to VirtualAlloc, making your application run faster, because your code can determine more quickly whether Windows NT has already committed the page. The disadvantage is that you must keep track of the page commit information somehow, which could be either a lot of work or very simple depending on your specific situation.

4. The best method takes advantage of structured exception handling (SEH). SEH is a feature in Windows NT that allows your application to be notified when "bad" things happen. Essentially, you set up your application with an exception handler, and then, whenever an attempt is made to access uncommitted memory, Windows NT notifies your application of the problem. Your application then commits the memory and tells Windows NT to retry the instruction that caused the exception. This time, the memory access succeeds, and the program continues running as though nothing ever went wrong. This is the best method because it requires the least amount of work from you (meaning less code) and because your program will run at full speed. A complete discussion of the SEH mechanism is saved for Chapter 10 in this book.

Freeing an Address Space

When your process no longer needs the committed memory and/or reserved address space, it must free it by calling VirtualFree:

```
BOOL VirtualFree(LPVOID lpAddress, DWORD dwSize,
    DWORD dwFreeType);
```

Let's examine a situation in which you want to decommit physical storage but keep the address space reserved. The *lpAddress* parameter specifies the base address of the region of pages to be freed, and the *dwSize* parameter indicates the number of bytes that you want to free. *dwFreeType* must be MEM_DECOMMIT.

Like committing, decommitting is done with page granularity. That is, specifying a base address that is in the middle of a page decommits the entire page. And, of course, if *lpAddress + dwSize* falls in the middle of a page, the whole page at this address is decommitted as well. All pages that fall within the range of *lpAddress* to *lpAddress + dwSize* are also decommitted. If *dwSize* is 0 (zero) and *lpAddress* is the base address for the allocated region, VirtualFree will decommit the complete range of allocated pages.

After the pages have been decommitted, the freed physical storage is available to any other process in the system. The protection attribute for the decommitted memory is unaltered, but any attempt to access decommitted memory results in an access violation.

In practice, knowing when it's OK to decommit memory is a very tricky thing. Consider the spreadsheet example again. If you're using an Intel CPU, each page of memory is 4 KB and can hold 32 (4096 / 128) CELLDATA structures. If the user deletes the contents of Cell-Data[0][1], you might be able to decommit the memory as long as cells CellData[0][0] through CellData[0][31] are also not in use. But how do you know? There are many different ways to tackle this problem.

Without a doubt, the easiest solution is to design a CELLDATA structure that is exactly a page. Then because there is always one structure per page, when you don't need the data in the structure any longer, you can decommit the physical page of storage. If your data structures were multiples of a page, say, 8 KB or 12 KB for Intel CPUs (these would be unusually large structures), decommitting memory would also be pretty easy.

A more practical solution is to keep a record of which structures are in use. To save memory, you might use a bitmap. So if you have an array of 100 structures, you also maintain an array of 100 bits. Initially, all the bits are set to 0 (zero), indicating that no structures are in use. As you use the structures, you set the corresponding bits to 1. Then whenever you don't need a structure and change its bit back to 0 (zero), you check the bits of the adjacent structures that fall into the same physical page of memory. If none of the adjacent structures are in use, you can decommit the page.

The last solution implements a garbage collection function. This scheme relies on the fact that Windows NT sets all the bytes in a page to 0 (zero) when physical storage is first committed. To use this scheme, you must first set aside a BOOL (called something like *fInUse*) in your structure. Then, every time you put a structure in committed memory, you need to ensure that *fInUse* is set to TRUE.

As your application runs, you'll want to call the garbage collection function periodically. This function should traverse all the potential data structures. For each structure, the function first determines whether storage is committed for the structure; if so, the function checks the *fInUse* member to see if it is 0 (zero). A value of 0 (zero) means that the structure is not in use, and a value of TRUE means that the structure is in use. After the function has checked all the structures that fall within a given page, if all of the structures are not in use, the garbage collection function calls VirtualFree to decommit the storage.

You could call the garbage collection function immediately after a structure is no longer considered in use, but, because the function cycles through all the possible structures, doing so might take more time than you want to spend. An excellent way to implement this function is to have it run as its own lower-priority thread. In this way, you don't take time away from the thread executing the main application. Whenever the user is idle with the main application or the main application's thread is performing file I/O, Windows NT can schedule time to the garbage collection function.

Of all the methods listed above, the first two are my personal favorites. However, if your structures are not big (less than a page), I recommend using the last method.

Now let's take a look at a case in which you want to release the address space as well. Here you also call VirtualFree, but instead of specifying MEM_DECOMMIT as the *dwFreeType* parameter, you specify MEM_RELEASE.

When releasing address space, you must release all the address space that was reserved. For example, you cannot reserve a 500-MB address space and then decide to release only 200 MB of it. All 500 MB must be released. When you release an address space, you must call VirtualFree, passing the base address of the virtual space in *lpAddress* and 0 (zero) as the *dwSize* parameter. Passing any other values for these parameters will result in the function failing.

The Virtual Memory Allocation Sample Application

The VMAlloc application (VMALLOC.EXE), listed in Figure 3-2 beginning on page 97, demonstrates how to use virtual memory techniques for manipulating an array of structures. When you start the program, the following window appears:

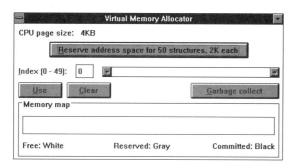

Initially, no address space has been reserved for the array, and all the address space that would be reserved for it is free, as shown by the memory map. When you press the *Reserve address space for 50 structures, 2K each* button, VMAlloc calls VirtualAlloc to reserve the space for the array, and the memory map is updated to reflect this. After address space has been reserved, the remaining buttons become active.

You can now type an index into the edit control or use the scroll bar to select an index and click on the *Use* button. This has the effect of committing a page of physical storage into the address space where the array element is to be placed. When a page of storage is committed, the memory map is redrawn to reflect the state of the address space reserved for the entire array. So if, after reserving the address space, you mark array elements 7 and 46 as in use, the window looks like this:

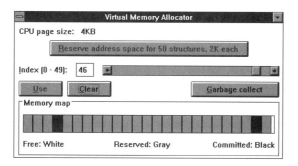

Any element that is marked as *in use* can be cleared by clicking on the *Clear* button. But doing so does not decommit the memory page occupied by the array element. This is because each page contains room for multiple structures—just because one is clear doesn't mean the others are too. If the memory is decommitted here, the data in the other structures is lost. So the memory map is not updated when an array element is cleared.

However, when a structure is cleared, its *fInUse* member is set to FALSE. This is necessary so that the garbage collection routine can make its pass over all the structures and decommit memory that's no longer in use. If you haven't guessed it by now, the *Garbage collect* button tells VMAlloc to execute its garbage collection routine. To keep things simple, I have not implemented the garbage collection function as its own thread.

To demonstrate the garbage collection function, clear the array element at index 46. Notice that the memory map does not change. Now if you click on the *Garbage collect* button, the program does decommit the page containing element 46, and the memory map is updated to reflect this:

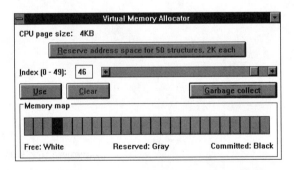

Finally, even though there is nothing visual about it, all the committed memory is decommitted and all of the address space is freed when the window is destroyed.

There is another element to this program that I haven't described yet. The program needs to determine the state of memory in the address space in three places:

- After changing the index, the program needs to enable the *Use* button and disable the *Clear* button or vice versa.

■ In the garbage collection function, the program needs to see if a page is committed before actually testing to see if the *fInUse* flag is set.

■ When updating the memory map, the program needs to know which pages are free, reserved, or committed.

You can determine the state of an address space by placing a call to VirtualQuery, a function that we'll discuss shortly.

VMAlloc.ico

```
VMALLOC.C
/*****************************************************************
Module name: VMAlloc.C
Notices: Copyright (c) 1993 Jeffrey Richter
*****************************************************************/

#include <windows.h>
#include <windowsx.h>
#include <tchar.h>
#include <stdio.h>        // for sprintf
#include "VMAlloc.H"


///////////////////////////////////////////////////////////////

UINT g_uPageSize = 0;

typedef struct {
   BOOL fAllocated;
   BYTE bOtherData[2048 - sizeof(BOOL)];
} SOMEDATA, *PSOMEDATA;

#define MAX_SOMEDATA     (50)
PSOMEDATA g_pSomeData = NULL;

RECT g_rcMemMap;
```

Figure 3-2.
The VMAlloc application.

(continued)

Figure 3-2. *continued*

```
/////////////////////////////////////////////////////////////////

BOOL Dlg_OnInitDialog (HWND hwnd, HWND hwndFocus,
   LPARAM lParam) {

   TCHAR szBuf[10];

   // Associate an icon with the dialog box.
   SetClassLong(hwnd, GCL_HICON, (LONG)
      LoadIcon((HINSTANCE) GetWindowLong(hwnd, GWL_HINSTANCE),
      __TEXT("VMAlloc")));

   // Initialize the dialog box by disabling all
   // the nonsetup controls.
   EnableWindow(GetDlgItem(hwnd, ID_INDEXTEXT), FALSE);
   EnableWindow(GetDlgItem(hwnd, ID_INDEX), FALSE);
   ScrollBar_SetRange(GetDlgItem(hwnd, ID_INDEXSCRL),
      0, MAX_SOMEDATA - 1, FALSE);
   ScrollBar_SetPos(GetDlgItem(hwnd, ID_INDEXSCRL), 0,TRUE);
   EnableWindow(GetDlgItem(hwnd, ID_INDEXSCRL), FALSE);
   EnableWindow(GetDlgItem(hwnd, ID_USE), FALSE);
   EnableWindow(GetDlgItem(hwnd, ID_CLEAR), FALSE);
   EnableWindow(GetDlgItem(hwnd, ID_GARBAGECOLLECT), FALSE);

   // Get the coordinates of the memory map display.
   GetWindowRect(GetDlgItem(hwnd, ID_MEMMAP), &g_rcMemMap);
   MapWindowPoints(NULL, hwnd, (LPPOINT) &g_rcMemMap, 2);

   // Destroy the temporary window that identifies the
   // location of the memory map display.
   DestroyWindow(GetDlgItem(hwnd, ID_MEMMAP));

   // Put the page size in the dialog box just
   // for the user's information.
   _stprintf(szBuf, __TEXT("%dKB"), g_uPageSize / 1024);
   SetDlgItemText(hwnd, ID_PAGESIZE, szBuf);

   // Initialize the edit control.
   SetDlgItemInt(hwnd, ID_INDEX, 0, FALSE);

   return(TRUE);
}
```

(continued)

Figure 3-2. *continued*

```
//////////////////////////////////////////////////////////////////////

void Dlg_OnDestroy (HWND hwnd) {
   if (g_pSomeData != NULL)
      VirtualFree(g_pSomeData, 0, MEM_RELEASE);
}


//////////////////////////////////////////////////////////////////////

void Dlg_OnCommand (HWND hwnd, int id, HWND hwndCtl,
   UINT codeNotify) {

   UINT uIndex, uIndexLast, uPage, uMaxPages;
   BOOL fTranslated, fOk, fAnyAllocs;
   MEMORY_BASIC_INFORMATION MemoryBasicInfo;

   switch (id) {
      case ID_RESERVE:
         // Reserve enough address space to hold MAX_SOMEDATA
         // SOMEDATA structures.
         g_pSomeData = VirtualAlloc(NULL,
            MAX_SOMEDATA * sizeof(SOMEDATA),.MEM_RESERVE,
            PAGE_READWRITE);

         // Disable the Reserve button and
         // enable all the other controls.
         EnableWindow(GetDlgItem(hwnd, ID_RESERVE), FALSE);
         EnableWindow(GetDlgItem(hwnd, ID_INDEXTEXT), TRUE);
         EnableWindow(GetDlgItem(hwnd, ID_INDEX), TRUE);
         EnableWindow(GetDlgItem(hwnd, ID_INDEXSCRL), TRUE);
         EnableWindow(GetDlgItem(hwnd, ID_USE), TRUE);
         EnableWindow(GetDlgItem(hwnd, ID_GARBAGECOLLECT),
            TRUE);

         // Force the index edit control to have the focus.
         SetFocus(GetDlgItem(hwnd, ID_INDEX));

         // Invalidate the memory map display.
         InvalidateRect(hwnd, &g_rcMemMap, FALSE);
         break;

      case ID_INDEX:
         if (codeNotify != EN_CHANGE)
            break;
```

(continued)

Figure 3-2. *continued*

```
        uIndex = GetDlgItemInt(hwnd, id, &fTranslated,
           FALSE);
        if ((g_pSomeData == NULL) ||
           (uIndex >= MAX_SOMEDATA)) {
           // If the index is out of range, assume the
           // translation was unsuccessful.
           fTranslated = FALSE;
        }

        if (fTranslated) {
           VirtualQuery(&g_pSomeData[uIndex],
              &MemoryBasicInfo, sizeof(MemoryBasicInfo));
           fOk = (MemoryBasicInfo.State == MEM_COMMIT);
           if (fOk)
              fOk = g_pSomeData[uIndex].fAllocated;

           EnableWindow(GetDlgItem(hwnd, ID_USE), !fOk);
           EnableWindow(GetDlgItem(hwnd, ID_CLEAR), fOk);
           ScrollBar_SetPos(GetDlgItem(hwnd, ID_INDEXSCRL),
              uIndex, TRUE);

        } else {
           EnableWindow(GetDlgItem(hwnd, ID_USE),   FALSE);
           EnableWindow(GetDlgItem(hwnd, ID_CLEAR), FALSE);
        }
        break;


    case ID_USE:
        uIndex = GetDlgItemInt(hwnd, ID_INDEX, &fTranslated,
           FALSE);

        if (uIndex >= MAX_SOMEDATA) {
           // If the index is out of range, assume the
           // translation was unsuccessful.
           fTranslated = FALSE;
        }

        if (fTranslated) {
           VirtualAlloc(&g_pSomeData[uIndex],
              sizeof(SOMEDATA), MEM_COMMIT, PAGE_READWRITE);

           // When pages are committed, Windows NT ensures
           // that they are zeroed.
           g_pSomeData[uIndex].fAllocated = TRUE;
```

(continued)

Figure 3-2. *continued*

```
        EnableWindow(GetDlgItem(hwnd, ID_USE),   FALSE);
        EnableWindow(GetDlgItem(hwnd, ID_CLEAR), TRUE);

        // Force the Clear button control to
        // have the focus.
        SetFocus(GetDlgItem(hwnd, ID_CLEAR));

        // Invalidate the memory map display.
        InvalidateRect(hwnd, &g_rcMemMap, FALSE);
    }
    break;

case ID_CLEAR:
    uIndex = GetDlgItemInt(hwnd, ID_INDEX, &fTranslated,
        FALSE);

    if (uIndex >= MAX_SOMEDATA) {
        // If the index is out of range, assume the
        // translation was unsuccessful.
        fTranslated = FALSE;
    }

    if (fTranslated) {
        g_pSomeData[uIndex].fAllocated = FALSE;
        EnableWindow(GetDlgItem(hwnd, ID_USE),   TRUE);
        EnableWindow(GetDlgItem(hwnd, ID_CLEAR), FALSE);

        // Force the Use button control to have the focus.
        SetFocus(GetDlgItem(hwnd, ID_USE));
    }
    break;

case ID_GARBAGECOLLECT:
    uMaxPages = MAX_SOMEDATA * sizeof(SOMEDATA) /
        g_uPageSize;

    for (uPage = 0; uPage < uMaxPages; uPage++) {
        fAnyAllocs = FALSE;

        uIndex = uPage * g_uPageSize / sizeof(SOMEDATA);

        uIndexLast = uIndex + g_uPageSize /
            sizeof(SOMEDATA);
```

(continued)

Figure 3-2. *continued*

```
            for (; uIndex < uIndexLast; uIndex++) {
                VirtualQuery(&g_pSomeData[uIndex],
                    &MemoryBasicInfo, sizeof(MemoryBasicInfo));

                if ((MemoryBasicInfo.State == MEM_COMMIT) &&
                        g_pSomeData[uIndex].fAllocated) {

                    fAnyAllocs = TRUE;
                    break;
                }
            }

            if (!fAnyAllocs) {
                // No allocated structures exist in the page.
                // We can safely decommit it.
                VirtualFree(&g_pSomeData[uIndexLast - 1],
                    sizeof(SOMEDATA), MEM_DECOMMIT);
            }
        }

        // Invalidate the memory map display.
        InvalidateRect(hwnd, &g_rcMemMap, FALSE);
        break;

    case IDCANCEL:
        EndDialog(hwnd, id);
        break;
    }
}

/////////////////////////////////////////////////////////////////

void Dlg_OnHScroll (HWND hwnd, HWND hwndCtl,
    UINT code, int pos) {

    INT nScrlPos;
    if (hwndCtl != GetDlgItem(hwnd, ID_INDEXSCRL))
        return;

    nScrlPos = ScrollBar_GetPos(hwndCtl);
    switch (code) {
        case SB_LINELEFT:
            nScrlPos--;
            break;
```

(continued)

Figure 3-2. *continued*

```
      case SB_LINERIGHT:
        nScrlPos++;
        break;

      case SB_PAGELEFT:
        nScrlPos -= g_uPageSize / sizeof(SOMEDATA);
        break;

      case SB_PAGERIGHT:
        nScrlPos += g_uPageSize / sizeof(SOMEDATA);
        break;

      case SB_THUMBTRACK:
        nScrlPos = pos;
        break;

      case SB_LEFT:
        nScrlPos = 0;
        break;

      case SB_RIGHT:
        nScrlPos = MAX_SOMEDATA - 1;
        break;
    }
  if (nScrlPos < 0)
    nScrlPos = 0;

  if (nScrlPos >= MAX_SOMEDATA)
    nScrlPos = MAX_SOMEDATA - 1;

  ScrollBar_SetPos(hwndCtl, nScrlPos, TRUE);
  SetDlgItemInt(hwnd, ID_INDEX, nScrlPos, TRUE);
}

//////////////////////////////////////////////////////////

void Dlg_OnPaint (HWND hwnd) {
  UINT uPage, uIndex, uIndexLast, uMemMapWidth;
  UINT uMaxPages = MAX_SOMEDATA * sizeof(SOMEDATA) /
    g_uPageSize;

  MEMORY_BASIC_INFORMATION MemoryBasicInfo;
  PAINTSTRUCT ps;

  BeginPaint(hwnd, &ps);
```

(continued)

Figure 3-2. *continued*

```
if (g_pSomeData == NULL) {
   // The memory has yet to be reserved.
   Rectangle(ps.hdc, g_rcMemMap.left, g_rcMemMap.top,
      g_rcMemMap.right, g_rcMemMap.bottom);
}

// Walk the virtual address space, adding
// entries to the list box.
uPage = 0;
while ((g_pSomeData != NULL) && uPage < uMaxPages) {

   uIndex = uPage * g_uPageSize / sizeof(SOMEDATA);

   uIndexLast = uIndex + g_uPageSize / sizeof(SOMEDATA);

   for (; uIndex < uIndexLast; uIndex++) {

      VirtualQuery(&g_pSomeData[uIndex], &MemoryBasicInfo,
         sizeof(MemoryBasicInfo));

      switch (MemoryBasicInfo.State) {
         case MEM_FREE:
            SelectObject(ps.hdc,
               GetStockObject(WHITE_BRUSH));
            break;

         case MEM_RESERVE:
            SelectObject(ps.hdc,
               GetStockObject(GRAY_BRUSH));
            break;

         case MEM_COMMIT:
            SelectObject(ps.hdc,
               GetStockObject(BLACK_BRUSH));
            break;
      }

      uMemMapWidth = g_rcMemMap.right - g_rcMemMap.left;
      Rectangle(ps.hdc,
         g_rcMemMap.left +
            uMemMapWidth / uMaxPages * uPage,
         g_rcMemMap.top,
         g_rcMemMap.left +
            uMemMapWidth / uMaxPages * (uPage + 1),
         g_rcMemMap.bottom);
```

(continued)

Figure 3-2. *continued*

```
    }

    uPage++;
  }

  EndPaint(hwnd, &ps);
}

//////////////////////////////////////////////////////////////

BOOL CALLBACK Dlg_Proc (HWND hDlg, UINT uMsg,
  WPARAM wParam, LPARAM lParam) {

  BOOL fProcessed = TRUE;

  switch (uMsg) {
    HANDLE_MSG(hDlg, WM_INITDIALOG,  Dlg_OnInitDialog);
    HANDLE_MSG(hDlg, WM_COMMAND,  Dlg_OnCommand);
    HANDLE_MSG(hDlg, WM_HSCROLL,  Dlg_OnHScroll);
    HANDLE_MSG(hDlg, WM_PAINT,    Dlg_OnPaint);
    HANDLE_MSG(hDlg, WM_DESTROY,  Dlg_OnDestroy);

    default:
      fProcessed = FALSE;
      break;
  }
  return(fProcessed);
}

//////////////////////////////////////////////////////////////

int APIENTRY WinMain (HINSTANCE hInstance,
  HINSTANCE hPrevInstance,
  LPSTR lpszCmdLine, int nCmdShow) {

  SYSTEM_INFO SystemInfo;

  // Get the page size used on this CPU.
  GetSystemInfo(&SystemInfo);
  g_uPageSize = SystemInfo.dwPageSize;

  DialogBox(hInstance, MAKEINTRESOURCE(DLG_VMALLOC),
    NULL, Dlg_Proc);
  return(0);
}

/////////////////////////// End Of File ///////////////////////
```

(continued)

Figure 3-2. *continued*

```
VMALLOC.H
/****************************************************************
Module name: VMAlloc.H
Notices: Copyright (c) 1993 Jeffrey Richter
****************************************************************/

// Dialog and control IDs.
#define DLG_VMALLOC          1
#define ID_PAGESIZE        100
#define ID_RESERVE         101
#define ID_INDEXTEXT       102
#define ID_INDEX           103
#define ID_INDEXSCRL       104
#define ID_USE             105
#define ID_CLEAR           106
#define ID_GARBAGECOLLECT  107
#define ID_MEMMAP          108


/////////////////////// End Of File //////////////////////////
```

```
VMALLOC.RC
/****************************************************************
Module name: VMAlloc.RC
Notices: Copyright (c) 1993 Jeffrey Richter
****************************************************************/

#include <windows.h>
#include "VMAlloc.h"

VMAlloc  ICON  DISCARDABLE VMAlloc.Ico

DLG_VMALLOC DIALOG 15, 24, 243, 120
STYLE WS_BORDER | WS_POPUP | WS_VISIBLE | WS_CAPTION |
   WS_SYSMENU | WS_MINIMIZEBOX
CAPTION "Virtual Memory Allocator"
BEGIN
   CONTROL "CPU page size:", -1, "STATIC",
      SS_LEFT | WS_CHILD | WS_VISIBLE | WS_GROUP, 4, 4, 52, 8
   CONTROL "16KB", ID_PAGESIZE, "STATIC",
      SS_LEFTNOWORDWRAP | SS_NOPREFIX | WS_CHILD |
      WS_VISIBLE | WS_GROUP, 60, 4, 32, 8
```

(continued)

Figure 3-2. *continued*

```
    CONTROL "&Reserve address space for 50 structures,
2K each",
        ID_RESERVE, "BUTTON", BS_DEFPUSHBUTTON | WS_CHILD |
        WS_VISIBLE | WS_GROUP | WS_TABSTOP, 32, 16, 180, 14
    LTEXT "&Index (0 - 49):", ID_INDEXTEXT, 4, 38, 48, 8
    EDITTEXT ID_INDEX, 56, 36, 16, 12,
        ES_LEFT | WS_CHILD | WS_VISIBLE | WS_BORDER | WS_TABSTOP
    SCROLLBAR ID_INDEXSCRL, 80, 38, 160, 9,
        SBS_HORZ | WS_CHILD | WS_VISIBLE | WS_TABSTOP
    PUSHBUTTON "&Use", ID_USE, 4, 52, 40, 14,
        WS_CHILD | WS_VISIBLE | WS_TABSTOP
    PUSHBUTTON "&Clear", ID_CLEAR, 48, 52, 40, 14,
        WS_CHILD | WS_VISIBLE | WS_TABSTOP
    PUSHBUTTON "&Garbage collect", ID_GARBAGECOLLECT,
        160, 52, 80, 14
    CONTROL "Memory map", -1, "button",
        BS_GROUPBOX | WS_CHILD | WS_VISIBLE, 4, 66, 236, 52
    CONTROL "", ID_MEMMAP, "static",
        SS_BLACKRECT | WS_CHILD | WS_VISIBLE, 8, 82, 228, 16
    LTEXT "Free: White", -1, 8, 104, 44, 8
    CTEXT "Reserved: Gray", -1, 88, 104, 56, 8,
        WS_CHILD | WS_VISIBLE | WS_GROUP
    RTEXT "Committed: Black", -1, 176, 104, 60, 8,
        SS_RIGHT | WS_CHILD | WS_VISIBLE | WS_GROUP
END

/////////////////////// End Of File ///////////////////////
```

Altering Protection Attributes

While your process executes, it might want to change the protection rights of its data. For example, say you've developed code to manage a linked list, the nodes of which you are keeping in virtual memory. You could design the functions that process the linked list so that they change the protection rights of the memory to PAGE_READWRITE at the start of each function and change the memory back to PAGE_NO-ACCESS just before each function terminates.

By doing this, you protect your linked-list data from other bugs. If any other code in your process has a stray pointer that attempts to access your linked-list data, an access violation occurs. This can be incredibly useful when trying to locate hard-to-find bugs in your application.

You can alter the protection rights of a page of memory by calling VirtualProtect:

```
BOOL VirtualProtect(LPVOID lpAddress, DWORD dwSize,
    DWORD flNewProtect, PDWORD lpflOldProtect);
```

Here *lpAddress* points to the base address of the memory, *dwSize* indicates the number of bytes for which you want to change the protection rights, and *flNewProtect* is one of the PAGE_* protection identifiers.

The last parameter, *lpflOldProtect*, is the address of a DWORD that VirtualProtect will fill in with the old protection rights for the memory. You must pass a valid address as this parameter, or the function will fail. If you are changing the protection attribute of more than one page, the DWORD pointed to by *lpflOldProtect* will receive the old protection attribute for the first page only. The function returns TRUE if it's successful.

Determining the State of an Address Space

There might be times when you need to find out information about a given range of pages. You can do so by using the VirtualQuery function:

```
DWORD VirtualQuery(LPVOID lpAddress,
    PMEMORY_BASIC_INFORMATION lpBuffer, DWORD dwLength);
```

lpAddress points to an address somewhere within the range of virtual address space for which you want information. The *lpBuffer* parameter is the address to a MEMORY_BASIC_INFORMATION structure as defined in WINNT.H:

```
typedef struct _MEMORY_BASIC_INFORMATION {
    PVOID BaseAddress;
    PVOID AllocationBase;
    DWORD AllocationProtect;
    DWORD RegionSize;
    DWORD State;
    DWORD Protect;
    DWORD Type;
} MEMORY_BASIC_INFORMATION, *PMEMORY_BASIC_INFORMATION;
```

The last parameter, *dwLength*, specifies the size of a MEMORY-_BASIC_INFORMATION structure. VirtualQuery returns the number of bytes copied into the buffer.

Based on the address that you pass in the *lpAddress* parameter, VirtualQuery fills the MEMORY_BASIC_INFORMATION structure with information about the range of adjoining pages that all share the same attributes. Here is a description of the structure's members:

Member Name	Description
BaseAddress	For all adjoining pages sharing the same attributes, identifies the base address of the virtual address space containing *lpAddress*.
AllocationBase	Identifies the base address of the reserved virtual address space containing *lpAddress*.
AllocationProtect	Identifies the protection status given to the reserved address space when it was initially reserved.
RegionSize	Gives the size, in bytes, of the region beginning at the page containing *lpAddress*. A region consists of consecutive pages having the same attributes.
State	Specifies the state of the pages: MEM_FREE, MEM_RESERVE, or MEM_COMMIT.
Protect	Identifies the protection status currently given to the adjoining pages.
Type	Identifies the type of pages: MEM_MAPPED, MEM_PRIVATE, or MEM_IMAGE.

The Virtual Memory Map Sample Application

The VMMap application (VMMAP.EXE), listed in Figure 3-4 beginning on page 115, walks the entire address space for its own process and shows the state of all the memory. When you start the program, the following window appears:

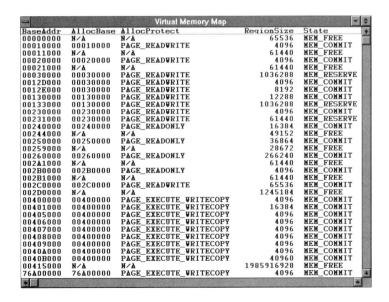

Each entry in the list box shows the result of a single call to Virtual-Query. The main loop looks like this:

```
// Start the memory walk at address zero.
PVOID lpAddress = 0;

MEMORY_BASIC_INFORMATION MemoryBasicInfo;

do {
    int x = VirtualQuery(lpAddress, &MemoryBasicInfo,
        sizeof(MemoryBasicInfo));

    if (x != sizeof(MemoryBasicInfo)) {
        // If a full structure was not returned, we are done.
        break;
    }


    // Examine the members of MemoryBasicInfo,
    // construct the string, and add it to the list box.
    .
    .
    .

    // Calculate the address of the next region to check.
    lpAddress = ((char *) MemoryBasicInfo.BaseAddress) +
        MemoryBasicInfo.RegionSize;

    // Continue checking until we wrap around to address
    // zero again.
} while (lpAddress != 0);
```

The entire content of this list box is shown in Figure 3-3 on the following pages:

There are two interesting things to note about this list. First, the address range from 0x00000000 to 0x00007FFF (the first 64 KB) always has a type of MEM_FREE. This region is reserved by the system and can never be allocated by a process. The system does this in order to help the application trap writes to NULL.

Second, the address range from 0x7FFF0000 to 0xFFFFFFFF (the 64 KB just below the 2-GB line) is also always reserved by the system and can never have memory committed to it. This is to catch wild writes that occur just below the 2-GB address. VMMap stops walking when it hits this address (0x7FFEF000 + 4096).

BaseAddr	AllocBase	AllocProtect	RegionSize	State	Protect	Type
00000000	N/A	N/A	65536	MEM_FREE	N/A	N/A
00010000	00010000	PAGE_EXECUTE_WRITECOPY	4096	MEM_COMMIT	PAGE_READONLY	Unknown (16777216)
00011000	00010000	PAGE_EXECUTE_WRITECOPY	12288	MEM_COMMIT	PAGE_EXECUTE_READ	Unknown (16777216)
00014000	00010000	PAGE_EXECUTE_WRITECOPY	4096	MEM_COMMIT	PAGE_READWRITE	Unknown (16777216)
00015000	00010000	PAGE_EXECUTE_WRITECOPY	4096	MEM_COMMIT	PAGE_READONLY	Unknown (16777216)
00016000	00010000	PAGE_EXECUTE_WRITECOPY	4096	MEM_COMMIT	PAGE_READONLY	Unknown (16777216)
00017000	00010000	PAGE_EXECUTE_WRITECOPY	4096	MEM_COMMIT	PAGE_WRITECOPY	Unknown (16777216)
00018000	00010000	PAGE_EXECUTE_WRITECOPY	4096	MEM_COMMIT	PAGE_READWRITE	Unknown (16777216)
00019000	00010000	PAGE_EXECUTE_WRITECOPY	4096	MEM_COMMIT	PAGE_WRITECOPY	Unknown (16777216)
0001A000	00010000	PAGE_EXECUTE_WRITECOPY	4096	MEM_COMMIT	PAGE_READONLY	Unknown (16777216)
0001B000	N/A	N/A	20480	MEM_FREE	N/A	N/A
00020000	00020000	PAGE_READWRITE	4096	MEM_COMMIT	PAGE_READWRITE	MEM_PRIVATE
00021000	N/A	N/A	61440	MEM_FREE	N/A	N/A
00030000	00030000	PAGE_READWRITE	4096	MEM_COMMIT	PAGE_READWRITE	MEM_PRIVATE
00031000	N/A	N/A	61440	MEM_FREE	N/A	N/A
00040000	00040000	PAGE_READWRITE	1036288	MEM_RESERVE	N/A	MEM_PRIVATE
0013D000	00040000	PAGE_READWRITE	4096	MEM_COMMIT	Unknown (260)	MEM_PRIVATE
0013E000	00040000	PAGE_READWRITE	8192	MEM_COMMIT	PAGE_READWRITE	MEM_PRIVATE
00140000	00140000	PAGE_READWRITE	12288	MEM_COMMIT	PAGE_READWRITE	MEM_PRIVATE
00143000	00140000	PAGE_READWRITE	1036288	MEM_RESERVE	N/A	MEM_PRIVATE
00240000	00240000	PAGE_READWRITE	4096	MEM_COMMIT	PAGE_READWRITE	MEM_MAPPED

Figure 3-3.
Contents of the Virtual Memory Map list box.

(continued)

Figure 3-3. *continued*

BaseAddr	AllocBase	AllocProtect	RegionSize	State	Protect	Type
00241000	00240000	PAGE_READWRITE	61440	MEM_RESERVE	N/A	MEM_MAPPED
00250000	00250000	PAGE_READONLY	16384	MEM_COMMIT	PAGE_READONLY	MEM_MAPPED
00254000	N/A	N/A	49152	MEM_FREE	N/A	N/A
00260000	00260000	PAGE_READONLY	36864	MEM_COMMIT	PAGE_READONLY	MEM_MAPPED
00269000	N/A	N/A	28672	MEM_FREE	N/A	N/A
00270000	00270000	PAGE_READONLY	266240	MEM_COMMIT	PAGE_READONLY	MEM_MAPPED
002B1000	N/A	N/A	61440	MEM_FREE	N/A	N/A
002C0000	002C0000	PAGE_READONLY	4096	MEM_COMMIT	PAGE_READONLY	MEM_MAPPED
002C1000	N/A	N/A	61440	MEM_FREE	N/A	N/A
002D0000	002D0000	PAGE_READWRITE	65536	MEM_COMMIT	PAGE_READWRITE	MEM_PRIVATE
002E0000	002D0000	PAGE_READWRITE	983040	MEM_RESERVE	N/A	MEM_PRIVATE
003D0000	003D0000	PAGE_READWRITE	4096	MEM_COMMIT	PAGE_READWRITE	MEM_PRIVATE
003D1000	N/A	N/A	61440	MEM_FREE	N/A	N/A
003E0000	003E0000	PAGE_READWRITE	65536	MEM_COMMIT	PAGE_READWRITE	MEM_MAPPED
003F0000	N/A	N/A	1607532544	MEM_FREE	N/A	N/A
60100000	60100000	PAGE_EXECUTE_WRITECOPY	4096	MEM_COMMIT	PAGE_READONLY	Unknown (16777216)
60101000	60100000	PAGE_EXECUTE_WRITECOPY	147456	MEM_COMMIT	PAGE_EXECUTE_READ	Unknown (16777216)
60125000	60100000	PAGE_EXECUTE_WRITECOPY	8192	MEM_COMMIT	PAGE_READWRITE	Unknown (16777216)
60127000	60100000	PAGE_EXECUTE_WRITECOPY	28672	MEM_COMMIT	PAGE_READONLY	Unknown (16777216)
6012E000	60100000	PAGE_EXECUTE_WRITECOPY	4096	MEM_COMMIT	PAGE_READWRITE	Unknown (16777216)
6012F000	60100000	PAGE_EXECUTE_WRITECOPY	65536	MEM_COMMIT	PAGE_WRITECOPY	Unknown (16777216)

BaseAddr	AllocBase	AllocProtect	RegionSize	State	Protect	Type
6013F000	60100000	PAGE_EXECUTE_WRITECOPY	135168	MEM_COMMIT	PAGE_READONLY	Unknown (16777216)
60160000	N/A	N/A	4849664	MEM_FREE	N/A	N/A
60600000	60600000	PAGE_EXECUTE_WRITECOPY	4096	MEM_COMMIT	PAGE_READONLY	Unknown (16777216)
60601000	60600000	PAGE_EXECUTE_WRITECOPY	212992	MEM_COMMIT	PAGE_EXECUTE_READ	Unknown (16777216)
60635000	60600000	PAGE_EXECUTE_WRITECOPY	8192	MEM_COMMIT	PAGE_READWRITE	Unknown (16777216)
60637000	60600000	PAGE_EXECUTE_WRITECOPY	20480	MEM_COMMIT	PAGE_READONLY	Unknown (16777216)
6063C000	60600000	PAGE_EXECUTE_WRITECOPY	61440	MEM_COMMIT	PAGE_WRITECOPY	Unknown (16777216)
6064B000	60600000	PAGE_EXECUTE_WRITECOPY	4096	MEM_COMMIT	PAGE_READWRITE	Unknown (16777216)
6064C000	60600000	PAGE_EXECUTE_WRITECOPY	4096	MEM_COMMIT	PAGE_WRITECOPY	Unknown (16777216)
6064D000	60600000	PAGE_EXECUTE_WRITECOPY	4096	MEM_COMMIT	PAGE_READWRITE	Unknown (16777216)
6064E000	60600000	PAGE_EXECUTE_WRITECOPY	12288	MEM_COMMIT	PAGE_WRITECOPY	Unknown (16777216)
60651000	60600000	PAGE_EXECUTE_WRITECOPY	233472	MEM_COMMIT	PAGE_READONLY	Unknown (16777216)
6068A000	N/A	N/A	3629056	MEM_FREE	N/A	N/A
60A00000	60A00000	PAGE_EXECUTE_WRITECOPY	4096	MEM_COMMIT	PAGE_READONLY	Unknown (16777216)
60A01000	60A00000	PAGE_EXECUTE_WRITECOPY	188416	MEM_COMMIT	PAGE_EXECUTE_READ	Unknown (16777216)
60A2F000	60A00000	PAGE_EXECUTE_WRITECOPY	4096	MEM_COMMIT	PAGE_READWRITE	Unknown (16777216)
60A30000	60A00000	PAGE_EXECUTE_WRITECOPY	20480	MEM_COMMIT	PAGE_READONLY	Unknown (16777216)
60A35000	60A00000	PAGE_EXECUTE_WRITECOPY	4096	MEM_COMMIT	PAGE_WRITECOPY	Unknown (16777216)
60A36000	60A00000	PAGE_EXECUTE_WRITECOPY	4096	MEM_COMMIT	PAGE_READWRITE	Unknown (16777216)
60A37000	60A00000	PAGE_EXECUTE_WRITECOPY	16384	MEM_COMMIT	PAGE_WRITECOPY	Unknown (16777216)
60A3B000	60A00000	PAGE_EXECUTE_WRITECOPY	249856	MEM_COMMIT	PAGE_READONLY	Unknown (16777216)

(continued)

Figure 3-3. *continued*

BaseAddr	AllocBase	AllocProtect	RegionSize	State	Protect	Type
60A78000	N/A	N/A	56131584	MEM_FREE	N/A	N/A
64000000	64000000	PAGE_EXECUTE_WRITECOPY	4096	MEM_COMMIT	PAGE_READONLY	Unknown (16777216)
64001000	64000000	PAGE_EXECUTE_WRITECOPY	188416	MEM_COMMIT	PAGE_EXECUTE_READ	Unknown (16777216)
6402F000	64000000	PAGE_EXECUTE_WRITECOPY	4096	MEM_COMMIT	PAGE_READWRITE	Unknown (16777216)
64030000	64000000	PAGE_EXECUTE_WRITECOPY	16384	MEM_COMMIT	PAGE_READONLY	Unknown (16777216)
64034000	64000000	PAGE_EXECUTE_WRITECOPY	4096	MEM_COMMIT	PAGE_READWRITE	Unknown (16777216)
64035000	64000000	PAGE_EXECUTE_WRITECOPY	8192	MEM_COMMIT	PAGE_WRITECOPY	Unknown (16777216)
64037000	64000000	PAGE_EXECUTE_WRITECOPY	143360	MEM_COMMIT	PAGE_READONLY	Unknown (16777216)
6405A000	N/A	N/A	457269248	MEM_FREE	N/A	N/A
7F470000	7F470000	PAGE_EXECUTE_READ	102400	MEM_COMMIT	PAGE_EXECUTE_READ	MEM_MAPPED
7F489000	7F470000	PAGE_EXECUTE_READ	1470464	MEM_RESERVE	N/A	MEM_MAPPED
7F5F0000	7F5F0000	PAGE_EXECUTE_READ	1048576	MEM_RESERVE	N/A	MEM_MAPPED
7F6F0000	7F5F0000	PAGE_EXECUTE_READ	24576	MEM_COMMIT	PAGE_EXECUTE_READ	MEM_MAPPED
7F6F6000	7F5F0000	PAGE_EXECUTE_READ	1024000	MEM_RESERVE	N/A	MEM_MAPPED
7F7F0000	N/A	N/A	7929856	MEM_FREE	N/A	N/A
7FF80000	7FF80000	PAGE_READWRITE	4096	MEM_COMMIT	PAGE_READWRITE	MEM_PRIVATE
7FF81000	7FF80000	PAGE_READWRITE	258048	MEM_RESERVE	N/A	MEM_PRIVATE
7FFC0000	7FFC0000	PAGE_READONLY	147456	MEM_COMMIT	PAGE_READONLY	MEM_MAPPED
7FFE4000	N/A	N/A	40960	MEM_FREE	N/A	N/A
7FFEE000	7FFEE000	PAGE_READWRITE	4096	MEM_COMMIT	PAGE_READWRITE	MEM_PRIVATE
7FFEF000	7FFEF000	PAGE_READWRITE	4096	MEM_COMMIT	PAGE_READWRITE	MEM_PRIVATE

VMMap.ico

VMMAP.C

```
/****************************************************************
Module name: VMMap.C
Notices: Copyright (c) 1993 Jeffrey Richter
****************************************************************/

#include <windows.h>
#include <windowsx.h>
#include <tchar.h>
#include <stdio.h>        // for sprintf
#include <string.h>       // for strchr
#include "VMMap.H"

// If you also want the map info written to a file,
// change FALSE to TRUE.
#define WRITETOFILE FALSE

#if WRITETOFILE
HANDLE g_hFile;
#endif


//////////////////////////////////////////////////////////////

typedef struct {
   const DWORD dwValue;
   LPCTSTR szText;
} LONGDATA;

#define TABLEENTRY(Value)          Value, __TEXT(#Value)

LONGDATA PageFlags[] = {
   TABLEENTRY(PAGE_NOACCESS),
   TABLEENTRY(PAGE_READONLY),
   TABLEENTRY(PAGE_READWRITE),
   TABLEENTRY(PAGE_WRITECOPY),
   TABLEENTRY(PAGE_EXECUTE),
   TABLEENTRY(PAGE_EXECUTE_READ),
```

Figure 3-4.   *(continued)*
The VMMap application.

Figure 3-4. *continued*

```
     TABLEENTRY(PAGE_EXECUTE_READWRITE),
     TABLEENTRY(PAGE_EXECUTE_WRITECOPY),
     TABLEENTRY(PAGE_GUARD),
     TABLEENTRY(PAGE_NOCACHE),
     TABLEENTRY(0)
};

LONGDATA MemFlags[] = {
     TABLEENTRY(MEM_COMMIT),
     TABLEENTRY(MEM_RESERVE),
     TABLEENTRY(MEM_DECOMMIT),
     TABLEENTRY(MEM_RELEASE),
     TABLEENTRY(MEM_FREE),
     TABLEENTRY(MEM_PRIVATE),
     TABLEENTRY(MEM_MAPPED),
     TABLEENTRY(MEM_TOP_DOWN),
     TABLEENTRY(MEM_IMAGE),
     TABLEENTRY(0)
};

//////////////////////////////////////////////////////////////

LPCTSTR GetFlagStr (DWORD dwFlag, LONGDATA FlagList[],
     LPTSTR pszBuf) {

     int x;

     for (x = 0; FlagList[x].dwValue != 0; x++) {
          if (FlagList[x].dwValue == dwFlag)
               return(FlagList[x].szText);
     }

     _stprintf(pszBuf, __TEXT("Unknown (%d)"), dwFlag);
     return(pszBuf);
}

//////////////////////////////////////////////////////////////

void ConstructMemInfoLine (PMEMORY_BASIC_INFORMATION pMBI,
     LPTSTR szLine) {

     LPCTSTR sz;
     TCHAR szBuf[50];
```

(continued)

116

Figure 3-4. *continued*

```
// BaseAddress
_stprintf(szLine, __TEXT("%08X  "), pMBI->BaseAddress);

// AllocationBase
_stprintf(_tcschr(szLine, 0),
   (pMBI->State != MEM_FREE) ?
      __TEXT("%08X") : __TEXT("N/A     "),
      pMBI->AllocationBase);

// AllocationProtect
if (pMBI->State != MEM_FREE) {
   sz = GetFlagStr(pMBI->AllocationProtect, PageFlags,
      szBuf);
} else {
   sz = __TEXT("N/A");
}

_stprintf(_tcschr(szLine, 0), __TEXT("  %-23s  "), sz);

// RegionSize
_stprintf(_tcschr(szLine, 0), __TEXT("%10u  "),
   pMBI->RegionSize);

// State
_stprintf(_tcschr(szLine, 0), __TEXT("%-16s  "),
   GetFlagStr(pMBI->State, MemFlags, szBuf));

// Protect
if ((pMBI->State != MEM_FREE) &&
   (pMBI->State != MEM_RESERVE)) {
   sz = GetFlagStr(pMBI->Protect, PageFlags, szBuf);
} else {
   sz = __TEXT("N/A");
}

_stprintf(_tcschr(szLine, 0), __TEXT("%-24s  "), sz);

// Type
if (pMBI->State != MEM_FREE) {
   sz = GetFlagStr(pMBI->Type, MemFlags, szBuf);
} else {
   sz = __TEXT("N/A");
}
```

(continued)

Figure 3-4. *continued*

```
   _stprintf(_tcschr(szLine, 0), __TEXT("%-16s"), sz);
}


/////////////////////////////////////////////////////////////

void Dlg_OnSize (HWND hwnd, UINT state, int cx, int cy) {
   SetWindowPos(GetDlgItem(hwnd, ID_LISTBOX), NULL, 0, 0,
      cx, cy, SWP_NOZORDER);
}


/////////////////////////////////////////////////////////////

BOOL Dlg_OnInitDialog (HWND hwnd, HWND hwndFocus,
   LPARAM lParam) {

   HWND hWndLB = GetDlgItem(hwnd, ID_LISTBOX);
   MEMORY_BASIC_INFORMATION MemoryBasicInfo;
   PVOID lpAddress = 0;
   TCHAR szLine[200];
   RECT rc;

   // Associate an icon with the dialog box.
   SetClassLong(hwnd, GCL_HICON, (LONG)
      LoadIcon((HINSTANCE) GetWindowLong(hwnd, GWL_HINSTANCE),
      __TEXT("VMMap")));

   // Make a horizontal scroll bar appear in the list box.
   ListBox_SetHorizontalExtent(hWndLB,
      150 * LOWORD(GetDialogBaseUnits()));

   // The list box has to be sized initially because
   // Windows NT won't send a WM_SIZE message to the
   // dialog box when it's first created.
   GetClientRect(hwnd, &rc);
   SetWindowPos(hWndLB, NULL, 0, 0, rc.right, rc.bottom,
      SWP_NOZORDER);

   // Add the caption heading as the first
   // entry in the list box.
   ListBox_AddString(hWndLB,
      __TEXT("BaseAddr  AllocBase AllocProtect            ")
      __TEXT("RegionSize  State             Protect")
      __TEXT("                     Type"));
```

(continued)

Figure 3-4.   *continued*

```
#if WRITETOFILE
    g_hFile = CreateFile(__TEXT("VMMAP.DAT"), GENERIC_WRITE, 0,
        NULL, CREATE_ALWAYS, 0, NULL);
#endif

    // Walk the virtual address space, adding
    // entries to the list box.
    do {
        int x = VirtualQuery(lpAddress, &MemoryBasicInfo,
            sizeof(MemoryBasicInfo));

        if (x != sizeof(MemoryBasicInfo)) {
            // Attempt to walk beyond the range
            // that Windows NT allows.
            break;
        }

        // Construct the line to be displayed, and
        // add it to the list box.
        ConstructMemInfoLine(&MemoryBasicInfo, szLine);
        ListBox_AddString(hWndLB, szLine);

#if WRITETOFILE
        {
            DWORD dw;
            WriteFile(g_hFile, szLine, lstrlen(szLine),
                &dw, NULL);
            WriteFile(g_hFile, __TEXT("\r\n"), 2 * sizeof(TCHAR),
                &dw, NULL);
        }
#endif

        // Get the address of the next region to test.
        lpAddress = ((BYTE *) MemoryBasicInfo.BaseAddress) +
            MemoryBasicInfo.RegionSize;

    } while (lpAddress != 0);

#if WRITETOFILE
    CloseHandle(g_hFile);
#endif

    return(TRUE);
}
```

(continued)

Figure 3-4. *continued*

```
////////////////////////////////////////////////////////////

void Dlg_OnCommand (HWND hwnd, int id, HWND hwndCtl,
   UINT codeNotify) {

   switch (id) {
      case IDCANCEL:
         EndDialog(hwnd, id);
         break;
   }
}


////////////////////////////////////////////////////////////

BOOL CALLBACK Dlg_Proc (HWND hDlg, UINT uMsg,
   WPARAM wParam, LPARAM lParam) {

   BOOL fProcessed = TRUE;
   switch (uMsg) {
      HANDLE_MSG(hDlg, WM_INITDIALOG, Dlg_OnInitDialog);
      HANDLE_MSG(hDlg, WM_COMMAND, Dlg_OnCommand);
      HANDLE_MSG(hDlg, WM_SIZE, Dlg_OnSize);

      default:
         fProcessed = FALSE;
         break;
   }
   return(fProcessed);
}


////////////////////////////////////////////////////////////

int APIENTRY WinMain (HINSTANCE hInstance,
   HINSTANCE hPrevInstance, LPSTR lpszCmdLine, int nCmdShow) {

   DialogBox(hInstance, MAKEINTRESOURCE(DLG_VMMAP),
      NULL, Dlg_Proc);
   return(0);
}

/////////////////////// End Of File ///////////////////////
```

(continued)

Figure 3-4.   *continued*

VMMAP.H

```
/***********************************************************
Module name: VMMap.H
Notices: Copyright (c) 1993 Jeffrey Richter
***********************************************************/


// Dialog and control IDs.
#define DLG_VMMAP                  1
#define ID_LISTBOX                 100


//////////////////////// End Of File ////////////////////////
```

VMMAP.RC

```
/***********************************************************
Module name: VMMap.RC
Notices: Copyright (c) 1993 Jeffrey Richter
***********************************************************/


#include <windows.h>
#include "VMMap.h"

VMMap  ICON  DISCARDABLE VMMap.Ico

DLG_VMMAP DIALOG 10, 18, 250, 250
STYLE WS_THICKFRAME | WS_POPUP | WS_VISIBLE | WS_CAPTION |
    WS_SYSMENU | WS_MAXIMIZEBOX | WS_MINIMIZEBOX
CAPTION "Virtual Memory Map"
FONT 8, "Courier"
BEGIN
    CONTROL "", ID_LISTBOX, "LISTBOX",
        LBS_NOINTEGRALHEIGHT | WS_CHILD | WS_VISIBLE |
        WS_HSCROLL | WS_VSCROLL | WS_GROUP | WS_TABSTOP,
        0, 0, 0, 0
END


//////////////////////// End Of File ////////////////////////
```

The System Status Sample Application

The SysStat application (SYSSTAT.EXE), listed in Figure 3-5 beginning on the next page, is a very simple program that calls GetSystemInfo and displays the information returned in the SYSTEM_INFO structure. The dialog box below shows the results of running the SysStat application on an Intel 486:

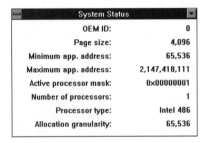

The fields of interest here are:

Field	Meaning
Page size	Shows the size of a memory page. The Intel processor uses 4-KB pages.
Min application address	Gives the minimum memory address that can be used by an application. Because the first 64 KB of every process are reserved, this value is 65,536.
Max application address	Gives the maximum memory address that can be used by an application. Because the top 2 GB are reserved for the system and the 64 KB just below the 2-GB line are also reserved, the maximum memory address is 2,147,418,111 (0x7FFEFFFF).
Allocation granularity	Shows the smallest amount of address space that can be reserved. This value used to be hard-coded in the system as 64 KB, but, since it might change for different machines in the future, Microsoft added it to the system information.

THREE: Virtual Memory Management

SysStat.ico

SYSSTAT.C

```
/*****************************************************************
Module name: SysStat.C
Notices: Copyright (c) 1993 Jeffrey Richter
*****************************************************************/

#include <windows.h>
#include <windowsx.h>
#include <tchar.h>
#include <stdio.h>
#include <string.h>      // for strrev
#include "SysStat.H"


///////////////////////////////////////////////////////////////

typedef struct {
    const DWORD dwValue;
    LPCTSTR szText;
} LONGDATA;

LONGDATA CPUFlags[] = {
    { PROCESSOR_INTEL_386,     __TEXT("Intel 386") },
    { PROCESSOR_INTEL_486,     __TEXT("Intel 486") },
    { PROCESSOR_INTEL_PENTIUM, __TEXT("Intel Pentium") },
    { PROCESSOR_INTEL_860,     __TEXT("Intel 860") },
    { PROCESSOR_MIPS_R2000,    __TEXT("MIPS R2000") },
    { PROCESSOR_MIPS_R3000,    __TEXT("MIPS R3000") },
    { PROCESSOR_MIPS_R4000,    __TEXT("MIPS R4000") },
    { PROCESSOR_ALPHA_21064,   __TEXT("DEC Alpha 21064") },
    { 0, NULL }
};



///////////////////////////////////////////////////////////////

LPCTSTR GetFlagStr (DWORD dwFlag, LONGDATA FlagList[],
    LPTSTR pszBuf) {
```

Figure 3-5.
The SysStat application.

(continued)

Figure 3-5. *continued*

```
    int x;

    for (x = 0; FlagList[x].dwValue != 0; x++) {
       if (FlagList[x].dwValue == dwFlag)
          return(FlagList[x].szText);
    }

    _stprintf(pszBuf, __TEXT("Unknown (%d)"), dwFlag);
    return(pszBuf);
}


///////////////////////////////////////////////////////////////

// This function accepts a number and converts it to a
// string, inserting commas where appropriate.
LPTSTR WINAPI BigNumToString (LONG lNum, LPTSTR szBuf) {
    WORD wNumDigits = 0, wNumChars = 0;

    do {
       // Put the last digit of the string
       // in the character buffer.
       szBuf[wNumChars++] = lNum % 10 + '0';

       // Increment the number of digits
       // that we put in the string.
       wNumDigits++;

       // For every three digits put in
       // the string, add a comma (,).
       if (wNumDigits % 3 == 0)
          szBuf[wNumChars++] - __TEXT(',');

       // Divide the number by 10, and repeat the process.
       lNum /= 10;

       // Continue adding digits to the
       // string until the number is zero.
    } while (lNum != 0);

    // If the last character added to
    // the string was a comma, truncate it.
    if (szBuf[wNumChars - 1] == __TEXT(','))
       szBuf[wNumChars - 1] = 0;
```

(continued)

Figure 3-5. *continued*

```
    // Ensure that the string is zero-terminated.
    szBuf[wNumChars] = 0;

    // We added all the characters to the string in
    // reverse order. We must reverse the contents
    // of the string.
    _tcsrev(szBuf);

    // Returns the address of the string.  This is the same
    // value that was passed to us initially.  Returning it
    // here makes it easier for the calling function to
    // use the string.
    return(szBuf);
}


/////////////////////////////////////////////////////////////

BOOL Dlg_OnInitDialog (HWND hwnd, HWND hwndFocus,
    LPARAM lParam) {

    TCHAR szBuf[50];
    SYSTEM_INFO si;

    // Associate an icon with the dialog box.
    SetClassLong(hwnd, GCL_HICON, (LONG)
        LoadIcon((HINSTANCE) GetWindowLong(hwnd,
        GWL_HINSTANCE), __TEXT("SysStat")));

    GetSystemInfo(&si);

    // Fill the static controls in the
    // list box with the appropriate number.
    SetDlgItemText(hwnd, ID_OEMID,
        BigNumToString(si.dwOemId, szBuf));

    SetDlgItemText(hwnd, ID_PAGESIZE,
        BigNumToString(si.dwPageSize, szBuf));

    SetDlgItemText(hwnd, ID_MINAPPADDR,
        BigNumToString((LONG) si.lpMinimumApplicationAddress,
        szBuf));
```

(continued)

Figure 3-5. *continued*

```
    SetDlgItemText(hwnd, ID_MAXAPPADDR,
        BigNumToString((LONG) si.lpMaximumApplicationAddress,
        szBuf));

    _stprintf(szBuf, __TEXT("0x%08X"),
        si.dwActiveProcessorMask);
    SetDlgItemText(hwnd, ID_ACTIVEPROCMASK, szBuf);

    SetDlgItemText(hwnd, ID_NUMOFPROCS,
        BigNumToString(si.dwNumberOfProcessors, szBuf));

    SetDlgItemText(hwnd, ID_PROCTYPE,
        GetFlagStr(si.dwProcessorType, CPUFlags, szBuf));

    SetDlgItemText(hwnd, ID_ALLOCGRAN,
        BigNumToString(si.dwAllocationGranularity, szBuf));

    return(TRUE);
}

///////////////////////////////////////////////////////////

void Dlg_OnCommand (HWND hwnd, int id, HWND hwndCtl,
    UINT codeNotify) {

    switch (id) {
        case IDCANCEL:
            EndDialog(hwnd, id);
            break;
    }
}

///////////////////////////////////////////////////////////

BOOL CALLBACK Dlg_Proc (HWND hDlg, UINT uMsg,
    WPARAM wParam, LPARAM lParam) {

    BOOL fProcessed = TRUE;

    switch (uMsg) {
        HANDLE_MSG(hDlg, WM_INITDIALOG, Dlg_OnInitDialog);
        HANDLE_MSG(hDlg, WM_COMMAND, Dlg_OnCommand);
```

(continued)

Figure 3-5. *continued*

```
    default:
        fProcessed = FALSE;
        break;
    }
    return(fProcessed);
}


//////////////////////////////////////////////////////////////

int APIENTRY WinMain (HINSTANCE hInstance,
    HINSTANCE hPrevInstance, LPSTR lpszCmdLine,
        int nCmdShow) {

    DialogBox(hInstance, MAKEINTRESOURCE(DLG_SYSSTAT),
        NULL, Dlg_Proc);
    return(0);
}


/////////////////////// End Of File ///////////////////////
```

SYSSTAT.H

```
/**********************************************************
Module name: SysStat.H
Notices: Copyright (c) 1993 Jeffrey Richter
**********************************************************/

// Dialog and control IDs.
#define DLG_SYSSTAT           1
#define ID_OEMID            100
#define ID_PAGESIZE         101
#define ID_MINAPPADDR       102
#define ID_MAXAPPADDR       103
#define ID_ACTIVEPROCMASK   104
#define ID_NUMOFPROCS       105
#define ID_PROCTYPE         106
#define ID_ALLOCGRAN        107


/////////////////////// End Of File ///////////////////////
```

(continued)

Figure 3-5. *continued*

SYSSTAT.RC

```
/**************************************************************
Module name: SysStat.RC
Notices: Copyright (c) 1993 Jeffrey Richter
**************************************************************/

#include <windows.h>
#include "SysStat.h"


SysStat  ICON  DISCARDABLE SysStat.Ico

DLG_SYSSTAT DIALOG 18, 18, 170, 103
STYLE WS_POPUP | WS_VISIBLE | WS_CAPTION | WS_SYSMENU |
   WS_MINIMIZEBOX
CAPTION "System Status"
BEGIN
   CONTROL "OEM ID:", -1, "STATIC",
      SS_RIGHT | SS_NOPREFIX | WS_CHILD | WS_VISIBLE |
      WS_GROUP, 4, 4, 88, 8
   CONTROL "ID_OEMID", ID_OEMID, "STATIC",
      SS_RIGHT | SS_NOPREFIX | WS_CHILD | WS_VISIBLE |
      WS_GROUP, 96, 4, 68, 8
   CONTROL "Page size:", -1, "STATIC",
      SS_RIGHT | SS_NOPREFIX | WS_CHILD | WS_VISIBLE |
      WS_GROUP, 4, 16, 88, 8
   CONTROL "ID_PAGESIZE", ID_PAGESIZE, "STATIC",
      SS_RIGHT | SS_NOPREFIX | WS_CHILD | WS_VISIBLE |
      WS_GROUP, 96, 16, 68, 8
   CONTROL "Minimum app. address:", -1, "STATIC",
      SS_RIGHT | SS_NOPREFIX | WS_CHILD | WS_VISIBLE |
      WS_GROUP, 4, 28, 88, 8
   CONTROL "ID_MINAPPADDR", ID_MINAPPADDR, "STATIC",
      SS_RIGHT | SS_NOPREFIX | WS_CHILD | WS_VISIBLE |
      WS_GROUP, 96, 28, 68, 8
   CONTROL "Maximum app. address:", -1, "STATIC",
      SS_RIGHT | SS_NOPREFIX | WS_CHILD | WS_VISIBLE |
      WS_GROUP, 4, 40, 88, 8
   CONTROL "ID_MAXAPPADDR", ID_MAXAPPADDR, "STATIC",
      SS_RIGHT | SS_NOPREFIX | WS_CHILD | WS_VISIBLE |
      WS_GROUP, 96, 40, 68, 8
   CONTROL "Active processor mask:", -1, "STATIC",
      SS_RIGHT | SS_NOPREFIX | WS_CHILD | WS_VISIBLE |
      WS_GROUP, 4, 52, 88, 8
```

(continued)

Figure 3-5. *continued*

```
    CONTROL "ID_ACTIVEPROCMASK", ID_ACTIVEPROCMASK,
        "STATIC",
        SS_RIGHT | SS_NOPREFIX | WS_CHILD | WS_VISIBLE |
        WS_GROUP, 96, 52, 68, 8
    CONTROL "Number of processors:", -1, "STATIC",
        SS_RIGHT | SS_NOPREFIX | WS_CHILD | WS_VISIBLE |
        WS_GROUP, 4, 64, 88, 8
    CONTROL "ID_NUMOFPROCS", ID_NUMOFPROCS, "STATIC",
        SS_RIGHT | SS_NOPREFIX | WS_CHILD | WS_VISIBLE |
        WS_GROUP, 96, 64, 68, 8
    CONTROL "Processor type:", -1, "STATIC",
        SS_RIGHT | SS_NOPREFIX | WS_CHILD | WS_VISIBLE |
        WS_GROUP, 4, 76, 88, 8
    CONTROL "ID_PROCTYPE", ID_PROCTYPE, "STATIC",
        SS_RIGHT | SS_NOPREFIX | WS_CHILD | WS_VISIBLE |
        WS_GROUP, 96, 76, 68, 8
    CONTROL "Allocation granularity:", -1, "STATIC",
        SS_RIGHT | SS_NOPREFIX | WS_CHILD | WS_VISIBLE |
        WS_GROUP, 4, 88, 88, 8
    CONTROL "ID_ALLOCGRAN", ID_ALLOCGRAN, "STATIC",
        SS_RIGHT | SS_NOPREFIX | WS_CHILD | WS_VISIBLE |
        WS_GROUP, 96, 88, 68, 8
END

///////////////////////// End Of File /////////////////////////
```

Keeping Memory Out of the Paging File

There might be rare occasions when you want to have an entire range of
memory locked in RAM instead of being paged out to the hard disk.
This type of memory use is required by device drivers that are responding to hardware interrupts from the user. When a device driver is invoked via a hardware interrupt, it must respond to that interrupt as
quickly as possible and return from its interrupt service routine. For the
device driver to accomplish this task, it might need immediate access to
its memory. The device driver can tell Windows NT that it wants its
memory to be resident at all times so that the operating system does not
page the memory to the paging file on the hard disk. Any Win32 application can request that Windows NT not swap its memory (or a portion
of it) to disk by calling VirtualLock:

```
BOOL VirtualLock(LPVOID lpvMem, DWORD cbMem);
```

This function locks the *cbMem* bytes starting at address *lpvMem* in memory. If it is successful, TRUE is returned. For an application, Windows NT allows the locked address space to remain locked only when the process is running. If another process becomes active, Windows NT allows the first process's locked memory to be swapped to disk. When the process becomes active again, Windows NT automatically reloads the locked pages from disk into RAM and keeps them there.

It is important to note that all the pages that you attempt to lock must be committed to physical storage. In addition, VirtualLock cannot be used to lock memory allocated with a PAGE_NOACCESS protection attribute. When it is no longer necessary for your application to keep the memory locked, you can unlock it with VirtualUnlock:

```
BOOL VirtualUnlock(LPVOID lpvMem, DWORD cbMem);
```

This function unlocks the *cbMem* bytes of memory starting at address *lpvMem*. When unlocking memory, it is not necessary to unlock the exact amount that was locked with VirtualLock—you can unlock a portion of the address space. If the range of memory is unlocked successfully, VirtualUnlock returns TRUE.

As with all of the virtual functions, operations are performed on a page basis. So if you lock a range of bytes that straddle a series of pages, all pages affected by the range are locked or unlocked.

I should stress that the use of the locking functions is discouraged, and here's why. If you lock a range of virtual memory in your process, Windows NT must force all those pages to be reloaded whenever there is a context switch to your process. Your application might take an immediate performance hit every time there is a context switch. If, instead, you didn't lock any of your pages, Windows NT would reload them as your application required. You are much better off allowing Windows NT to perform the page swapping rather than getting involved with it yourself. After all, only the operating system knows how other applications are behaving and what toll they are taking on the system's memory. Windows NT's memory management system has been fine-tuned for this—let it do its job.

Virtual Memory Statistics

Win32 offers one function, GlobalMemoryStatus, that allows your application to get memory information about the system that it is running on.

```
VOID GlobalMemoryStatus(LPMEMORYSTATUS lpms);
```

The only parameter to this function, *lpms*, is a pointer to a MEM-ORYSTATUS structure that you must allocate (or create on the stack):

```
typedef struct _MEMORYSTATUS {
    DWORD dwLength;
    DWORD dwMemoryLoad;
    DWORD dwTotalPhys;
    DWORD dwAvailPhys;
    DWORD dwTotalPageFile;
    DWORD dwAvailPageFile;
    DWORD dwTotalVirtual;
    DWORD dwAvailVirtual;
} MEMORYSTATUS, *LPMEMORYSTATUS;
```

The first member in this structure, *dwLength*, represents the size of the structure in bytes. Your application must initialize this member before it places the call to GlobalMemoryStatus.

The Virtual Memory Status Sample Application

The VMStat application (VMSTAT.EXE), listed in Figure 3-6 beginning on page 132, displays a simple dialog box that lists the results of a call to GlobalMemoryStatus. The result of running this program on my 20-MB Intel 486 machine is shown below:

Virtual Memory Status	
Memory load:	0
TotalPhys:	20,512,768
AvailPhys:	7,540,736
TotalPageFile:	45,469,696
AvailPageFile:	27,582,464
TotalVirtual:	2,147,352,576
AvailVirtual:	2,138,427,392

The *dwMemoryLoad* member gives a rough estimate of how busy the memory management system has been. This number can be anywhere from 0 to 100. A value of 0 indicates that the memory system is not busy, whereas a value of 100 indicates that the system is very busy.

The *dwTotalPhys* member indicates the total number of bytes of physical memory that exists. On my 20-MB machine, this value is 20,512,768, which is just over 19.5 MB. This value is the exact amount of memory, including any holes in the address space between the low 640 KB and 1 MB of physical memory. The *dwAvailPhys* member indicates the total number of bytes of physical memory available for allocation.

The *dwTotalPageFile* member indicates the maximum number of bytes that can be contained in the paging file on your hard disk. Although VMStat reported that my swap file is currently 45,469,696 bytes, Windows NT can expand the paging file if it needs to. The *dwAvailPageFile* member indicates that 27,582,464 bytes in the paging file are not committed to any process and are currently available should a process decide to commit any memory.

The *dwTotalVirtual* and *dwAvailVirtual* members indicate the total number of bytes that are addressable in your process's address space. Note that these are the only two members of this structure that are process specific, whereas all the other members are system specific. The value of 2,138,427,392 is just 128 KB short of being exactly 2 GB. The 128-KB difference exists because Windows NT never lets an application gain access to the first 64 KB and the last 64 KB before the 2-GB mark of address space. Of this space, the *dwAvailVirtual* member indicates that 2,138,714,112 bytes of address space are available for VMStat to do with what it wants. If you do the subtraction, you'll see that VMStat has 8,925,184 bytes reserved in its virtual address space.

VMStat.ico

VMSTAT.C

```
/************************************************************
Module name: VMStat.C
Notices: Copyright (c) 1993 Jeffrey Richter
*************************************************************/

#include <windows.h>
#include <windowsx.h>
#include <tchar.h>
#include <string.h>      // for strrev
#include "VMStat.H"


//////////////////////////////////////////////////////////////////
```

Figure 3-6.   *(continued)*
The VMStat application.

Figure 3-6. *continued*

```
// This function accepts a number and converts it to a string,
// inserting commas where appropriate.
LPTSTR WINAPI BigNumToString (LONG lNum, LPTSTR szBuf) {
   WORD wNumDigits = 0, wNumChars = 0;

   do {
      // Put the last digit of the string
      // in the character buffer.
      szBuf[wNumChars++] = lNum % 10 + __TEXT('0');

      // Increment the number of digits
      // that we put in the string.
      wNumDigits++;

      // For every three digits put in
      // the string, add a comma (,).
      if (wNumDigits % 3 == 0)
         szBuf[wNumChars++] = __TEXT(',');

      // Divide the number by 10, and repeat the process.
      lNum /= 10;
      // Continue adding digits to
      // the string until the number is zero.
   } while (lNum != 0);

   // If the last character added to
   // the string was a comma, truncate it.
   if (szBuf[wNumChars - 1] == __TEXT(','))
      szBuf[wNumChars - 1] = 0;

   // Ensure that the string is zero-terminated.
   szBuf[wNumChars] = 0;

   // We added all the characters to the
   // string in reverse order. We must reverse
   // the contents of the string.
   _tcsrev(szBuf);

   // Returns the address of the string.  This is the same
   // value that was passed to us initially.  Returning it
   // here makes it easier for the calling function
   // to use the string.
   return(szBuf);
}
```

(continued)

Figure 3-6. *continued*

```
///////////////////////////////////////////////////////////

BOOL Dlg_OnInitDialog (HWND hwnd, HWND hwndFocus,
   LPARAM lParam) {

   TCHAR szBuf[50];
   MEMORYSTATUS ms;

   // Associate an icon with the dialog box.
   SetClassLong(hwnd, GCL_HICON, (LONG)
      LoadIcon((HINSTANCE) GetWindowLong(hwnd, GWL_HINSTANCE),
      __TEXT("VMStat")));

   // Initialize the structure length before
   // calling GlobalMemoryStatus.
   ms.dwLength = sizeof(ms);
   GlobalMemoryStatus(&ms);

   // Fill the static controls in the
   // list box with the appropriate number.
   SetDlgItemText(hwnd, ID_MEMLOAD,
      BigNumToString(ms.dwMemoryLoad, szBuf));

   SetDlgItemText(hwnd, ID_TOTALPHYS,
      BigNumToString(ms.dwTotalPhys, szBuf));

   SetDlgItemText(hwnd, ID_AVAILPHYS,
      BigNumToString(ms.dwAvailPhys, szBuf));

   SetDlgItemText(hwnd, ID_TOTALPAGEFILE,
      BigNumToString(ms.dwTotalPageFile, szBuf));

   SetDlgItemText(hwnd, ID_AVAILPAGEFILE,
      BigNumToString(ms.dwAvailPageFile, szBuf));

   SetDlgItemText(hwnd, ID_TOTALVIRTUAL,
      BigNumToString(ms.dwTotalVirtual, szBuf));

   SetDlgItemText(hwnd, ID_AVAILVIRTUAL,
      BigNumToString(ms.dwAvailVirtual, szBuf));

   return(TRUE);
}
```

(continued)

Figure 3-6. *continued*

```
///////////////////////////////////////////////////////////

void Dlg_OnCommand (HWND hwnd, int id, HWND hwndCtl,
   UINT codeNotify) {

   switch (id) {
      case IDCANCEL:
         EndDialog(hwnd, id);
         break;
   }
}


///////////////////////////////////////////////////////////

BOOL CALLBACK Dlg_Proc (HWND hDlg, UINT uMsg,
   WPARAM wParam, LPARAM lParam) {

   BOOL fProcessed = TRUE;

   switch (uMsg) {
      HANDLE_MSG(hDlg, WM_INITDIALOG, Dlg_OnInitDialog);
      HANDLE_MSG(hDlg, WM_COMMAND, Dlg_OnCommand);

      default:
         fProcessed = FALSE;
         break;
   }
   return(fProcessed);
}


///////////////////////////////////////////////////////////

int APIENTRY WinMain (HINSTANCE hInstance,
   HINSTANCE hPrevInstance, LPSTR lpszCmdLine, int nCmdShow) {

   DialogBox(hInstance, MAKEINTRESOURCE(DLG_VMSTAT),
      NULL, Dlg_Proc);
   return(0);
}

/////////////////////// End Of File ///////////////////////
```

(continued)

Figure 3-6. *continued*

VMSTAT.H

```
/*****************************************************************
Module name: VMStat.H
Notices: Copyright (c) 1993 Jeffrey Richter
*****************************************************************/

// Dialog and control IDs.
#define DLG_VMSTAT          1
#define ID_MEMLOAD          100
#define ID_TOTALPHYS        101
#define ID_AVAILPHYS        102
#define ID_TOTALPAGEFILE    103
#define ID_AVAILPAGEFILE    104
#define ID_TOTALVIRTUAL     105
#define ID_AVAILVIRTUAL     106


///////////////////////// End Of File /////////////////////////
```

VMSTAT.RC

```
/*****************************************************************
Module name: VMStat.RC
Notices: Copyright (c) 1993 Jeffrey Richter
*****************************************************************/

#include <windows.h>
#include "VMStat.h"

VMStat  ICON  DISCARDABLE VMStat.Ico

DLG_VMSTAT DIALOG 60, 27, 129, 101
STYLE WS_BORDER | WS_POPUP | WS_VISIBLE | WS_CAPTION |
   WS_SYSMENU | WS_MINIMIZEBOX
CAPTION "Virtual Memory Status"
BEGIN
   CONTROL "Memory load:", -1, "STATIC",
      SS_RIGHT | WS_CHILD | WS_VISIBLE | WS_GROUP,
      4, 4, 52, 8
   CONTROL "Text", ID_MEMLOAD, "STATIC",
      SS_RIGHT | WS_CHILD | WS_VISIBLE | WS_GROUP,
      60, 4, 60, 8
   CONTROL "TotalPhys:", -1, "STATIC",
```

(continued)

Figure 3-6. *continued*

```
         SS_RIGHT | WS_CHILD | WS_VISIBLE | WS_GROUP,
         4, 20, 52, 8
    CONTROL "Text", ID_TOTALPHYS, "STATIC",
         SS_RIGHT | WS_CHILD | WS_VISIBLE | WS_GROUP,
         60, 20, 60, 8
    CONTROL "AvailPhys:", -1, "STATIC",
         SS_RIGHT | WS_CHILD | WS_VISIBLE | WS_GROUP,
         4, 32, 52, 8
    CONTROL "Text", ID_AVAILPHYS, "STATIC",
         SS_RIGHT | WS_CHILD | WS_VISIBLE | WS_GROUP,
         60, 32, 60, 8
    CONTROL "TotalPageFile:", -1, "STATIC",
         SS_RIGHT | WS_CHILD | WS_VISIBLE | WS_GROUP,
         4, 48, 52, 8
    CONTROL "Text", ID_TOTALPAGEFILE, "STATIC",
         SS_RIGHT | WS_CHILD | WS_VISIBLE | WS_GROUP,
         60, 48, 60, 8
    CONTROL "AvailPageFile:", -1, "STATIC",
         SS_RIGHT | WS_CHILD | WS_VISIBLE | WS_GROUP,
         4, 60, 52, 8
    CONTROL "Text", ID_AVAILPAGEFILE, "STATIC",
         SS_RIGHT | WS_CHILD | WS_VISIBLE | WS_GROUP,
         60, 60, 60, 8
    CONTROL "TotalVirtual:", -1, "STATIC",
         SS_RIGHT | WS_CHILD | WS_VISIBLE | WS_GROUP,
         4, 76, 52, 8
    CONTROL "Text", ID_TOTALVIRTUAL, "STATIC",
         SS_RIGHT | WS_CHILD | WS_VISIBLE | WS_GROUP,
         60, 76, 60, 8
    CONTROL "AvailVirtual:", -1, "STATIC",
         SS_RIGHT | WS_CHILD | WS_VISIBLE | WS_GROUP,
         4, 88, 52, 8
    CONTROL "Text", ID_AVAILVIRTUAL, "STATIC",
         SS_RIGHT | WS_CHILD | WS_VISIBLE | WS_GROUP,
         60, 88, 60, 8
END

//////////////////////// End Of File ////////////////////////
```

Writing Robust Applications

To make your applications as robust as possible, you should verify that each address passed to your functions actually points to valid data. Win32 offers a series of functions, listed in Figure 3-7 on the following page, that allow you to verify the validity of a virtual address. For all of the functions listed, Win32 returns FALSE if the memory can be accessed successfully and TRUE if an access violation occurs.

One problematic situation to be aware of occurs because Windows NT is a multitasking environment. It's a timing problem that creates an interesting bug. First, an address to a string is passed to your thread. Then you call *IsBadStringPtr* to determine if the string is readable. Next, another thread frees the memory occupied by the string or changes the protection status attribute of the page that contains the string to PAGE_NOACCESS.

If this situation occurs, any access to the string will fail. Fortunately, this type of bug occurs very infrequently. When it does, it is almost impossible to find and fix. The problem cannot occur if only one thread operates on the string at any given time. By carefully designing and implementing your code, you can avoid having another thread in your process pull the rug out from under you.

Win32 Function	What It Does
BOOL IsBadReadPtr (CONST VOID *lp, UINT ucb);	Determines if the *ucb* bytes of memory starting at address *lp* are readable.
BOOL IsBadWritePtr (LPVOID lp, UINT ucb);	Determines if the *ucb* bytes of memory starting at address *lp* are writable.
BOOL IsBadHugeReadPtr (CONST VOID *lp, UINT ucb);	Same as IsBadReadPtr. Supplied for backward compatibility with 16-bit Windows.
BOOL IsBadHugeWritePtr (LPVOID lp, UINT ucb);	Same as IsBadWritePtr. Supplied for backward compatibility with 16-bit Windows.
BOOL IsBadCodePtr(FARPROC lpfn);	Same as IsBadReadPtr with *ucb* passed as 1.
BOOL IsBadStringPtr (LPCSTR lpsz, UINT ucchMax);	Determines if the string at address *lpsz* can be read. The function continues checking characters from the string until either a zero byte is found or *ucchMax* characters have been checked. This function does not check if the memory occupied by the string can be written to.

Figure 3-7.
Functions that validate virtual addresses.

You can make your functions robust by using structured exception handling (SEH). Using SEH, you can write the body of your functions assuming that nothing will go wrong. Then, at the bottom of your function, you can include special code that addresses problems that might have come up while executing the body. Illegal accesses to memory are only one type of problem that structured exception handling can catch for you.

The IsBad* functions are implemented using structured exception handling. They traverse the memory that you have specified, and, if an access violation occurs, the functions stop and return TRUE (the memory block is bad). If the functions complete without generating an exception, they return FALSE (all data accessed successfully). See Chapter 10 for more complete information about structured exception handling.

CHAPTER FOUR

MEMORY-MAPPED FILES

Working with files is something almost every application must do, and it's always a hassle. Should your application open the file, read it, and close the file, or should it open the file and use a buffering algorithm to read from and write to different portions of the file? Windows NT offers the best of both worlds: memory-mapped files.

Memory-mapped files allow you to allocate an address space and associate a disk file with the space. In a sense, you tell Windows NT that the disk file is where the committed storage is. Once the file has been mapped, you can access it as if the whole file were sitting right in memory.

Memory-mapped files are used in Windows NT in three ways. First, Windows NT uses them internally to load and execute EXEs and DLLs. Second, you can use memory-mapped files to access a data file on disk as though it were in memory for a single application. Your application does not have to buffer the data or perform file I/O to access this data, and just about the only restriction Windows NT places on the kind of data or object that you can map is a size limit of 2 GB. Third, you can use memory-mapped files to share blocks of data in memory between multiple processes. Windows NT uses this same mechanism internally when a user tries to run a second instance of an application.

Memory-mapped files are an extremely important component of Windows NT for two reasons. First, whenever you attempt to execute an application, Windows NT doesn't actually load the complete file into memory. Instead, it reserves a portion of the application's 2-GB address space and maps the executable file into that reserved space. Once the file has been mapped, Windows NT takes care of all the paging, buffering, and caching. For example, if your application begins executing and tries to jump to the address of an instruction that hasn't been loaded into memory, Windows NT sees that the page of code is not loaded into memory. So Windows NT finds a page of physical memory (discarding or paging other code or data if necessary), loads the page of code into physical memory, maps it into your virtual address space, and jumps to the proper instruction. This process is repeated each time your application tries to access code or data that's not loaded into physical memory.

Second, memory-mapped files are important because they are the only method supported by Windows NT for sharing blocks of memory between processes.

Manipulating a File's Data: A Case Study

To understand the power of memory-mapped files, let's look at four possible ways of implementing a program to reverse the order of all the bytes in a file.

Method 1: One File, One Buffer

The first and theoretically simplest method involves allocating a block of memory large enough to hold the entire file. The file is opened, its contents are read into the memory block, and the file is closed. With the contents in memory, we can now reverse all the bytes by swapping the first byte with the last, the second byte with the second-to-last, and so on. This swapping continues until you swap the two middle bytes in the file. After all the bytes have been swapped, you reopen the file and overwrite its contents with the contents of the memory block.

This method is pretty easy to implement but has two major drawbacks. First, a memory block the size of the file must be allocated. This might not be too bad if the file is small, but if the file is huge—say, 2 GB—Windows NT will not allow the application to commit a block of memory that large. Large files require a different method.

Second, if the process is interrupted in the middle, while the reversed bytes are being written back out to the file, the contents of the file will be corrupted. The simplest way to guard against this is to make a copy of the original file before reversing its contents. Thus, if the whole process succeeds, the copy of the file can be deleted. Unfortunately, this safeguard requires additional disk space.

Method 2: Two Files, One Buffer

In the second method, you open the existing file and create a new file of 0 (zero) length on the disk. Then you allocate a small internal buffer—say, 8 KB. You seek to the end of the original file minus 8 KB, read the last 8 KB into the buffer, reverse the bytes, and write the buffer's contents to the newly created file. The process of seeking, reading, reversing, and writing repeats until you reach the beginning of the original file. Some special handling is required if the file's length is not an exact multiple of 8 KB, but it's not extensive. After the original file is fully processed, both files are closed and the original file is deleted.

This method is a bit more complicated to implement than the first one. It uses memory much more efficiently because only an 8-KB chunk is ever allocated, but there are two big problems. First, the processing is slower than in the first method. On each iteration, you must perform a seek on the original file before performing a read.

The second problem is that this method can potentially use an enormous amount of hard disk space. If the original file is 400 MB, the new file will grow to be 400 MB as the process continues. Just before the original file is deleted, the two files occupy 800 MB of disk space. This is 400 MB more than should be required and leads us to the next method.

Method 3: One File, Two Buffers

For this method, let's say that the program initializes by allocating two separate 8-KB buffers. The program reads the first 8 KB of the file into one buffer and the last 8 KB of the file into the other buffer. The process then reverses the contents of both buffers and writes the contents of the first buffer back to the end of the file and the contents of the second buffer back to the beginning of the same file. Each iteration continues by moving blocks from the front and back of the file in 8-KB chunks. Some special handling is required if the file's length is not an exact multiple of 16 KB and the two 8-KB chunks overlap. This special handling is more complex than the special handling in the previous method, but it's nothing that should scare off a seasoned programmer.

Compared with the previous two methods, this method is better at conserving hard disk space. Because everything is read and written to the same file, no additional disk space is required. As for memory use, this method is also not too bad, using only 16 KB. Of course, this is probably the most difficult method to implement. Like the first method, this method may result in corruption of the data file if the process is somehow interrupted. Now let's take a look at how this process might be accomplished using memory-mapped files.

Method 4: One File, Zero Buffers

When using memory-mapped files to reverse the contents of a file, you open the file and then tell Windows NT to reserve a region of virtual address space. You tell Windows NT to pretend that the first byte of the file is mapped to the first byte of this address space. You can now access the region of virtual memory as though it were actually the file. In fact, if there were a single zero byte at the end of the file, you could simply call the C Runtime function *strrev* to reverse the data in the file.

This method's great advantage is that Windows NT manages all the file caching for you. You don't have to allocate any memory, load file data into memory, write data back to the file, or free any memory blocks at all. Unfortunately, the possibility of an interruption such as a power failure corrupting data still exists with memory-mapped files.

Using Memory-Mapped Files

Normally, when Windows NT commits memory, it sets aside pages from the paging file on the user's hard disk. However, when virtual memory is committed to memory-mapped files, Windows NT doesn't need to commit any memory from the paging file because the file's data is already available to Windows NT on the hard disk. If Windows NT needs to discard a physical page of memory containing memory-mapped file data, it writes any changes in the memory back to the disk file and frees the physical page. When your process attempts to access the data again, Windows NT allocates another physical page of RAM for the data and reads the data back into this page. Your process can now continue working with the file.

The first step in mapping a file is to open the file by calling CreateFile:

```
HANDLE CreateFile(LPCSTR lpFileName, DWORD dwDesiredAccess,
    DWORD dwShareMode, LPSECURITY_ATTRIBUTES lpSecurityAttributes,
    DWORD dwCreationDisposition, DWORD dwFlagsAndAttributes,
    HANDLE hTemplateFile);
```

This function takes quite a few parameters. For this discussion, I'll concentrate on only the first three: *lpFileName, dwDesiredAccess,* and *dwShareMode*. CreateFile is discussed in more detail in Chapter 9 of this book. As you might guess, the *lpFileName* parameter is where you pass the name of the file that you want to open. The *dwDesiredAccess* parameter can be GENERIC_READ, GENERIC_WRITE, or both (GENERIC-_READ *OR*ed with GENERIC_WRITE). These flags indicate how you are allowing the rest of your program to access the data in the file. Don't make the same mistake I did when I first used this function. I assumed that GENERIC_WRITE implied GENERIC_READ. It seemed strange to me that you could write to a file without also being able to read from it. If you want to both read and write (the most common case by far), you must specify both flags *OR*ed together.

The *dwShareMode* parameter tells Windows NT how you want to share this file with other processes, including your own. A value of 0 (zero) means that Windows NT will not share the file with any other process. If a process attempts to open this file, Windows NT will return INVALID_HANDLE_VALUE back to the process.

Specifying the FILE_SHARE_READ flag tells Windows NT to allow other processes to open the file for reading only. Windows NT returns a file handle of INVALID_HANDLE_VALUE to any process that attempts to open the file for writing. The last value that can be specified for *dwShareMode* is FILE_SHARE_WRITE, which indicates that the file can be opened for writing only. If you want other applications to open this file for reading and writing, specify FILE-_SHARE_READ *OR*ed with FILE_SHARE_WRITE.

If CreateFile is successful, a file handle is returned; otherwise IN-VALID_HANDLE_VALUE is returned. With the returned file handle, you can create a file-mapping object using CreateFileMapping:

```
HANDLE CreateFileMapping(HANDLE hFile, LPSECURITY_ATTRIBUTES lpsa,
    DWORD fdwProtect, DWORD dwMaximumSizeHigh,
    DWORD dwMaximumSizeLow, LPSTR lpszMapName);
```

A file-mapping object describes the full size of the file being mapped as well as its access rights. The first parameter, *hFile,* specifies the file handle returned from the previous call to CreateFile. The *lpsa* parameter is a pointer to a SECURITY_ATTRIBUTES structure. The *fdwProtect* parameter specifies the protection on the file's data and can be either PAGE_READONLY or PAGE_READWRITE. If you are planning only to read from the file and don't plan to write to it at all, use

PAGE_READONLY. In addition, the call to CreateFile earlier must have specified GENERIC_READ in the *dwDesiredAccess* parameter. If you are planning to write to the file, you must specify PAGE_READWRITE in CreateFileMapping's *fdwProtect* parameter. You must also have specified GENERIC_READ | GENERIC_WRITE in CreateFile's *fdwProtect* parameter. This means that you will not be able to create a file-mapping object if the file handle you are attempting to map was created by calling CreateFile and passing GENERIC_WRITE by itself as the *dwDesiredAccess* parameter.

CreateFileMapping's next two parameters, *dwMaximumSizeHigh* and *dwMaximumSizeLow*, tell the system the file's size in bytes. Because files under Windows NT might become extremely large—much larger than 4 GB—and because 32 bits can't specify anything larger than 4 GB, CreateFileMapping has two parameters that it concatenates to calculate the file's size. The *dwMaximumSizeHigh* parameter specifies the high 32 bits, and the *dwMaximumSizeLow* parameter specifies the low 32 bits. For files that are 4 GB or less, *dwMaximumSizeHigh* will always be 0 (zero).

Using two 32-bit values means that Windows NT can process files as large as 18 billion GB (or 18 quintillion bytes or 1.8×10^{19} bytes). If you want Windows NT to use the current size of the file as the limit, you can pass 0 (zero) for both parameters. If you intend only to read from the file, this is what you will most likely do. If you intend to write to the file, you will want to make the number larger so that you leave yourself some breathing room.

You are probably thinking that there must be something terribly wrong here. It's nice that Windows NT lets you create files that are 18-quintillion bytes large, but how are you ever going to map a file that huge into your process's address space, which has a maximum limit of 2 GB? I'll explain the answer shortly.

CreateFileMapping's last parameter, *lpszMapName*, is a zero-terminated string that assigns a name to this file-mapping object. The name is used to share the object with another process and is discussed later in this chapter. If all is successful, CreateFileMapping returns a handle to a file-mapping object. If CreateFileMapping fails, the return value is NULL. Note that this is different from the return value from CreateFile. If CreateFile fails to open the specified file, CreateFile returns INVALID_HANDLE_VALUE (which is defined as −1).

Once you have created a file-mapping object, you still need to tell Windows NT that you want to map the file into an address space. This is done by calling MapViewOfFile:

```
LPVOID MapViewOfFile(HANDLE hFileMappingObject,
    DWORD dwDesiredAccess, DWORD dwFileOffsetHigh,
    DWORD dwFileOffsetLow, DWORD dwNumberOfBytesToMap);
```

The *hFileMappingObject* parameter identifies the handle of the file-mapping object, which was returned by the previous call to either CreateFileMapping or OpenFileMapping (discussed later). The *dwDesired-Access* parameter identifies how the data can be accessed: FILE_MAP_WRITE for read/write access and FILE_MAP_READ for read-only access. Of course, to use FILE_MAP_WRITE, the file-mapping object must have been created with PAGE_READWRITE passed in Create-FileMapping's *fdwProtect* parameter. Using FILE_MAP_READ requires that PAGE_READWRITE or PAGE_READONLY were passed in the *fdwProtect* parameter. It seems strange and annoying that Windows NT requires all these protection attributes to be set over and over again. I assume this was done to give an application as much control over data protection as possible.

Earlier, I said that I would tell you how Windows NT maps an 18 quintillion-byte file into a 2-GB address space. Well, here is the answer: It doesn't. The solution allows you to map only portions of the file into your process's address space at any one time. Each portion is called a view of the file, which explains how the MapViewOfFile function got its name. The *dwFileOffsetHigh* and *dwFileOffsetLow* parameters tell Windows NT which byte in the file should be mapped as the first byte into the address space region. Note that when mapping a portion of a file into memory this way, you must map in *allocation granularity* boundaries. (One allocation granularity boundary is the minimum amount of address space that can be reserved; on most CPUs, it is 64 KB.) The last parameter, *dwNumberOfBytesToMap*, specifies the size of the virtual address space that should be reserved by the view. You'll notice that this parameter is a single 32-bit value because it could never be larger than 2 GB.

Let's look at an example using a 2-GB file. A routine that counts all the J characters (one of my favorite characters) in this file requires three steps. First call CreateFile to open the file. Then call CreateFileMapping to create a file-mapping object for the entire file. Next call Map-ViewOfFile:

```
LPBYTE lpByte = (LPBYTE) MapViewOfFile(hFileMapping,
    FILE_MAP_WRITE              // Desired access
    0, 0,                       // Starting byte in file
    1 * 1024 * 1024 * 1024);  // Numbytes to map
```

The return value indicates the virtual address where the file has been mapped. Notice that in the call above I passed 1 GB as the *dwNumberOfBytesToMap* parameter. This reserves a 1-GB address space starting at the address in *lpByte*. You can now process the first half of the file, searching for J's. After the search is complete, remove this view of the file and map another view of the file into the virtual address space.

Unmapping a view of a file is done by calling UnmapViewOfFile:

```
BOOL UnmapViewOfFile(LPVOID lpBaseAddress);
```

The only parameter, *lpBaseAddress*, must be the same value returned from the call to MapViewOfFile. Here you'd pass *lpByte*. This step is necessary. If, as follows, you simply called MapViewOfFile to map in a view of the file containing the second half of the file, you would actually be requesting that the system map in multiple views of the same file:

```
LPBYTE lpByte = (LPBYTE) MapViewOfFile(hFileMapping,
    FILE_MAP_WRITE,                 // Desired access
    0, 1 * 1024 * 1024 * 1024,    // Starting byte in file
    1 * 1024 * 1024 * 1024);      // NumBytes to map
```

Because each view is requesting a size of 1 GB, the second mapping is guaranteed to fail. If you were mapping smaller views of files, it would be possible to map multiple views of the same file into your process's address space simultaneously. Windows NT allows you to map multiple views of the same section of a file. For example, you could map the first 10 KB of a file into a view, and you could also map the first 4 KB of the same file into a separate view. If your application alters the contents of the file in one view, the data in the other view is updated to reflect the changes automatically. This happens because Windows NT really has the data in only a single page of physical memory, but the page is mapped into the process's virtual address space more than once.

Now, with a view of the second half of the file mapped into the address space, you can continue your scan for J's. When finished, it's time to tidy up. Unmap your view of the file by calling UnmapViewOfFile. In addition to freeing the reserved address space, UnmapViewOfFile also flushes any changes to the data file back to disk.

In the interest of speed, Windows NT buffers writes to the data in memory and doesn't update the disk image of the file immediately. However, a call to UnmapViewOfFile forces all the modified data in memory to be written back to the disk image. If you need to ensure that your updates have been written to disk, you can force Windows NT to write all the modified data back to the disk image by calling FlushViewOfFile:

```
BOOL FlushViewOfFile(LPVOID lpBaseAddress,
    DWORD dwNumberOfBytesToFlush);
```

This function requires the address of the mapped view as returned by the previous call to MapViewOfFile and also requires the number of bytes to write to disk. If you call FlushViewOfFile and none of the data has been changed, the function simply returns without writing anything to the disk.

Finally, close the file-mapping object as well as the file object. You can do so by calling CloseHandle:

```
CloseHandle(hFileMapping);
CloseHandle(hFile);
```

Memory-Mapped File Considerations

Now that you have the gist of using memory-mapped files, let me mention a few issues to consider. Memory mapping is simply great when the file that is mapped into view is a read-only file: A memory-mapped file uses few system resources because Windows NT doesn't need to commit any page space in the paging file. On the other hand, if a memory-mapped file is writable, manipulating the file can be far more complicated because you need to calculate the maximum possible size to which the file might grow. In addition, you might even need to call the Win32 SetFilePointer and SetEndOfFile functions to adjust the end of the file before you close it. These functions need to be used in the FileRev program, which I'll discuss next.

Memory-mapped files shouldn't be used to share writable files over a network because Windows NT cannot guarantee coherent views of the data. If someone's computer updates the contents of the file, someone else's computer might have the original data in memory and will not see that the information has changed.

The File Reverse Sample Application

The FileRev application (FILEREV.EXE), listed in Figure 4-1 beginning on page 152, demonstrates how to use memory-mapped files to reverse the contents of an ANSI text file. FileRev doesn't create any windows or do anything visual, and it won't work correctly for binary or Unicode files.

When WinMain begins executing, it takes whatever filename was specified on FileRev's command line and makes a copy of that file called FILEREV.DAT. It does this so that the original file won't become unusable by reversing its contents. Next, FileRev opens the FILEREV.DAT file for reading and writing by using the CreateFile function.

As I said earlier, the easiest way to reverse the contents of the file is to call the C Runtime function *strrev*. As with all C strings, the last byte of the string must be a zero terminator. Because text files do not end with a zero byte, FileRev must append one to the end of the file. It does so by first calling GetFileSize:

```
dwFileSize = GetFileSize(hFile, NULL);
```

Now that you're armed with the length of the file, you can create the file-mapping object by calling CreateFileMapping. The file-mapping object is created with a length of *dwFileSize* plus 1 (for the zero byte). If there is a bug in FileRev that overwrites the address space occupied by the file-mapping object, an access violation will occur. After the file-mapping object is created, a view of the object is mapped into FileRev's address space. The *lpvFile* variable contains the return value from MapViewOfFile and points to the first byte of the text file.

The next step is to write a zero byte at the end of the file and to reverse the string:

```
((LPSTR) lpvFile)[dwFileSize] = 0;
strrev(lpvFile);
```

In a text file, every line is terminated by a return character ('\r') followed by a newline character ('\n'). Unfortunately, when we call *strrev* to reverse the file, these characters also get reversed. So that the reversed text file can be loaded into an editor, every occurrence of the '\n\r' pair needs to be converted back to its original '\r\n' order. This is the job of the following loop:

```
// Find first occurrence of '\n'.
lpch = strchr(lpvFile, '\n');

while (lpch != NULL) {
   *lpch++ = '\r';    // Change the '\n' to '\r'.
   *lpch++ = '\n';    // Change the '\r' to '\n'.

   // Find the next occurrence.
   lpch = strchr(lpch, '\n');
}
```

When you examine simple code like this, it is easy to forget that you are actually manipulating the contents of a file on the hard disk, which shows you how powerful memory-mapped files are.

After the file has been adjusted, the only job remaining is to remove the zero byte added earlier. If you don't remove the zero byte, the reversed file would be 1 byte larger, and calling FileRev again would not reverse the file back to its original form. To remove the trailing zero byte, you need to drop back a level and use the file-management functions instead of manipulating the file through memory mapping.

Forcing the reversed file to end at a specific location requires positioning the file pointer at the desired location (the end of the original file) and calling the SetEndOfFile function:

```
SetFilePointer(hFile, dwFileSize, NULL, FILE_BEGIN);
SetEndOfFile(hFile);
```

The last thing FileRev does is unmap the view of the file, close all the object handles, and spawn an instance of the NotePad applet so that you can look at the reversed file. Below is the result of running FileRev on its own FILEREV.C file:

151

FileRev.ico

FILEREV.C

```
/**************************************************************
Module name: FileRev.C
Notices: Copyright (c) 1993 Jeffrey Richter
**************************************************************/

#include <windows.h>
#include <windowsx.h>
#include <tchar.h>
#include <string.h>        // for strrev


///////////////////////////////////////////////////////////////

#define FILENAMEA "FileRev.Dat"
#define FILENAME  __TEXT("FileRev.Dat")


///////////////////////////////////////////////////////////////

int APIENTRY WinMain (HINSTANCE hInstance,
   HINSTANCE hPrevInstance, LPSTR lpszCmdLine, int nCmdShow) {

   HANDLE hFile, hFileMap;
   LPVOID lpvFile;
   LPSTR lpch;      // Always ANSI regardless of how application
                    // compiled.
   DWORD dwFileSize;
   LPTSTR lpszCmdLineT;

   // Get the name of the file the user wants to reverse.
   // We must use GetCommandLine here instead of WinMain's
   // lpszCmdLine parameter because lpszCmdLine is always an
   // ANSI string, never a Unicode string.  GetCommandLine
   // returns ANSI or Unicode depending
   // on how we've compiled.
   lpszCmdLineT = _tcschr(GetCommandLine(), __TEXT(' '));
```

Figure 4-1.   *(continued)*

The FileRev application.

Figure 4-1. *continued*

```
if (lpszCmdLineT != NULL) {
   // We found a space after the executable file's name.
   // Now let's skip over any white space to get to
   // the first argument.
   while (*lpszCmdLineT == __TEXT(' '))
      lpszCmdLineT++;
}

if ((lpszCmdLineT == NULL) || (*lpszCmdLineT == 0)) {
   // If no space was found or there are no arguments
   // after the executable file's name, display an
   // error message.
   MessageBox(NULL,
      __TEXT("You must enter a filename on ")
      __TEXT("the command line."),
      __TEXT("FileRev"), MB_OK);
   return(0);
}

// Copy input file to FILEREV.DAT so that the original is
// not destroyed.
if (!CopyFile(lpszCmdLineT, FILENAME, FALSE)) {
   // Copy failed.
   MessageBox(NULL,
      __TEXT("New file could not be created."),
      __TEXT("FileRev"), MB_OK);
   return(0);
}

// Open the file for reading and writing.
hFile = CreateFile(FILENAME, GENERIC_WRITE | GENERIC_READ,
   0, NULL, OPEN_EXISTING, FILE_ATTRIBUTE_NORMAL, NULL);
if (hFile == INVALID_HANDLE_VALUE) {
   // File open failed.
   MessageBox(NULL, __TEXT("File could not be opened."),
      __TEXT("FileRev"), MB_OK);
   return(0);
}

// Get the size of the file.  I am assuming here that the
// file is smaller than 4 GB.
dwFileSize = GetFileSize(hFile, NULL);

// Create the file-mapping object.  The file-mapping object
// is one byte bigger than the file size so
```

(continued)

Figure 4-1. *continued*

```
// that a zero byte can be placed at the end to
// terminate the string (file).
hFileMap = CreateFileMapping(hFile, NULL, PAGE_READWRITE,
    0, dwFileSize + 1, NULL);
if (hFileMap == NULL) {
    // File-mapping open failed.
    MessageBox(NULL, __TEXT("File map could not be opened."),
        __TEXT("FileRev"), MB_OK);
    CloseHandle(hFile);
    return(0);
}

// Get the address where the first byte of the file
// is mapped into memory.
lpvFile = MapViewOfFile(hFileMap, FILE_MAP_WRITE, 0, 0, 0);
if (lpvFile == NULL) {
    // Map view of file failed.
    MessageBox(NULL, __TEXT("Could not map view of file."),
        __TEXT("FileRev"), MB_OK);
    CloseHandle(hFileMap);
    CloseHandle(hFile);
    return(0);
}

// For all the file manipulations below, we
// explicitly use ANSI functions instead of Unicode
// functions because, even though the application
// can be ANSI or Unicode, it can process only
// ANSI files.

// Put a zero character at the very end of the file.
((LPSTR) lpvFile)[dwFileSize] = 0;

// Reverse the contents of the file.
strrev(lpvFile);

// Convert all "\n\r" combinations back
// to "\r\n" to preserve the normal
// end-of-line sequence.
lpch = strchr(lpvFile, '\n'); // Find first '\n'.
while (lpch != NULL) {
    // We have found an occurrence...
    *lpch++ = '\r';    // Change '\n' to '\r'.
    *lpch++ = '\n';    // Change '\r' to '\n'.
    lpch = strchr(lpch, '\n'); // Find the next occurrence.
```

(continued)

Figure 4-1.   *continued*

```
    }

    // Remove the trailing zero byte added earlier by
    // positioning the file pointer at the end of the file,
    // not including the zero byte, and setting
    // the end-of-file.
    SetFilePointer(hFile, dwFileSize, NULL, FILE_BEGIN);
    SetEndOfFile(hFile);

    // Clean up everything before exiting.
    UnmapViewOfFile(lpvFile);
    CloseHandle(hFileMap);
    CloseHandle(hFile);

    // Spawn NOTEPAD to see the fruits of our labors.
    // WinExec exists only in ANSI form, not Unicode.
    WinExec("NOTEPAD.EXE " FILENAMEA, SW_SHOW);
    return(0);
}


////////////////////// End Of File //////////////////////
```

FILEREV.H

```
/****************************************************************
Module name: FileRev.H
Notices: Copyright (c) 1993 Jeffrey Richter
****************************************************************/

// Dialog and control IDs.

////////////////////// End Of File //////////////////////
```

FILEREV.RC

```
/****************************************************************
Module name: FileRev.RC
Notices: Copyright (c) 1993 Jeffrey Richter
****************************************************************/

FileRev  ICON  DISCARDABLE FileRev.Ico

////////////////////// End Of File //////////////////////
```

155

Mapping a File with a Twist

Just as the VirtualAlloc function allows you to suggest an initial address to reserve address space, you can suggest that a file be mapped into a particular address by using the MapViewOfFileEx function instead of the MapViewOfFile function:

```
LPVOID MapViewOfFileEx(HANDLE hFileMappingObject,
    DWORD dwDesiredAccess, DWORD dwFileOffsetHigh,
    DWORD dwFileOffsetLow, DWORD dwNumberOfBytesToMap,
    LPVOID lpBaseAddress);
```

All the parameters and the return value for this function are identical to that of the MapViewOfFile function with the single exception of the last parameter, *lpBaseAddress*. In this parameter, you specify a target address for the file you're mapping. Like VirtualAlloc, the address you specify must be on an even allocation granularity boundary (usually 64 KB); otherwise, MapViewOfFileEx returns NULL, indicating an error.

If Windows NT can't map the file at this location (usually because the file is too large and would overlap another reserved address space), the function fails and returns NULL. MapViewOfFileEx does not attempt to locate another address space that can accommodate the file. Of course, you can specify NULL as the *lpBaseAddress* parameter, in which case MapViewOfFileEx behaves exactly the same as MapViewOfFile. This function is useful when using memory-mapped files to share data with other processes.

As an example, you might need a memory-mapped file to be mapped at a particular address when you're sharing a group of data structures containing pointers to other data structures between two or more applications. A linked list is a perfect example. In a linked list, each node, or element, of the list contains the memory address to another element in the list. To walk the list, you must know the address of the first element and then reference the member of the element that contains the address of the next element. This can be a problem when using memory-mapped files.

If one application prepares the linked list in a memory-mapped file and then shares this file with another process, it is possible that the other process will map the file into a completely different location in its address space. When the second process attempts to walk the linked list, it looks at the first element of the list, pulls out the memory address of the next element, and then tries to reference this next element. However, the address of the next element in the first node will be incorrect for this second process.

There are two ways to solve this problem. First, the second process can simply call MapViewOfFileEx instead of MapViewOfFile when it maps the memory-mapped file containing the linked list into its own address space. Of course, this requires that the second process know where the first process had originally mapped the file when constructing the linked list. This usually isn't a problem because both applications were probably designed to interact with each other, and the address can be hard-coded into both. Or one process can notify the other process using another form of interprocess communication, such as sending a message to a window.

The second method for solving the problem involves the process that creates the linked list storing in each node the offset from within the address space where the next node is located. This requires that the application add the offset to the base address of the memory-mapped file to access each node. This method is not great because it can be slow, it requires more code space (for all of the calculations), and it can be quite error prone.

Sharing Data with Memory-Mapped Files

Microsoft Windows has always offered several methods for a process to communicate information to another process. Probably the most common method is to call either SendMessage or PostMessage, using a window belonging to another process. Unfortunately, in 16-bit Windows, doing so allows only one 32-bit value and one 16-bit value to be passed. (Win32 allows two 32-bit values.)

For passing data that requires substantially more than 48 bits in 16-bit Windows, it is possible to allocate a global block of memory using the GMEM_SHARE flag and passing the handle (as *wParam* or *lParam*) in a call to SendMessage or PostMessage. The receiver of this message can then call GlobalLock to get an address to the memory block and read or write the data. This method doesn't work in Win32, however. When your process gets a handle to a memory block allocated with GlobalAlloc, the handle is specific to your process. If another process attempts to call GlobalLock using this handle, the call fails.

At first you might think the solution would require that the originator of the message call GlobalLock to get the address of the memory block. Then the originator could call SendMessage, passing the address in *lParam* to the window of the other process. This works in 16-bit Windows but fails under Win32. The reason is that the address is relative to the originating process's address space. If the other process gets the address from the message and attempts to use it, this process will be attempting to write in its own address space, which doesn't even contain the data. This will cause either memory corruption in the receiving process's address space or, more likely, an access violation.

Memory-mapped files are the only means for multiple processes to share a block of data simultaneously in Win32. Let's look at an example: starting an application. When Windows NT starts an application, it calls CreateFile to open the EXE file on the disk. It then calls CreateMappingFile to create a file-mapping object. Finally, it calls MapViewOfFile on behalf of the newly created process so that the EXE file is mapped into the process's address space. Windows NT then sets the CPU's instruction pointer to point to the first byte of executable code in this mapped view of the file and lets the CPU start executing the code.

If the user runs a second instance of the same application, Windows NT sees that a file-mapping object already exists for the desired application and doesn't create a new file object or file-mapping object. Instead, Windows NT maps a view of the file a second time, this time in the context of the newly created process's address space. What the system has done is map the identical file into two address spaces simultaneously. Obviously, this is a more efficient use of memory because both processes are sharing the same physical memory pages, containing portions of the code that are executing.

How to Share Memory with Memory-Mapped Files

Now let's look at how you can use the memory-mapping file functions to share memory between multiple processes. The first function is CreateFileMapping:

```
HANDLE CreateFileMapping(HANDLE hFile, LPSECURITY_ATTRIBUTES lpsa,
    DWORD fdwProtect, DWORD dwMaximumSizeHigh,
    DWORD dwMaximumSizeLow, LPSTR lpName);
```

If you call this function to create a file-mapping object and if a file-mapping object using the same parameters already exists, CreateFileMapping doesn't create a new object. Instead, it returns a process-relative handle that identifies the already existing file-mapping object.

You can determine whether a new file-mapping object was created by calling GetLastError. Usually, you would call GetLastError to determine why a function call failed. However, in the case of CreateFileMapping, you can call GetLastError if the function is successful. If GetLastError returns ERROR_ALREADY_EXISTS, CreateFileMapping has returned a handle to a previously existing object. If you don't want to use this object, you need to close the handle. The following code fragment guarantees that CreateFileMapping creates a new object or none at all:

```
HANDLE hFileMap = CreateFileMapping(...);
if ((hFileMap != NULL) &&
    (GetLastError() ==
    ERROR_ALREADY_EXISTS)) {
    CloseHandle(hFileMap);
    hFileMap = NULL;
}
return(hFileMap);
```

The last parameter to CreateFileMapping, *lpName*, allows you to assign a name to an object. For example, one process might create a file-mapping object and assign it the name MyFileMapObj:

```
HANDLE hFileMap = CreateFileMapping(..., "MyFileMapObj");
```

Another process can use this name. If you want to share this memory-mapped file with another process, both processes use the same name. The first process calls CreateFileMapping to create the object and assign it a name. The second process then calls OpenFileMapping:

```
HANDLE OpenFileMapping(DWORD dwDesiredAccess, BOOL bInheritHandle,
    LPSTR lpName);
```

In this call, the second process specifies the same name that the first process used—in this example, MyFileMapObj. The second process can also specify access rights, such as FILE_MAP_READ and/or FILE_MAP_WRITE, using the *dwDesiredAccess* parameter. The second process can use the *bInheritHandle* parameter to indicate whether it wants any child processes to automatically inherit the handle to this file-mapping object. The handle that OpenFileMapping returns identifies the process-relative handle to the file-mapping object created by the first process.

If the function cannot find a file-mapping object that has the passed name, NULL is returned. If you want to share this file with several processes, note that all the processes but the first can call Open-

FileMapping to get their own process-relative handle. With these handles, mapping the data into each process's own address space is simply a matter of each process calling MapViewOfFile.

There's one more issue to consider: coherence. When multiple processes map the same file-mapping object into their respective address spaces, all the processes are looking at exactly the same data. This must be true because there is only one physical page of memory containing the information; it is simply mapped to different address spaces for each process. However, we're working with files here, and there is no reason why another application can't call CreateFile to open the same file that another process has mapped. This new process can then read from and write to the file using the ReadFile and WriteFile functions. Of course, whenever a process makes these calls, it must be either reading or writing file data to and from a memory buffer. This memory buffer is one that the process must have created and is not the same memory that is being used by the mapped files. This situation can cause problems: A process can call ReadFile to read a portion of a file, modify the data, and write it back out using WriteFile, without the file-mapping object being aware of this. For this reason, it is recommended that when you call CreateFile for files that will be memory-mapped, you specify 0 (zero) as the value of the *fdwShareMode* parameter. Doing so tells Windows NT that you want exclusive access to the file and that no other process may open it.

I know what you're thinking: Using files to communicate data from one process to another could be annoying if the data you want to share is not already in a file! This is true. However, there is a small part that I have left out of the equation until now. If you want to share data between processes and that data is not already in a disk file, you can call CreateFileMapping and pass (HANDLE) 0xFFFFFFFF as the *hFile* parameter. Doing so tells Windows NT that you are not mapping on disk; instead you want Windows NT to treat a region of memory as though it were a file. In fact, when you place this call, Windows NT sets aside a region of bytes in the disk's paging file to accommodate your request. The amount of memory is determined by the *dwMaximumSizeHigh* and *dwMaximumSizeLow* parameters of CreateFileMapping.

Once you have created this file-mapping object and mapped a view of it into your process's address space, you can use it as you would any region of memory. If other processes want to share this memory, they can't call CreateFileMapping in the hope that Windows NT will find the handle of the already existing file-mapping object and return it.

If another process calls CreateFileMapping, passing (HANDLE) 0xFFFFFFFF as the *hFile* parameter, Windows NT assumes that the process wants to create an in-memory file mapping.

One way to share an in-memory file mapping is for the second process to use the DuplicateHandle function to get a process-relative handle to the same object. This is the most difficult method. An application can also gain access to the handle by using inheritance. The best method is for the process creating the in-memory file-mapping object to assign it a name. Then the process wanting to share the object can call OpenFileMapping using the same name. This is the same procedure that was discussed earlier.

When each process sharing the file-mapping object no longer has a need to access it, CloseHandle must be called. Only after all the processes have closed their handles to the file-mapping object does Windows NT delete the object from its memory. In the case of in-memory mapped files, the committed pages in the paging file are also decommited at this time.

Here is an interesting problem that has caught unsuspecting programmers by surprise. Can you guess what is wrong with the following code fragment:

```
HANDLE hFile = CreateFile(...);
HANDLE hMap = CreateFileMapping(hFile, ...);
if (hMap == NULL)
   return(GetLastError());
.
.
.
```

If the call to CreateFile above fails, it returns 0xFFFFFFFF (INVALID_HANDLE_VALUE). However, the unsuspecting programmer who wrote the code above didn't test to check whether the file was created successfully. When CreateFileMapping is called, 0xFFFFFFFF is passed in the *hFile* parameter, which causes the system to create a file mapping using pages from the paging file instead of the intended disk file.

The Memory-Mapped File Sharing Sample Application

The MMFShare application (MMFSHARE.EXE), listed in Figure 4-2 beginning on page 163, demonstrates how to use memory-mapped files to transfer data between two or more separate processes.

You're going to need to execute at least two instances of the MMFSHARE.EXE program. When each instance is invoked, it creates its own dialog box, shown on the following page.

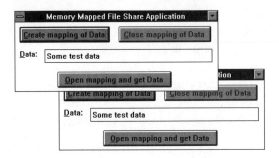

To transfer data from one instance of MMFShare to another, type the data to be transferred into the *Data* edit field. Then click on the *Create mapping of Data* button. When you do, MMFShare calls Create-FileMapping to create a 4-KB in-memory file and names the object MMFSharedData. If MMFShare sees that a file-mapping object with this name already exists, it displays a message box notifying you that it could not create the object. If, on the other hand, MMFShare succeeds in creating the object, it proceeds to map a view of the file into the process's address space and copies the data from the Edit control into the memory-mapped file.

After the data has been copied, MMFShare unmaps the view of the file, disables the *Create mapping of Data* button, and enables the *Close mapping of Data* button. At this point, there is a memory-mapped file named *MMFSharedData* just sitting somewhere in the system. No processes have mapped a view to the data contained in the file.

If you now go to another instance of MMFShare and click on this instance's *Open mapping and get Data* button, MMFShare attempts to locate a file-mapping object called MMFSharedData by calling Open-FileMapping. If an object of this name cannot be found, MMFShare displays another message box notifying you. If MMFShare finds the object, it maps a view of the object into its process's address space and copies the data from the memory-mapped file into the Edit control of the dialog box. Voilà! You have transferred data from one process to another.

The last button in the dialog box, *Close mapping of Data*, is used to close the file-mapping object by destroying the data contained within it. If no file-mapping object exists, no other instance of MMFShare will be able to open one and get data from it. Also, if one instance has created a memory-mapped file, no other instance is allowed to create one and overwrite the data contained within.

MMFShare.ico

MMFSHARE.C

```
/*****************************************************************
Module name: MMFShare.C
Notices: Copyright (c) 1993 Jeffrey Richter
*****************************************************************/

#include <windows.h>
#include <windowsx.h>
#include "MMFShare.H"


///////////////////////////////////////////////////////////////

BOOL Dlg_OnInitDialog (HWND hwnd, HWND hwndFocus,
   LPARAM lParam) {

   // Associate an icon with the dialog box.
   SetClassLong(hwnd, GCL_HICON, (LONG)
      LoadIcon((HINSTANCE) GetWindowLong(hwnd, GWL_HINSTANCE),
      __TEXT("MMFShare")));

   // Initialize the Edit control with some test data.
   Edit_SetText(GetDlgItem(hwnd, ID_DATA),
      __TEXT("Some test data"));

   // Disable the "Close file" button because the file can't
   // be closed if it was never created or opened.
   Button_Enable(GetDlgItem(hwnd, ID_CLOSEFILE), FALSE);
   return(TRUE);
}


///////////////////////////////////////////////////////////////

void Dlg_OnCommand (HWND hwnd, int id, HWND hwndCtl,
   UINT codeNotify) {

   // Handle of the open memory-mapped file.
   static HANDLE s_hFileMap = NULL;
```

Figure 4-2. *(continued)*
The MMFShare application.

163

Figure 4-2. *continued*

```
HANDLE hFileMapT;

switch (id) {
   case ID_CREATEFILE:
      if (codeNotify != BN_CLICKED)
         break;

      // Create an in-memory memory-mapped
      // file that contains the
      // contents of the Edit control. The file is
      // 4-KB at most and is named
      // MMFSharedData.
      s_hFileMap = CreateFileMapping((HANDLE) 0xFFFFFFFF,
         NULL, PAGE_READWRITE, 0, 4 * 1024,
         __TEXT("MMFSharedData"));

      if (s_hFileMap != NULL) {

         if (GetLastError() == ERROR_ALREADY_EXISTS) {
            MessageBox(hwnd,
               __TEXT("Mapping already exists - ")
               __TEXT("not created."),
               NULL, MB_OK);
            CloseHandle(s_hFileMap);

         } else {

            // File mapping created successfully.

            // Map a view of the file
            // into the address space.
            LPVOID lpView = MapViewOfFile(s_hFileMap,
               FILE_MAP_READ | FILE_MAP_WRITE, 0, 0, 0);

            if ((BYTE *) lpView != NULL) {
               // View mapped successfully; put contents
               // of Edit control in the
               // memory-mapped file.
               Edit_GetText(GetDlgItem(hwnd, ID_DATA),
                  (LPTSTR) lpView, 4 * 1024);
```

(continued)

Figure 4-2. *continued*

```
                        // Unmap the view. This protects the
                        // data from wayward pointers.
                        UnmapViewOfFile((LPVOID) lpView);

                        // The user can't create
                        // another file right now.
                        Button_Enable(hwndCtl, FALSE);

                        // The user closed the file.
                        Button_Enable(GetDlgItem(hwnd, ID_CLOSEFILE),
                            TRUE);

                    } else {
                        MessageBox(hwnd,
                            __TEXT("Can't map view of file."),
                            NULL, MB_OK);
                    }
                }

            } else {
                MessageBox(hwnd,
                    __TEXT("Can't create file mapping."),
                    NULL, MB_OK);
            }
            break;

        case ID_CLOSEFILE:
            if (codeNotify != BN_CLICKED)
                break;

            if (CloseHandle(s_hFileMap)) {
                // User closed the file.  A new file can be
                // created, but the new file can't be closed.
                Button_Enable(GetDlgItem(hwnd, ID_CREATEFILE),
                    TRUE);
                Button_Enable(hwndCtl, FALSE);
            }
            break;

        case ID_OPENFILE:
            if (codeNotify != BN_CLICKED)
                break;
```

(continued)

Figure 4-2. *continued*

```
         // See if a memory-mapped file named
         // MMFSharedData already exists.
         hFileMapT = OpenFileMapping(
            FILE_MAP_READ | FILE_MAP_WRITE,
            FALSE, __TEXT("MMFSharedData"));

         if (hFileMapT != NULL) {
            // Memory-mapped file does exist.  Map a view
            // of it into the process's address space.
               LPVOID lpView = MapViewOfFile(hFileMapT,
                  FILE_MAP_READ | FILE_MAP_WRITE, 0, 0, 0);

            if ((BYTE *) lpView != NULL) {

               // Put the contents of the
               // file into the Edit control.
               Edit_SetText(GetDlgItem(hwnd, ID_DATA),
                  (LPTSTR) lpView);
               UnmapViewOfFile((LPVOID) lpView);

            } else {
               MessageBox(hwnd,
                  __TEXT("Can't map view."), NULL, MB_OK);
            }

            CloseHandle(hFileMapT);

         } else {
            MessageBox(hwnd,
               __TEXT("Can't open mapping."), NULL, MB_OK);
         }
         break;

      case IDCANCEL:
         EndDialog(hwnd, id);
         break;
   }
}
```

(continued)

Figure 4-2. *continued*

```
/////////////////////////////////////////////////////////////

BOOL CALLBACK Dlg_Proc (HWND hDlg, UINT uMsg,
   WPARAM wParam, LPARAM lParam) {

   BOOL fProcessed = TRUE;

   switch (uMsg) {
      HANDLE_MSG(hDlg, WM_INITDIALOG, Dlg_OnInitDialog);
      HANDLE_MSG(hDlg, WM_COMMAND, Dlg_OnCommand);

      default:
         fProcessed = FALSE;
         break;
   }
   return(fProcessed);
}


/////////////////////////////////////////////////////////////

int APIENTRY WinMain (HINSTANCE hInstance,
   HINSTANCE hPrevInstance, LPSTR lpszCmdLine, int nCmdShow) {

   DialogBox(hInstance, MAKEINTRESOURCE(DLG_MMFSHARE),
      NULL, Dlg_Proc);
   return(0);
}

////////////////////// End Of File //////////////////////
```

MMFSHARE.H

```
/************************************************************
Module name: MMFShare.H
Notices: Copyright (c) 1993 Jeffrey Richter
************************************************************/

// Dialog and control IDs.
#define DLG_MMFSHARE      1
#define ID_DATA          100
#define ID_CREATEFILE    101
#define ID_OPENFILE      102
#define ID_CLOSEFILE     103

////////////////////// End Of File //////////////////////
```

```
MMFSHARE.RC
/***************************************************************
Module name: MMFShare.RC
Notices: Copyright (c) 1993 Jeffrey Richter
***************************************************************/

#include <windows.h>
#include "MMFShare.H"

MMFShare ICON DISCARDABLE MMFShare. Ico

DLG_MMFSHARE DIALOG 38, 36, 186, 61
STYLE WS_BORDER | WS_POPUP | WS_VISIBLE | WS_CAPTION |
  WS_SYSMENU | WS_MINIMIZEBOX
CAPTION "Memory Mapped File Share Application"
BEGIN
    CONTROL "&Create mapping of Data", ID_CREATEFILE, "BUTTON",
       BS_PUSHBUTTON | WS_CHILD | WS_VISIBLE | WS_GROUP |
       WS_TABSTOP, 4, 4, 84, 14
    CONTROL "&Close mapping of Data", ID_CLOSEFILE, "BUTTON",
       BS_PUSHBUTTON | WS_CHILD | WS_VISIBLE | WS_TABSTOP,
       96, 4, 84, 14
    CONTROL "&Data:", -1, "STATIC",
       SS_LEFT | WS_CHILD | WS_VISIBLE | WS_GROUP,
       4, 24, 24, 12
    CONTROL "", ID_DATA, "EDIT",
       ES_LEFT | WS_CHILD | WS_VISIBLE | WS_BORDER |
       WS_TABSTOP, 28, 24, 153, 12
    CONTROL "&Open mapping and get Data", ID_OPENFILE,
       "BUTTON", BS_PUSHBUTTON | WS_CHILD | WS_VISIBLE |
       WS_GROUP | WS_TABSTOP, 40, 44, 104, 14
END

///////////////////// End Of File /////////////////////////
```

How Executables and DLLs Are Managed with Memory-Mapped Files

When you create a new process for an application that's already running, Windows NT simply opens another memory-mapped view of the file-mapping object that identifies the executable file's image and creates a new process object and a new thread object (for the primary thread). Windows NT also assigns new process and thread IDs to these objects. By using memory-mapped files, multiple running instances of the same application can share the same code and data in memory.

Note one small problem here. Windows NT is a true 32-bit operating system that uses the flat memory model. When you compile and link your program, all the code and data is thrown together as one large entity. The data is separated from the code but only to the extent that it follows the code in the executable file.[1] The illustration below shows a simplified view of how the code and data for an application are loaded into virtual memory and then mapped into a process's address space.

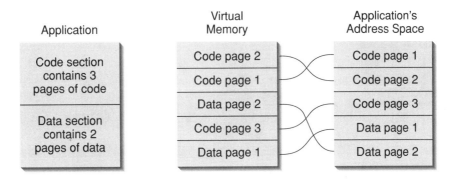

As an example, let's say that a second instance of an application is run. Windows NT simply maps the pages of virtual memory containing the file's code and data into the second process's address space, as shown here:

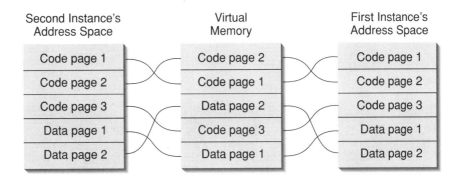

---

1. Actually, the contents of a file are broken down into sections. The code is in one section, and the global variables are in another section. Sections are aligned on page boundaries. Pages are 4 KB on MIPS and Intel *x*86 CPUs, 8 KB on the DEC Alpha CPU, and 16 KB on other CPUs. An application can determine the page size being used by calling GetSystemInfo. In the executable or DLL file, the code section usually precedes the data section.

If one instance of the application alters some of its global variables (residing in a data page), the memory contents for all instances of the application change. This type of change could cause disastrous effects and must not be allowed. Windows NT prohibits this by using the copy-on-write feature of the memory management system. Any time an application attempts to write to its memory-mapped file, Windows NT catches the attempt, allocates a new block of memory for the page containing the memory that is about to be written to, copies the contents of the page, and allows the application to write to this newly allocated memory block. As a result, no other instances of the same application are affected. The illustration below shows the effect of the first instance of the application attempting to change a global variable in data page 2.

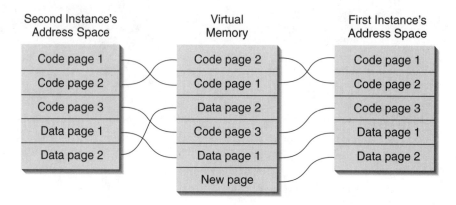

Windows NT allocated a new page of virtual memory and copied the contents of data page 2 into it. The first instance's address space is changed so that the new data page is mapped into the address space at the same location as that of the original address page. Now Windows NT can let the process alter the global variable without fear of altering the data for another instance of the same application.

A similar sequence of events occurs when an application is being debugged. Let's say that you're running multiple instances of an application and want to debug only one instance. You access your debugger and set a breakpoint in a line of source code. The debugger actually modifies your code by changing one of your assembly-language instructions to an instruction that causes the debugger to activate itself. So we have the same problem again. When the debugger modifies the code, it causes all instances of the application to activate the debugger when the changed assembly instruction is executed. To fix this situation, Windows NT again uses copy-on-write memory. When Windows NT senses that the debugger is attempting to change the code, it allocates a new block of memory, copies the relevant page containing the instruction into the new page, and allows the debugger to modify the code in the page copy.

Note that you can create global variables in an executable or DLL file and share them among all instances of the file. Briefly, the method requires placing the variables you want to share in their own section by using the *#pragma data_seg()* compiler directive. Then you must use the *-SECTION:name, attributes* switch to tell the linker that you want the data in the section to be shared for all instances or mappings of the file. The *name* argument identifies the name of the section containing the data variables you want to share, and the *attributes* argument specifies the attributes of data in this section. To share variables, you'll need to use RSW for Read, Shared, and Write.

(See Chapter 7 for more information about sharing global variables among multiple instances of a DLL.)

THREAD SYNCHRONIZATION

In an environment in which several threads are running concurrently, it becomes important to be able to synchronize the activities of various threads. Windows NT provides several synchronization objects that allow threads to synchronize their actions with one another. In this chapter, I'll concentrate on the four main synchronization objects: critical sections, mutexes, semaphores, and events. Other objects also exist for synchronization, and some of these are discussed and demonstrated in other chapters in this book.

This chapter offers numerous techniques for using the four main synchronization objects. For the most part, all the synchronization objects behave similarly. However, it is the differences among the types of objects that make one type of object more suitable for a particular task than another.

Of these four types of synchronization objects, a critical section is not a Windows NT object. That is, a critical section is not managed by the Windows NT Executive and you don't manipulate it using handles. A critical section is the easiest synchronization object to use and understand and, therefore, we'll discuss it first.

However, before we move directly on to critical sections, let's discuss the general concept of thread synchronization.

Thread Synchronization in a Nutshell

In general, a thread synchronizes itself with another thread by putting itself to sleep. However, just before the thread puts itself to sleep, it tells the operating system what "special event" has to occur in order for the thread to continue execution. When the thread is sleeping, it is no longer scheduled time by the operating system and therefore stops executing.

The operating system remains aware of the thread's request and watches to see if and when this "special event" occurs. When it occurs, the operating system wakes up the thread and allows the thread to continue execution—the thread has now synchronized its execution with the occurrence of the event.

As we discuss the various synchronization objects throughout this chapter, I'll show you how to specify what a "special event" is and how to put your thread to sleep after notifying the system to watch for the event on your thread's behalf.

One of the Worst Things You Can Do

Without the synchronization objects and the help from the operating system to watch for "special events," a thread would be forced to synchronize itself with "special events" by using a technique that has negative effects. Because Windows NT has built-in support for thread synchronization, you should *never* use the technique I am about to demonstrate.

In this technique, one thread synchronizes itself with the completion of a task in another thread by continuously polling the state of a variable that is shared or accessible by multiple threads. The code fragment below illustrates:

```
BOOL g_fFinishedCalculation = FALSE;

int WinMain (...) {
   CreateThread(..., RecalcFunc, ...);
   .
   .
   .
   // Wait for the recalculation to complete.
   while (!g_fFinishedCalculation)
      ;
   .
   .
   .
}

DWORD WINAPI RecalcFunc (LPVOID lpvThreadParm) {
   // Perform the recalculation.
   .
   .
   .
   g_fFinishedCalculation = TRUE;
   return(0);
}
```

As you can see, the primary thread (executing WinMain) doesn't put itself to sleep when it needs to synchronize itself with the completion of the RecalcFunc function. Because the primary thread does not sleep, it is being scheduled time by the operating system. This takes precious time cycles away from other threads that could be executing code that does something more useful.

Another problem with the polling method as used in the previous code fragment is that the Boolean variable *g_fFinishedCalculation* may never be set to TRUE. This could happen if the primary thread has a higher priority than the thread executing the RecalcFunc function. In this case, the system never assigns any time slices to the RecalcFunc thread, which will never execute the statement that sets *g_fFinished-Calculation* to TRUE. If the thread executing the WinMain function were put to sleep instead of polling, it would not be scheduled time, and the system would have an opportunity to schedule time to lower priority threads like the RecalcFunc thread, allowing it to execute.

I can't be any clearer than this: Synchronize threads by putting them to sleep. Do not synchronize threads by having them continuously poll for special events.

Critical Sections

A critical section is a small section of code that requires exclusive access to some shared data before the code can execute. Of all the synchronization objects, critical sections are the simplest to use, but they can be used to synchronize only threads within a single process. Critical sections allow only one thread at a time to gain access to a region of data. Examine the following code fragment:

```
int   g_nIndex = 0;
const int MAX_TIMES = 1000;
DWORD g_dwTimes[MAX_TIMES];

DWORD WINAPI FirstThread (LPVOID lpvThreadParm) {
   BOOL fDone = FALSE;

   while (!fDone) {
      if (g_nIndex >= MAX_TIMES) {
         fDone = TRUE;
      } else {
         g_dwTimes[g_nIndex] == GetTickCount();
         g_nIndex++;
      }
```

```
    }
    return(0);
}

DWORD WINAPI SecondThread (LPVOID lpvThreadParm) {
    BOOL fDone = FALSE;

    while (!fDone) {
        if (g_nIndex >= MAX_TIMES) {
            fDone = TRUE;
        } else {
            g_nIndex++;
            g_dwTimes[g_nIndex - 1] == GetTickCount();
        }
    }
    return(0);
}
```

Both of the thread functions here are supposed to produce the same result although each is coded slightly differently. If the First-Thread function were running by itself, it would fill the $g\_dwTimes$ array with ascending values. The same is true if we were to run the Second-Thread function by itself. Ideally, we would like to have both threads running concurrently and still have the $g\_dwTimes$ array produce ascending values. However, there is a problem with the code above. The problem is that the $g\_dwTimes$ array won't be filled properly because the two thread functions are accessing the same global variables simultaneously. Here is an example of how this could happen.

Let's say that we have just started executing both threads on a system with one CPU. Windows NT starts running SecondThread first (which could very well happen), and right after SecondThread increments g_nIndex to 1, Windows NT preempts the thread and allows First-Thread to run. FirstThread then sets $g\_dwTimes[1]$ to the system time, and Windows NT preempts the thread and gives time back to Second-Thread. SecondThread now sets $g\_dwTimes[1 - 1]$ to the new system time. Because this operation occurred later, the new system time is a higher value than that of the time placed into FirstThread's array. Also, notice that index 1 of $g\_dwTimes$ was filled in before index 0 (zero). The data in the array is corrupted.

I admit that this example is a bit contrived. It is difficult to come up with a real-life example that doesn't require several pages of source code. However, you can easily see how this problem can extend itself to real-life examples. Consider the case of managing a linked list of objects.

If access to the linked list was not synchronized, one thread would be adding an item to the list while another thread was simultaneously trying to search for an item in the list. The situation could become more chaotic if the two threads were both adding items to the list at the same time. By using critical sections, you can ensure that access to the data structures are coordinated between threads.

Creating a Critical Section

To create a critical section, you must first allocate a CRITICAL-_SECTION data structure in your own process. The allocation of the critical section structure must be global so that different threads can gain access to it. Usually critical sections are simply global variables. Although the CRITICAL_SECTION structure and its members appear in WINNT.H,[1] you should think of the members of this structure as being off-limits. The Win32 functions that manipulate critical sections initialize and maintain all the members in the structure for you. You should not access or modify any of the members yourself.

After adding critical sections to our example program, the code looks like this:

```
int    g_nIndex = 0;
const int MAX_TIMES = 1000;
DWORD g_dwTimes[MAX_TIMES];
CRITICAL_SECTION g_CriticalSection;

int WinMain (...) {
   HANDLE hThreads[2];

   // Initialize the critical section before the threads so
   // that it is ready when the threads execute.
   InitializeCriticalSection(&g_CriticalSection);

   hThreads[0] = CreateThread(...);
   hThreads[1] = CreateThread(...);

   // Wait for both threads to terminate.
   // Don't worry about this line, it will be explained shortly.
   WaitForMultipleObjects(2, hThreads, TRUE, INFINITE);

   // Close the thread handles.
   CloseHandle(hThreads[0]);
```

(continued)

---

1. CRITICAL_SECTION itself is in WINBASE.H as RTL_CRITICAL_SECTION. The RTL_CRITICAL_SECTION structure is typedefed in WINNT.H.

177

```
        CloseHandle(hThreads[1]);

        // Delete the critical section.
        DeleteCriticalSection(&g_CriticalSection);
}
DWORD WINAPI FirstThread (LPVOID lpvThreadParm) {
        BOOL fDone = FALSE;

        while (!fDone) {
            EnterCriticalSection(&g_CriticalSection);
            if (g_nIndex >= MAX_TIMES) {
                fDone = TRUE;
            } else {
                g_dwTimes[g_nIndex] == GetTickCount();
                g_nIndex++;
            }
            LeaveCriticalSection(&g_CriticalSection);
        }
        return(0);
}


DWORD WINAPI SecondThread (LPVOID lpvThreadParm) {
        BOOL fDone = FALSE;

        while (!fDone) {
            EnterCriticalSection(&g_CriticalSection);
            if (g_nIndex >= MAX_TIMES) {
                fDone = TRUE;
            } else {
                g_nIndex++;
                g_dwTimes[g_nIndex - 1] == GetTickCount();
            }
            LeaveCriticalSection(&g_CriticalSection);
        }
        return(0);
}
```

Using a Critical Section

Before you can synchronize threads with a critical section, you must initialize it by calling InitializeCriticalSection, passing in the address to the CRITICAL_SECTION structure as the *lpCriticalSection* parameter:

```
VOID InitializeCriticalSection
        (LPCRITICAL_SECTION lpCriticalSection);
```

This initializes the members of the structure so that they have useful meanings when EnterCriticalSection is called. The code above shows the critical section being initialized in WinMain. Both thread functions are expecting that the *g_CriticalSection* structure variable has been initialized by calling InitializeCriticalSection before they begin executing. Let's see what happens next.

Referring again to our code example on the previous page, let's say that SecondThread executes first. It calls EnterCriticalSection, passing it the address to the *g_CriticalSection* structure variable:

```
VOID EnterCriticalSection(LPCRITICAL_SECTION lpCriticalSection);
```

EnterCriticalSection sees that this is the first time that EnterCriticalSection has been called for this variable, changes some members in the data structure, and lets the *g_nIndex++;* line execute. After this line executes, Windows NT might preempt SecondThread and assign processor time to FirstThread. FirstThread calls EnterCriticalSection, passing the address of the same object that SecondThread had used. This time, EnterCriticalSection sees that the *g_CriticalSection* structure variable is in use and puts FirstThread to sleep. Because FirstThread is asleep, Windows NT can assign the remainder of its time slice to another thread. Windows NT will stop trying to assign time slices to FirstThread until FirstThread is awakened.

Eventually, SecondThread will be assigned another time slice. Then it will execute the following statement:

```
g_dwTimes[g_nIndex - 1] = GetTickCount();
```

This causes *g_dwTimes[0]* to be assigned the current system time. This is different from our first scenario, in which *g_dwTimes[1]* was assigned a lesser value than *g_dwTimes[0]*. At this point, if Windows NT wants to preempt the second thread it can do so, but it can't assign time to FirstThread because FirstThread is still sleeping. Eventually, SecondThread will be assigned a time slice again and will execute the following statement:

```
LeaveCriticalSection(&g_CriticalSection);
```

The *g_CriticalSection* variable indicates that the protected data structures are no longer protected and are available to any other thread that wants access to them. FirstThread was waiting on *g_CriticalSection*, so it can now be awakened. Its call to EnterCriticalSection sets ownership of *g_CriticalSection* to FirstThread, and EnterCriticalSection finally returns so that FirstThread can continue execution.

As you can see, using critical sections allows access of data to only one thread at a time. It is possible to have more than two threads requiring access to the same data at the same time. When this happens, all the threads must call EnterCriticalSection before they attempt to manipulate the data. If one of the threads already has ownership of the critical section, any thread waiting to gain access is put to sleep. When ownership is relinquished by calling LeaveCriticalSection, Windows NT wakes up just one of the waiting threads and gives that thread ownership. All the other sleeping threads continue to sleep.

Note that it is legal and even useful for a single thread to own a critical section several times. This is possible because calls to EnterCriticalSection from the thread owning the critical section increment a reference count. Before another thread can own the critical section, the thread currently owning it must call LeaveCriticalSection enough times so that the reference count drops back to 0 (zero). Let's see how this works using the following example:

```
int g_nNums[100];
CRITICAL_SECTION CriticalSection;
  .
  .
  .
LRESULT WINAPI Thread (LPVOID lpvParam) {
    int nIndex = (int) *lpvParam;
    EnterCriticalSection(&CriticalSection);

    if (g_nNums[nIndex] < MIN_VAL)
       IncrementNum(nIndex);
    else
       g nNums[nIndex] = MIN_VAL;

    LeaveCriticalSection(&CriticalSection);
}

void IncrementNum (int nIndex) {
    EnterCriticalSection(&CriticalSection);
    g_nNums[nIndex]++;
    LeaveCriticalSection(&CriticalSection);
}
```

In this code fragment, the Thread function acquires ownership of the critical section when it first begins executing. In this way, it can test *g_nNums[nIndex]*, knowing that no other thread can change *g_nNums-[nIndex]* during the test. Then, if *g_nNums[nIndex]* contains a value less than MIN_VAL, the IncrementNum function is called.

IncrementNum is an independent function. It is implemented without any knowledge of what calls it. Because the function will alter the *g_nNums* array, it requests access to the array by calling Enter-CriticalSection. Because IncrementNum is executing under the thread that already owns the critical section, EnterCriticalSection increments only the reference count of the critical section and allows the thread to continue execution. If IncrementNum were called from another thread, the call to EnterCriticalSection would put that thread to sleep until the thread executing the Thread function called LeaveCriticalSection.

If you have several unrelated data structures in your application, you would create CRITICAL_SECTION variables for each of the data structures. Then in your code you would first have to call Initialize-CriticalSection once for each of the CRITICAL_SECTION variables. Your threads would also need to call EnterCriticalSection, passing the address of the CRITICAL_SECTION variable that applies to the data structures to which the thread wants access. Examine this code fragment:

```
int g_nNum[100];
char g_cChars[100];
CRITICAL_SECTION g_CriticalSection;
.
.
.
LRESULT WINAPI ThreadFunc (LPVOID lpvParam) {
   int x;

   EnterCriticalSection(&g_CriticalSection);

   for (x = 0; x < 100; x++) {
      g_nNums[x] = 0;
      g_cChars[x] = 'X';
   }

   LeaveCriticalSection(&g_CriticalSection);
}
```

In this case, you enter a single critical section whose job it is to protect both the *g_nNums* array and the *g_cChars* array while they are being initialized. But the two arrays have nothing to do with one another. While this loop executes, no thread can gain access to either array. If the ThreadFunc function is implemented as shown at the top of the following page, the initialization of the two arrays is separated.

```
LRESULT WINAPI ThreadFunc (LPVOID lpvParam) {
   int x;

   EnterCriticalSection(&g_CriticalSection);

   for (x = 0; x < 100; x++)
      g_nNums[x] = 0;

   for (x = 0; x < 100; x++)
      g_cChars[x] = 'X';

   LeaveCriticalSection(&g_CriticalSection);
}
```

So, theoretically, after the *g_nNums* array has been initialized, another thread that needs access only to the *g_nNums* array and not to the *g_cChars* array can begin executing while ThreadFunc continues to initialize the *g_cChars* array. But, alas, this cannot happen because both data structures are being protected by a single critical section. To fix this, you can create two critical sections, as follows:

```
int g_nNums[100];
char g_cChars[100];
CRITICAL_SECTION g_CriticalSectionForNums;
CRITICAL_SECTION g_CriticalSectionForChars;
   .
   .
   .
LRESULT WINAPI ThreadFunc (LPVOID lpvParam) {
   int x;

   EnterCriticalSection(&g_CriticalSectionForNums);

   for (x = 0; x < 100; x++)
      g_nNums[x] = 0;

   LeaveCriticalSection(&g_CriticalSectionForNums);

   EnterCriticalSection(&g_CriticalSectionForChars);

   for (x = 0; x < 100; x++)
      g_cChars[x] = 'X';

   LeaveCriticalSection(&g_CriticalSectionForChars);
}
```

Now this function has been implemented so that another thread can start using the *g_nNums* array as soon as ThreadFunc has finished initializing it. Sometimes, you will need to access two data structures simultaneously. If this were a requirement of ThreadFunc, it would be implemented like this:

```
LRESULT WINAPI ThreadFunc (LPVOID lpvParam) {
   int x;

   EnterCriticalSection(&g_CriticalSectionForNums);
   EnterCriticalSection(&g_CriticalSectionForChars);

   for (x = 0; x < 100; x++)
      g_nNums[x] = 0;

   for (x = 0; x < 100; x++)
      g_cChars[x] = 'X';

   LeaveCriticalSection(&g_CriticalSectionForChars);
   LeaveCriticalSection(&g_CriticalSectionForNums);
}
```

Suppose that another thread in the process also requires access to the two arrays and it is written as follows:

```
LRESULT WINAPI OtherThreadFunc (LPVOID lpvParam) {
   int x;

   EnterCriticalSection(&g_CriticalSectionForChars);
   EnterCriticalSection(&g_CriticalSectionForNums);

   for (x = 0; x < 100; x++)
      g_nNums[x] = 0;

   for (x = 0; x < 100; x++)
      g_cChars[x] = 'X';

   LeaveCriticalSection(&g_CriticalSectionForNums);
   LeaveCriticalSection(&g_CriticalSectionForChars);
}
```

All I did in the function above was switch the order of the calls to EnterCriticalSection and LeaveCriticalSection. But because the two functions are written like this, there's a chance for *deadlock* to occur. Deadlock occurs when a thread will never execute because the thing it is waiting for (the critical sections, in this example) will never be available.

Suppose that ThreadFunc begins executing and gains ownership of the *g_CriticalSectionForNums* critical section. Then the thread executing the OtherThreadFunc function thread is given some CPU time and gains ownership of the *g_CriticalSectionForChars* critical section. Now you

183

have a deadlock situation. When either ThreadFunc or OtherThreadFunc tries to continue executing, neither will be able to gain ownership of the other critical section they require before they can continue execution.

In the example on the previous page, the problem can be fixed easily by writing the functions so that they call EnterCriticalSection in the same order. This will keep one thread from locking the other one out of a needed resource.

Here is a technique you can use to minimize the time spent inside a critical section. The following code prevents other threads from changing the value in *g_nNums[3]* before the WM_SOMEMSG is sent to a window:

```
int g_nNums[100];
CRITICAL_SECTION g_CriticalSection;

LRESULT WINAPI SomeThread (LPVOID lpvParam) {
   EnterCriticalSection(&g_CriticalSection);

   // Send a message to a window.
   SendMessage(hwndSomeWnd, WM_SOMEMSG, g_nNums[3], 0);

   LeaveCriticalSection(&g_CriticalSection);
}
```

From examining the code above, you couldn't know how much time the window procedure requires to process the WM_SOMEMSG message—it could take a few microseconds or a few years.[2] During that time, no other threads can gain access to the *g_nNums* array. It would be much better to write the code as follows:

```
int g_nNums[100];
CRITICAL_SECTION g_CriticalSection;

LRESULT WINAPI SomeThread (LPVOID lpvParam) {
   int nTemp;

   EnterCriticalSection(&g_CriticalSection);

   nTemp = g_nNums[3];

   LeaveCriticalSection(&g_CriticalSection);

   // Send a message to a window.
   SendMessage(hwndSomeWnd, WM_SOMEMSG, nTemp, 0);
}
```

---

2. Hopefully, the window procedure is written a bit more efficiently than I suggest here and, at most, will not require more than a couple seconds to run.

This code saves the value in *g_nNums[3]* in a temporary integer variable *nTemp*. You can probably guess how long the CPU requires to execute this line—just a few microseconds. Immediately after saving the temporary variable, LeaveCriticalSection is called because the array no longer needs to be protected. This second implementation is much better than the first because other threads are stopped from using the *g_nNums* array for only a few microseconds instead of a few years.

While an application terminates, all the CRITICAL_SECTION variables should be cleaned up by calling DeleteCriticalSection:

```
VOID DeleteCriticalSection(LPCRITICAL_SECTION lpCriticalSection);
```

This function releases all the resources owned by the critical section. Naturally, you should not call EnterCriticalSection or LeaveCritical-Section using a deleted *CRITICAL_SECTION* variable unless it has been initialized again with InitializeCriticalSection. Also, be sure that you don't delete a critical section if a thread is waiting on a call to EnterCriticalSection.

Synchronizing GDI Objects with Critical Sections

Before moving on, let me state something very important: The use of GDI objects is not synchronized—that is, two or more threads cannot use the same GDI object simultaneously. For example, let's say that you have a thread that creates a font and saves the font's handle in a global variable. You also have two other threads that each receive a WM_PAINT message at the same time. If both threads call BeginPaint followed by SelectObject (to select the same global font), the second thread's call to SelectObject will fail. Microsoft didn't want to build GDI object synchronization into Windows NT because it would slow the system down too much.

A good way to synchronize shared GDI objects is to use a global CRITICAL_SECTION structure in your application. Then, in each thread's WM_PAINT processing, place a call to EnterCriticalSection before the call to BeginPaint and place another call to LeaveCritical-Section after the call to EndPaint. This will guarantee that only one thread has access to the shared GDI object at a time.

Of course, you could also have each thread create its very own GDI objects that are not shared with any other threads. In this way, you would avoid all the potential problems of synchronizing access to GDI objects.

The Critical Sections Sample Application

The CritSecs (CRITSECS.EXE) application, listed in Figure 5-1 beginning on page 190, demonstrates the importance of using critical sections in a multithreaded application. When the program starts, WinMain invokes a modal dialog box. This dialog box serves as the interface to the application. When the dialog box function receives the WM_INITDIALOG message, the Dlg_OnInitDialog function initializes a global CRITICAL_SECTION structure, initializes all the child controls in the dialog box and creates two threads—CounterThread and DisplayThread. At this point, three threads are running in this process: the primary thread that's handling the input to the dialog box and its controls, CounterThread, and DisplayThread.

Toward the top of CritSecs.C, the following variable appears:

```
// The "Data" that needs protecting.
char g_szNumber[10] = "0";
```

This is a character array that is initialized to a string containing the number 0 (zero). CounterThread converts the number in this character array to an integer, increments the integer by one, and converts the integer back to a character array so that it can be stored in the $g\_szNumber$ array. DisplayThread reads the number in the $g\_szNumber$ array and adds the number to a list box control in the dialog box.

When CritSecs is invoked, its list box starts filling with numbers. The CritSecs dialog box appears as follows:

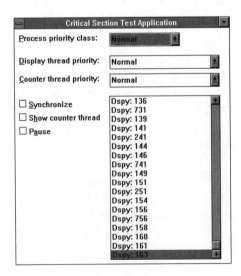

You might notice that the numbers in the list box don't appear in ascending order because CritSecs, by default, does not synchronize access to the *g_ szNumber* array. While CounterThread is converting the array to an integer, incrementing it, and copying the number back, DisplayThread is reading the *g_ szNumber* array and adding its contents to the list box.

To see what a big difference the critical sections make, click on the *Synchronize* check box. CritSecs immediately starts making use of the *g_CriticalSection* variable that was created to guard access to the *g_ sz-Number* array. The result is that the list box now shows numbers that are in ascending order:

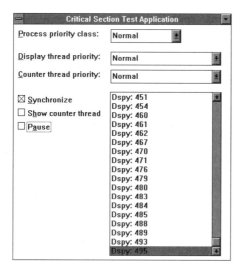

I have added a few other capabilities to CritSecs. The *Process priority class*, *Display thread priority*, and *Counter thread priority* combo boxes let you fiddle with the priority class of the whole CritSecs application as well as the relative priorities of the two threads executing the DisplayThread and CounterThread functions.

The *Pause* check box demonstrates how to suspend the threads executing CounterThread and DisplayThread by calling the SuspendThread and ResumeThread functions.

The last check box, *Show counter thread*, causes CounterThread to add the following line to the list box every time it completes its increment of the number and store it back in the *g_ szNumber* array:

```
Cntr: Increment
```

When this check box is on, the list box appears as follows:

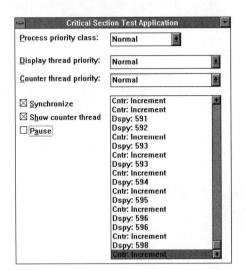

You can see that each iteration of DisplayThread's loop executes faster than each iteration of CounterThread's loop. In some cases Display-Thread's loop completes three iterations for just one iteration of CounterThread's loop. This shows that you should get into the habit of anticipating how the system schedules time to threads. By altering the relative priorities of the two threads, you can alter the order and frequency of this behavior.

CritSecs might produce different results on your computer system. Here are some reasons why:

- the number of CPUs in your system

- the speed of your system

- the number of threads created by other processes also running

- the priority class of other processes running

- the relative priorities of the threads running in these other processes

Two more things to note about the CritSecs program: First, Counter-Thread calls the Win32 Sleep function after it stores the number back into the *g_szNumber* array. The prototype for the Sleep function is shown below:

```
VOID Sleep(DWORD cMilliseconds);
```

When a thread calls Sleep, it tells Windows NT that it doesn't need any processor time for the number of milliseconds specified by the *cMilliseconds* parameter. CounterThread calls Sleep, passing a value of 0 (zero) for *cMilliseconds*. This tells Windows NT that the thread doesn't need any processor time for the next 0 (zero) milliseconds. This might seem like a useless thing to do, but a side effect of the Sleep function exaggerates the results of CritSecs; Sleep also tells Windows NT that the thread would like to voluntarily give up the remainder of its time slice. I put the call to Sleep(0) in CounterThread to dramatize the effect of un-synchronized threads in CritSecs. Without the call to Sleep(0), CritSecs would still have behaved improperly without synchronizing the threads, but the problems would not have been as pronounced.

The second note of interest in the CritSecs application is how it turns synchronization on and off. You'll see the following line at the beginning of both CounterThread's and DisplayThread's loop:

```
fSyncChecked = IsDlgButtonChecked(g_hwndDlg, ID_SYNCHRONIZE);
```

This line retrieves and saves the status of the *Synchronize* check box at the beginning of each loop's iteration. Elsewhere in the loop, I included code such as the following:

```
if (fSyncChecked) {
    EnterCriticalSection(&g_CriticalSection);
}
    .
    .
    .
if (fSyncChecked) {
    LeaveCriticalSection(&g_CriticalSection);
}
```

When I first developed CritSecs, the code above originally looked like this:

```
if (IsDlgButtonChecked(g_hwndDlg, ID_SYNCHRONIZE)) {
    EnterCriticalSection(&g_CriticalSection);
}
    .
    .
    .
if (IsDlgButtonChecked(g_hwndDlg, ID_SYNCHRONIZE)) {
    LeaveCriticalSection(&g_CriticalSection);
}
```

189

The differences here caused a bug in CritSecs that made the program hang sometimes but not every time, and it took me some time to track down the problem. This problem occurs often in multithreaded applications even when you're extremely careful. Eventually, I fixed the problem by using the first set of code.

What had been happening was the CounterThread loop would start and see that the *Synchronize* check box was on. So CounterThread would call EnterCriticalSection. Then DisplayThread, seeing that the *Synchronize* check box was on, would also call EnterCriticalSection. But Windows NT would not let DisplayThread's call to EnterCriticalSection return because CounterThread currently had ownership of it. While CounterThread was reading the number, I would turn the *Synchronize* check box off. When CounterThread made its call to IsDlgButton-Checked, it saw that the check box was off and would not call Leave-CriticalSection. As long as the check box remained off, CounterThread would never release the critical section and DisplayThread would stay forever hung waiting for the critical section.

By saving the state of the check box in a variable and testing the variable before calling Enter/LeaveCriticalSection, I removed the possibility of executing unmatched EnterCriticalSection and LeaveCritical-Section calls. As you can see, you must be very careful when designing and implementing multithreaded applications.

CritSecs.ico

CRITSECS.C

```
/******************************************************************
Module name: CritSecs.C
Notices: Copyright (c) 1993 Jeffrey Richter
******************************************************************/

#include <windows.h>
#include <windowsx.h>
#include <tchar.h>
```

Figure 5-1.   *(continued)*
The CritSecs application.

Figure 5-1.   *continued*

```
#include <stdio.h>        // for sprintf
#include <string.h>       // for strrev
#include "CritSecs.H"

///////////////////////////////////////////////////////////////

// Global variables
HWND     g_hwndDlg = NULL;
HANDLE   g_hThreadCntr = NULL;
HANDLE   g_hThreadDspy = NULL;

// The "Data" that needs protecting.
TCHAR    g_szNumber[10] = __TEXT("0");

// The "Critical section" used to protect the "Data".
CRITICAL_SECTION g_CriticalSection;

///////////////////////////////////////////////////////////////

// Add a string to a list box.
void AddToListBox (LPCTSTR szBuffer) {
   HWND hwndDataBox = GetDlgItem(g_hwndDlg, ID_DATABOX);

   int x = ListBox_AddString(hwndDataBox, szBuffer);
   ListBox_SetCurSel(hwndDataBox, x);

   if (ListBox_GetCount(hwndDataBox) > 100)
      ListBox_DeleteString(hwndDataBox, 0);
}

///////////////////////////////////////////////////////////////

// Thread to increment the protected counter data.
DWORD WINAPI CounterThread (LPVOID lpThreadParameter) {
   unsigned int nNumber, nDigit;
   BOOL fSyncChecked;

   while (TRUE) {
      // Get the status of the "Synchronize" button and save it.
      fSyncChecked =
         IsDlgButtonChecked(g_hwndDlg, ID_SYNCHRONIZE);

      if (fSyncChecked) {
         // If the user wants us synchronized, do it.
         EnterCriticalSection(&g_CriticalSection);
      }
```

(continued)

191

Figure 5-1. *continued*

```
// Convert the string number to an integer and add one.
_stscanf(g_szNumber, __TEXT("%d"), &nNumber);
nNumber++;

// Convert the new integer back to a string.
nDigit = 0;
while (nNumber != 0) {
    // Put a digit into the string.
    g_szNumber[nDigit++] = __TEXT('0') + (nNumber % 10);

    // A call to sleep here tells Windows NT that we
    // wish to relinquish the remainder of our time
    // slice to another thread.  This call is needed for
    // single-CPU systems so that the results of the
    // synchronization and lack thereof is obvious.
    // Normally, your programs would NOT call Sleep.
    Sleep(0);

    // Get ready to get the next digit.
    nNumber /= 10;
}

// All digits converted to characters.
// Terminate the string.
g_szNumber[nDigit] = 0;

// Characters were generated in reverse order,
// reverse the string.
// Call strrev if ANSI, Call _wcsrev if UNICODE.
_tcsrev(g_szNumber);

if (fSyncChecked) {
    // If the user wants synchronization, do it.
    // In earlier versions of this program, I was calling
    // IsDlgButtonChecked as I did earlier instead of
    // using the fSyncChecked variable.  This caused
    // problems because the user could check or uncheck
    // the button in between the calls to
    // EnterCriticalSection and LeaveCriticalSection.
    // This meant that I was sometimes leaving a critical
    // section that was never entered into.  And I was
    // sometimes entering a critical section that
    // I never left.
    LeaveCriticalSection(&g_CriticalSection);
}
```

(continued)

Figure 5-1. *continued*

```
      // If the user wants to display something
      // after each iteration, do it.
      if (IsDlgButtonChecked(g_hwndDlg, ID_SHOWCNTRTHRD))
         AddToListBox(__TEXT("Cntr: Increment"));
   }
   return(0);  // We will never get here.
}


/////////////////////////////////////////////////////////////////

// Thread to add the current value of
// the counter (Data) to the list box.
DWORD WINAPI DisplayThread (LPVOID lpThreadParameter) {
   BOOL fSyncChecked;
   TCHAR szBuffer[50];

   while (TRUE) {

      // Determine if the user wants us to synchronize ourself.
      fSyncChecked =
         IsDlgButtonChecked(g_hwndDlg, ID_SYNCHRONIZE);

      if (fSyncChecked)
         EnterCriticalSection(&g_CriticalSection);

      // Construct a string with the string form of the number.
      _stprintf(szBuffer, __TEXT("Dspy: %s"), g_szNumber);

      if (fSyncChecked)
         LeaveCriticalSection(&g_CriticalSection);

      // Add the string form of the number to the list box.
      AddToListBox(szBuffer);
   }
   return(0);  // We will never get here.
}


/////////////////////////////////////////////////////////////////

BOOL Dlg_OnInitDialog (HWND hwnd, HWND hwndFocus,
   LPARAM lParam) {
   HWND hWndCtl;
   DWORD dwThreadCntr, dwThreadDspy;
```

(continued)

Figure 5-1. *continued*

```
// Save the handle of the dialog box in a global so that
// the threads can easily gain access to it.  This must be
// done before creating the threads.
g_hwndDlg = hwnd;

// Associate an icon with the dialog box.
SetClassLong(hwnd, GCL_HICON, (LONG)
   LoadIcon((HINSTANCE) GetWindowLong(hwnd,
      GWL_HINSTANCE), __TEXT("CritSecs")));

// Initialize the critical section.  This must also be
// done before any threads try to use it.
InitializeCriticalSection(&g_CriticalSection);

// Create our counter thread and let it start running.
g_hThreadCntr = CreateThread(NULL, 0, CounterThread, NULL,
   0, &dwThreadCntr);

// Create our display thread and let it start running.
g_hThreadDspy = CreateThread(NULL, 0, DisplayThread, NULL,
   0, &dwThreadDspy);

// Fill the Priority class combo box and select "Normal".
hWndCtl = GetDlgItem(hwnd, ID_PRIORITYCLASS);
ComboBox_AddString(hWndCtl, __TEXT("Idle"));
ComboBox_AddString(hWndCtl, __TEXT("Normal"));
ComboBox_AddString(hWndCtl, __TEXT("High"));
ComboBox_AddString(hWndCtl, __TEXT("Realtime"));
ComboBox_SetCurSel(hWndCtl, 1);  // Normal

// Fill the display thread's relative priority
// combo box and select "Normal".
hWndCtl = GetDlgItem(hwnd, ID_DSPYTHRDPRIORITY);
ComboBox_AddString(hWndCtl, __TEXT("Idle"));
ComboBox_AddString(hWndCtl, __TEXT("Lowest"));
ComboBox_AddString(hWndCtl, __TEXT("Below normal"));
ComboBox_AddString(hWndCtl, __TEXT("Normal"));
ComboBox_AddString(hWndCtl, __TEXT("Above normal"));
ComboBox_AddString(hWndCtl, __TEXT("Highest"));
ComboBox_AddString(hWndCtl, __TEXT("Realtime"));
ComboBox_SetCurSel(hWndCtl, 3);  // Normal
```

(continued)

Figure 5-1. *continued*

```
    // Fill the counter thread's relative priority
    // combo box and select "Normal".
    hWndCtl = GetDlgItem(hwnd, ID_CNTRTHRDPRIORITY);
    ComboBox_AddString(hWndCtl, __TEXT("Idle"));
    ComboBox_AddString(hWndCtl, __TEXT("Lowest"));
    ComboBox_AddString(hWndCtl, __TEXT("Below normal"));
    ComboBox_AddString(hWndCtl, __TEXT("Normal"));
    ComboBox_AddString(hWndCtl, __TEXT("Above normal"));
    ComboBox_AddString(hWndCtl, __TEXT("Highest"));
    ComboBox_AddString(hWndCtl, __TEXT("Realtime"));
    ComboBox_SetCurSel(hWndCtl, 3);   // Normal

    return(TRUE);
}


///////////////////////////////////////////////////////////////

void Dlg_OnDestroy (HWND hwnd) {
    // When the dialog box is destroyed, terminate the
    // two threads and delete the critical section.
    TerminateThread(g_hThreadDspy, 0);
    TerminateThread(g_hThreadCntr, 0);
    DeleteCriticalSection(&g_CriticalSection);
}


///////////////////////////////////////////////////////////////

void Dlg_OnCommand (HWND hwnd, int id, HWND hwndCtl,
    UINT codeNotify) {

    HANDLE hThread;
    DWORD dw;

    switch (id) {
        case IDCANCEL:
            EndDialog(hwnd, id);
            break;

        case ID_PRIORITYCLASS:
            if (codeNotify != CBN_SELCHANGE)
                break;
```

(continued)

Figure 5-1. *continued*

```
        // User is changing priority class.
        switch (ComboBox_GetCurSel(hwndCtl)) {
            case 0:
                dw = IDLE_PRIORITY_CLASS;
                break;

            case 1:
                dw = NORMAL_PRIORITY_CLASS;
                break;

            case 2:
                dw = HIGH_PRIORITY_CLASS;
                break;

            case 3:
                dw = REALTIME_PRIORITY_CLASS;
                break;
        }
        SetPriorityClass(GetCurrentProcess(), dw);
        break;

    case ID_DSPYTHRDPRIORITY:
    case ID_CNTRTHRDPRIORITY:
        if (codeNotify != CBN_SELCHANGE)
            break;

        switch (ComboBox_GetCurSel(hwndCtl)) {
            case 0:
                dw = (DWORD) THREAD_PRIORITY_IDLE;
                break;

            case 1:
                dw = (DWORD) THREAD_PRIORITY_LOWEST;
                break;

            case 2:
                dw = (DWORD) THREAD_PRIORITY_BELOW_NORMAL;
                break;

            case 3:
                dw = (DWORD) THREAD_PRIORITY_NORMAL;
                break;
```

(continued)

Figure 5-1. *continued*

```
        case 4:
            dw = (DWORD) THREAD_PRIORITY_ABOVE_NORMAL;
            break;

        case 5:
            dw = (DWORD) THREAD_PRIORITY_HIGHEST;
            break;

        case 6:
            dw = (DWORD) THREAD_PRIORITY_TIME_CRITICAL;
            break;
        }
        // User is changing the relative priority
        // of one of the threads.
        hThread = (id == ID_CNTRTHRDPRIORITY) ?
            g_hThreadCntr : g_hThreadDspy;

        SetThreadPriority(hThread, dw);
        break;

    case ID_PAUSE:
        // User is pausing or resuming both threads.
        if (Button_GetCheck(hwndCtl)) {

            SuspendThread(g_hThreadCntr);
            SuspendThread(g_hThreadDspy);

        } else {

            ResumeThread(g_hThreadCntr);
            ResumeThread(g_hThreadDspy);

        }
        break;
    }
}

//////////////////////////////////////////////////////////////////

BOOL CALLBACK Dlg_Proc (HWND hDlg, UINT uMsg,
    WPARAM wParam, LPARAM lParam) {

    BOOL fProcessed = TRUE;
```

(continued)

Figure 5-1. *continued*

```
    switch (uMsg) {
        HANDLE_MSG(hDlg, WM_INITDIALOG, Dlg_OnInitDialog);
        HANDLE_MSG(hDlg, WM_DESTROY, Dlg_OnDestroy);
        HANDLE_MSG(hDlg, WM_COMMAND, Dlg_OnCommand);

        default:
            fProcessed = FALSE;
            break;
    }
    return(fProcessed);
}


///////////////////////////////////////////////////////////////////

int APIENTRY WinMain (HINSTANCE hInstance,
    HINSTANCE hPrevInstance, LPSTR lpszCmdLine, int nCmdShow) {

    DialogBox(hInstance, MAKEINTRESOURCE(DLG_CRITSECS),
        NULL, Dlg_Proc);
    return(0);
}


//////////////////////// End Of File ////////////////////////
```

CRITSECS.H

```
/************************************************************
Module name: CritSecs.H
Notices: Copyright (c) 1993 Jeffrey Richter
*************************************************************/

// Dialog and control IDs.
#define DLG_CRITSECS              1
#define ID_PRIORITYCLASS        100
#define ID_DSPYTHRDPRIORITY     101
#define ID_CNTRTHRDPRIORITY     102
#define ID_PAUSE                103
#define ID_SYNCHRONIZE          104
#define ID_SHOWCNTRTHRD         105
#define ID_DATABOX              106


//////////////////////// End Of File ////////////////////////
```

(continued)

Figure 5-1.   *continued*

CRITSECS.RC

```
/****************************************************************
Module name: CritSecs.RC
Notices: Copyright (c) 1993 Jeffrey Richter
****************************************************************/

#include <windows.h>
#include "CritSecs.h"


CritSecs  ICON  DISCARDABLE CritSecs.Ico

DLG_CRITSECS DIALOG 29, 28, 197, 208
STYLE WS_BORDER | WS_POPUP | WS_VISIBLE | WS_CAPTION |
   WS_SYSMENU | WS_MINIMIZEBOX
CAPTION "Critical Section Test Application"
BEGIN
   CONTROL "&Process priority class:", -1, "STATIC",
      SS_LEFT | WS_CHILD | WS_VISIBLE | WS_GROUP, 4, 4, 88, 8
   CONTROL "", ID_PRIORITYCLASS, "COMBOBOX",
      CBS_DROPDOWNLIST | WS_CHILD | WS_VISIBLE | WS_GROUP |
      WS_TABSTOP, 88, 4, 64, 48
   CONTROL "&Display thread priority:", -1, "STATIC",
      SS_LEFTNOWORDWRAP | WS_CHILD | WS_VISIBLE | WS_GROUP |
      WS_TABSTOP, 4, 24, 84, 8
   CONTROL "", ID_DSPYTHRDPRIORITY, "COMBOBOX",
      CBS_DROPDOWNLIST | WS_CHILD | WS_VISIBLE | WS_GROUP |
      WS_TABSTOP, 88, 24, 100, 76
   CONTROL "&Counter thread priority:", -1, "STATIC",
      SS_LEFTNOWORDWRAP | WS_CHILD | WS_VISIBLE | WS_GROUP |
      WS_TABSTOP, 4, 40, 88, 8
   CONTROL "", ID_CNTRTHRDPRIORITY, "COMBOBOX",
      CBS_DROPDOWNLIST | WS_CHILD | WS_VISIBLE | WS_GROUP |
      WS_TABSTOP, 88, 40, 100, 76
   CONTROL "&Synchronize", ID_SYNCHRONIZE, "BUTTON",
      BS_AUTOCHECKBOX | WS_CHILD | WS_VISIBLE | WS_TABSTOP,
      4, 60, 64, 12
   CONTROL "S&how counter thread", ID_SHOWCNTRTHRD, "BUTTON",
      BS_AUTOCHECKBOX | WS_CHILD | WS_VISIBLE | WS_TABSTOP,
      4, 72, 80, 12
   CONTROL "P&ause", ID_PAUSE, "BUTTON",
      BS_AUTOCHECKBOX | WS_CHILD | WS_VISIBLE | WS_TABSTOP,
```

(continued)

Figure 5-1. *continued*

```
    4, 84, 44, 12
  CONTROL "", ID_DATABOX, "LISTBOX", LBS_NOTIFY | WS_CHILD |
    WS_VISIBLE | WS_BORDER | WS_VSCROLL | WS_GROUP |
    WS_TABSTOP, 88, 60, 100, 144
END


//////////////////////// End Of File ////////////////////////
```

Synchronizing with Windows NT Objects

Critical sections are great for serializing access to data within a process because they are very fast. However, you might want to synchronize some applications with other events occurring in the machine or with operations being performed in other processes. For example, you might want to create a child process to help accomplish some work, and as a result, the parent process might need to wait until the child process completes before continuing.

The following Windows NT objects can be used to synchronize threads:

- Processes
- Threads
- Files
- File change notifications
- Console input
- Mutexes
- Semaphores
- Events

Each object can be in one of two states at any time: *signaled* and *not signaled*. Threads can be put to sleep until an object becomes signaled. If a parent process needs to wait for the child process to finish, the parent puts itself to sleep until the child process becomes signaled. You may recall from Chapter 1 that processes become signaled when they terminate. The same is true for threads. When a thread is created and running, it is not signaled. As soon as the thread terminates, it becomes signaled.

I like to think of the signaled state as a flag being raised. Threads sleep while the objects they are waiting for are not signaled (the flag is lowered). However, as soon as the object becomes signaled (the flag goes up), the sleeping thread sees the flag, wakes up, and continues to execute.

Of all these Windows NT objects, some exist for no other purpose than to help with the synchronization of threads. For example, if a thread has a handle to a process, the thread can call various Win32 functions to change the priority class of the process or get the exit code of the process. In addition, a thread can use the handle of a process to synchronize itself with the termination of the process.

Thread handles also serve the same two purposes. You can use a thread handle to manipulate a thread, and you can use a handle of a thread to synchronize a thread with the termination of another thread.

Like process handles and thread handles, file handles can also be used for two purposes: You can read from and write to a file using its handle, and you can set a thread to synchronize itself with the completion of an asynchronous file I/O operation. Asynchronous file I/O and this type of thread synchronization is discussed in Chapter 9.

The last type of Windows NT object that serves two purposes is the console input object. This object is very similar to a file, and, in fact, you call the CreateFile function to create a console input object. A console-based application can use a handle of this object to read input from the application's input buffer, and a thread can use this handle to put itself to sleep until input is available to process.

The other objects—file change notifications, mutexes, semaphores, and events—exist for the sole purpose of thread synchronization. Win32 functions exist to create these objects, open these objects, synchronize threads with these objects, and close these objects. There are no other operations that can be performed with them. The remainder of this chapter discusses how to use mutexes, semaphores, and events. File change notification objects are discussed in Chapter 9.

There are two main functions that threads can use to wait for objects:

```
DWORD WaitForSingleObject(HANDLE hObject, DWORD dwTimeout);
```

and

```
DWORD WaitForMultipleObjects(DWORD cObjects, LPHANDLE lpHandles,
    BOOL bWaitAll, DWORD dwTimeout);
```

201

The WaitForSingleObject function tells Windows NT that you are waiting for the object identified by the *hObject* parameter to be signaled. The *dwTimeout* parameter tells Windows NT how long you are willing to wait in milliseconds.

WaitForSingleObject returns one of the following values:

Return Value	Meaning
WAIT_OBJECT_0	Object reached the signaled state.
WAIT_TIMEOUT	Object did not reach the signaled state in *dwTimeout* milliseconds.
WAIT_ABANDONED	The object was a mutex that reached the signaled state because it was abandoned. (See "Mutexes" later in this chapter.)
WAIT_FAILED	An error occurred. Call GetLastError to get extended error information.

You can pass two special values as the *dwTimeout* parameter to Wait-ForSingleObject. Passing 0 (zero) tells Windows NT that you don't want to wait at all and that Windows NT should simply tell you if the object is signaled or not. A return value of WAIT_OBJECT_0 indicates that the object is signaled, and a return value of WAIT_TIMEOUT indicates the object is not signaled. Passing a value of INFINITE (defined as 0xFFFFFFFF) causes WaitForSingleObject to wait until the object reaches the signaled state.

The WaitForMultipleObjects function is similar to the WaitFor-SingleObject function except that it waits for either several objects to be signaled or one object from a list of objects to be signaled. When calling this function, the *cObjects* parameter indicates the number of objects you want the function to check. This value cannot be larger than MAXI-MUM_WAIT_OBJECTS, which is defined as 64. The *lpHandles* parameter is a pointer to an array of handles identifying these objects. An error occurs if the same object appears more than once in this list even if the object is being identified by two different handle values.

The *bWaitAll* parameter indicates whether you want to wait for just one of the objects in the list to become signaled or if you want all the objects in the list to become signaled. If *bWaitAll* is TRUE, WaitForMul-tipleObjects waits for all the objects to be signaled at the same time. If *bWaitAll* is FALSE, WaitForMultipleObjects waits until at least one of the objects becomes signaled. The *dwTimeout* parameter is identical to the *dwTimeout* parameter for the WaitForSingleObject function. If multiple objects become signaled simultaneously, WaitForMultipleObjects returns the index of the lowest handle value in the array identifying the object that became signaled.

WaitForMultipleObjects returns one of the following values:

Return Value	Meaning
WAIT_OBJECT_0 to (WAIT_OBJECTS_0 + cOBJECTS – 1)	When waiting for all objects, this value indicates that the wait was completed successfully.
	When waiting for any object, this value indicates the index of the handle in the *lpHandles* array belonging to the object that became signaled.
WAIT_TIMEOUT	The object or objects did not reach the signaled state in *dwTimeout* milliseconds.
WAIT_ABANDONED_0 to WAIT_ABANDONED_0 + cOBJECTS – 1	When waiting for all objects, this value indicates that the wait was completed successfully and that at least one object was a mutex that was signaled because it was abandoned.
	When waiting for any object, this value indicates that index of the handle in the *lpHandles* array belonging to the mutex object that became signaled because it was abandoned.
WAIT_FAILED	An error occurred. Call GetLastError to get extended error information.

The WaitForSingleObject and WaitForMultipleObjects functions have important effects on objects. For processes and threads, they do nothing. Once processes and threads become signaled, they stay signaled. For example, if ten threads are calling WaitForSingleObject and waiting for the same process to become signaled, when the process terminates, the process object becomes signaled and all the waiting threads wake up to continue execution. The same is true for thread objects; once they become signaled, they stay that way.

For mutex, semaphore, and (auto-reset) event objects, the WaitForSingleObject and WaitForMultipleObjects functions change their states to not signaled. Once these objects become signaled and another thread is awakened, the object is immediately reset to its not signaled state.

Because of this, only one thread waiting for a mutex or an (auto-reset) event will awaken; other waiting threads will continue to sleep. Semaphores behave a little differently in that they allow several threads to awaken simultaneously. These concepts will be made clearer as we go on.

One more point to know about the WaitForMultipleObjects function: When WaitForMultipleObjects is called with *bWaitAll* passed as TRUE, none of the objects being waited for are reset to not signaled until all the objects being waited for are signaled. Let's say that Thread-1 is waiting for a mutex object and a semaphore object. And let's say that Thread-2 is executing code and is just about to enter a wait for the same mutex object that Thread-1 is waiting for. If the mutex now becomes signaled, Thread-1 has half of what it needs to stop waiting and continue execution. It still needs to wait for the semaphore. If Thread-2 now calls WaitForSingleObject, specifying the mutex, Windows NT will give ownership of the mutex to Thread-2. Thread-1 must still wait for the semaphore to become available but it must now also wait for Thread-2 to release the mutex.

You might ask yourself why Windows NT does not assign "ownership" of a synchronization object to a waiting thread as soon as the object becomes signaled? The answer is easy—to avoid a deadlock situation.

Imagine the following scenario: Thread-1 and Thread-2 are both suspended on a call to WaitForMultipleObjects, waiting for the same mutex and semaphore objects to become signaled. Now a third thread releases the mutex object. Windows NT sees this and gives ownership of the mutex object to Thread-1. The same third thread now releases the semaphore object. Windows NT sees this and gives the semaphore to Thread-2. At this point, both Thread-1 and Thread-2 are still suspended waiting for the other synchronization object to become signaled. But we have a problem here because Thread-1 has ownership of the mutex but can't resume itself, so the mutex can never be released. This means that Thread-2 will never gain ownership of the mutex and is also stuck in its suspended state forever. Thread-1 could actually resume execution if the semaphore that it is waiting for was created with a maximum count of 2 or more and if another thread releases the semaphore. However, if both Thread-1 and Thread-2 were waiting for two mutexes instead of a mutex and a semaphore, the deadlock situation would occur and would also be permanent.

Thread synchronization is a complex topic. If the paragraphs above don't make total sense to you yet, don't worry. Read the next two sections, and all will become clear.

Mutexes

Mutexes are very much like critical sections except they can be used to synchronize data access across multiple processes. To use a mutex, one process must first create the mutex with the CreateMutex function:

```
HANDLE CreateMutex(LPSECURITY_ATTRIBUTES lpsa, BOOL fInitialOwner,
    LPTSTR lpszMutexName);
```

The *lpsa* parameter points to a SECURITY_ATTRIBUTES structure. The *fInitialOwner* parameter indicates whether the thread creating the mutex should be the initial owner of the mutex. The value TRUE means that the thread will own the mutex and therefore the mutex will be in the not-signaled state. Any thread that waits on the mutex will be suspended until the thread that created the mutex releases it. Passing FALSE for the *fInitialOwner* parameter of CreateMutex means that the mutex is not owned by any thread and is therefore created in the signaled state. The first thread to wait for the mutex will immediately gain ownership of the mutex and continue execution.

The *lpszMutexName* parameter is either NULL or an address of a zero-terminated string that identifies the mutex. When an application calls CreateMutex, Windows NT allocates a mutex object and assigns it the name indicated by *lpszMutexName*. CreateMutex then returns the process-specific handle of the new mutex.

One of the main reasons to use a mutex is to synchronize data across multiple processes. To do this, both processes must have handles to the same mutex object. These handles can be obtained in several ways. The first and most common way is for the second process to also call CreateMutex using the same name that was specified in the *lpszMutexName* parameter when the first process created the mutex. After this call, Windows NT determines that a mutex with the specified name already exists, and it does not create a new mutex but returns a process-specific handle identifying the previously created mutex.

A process can determine whether CreateMutex actually created a new mutex by calling GetLastError immediately after the call to CreateMutex. If GetLastError reports ERROR_ALREADY_EXISTS, a new mutex object was not created. If you are expecting to share this mutex with other processes, you can ignore this last step.

Another method for obtaining the handle of a mutex involves a call to the OpenMutex function:

```
HANDLE OpenMutex(DWORD fdwAccess, BOOL fInherit, LPTSTR lpszName);
```

The *fdwAccess* parameter can be either SYNCHRONIZE or MUTEX-_ALL_ACCESS. The *fInherit* parameter indicates whether any child process created by this process should inherit this mutex. The *lpszName* parameter is the zero-terminated string name of the mutex.

When the call to OpenMutex is made, Windows NT scans all the existing mutexes to see if any of them have the name indicated by *lpszName*. If it finds a mutex with the specified name, Windows NT creates a process-specific handle identifying the mutex and returns the handle to the calling thread. The thread can now use this handle in any function that accepts a mutex handle. If a mutex with the specified name cannot be found, NULL is returned.

Both methods described above require that the mutex be named. Two other methods don't require naming—one involves the use of the DuplicateHandle function and the other involves parent-child process inheritance.

Using Mutexes Instead of Critical Sections

Let's rewrite the critical section example using mutexes, and you will see how similar the code is. See Figure 5-2.

```
int    g_nIndex = 0;
const int MAX_TIMES = 1000;
DWORD g_dwTimes[MAX_TIMES];
HANDLE g_hMutex = NULL;

int WinMain (...) {
   HANDLE hThreads[2];

   // Create the mutex before the threads so that it
   // exists when the thread executes.
   g_hMutex = CreateMutex(NULL, FALSE, NULL);

   // Save the handles of the threads in an array.
   hThreads[0] = CreateThread(...);
   hThreads[1] = CreateThread(...);

   // Wait for both threads to terminate.
   WaitForMultipleObjects(2, hThreads, TRUE, INFINITE);

   // Close the thread handles.
   CloseHandle(hThreads[0]);
   CloseHandle(hThreads[1]);
```

Figure 5-2.

(continued)

Using mutexes instead of critical sections.

Figure 5-2. *continued*

```
   // Close the mutex.
   CloseHandle(g_hThread);
}

DWORD WINAPI FirstThread (LPVOID lpvThreadParm) {
   BOOL fDone = FALSE;
   DWORD dw;

   while (!fDone) {
      // Wait forever for the mutex to become signaled.
      dw = WaitForSingleObject(g_hMutex, INFINITE);

      if (dw == WAIT_OBJECT_0) {
         // Mutex reached the signaled state.
         if (g_nIndex >= MAX_TIMES) {
            fDone = TRUE;
         } else {
            g_dwTimes[g_nIndex] == GetTickCount();
            g_nIndex++;
         }

         // Reset the mutex to the not-signaled state.
         ResetMutex(g_hMutex);
      } else {

         // The mutex was abandoned.
         break;   // Exit the while loop.
      }
   }
   return(0);
}

DWORD WINAPI SecondThread (LPVOID lpvThreadParm) {
   BOOL fDone = FALSE;
   DWORD dw;

   while (!fDone) {
      // Wait forever for the mutex to become signaled.
      dw = WaitForSingleObject(g_hMutex, INFINITE);

      if (dw == WAIT_OBJECT_0) {
         // Mutex reached the signaled state.
         if (g_nIndex >= MAX_TIMES) {
            fDone = TRUE;
```

Figure 5-2. *continued*

```
        } else {
            g_nIndex++;
            g_dwTimes[g_nIndex - 1] == GetTickCount();
        }

        // Reset the mutex to the not-signaled state.
        ResetMutex(g_hMutex);
    } else {
        // The mutex was abandoned.
        break;   // Exit the while loop.
    }
    }
    return(0);
}
```

Notice that I created the mutex before creating the threads. This is important because, if it were done the other way around, the threads could attempt to call WaitForSingleObject passing the handle NULL because the mutex had not been created yet. You can write the code differently so that you create the threads first. It would look like this:

```
.
.
.
// Create both threads but do not allow them to begin executing.
hThreads[0] = CreateThread(..., CREATE_SUSPENDED, ...);
hThreads[1] = CreateThread(..., CREATE_SUSPENDED, ...);

// Create the mutex.
g_hMutex = CreateMutex(NULL, FALSE, NULL);

// Allow the threads to run.
ResumeThread(hThreads[0]);
ResumeThread(hThreads[1]);
.
.
.
```

Here I created both threads, but they are suspended. They won't run until they are resumed. Then I created the mutex and saved its handle in the global *g_hMutex* variable. Now that I know this handle is not NULL, I resume both of the suspended threads by calling Resume-Thread. The order here is very important. I've gotten burned waiting for NULL handles more often than I'd like to remember.

Back in Figure 5-2, in WinMain, I showed how the program waits for the two threads to terminate by calling WaitForMultipleObjects. In this call, the value 2 indicates that I'm waiting for two objects to be signaled, *hThread* identifies the array of handles, and TRUE means that I want to wait until all the objects are signaled, which will tell me that both threads have terminated. The inclusion of the INFINITE identifier means that I will wait forever for both threads to terminate. When Wait-ForMultipleObjects returns, WinMain calls CloseHandle so that the mutex is destroyed.

Both thread functions have been modified to use mutexes instead of critical sections. The calls to EnterCriticalSection have been replaced by calls to WaitForSingleObject. WaitForSingleObject can return WAIT-_OBJECT_0, WAIT_ABANDONED, or WAIT_TIMEOUT. WAIT_TIME-OUT can never occur here because INFINITE was specified in the call. A return value of WAIT_OBJECT_0 means that the mutex was signaled and the thread can continue executing. When WaitForSingleObject sees that the mutex has reached a signaled state, the thread immediately grabs ownership of the mutex, which places the mutex back into the not-signaled state again. The thread can then manipulate the data structure, and, when it no longer needs access to the structure, it calls the ReleaseMutex function:

```
BOOL ReleaseMutex(HANDLE hMutex);
```

ReleaseMutex is the function that changes the mutex from the not-signaled state to the signaled state just like the LeaveCriticalSection function does for critical sections. One important thing to note is that this function has an effect only if the same thread that is calling ReleaseMutex also has ownership of the mutex. Immediately after this function is called, any thread that is waiting for this mutex can grab hold of it and begin executing. Of course, when the thread grabs the mutex, the mutex again becomes not signaled. If no threads are waiting on the mutex, the mutex remains in the signaled state, indicating that no thread is accessing the protected data. If a thread comes along and waits on the mutex, it will immediately grab the mutex, locking other threads out if they try to wait on the mutex.

Let me reiterate that when working with any kind of synchronization object, you always want to maintain ownership of that object for as short a time as possible. If other threads are waiting for the object, they are all sleeping and not doing their work.

Mutex objects are different from all other Windows NT synchronization objects because mutex objects are owned by a thread. All other synchronization objects are either signaled or not signaled, period. Mutex objects, in addition to being signaled or not signaled, remember which thread owns them. A mutex is abandoned if a thread waits for a mutex object, grabs the object putting it in the not-signaled state, and then terminates. In this scenario, the mutex is not signaled and will never be signaled because no other thread can release the mutex by calling ReleaseMutex.

When Windows NT sees that this has happened, it automatically sets the mutex back to the signaled state. Any threads that are currently waiting for the mutex with a call to WaitForSingleObject get awakened, and WaitForSingleObject returns WAIT_ABANDONED instead of WAIT_OBJECT_0. In this way, a thread knows that the mutex had not been released gracefully. This is usually an indication that a bug exists in the application. There is no way to know if the thread that owned the mutex had finished what it was doing to the data before it terminated. Remember that threads can be forcibly terminated by calling Exit-Thread or TerminateThread.

In the code fragment, I check to see whether the mutex has been abandoned, and if it is, I break out of the *while* loop, causing the thread to end. WinMain will eventually see that both threads have terminated, causing the mutex to be destroyed and the process to terminate. I could have ignored the possibility for WAIT_ABANDONED to be returned from WaitForSingleObject, but I don't know what state the protected data might be in.

One last thing about mutexes: Mutexes have an ownership count associated with them. So, if a thread calls WaitForSingleObject for a mutex object that the thread already owns, the call succeeds immediately every time because Windows NT knows that this thread already owns the mutex. In addition, the reference count for the mutex is incremented each time. This means that the thread must call ReleaseMutex the same number of times before the mutex will be in the signaled state again. This is identical to the way that EnterCriticalSection and Leave-CriticalSection work for critical sections.

The Mutexes Sample Application

The Mutexes application (MUTEXES.EXE), listed in Figure 5-3 beginning on the following page, is simply the CritSecs program modified to use mutexes instead of critical sections. On the outside, the program actually behaves identically to the CritSecs program. However, by using mutexes instead of critical sections, it would now be possible to put the CounterThread function in one process and the DisplayThread function in another process.

Mutexes.ico

MUTEXES.C

```
/*********************************************************
Module name: Mutexes.C
Notices: Copyright (c) 1993 Jeffrey Richter
*********************************************************/

#include <windows.h>
#include <windowsx.h>
#include <tchar.h>
#include <stdio.h>        // for sprintf
#include <string.h>       // for strrev
#include "Mutexes.H"


///////////////////////////////////////////////////////////

// Global variables.
HWND      g_hwndDlg = NULL;
HANDLE    g_hThreadCntr = NULL;
HANDLE    g_hThreadDspy = NULL;

// The "Data" that needs protecting.
TCHAR     g_szNumber[10] = __TEXT("0");

// The "Mutex" used to protect the "Data".
HANDLE g_hMutex;

///////////////////////////////////////////////////////////

// Add a string to a list box.
void AddToListBox (LPCTSTR szBuffer) {
   HWND hwndDataBox = GetDlgItem(g_hwndDlg, ID_DATABOX);

   int x = ListBox_AddString(hwndDataBox, szBuffer);
   ListBox_SetCurSel(hwndDataBox, x);

   if (ListBox_GetCount(hwndDataBox) > 100)
      ListBox_DeleteString(hwndDataBox, 0);
}
```

Figure 5-3.   *(continued)*
The Mutexes application.

Figure 5-3. *continued*

```
///////////////////////////////////////////////////////////////

// Thread to increment the protected counter data.
DWORD WINAPI CounterThread (LPVOID lpThreadParameter) {
   unsigned int nNumber, nDigit;
   BOOL fSyncChecked;

   while (TRUE) {

      // Get the status of the "Synchronize" button and save it.
      fSyncChecked =
         IsDlgButtonChecked(g_hwndDlg, ID_SYNCHRONIZE);

      if (fSyncChecked) {
         // If the user wants us synchronized, do it.
         WaitForSingleObject(g_hMutex, INFINITE);
      }

      // Convert the string number to an integer and add one.
      _stscanf(g_szNumber, __TEXT("%d"), &nNumber);
      nNumber++;

      // Convert the new integer back to a string.
      nDigit = 0;
      while (nNumber != 0) {
         // Put a digit into the string.
         g_szNumber[nDigit++] = __TEXT('0') + (nNumber % 10);

         // A call to sleep here tells Windows NT that we
         // wish to relinquish the remainder of our time
         // slice to another thread.  This call is needed for
         // single-CPU systems so that the results of the
         // synchronization and lack thereof is obvious.
         // Normally, your programs would NOT call Sleep.
         Sleep(0);

         // Get ready to get the next digit.
         nNumber /= 10;
      }

      // All digits converted to characters.
      // Terminate the string.
      g_szNumber[nDigit] = 0;
```

(continued)

Figure 5-3. *continued*

```
        // Characters were generated in reverse order;
        // reverse the string.
        // Call strrev if ANSI, Call _wcsrev if UNICODE.
        _tcsrev(g_szNumber);

        if (fSyncChecked) {
            // If the user wants synchronization, do it.
            ReleaseMutex(g_hMutex);
        }

        // If the user wants to display something
        // after each iteration, do it.
        if (IsDlgButtonChecked(g_hwndDlg, ID_SHOWCNTRTHRD))
            AddToListBox(__TEXT("Cntr: Increment"));
    }
    return(0);  // We will never get here.
}


/////////////////////////////////////////////////////////////////

// Thread to add the current value of
// the counter (Data) to the list box.
DWORD WINAPI DisplayThread (LPVOID lpThreadParameter) {
    BOOL fSyncChecked;
    TCHAR szBuffer[50];

    while (TRUE) {

        // Determine if the user wants us to synchronize ourself.
        fSyncChecked =
            IsDlgButtonChecked(g_hwndDlg, ID_SYNCHRONIZE);

        if (fSyncChecked)
            WaitForSingleObject(g_hMutex, INFINITE);

        // Construct a string with the string form of the number.
        _stprintf(szBuffer, __TEXT("Dspy: %s"), g_szNumber);

        if (fSyncChecked)
            ReleaseMutex(g_hMutex);

        // Add the string form of the number to the list box.
        AddToListBox(szBuffer);
```

(continued)

213

Figure 5-3. *continued*

```
    }
    return(0);   // We will never get here.
}


//////////////////////////////////////////////////////////////

BOOL Dlg_OnInitDialog (HWND hwnd, HWND hwndFocus,
    LPARAM lParam) {

    HWND hWndCtl;
    DWORD dwThreadCntr, dwThreadDspy;

    // Save the handle of the dialog box in a global so that
    // the threads can easily gain access to it.  This must be
    // done before creating the threads.
    g_hwndDlg = hwnd;

    // Associate an icon with the dialog box.
    SetClassLong(hwnd, GCL_HICON, (LONG)
        LoadIcon((HINSTANCE) GetWindowLong(hwnd, GWL_HINSTANCE),
        __TEXT("Mutexes")));

    // Initialize the mutex object.  This must also be done
    // before any threads try to use it.  There should be error
    // checking here.
    g_hMutex = CreateMutex(NULL, FALSE, NULL);

    // Create our counter thread and let it start running.
    g_hThreadCntr = CreateThread(NULL, 0, CounterThread, NULL,
        0, &dwThreadCntr);

    // Create our display thread and let it start running.
    g_hThreadDspy = CreateThread(NULL, 0, DisplayThread, NULL,
        0, &dwThreadDspy);

    // Fill the Priority class combo box and select "Normal".
    hWndCtl = GetDlgItem(hwnd, ID_PRIORITYCLASS);
    ComboBox_AddString(hWndCtl, __TEXT("Idle"));
    ComboBox_AddString(hWndCtl, __TEXT("Normal"));
    ComboBox_AddString(hWndCtl, __TEXT("High"));
    ComboBox_AddString(hWndCtl, __TEXT("Realtime"));
    ComboBox_SetCurSel(hWndCtl, 1);   // Normal
```

(continued)

Figure 5-3.   *continued*

```
        // Fill the display thread's relative priority
        // combo box and select "Normal".
        hWndCtl = GetDlgItem(hwnd, ID_DSPYTHRDPRIORITY);
        ComboBox_AddString(hWndCtl, __TEXT("Idle"));
        ComboBox_AddString(hWndCtl, __TEXT("Lowest"));
        ComboBox_AddString(hWndCtl, __TEXT("Below normal"));
        ComboBox_AddString(hWndCtl, __TEXT("Normal"));
        ComboBox_AddString(hWndCtl, __TEXT("Above normal"));
        ComboBox_AddString(hWndCtl, __TEXT("Highest"));
        ComboBox_AddString(hWndCtl, __TEXT("Realtime"));
        ComboBox_SetCurSel(hWndCtl, 3);   // Normal

        // Fill the counter thread's relative priority
        // combo box and select "Normal".
        hWndCtl = GetDlgItem(hwnd, ID_CNTRTHRDPRIORITY);
        ComboBox_AddString(hWndCtl, __TEXT("Idle"));
        ComboBox_AddString(hWndCtl, __TEXT("Lowest"));
        ComboBox_AddString(hWndCtl, __TEXT("Below normal"));
        ComboBox_AddString(hWndCtl, __TEXT("Normal"));
        ComboBox_AddString(hWndCtl, __TEXT("Above normal"));
        ComboBox_AddString(hWndCtl, __TEXT("Highest"));
        ComboBox_AddString(hWndCtl, __TEXT("Realtime"));
        ComboBox_SetCurSel(hWndCtl, 3);   // Normal

        return(TRUE);
}


/////////////////////////////////////////////////////////////////

void Dlg_OnDestroy (HWND hwnd) {
        // When the dialog box is destroyed, terminate the
        // two threads and delete the mutex object.
        TerminateThread(g_hThreadDspy, 0);
        TerminateThread(g_hThreadCntr, 0);
        CloseHandle(g_hMutex);
}


/////////////////////////////////////////////////////////////////

void Dlg_OnCommand (HWND hwnd, int id, HWND hwndCtl,
    UINT codeNotify) {

    HANDLE hThread;
    DWORD dw;
```

(continued)

Figure 5-3. *continued*

```
switch (id) {
   case IDCANCEL:
      EndDialog(hwnd, id);
      break;

   case ID_PRIORITYCLASS:
      if (codeNotify != CBN_SELCHANGE)
         break;

      // User is changing priority class.
      switch (ComboBox_GetCurSel(hwndCtl)) {
         case 0:
            dw = IDLE_PRIORITY_CLASS;
            break;

         case 1:
            dw = NORMAL_PRIORITY_CLASS;
            break;

         case 2:
            dw = HIGH_PRIORITY_CLASS;
            break;

         case 3:
            dw = REALTIME_PRIORITY_CLASS;
            break;
      }
      SetPriorityClass(GetCurrentProcess(), dw);
      break;

   case ID_DSPYTHRDPRIORITY:
   case ID_CNTRTHRDPRIORITY:
      if (codeNotify != CBN_SELCHANGE)
         break;

      switch (ComboBox_GetCurSel(hwndCtl)) {
         case 0:
            dw = (DWORD) THREAD_PRIORITY_IDLE;
            break;

         case 1:
            dw = (DWORD) THREAD_PRIORITY_LOWEST;
            break;
```

(continued)

Figure 5-3. *continued*

```
            case 2:
                dw = (DWORD) THREAD_PRIORITY_BELOW_NORMAL;
                break;

            case 3:
                dw = (DWORD) THREAD_PRIORITY_NORMAL;
                break;

            case 4:
                dw = (DWORD) THREAD_PRIORITY_ABOVE_NORMAL;
                break;

            case 5:
                dw = (DWORD) THREAD_PRIORITY_HIGHEST;
                break;

            case 6:
                dw = (DWORD) THREAD_PRIORITY_TIME_CRITICAL;
                break;
        }
        // User is changing the relative priority
        // of one of the threads.
        hThread = (id == ID_CNTRTHRDPRIORITY) ?
            g_hThreadCntr : g_hThreadDspy;

        SetThreadPriority(hThread, dw);
        break;

    case ID_PAUSE:
        // User is pausing or resuming both threads.
        if (Button_GetCheck(hwndCtl)) {

            SuspendThread(g_hThreadCntr);
            SuspendThread(g_hThreadDspy);

        } else {

            ResumeThread(g_hThreadCntr);
            ResumeThread(g_hThreadDspy);

        }
        break;
    }
}
```

(continued)

Figure 5-3. *continued*

```
///////////////////////////////////////////////////////////////

BOOL CALLBACK Dlg_Proc (HWND hDlg, UINT uMsg,
   WPARAM wParam, LPARAM lParam) {

   BOOL fProcessed = TRUE;

   switch (uMsg) {
      HANDLE_MSG(hDlg, WM_INITDIALOG, Dlg_OnInitDialog);
      HANDLE_MSG(hDlg, WM_DESTROY, Dlg_OnDestroy);
      HANDLE_MSG(hDlg, WM_COMMAND, Dlg_OnCommand);

      default:
         fProcessed = FALSE;
         break;
   }
   return(fProcessed);
}


///////////////////////////////////////////////////////////////

int APIENTRY WinMain (HINSTANCE hInstance,
   HINSTANCE hPrevInstance, LPSTR lpszCmdLine, int nCmdShow) {

   DialogBox(hInstance, MAKEINTRESOURCE(DLG_MUTEXES),
      NULL, Dlg_Proc);
   return(0);
}

/////////////////////// End Of File ///////////////////////////
```

MUTEXES.H

```
/***************************************************************
Module name: Mutexes.H
Notices: Copyright (c) 1993 Jeffrey Richter
***************************************************************/

// Dialog and control IDs.
#define DLG_MUTEXES              1
#define ID_PRIORITYCLASS         100
#define ID_DSPYTHRDPRIORITY      101
#define ID_CNTRTHRDPRIORITY      102
```

(continued)

Figure 5-3. *continued*

```
#define ID_PAUSE              103
#define ID_SYNCHRONIZE        104
#define ID_SHOWCNTRTHRD       105
#define ID_DATABOX            106


///////////////////////// End Of File /////////////////////////
```

MUTEXES.RC

```
/****************************************************************
Module name: Mutexes.RC
Notices: Copyright (c) 1993 Jeffrey Richter
****************************************************************/

#include <windows.h>
#include "Mutexes.h"

Mutexes  ICON  DISCARDABLE Mutexes.Ico

DLG_MUTEXES DIALOG 29, 28, 197, 208
STYLE WS_BORDER | WS_POPUP | WS_VISIBLE | WS_CAPTION |
  WS_SYSMENU | WS_MINIMIZEBOX
CAPTION "Mutex Test Application"
BEGIN
    CONTROL "&Process priority class:", -1, "STATIC",
        SS_LEFT | WS_CHILD | WS_VISIBLE | WS_GROUP, 4, 4, 88, 8
    CONTROL "", ID_PRIORITYCLASS, "COMBOBOX",
        CBS_DROPDOWNLIST | WS_CHILD | WS_VISIBLE | WS_GROUP |
        WS_TABSTOP, 88, 4, 64, 48
    CONTROL "&Display thread priority:", -1, "STATIC",
        SS_LEFTNOWORDWRAP | WS_CHILD | WS_VISIBLE | WS_GROUP |
        WS_TABSTOP, 4, 24, 84, 8
    CONTROL "", ID_DSPYTHRDPRIORITY, "COMBOBOX",
        CBS_DROPDOWNLIST | WS_CHILD | WS_VISIBLE | WS_GROUP |
        WS_TABSTOP, 88, 24, 100, 76
    CONTROL "&Counter thread priority:", -1, "STATIC",
        SS_LEFTNOWORDWRAP | WS_CHILD | WS_VISIBLE | WS_GROUP |
        WS_TABSTOP, 4, 40, 88, 8
    CONTROL "", ID_CNTRTHRDPRIORITY, "COMBOBOX",
        CBS_DROPDOWNLIST | WS_CHILD | WS_VISIBLE | WS_GROUP |
        WS_TABSTOP, 88, 40, 100, 76
```

(continued)

Figure 5-3. *continued*

```
    CONTROL "&Synchronize", ID_SYNCHRONIZE, "BUTTON",
        BS_AUTOCHECKBOX | WS_CHILD | WS_VISIBLE | WS_TABSTOP,
        4, 60, 64, 12
    CONTROL "S&how counter thread", ID_SHOWCNTRTHRD, "BUTTON",
        BS_AUTOCHECKBOX | WS_CHILD | WS_VISIBLE | WS_TABSTOP,
        4, 72, 80, 12
    CONTROL "P&ause", ID_PAUSE, "BUTTON",
        BS_AUTOCHECKBOX | WS_CHILD | WS_VISIBLE | WS_TABSTOP,
        4, 84, 44, 12
    CONTROL "", ID_DATABOX, "LISTBOX", LBS_NOTIFY | WS_CHILD |
        WS_VISIBLE | WS_BORDER | WS_VSCROLL | WS_GROUP |
        WS_TABSTOP, 88, 60, 100, 144
END

//////////////////////// End Of File ////////////////////////
```

Semaphores

In many respects, semaphores are similar to mutexes. The main difference is that Windows NT doesn't keep track of which thread owns a semaphore. Therefore, it's possible for one thread to wait for the semaphore object and another thread to release the object. Another difference is that semaphores have a resource count associated with them. Whereas a mutex allows only one thread to gain access to it, a semaphore allows multiple threads to gain access to it simultaneously.

For example, let's say that a computer has three serial ports. No more than three threads can use the serial ports at any given time. This situation provides a perfect opportunity to use a semaphore. A semaphore is signaled when its reference count is greater than 0 (zero), and is not-signaled when the count is equal to 0 (zero). Every time a thread calls WaitForSingleObject and passes the handle of a semaphore, Windows NT checks whether the reference count for the semaphore is greater than 0 (zero). If it is, Windows NT decrements the reference count and wakes the thread. If the reference count is 0 (zero) when the thread calls WaitForSingleObject, Windows NT puts the thread to sleep until another thread releases the semaphore.

The functions for manipulating semaphores are similar to the ones for manipulating mutexes. You create a semaphore by calling the CreateSemaphore function:

```
HANDLE CreateSemaphore(LPSECURITY_ATTRIBUTE lpsa,
    LONG cSemInitial, LONG cSemMax, LPTSTR lpszSemName);
```

This function creates a semaphore that has a maximum reference count of *cSemMax*. So, in the example on the previous page, you would pass the value 3 to represent the three serial ports. The *cSemInitial* parameter lets you specify the starting reference count for the semaphore. When the system starts, all three serial ports are available, so we would set this value to 3 as well. When the operating system initializes, you might want it to indicate that there are three serial ports but none are available. To do this, you would pass 0 (zero) as the *cSemInitial* parameter.

The last parameter of CreateSemaphore, *lpszSemName*, assigns a string name to the semaphore. You can use this string name in other processes to get the handle of the semaphore by calling Create-Semaphore or OpenSemaphore:

```
HANDLE OpenSemaphore(DWORD fdwAccess, BOOL fInherit,
   LPTSTR lpszName);
```

This function's semantics are identical to those of the OpenMutex function, discussed in the previous section.

To release a semaphore, you call the ReleaseSemaphore function:

```
BOOL ReleaseSemaphore(HANDLE hSemaphore, LONG cRelease,
   LPLONG lplPrevious);
```

This function is similar to the ReleaseMutex function except for a few differences. First, any thread can call this function at any time. Windows NT does not keep track of which thread owns the semaphore (especially because semaphores are not owned). Second, the ReleaseSemaphore function can be used to change the reference count of the semaphore by more than 1. The *cRelease* parameter indicates by how much the semaphore should be released. For example, let's say that we have an application that copies data from one serial port to another. The application would have to acquire the semaphore twice by calling WaitForSingleObject twice:

```
// Get two serial ports.
WaitForSingleObject(g_hSemSerialPort, INFINITE);
WaitForSingleObject(g_hSemSerialPort, INFINITE);
.
.
.
// Use the serial ports to do the copy.
.
.
.
// Release the serial ports so that other applications
// can use them.
ReleaseSemaphore(g_hSemSerialPort, 2, NULL);
```

It would be nice if you could call WaitForMultipleObjects once instead of calling WaitForSingleObject twice, as on the previous page. However, WaitForMultipleObjects does not allow the same handle to be used more than once in a single call. So, although we must call WaitForSingleObject twice, it is convenient that we can call ReleaseSemaphore once at the end to increment the semaphore's count by 2.

ReleaseSemaphore's last parameter, *lplPrevious*, is a pointer to a long, which ReleaseSemaphore fills with the reference count of the semaphore *before* adding *cRelease* back to it. If you are not interested in this value, you can simply pass NULL.

It would be nice if there were a Win32 function for determining the reference count of a semaphore without actually altering the semaphore's count. At first, I thought that calling ReleaseSemaphore and passing 0 (zero) for the second parameter might work by returning the actual count in the long pointed to by the *lplPrevious* parameter. But, unfortunately, this doesn't work; ReleaseSemaphore fills the long with 0 (zero). Next I tried passing a really big number as the second parameter, but ReleaseSemaphore still fills the long with 0 (zero). There is no way to get the count of a semaphore without altering it.

The Supermarket Sample Application

The Sprmrkt (SPRMRKT.EXE) application, listed in Figure 5-5 beginning on page 235, demonstrates the use of mutexes and semaphores to control a supermarket simulation. When you run Sprmrkt, the following dialog box appears:

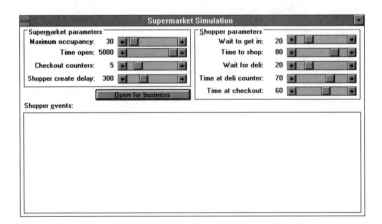

Using this dialog box, you can set up all the initial parameters before executing the simulation. When you have finished configuring the simulation parameters, click on the *Open for business* button. This creates a thread that represents the supermarket and starts executing it. The function that identifies this thread is called ThreadSuperMarket.

The supermarket thread is responsible for:

1. Opening the supermarket

2. Creating threads that represent individual shoppers

3. Closing the front doors when the store closes so that no more shoppers can enter

4. Waiting until all the shoppers in the store have checked out their groceries before ending the simulation

5. Notifying the GUI-thread (or primary thread) that the simulation has ended so that the dialog box can reenable the simulation parameter controls and another simulation can be executed

As mentioned in number 2 above, each shopper is represented by his own thread. Every so often, the supermarket thread creates a new shopper thread by calling CreateThread:

```
hThread = CreateThread(
    NULL,                       // Security attributes
    0,                          // Stack
    ThreadShopper,              // Thread function
    (LPVOID) ++nShopperNum,     // Shopper number as lpvParam
    0,                          // Flags
    &dwThreadId);               // Thread ID

CloseHandle(hThread);
```

The call to CloseHandle tells Windows NT that the shopper thread isn't referenced directly from within the supermarket thread. After the supermarket thread creates a shopper thread, the shopper thread executes. When the shopper thread is finished and exits the supermarket, the shopper thread terminates. If you didn't call CloseHandle, Windows NT would see that you still had an outstanding handle to the shopper thread. Because of this outstanding handle, Windows NT would not be able to free up its internal memory associated with the thread until the whole process terminated. Because shoppers are created frequently and because the user can run the simulation several times in a row without exiting and restarting the program, Windows NT's internal record-keeping responsibility for the created threads can really add up, causing your application to hit its allowed quota of resources. So the call to CloseHandle above is really quite necessary.

After the supermarket has created a shopper, it waits a random amount of time before creating another. The maximum duration of this wait is specified by the *Shopper create delay* setting in the dialog box.

By having the supermarket running as its own thread and each shopper also executing as his own thread, you create the feeling that every shopper can move around the supermarket at his own pace and that the supermarket itself is operating at its own pace.

Shoppers perform the following actions:

1. Wait to get into the store

2. Perform a random amount of shopping

3. Go to the deli counter to order luncheon meats

4. Stand in line at the checkout counter to pay for items

5. Spend a random amount of time at the checkout counter

6. Leave the checkout counter

7. Leave the supermarket

After a shopper thread leaves the supermarket, it terminates.

As the simulation progresses, the *Shopper events* list box notifies you of the various events that are occurring in the supermarket. By examining this information, you can see where potential bottlenecks occur and how a change to the configuration parameters might alter the scenario for the next run. This information might be used by a manager to determine the best number of open checkout registers or number of workers attending the deli counters. Figure 5-4 shows the results of a sample run using the parameter settings shown in the dialog box:

```
---> Opening the supermarket to shoppers.
0001: Waiting to get in store (11).
0002: Waiting to get in store (16).
0001: In supermarket, shopping for 46.
0002: In supermarket, shopping for 38.
0003: Waiting to get in store (17).
```

Figure 5-4. *(continued)*
Simulation results using the dialog box settings.

224

Figure 5-4. *continued*

```
0003: In supermarket, shopping for 65.
0002: Not going to the Deli counter.
0001: Waiting for service at Deli Counter (17).
0002: Waiting for an empty checkout counter.
0001: Being served at Deli (49).
0002: Checking out (30).
0003: Waiting for service at Deli Counter (0).
0003: Tired of waiting at Deli.
0004: Waiting to get in store (7).
0002: Leaving checkout counter.
0001: Waiting for an empty checkout counter.
0005: Waiting to get in store (3).
0003: Waiting for an empty checkout counter.
0004: In supermarket, shopping for 9.
0006: Waiting to get in store (8).
0002: Left the supermarket.
0001: Checking out (0).
0005: In supermarket, shopping for 0.
0003: Checking out (22).
0006: In supermarket, shopping for 42.
0004: Not going to the Deli counter.
0001: Leaving checkout counter.
0005: Not going to the Deli counter.
0003: Leaving checkout counter.
0004: Waiting for an empty checkout counter.
0001: Left the supermarket.
0005: Waiting for an empty checkout counter.
0004: Checking out (36).
0003: Left the supermarket.
0006: Waiting for service at Deli Counter (13).
0007: Waiting to get in store (7).
0005: Checking out (3).
0006: Being served at Deli (42).
0004: Leaving checkout counter.
0007: In supermarket, shopping for 41.
0008: Waiting to get in store (16).
0005: Leaving checkout counter.
0006: Waiting for an empty checkout counter.
0005: Left the supermarket.
0004: Left the supermarket.
0008: In supermarket, shopping for 24.
0007: Not going to the Deli counter.
0006: Checking out (43).
0007: Waiting for an empty checkout counter.
```

(continued)

Figure 5-4. *continued*

```
0008: Not going to the Deli counter.
0007: Checking out (8).
0009: Waiting to get in store (10).
0008: Waiting for an empty checkout counter.
0008: Checking out (27).
0006: Leaving checkout counter.
0009: In supermarket, shopping for 18.
0007: Leaving checkout counter.
0006: Left the supermarket.
0007: Left the supermarket.
0009: Not going to the Deli counter.
0008: Leaving checkout counter.
0008: Left the supermarket.
0009: Waiting for an empty checkout counter.
0009: Checking out (46).
0010: Waiting to get in store (16).
0010: In supermarket, shopping for 79.
0009: Leaving checkout counter.
0009: Left the supermarket.
0011: Waiting to get in store (12).
0011: In supermarket, shopping for 31.
0010: Waiting for service at Deli Counter (5).
0011: Not going to the Deli counter.
0010: Being served at Deli (1).
0011: Waiting for an empty checkout counter.
0010: Waiting for an empty checkout counter.
0010: Checking out (22).
0011: Checking out (5).
0012: Waiting to get in store (1).
0011: Leaving checkout counter.
0010: Leaving checkout counter.
0012: In supermarket, shopping for 0.
0011: Left the supermarket.
0010: Left the supermarket.
0012: Not going to the Deli counter.
0013: Waiting to get in store (5).
0012: Waiting for an empty checkout counter.
0012: Checking out (35).
0013: In supermarket, shopping for 55.
0014: Waiting to get in store (14).
0014: In supermarket, shopping for 38.
0012: Leaving checkout counter.
0013: Waiting for service at Deli Counter (14).
0013: Being served at Deli (32).
```

(continued)

Figure 5-4. *continued*

```
0012: Left the supermarket.
0014: Waiting for service at Deli Counter (18).
0013: Waiting for an empty checkout counter.
0014: Tired of waiting at Deli.
0014: Waiting for an empty checkout counter.
0015: Waiting to get in store (2).
0013: Checking out (35).
0014: Checking out (23).
0015: In supermarket, shopping for 58.
0013: Leaving checkout counter.
0013: Left the supermarket.
0014: Leaving checkout counter.
0015: Not going to the Deli counter.
0014: Left the supermarket.
0015: Waiting for an empty checkout counter.
0016: Waiting to get in store (7).
0015: Checking out (9).
0016: In supermarket, shopping for 18.
0015: Leaving checkout counter.
0015: Left the supermarket.
0016: Waiting for service at Deli Counter (16).
0016: Being served at Deli (36).
0017: Waiting to get in store (15).
0016: Waiting for an empty checkout counter.
0017: In supermarket, shopping for 27.
0016: Checking out (10).
0017: Not going to the Deli counter.
0016: Leaving checkout counter.
0017: Waiting for an empty checkout counter.
0017: Checking out (29).
0016: Left the supermarket.
0017: Leaving checkout counter.
0017: Left the supermarket.
0018: Waiting to get in store (13).
0018: In supermarket, shopping for 75.
0019: Waiting to get in store (2).
0019: In supermarket, shopping for 11.
0019: Not going to the Deli counter.
0018: Not going to the Deli counter.
0020: Waiting to get in store (8).
0019: Waiting for an empty checkout counter.
0018: Waiting for an empty checkout counter.
0019: Checking out (4).
0020: In supermarket, shopping for 54.
```

(continued)

Figure 5-4. *continued*

```
0021: Waiting to get in store (3).
0018: Checking out (52).
0019: Leaving checkout counter.
0021: In supermarket, shopping for 65.
0019: Left the supermarket.
0020: Not going to the Deli counter.
0020: Waiting for an empty checkout counter.
0018: Leaving checkout counter.
0021: Waiting for service at Deli Counter (3).
0020: Checking out (49).
0018: Left the supermarket.
0021: Being served at Deli (35).
0022: Waiting to get in store (3).
0020: Leaving checkout counter.
0020: Left the supermarket.
0021: Waiting for an empty checkout counter.
0022: In supermarket, shopping for 58.
0023: Waiting to get in store (5).
0021: Checking out (34).
0023: In supermarket, shopping for 54.
0022: Not going to the Deli counter.
0024: Waiting to get in store (9).
0021: Leaving checkout counter.
0023: Waiting for service at Deli Counter (7).
0022: Waiting for an empty checkout counter.
0024: In supermarket, shopping for 66.
0021: Left the supermarket.
0023: Being served at Deli (2).
0022: Checking out (31).
0023: Waiting for an empty checkout counter.
0022: Leaving checkout counter.
0024: Not going to the Deli counter.
0023: Checking out (56).
0025: Waiting to get in store (2).
0022: Left the supermarket.
0024: Waiting for an empty checkout counter.
0025: In supermarket, shopping for 73.
0024: Checking out (32).
0023: Leaving checkout counter.
0026: Waiting to get in store (9).
0023: Left the supermarket.
0025: Waiting for service at Deli Counter (16).
0024: Leaving checkout counter.
0026: In supermarket, shopping for 21.
```

(continued)

Figure 5-4. *continued*

```
0027: Waiting to get in store (9).
0025: Being served at Deli (68).
0024: Left the supermarket.
0027: In supermarket, shopping for 45.
0028: Waiting to get in store (14).
0026: Waiting for service at Deli Counter (15).
0025: Waiting for an empty checkout counter.
0028: In supermarket, shopping for 67.
0026: Being served at Deli (27).
0029: Waiting to get in store (17).
0027: Waiting for service at Deli Counter (19).
0025: Checking out (34).
0026: Waiting for an empty checkout counter.
0029: In supermarket, shopping for 4.
0028: Not going to the Deli counter.
---> Waiting for shoppers to checkout so store can close.
0027: Being served at Deli (13).
0025: Leaving checkout counter.
0026: Checking out (50).
---> 0 shoppers NOT in store.
0028: Waiting for an empty checkout counter.
0029: Not going to the Deli counter.
0027: Waiting for an empty checkout counter.
---> 1 shoppers NOT in store.
0025: Left the supermarket.
0028: Checking out (39).
0027: Checking out (11).
0029: Waiting for an empty checkout counter.
0026: Leaving checkout counter.
---> 2 shoppers NOT in store.
0027: Leaving checkout counter.
---> 3 shoppers NOT in store.
0029: Checking out (50).
0026: Left the supermarket.
0028: Leaving checkout counter.
0027: Left the supermarket.
---> 4 shoppers NOT in store.
0028: Left the supermarket.
0029: Leaving checkout counter.
---> 5 shoppers NOT in store.
0029: Left the supermarket.
---> 6 shoppers NOT in store.
---> 7 shoppers NOT in store.
---> 8 shoppers NOT in store.
```

(continued)

Figure 5-4. *continued*

```
---> 9 shoppers NOT in store.
---> 10 shoppers NOT in store.
---> 11 shoppers NOT in store.
---> 12 shoppers NOT in store.
---> 13 shoppers NOT in store.
---> 14 shoppers NOT in store.
---> 15 shoppers NOT in store.
---> 16 shoppers NOT in store.
---> 17 shoppers NOT in store.
---> 18 shoppers NOT in store.
---> 19 shoppers NOT in store.
---> 20 shoppers NOT in store.
---> 21 shoppers NOT in store.
---> 22 shoppers NOT in store.
---> 23 shoppers NOT in store.
---> 24 shoppers NOT in store.
---> 25 shoppers NOT in store.
---> 26 shoppers NOT in store.
---> 27 shoppers NOT in store.
---> 28 shoppers NOT in store.
---> 29 shoppers NOT in store.
---> Store closed -- end of simulation.
```

Now let's imagine that this supermarket is open for business, and inside the supermarket several shoppers are going about their business. With all this going on simultaneously, there must be some way to synchronize the actions of these executing threads. In this example, there are several forms of synchronization being used.

When the supermarket thread starts executing, it immediately creates a semaphore object that is identified by the global *g_hSem-Entrance* variable:

```
g_hSemEntrance = CreateSemaphore(
    NULL,              // Security attributes.
    0,                 // Initial lock count.
    g_nMaxOccupancy,   // Maximum people allowed in store.
    NULL);             // Do not name the semaphore.
```

This object is used to monitor the number of shoppers that are allowed into the supermarket at any one time. This maximum number of shoppers is identified by the *Maximum occupancy* setting specified in the dialog box. For a brief moment after opening for business, the supermarket is still closed, not allowing any shoppers into the store. This closed

230

state is indicated by passing 0 (zero) as the initial lock count. When the store is ready to allow shoppers in, it calls:

```
ReleaseSemaphore(g_hSemEntrance, g_nMaxOccupancy, NULL);
```

When a new shopper thread is created, the first thing it does is call:

```
dwResult = WaitForSingleObject(g_hSemEntrance, nDuration);
```

This causes the shopper thread to suspend its execution if the store is already filled with shoppers to maximum occupancy. If the supermarket is not filled with shoppers, WaitForSingleObject returns immediately, granting the shopper admittance to the store. The count of the semaphore is also decremented so that one fewer shopper is allowed into the store.

You'll notice that I specified a duration value in the call on the previous page using the *nDuration* parameter. Shoppers will wait only so long to get into the supermarket before getting tired and going home. The maximum value of this duration can be set by using the *Wait to get in* setting in the dialog box. If the shopper gets tired of waiting to enter the market, WaitForSingleObject returns WAIT_TIMEOUT. The shopper thread places the notification of this event into the *Shopper events* list box and returns from the shopper thread, causing the thread to be terminated.

Once the shopper has entered the store, some shopping must occur. The maximum duration of this shopping can be set by the *Time to shop* setting in the dialog box. In the shopper thread, the action of shopping is performed by simply placing a call to the Sleep function and passing the value of the shopping duration.

After the shopper has picked up a few items (Sleep has returned), the shopper heads on over to the deli counter to buy roast beef (yummy—my favorite). Actually, as was pointed out to me by a friend, most people go to the market without stopping at the deli counter at all. So, in the shopper thread, the shopper has only a one-in-three chance of going to the deli counter (which leaves more roast beef for me).

If, as luck would have it, the shopper does go to the deli counter, the shopper must be waited on. In the simulation, the deli counter is attended by only one worker. So the synchronization of shoppers with the deli counter is guarded by a mutex object. Only one shopper thread can own the mutex at any one time. If another shopper goes to the deli counter while another shopper is being waited on, the newly arriving shopper must wait until the first shopper completes her business at the counter. Completing her business means releasing the mutex so that another shopper can complete his business. A shopper thread spends time at the deli counter by calling Sleep, passing in a random duration whose maximum value is specified by the *Time at deli counter* setting in the dialog box.

It is also quite possible that the shopper currently being waited on is taking too long and a waiting shopper gets frustrated and leaves the deli counter. The maximum duration for waiting for service at the deli counter can be specified using the *Wait for deli* setting in the dialog box.

There are two problems with this part of the simulation. One, there is only one worker attending the deli counter. It is quite possible that you might want to add a simulation parameter in which the user controlling the simulation can specify the number of workers attending the deli counter. In this way, several shoppers could be served simultaneously. If you decide to do this, you could simply change the use of the mutex object controlling the deli counter to a semaphore object in which the maximum count of the semaphore represents the number of people working at the deli counter. I chose not to do this so that you would see another programming example using mutexes.

The second problem with this scheme is that shoppers are not necessarily waited on in the order in which they appear at the deli counter. In other words, let's say that Shopper-1 is currently being waited on when Shopper-2 appears, followed shortly by Shopper-3. When Shopper-1 leaves the counter, both Shopper-2 and Shopper-3 are still waiting to gain ownership of the mutex. There is no guarantee that Windows NT will give the mutex to Shopper-2 because it was waiting for the mutex first. If you wanted to add this type of control for synchronizing threads, you would have to add the logic yourself. Windows NT and the Win32 API don't support any direct means of doing this for you automatically.

Regardless of how the shopper dealt with the deli counter, the next step is for the shopper to stand in line at the checkout counter. You can specify the number of checkout counters in the supermarket using the *Checkout counters* setting in the dialog box.

Here is another place in which the simulation differs a little bit from reality. A standard pattern in all the supermarkets I've ever been in involves sauntering up to the checkout area and selecting the checkout line you intend to stand in. This is usually a matter of examining what everyone else is buying to see which lines have the least number of items to be rung up before the cashier gets to your stuff. Then you see which lines contain people who have their checkbooks out—you know that these are the bad lines. And then, after you have factored all this into your decision, you take a quick glance to see which cashier looks friendliest and go with that line.

In the supermarket simulation, things are a little less detailed. Waiting for a checkout counter is more like raising your hand and hoping the teacher will call on you. When the teacher asks a question, all the students who think they know the answer raise their hand. But the teacher selects only one student (at random) to answer. In the supermarket simulation, there are a fixed number of checkout counters. These are guarded by a semaphore which was created by the supermarket thread, as shown below:

```
g_hSemCheckout = CreateSemaphore(
    NULL,                    // Security attributes.
    g_nCheckoutRegisters,    // All registers are free.
    g_nCheckoutRegisters,    // The # of registers at the store.
    NULL);                   // No name for the semaphore.
```

When a shopper is ready to check out, the shopper thread waits for this semaphore. If a checkout counter is available, the shopper immediately starts checking out, and the semaphore is decremented. If all the checkout counters are in use, the shopper must wait. I designed the simulation so that a shopper cannot get tired of waiting for a checkout counter and leave the supermarket. Once a shopper begins waiting, he must continue waiting until he has checked out:

```
WaitForSingleObject(g_hSemCheckout, INFINITE);
```

Once the shopper has gained access to a checkout counter, it takes some time for the cashier to ring up all his purchases. This time is determined by placing a call to Sleep, again passing it a random duration whose maximum value is specified by the *Time at checkout* setting in the dialog box.

When all of the shopper's items have been totaled, the shopper leaves the checkout counter by releasing the *g_hSemCheckout* semaphore:

```
ReleaseSemaphore(g_hSemCheckout, 1, NULL);
```

This release allows a shopper waiting for a checkout counter to gain access to one. Now that the shopper has checked out, the shopper must also exit the supermarket by releasing the *g_hSemEntrance* semaphore, as shown at the top of the following page.

```
ReleaseSemaphore(g_hSemEntrance, 1, NULL);
```

This release tells the semaphore guarding the admittance of shoppers into the market that one shopper has left and that another shopper can enter.

Once the shopper has left the market, the shopper no longer has a reason for being and returns from the thread. Perhaps this is where the phrase "shop till you drop" comes from.

We have spent a good bit of time talking about the shopper threads. Let's return now to the supermarket thread. As mentioned at the beginning of this discussion, the supermarket thread is responsible for randomly creating shoppers. However, the supermarket also stays open for some amount of time and then closes. The amount of time that the supermarket stays open is set using the *Time open* setting in the dialog box.

When the supermarket thread sees that the set amount of time has been reached, it stops creating shoppers. But the supermarket cannot close until all the existing shoppers have been served. The supermarket executes the following loop:

```
for (nMaxOccupancy = 0;
    nMaxOccupancy < g_nMaxOccupancy; nMaxOccupancy++) {
    WaitForSingleObject(g_hSemEntrance, INFINITE);
}
```

The loop simply calls WaitForSingleObject repeatedly until the supermarket has gained control of the entrance semaphore *g_nMaxOccupancy* times, which can happen only after every shopper has left the supermarket. You could have a problem here if a shopper thread was created just before the supermarket closed. In this case, the supermarket is waiting for the semaphore and the shopper thread is also waiting for the semaphore. Windows NT makes no guarantee as to which thread will gain the semaphore when it becomes signaled. So, it is possible that a waiting shopper can enter the supermarket even though the supermarket is closed.

It is also possible that the supermarket thread can gain all of the semaphore. In this case, any created shoppers that have not entered the store yet would just get tired of waiting to enter and terminate themselves anyway. In a real simulation, these areas would need to be cleaned up a bit.

It might be nice if the supermarket simply called WaitForMultiple-Objects once instead of calling WaitForSingleObject repeatedly in a loop. But this can't be done for two reasons. First, you can't pass a handle identifying a single object to WaitForMultipleObjects more than once. Second, WaitForMultipleObjects lets you wait for only MAXIMUM-

_WAIT_OBJECTS number of objects, which is currently defined as 64. Because we could set the maximum occupancy to be well over 64— maybe 500—calling WaitForMultipleObjects wouldn't work even if we could specify the handle to the semaphore more than one time.

After the supermarket thread captures the *g_hSemEntrance* semaphore *g_nMaxOccupancy* number of times, it makes the following calls to make sure that all the synchronization objects are destroyed by the system:

```
CloseHandle(g_hSemCheckout);
CloseHandle(g_hMtxDeliCntr);
CloseHandle(g_hSemEntrance);
```

Sprmrkt.ico

SPRMRKT.C

```
/***********************************************************
Module name: SprMrkt.C
Notices: Copyright (c) 1993 Jeffrey Richter
***********************************************************/

#include <windows.h>
#include <windowsx.h>
#include <tchar.h>
#include <stdio.h>
#include <stdlib.h>   // For random number stuff
#include <string.h>
#include <stdarg.h>
#include "SprMrkt.H"


// This is the correction to a bug in windowsx.h:
#undef FORWARD_WM_HSCROLL
#define FORWARD_WM_HSCROLL(hwnd, hwndCtl, code, pos, fn) \
    (void)(fn)((hwnd), WM_HSCROLL, \
        MAKEWPARAM((UINT)(code),(UINT)(pos)), \
        (LPARAM)(UINT)(hwndCtl))


///////////////////////////////////////////////////////////
```

Figure 5-5.
The Supermarket application.

(continued)

Figure 5-5. *continued*

```
// Forward references to the supermarket
// and shopper thread functions.
DWORD WINAPI ThreadSuperMarket (LPVOID lpvParam);
DWORD WINAPI ThreadShopper (LPVOID lpvParam);

///////////////////////////////////////////////////////////////

// Global variables.
HWND g_hwndLB = NULL;    // List box for shopper events.

// User-settable simulation parameters.
int g_nMaxOccupancy;
int g_nTimeOpen;
int g_nCheckoutCounters;
int g_nMaxDelayBetweenShopperCreation;
int g_nMaxWaitToGetInMarket;
int g_nMaxTimeShopping;
int g_nMaxWaitForDeliCntr;
int g_nMaxTimeSpentAtDeli;
int g_nMaxTimeAtCheckout;

// Synchronization objects used to control the simulation.
HANDLE g_hSemEntrance;
HANDLE g_hMtxDeliCntr;
HANDLE g_hSemCheckout;

///////////////////////////////////////////////////////////////

// This function constructs a string using the format string
// passed and the variable number of arguments and adds the
// string to the shopper events list box identified by the
// global g_hwndLB variable.
void AddStr (LPCTSTR szFmt, ...) {
   TCHAR szBuf[150];
   int nIndex;
   va_list va_params;

   // Make va_params point to the first argument after szFmt.
   va_start(va_params, szFmt);

   // Build the string to be displayed.
   _vstprintf(szBuf, szFmt, va_params);

   do {
      // Add the string to the end of the list box.
      nIndex = ListBox_AddString(g_hwndLB, szBuf);
```

(continued)

Figure 5-5. *continued*

```
    // If the list box is full, delete the first item in it.
    if (nIndex == LB_ERR)
        ListBox_DeleteString(g_hwndLB, 0);

  } while (nIndex == LB_ERR);

  // Select the newly added item.
  ListBox_SetCurSel(g_hwndLB, nIndex);

  // Indicate that we are done referencing
  // the variable arguments.
  va_end(va_params);
}


///////////////////////////////////////////////////////////////

// This function returns a random number
// between 0 and nMaxValue inclusive.
int Random (int nMaxValue) {
  return(((2 * rand() * nMaxValue + RAND_MAX) /
     RAND_MAX - 1) / 2);
}


///////////////////////////////////////////////////////////////

BOOL Dlg_OnInitDialog (HWND hwnd, HWND hwndFocus,
   LPARAM lParam) {

  HWND hwndSB;

  // Associate an icon with the dialog box.
  SetClassLong(hwnd, GCL_HICON, (LONG)
     LoadIcon((HINSTANCE) GetWindowLong(hwnd, GWL_HINSTANCE),
     __TEXT("SprMrkt")));

  // Save the window handle to the shopper events list box
  // in a global variable so that the AddStr function has
  // access to it.
  g_hwndLB = GetDlgItem(hwnd, ID_SHOPPEREVENTS);

  // Set the scroll bar range and default positions for all
  // the simulation parameters.
  hwndSB = GetDlgItem(hwnd, ID_MAXOCCUPANCY);
  ScrollBar_SetRange(hwndSB, 0, 500, TRUE);
```

(continued)

Figure 5-5. *continued*

```
    // Set the initial value of the SCROLLBAR.
    FORWARD_WM_HSCROLL(hwnd, hwndSB, SB_THUMBTRACK,
        30, SendMessage);

    hwndSB = GetDlgItem(hwnd, ID_TIMEOPEN);
    ScrollBar_SetRange(hwndSB, 0, 5000, TRUE);
    FORWARD_WM_HSCROLL(hwnd, hwndSB, SB_THUMBTRACK,
        5000, SendMessage);

    hwndSB = GetDlgItem(hwnd, ID_NUMCOUNTERS);
    ScrollBar_SetRange(hwndSB, 0, 30, TRUE);
    FORWARD_WM_HSCROLL(hwnd, hwndSB, SB_THUMBTRACK,
        5, SendMessage);

    hwndSB = GetDlgItem(hwnd, ID_SHOPPERCREATIONDELAY);
    ScrollBar_SetRange(hwndSB, 0, 1000, TRUE);
    FORWARD_WM_HSCROLL(hwnd, hwndSB, SB_THUMBTRACK,
        300, SendMessage);

    hwndSB = GetDlgItem(hwnd, ID_DELAYTOGETIN);
    ScrollBar_SetRange(hwndSB, 0, 100, TRUE);
    FORWARD_WM_HSCROLL(hwnd, hwndSB, SB_THUMBTRACK,
        20, SendMessage);

    hwndSB = GetDlgItem(hwnd, ID_TIMETOSHOP);
    ScrollBar_SetRange(hwndSB, 0, 100, TRUE);
    FORWARD_WM_HSCROLL(hwnd, hwndSB, SB_THUMBTRACK,
        80, SendMessage);

    hwndSB = GetDlgItem(hwnd, ID_WAITDELICNTR);
    ScrollBar_SetRange(hwndSB, 0, 100, TRUE);
    FORWARD_WM_HSCROLL(hwnd, hwndSB, SB_THUMBTRACK,
        20, SendMessage);

    hwndSB = GetDlgItem(hwnd, ID_TIMEATDELICNTR);
    ScrollBar_SetRange(hwndSB, 0, 100, TRUE);
    FORWARD_WM_HSCROLL(hwnd, hwndSB, SB_THUMBTRACK,
        70, SendMessage);

    hwndSB = GetDlgItem(hwnd, ID_TIMEATCHECKOUT);
    ScrollBar_SetRange(hwndSB, 0, 100, TRUE);
    FORWARD_WM_HSCROLL(hwnd, hwndSB, SB_THUMBTRACK,
        60, SendMessage);

    return(TRUE);
}
```

(continued)

Figure 5-5. *continued*

```
///////////////////////////////////////////////////////////

void Dlg_OnHScroll(HWND hwnd, HWND hwndCtl,
   UINT code, int pos) {

   TCHAR szBuf[10];
   int nPosCrnt, nPosMin, nPosMax;

   // Get the current position and the legal range for the
   // scroll bar that the user is changing.
   nPosCrnt = ScrollBar_GetPos(hwndCtl);
   ScrollBar_GetRange(hwndCtl, &nPosMin, &nPosMax);

   switch (code) {
      case SB_LINELEFT:
         nPosCrnt--;
         break;

      case SB_LINERIGHT:
         nPosCrnt++;
         break;

      case SB_PAGELEFT:
         nPosCrnt += (nPosMax - nPosMin + 1) / 10;
         break;

      case SB_PAGERIGHT:
         nPosCrnt -= (nPosMax - nPosMin + 1) / 10;
         break;

      case SB_THUMBTRACK:
         nPosCrnt = pos;
         break;

      case SB_LEFT:
         nPosCrnt = nPosMin;
         break;

      case SB_RIGHT:
         nPosCrnt = nPosMax;
         break;
   }
```

(continued)

Figure 5-5. *continued*

```
    // Make sure that the new scroll position
    // is within the legal range.
    if (nPosCrnt < nPosMin)
        nPosCrnt = nPosMin;

    if (nPosCrnt > nPosMax)
        nPosCrnt = nPosMax;

    // Set the new scroll position.
    ScrollBar_SetPos(hwndCtl, nPosCrnt, TRUE);

    // Change the value displayed in the text box to
    // reflect the value in the scroll bar.
    _stprintf(szBuf, __TEXT("%d"), nPosCrnt);
    SetWindowText(GetPrevSibling(hwndCtl), szBuf);
}

///////////////////////////////////////////////////////////////////

void Dlg_OnCommand (HWND hwnd, int id, HWND hwndCtl,
    UINT codeNotify) {

    DWORD dwThreadId;
    HANDLE hThread;

    switch (id) {
        case IDOK:
            // Load the scroll bar settings into the global
            // variables so that they can be used
            // by the simulation.
            g_nMaxOccupancy = ScrollBar_GetPos(
                GetDlgItem(hwnd, ID_MAXOCCUPANCY));

            g_nTimeOpen = ScrollBar_GetPos(
                GetDlgItem(hwnd, ID_TIMEOPEN));

            g_nCheckoutCounters = ScrollBar_GetPos(
                GetDlgItem(hwnd, ID_NUMCOUNTERS));

            g_nMaxDelayBetweenShopperCreation = ScrollBar_GetPos(
                GetDlgItem(hwnd, ID_SHOPPERCREATIONDELAY));

            g_nMaxWaitToGetInMarket = ScrollBar_GetPos(
                GetDlgItem(hwnd, ID_DELAYTOGETIN));

            g_nMaxTimeShopping = ScrollBar_GetPos(
                GetDlgItem(hwnd, ID_TIMETOSHOP));
```

(continued)

240

Figure 5-5. *continued*

```
        g_nMaxWaitForDeliCntr = ScrollBar_GetPos(
           GetDlgItem(hwnd, ID_WAITDELICNTR));

        g_nMaxTimeSpentAtDeli = ScrollBar_GetPos(
           GetDlgItem(hwnd, ID_TIMEATDELICNTR));

        g_nMaxTimeAtCheckout = ScrollBar_GetPos(
           GetDlgItem(hwnd, ID_TIMEATCHECKOUT));

        // Clear out everything in the list box.
        ListBox_ResetContent(
           GetDlgItem(hwnd, ID_SHOPPEREVENTS));

        // Disable the "Open for business" button
        // while simulation is in progress.

        EnableWindow(hwndCtl, FALSE);

        if (NULL == GetFocus()) {
           SetFocus(GetDlgItem(hwnd, ID_MAXOCCUPANCY));
        }

        // The overhead of the system will cause the
        // results of the simulation to be stilted.  To help
        // minimize this effect, we boost the priority class
        // of this process.
        SetPriorityClass(GetCurrentProcess(),
           HIGH_PRIORITY_CLASS);

        // Create the thread representing the supermarket.
        hThread = CreateThread(
           NULL,               // Security attributes
           0,                  // Stack
           ThreadSuperMarket,  // Thread function
           (LPVOID) hwnd,      // Thread function parameter
           0,                  // Flags
           &dwThreadId);       // Thread ID

        // Since we are not interested in manipulating the
        // thread object from this function, we can close
        // our handle to it.
        CloseHandle(hThread);
        break;
```

(continued)

241

Figure 5-5. *continued*

```
      case IDCANCEL:
         EndDialog(hwnd, id);
         break;
   }
}


//////////////////////////////////////////////////////////////////

BOOL CALLBACK Dlg_Proc (HWND hDlg, UINT uMsg,
   WPARAM wParam, LPARAM lParam) {

   BOOL fProcessed = TRUE;

   switch (uMsg) {
      HANDLE_MSG(hDlg, WM_INITDIALOG,  Dlg_OnInitDialog);
      HANDLE_MSG(hDlg, WM_COMMAND,  Dlg_OnCommand);
      HANDLE_MSG(hDlg, WM_HSCROLL,  Dlg_OnHScroll);

      case WM_USER:
         // This message is sent by the SuperMarketThread to
         // notify us that the simulation has completed.

         // Return the priority class of the simulation
         // back to normal.
         SetPriorityClass(GetCurrentProcess(),
            NORMAL_PRIORITY_CLASS);

         // Enable the "Open for business" button so that
         // the user can run the simulation again with
         // new parameters.
         EnableWindow(GetDlgItem(hDlg, IDOK), TRUE);
         break;

      default:
         fProcessed = FALSE;
         break;
   }
   return(fProcessed);
}

//////////////////////////////////////////////////////////////////
```

(continued)

Figure 5-5. *continued*

```
int APIENTRY WinMain (HINSTANCE hInstance,
    HINSTANCE hPrevInstance, LPSTR lpszCmdLine, int nCmdShow) {

    DialogBox(hInstance, MAKEINTRESOURCE(DLG_SPRMRKT),
        NULL, Dlg_Proc);
    return(0);
}


//////////////////////////////////////////////////////////////////

DWORD WINAPI ThreadSuperMarket (LPVOID lpvParam) {
    DWORD dwCloseTime;
    HANDLE hThread;
    DWORD dwThreadId;
    int nShopperNum = 0, nMaxOccupancy;

    g_hSemEntrance = CreateSemaphore(
        NULL,               // Security attributes.
        0,                  // Initial lock count.
        g_nMaxOccupancy,    // Maximum people allowed in store.
        NULL);              // Do not name the semaphore.

    g_hMtxDeliCntr = CreateMutex(
        NULL,               // Security attributes.
        FALSE,              // Initially, no one is at the Deli.
        NULL);              // Do not name the mutex.

    g_hSemCheckout = CreateSemaphore(
        NULL,               // Security attributes.
        g_nCheckoutCounters, // All counters are free.
        g_nCheckoutCounters, // The # of counters at the store.
        NULL);              // No name for the semaphore.

    // Open the store to the shoppers.
    AddStr(__TEXT("---> Opening the supermarket to shoppers."));
    ReleaseSemaphore(g_hSemEntrance, g_nMaxOccupancy, NULL);

    // Get the time that the store should not
    // allow new customers into the store.
    dwCloseTime = GetTickCount() + g_nTimeOpen;

    // Continue loop until the store closes.
    while (GetTickCount() < dwCloseTime) {
```

(continued)

243

Figure 5-5. *continued*

```
        // Create the thread representing a shopper.
        hThread = CreateThread(
            NULL,                     // Security attributes
            0,                        // Stack
            ThreadShopper,            // Thread function
            (LPVOID) ++nShopperNum,   // Shopper number as lpvParam
            0,                        // Flags
            &dwThreadId);             // Thread ID

        // Since we are not interested in manipulating the
        // thread object from this function, we can close
        // our handle to it.
        CloseHandle(hThread);

        // Wait until another shopper comes to the supermarket.
        Sleep(Random(g_nMaxDelayBetweenShopperCreation));
    }
    // The supermarket wants to close;
    // wait for all the shoppers to leave.
    AddStr(__TEXT("---> Waiting for shoppers to check out ")
        __TEXT("so store can close."));

    nMaxOccupancy = 1;
    for (; nMaxOccupancy <=g_nMaxOccupancy; nMaxOccupancy++) {
        WaitForSingleObject(g_hSemEntrance, INFINITE);
        AddStr(__TEXT("---> %d shoppers NOT in store."),
        nMaxOccupancy);
    }

    AddStr(__TEXT("---> Store closed - end of simulation."));

    // Everybody has left the market - end of simulation.
    CloseHandle(g_hSemCheckout);
    CloseHandle(g_hMtxDeliCntr);
    CloseHandle(g_hSemEntrance);

    // Notify the GUI thread that the simulation has completed.
    // The window handle of the GUI thread's dialog box was
    // passed in the lpvParam parameter to this thread when
    // it was created.
    SendMessage((HWND) lpvParam, WM_USER, 0, 0);

    return(0);
}
```

(continued)

Figure 5-5. *continued*

```
//////////////////////////////////////////////////////////////

DWORD WINAPI ThreadShopper (LPVOID lpvParam) {
   int nShopperNum = (int) lpvParam;
   DWORD dwResult;
   int nDuration;

   // Wait till the shopper can enter the supermarket.
   nDuration = Random(g_nMaxWaitToGetInMarket);
   AddStr(__TEXT("%04lu: Waiting to get in store (%lu)."),
      nShopperNum, nDuration);

   dwResult = WaitForSingleObject(g_hSemEntrance, nDuration);
   if (dwResult == WAIT_TIMEOUT) {
      // The shopper got tired of
      // waiting to be let in and left.
      AddStr(__TEXT("%04lu: Tired of waiting, went home."),
         nShopperNum);
      return(0);
   }

   // Shopper entered the supermarket.  Time to go shopping.
   nDuration = Random(g_nMaxTimeShopping);
   AddStr(__TEXT("%04lu: In supermarket, shopping for %lu."),
      nShopperNum, nDuration);
   Sleep(nDuration);

   // Done initial shopping. Shopper has a one in three
   // chance of going to the Deli counter.
   if (Random(2) == 0) {

      // Shopper going to Deli counter.
      nDuration = Random(g_nMaxWaitForDeliCntr);
      AddStr(
         __TEXT("%04lu: Waiting for service at ")
         __TEXT("Deli Counter (%lu)."),
         nShopperNum, nDuration);
      dwResult =
         WaitForSingleObject(g_hMtxDeliCntr, nDuration);

      if (dwResult == 0) {
         // Got attention at Deli; order stuff.
         nDuration = Random(g_nMaxTimeSpentAtDeli);
```

(continued)

Figure 5-5. *continued*

```
            AddStr(__TEXT("%04lu: Being served at Deli (%lu)."),
                nShopperNum, nDuration);
            Sleep(nDuration);

            // Leave the Deli counter
            ReleaseMutex(g_hMtxDeliCntr);

        } else {
            // Tired of waiting at Deli counter;
            // leave and continue shopping.
            AddStr(__TEXT("%04lu: Tired of waiting at Deli."),
                nShopperNum);
        }

    } else {
        AddStr(__TEXT("%04lu: Not going to the Deli counter."),
            nShopperNum);
    }

    // Waiting for a checkout counter.
    AddStr(
        __TEXT("%04lu: Waiting for an empty checkout counter."),
        nShopperNum);
    WaitForSingleObject(g_hSemCheckout, INFINITE);

    // Checking out.
    nDuration = Random(g_nMaxTimeAtCheckout);
    AddStr(__TEXT("%04lu: Checking out (%lu)."),
        nShopperNum, nDuration);
    Sleep(nDuration);

    // Leaving the checkout counter.
    AddStr(__TEXT("%04lu: Leaving checkout counter."),
        nShopperNum);
    ReleaseSemaphore(g_hSemCheckout, 1, NULL);

    // Leaving the store.
    AddStr(__TEXT("%04lu: Left the supermarket."),
        nShopperNum);
    ReleaseSemaphore(g_hSemEntrance, 1, NULL);

    // Shopper shopped till he/she dropped.  Shopper dead.
    return(0);
}

//////////////////////// End Of File ////////////////////////
```

(continued)

Figure 5-5. *continued*

SPRMRKT.H

```
/*****************************************************************
Module name: SprMrkt.H
Notices: Copyright (c) 1993 Jeffrey Richter
*****************************************************************/

// Dialog and control IDs.
#define DLG_SPRMRKT                    1
#define ID_MAXOCCUPANCY                100
#define ID_TIMEOPEN                    101
#define ID_NUMCOUNTERS                 102
#define ID_SHOPPERCREATIONDELAY        103
#define ID_DELAYTOGETIN                104
#define ID_TIMETOSHOP                  105
#define ID_WAITDELICNTR                106
#define ID_TIMEATDELICNTR              107
#define ID_TIMEATCHECKOUT              108
#define ID_SHOPPEREVENTS               109


///////////////////////// End Of File /////////////////////////
```

SPRMRKT.RC

```
/*****************************************************************
Module name: SprMrkt.RC
Notices: Copyright (c) 1993 Jeffrey Richter
*****************************************************************/

#include <windows.h>
#include "SprMrkt.h"

SprMrkt   ICON  DISCARDABLE SprMrkt.Ico

DLG_SPRMRKT DIALOG 4, 58, 360, 206
LANGUAGE LANG_NEUTRAL, SUBLANG_NEUTRAL
STYLE WS_BORDER | WS_MINIMIZEBOX | WS_POPUP | WS_VISIBLE |
  WS_CAPTION | WS_SYSMENU
CAPTION "Supermarket Simulation"
FONT 8, "MS Sans Serif"
BEGIN
    GROUPBOX          "Super&market parameters", -1,
                      4, 0, 176, 66, WS_GROUP
    RTEXT             "Maximum occupancy:",
                      -1, 8, 12, 72, 8, NOT WS_GROUP
```

(continued)

Figure 5-5. *continued*

```
RTEXT             "MO", -1,
                  84, 12, 16, 8, SS_NOPREFIX | NOT WS_GROUP
SCROLLBAR         ID_MAXOCCUPANCY,
                  104, 12, 72, 10, WS_TABSTOP
RTEXT             "Time open:", -1,
                  8, 24, 72, 8, NOT WS_GROUP
RTEXT             "TO", -1,
                  84, 24, 16, 8, SS_NOPREFIX | NOT WS_GROUP
SCROLLBAR         ID_TIMEOPEN, 104, 24, 72, 10, WS_TABSTOP
RTEXT             "Checkout counters:", -1,
                  12, 38, 68, 8, NOT WS_GROUP
RTEXT             "CC", -1,
                  84, 38, 16, 8, SS_NOPREFIX | NOT WS_GROUP
SCROLLBAR         ID_NUMCOUNTERS,
                  104, 38, 72, 10, WS_TABSTOP
RTEXT             "Shopper create delay:", -1,
                  8, 52, 72, 8, NOT WS_GROUP
RTEXT             "SC", -1,
                  84, 52, 16, 8, SS_NOPREFIX | NOT WS_GROUP
SCROLLBAR         ID_SHOPPERCREATIONDELAY,
                  104, 52, 72, 10, WS_TABSTOP
GROUPBOX          "&Shopper parameters", -1,
                  184, 0, 172, 80, WS_GROUP
RTEXT             "Wait to get in market:", -1,
                  188, 12, 68, 8, NOT WS_GROUP
RTEXT             "WTGI", -1,
                  260, 12, 16, 8, SS_NOPREFIX | NOT WS_GROUP
SCROLLBAR         ID_DELAYTOGETIN,
                  280, 10, 72, 10, WS_TABSTOP
RTEXT             "Time to shop:", -1,
                  208, 24, 48, 8, NOT WS_GROUP
RTEXT             "TTS", -1,
                  260, 24, 16, 8, SS_NOPREFIX | NOT WS_GROUP
SCROLLBAR         ID_TIMETOSHOP,
                  280, 24, 72, 10, WS_TABSTOP
RTEXT             "Wait for deli counter:", -1,
                  188, 38, 68, 8, NOT WS_GROUP
RTEXT             "WFDC", -1,
                  260, 38, 16, 8, SS_NOPREFIX | NOT WS_GROUP
SCROLLBAR         ID_WAITDELICNTR,
                  280, 38, 72, 10, WS_TABSTOP
RTEXT             "Time at deli counter:", -1,
                  188, 52, 68, 8, NOT WS_GROUP
```

(continued)

Figure 5-5. *continued*

```
        RTEXT               "TADC", -1,
                            260, 52, 16, 8, SS_NOPREFIX | NOT WS_GROUP
        SCROLLBAR           ID_TIMEATDELICNTR,
                            280, 52, 72, 10, WS_TABSTOP
        RTEXT               "Time at checkout:", -1,
                            196, 66, 60, 8, NOT WS_GROUP
        RTEXT               "TAC", -1,
                            260, 66, 16, 8, SS_NOPREFIX | NOT WS_GROUP
        SCROLLBAR           ID_TIMEATCHECKOUT,
                            280, 66, 72, 10, WS_TABSTOP
        PUSHBUTTON          "&Open for business", DLG_SPRMRKT,
                            80, 68, 100, 12, WS_GROUP
        LTEXT               "Shopper &events:", -1, 4, 82, 60, 8
        LISTBOX             ID_SHOPPEREVENTS, 4, 94, 352, 108,
                            LBS_NOINTEGRALHEIGHT | WS_VSCROLL |
                            WS_TABSTOP
    END

//////////////////////// End Of File ////////////////////////
```

Events

Event objects are quite different from mutexes and semaphores. Mutexes and semaphores are usually used to control access to data, but events are used to signal that some operation has completed. There are two different types of event objects: manual-reset events and auto-reset events. A manual-reset event is used to signal several threads simultaneously that an operation has completed, and an auto-reset event is used to signal a single thread that an operation has completed.

Events are most commonly used when one thread performs initialization work and, when it completes, it signals another thread to perform the remaining work. The initialization thread sets the event to the not-signaled state and begins to perform the initialization. Then, after the initialization has completed, the thread sets the event to the signaled state. When the worker thread starts executing, it immediately suspends itself, waiting for the event to become signaled. When the initialization thread signals the event, the worker thread wakes up and performs the rest of the work necessary.

For example, a process might be running two threads. The first thread reads data from a file into a memory buffer. Once the data has been read, the first thread signals the second thread that it can process

249

the data. When the second thread finishes processing the data, it might need to signal the first thread again so that the first thread can read the next block of data from the file.

Let's start our discussion with how to create an event. The semantics for creating, opening, and closing events are identical to those for mutexes and semaphores. Events can be created using the CreateEvent function:

```
HANDLE CreateEvent(LPSECURITY_ATTRIBUTES lpsa,
   BOOL fManualReset, BOOL fInitialState, LPTSTR lpszEventName);
```

The *fManualReset* parameter is a boolean value that tells Windows NT whether you want to create a manual-reset event (TRUE) or an auto-reset event (FALSE). The *fInitalState* parameter indicates whether the event should be initialized as signaled (TRUE) or not signaled (FALSE). After Windows NT creates the event object, CreateEvent returns the process-specific handle to the event. Other processes can gain access to the object by calling CreateEvent using the same value in the *lpszEventName* parameter; by using inheritance; by using the DuplicateHandle function; or by calling OpenEvent (as shown below), specifying a name in the *lpszName* parameter that matches the name specified in the call to CreateEvent:

```
HANDLE OpenEvent(DWORD fdwAccess, BOOL fInherit, LPTSTR lpszName);
```

As always, events are closed by calling the very popular CloseHandle function.

Manual-Reset Events

Manual-reset events are not automatically reset to the not-signaled state by the WaitForSingleObject and WaitForMultipleObjects functions. For mutexes, when a thread calls WaitForSingleObject or WaitForMultiple-Objects, the functions wait for the mutex to be signaled and then automatically reset the mutex to not signaled. This is important because it guarantees that no more than one thread waiting on the mutex will be able to wake up and continue executing. If threads were responsible for manually resetting the mutex back to the not-signaled state, it would be possible for two or more threads to have their waits satisfied before each one would reset the mutex to not signaled.

For manual-reset events, the story is quite different. You might have several threads, all of them waiting for the same event to occur. When the event does occur, all the waiting threads might be able to perform their own processing. Let's go back to our file reading and processing example. It might be the case that one thread is responsible for reading data from a file into a buffer. Once the data has been read, we might want to start 9 other threads. Each of these 9 threads might process the data in a slightly different way. Let's say the file contains a word processing document. The first thread could count characters, the second thread could count words, the third thread could count pages, a fourth thread could perform a spell check, a fifth thread could print the document, and so on. The one extremely important thing that all of these threads have in common is that none of them write to the data. All of them consider the data to be a read-only source.

In this example, you most certainly would want to allow all the waiting threads to be satisfied when the event occurred. This is the reason for manual-reset events. When a manual-reset event is signaled, all threads waiting on the event are allowed to run. A thread sets an event object to the signaled state by calling:

```
BOOL SetEvent(HANDLE hEvent);
```

This function takes the handle to an event object and simply sets it to the signaled state. SetEvent returns TRUE if the function is successful. Once the manual-reset event has been signaled, it remains signaled until one thread explicitly resets the event by calling:

```
BOOL ResetEvent(HANDLE hEvent);
```

This function takes the handle to an event object and resets it to the not-signaled state. ResetEvent returns TRUE if the function is successful.

For the file reading and processing example, the thread that reads the file data and puts it into the shared memory buffer would call ResetEvent just before reading the data into the buffer. It would then call SetEvent when the reading was completed.

I've left out one small issue: How does the file-read thread know when to read the next block of data? We know that it should do it when all the other threads have finished their work with it. But the other threads need a way to signal that they've finished. The best method is for each of the data processing threads to create their own event object. If all the handles for these event objects were stored in an array, the file-read thread could call WaitForMultipleObjects, indicating that it wants to wait for all the event handles.

Because calling SetEvent, releasing waiting events, and immediately calling ResetEvent is quite common, Win32 offers another function (shown at the top of the following page) that performs all three of these steps.

```
BOOL PulseEvent(HANDLE hEvent);
```

When PulseEvent returns, the event is left in the not-signaled state. If the function is successful, TRUE is returned.

The Bucket of Balls Sample Application A basic synchronization problem, commonly referred to as the classic multiple-readers/multiple-writers scenario, exists for many different applications. The problem involves an arbitrary number of threads attempting to access a global resource. Some of these threads (the writers) need to modify the contents of the global data, and some of the threads (the readers) need only to read the data. Synchronization is necessary because of the following rules:

1. When one thread is writing to the data, no other thread can write to the data.

2. When one thread is writing to the data, no other thread can read from the data.

3. When one thread is reading from the data, no other thread can write to the data.

4. When one thread is reading from the data, other threads can also read from the data.

Let's look at this problem in the context of a database application in which we have five end-users all working on the same database: two employees are entering records into the database and three employees are retrieving records from the database.

In this scenario, rule 1 is necessary because we certainly can't have both Employee 1 and Employee 2 updating record 3,457 at the same time. If both employees attempt to modify the same record, Employee 1's changes might be made to the database, and Employee 2's changes would overwrite Employee 1's changes. We wouldn't want to the have a situation in which a record in the database contained conflicting information.

Rule 2 prohibits an employee from accessing a record in the database if another employee is updating a record in the database. If this situation were not prevented, it would be possible for Employee 4 to read the contents of record 2,543 while Employee 1 was altering the same record. When Employee 4's computer displayed the record, the record would contain some of the old information and some of the updated information—this is certainly unacceptable. Rule 3 is needed in order to solve the same problem. The difference in the wording of rules 2 and 3 prevents the situation regardless of who gains access to the database record first—an employee who is trying to write or an employee who is attempting to read.

The last rule, rule 4, exists for performance reasons. It makes sense that if no employees are attempting to modify records in the database, the content of the database is not changing and, therefore, any and all employees who are simply retrieving records from the database should be allowed to do so.

OK, there you have the gist of the problem. Now the question is how do we solve it?

The Bucket (BUCKET.EXE) application, listed in Figure 5-6 beginning on page 261, demonstrates the solution by synchronizing the access to a small database by five threads. In order to accomplish this synchronization, Bucket uses three of the Windows NT synchronization objects discussed in this chapter: manual-reset events, semaphores, and mutexes. Although Bucket manages only five threads (two updating the database and three reading the database), the groundwork presented easily extends itself to a situation in which virtually any number of threads (readers and/or writers) can be synchronized.

When you invoke Bucket, the following dialog box appears:

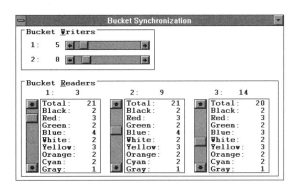

The database being managed is a bucket that can contain no more than 100 balls. Initially, the bucket is empty. The *Bucket Writers* section, in the upper portion of the dialog box, represents the two threads that add, remove, or change the different colored balls in the bucket. To the right of the thread number is a time value specified in seconds. For

Writer 1, this value is 5. This means that every 5 seconds, Writer 1 attempts to gain access to the bucket and add another ball. The scroll bar at the right of the seconds value allows you to change this delay time, which can range from zero all the way to 60 seconds. Writer 2 operates in the same way except that it starts out with an initial delay time of 8 seconds.

The bottom portion of the dialog box represents the three Reader threads. These threads work similarly to the Writer threads. After every specified number of seconds (0 to 60), each of the three Reader threads erases the contents of its list box, counts the different colored balls in the bucket, and updates the list box to display the results.

The important thing to remember here is that all the threads are being synchronized. If a Writer currently has permission to add, remove, or change a ball in the bucket, neither the other Writer nor any of the Readers will be granted permission to the bucket. On the other hand, if a Reader has access to the bucket and is counting the balls, any of the other Readers requesting access to do the same will gain access, but none of the Writers will be allowed to dip into the bucket until all the Readers are finished.

Now that you see how the program operates, let's turn our attention to the source code, listed in Figure 5-6 beginning on page 261. When you invoke Bucket, it immediately calls DialogBox to display the dialog box shown earlier and performs all its initialization during the WM_INITDIALOG message processing. The first several lines of the Dlg_OnInitDialog function prepare all the scroll bars for the Writers and Readers by setting their legal ranges and their initial values.

Next, three different synchronization objects are created. Each object serves a special purpose and each was chosen specifically to take advantage of its particular behavior.

The first object created is a manual-reset event. This manual-reset event is not signaled when a Writer starts to modify the bucket and is signaled when the Writer finishes. The Reader threads can access the bucket only when this event is signaled. When created, this manual-reset event is initialized to be not signaled.

The second synchronization object, which is a semaphore, indicates whether any Readers are currently accessing the bucket. The semaphore is created with a maximum count of 1 and is initialized to 1 as well. This means that the semaphore is created in the signaled state, indicating that no Readers are currently accessing the bucket. The semaphore is used only to indicate whether any Readers are accessing the bucket—not the number of Readers accessing the bucket.

When a Reader gains access to the bucket, the semaphore will be given a count of 0 (zero). Other Readers don't wait on the semaphore to gain access to the bucket. Instead, a global counter is maintained that reflects the number of simultaneous Readers accessing the bucket. When the last Reader finishes, it releases the semaphore. This causes the semaphore to become signaled again, and it is then available to a Writer or a new Reader if one should happen along.

You'll notice that I use a semaphore here instead of a mutex. With this setup, it is very likely that one of the Readers will gain ownership of the semaphore. Once the semaphore is obtained, other Readers can also start accessing the bucket. Meanwhile, the first Reader, the one that originally obtained ownership of the semaphore, can finish what it needs to do. However, because other Readers are not finished accessing the bucket, the semaphore is still not signaled and cannot be released. Eventually, all the Readers will finish accessing the bucket and the last Reader finished must turn out the lights (or, in layman's terms, release the semaphore).

Here we have a situation in which the thread that originally gained ownership of the semaphore is *not* the same thread that will release it, which is why I used a semaphore instead of a mutex. You might recall that a mutex is owned by a thread, whereas a semaphore has no concept of ownership. The thread that acquires ownership of a mutex must also release it. If another thread attempts to release the mutex (by calling ReleaseMutex), the call will fail.

The third and last synchronization object created is a mutex. This mutex is used to guard against multiple Writers accessing the bucket simultaneously. The mutex is initialized to the not-signaled state, indicating that no Writers are accessing the bucket. When a Writer wants to modify the contents of the bucket, the Writer must wait for the mutex. When it gains ownership of the mutex, the mutex becomes signaled, indicating to other Writers that another thread is modifying the contents of the bucket. These other Writers will continue to wait on the mutex. When the thread owning the mutex is no longer modifying the bucket, it releases the mutex, allowing one other waiting Writer to manipulate the bucket.

Notice that the thread that gains ownership of the mutex is guaranteed to be the same thread that releases the mutex, which is why I used a mutex in this case instead of a semaphore. Actually, it would be possible to use a semaphore here if you wanted to; however, a mutex offers a little more robustness. If the thread owning the mutex were to somehow terminate or be terminated, the mutex would become abandoned. Other threads waiting for the mutex would be notified of this situation and could decide whether it was safe to access the bucket or not. When a mutex is abandoned, it is an indication that something has gone wrong. It is almost always a bad idea to access the data protected by a mutex if that mutex is abandoned.

Although the Bucket application doesn't check for the possible abandonment of a mutex, you should explicitly check for it in your own applications.

At the end of the Dlg_OnInitDialog function, with everything initialized, the two Writer and three Reader threads are created. A mistake that I just can't seem to avoid is creating the threads before creating the various synchronization objects. If you create the threads first, they will attempt to reference the synchronization objects, all of whose handles will be NULL because they haven't been created yet. Maybe you can break yourself of this habit before you start. I'm afraid it's too late for me—save yourself.

Only one Writer function is used by the two Writer threads. This function performs some initialization so that it can interact with the dialog box controls and then enters an infinite *while* loop. A Writer thread's first action in this loop is to suspend itself for the number of seconds specified in the dialog box. This simulates the thread performing some additional work and helps to drive home the idea that different threads access the bucket at different times.

```
// Go to sleep for the user-defined time.
Sleep(1000 * GetDlgItemInt(g_hwndDlg, nNumID, NULL, FALSE));
```

After this time period, the Writer thread resumes execution with the intention of modifying the contents of the bucket. But, before it can modify the bucket, it must be granted access to do so. A series of things must be true in order for this to happen.

First, the thread must check that no other Writer threads are currently accessing the bucket. The thread does this by waiting for the mutex that was created for just this purpose.

```
// Wait for no other writers to be altering the bucket (data).
WaitForSingleObject(g_hMutexWriters, INFINITE);
```

When the Writer thread gains ownership of the mutex, it knows that no other Writer thread has access to the bucket and that no other

Writer thread will gain access to the bucket until this Writer thread releases the mutex.

Second, the Writer thread must block any new Reader threads from attempting to examine the contents of the bucket. It does this by resetting the manual-reset event object to its not-signaled state. As you'll see later, Reader threads make sure that this event is signaled before they start accessing the bucket.

```
// Block any new readers from beginning to read the
// contents of the bucket (data).
ResetEvent(g_hEventDataReady);
```

This event stops only new Readers from accessing the bucket. But some Readers might already be accessing the bucket. This Writer thread must wait until all the Readers are done. The Writer does this by waiting for the semaphore to become signaled. When the Writer gains ownership of the semaphore, the semaphore is automatically placed in the not-signaled state.

```
// Wait for any readers still reading the
// contents of the bucket to finish.
WaitForSingleObject(g_hSemReaders, INFINITE);
```

At this point, the Writer knows that no other Writer threads can access the bucket and that no Reader threads can access the bucket. So the Writer thread can now feel free to manipulate the bucket on its own by calling Bucket_AlterContents.

```
// No readers can start reading and all readers that were reading
// have finished.  We can now alter the contents of the bucket.
Bucket_AlterContents();
```

When Bucket_AlterContents returns, the Writer thread must indicate that it's finished and allow the rest of the threads access; it does this by calling SetEvent to signal the manual-reset event.

```
// The contents of the bucket have been altered; let readers know
// that the bucket (data) is available to process.
SetEvent(g_hEventDataReady);
```

This tells all waiting Readers that the contents of the bucket are up-to-date and ready for processing. Then the Writer calls ReleaseSemaphore to allow any Readers to start reading the data. And finally the Writer releases the mutex, allowing another Writer thread to alter the contents of the bucket.

```
// Allow any waiting readers to examine the
// contents of the bucket.
ReleaseSemaphore(g_hSemReaders, 1, NULL);
```

```
// Allow another writer to reserve its access to the
// bucket, which will occur when all the readers
// have finished with this pass.
ReleaseMutex(g_hMutexWriters);
```

This Writer thread then loops around, back to the top, and repeats the whole cycle again.

Only one Reader function is used by the three Reader threads. Like the Writer function, this function also performs some initialization so that it can interact with the dialog box controls and then enters an infinite *while* loop. A Reader thread's first action in this loop is to suspend itself for the number of seconds specified in the dialog box.

```
// Go to sleep for the user-defined time.
Sleep(1000 * GetDlgItemInt(g_hwndDlg, nNumID, NULL, FALSE));
```

After this time period, the Reader thread resumes execution with the intention of examining the contents of the bucket. But, before it can examine the bucket, it must be granted access to do so. A series of things must be true in order for this to happen.

First, the Reader must wait until the bucket contains data worth examining. By checking the manual-reset event, the Reader determines when to stop waiting. The state of this event is changed only by Writer threads, never by Reader threads.

```
// Wait for the contents of the bucket to be ready for examining.
WaitForSingleObject(g_hEventDataReady, INFINITE);
```

Second, the Reader must increment a global counter, *g_lNumReaders*. This counter indicates the number of Reader threads that are currently examining the contents of the bucket. Unfortunately, this counter is a global variable that is incremented and decremented by the three Reader threads, so there should be some form of synchronization guarding this variable. Although it is possible to use a mutex to guard *g_lNumReaders*, I chose to use the InterlockedIncrement function instead.

```
// Number of Reader threads examining the bucket.
LONG g_lNumReaders = -1;
    .
    .
    .
```

```
// We want to examine the bucket; increment the number of readers.
if (InterlockedIncrement(&g_lNumReaders) == 0) {
   // We are the first reader, wait for the semaphore.
   WaitForSingleObject(g_hSemReaders, INFINITE);
}
```

This function and its counterpart, InterlockedDecrement, are discussed in detail at the end of this chapter. For now though, I'll just say that these two functions either increment or decrement a long variable whose address is passed to them. These functions guarantee that only one thread at a time can access the long variable. The functions return 0 (zero) if the new value of the variable is 0, less than 0 if the new value is less than 0, or greater than 0 if the new value is greater than 0.

When Bucket starts executing, the $g\_lNumReaders$ variable is initialized to −1. So, for the first Reader, calling InterlockedIncrement changes $g\_lNumReaders$ to 0 (zero). When the Reader thread sees that $g\_lNumReaders$ is 0, it waits for the semaphore. Remember, the semaphore indicates whether the bucket is being accessed by any Reader. If the semaphore is not signaled, no Reader has access and the Reader must wait until the Writer owning the semaphore releases it, allowing Readers to start examining the bucket.

If the value in $g\_lNumReaders$ is already 0 (zero) or greater, the new Reader does not have to wait for the semaphore because at least one other Reader is already examining the contents of the bucket.

Now that all of this checking is done, the Reader examines the bucket and displays its results by calling Bucket_DumpToLB.

```
// Examine the contents of the bucket and dump it to the list box.
Bucket_DumpToLB(hwndLB);
```

After accessing the bucket, the Reader must decrement the number of Readers by calling InterlockedDecrement. If the new value of $g\_lNumReaders$ is less than 0 (zero), the Reader thread knows that it is the last Reader examining the bucket. To indicate this to any waiting Writer threads, the Reader must release the semaphore.

```
// We are done examining the bucket;
// decrement the number of readers.
if (InterlockedDecrement(&g_lNumReaders) < 0) {
   // We are the last reader; release the semaphore.
   ReleaseSemaphore(g_hSemReaders, 1, NULL);
}
```

This Reader thread then loops around, back to the top, and repeats the whole cycle again.

I'd like to point out just a few more issues about Bucket. First, you can terminate Bucket by choosing Close from the system menu. When you do this, the dialog box receives a WM_DESTROY message, and the Dlg_OnDestroy function simply closes some handles and returns. Since the thread that handles all the processing for the dialog box is the process's primary thread, the process terminates. This is because the C Runtime's startup code implicitly calls ExitProcess.

If the processing for the dialog box was handled by another thread, only that thread would terminate, and the other threads in the Bucket process would continue to execute. After the thread that handles the dialog box is destroyed, the dialog box disappears. So Bucket would continue to run even without a user interface. Also, if you displayed the task list by pressing Ctrl+Esc, Bucket wouldn't appear in the list. This is an easy way to unintentionally use up system resources. The only way to terminate the Bucket application would be to log out or to invoke the Process Viewer (PVIEW.EXE) application and forcibly terminate the Bucket application.

Second, I'd like to point out that this example shows how to synchronize Writer and Reader threads that are all contained within the same process. Extending this example so that it works with threads in multiple processes is pretty straightforward. You'd simply need to name each of the three synchronization objects so that handles to them can be obtained in the other processes. Next, you'd need to put the *g_lNumReaders* variable into a block of shared memory. The easiest way to do this would be to use a memory-mapped file.

The third point involves cleanup. You should be sure to clean up when the user terminates one of the processes. This can be a little tricky. For example, the following situation can occur: A Reader thread increments the global counter and starts examining the data, but before the Reader thread finishes, the user terminates the application. This would cause the global counter variable to become invalid. Bucket doesn't address this situation because it involves only one process. If the global variable were to become invalid, it wouldn't matter because all the other threads would be terminated.

Fixing these cleanup problems should be much easier for you to accomplish in a real application because you'll probably structure your application's code quite differently than Bucket's.

Bucket.ico

BUCKET.C

```
/***************************************************************
Module name: Bucket.C
Notices: Copyright (c) 1993 Jeffrey Richter
***************************************************************/

#include <windows.h>
#include <windowsx.h>
#include <tchar.h>
#include <stdio.h>   // for sprintf
#include <stdlib.h>  // for rand
#include "Bucket.h"


//////////////////////////////////////////////////////////////

// Number of Reader threads examining the bucket.
LONG   g_lNumReaders = -1;

// Synchronization handles.
HANDLE g_hEventDataReady;
HANDLE g_hSemReaders;
HANDLE g_hMutexWriters;

// Window handle of dialog box.
HWND g_hwndDlg = NULL;


//////////////////////////////////////////////////////////////
////// Data and routines for manipulating the Bucket. ///////
//////////////////////////////////////////////////////////////

typedef enum {
   BC_FIRSTBALLCLR,
   // BC_NULL Indicates an empty space in the bucket.
   BC_NULL = BC_FIRSTBALLCLR,
   BC_BLACK,
   BC_RED,
   BC_GREEN,
```

Figure 5-6.   *(continued)*
The Bucket application.

Figure 5-6. *continued*

```
    BC_BLUE,
    BC_WHITE,
    BC_YELLOW,
    BC_ORANGE,
    BC_CYAN,
    BC_GRAY,
    BC_LASTBALLCLR = BC_GRAY
} BALLCOLOR;

const TCHAR *szBallColors[] = {
  NULL,
    __TEXT("Black"),
    __TEXT("Red"),
    __TEXT("Green"),
    __TEXT("Blue"),
    __TEXT("White"),
    __TEXT("Yellow"),
    __TEXT("Orange"),
    __TEXT("Cyan"),
    __TEXT("Gray")
};

#define MAX_BALLS    100

// Initially, the bucket is empty.
BALLCOLOR g_Bucket[MAX_BALLS] = { BC_NULL };

///////////////////////////////////////////////////////////////

void Bucket_AlterContents (void) {

    // Add/remove a randomly colored ball to/from the bucket.
    g_Bucket[rand() % MAX_BALLS] = (BALLCOLOR) (rand() % 10);
}

///////////////////////////////////////////////////////////////

void Bucket_DumpToLB (HWND hwndLB) {

    int nBallNum;
    int nBallColor[BC_LASTBALLCLR - BC_FIRSTBALLCLR + 1] =
        { 0 };

    BALLCOLOR BallColor;
    TCHAR szBuf[50];
```

(continued)

Figure 5-6. *continued*

```
    // Calculate the number of each colored ball in the bucket.
    for (nBallNum = 0; nBallNum < MAX_BALLS; nBallNum++) {
        // Get the color of the nBallNum'th ball.
        BallColor = g_Bucket[nBallNum];

        // Increment the number of balls of this color.
        nBallColor[BallColor]++;
    }

    // Empty the list box.
    ListBox_ResetContent(hwndLB);

    // Build the contents of the list box
    BallColor = BC_FIRSTBALLCLR;
    for (; BallColor <= BC_LASTBALLCLR; BallColor++) {

        if (szBallColors[BallColor] != NULL) {
            _stprintf(szBuf, __TEXT("%s: %*s%2d"),
                szBallColors[BallColor],
                7 - lstrlen(szBallColors[BallColor]), __TEXT(" "),
                nBallColor[BallColor]);
        } else {
            _stprintf(szBuf, __TEXT("Total:   %2d"),
                MAX_BALLS - nBallColor[BallColor]);
        }

        ListBox_AddString(hwndLB, szBuf);
    }
}


//////////////////////////////////////////////////////////////

DWORD WINAPI Writer (LPVOID lpvParam) {
    int nWriterNum = (int) lpvParam, nNumID;

    switch (nWriterNum) {
        case 1:
            nNumID = ID_WRITE1NUM;
            break;

        case 2:
            nNumID = ID_WRITE2NUM;
            break;
    }
```

(continued)

Figure 5-6. *continued*

```
    while (TRUE) {
        // Go to sleep for the user-defined time.
        Sleep(1000 *
            GetDlgItemInt(g_hwndDlg, nNumID, NULL, FALSE));

        // Wait for no other writers to
        // alter the bucket (data).
        WaitForSingleObject(g_hMutexWriters, INFINITE);

        // Block any new readers from beginning to read the
        // contents of the bucket (data).
        ResetEvent(g_hEventDataReady);

        // Wait for any readers still reading the
        // contents of the bucket to finish.
        WaitForSingleObject(g_hSemReaders, INFINITE);

        // No readers can start reading and all readers that
        // were reading have finished.  We can now alter the
        // contents of the bucket.
        Bucket_AlterContents();

        // The contents of the bucket have been altered.
        // Let readers know that the bucket (data) is
        // available to process.
        SetEvent(g_hEventDataReady);

        // Allow any waiting readers to examine the
        // contents of the bucket.
        ReleaseSemaphore(g_hSemReaders, 1, NULL);

        // Allow another writer to reserve its access to the
        // bucket, which will occur when all the readers
        // have finished this pass.
        ReleaseMutex(g_hMutexWriters);
    }

    return(0);
}

//////////////////////////////////////////////////////////////

DWORD WINAPI Reader (LPVOID lpvParam) {
    int nReaderNum = (int) lpvParam, nNumID;
    HWND hwndLB;
```

(continued)

Figure 5-6. *continued*

```
// Get the window handle of the reader's display list box.
// Get the ID of the reader's number static control.
switch (nReaderNum) {
    case 1:
        hwndLB  = GetDlgItem(g_hwndDlg, ID_READ1LIST);
        nNumID = ID_READ1NUM;
        break;

    case 2:
        hwndLB  = GetDlgItem(g_hwndDlg, ID_READ2LIST);
        nNumID = ID_READ2NUM;
        break;

    case 3:
        hwndLB  = GetDlgItem(g_hwndDlg, ID_READ3LIST);
        nNumID = ID_READ3NUM;
        break;
}

while (TRUE) {

    // Go to sleep for the user-defined time.
    Sleep(1000 *
        GetDlgItemInt(g_hwndDlg, nNumID, NULL, FALSE));

    // Wait for the contents of the bucket to be
    // ready for examining.
    WaitForSingleObject(g_hEventDataReady, INFINITE);

    // We want to examine the bucket; increment the
    // number of readers.
    if (InterlockedIncrement(&g_lNumReaders) == 0) {
        // We are the first reader; wait for the semaphore.
        WaitForSingleObject(g_hSemReaders, INFINITE);
    }

    // Examine the contents of the bucket and dump
    // it to the list box.
    Bucket_DumpToLB(hwndLB);

    // We are done examining the bucket; decrement the
    // number of readers.
    if (InterlockedDecrement(&g_lNumReaders) < 0) {
        // We are the last reader; release the semaphore.
        ReleaseSemaphore(g_hSemReaders, 1, NULL);
    }
```

(continued)

Figure 5-6. *continued*

```
   }
   return(0);
}


/////////////////////////////////////////////////////////////

BOOL Dlg_OnInitDialog (HWND hwnd, HWND hwndFocus,
   LPARAM lParam) {

   HANDLE hThread;
   DWORD dwThreadID;

   // Save the handle of the dialog box in a global so that
   // the threads can easily gain access to it.  This must
   // be done before creating the threads.
   g_hwndDlg = hwnd;

   // Associate an icon with the dialog box.
   SetClassLong(hwnd, GCL_HICON, (LONG)
      LoadIcon((HINSTANCE) GetWindowLong(hwnd, GWL_HINSTANCE),
      __TEXT("Bucket")));

   // Initialize the scroll bar values for the bucket writers.
   ScrollBar_SetRange(GetDlgItem(hwnd, ID_WRITE1SCRL),
      0, 60, FALSE);
   ScrollBar_SetPos(GetDlgItem(hwnd, ID_WRITE1SCRL), 5, TRUE);
   SetDlgItemInt(hwnd, ID_WRITE1NUM, 5, FALSE);

   ScrollBar_SetRange(GetDlgItem(hwnd, ID_WRITE2SCRL),
      0, 60, FALSE);
   ScrollBar_SetPos(GetDlgItem(hwnd, ID_WRITE2SCRL), 8, TRUE);
   SetDlgItemInt(hwnd, ID_WRITE2NUM, 8, FALSE);

   // Initialize the scroll bar values for the bucket reader.
   ScrollBar_SetRange(GetDlgItem(hwnd, ID_READ1SCRL),
      0, 60, FALSE);
   ScrollBar_SetPos(GetDlgItem(hwnd, ID_READ1SCRL), 7, TRUE);
   SetDlgItemInt(hwnd, ID_READ1NUM, 3, FALSE);

   ScrollBar_SetRange(GetDlgItem(hwnd, ID_READ2SCRL),
      0, 60, FALSE);
   ScrollBar_SetPos(GetDlgItem(hwnd, ID_READ2SCRL), 23, TRUE);
   SetDlgItemInt(hwnd, ID_READ2NUM, 9, FALSE);
```

(continued)

Figure 5-6.   *continued*

```
    ScrollBar_SetRange(GetDlgItem(hwnd, ID_READ3SCRL),
      0, 60, FALSE);
    ScrollBar_SetPos(GetDlgItem(hwnd, ID_READ3SCRL), 38, TRUE);
    SetDlgItemInt(hwnd, ID_READ3NUM, 14, FALSE);

    // Create all the synchronization objects necessary to
    // coordinate the access to the bucket.
    g_hEventDataReady = CreateEvent(NULL, TRUE, FALSE, NULL);
    g_hSemReaders     = CreateSemaphore(NULL, 1, 1, NULL);
    g_hMutexWriters   = CreateMutex(NULL, FALSE, NULL);

    // Create the two writer and three reader threads.
    // Threads MUST be created AFTER all other
    // synchronization objects.
    hThread = CreateThread(NULL, 0, Writer, (LPVOID) 1,
      0, &dwThreadID);
    CloseHandle(hThread);
    hThread = CreateThread(NULL, 0, Writer, (LPVOID) 2,
      0, &dwThreadID);
    CloseHandle(hThread);
    hThread = CreateThread(NULL, 0, Reader, (LPVOID) 1,
      0, &dwThreadID);
    CloseHandle(hThread);
    hThread = CreateThread(NULL, 0, Reader, (LPVOID) 2,
      0, &dwThreadID);
    CloseHandle(hThread);
    hThread = CreateThread(NULL, 0, Reader, (LPVOID) 3,
      0, &dwThreadID);
    CloseHandle(hThread);

    return(TRUE);
}


////////////////////////////////////////////////////////////////

void Dlg_OnDestroy (HWND hwnd) {
    // When the dialog box is destroyed, clean up
    // the created objects.
    CloseHandle(g_hEventDataReady);
    CloseHandle(g_hSemReaders);
    CloseHandle(g_hMutexWriters);
```

(continued)

Figure 5-6. *continued*

```
    // This sample application doesn't clean up as nicely
    // as it should.  I rely on Windows NT to perform all
    // necessary cleanup, including thread destruction and
    // synchronization object destruction.
}


/////////////////////////////////////////////////////////////

void Dlg_OnHScroll (HWND hwnd, HWND hwndCtl,
   UINT code, int pos) {

   int posCrnt, posMin, posMax;

   posCrnt = ScrollBar_GetPos(hwndCtl);
   ScrollBar_GetRange(hwndCtl, &posMin, &posMax);

   switch (code) {
      case SB_LINELEFT:
         posCrnt--;
         break;

      case SB_LINERIGHT:
         posCrnt++;
         break;

      case SB_PAGELEFT:
         posCrnt -= 10;
         break;

      case SB_PAGERIGHT:
         posCrnt != 10;
         break;

      case SB_THUMBTRACK:
         posCrnt = pos;
         break;

      case SB_LEFT:
         posCrnt = 0;
         break;
```

(continued)

Figure 5-6. *continued*

```
    case SB_RIGHT:
        posCrnt = posMax;
        break;
}

if (posCrnt < 0)
    posCrnt = 0;

if (posCrnt > posMax)
    posCrnt = posMax;

ScrollBar_SetPos(hwndCtl, posCrnt, TRUE);

SetDlgItemInt(hwnd, GetDlgCtrlID(hwndCtl) - 1,
    posCrnt, FALSE);
}

///////////////////////////////////////////////////////////////

void Dlg_OnVScroll (HWND hwnd, HWND hwndCtl,
    UINT code, int pos) {

    int posCrnt, posMin, posMax;

    posCrnt = ScrollBar_GetPos(hwndCtl);
    ScrollBar_GetRange(hwndCtl, &posMin, &posMax);

    switch (code) {
        case SB_LINEUP:
            posCrnt--;
            break;

        case SB_LINEDOWN:
            posCrnt++;
            break;

        case SB_PAGEUP:
            posCrnt -= 10;
            break;

        case SB_PAGEDOWN:
            posCrnt += 10;
            break;
```

(continued)

Figure 5-6.   *continued*

```
        case SB_THUMBTRACK:
            posCrnt = pos;
            break;

        case SB_TOP:
            posCrnt = 0;
            break;

        case SB_BOTTOM:
            posCrnt = posMax;
            break;
    }

    if (posCrnt < 0)
        posCrnt = 0;

    if (posCrnt > posMax)
        posCrnt = posMax;

    ScrollBar_SetPos(hwndCtl, posCrnt, TRUE);

    SetDlgItemInt(hwnd, GetDlgCtrlID(hwndCtl) - 1,
        posCrnt, FALSE);
}


///////////////////////////////////////////////////////////////

void Dlg_OnCommand (HWND hwnd, int id,
    HWND hwndCtl, UINT codeNotify) {

    switch (id) {
        case IDCANCEL:
            EndDialog(hwnd, id);
            break;
    }
}



///////////////////////////////////////////////////////////////

BOOL CALLBACK Dlg_Proc (HWND hDlg, UINT uMsg,
    WPARAM wParam, LPARAM lParam) {

    BOOL fProcessed = TRUE;
```

(continued)

Figure 5-6. *continued*

```
   switch (uMsg) {
      HANDLE_MSG(hDlg, WM_INITDIALOG, Dlg_OnInitDialog);
      HANDLE_MSG(hDlg, WM_DESTROY, Dlg_OnDestroy);
      HANDLE_MSG(hDlg, WM_COMMAND, Dlg_OnCommand);
      HANDLE_MSG(hDlg, WM_HSCROLL, Dlg_OnHScroll);
      HANDLE_MSG(hDlg, WM_VSCROLL, Dlg_OnVScroll);

      default:
         fProcessed = FALSE;
         break;
   }

   return(fProcessed);
}

//////////////////////////////////////////////////////////////

int APIENTRY WinMain (HINSTANCE hInstance,
   HINSTANCE hPrevInstance, LPSTR lpszCmdLine, int nCmdShow) {

   DialogBox(hInstance, MAKEINTRESOURCE(DLG_BUCKET),
      NULL, Dlg_Proc);
   return(0);
}

//////////////////////// End Of File ////////////////////////
```

BUCKET.H
```
/************************************************************
Module name: Bucket.H
Notices: Copyright (c) 1993 Jeffrey Richter
************************************************************/

// Dialog and control IDs.
#define DLG_BUCKET       1
#define ID_WRITE1NUM     100
#define ID_WRITE1SCRL    101
#define ID_WRITE2NUM     102
#define ID_WRITE2SCRL    103
#define ID_READ1NUM      104
#define ID_READ1SCRL     105
```

(continued)

Figure 5-6. *continued*

```
#define ID_READ1LIST      106
#define ID_READ2NUM       107
#define ID_READ2SCRL      108
#define ID_READ2LIST      109
#define ID_READ3NUM       110
#define ID_READ3SCRL      111
#define ID_READ3LIST      112


///////////////////////// End Of File /////////////////////////
```

BUCKET.RC

```
/*****************************************************************
Module name: Bucket.RC
Notices: Copyright (c) 1993 Jeffrey Richter
*****************************************************************/

#include <windows.h>
#include "Bucket.h"

Bucket  ICON  DISCARDABLE Bucket.Ico

DLG_BUCKET DIALOG 12, 48, 216, 168
STYLE WS_POPUP | WS_VISIBLE | WS_CAPTION | WS_SYSMENU |
   WS_BORDER | WS_MINIMIZEBOX
CAPTION "Bucket Synchronization"
FONT 8, "Courier"
BEGIN
   GROUPBOX        "Bucket &Writers", -1, 4, 0, 108, 48
   RTEXT           "1:", -1, 8, 16, 12, 8, SS_NOPREFIX
   RTEXT           "100", ID_WRITE1NUM, 20, 16, 16, 8,
                   SS_NOPREFIX
   SCROLLBAR       ID_WRITE1SCRL, 40, 16, 68, 10
   RTEXT           "2:", -1, 8, 32, 12, 8, SS_NOPREFIX
   RTEXT           "100", ID_WRITE2NUM, 20, 32, 16, 8,
                   SS_NOPREFIX
   SCROLLBAR       ID_WRITE2SCRL, 40, 32, 68, 10
   GROUPBOX        "Bucket &Readers", -1, 4, 56, 208, 108
   RTEXT           "1:", -1, 20, 68, 12, 8, SS_NOPREFIX
   RTEXT           "100", ID_READ1NUM, 36, 68, 16, 8,
                   SS_NOPREFIX
   SCROLLBAR       ID_READ1SCRL, 8, 80, 10, 80, SBS_VERT
```

(continued)

Figure 5-6. *continued*

```
      LISTBOX          ID_READ1LIST, 20, 80, 48, 80,
                       LBS_NOINTEGRALHEIGHT |
                       WS_VSCROLL | WS_TABSTOP
      RTEXT            "2:", -1, 88, 68, 12, 8, SS_NOPREFIX
      RTEXT            "100", ID_READ2NUM, 104, 68, 16, 8,
                       SS_NOPREFIX
      SCROLLBAR        ID_READ2SCRL, 76, 80, 10, 80, SBS_VERT
      LISTBOX          ID_READ2LIST, 88, 80, 48, 80,
                       LBS_NOINTEGRALHEIGHT |
                       WS_VSCROLL | WS_TABSTOP
      RTEXT            "3:", -1, 156, 68, 12, 8, SS_NOPREFIX
      RTEXT            "100", ID_READ3NUM, 172, 68, 16, 8,
                       SS_NOPREFIX
      SCROLLBAR        ID_READ3SCRL, 144, 80, 10, 80, SBS_VERT
      LISTBOX          ID_READ3LIST, 156, 80, 48, 80,
                       LBS_NOINTEGRALHEIGHT |
                       WS_VSCROLL | WS_TABSTOP
   END


///////////////////////// End Of File /////////////////////////
```

Auto-Reset Events

Auto-reset events behave more like mutexes and semaphores than manual-reset events do. When a thread calls SetEvent to signal an event, the event stays signaled until another thread that is waiting for the event is awakened. Just before the waiting thread is resumed, the system automatically resets the event to the not-signaled state. Using an auto-reset event in this way has the effect of allowing only one thread waiting for the event to resume execution. Any other threads waiting for the event are left suspended, still waiting for the event. You also have no control over which of the suspended threads will resume execution—the operating system has total control. This statement is true of not only events but of all synchronization objects. If multiple waits are satisfied, the highest priority thread will run.

You can manipulate an auto-reset event by using the same functions that manipulate a manual-reset event: SetEvent, ResetEvent, and PulseEvent. Usually, you don't use the ResetEvent function, however, because the system automatically resets an auto-reset event before WaitForSingleObject and WaitForMultipleObjects return.

The PulseEvent function performs the same operations for manual-reset events as it does for auto-reset events; that is, PulseEvent signals the event, releases a thread waiting for the event, and resets the

273

event. However, there is one small difference between calling Pulse-Event for an auto-reset event and calling it for a manual-reset event: Pulsing an auto-reset event releases only a single thread that is waiting for the event, even if several threads are waiting. By contrast, pulsing a manual-reset event releases all the threads waiting for the event.

The Document Statistics Sample Application   The Docstats (DOC-STATS.EXE) application, listed in Figure 5-7 beginning on page 277, demonstrates the use of auto-reset events. To run DocStats, enter the following line from a command shell:

```
DOCSTATS PathName
```

PathName indicates any ANSI text file available on your system.

DocStats analyzes the specified file and generates a message box that indicates the number of characters, words, and lines in the file. What makes DocStats exciting is the way it accomplishes this heroic task.

First, DocStats creates three threads—one for each of the items to be counted (characters, words, and lines). These threads will be suspended until a global buffer contains data for them to process. Next, DocStats opens the specified file and loads the first 1024 bytes of the file into the global data buffer. Now that the data is ready to be processed, DocStats must notify the three suspended threads that they can resume execution to process the global data.

While the three threads are processing the file data, the primary thread must suspend itself so that it won't immediately loop around and read the next 1024 bytes from the data file. The primary thread must wait until all three counting threads have completed processing the data before reading the next chunk of data from the file. If the primary thread doesn't wait, reading the next chunk of data overwrites the contents of the global buffer while the three secondary threads are processing it—a big no-no.

When the primary thread has read the last chunk of the file's data, it closes the file, retrieves the results calculated by the three secondary threads, and displays the results of processing the file.

The most interesting aspect of DocStats is how it synchronizes the execution of the primary thread with the three secondary threads. Initially, when the primary thread starts executing, it creates six auto-reset events—two for each secondary thread. One of these events signals a single secondary thread that the primary thread has read the data from the file and that this data can now be processed. The handles to these events are stored in the *g_hEventsDataReady* array. When these events are created, they are initially set to not signaled, which indicates that the data buffer is not ready for processing.

The other event indicates that the secondary thread has processed the file's data contained in the global buffer and that it's suspending itself, waiting for the primary thread to indicate that the next chunk of data has been read and is ready to be processed. The handles to these events are stored in the *g_hEventsProcIdle* array. When these events are created, they are initially set to signaled, which indicates that the secondary threads are idle.

Next, the primary thread creates the three secondary threads. None of these threads are created in the suspended state—all are allowed to begin executing. The handles to these three threads are stored in the *hThread* array. All the threads operate in the same way. After they begin executing, they immediately enter a loop, which will iterate with each chunk of file data read by the primary thread. However, before any of the secondary threads can start processing the global buffer, they must wait until the buffer has been initialized. So, the first action in this loop is a call to WaitForSingleObject, passing in the handle of an event contained in the *g_hEventsDataReady* array.

The primary thread now opens the file and waits for all three of the secondary threads to indicate that they are not processing the data in the global buffer. For the first iteration, all the event handles in the *g_hEventsProcIdle* array are signaled, so the primary thread won't need to wait at all. Now the primary thread reads the first 1024 bytes into the global buffer and, after reading the data, signals the three waiting threads that the data is ready by calling SetEvent three times, once for each event in the *g_hEventsDataReady* array.

When these events become signaled, the secondary threads wake up and begin processing the file's data. Also, because these are auto-reset events, the events are automatically set back to the not-signaled state, indicating that the data is not ready for processing. So the secondary threads have indicated that the data is not ready for processing, but they have already resumed execution and are no longer checking the events. They are running thinking that the data is ready, and it is.

When I was first designing this application, I tried to get by with using only one event to signal that the data was ready. After all, there is only one block of data, and it seemed to me that one event should be able to indicate to all of the secondary threads that the block of data is ready. But, I wasn't able to solve this problem using only a single event.

The reason is because one of the secondary threads would see that the data is ready, and, because an auto-reset event was used, the event would be reset to the not-signaled state. This would happen before any of the other two secondary threads saw that the event had been signaled.

The other two secondary threads would never get a chance to process the data. By using three different events to represent the "data ready" event, each thread can look for its own event without affecting any other threads.

After each of the three secondary threads have scanned the whole buffer, they call SetEvent on their respective event contained in the *g_hEventsProcIdle* array. This call signals back to the primary thread that the secondary thread is finished accessing the buffer. Remember, the primary thread calls WaitForMultipleObjects at the top of its loop. This means that it will wait until all three of the secondary threads have completed processing the buffer and set their respective events to signaled before it reads the next chunk of the file's data.

When the primary thread's call to WaitForMultipleObjects returns, the three *g_hEventsProcIdle* events are automatically reset to their not-signaled state, indicating that the secondary threads are not idle and are processing data. In reality, they are still waiting for the data-ready events to be signaled.

Let's consider what would happen if the *g_hEventsProcIdle* events were not automatically reset to not signaled. And imagine that we're running the program on a single CPU system and that threads are allowed to execute for a full hour before being preempted.

In this case, the primary thread could read the file's data, set the three data-ready events to signaled, and loop back around to the top of its loop. This time, it would be waiting for the three *g_hEventsProcIdle* events to be signaled and, if they weren't automatically reset to not signaled, the wait would end and the primary thread would read the next chunk of data into the buffer all before the secondary threads had a chance to process the contents of the previous chunk—a bug in the program!

Hopefully, you see the problem here. I know that having the CPU dedicated to a single thread for a full hour before preempting it is a bit excessive, but extreme thinking is a good practice when creating multithreaded applications. Writing and designing multithreaded applications isn't easy. A number of possible gotchas can occur. I've found a tremendous help in imagining that the computer system I'm using to implement my application actually preempts threads once an hour.

As it turns out, it took me quite a few tries before I got DocStats to execute correctly. Even a machine that preempts threads every 20 milliseconds is enough for the application to fail. It's just always easier to consider the potential problem up front rather than let the system discover it for you.

Now, back to DocStats. After the primary thread has finished reading all the file's data, the secondary threads must return the results of their calculations. They do this by executing a return statement at the end of their thread functions using the result as the function's return value. Once again, the primary thread calls WaitForMultipleObjects suspending itself until all three secondary threads have terminated. The suspending is done by waiting for the thread handles contained in the *hThreads* array rather than waiting for any events.

After all three of the secondary threads have terminated, the primary thread calls GetExitCodeThread to get each of the thread's return values. The primary thread then calls CloseHandle for all six events and all three threads so that the system resources are freed. Finally, DocStats constructs a string using the three threads' exit codes and displays the results in a message box.

DocStats.ico

DOCSTATS.C

```
/******************************************************************
Module name: DocStats.C
Notices: Copyright (c) 1993 Jeffrey Richter
******************************************************************/

#include <windows.h>
#include <windowsx.h>
#include <tchar.h>
#include <stdio.h>          // for sprintf
#include <string.h>


///////////////////////////////////////////////////////////////////

#define ARRAY_SIZE(A)  (sizeof(A) / sizeof((A)[0]))
```

Figure 5-7.   *(continued)*
The DocStats application.

Figure 5-7. *continued*

```
typedef enum {
    STAT_FIRST = 0,
    STAT_LETTERS = STAT_FIRST,
    STAT_WORDS,
    STAT_LINES,
    STAT_LAST = STAT_LINES
} STATTYPE;

HANDLE g_hEventsDataReady[STAT_LAST - STAT_FIRST + 1];
HANDLE g_hEventsProcIdle[STAT_LAST - STAT_FIRST + 1];

BYTE g_bFileBuf[1024];
DWORD g_dwNumBytesInBuf;

DWORD WINAPI LetterStats (LPVOID lpvParam);
DWORD WINAPI WordStats (LPVOID lpvParam);
DWORD WINAPI LineStats (LPVOID lpvParam);

///////////////////////////////////////////////////////////////////

int APIENTRY WinMain (HINSTANCE hInstance,
    HINSTANCE hPrevInstance, LPSTR lpszCmdLine, int nCmdShow) {

    HANDLE hThreads[STAT_LAST - STAT_FIRST + 1];
    HANDLE hFile;
    DWORD dwNumLetters = 0, dwNumWords = 0, dwNumLines = 0;
    DWORD dwThreadID;
    TCHAR szBuf[150];
    LPTSTR lpszCmdLineT;

    // Get the name of the file the user wants to reverse.
    // We must use GetCommandLine here instead of WinMain's
    // lpszCmdLine parameter because lpszCmdLine is always an
    // ANSI string -- never a Unicode string.  GetCommandLine
    // returns ANSI or Unicode depending on how we
    // have compiled.
    lpszCmdLineT = _tcschr(GetCommandLine(), __TEXT(' '));

    if (lpszCmdLineT != NULL) {
        // We found a space after the executable's filename.
        // Now, let's skip over any white space to get to the
        // first argument.
        while (*lpszCmdLineT == __TEXT(' '))
            lpszCmdLineT++;
    }
```

(continued)

Figure 5-7. *continued*

```
if ((lpszCmdLineT == NULL) || (*lpszCmdLineT == 0)) {
    // If a space was not found or there are no arguments
    // after the executable's filename, display an
    // error message.

    MessageBox(NULL,
        __TEXT("You must enter a filename on ")
        __TEXT("the command line."),
        __TEXT("DocStats"), MB_OK);
    return(0);
}

// Open the file for reading.
hFile = CreateFile(lpszCmdLineT, GENERIC_READ, 0,
    NULL, OPEN_EXISTING, FILE_ATTRIBUTE_NORMAL, NULL);
if (hFile == INVALID_HANDLE_VALUE) {
    // File open failed.
    MessageBox(NULL, __TEXT("File could not be opened."),
        __TEXT("DocStats"), MB_OK);
    return(0);
}

// Signalled when not processing buffer.
g_hEventsDataReady[STAT_LETTERS] =
    CreateEvent(NULL, FALSE, FALSE, NULL);
g_hEventsProcIdle[STAT_LETTERS] =
    CreateEvent(NULL, FALSE, TRUE, NULL);

g_hEventsDataReady[STAT_WORDS] =
    CreateEvent(NULL, FALSE, FALSE, NULL);
g_hEventsProcIdle[STAT_WORDS] =
    CreateEvent(NULL, FALSE, TRUE, NULL);

g_hEventsDataReady[STAT_LINES] =
    CreateEvent(NULL, FALSE, FALSE, NULL);
g_hEventsProcIdle[STAT_LINES] =
    CreateEvent(NULL, FALSE, TRUE, NULL);

// Create all the threads.  Threads MUST be
// created AFTER the event objects.
hThreads[STAT_LETTERS] =
    CreateThread(NULL, 0, LetterStats, NULL, 0, &dwThreadID);
hThreads[STAT_WORDS]   =
    CreateThread(NULL, 0, WordStats,   NULL, 0, &dwThreadID);
hThreads[STAT_LINES]   =
    CreateThread(NULL, 0, LineStats,   NULL, 0, &dwThreadID);
```

(continued)

Figure 5-7. *continued*

```
do {
   // Wait for the worker threads to be idle.
   WaitForMultipleObjects(STAT_LAST - STAT_FIRST + 1,
      g_hEventsProcIdle, TRUE, INFINITE);

   // Read part of the file into the global memory buffer.
   ReadFile(hFile, g_bFileBuf, ARRAY_SIZE(g_bFileBuf),
      &g_dwNumBytesInBuf, NULL);

   // Signal the works that the data is ready.
   SetEvent(g_hEventsDataReady[STAT_LETTERS]);
   SetEvent(g_hEventsDataReady[STAT_WORDS]);
   SetEvent(g_hEventsDataReady[STAT_LINES]);

} while (g_dwNumBytesInBuf != 0);

// All the statistics for the file have been accumulated;
// time to clean up.
CloseHandle(hFile);

// Wait for all of the threads to return.
WaitForMultipleObjects(STAT_LAST - STAT_FIRST + 1, hThreads,
   TRUE, INFINITE);

GetExitCodeThread(hThreads[STAT_LETTERS], &dwNumLetters);
CloseHandle(hThreads[STAT_LETTERS]);
CloseHandle(g_hEventsDataReady[STAT_LETTERS]);
CloseHandle(g_hEventsProcIdle[STAT_LETTERS]);

GetExitCodeThread(hThreads[STAT_WORDS], &dwNumWords);
CloseHandle(hThreads[STAT_WORDS]);
CloseHandle(g_hEventsDataReady[STAT_WORDS]);
CloseHandle(g_hEventsProcIdle[STAT_WORDS]);

GetExitCodeThread(hThreads[STAT_LINES], &dwNumLines);
CloseHandle(hThreads[STAT_LINES]);
CloseHandle(g_hEventsDataReady[STAT_LINES]);
CloseHandle(g_hEventsProcIdle[STAT_LINES]);

_stprintf(szBuf,
   __TEXT("Num letters = %d, Num words = %d, ")
   __TEXT("Num lines = %d"),
   dwNumLetters, dwNumWords, dwNumLines);
```

(continued)

Figure 5-7.   *continued*

```
   MessageBox(NULL, szBuf, __TEXT("DocStats"), MB_OK);
   return(0);
}


//////////////////////////////////////////////////////////////

DWORD WINAPI LetterStats (LPVOID lpvParam) {
   DWORD dwNumLetters = 0, dwByteIndex;
   BYTE bByte;

   do {
      // Wait for the data to be ready.
      WaitForSingleObject(g_hEventsDataReady[STAT_LETTERS],
         INFINITE);

      dwByteIndex = 0;
      for (; dwByteIndex < g_dwNumBytesInBuf; dwByteIndex++) {

         bByte = g_bFileBuf[dwByteIndex];

         // This program works only on ANSI files.  Regardless
         // of whether we compile DOCSTATS for ANSI or
         // UNICODE, we must always call the ANSI version of
         // IsCharAlpha.
         if (IsCharAlphaA(bByte))
            dwNumLetters++;
      }

      // Data processed; signal that we are done.
      SetEvent(g_hEventsProcIdle[STAT_LETTERS]);
   } while (g_dwNumBytesInBuf > 0);

   return(dwNumLetters);
}


//////////////////////////////////////////////////////////////

DWORD WINAPI WordStats (LPVOID lpvParam) {
   DWORD dwNumWords = 0, dwByteIndex;
   BYTE bByte;
   BOOL fInWord = FALSE, fIsWordSep;
```

(continued)

Figure 5-7. *continued*

```
    do {
        // Wait for the data to be ready.
        WaitForSingleObject(g_hEventsDataReady[STAT_WORDS],
            INFINITE);

        dwByteIndex = 0;
        for (; dwByteIndex < g_dwNumBytesInBuf; dwByteIndex++) {

            bByte = g_bFileBuf[dwByteIndex];

            // This program only works on ANSI files.  Regardless
            // of whether we compile DOCSTATS for ANSI or
            // UNICODE, we must always call the ANSI version
            // of strchr.
            fIsWordSep = (strchr(" \t\n\r", bByte) != NULL);

            if (!fInWord && !fIsWordSep) {
                dwNumWords++;
                fInWord = TRUE;
            } else {
                if (fInWord && fIsWordSep) {
                    fInWord = FALSE;
                }
            }
        }

        // Data processed; signal that we are done.
        SetEvent(g_hEventsProcIdle[STAT_WORDS]);
    } while (g_dwNumBytesInBuf > 0);

    return(dwNumWords);
}


//////////////////////////////////////////////////////////////////

DWORD WINAPI LineStats (LPVOID lpvParam) {
    DWORD dwNumLines = 0, dwByteIndex;
    BYTE bByte;

    do {
        // Wait for the data to be ready.
        WaitForSingleObject(g_hEventsDataReady[STAT_LINES],
            INFINITE);
```

(continued)

Figure 5-7. *continued*

```
     dwByteIndex = 0;
     for (; dwByteIndex < g_dwNumBytesInBuf; dwByteIndex++) {

        bByte = g_bFileBuf[dwByteIndex];

        // This program works only on ANSI files.  Regardless
        // of whether we compile DOCSTATS for ANSI or
        // UNICODE, we must always compare the byte to an
        // ANSI version of '\n'.
        if ('\n' == bByte)
           dwNumLines++;
     }

     // Data processed; signal that we are done.
     SetEvent(g_hEventsProcIdle[STAT_LINES]);

  } while (g_dwNumBytesInBuf > 0);

  return(dwNumLines);
}

//////////////////////// End Of File ////////////////////////
```

DOCSTATS.H

```
/*************************************************************
Module name: DocStats.H
Notices: Copyright (c) 1993 Jeffrey Richter
*************************************************************/

// Dialog and control IDs.

//////////////////////// End Of File ////////////////////////
```

DOCSTATS.RC

```
/*************************************************************
Module name: DocStats.RC
Notices: Copyright (c) 1993 Jeffrey Richter
*************************************************************/

DocStats  ICON  DISCARDABLE DocStats.Ico

//////////////////////// End Of File ////////////////////////
```

Thread Suspension

WaitForSingleObject and WaitForMultipleObjects are definitely the most commonly used functions that a thread can call to suspend itself until certain criteria are met. However, there are a few other functions that a thread can call to suspend itself. The following sections discuss these briefly.

Sleep

The simplest of these functions is Sleep:

```
VOID Sleep(DWORD cMilliseconds);
```

This function causes the thread to suspend itself until *cMilliseconds* have elapsed. Note that Sleep allows a thread to voluntarily give up the remainder of its time slice. Even a call to Sleep passing in a value of 0 (zero) causes the CPU to stop executing the current thread and assign itself to the next waiting thread. The CritSecs program discussed earlier uses this technique.

Asynchronous File I/O

Windows NT offers asynchronous file I/O, which is an application's capability to start a file read or write operation without stopping the thread from executing. For example, if an application needs to load a large file into memory, the application could tell Windows NT to load the file into memory, and, as Windows NT loads the file, the application can be busy performing other tasks—creating windows, initializing internal data structures, and so on. When the initialization is complete, the application can suspend itself waiting for Windows NT to notify it that the file has been read.

File handles are synchronizable objects in Windows NT, which means that you can call WaitForSingleObject passing the handle of a file. While Windows NT is performing the asynchronous I/O, the handle is not signaled. As soon as the file operation is complete, Windows NT changes the handle to signaled so that the application knows the file operation has completed. At this point, the thread continues execution.

Asynchronous file I/O is discussed in more detail in Chapter 9.

WaitForInputIdle

A thread can also suspend itself by calling WaitForInputIdle:

```
DWORD WaitForInputIdle(HANDLE hProcess, DWORD dwTimeout);
```

This function waits until the process identified by *hProcess* has no input pending in the thread that created the application's first window. This function is useful for a parent process. The parent process spawns a child process to do some work. When the parent process calls CreateProcess, the parent process continues to execute while the child process is initializing. It might be that the parent process needs to get the handle of a window created by the child. The only way for the parent process to know when the child process has been fully initialized is for the parent to wait until the child is no longer processing any input. So, after the call to CreateProcess, the parent would place a call to WaitForInputIdle.

Another example of using WaitForInputIdle is when you need to force keystrokes into an application. Let's say that you post the following messages to the main window of an application:

WM_KEYDOWN	with a virtual key of VK_MENU
WM_KEYDOWN	with a virtual key of VK_F
WM_KEYUP	with a virtual key of VK_F
WM_KEYUP	with a virtual key of VK_MENU
WM_KEYDOWN	with a virtual key of VK_O
WM_KEYUP	with a virtual key of VK_O

This sequence has the effect of sending Alt+F, O to an application, which, for most English language applications, will select the application's File Open menu command. Selecting this command displays a dialog box; however, before the dialog box can appear, Windows must load the dialog box template from the file and cycle through all the controls in the template, calling CreateWindow for each one. This can take some time. So the application that posted the WM_KEY* messages can now call WaitForInputIdle, which causes the application to wait until the dialog box has been completely created and is ready for user input. The application can now force additional keys into the dialog box and its controls so that it can continue doing whatever it needs to do.

This particular problem was faced by many developers under 16-bit Windows. Applications wanted to post messages to a window but didn't know exactly when the window was created and ready. The WaitFor-InputIdle function solves this problem.

MsgWaitForMultipleObjects

A thread can call the MsgWaitForMultipleObjects function to cause the thread to wait for its own messages:

```
DWORD MsgWaitForMultipleObjects(DWORD dwCount, LPHANDLE lpHandles,
    BOOL bWaitAll, DWORD dwMilliseconds, DWORD dwWakeMask);
```

The MsgWaitForMultipleObjects function is similar to the WaitFor-MultipleObjects function with the addition of the *dwWakeMask* parameter. This parameter can be used by an application to determine if it should awaken to process certain types of messages. For example, if a thread wants to suspend itself until any keyboard or mouse messages are in the queue, the application can make the following call:

```
MsgWaitForMultipleObjects(0, NULL, TRUE, INFINITE,
    QS_KEY | QS_MOUSE);
```

This statement says that we're not passing any handles of synchronization objects, as indicated by passing 0 (zero) and NULL for the *dwCount* and *lpHandles* parameters. We're telling the function to wait for all objects to be signaled. But, because we're specifying only one object to wait on, the *fWaitAll* parameter could have easily been FALSE without altering the effect of this call. We are also telling Windows NT that we want to wait forever until either a keyboard message or a mouse message is available in the thread's input queue.

The legal domain of possible values that can be specified in the last parameter are the same as the values that can be passed to the Get-QueueStatus function, which is discussed in Chapter 6. The MsgWait-ForMultipleObjects function can be useful if you are waiting for a particular object to become signaled and you want to allow the user to interrupt the wait. If you are waiting for the object to become signaled and the user presses a key, the thread is awakened and the MsgWaitFor-MultipleObjects function returns. Normally, when the WaitForMultiple-Objects function returns, it returns the index of the object that became signaled to satisfy the call (0 to *dwCount* − 1). The addition of the *dwWakeMask* parameter is like adding an additional handle to the call. If MsgWaitForMultipleObjects is satisfied because of the wake mask, the return value will be *dwCount*. The FileChng application in Chapter 9 demonstrates how to use this function.

WaitForDebugEvent

Windows NT has very good debugging support built right into the operating system. When a debugger starts executing, it attaches itself to a debugee. The debugger simply sits idle waiting for the operating system to notify it of debug events related to the debugee. A debugger waits for these events by calling:

```
BOOL WaitForDebugEvent(LPDEBUG_EVENT lpde, DWORD dwTimeout);
```

When a debugger calls WaitForDebugEvent, the debugger's thread is suspended. Windows NT notifies the debugger that a debug event has occurred by allowing the call to WaitForDebugEvent to return. The structure pointed to by the *lpde* parameter is filled by Windows NT before it awakens the thread. This structure contains information regarding the debug event that has just occurred.

The Interlocked Family of Functions

The last three functions we'll discuss are InterlockedIncrement, InterlockedDecrement, and InterlockedExchange:

```
LONG InterlockedIncrement(LPLONG lplValue);

LONG InterlockedDecrement(LPLONG lplValue);

LONG InterlockedExchange(LPLONG lplTarget, LONG lValue);
```

The sole purpose of these functions is to change the value of a long variable. These functions guarantee that the thread changing the long variable has exclusive access to this variable—no other thread will be able to change this variable at the same time. This is true even if the two threads are executed simultaneously by two different CPUs in the same machine.

It is important to note that all the threads should attempt to modify the shared long variable by calling these functions; no thread should ever attempt to modify the shared variable by using simple C statements:

```
// The long variable shared by many threads.
LONG lValue;
    .
    .
    .
```

(continued)

```
// Incorrect way to increment the long.
lValue++;
.
.
.
// Correct way to increment the long.
InterlockedIncrement(&lValue);
```

Normally, the way to protect the long variable from being corrupted would be to use a form of synchronization, such as mutexes. But, because the manipulation of a long variable is so useful, Microsoft added these three functions to the Win32 API.

The calls to InterlockedIncrement and InterlockedDecrement add 1 to and subtract 1 from the long variable whose address you pass as the *lplValue* parameter to the functions. These functions *do not* return the new value of the long variable. Instead, they return a value that compares the new value of the long to 0 (zero). If the result of incrementing or decrementing the long variable causes the long variable to be 0, the function returns 0. If the value of the long becomes less than 0, the functions return a value that is less than 0. And you can probably guess that if the long variable becomes greater than 0, the functions return a value that is greater than 0. The return value is almost never the actual value of the long variable. I use both of these functions in the MULTINST.C and MODUSE.C source files, which are described in Chapter 7.

The third function, InterlockedExchange, is used to completely replace the current value of the long whose address is passed in the *lplTarget* parameter with a long value that is passed in the *lValue* parameter. Again, this function protects the long variable from any other thread that is attempting to change the variable at the same time.

Another point about using these functions: No Interlocked function is available so a thread can read the value of a long while another thread is attempting to change the long because the function isn't necessary. If one thread calls InterlockedIncrement while another thread reads the contents of the long, the value read from the long will always be valid. The thread might get the value of the long before InterlockedIncrement changes the variable, or the thread might get the value after InterlockedIncrement changes the value. The thread has no idea which value it gets, but it is guaranteed to get a valid value and not a value that is partially incremented.

THE WIN32 SUBSYSTEM ENVIRONMENT

Microsoft had some pretty big goals in mind when it started designing Windows NT: virtual memory management, preemptive multitasking, and security, just to name a few. Backward compatibility with 16-bit Windows was also very important. If Windows NT becomes successful, it will be so partly because it rides the coattails of 16-bit Windows. Of course, Windows NT also offers several improvements and enhancements over 16-bit Windows in order to make it more attractive and compelling to end users.

This chapter discusses the Win32 subsystem environment under Windows NT. As you will see, many things had to change from the 16-bit Windows environment. But, as you would expect, Microsoft attempted to make the changes as small as possible in order to preserve backward compatibility while making the system robust and immune to ill-behaved applications.

Multitasking

I think multitasking is the single most important new feature that separates 16-bit Windows from Windows NT. Although 16-bit Windows can run multiple applications simultaneously, it runs the applications non-preemptively. That is, one application must tell Windows it's finished processing before the scheduler can assign another application execution time, which creates problems for both users and application developers.

For users, it means that control of the system is lost for an arbitrary time period decided by the application (not the user). If an application takes a long time to execute a particular task, such as formatting a floppy disk, the user can't switch away from that task and work with a word processor while the formatting continues in the background. This situation is unfortunate because users want to make the most of their time and not wait for the machine to finish.

Developers for 16-bit Windows recognize this and try to implement their applications so that they execute tasks in spurts. For example, a formatting program might format a single track on a floppy disk and then return control to Windows. Once Windows has control, it can respond to other tasks for the user. When the user is idle, Windows returns control back to the format program so that another track can be formatted.

Well, this method of sharing time between tasks works, but it makes implementing a program significantly more difficult. One way the formatting program can accomplish its tasks is to set a timer for itself using the SetTimer function. The program is then notified with WM_TIMER messages when it's time to execute another part of the process. This type of implementation involves the following problems:

1. Windows offers a limited number of timers for application use. What should the program do if a timer is not available—not allow the user to format a disk until another application using a timer is terminated?

2. The program must keep track of its progress. The formatting program must save, either in global variables or in a dynamically allocated block of memory, information such as the letter of the drive it is formatting, the track that has just been formatted, etc.

3. The program code can't include a function that formats a disk; instead it must include a function that formats a single track of a disk. This means that the functions in the program must be broken up in a way that is not natural for a programmer to implement. You don't usually design an algorithm thinking that the processor needs to be able to jump into the middle of it. You can imagine how difficult implementation would be if your algorithm required a series of nested loops to perform its operations and the processor needed to jump into the innermost loop.

4. WM_TIMER messages occur at regular intervals. So if an application sets a timer to go off every second, WM_TIMER messages are received 60 times every minute. This is true whether a user is running the application on a 25-MHz 386 or a 50-MHz 486. If a user has a faster machine, the program should take advantage of that.

Another favorite method used by 16-bit Windows developers to help their applications behave more courteously towards other applications involves the PeekMessage function. When an application calls PeekMessage, it tells Windows, ''I have more work to process, but I'm willing to postpone doing it if another application needs to do something.''

Using this method makes the code easier to implement because the implementer can design the algorithms assuming that the computer won't jump into the middle of a process. This method also doesn't require any timers and doesn't have any special system resource requirements. It does have two problems, however: The implementer must sprinkle PeekMessage loops throughout the code, and the application must be written to handle all kinds of asynchronous events. For example, a spreadsheet might be recalculating cell values when another application attempts to initiate a DDE conversation with it. It is incredibly difficult to test your application to verify that it performs correctly in all possible scenarios.

As it turns out, even when developers use these methods to help their applications behave in a friendlier way, their programs still don't multitask smoothly. Sometimes a user might click on another application's window, and a full second or more might go by before Windows changes to the active application. More important though, if an application bug causes the application to never call PeekMessage or to never return control back to Windows, the entire 16-bit Windows system effectively hangs. At this point, the user can't switch to another application, can't save to disk any work that was in progress, and more often than not, is forced to reboot the computer. This is totally unacceptable!

Windows NT solves these problems (and more that I haven't even mentioned) with preemptive multitasking. By adding a preemptive multitasking capability to Windows NT, Microsoft has done much more than allow multiple applications to run simultaneously. The environment is much more robust because a single application can't control all the system resources.

Preemptive Time Scheduling

16-bit Windows has only one thread of execution. That is, the microprocessor travels in a linear path from functions in one application to functions in another application, frequently dipping into the operating system's code. Whenever the user moves from executing one application, or task, to another, the operating system code performs a task switch. A task switch simply means that the operating system saves the state of the CPU's registers before deactivating the current task and restores the registers for the newly activated task. Notice that I said the operating system is responsible for performing the task switch. Because the system has only one thread of execution, if any code enters an infinite loop the thread can never access the operating system code that performed the task switch, and the system hangs.

16-bit Windows uses the concepts of modules and tasks. A module identifies an executable file that is loaded into memory. Every time an instance of the executable file is invoked, 16-bit Windows calls this instance a task. With few exceptions, resources (that is, memory blocks or windows) created (allocated) when the task is executing become owned by the particular task. Some resources, such as icons and cursors, are actually owned by the module, which allows these resources to be shared by all of the module's tasks.

Windows NT still uses the term module to identify an executable file loaded into memory. However, Windows NT takes the concept of a task and breaks it down into two new concepts—*processes* and *threads.*

A process refers to an instance of a running program. For example, if a single instance of Clock and two instances of Notepad are running, three processes are running in the system. A thread describes a path of execution within a process. When an executable file is invoked, Windows NT creates both a process and a thread. For example, when the user invokes an application from the Program Manager, Windows NT locates the program's EXE file, creates a process and a thread for the new instance, and tells the CPU to start executing the thread beginning with the C Runtime startup code, which in turn calls your WinMain function. When the application terminates (returns from WinMain), Windows NT destroys the thread.

Every process has at least one thread. Windows NT schedules CPU time among threads of a process, not among processes themselves. After a thread begins executing, it can create additional threads within the process. These threads execute until they are destroyed or until they terminate on their own. The number of threads that can be created is limited only by system resources.

While a thread is executing, Windows NT can steal the CPU away from the thread and give the CPU to another thread. But the CPU cannot be interrupted while it is executing a single instruction (a CPU instruction, not a line of source code). The operating system's ability to interrupt a thread at (almost) any time and assign the CPU to a waiting thread is called *preemptive multitasking.*

The life span of a process is directly tied to the threads it owns. Threads within a process have lives of their own, too. New threads are created, existing threads are paused and restarted, and other threads are terminated. When all the threads in a process terminate, Windows NT terminates the process, frees any resources owned by the process, and removes the process from memory.

Most objects allocated by a thread are owned by the process that also owns the thread. For example, a block of memory allocated by a thread is owned by the process, not the thread. All the global and static variables in an application are also owned by the process. And all GDI objects (pens, brushes, bitmaps) are owned by the process. Most USER objects (windows, menus, accelerator tables) are owned by the thread that created or loaded them into memory. Only three USER objects—icons, cursors, and window classes—are owned by a process instead of by a thread.

An understanding of ownership is important so that you know what can be shared. If a process has seven threads operating within it and one thread makes a call to allocate a block of memory, the block of memory can then be accessed from any of the seven threads. This access can cause several problems if all the threads attempt to read and write from the same block simultaneously. Synchronizing several threads is discussed further in Chapter 5.

Ownership is also important because Windows NT is much better than 16-bit Windows about cleaning up after a thread or a process after it terminates. If a thread terminates and neglects to destroy a window that it created, the system ensures that the window is destroyed and isn't just sitting around somewhere soaking up precious memory and system resources. For example, if a thread creates or loads a cursor into memory and then the thread is terminated, the cursor is not destroyed. This is because the cursor is owned by the process and not by the thread. When the process terminates, the system ensures that the cursor is destroyed.

In 16-bit Windows, a task has the equivalent of one and only one thread. As a result, the concept of ownership is less complicated.

Windows NT's Client/Server Architecture

Windows NT makes extensive use of a client/server architecture, illustrated in Figure 6-1. The Windows NT Executive is responsible for process and thread management and memory allocation but doesn't have anything to do with the user interface. The Win32 subsystem provides the graphical user interface and controls all user input (USER) and application output (GDI). As the figure shows, the Win32 subsystem is really not much more than an application—like any application you write. It's special because the system loads the Win32 subsystem as soon as the operating system starts running and because the Win32 subsystem is used by all applications, including the OS/2 and POSIX subsystems.

In a Win32 application, threads frequently make calls to functions that need to have work performed by the subsystem. An application that creates a window is a classic example. The Win32 subsystem is responsible for maintaining a list of all the windows that have been created by any and all processes running in the system. When you create a window, the Win32 subsystem is responsible for allocating the internal data structure that describes the window and for adding this new data structure to its list of windows.

This relationship between your application and the Win32 subsystem is a client/server relationship. Your application is the client making requests of the Win32 subsystem, which acts as the server. In order for your application to make requests of the server, it needs the server to create an agent thread. In other words, if a thread in your process makes any function calls that require work to be performed by the Win32 subsystem, the subsystem creates a thread that runs in the subsystem's address space and has sole responsibility for servicing your thread's requests. So if you have three threads in your process and all three call CreateWindow, three agent threads will exist in the Win32 subsystem process acting on behalf of your threads. If your process contains a thread that simply performs some operations and never makes any calls that require the help of the Win32 subsystem, a complementary agent thread will not be created in the subsystem.

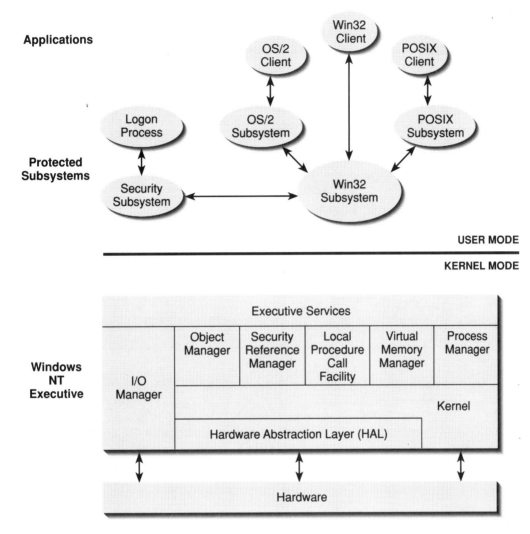

Figure 6-1.
Windows NT's client/server architecture.

How a Process Thread and an Agent Thread Work Together

In the example of an application that creates a window, your process creates a thread and the Win32 subsystem creates an agent thread. These two threads will never execute simultaneously—one of them is always suspended. The following describes how they work together.

The thread in your process attempts to create a window by calling CreateWindow. The code for the CreateWindow function is located in a dynamic-link library (DLL) called USER32.DLL. USER32.DLL was automatically mapped into the address space when the process loaded into memory. The code in this DLL doesn't do very much at all. It packages all the parameters passed to CreateWindow into a block of memory that is shared between your process and the Win32 subsystem, and it executes a *local procedure call* (LPC). A local procedure call is an internal system mechanism that allows a function in one process to call a function in another process, as shown in Figure 6-2. An LPC is faster than a *remote procedure call* (RPC), which allows functions to be called on another machine connected to a network.

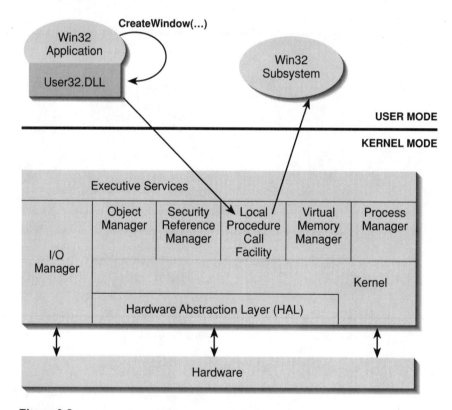

Figure 6-2.
A call to CreateWindow from a process's thread causes a local procedure call to the Win32 subsystem, which actually performs the work.

When USER32.DLL makes the LPC call, your thread becomes suspended and its corresponding agent thread in the Win32 subsystem is awakened. When the Win32 subsystem thread awakens, it unpacks the parameters from the shared memory block and performs the work necessary to create the window. This work requires it to allocate a data structure for the window object and initialize its values. Because the data structure is allocated while the Win32 subsystem is the active process, the structure is in the Win32 subsystem's address space. Your process has absolutely no direct access to the contents of this data block.

After the window has been created, the handle to the window is placed back into the shared block of memory, and the LPC call returns. When the call returns, the Win32 subsystem's thread is suspended and the thread in your process is awakened.[1] Your process's thread is still executing the code in the USER32.DLL CreateWindow function. Before CreateWindow returns, it unpacks the return value from the block of memory and then returns the window handle.

This is an awful lot of work just to create a window. LPC calls are necessary not only for creating windows but for almost all the USER and GDI functions.

You'll notice that I left Kernel (memory management) calls out of this discussion. When your process calls a function in KERNEL32.DLL, the code in the function interprets the call and in turn calls the Windows NT Executive. The Win32 subsystem doesn't get involved in any of your process's kernel-mode calls because of memory allocation and speed. For example, let's say that you want to allocate a block of memory. If a call to HeapAlloc were to make an LPC call to a function in the Win32 subsystem to allocate the memory, the memory would be allocated out of the subsystem's address space—not your process's. This is certainly not what you want. Also, the LPC mechanism is slow, and the fewer operations that need to be performed this way, the better.

LPC calls aren't necessary for all USER and GDI functions. Whenever possible, Microsoft implemented functions entirely in the USER32.DLL or GDI32.DLL so that applications can run faster. For example, the PtInRect function in USER32.DLL determines whether a specified point is contained within a specified rectangle. This function doesn't require any knowledge of server-side data structures, and its code is located in the USER32.DLL: No context switches need to be made to the subsystem to get PtInRect's return value.

---

1. These threads are synchronized by using a special form of an event object called an *event pair*. Events are discussed in Chapter 5.

Thread Information

At the time a thread is created, the Win32 subsystem associates a THREADINFO structure with the thread. THREADINFO is an internal (undocumented) data structure that identifies the thread's message queue, virtualized input queue, and wake flags. Figure 6-3 illustrates how THREADINFO structures are associated with three threads.

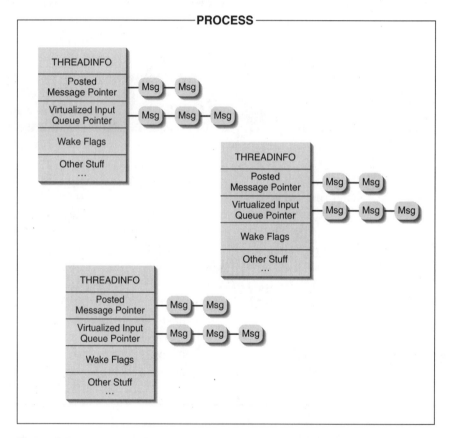

Figure 6-3.
Three threads with their THREADINFO structures.

In 16-bit Windows, each task has its own message queue so that every application doesn't have to process the messages destined for other applications. By default, this message queue is large enough to hold up to eight messages. An application is able to increase or decrease the queue size by calling SetMessageQueue. This function exists in the

Win32 API but is obsolete and doesn't do anything because messages are stored in a linked list with no limit on the number of messages that can be placed in the list. In the Win32 subsystem, each thread's message queue is maintained as a doubly-linked list. As messages are posted to the queue, MSG structures are linked onto the end of the linked list. When a message is pulled off the message queue, the Win32 subsystem returns the first message in the linked list. The THREADINFO structure actually contains the pointer to the first message in the linked list rather than the actual message queue.

In addition to maintaining the message queue, the THREAD-INFO structure maintains a pointer to a virtualized input queue, where hardware input events, such as WM_MOUSEMOVE and WM_KEY-DOWN, are stored. This queue is analogous to the system queue in 16-bit Windows.

The wake flags are a set of bits that are used when the thread has at least one window associated with it. The flags indicate that the thread should be awakened so that a message can be processed. The Get-QueueStatus function, shown below, returns the status of the wake flags:

```
DWORD GetQueueStatus(UINT fuFlags);
```

The *fuFlags* parameter is a flag or a series of flags *OR*ed together that allows you to test for specific wake bits. The table below shows the possible flag values and their meanings:

Flag	Message in the Queue
QS_KEY	WM_KEYUP, WM_KEYDOWN, WM_SYSKEYUP, or WM_SYSKEYDOWN
QS_MOUSE	Same as QS_MOUSEMOVE | QS_MOUSEBUTTON
QS_MOUSEMOVE	WM_MOUSEMOVE
QS_MOUSEBUTTON	WM_?BUTTON*[2]
QS_PAINT	WM_PAINT
QS_POSTMESSAGE	Posted message (other than from a hardware input event)
QS_SENDMESSAGE	Message sent by another thread or process
QS_TIMER	WM_TIMER
QS_HOTKEY	WM_HOTKEY

2. Where ? is L, M , or R and * is DOWN, UP, or DBLCLK.   *(continued)*

Flag	Message in the Queue
QS_INPUT	Same as QS_MOUSE | WS_KEY
QS_ALLEVENTS	Same as QS_INPUT | QS_POSTMESSAGE | QS_TIMER | QS_PAINT | QS_HOTKEY[3]
QS_ALLINPUT	Same as QS_ALLEVENTS | QS_SENDMESSAGE

When you call the GetQueueStatus function, the *fuFlags* parameter tells GetQueueStatus the types of messages to check for in the queues. The fewer the number of QS_* identifiers you *OR* together, the faster the call executes. Then, when GetQueueStatus returns, the types of messages currently in the queue can be found in the high-word of the return value. This returned set of flags will always be a subset of what you asked for. For example, if you make the following call,

```
BOOL fPaintMsgWaiting = GetQueueStatus(QS_TIMER) & QS_PAINT;
```

the value of *fPaintMsgWaiting* will always be FALSE whether or not a WM_PAINT message is waiting in the queue because QS_PAINT was not specified as a flag in the parameter passed to GetQueueStatus.

The low-word of GetQueueStatus's return value indicates the types of messages that have been added to the queue and that haven't been processed since the last call to GetQueueStatus, GetMessage, or PeekMessage.

Not all the wake flags are treated equally. For the QS_MOUSEMOVE flag, as long as an unprocessed WM_MOUSEMOVE message exists in the queue, the flag is turned on. When GetMessage or PeekMessage (with PM_REMOVE) pulls the last WM_MOUSEMOVE message from the queue, the flag is turned off until a new WM_MOUSEMOVE message is placed in the input queue. The QS_KEY, QS_MOUSEBUTTON, and QS_HOTKEY flags work in the same way for their respective messages.

The QS_PAINT flag is handled differently. If a window created by the thread has an invalid region, the QS_PAINT flag is turned on. When the area occupied by all windows created by this thread becomes validated (usually by a call to ValidateRect, ValidateRegion, or BeginPaint), the QS_PAINT flag is turned off. It's only when all windows are validated that this flag is turned off. Calling GetMessage or PeekMessage has no effect on this wake flag.

---

3. The QS_SENDMESSAGE flag is not *OR*ed into the QS_ALLEVENTS flag because it's reserved for internal use by the system.

The QS_POSTMESSAGE flag is set whenever at least one message is in the thread's message queue. This doesn't include hardware event messages that are in the thread's virtualized input queue. When all the messages in the thread's message queue have been processed and the queue is empty, this flag is reset.

The QS_TIMER flag is set whenever a timer (created by the thread) goes off. After the WM_TIMER event is returned by GetMessage or PeekMessage, the QS_TIMER flag is reset until the timer goes off again.

The QS_SENDMESSAGE flag indicates that another thread has sent a message to a window that was created by your thread. This flag is used by the system internally to identify and process messages being sent from one thread to another. It's not used for messages that a thread sends to itself. Although you can use the QS_SENDMESSAGE flag, it's very rare that you need to. I've never seen an application use this flag.

Inside the THREADINFO structure are some additional flags that are not returned by the GetQueueStatus function. For example, when an application calls PostQuitMessage, the QS_QUIT flag is turned on. A WM_QUIT message is not appended to the thread's message queue. This flag is simply turned on.

Now, you're probably wondering how Windows NT determines what message to return when you call GetMessage or PeekMessage. Figure 6-4 illustrates the process, and the following list describes the steps in the figure.

1. If the QS_SENDMESSAGE flag is turned on, Windows NT sends the message to the proper window procedure. Get-Message doesn't return to the application after the window procedure has processed the message; instead, it sits and waits for another message to process.

2. If there are messages in the thread's message queue, Windows NT fills the MSG structure passed to it when the application called GetMessage or PeekMessage and then returns. The application's message loop usually calls DispatchMessage at this point to have the message processed by the appropriate window procedure.

3. If the QS_QUIT flag is turned on, Windows NT returns a WM_QUIT message to the thread and resets the flag.

302

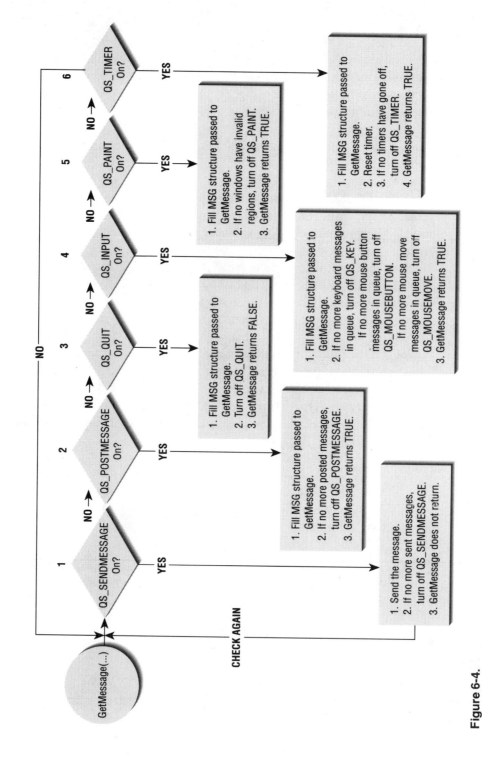

Figure 6-4.
How messages are retrieved for a thread.

4. If there are messages in the thread's virtualized input queue, Windows NT returns the hardware input message.

5. If the QS_PAINT flag is turned on, Windows NT returns a WM_PAINT message for the proper window.

6. If the QS_TIMER flag is turned on, Windows NT returns a WM_TIMER message.

It might be hard to believe, but there's a reason for this madness. The big assumption that Microsoft made when designing this algorithm was that applications should be user driven and that the user drives the applications by creating hardware inputs (keyboard and mouse operations). While using an application, the user might click a mouse button, which causes a sequence of events to occur. An application makes each of these events occur by posting messages to a thread's message queue.

So if you press the mouse button, the window that processes the WM_LBUTTONDOWN message might post three messages to different windows. Because it's the hardware event that sparks these three software events, the system processes the software events before sending the user's next hardware event. This explains why the message queue is checked before the input queue.

An excellent example of this is a call to TranslateMessage. The TranslateMessage function checks whether a WM_KEYDOWN or a WM_SYSKEYDOWN message was retrieved from the input queue, and if so, the system checks whether the virtual-key information can be converted into an ASCII-key equivalent. If the virtual-key information can be converted, TranslateMessage calls PostMessage to place a WM_CHAR message or a WM_SYSCHAR message in the message queue. The next time GetMessage is called, the system first checks the contents of the message queue, and if a message exists there, pulls the message from the queue and returns it. The returned message will be the WM_CHAR message or the WM_SYSCHAR message. Now, the next time GetMessage is called, the message queue is empty, and Windows NT checks the input queue. In this queue, the system finds the WM_(SYS)KEYUP message and returns it from GetMessage.

Because the system works this way, the following sequence of hardware events,

```
WM_KEYDOWN
WM_KEYUP
```

generates the following sequence of messages to your window procedure (assuming that the virtual-key information can be converted to an ASCII equivalent):

```
WM_KEYDOWN
WM_CHAR
WM_KEYUP
```

Now, let's get back to discussing how the system decides what messages to return from GetMessage. After the system checks the message queue and before it checks the virtualized input queue, it checks the QS-_QUIT flag. Remember that the QS_QUIT flag is set when the thread calls PostQuitMessage. Calling PostQuitMessage is similar to calling PostMessage, which places the message at the end of the message queue and causes the message to be processed before the input queue is checked. So why does PostQuitMessage set a flag instead of placing a WM_QUIT message in the message queue? There are two reasons.

First, in 16-bit Windows, queues can hold up to only eight messages. If the queue is full and the application attempts to post a WM_QUIT message to the queue, the WM_QUIT message gets lost and the application never terminates. By handling the WM_QUIT message as a special flag, the message never gets lost. The second reason for handling the QS_QUIT flag this way is to let the application finish processing all the other posted messages before terminating the application.

Now we come to the last two messages: WM_PAINT and WM-_TIMER. A WM_PAINT message has low priority because painting the screen under Windows NT is a slow process. If every time a window became invalid a WM_PAINT message was sent, Windows NT would be too slow to use. By placing WM_PAINT messages after keyboard input, Windows NT runs much faster. For example, you can select a menu item that invokes a dialog box, choose an item from the box, and press Enter all before the dialog box even appears on the screen. If you type fast enough, your keystroke messages will always be pulled from the queue before any WM_PAINT messages. When you press Enter to accept the dialog box options, the dialog box window is destroyed and Windows NT resets the QS_PAINT flag.

The last message, WM_TIMER, has an even lower priority than that of a WM_PAINT message. To understand why, think about the Clock application that ships with Windows NT. Clock updates its display every time it receives a WM_TIMER message. Imagine that WM-_TIMER messages are returned before WM_PAINT messages and that Clock sets a timer that has such short duration that it just goes off continuously, never allowing a WM_PAINT message to be returned from GetMessage. In this case, Clock would never paint itself—it would just keep updating its internal time but would never get a WM_PAINT message.

I want to point out here that 16-bit Windows uses this same algorithm for retrieving messages, except for two differences. First, in 16-bit Windows, all tasks share the same input queue (the system queue). So when a task calls GetMessage, 16-bit Windows examines the task's message queue and then its quit flag, and then it checks the system queue. If no messages exist in these places, GetMessage continues to check the task's QS_PAINT and QS_TIMER flags.

The second difference is that 16-bit Windows does not support preemptive multitasking. It allows switching to another task when there are no messages for a task to process. When a task calls GetMessage (or PeekMessage), if there are no posted messages, if the quit flag is turned off, if there are no system queue messages and no invalid windows to be painted, 16-bit Windows checks the message queue for another task (unless you called PeekMessage using the PM_NOYIELD flag). If another task has posted messages, a quit flag, or system messages, the system switches to the other task and allows the other task's call to GetMessage to return. Finally, when no tasks have any outstanding application or system queue messages to process, 16-bit Windows checks each task to see if any WM_TIMER messages need processing.

It should be pointed out that in Windows NT the GetMessage and PeekMessage functions check only in the calling thread's queue for messages, which means that threads can never retrieve messages from a queue that's attached to another thread, including messages for threads that are part of the same process.

Deserialized Input

Serialized input (used by 16-bit Windows) is a user's input (keyboard and mouse events) that enters into the system queue at one centralized location. Once there, the events are removed from the queue as various applications request them. For example, let's say that the user types *ABC*, *Alt+Tab*, *XYZ* at the keyboard. This means that seven keyboard hardware events are added to the system queue.[4] The application with keyboard

4. Actually, more than seven events are appended to the system queue. For example, each keystroke generates a WM_KEYDOWN and a WM_KEYUP event. I am just calling it seven events to simplify the discussion.

focus retrieves the *ABC* messages from the system queue and displays the characters in its client area. Let's say a bug in the program causes it to enter an infinite loop whenever it receives the letter *C*. At this point, the whole system is hung. Alt+Tab and *XYZ* will never be read from the system queue. In fact, if the user attempts to activate another application using the mouse, the mouse event will be appended to the system queue after the last keystroke event. And, as you might expect, this mouse event will never be retrieved from the system queue either. The user has no recourse now but to reboot the computer.

For 16-bit Windows, Microsoft tried to improve this situation. Support was added so that a user can press Ctrl+Alt+Del if an application is no longer responding to the system. When the system detects this input, it locates the currently active application and attempts to remove it from memory. My experience with this feature has shown that usually 16-bit Windows cannot recover from the hung application gracefully and I still need to reboot.

The solution to this serialized input problem is *deserialized input*. With deserialized input, one hardware event isn't necessarily processed before another event. I know what you're thinking: "Does this mean that if you type *ABC* at the keyboard the application will receive *CAB*?" No, of course not. However, it does mean that if you type *ABC*, Alt+Tab, *XYZ*, the application that becomes active after the Alt+Tab might process *XYZ* before the first application finishes processing *ABC*.

In Windows NT, input is applied on a thread-level basis instead of on the system-wide basis employed by 16-bit Windows. A thread receives hardware events in the order in which the user enters them, which is how Windows NT deserializes the hardware input.

How Windows NT Deserializes Input

When Windows NT starts running the Win32 subsystem, the Win32 subsystem creates a private thread for itself called the *raw input thread* (RIT). When the user presses and releases a key, presses and releases a mouse button, or moves the mouse, the device driver for the hardware device appends a hardware event to the RIT's queue. This causes the RIT to wake up, examine the event at the head of its queue, translate the event into the appropriate WM_KEY*, WM_?BUTTON*, or WM_MOUSEMOVE message, and post the message to the appropriate thread's virtualized input queue.

As stated earlier in this chapter, each thread has its very own message queue and virtualized input queue. Every time a thread creates a window, Windows NT places all messages posted for this window in the creating thread's queue.

Assume the following scenario: A process creates two threads, ThreadA and ThreadB. ThreadA creates a window—WinA—and ThreadB creates two windows—WinB and WinC. Figure 6-5 illustrates this scenario. If a thread in the system posts a message to WinA, this message is placed in ThreadA's queue. Any messages posted for either WinB or WinC are placed in ThreadB's queue.

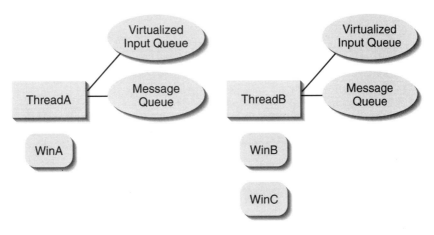

Figure 6-5.
Scenario in which ThreadA creates WinA, and ThreadB creates WinB and WinC.

When the RIT processes a hardware event, it must determine which virtualized input queue should receive the event. For a mouse event, the RIT first determines which window is under the mouse cursor and then places the mouse event (WM_?BUTTON* or WM-_MOUSEMOVE) in the input queue associated with the thread that created the window. For a keystroke event, the RIT determines which process is the foreground process. The foreground process is the process with which the user is currently working. The RIT then determines which thread within the process is the foreground thread. The appropriate keyboard message is placed in the input queue associated with this foreground thread.

In order for the system to switch applications, regardless of whether an application is processing input, the RIT must examine each hardware input event before posting the event to a thread's virtualized input queue. For example, the RIT checks whether the user has pressed Alt+Tab, Ctrl+Esc, or Ctrl+Alt+Del, and then the RIT switches active applications, invokes the Task Manager, or displays the Windows NT Security dialog box, shown below:

Sharing Thread Input Queues

You can force two or more threads to share the same input queue by using the AttachThreadInput function:

```
BOOL AttachThreadInput(DWORD idAttach, DWORD idAttachTo,
   BOOL fAttach);
```

This function tells Windows NT to let two threads share the same input queue, as illustrated in Figure 6-6. The first parameter, *idAttach*, is the ID of the thread containing the input queue you no longer want. The second parameter, *idAttachTo*, is the ID of the thread containing the input queue you want the threads to share. The last parameter, *fAttach*, is TRUE if you want the sharing to occur or FALSE if you want to separate the two threads' input queues again. You can tell several threads to share the same input queue by making successive calls to the Attach-ThreadInput function.

Returning to the example, let's say that ThreadB calls Attach-ThreadInput, passing ThreadB's ID as the first parameter, ThreadA's ID as the second parameter, and TRUE as the last parameter:

```
AttachThreadInput(idThreadB, idThreadA, TRUE);
```

Now every hardware input event destined for either WinB or WinC will be appended to ThreadA's input queue. ThreadB's input queue will no longer receive input events unless the two queues are detached by calling AttachThreadInput a second time, passing FALSE as the *fAttach* parameter.

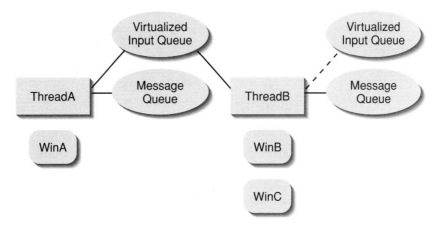

Figure 6-6.
Two threads sharing one input queue.

When you attach two threads to the same input queue, each thread maintains its own message queue; only the input queues are attached. Every time you attach another thread to the same input queue, you are making the system behave more and more like 16-bit Windows. After all, in 16-bit Windows, all the tasks are attached to a single input queue—the system queue. In fact, when you run 16-bit Windows applications under Windows NT, the system makes sure that all the 16-bit Windows applications share a single input queue for backward compatibility; 16-bit Windows applications expect this behavior.

If you make all threads share a single queue, you severely curtail the robustness of the system. If one application receives a keystroke and hangs, another application can't receive any input. So think twice or three times before using the AttachThreadInput function.

The system implicitly attaches the virtualized input queues of several threads, if an application installs a journal record hook or a journal playback hook. When the hook is uninstalled, the system automatically restores all the threads so that they are using the same input queues they were using before the hook was installed.

When an application installs a journal record hook, it tells the system that it wants to be notified of all hardware events entered by the user. The application usually saves or records this information. In another session, the application installs a journal playback hook, which causes the system to ignore the user's input and to expect the application that installed the hook to play back the events it recorded earlier.

Playing back the recorded events simulates the user repeating his or her hardware input. The Recorder applet that Microsoft ships with 16-bit Windows allows users to record events for later playback. You'll notice that Recorder is not shipped with Windows NT—perhaps Recorder compromises the robustness of the system.

The system implicitly calls AttachThreadInput on your behalf at one other time. Let's say that you have an application that creates two threads. The first thread creates a dialog box. After the dialog box has been created, the second thread calls CreateWindow, using the WS-_CHILD style, and passing the handle of the dialog box to be the child's parent. Windows NT implicitly calls AttachThreadInput with the child window's thread to tell the child's thread that it should use the same input queue that the dialog box thread is using. This action forces input to be synchronized among all the child windows in the dialog box. As you'll see later in this chapter, it's possible for windows created by different threads to look like they all have the input focus simultaneously, which can confuse an end user. By attaching the input queues together, only one window will appear to have focus.

Local Input State

Back when programmers were developing applications for MS-DOS, it could always be presumed that the running application would be the only application running. As a result, applications frequently assumed that the whole display was theirs for the writing, the memory theirs for the allocating, the disk space theirs for the accessing, the keystrokes theirs for the taking, and the CPU theirs for the computing—you get the idea.

Well, 16-bit Windows came around and programmers had to learn to cooperate with each other. Many programs, all running simultaneously, had to share the limited system resources. An application had to restrict its output to a small rectangular region on the display, allocate memory only when needed and try to make it discardable, relinquish control of itself to other applications on certain keystrokes, and purposely put itself to sleep so that other applications could get a little CPU time. If an application was not as friendly as it should be, a user had no recourse but to terminate the piggish application or run it alone, which obviously defeated the idea of a multitasking environment.

Under Windows NT, much of this is still true. Developers still design their applications to use a small rectangular region on the display for output so that they use as little memory as possible, etc. The big difference is that Windows NT makes the application behave courteously. Windows NT forces limits on the amount of memory that an application can hog. It monitors the keyboard and allows the user to switch to another application whether the currently active application wants to allow this or not. It preempts a running application and gives time to another application regardless of how hungry for processing time the current application is.[5]

Who are the winners now that Windows NT has so much control over the applications we write? Both the users and the developers. Because Windows NT does all this no matter what we as programmers might do to stop it, we can relax a little and don't have to worry about crowding out other applications. A big part of making this work is the concept of the *local input state.*

Each thread has its very own input state that is managed inside a thread's THREADINFO structure. This input state consists of the thread's virtualized input queue as well as a set of variables. These variables keep track of the following input state management information:

Keyboard input and window focus information such as

- which window has keyboard focus
- which window is active
- which keys are pressed on the keyboard
- the state of the caret

Mouse cursor management information such as

- which window has mouse capture
- the shape of the mouse cursor
- visibility of the mouse cursor

Because each thread gets its very own set of input state variables, each thread has a different notion of focus window, mouse capture window, and so on. So, as it appears to the thread, either one of its windows

---

5. You can set your process's priority class high; however, doing so might starve processes at a lower priority, making the lower priority processes unresponsive. But even if you set a process's priority class high, the system still gives the user the ability to terminate the process.

has keyboard focus or no window in the system has keyboard focus, either one of its windows has mouse capture or no window has mouse capture, etc. As you might expect, this separatism has several ramifications that we'll discuss in this chapter.

Keyboard Input and Focus

Windows NT and 16-bit Windows handle keyboard input in very different ways. When I was first getting started with Windows NT, I tried to understand how the system handles keyboard input by drawing on my knowledge of 16-bit Windows. As it turned out, my knowledge of how 16-bit Windows handles keyboard input made it more difficult to understand how Windows NT handles keyboard input and how it changes the input focus among windows.

In Windows NT, the RIT directs the user's keyboard input to a thread's virtualized input queue—not to a window. The RIT places the keyboard events into the thread's input queue without referring to a particular window. When the thread calls GetMessage, the keyboard event is removed from the queue and assigned to the window (created by the thread) that currently has input focus. Figure 6-7 illustrates this process.

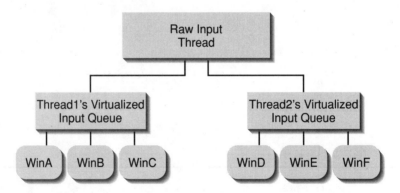

Figure 6-7.
The RIT directs the user's keyboard input to a thread's virtualized input queue.

To instruct a different window to accept keyboard input, you need to specify to which thread's virtualized input queue the RIT should direct keyboard input *and* tell the thread's input state variables which window will have keyboard focus. Calling SetFocus alone does not accomplish both tasks. If Thread1 is currently receiving input from the RIT, a call to SetFocus passing the handle of WinA, WinB, or WinC causes the focus to change. The window losing focus removes its focus rectangle or hides its caret, and the window gaining focus draws a focus rectangle or shows a caret.

However, let's say that Thread1 is still receiving input from the RIT and it calls SetFocus, passing the handle of WinE. In this case, the system prevents the call to SetFocus from doing anything because the window for which you are trying to set focus is not using the virtualized input queue that is currently "connected" to the RIT. After executing this call, there is no change in focus, and the appearance of the screen doesn't change.

In another situation, Thread1 might receive input from the RIT and Thread2 might call SetFocus, passing the handle of WinE. In this case, Thread2's local input state variables are updated to reflect that WinE is the window to receive keyboard input the next time the RIT directs keystrokes to Thread2. The call doesn't cause the RIT to direct input to Thread2's virtualized input queue.

Because WinE now has focus for Thread2, it receives a WM_SET-FOCUS message. If WinE is a pushbutton, it draws a focus rectangle for itself, so two windows with focus rectangles might appear on the screen. I found this very disconcerting at first, and now that I've seen it happen a few more times, I still find it disconcerting. You should be careful when you call SetFocus so that this situation doesn't occur.

By the way, if you give focus to a window that displays a caret when it receives a WM_SETFOCUS message, you can produce several windows on the screen displaying carets simultaneously. This can be a bit disconcerting to a user.

When focus is transferred from one window to another using conventional methods (such as clicking on a window with the mouse), the window losing focus receives a WM_KILLFOCUS message. If the window receiving focus belongs to a thread other than the thread associated with the window losing focus, the local input state variables of the thread that created the window losing focus are updated to reflect that no window has focus. Calling GetFocus at this time returns NULL, which makes the thread think that no window currently has focus. This can be problematic when porting a 16-bit Windows application to Windows NT because most 16-bit Windows applications never expect Get-Focus to return NULL.

The SetActiveWindow function activates a top-level window in the system.

```
HWND SetActiveWindow(HWND hwnd)
```

In 16-bit Windows, an application typically calls this function to bring another application to the foreground. In Windows NT, this function behaves just like the SetFocus function. That is, if a thread calls SetActiveWindow, passing the handle of a window owned by a different thread, the system does nothing. But if the window was created by the same thread making the call, the system changes the active window.

The complement of SetActiveWindow is the GetActiveWindow function:

```
HWND GetActiveWindow(VOID);
```

This function works just like the GetFocus function except it returns the handle of the active window indicated by the calling thread's local input state variables. So if the active window is owned by another thread, GetActiveWindow returns NULL.

These functions behave differently under Windows NT than they do when executed under 16-bit Windows for a reason: Microsoft is taking control away from applications and giving it back to the users. The assumption is that users find it disconcerting when windows pop up in the foreground under program control.

For example, a user might start a lengthy process in Application A and switch to Application B. When Application A is done, it may activate its main window. You certainly wouldn't want Application A's main window to pop up on top of Application B's window while the user is still working with Application B. This could catch the user by surprise. Also, the user might not immediately notice that Application A's window popped up over Application B's window, and the user might enter text into Application A by mistake. This could have disastrous effects.

However, sometimes an application really needs to bring a window to the foreground. These functions not only change the window focus for a thread but also instruct the RIT to direct keystrokes to a different thread. One of these functions, the SetForegroundWindow function, is new for Win32:

```
BOOL SetForegroundWindow(HWND hwnd);
```

This function brings the window identified by the *hwnd* parameter to the foreground. Windows NT also activates the window and gives it focus. This function sets the foreground window regardless of which thread created the window. The complementary function is Get-ForegroundWindow:

```
HWND GetForegroundWindow(VOID);
```

This function returns the handle of the window that is currently in the foreground.

Other functions that can alter a window's z-order, activation status, and focus status include BringWindowToTop and SetWindowPos. The BringWindowToTop function, shown below, exists in both 16-bit Windows and Windows NT:

```
BOOL BringWindowToTop(HWND hwnd);
```

When you call this function, Windows NT activates the window you specify regardless of which thread created the window, as long as the thread calling BringWindowToTop is in the foreground. Windows NT both redirects the RIT to the thread that created the window and sets the focus window for the thread's local input state variables. If the thread calling BringWindowToTop is not the foreground thread, the window order doesn't change.

The SetWindowPos function, shown below, brings a window to the foreground or the background by passing HWND_TOP or HWND-_BOTTOM as the second parameter:

```
BOOL SetWindowPos(HWND hwnd, HWND hwndInsertAfter,
    int x, int y, int cx, int cy, UINT fuFlags);
```

Actually, BringWindowToTop is implemented internally as a call to SetWindowPos passing HWND_TOP as the second parameter.

Another aspect of keyboard management and the local input state is that of the synchronous key state array. Every thread's local input state variables include a synchronous key state array, but all threads share a single asynchronous key state array. These arrays reflect the state of all keys on a keyboard at any given time. The GetAsyncKeyState function determines whether the user is currently pressing a key on the keyboard:

```
SHORT GetAsyncKeyState(int nVirtKey);
```

The *nVirtKey* parameter identifies the virtual-key code of the key to check. The high-bit of the result indicates whether the key is currently pressed (1) or not (0). I have often used this function during the processing of a single message to check whether the user has released the primary mouse button. I pass the virtual-key value VK_LBUTTON and wait for the high-bit of the return value to be 0 (zero). This function has changed slightly for Win32. In Win32, GetAsyncKeyState always returns 0 (not pressed) if the thread calling the function did not create the window that currently has input focus.

The GetKeyState function, shown below, differs from the Get-AsyncKeyState function because it returns the keyboard state at the time the most recent keyboard message was removed from the thread's queue:

```
SHORT GetKeyState(int nVirtKey);
```

This function is not affected by which window has input focus and can be called at any time. For a more detailed discussion of these two key state arrays and these functions, refer to my article about keystroke processing, "Simulating Keyboard Input Between Programs Requires a (Key)Stroke of Genius," in the December 1992 issue of *Microsoft Systems Journal.*

Mouse Cursor Management

Mouse cursor management is another component of the local input state. Because the mouse, like the keyboard, must be shared among all the different threads, Windows NT must not allow a single thread to monopolize the mouse cursor by altering its shape or confining it to a small area of the screen. In this section, we'll take a look at how the mouse cursor is managed by the system.

One aspect of mouse cursor management is the hide/show capability of the mouse cursor. Let's say that a 16-bit Windows application calls ShowCursor(FALSE), causing the mouse cursor to be hidden, and the application never calls ShowCursor(TRUE). The user wouldn't be able to see the mouse when using a different application.

Windows NT wouldn't allow this to happen. The system hides the cursor whenever the mouse is positioned over a window created by the thread that called ShowCursor(FALSE) and shows it whenever the cursor is positioned over a window not created by this thread.

Another aspect of mouse cursor management is the capability of clipping the cursor to a rectangular region of the screen. In 16-bit Windows, it is possible for an application to clip the mouse cursor by calling the ClipCursor function:

```
BOOL ClipCursor(CONST RECT *lprc);
```

This function causes the mouse to be contained within the screen coordinates specified in the rectangle pointed to by the *lprc* parameter. Again, we have the problem in which one application should not be able to limit the movement of the mouse cursor on the screen. But Windows NT must also allow an application to clip a mouse cursor's motion to a specified rectangle. So Windows NT allows the application to set the clipping rectangle and confines the mouse to that region of the screen. Then if an asynchronous activation event occurs (when the user clicks on another application, when a call to SetForegroundWindow is made, or when Ctrl+Esc is pressed), Windows NT stops clipping the cursor's movement, allowing it to move freely across the whole screen.

Now we move to the issue of mouse capture. When a window "captures" the mouse (by calling SetCapture), it requests that all mouse messages be directed from the RIT to the thread's virtualized input queue and that all mouse messages from the input queue be directed to the window that set capture. This capturing of mouse messages continues until the application later calls ReleaseCapture.

Under 16-bit Windows, if an application calls SetCapture but never calls ReleaseCapture, mouse messages can never be directed to any other window in the system. Again, we have a situation that Windows NT cannot allow, but solving this problem is a bit tricky. When an application calls SetCapture, the RIT is directed to place all mouse messages in the thread's virtualized input queue. SetCapture also sets the local input state variables for the thread that called SetCapture.

As soon as the user releases all mouse buttons, the RIT no longer directs mouse messages solely to the thread's virtualized input queue. Instead, the RIT directs mouse messages to the input queue associated with the window that is directly beneath the mouse. This is normal behavior when the mouse is not captured.

However, the thread that originally called SetCapture still thinks that mouse capture is in effect. This means that whenever the mouse is positioned over any window created by the thread that has capture set, the mouse messages will be directed to the capture window for that thread. In other words, when the user releases all mouse buttons, mouse capture is no longer performed on a system-wide level—it is now performed on a thread-local level.

The final local input state variable pertaining to the mouse is its shape. Whenever a thread calls SetCursor to change the shape of the mouse, the local input state variables are updated to reflect the mouse

317

shape. In other words, the local input state variables always remember the most recent shape of the mouse set by the thread.

Let's say that the user moves the mouse over your window, your window receives a WM_SETCURSOR message, and you call SetCursor to change the mouse cursor to an hourglass. After the call to SetCursor, you have code that enters into a lengthy process. (An infinite loop is a good example of a lengthy process.) Now the user moves the mouse out of your window and over the window belonging to another application. In 16-bit Windows, the mouse cursor doesn't change, but in Windows NT the mouse cursor can be changed by the other window procedure.

Local input state variables are not required in order for a thread to change the mouse cursor shape when another thread executes a lengthy procedure. But now let's move the mouse cursor back over our window that is still executing its lengthy procedure. The system wants to send WM_SETCURSOR messages to the window, but the window is unable to retrieve them because it is still looping. So the system looks at the most recently set mouse cursor shape (contained in the thread's local input state variables) and automatically sets the mouse cursor back to this shape (the hourglass, in this example). This gives the user visual feedback that the process is still working and that the user must wait.

Local Input State Laboratory Sample Application

The LISLab application (LISLAB.EXE), listed in Figure 6-8 beginning on page 324, is a laboratory that allows you to experiment with how local input states work in Windows NT. When you first invoke the application, the following dialog box appears:

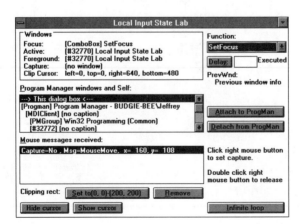

In the upper left corner is the *Windows* group box. The five entries in this box are updated once a second. That is, once every second, the dialog box receives a WM_TIMER message, and in response, it calls the following functions: GetFocus, GetActiveWindow, GetForegroundWindow, GetCapture, and GetClipCursor. The first four of these functions return window handles. From these window handles, I can determine the window's class and caption and display this information. Remember that these window handles are being retrieved from my own thread's local input state variables.

If I activate another application (like the Program Manager), the *Focus* and *Active* entries change to *(no window)* and the *Foreground* entry changes to *[Progman] Program Manager*. Notice that by activating another application you make LISLab think that no window has focus and that no window is active.

Next, you can experiment with changing the window focus. First select *SetFocus* from the combo box at the upper right of the LISLab dialog box. Then enter a delay time (in seconds) that you want LISLab to wait before calling SetFocus. For this experiment, you'll probably want to specify a delay of 0 (zero) seconds. I'll explain how the *Delay* field is used shortly.

Next, select a window that you want to pass in the call to SetFocus. You select a window using the *Program Manager windows and Self* list box on the left side of the LISLab dialog box. For this experiment, choose the Program Manager itself. Now you are ready to call SetFocus. Simply click on the *Delay* button, and watch what happens to the *Windows* group box—nothing. The system doesn't perform a focus change.

If you really want SetFocus to change focus to the Program Manager, you can click on the *Attach to ProgMan* button. Clicking on this button causes LISLab to call:

```
AttachThreadInput(GetWindowThreadProcessId(g_hwndPM, NULL),
    GetCurrentThreadId(), TRUE);
```

This call tells LISLab's thread to use the same virtualized input queue as that of the Program Manager. In addition, LISLab's thread will also share the same local input state variables used by the Program Manager.

If after clicking on the *Attach to ProgMan* button you click on the Program Manager window, LISLab's dialog box looks like the illustration at the top of the following page.

319

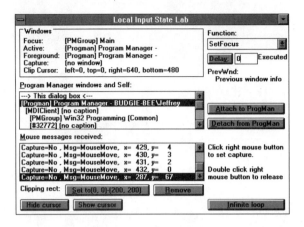

Notice that now, because the input queues are attached, LISLab can follow window focus changes made in the Program Manager. The dialog box above shows that the Main group currently has focus. If we continue to manipulate group windows in the Program Manager, LISLab will continue to update its display and show us which Program Manager window has focus, which window is active, etc.

Now we can move back to LISLab, click on the *Delay* button, and have SetFocus attempt to give the Program Manager focus. This time, however—again because the input queues are attached—the call to Set-Focus succeeds.

You can continue to experiment by placing calls to SetActiveWindow, SetForegroundWindow, BringWindowToTop, and SetWindowPos by selecting the desired function from the combo box. Try calling these functions both when the input queues are attached and when they are detached, and notice the differences.

Now I should explain why I include the delay option. The delay option causes LISLab to call the specified function after the number of seconds indicated. An example will help illustrate why you need it. First, make sure that LISLab is detached from the Program Manager. Then, select --> *This dialog box* <-- from the *Program Manager windows and Self* list box. Next, select *SetFocus* from the function combo box, and enter a delay of 10 seconds. Finally, click on the *Delay* button, and then quickly click on the Program Manager window to make it active. You must make the Program Manager active before the 10 seconds elapse.

While LISLab is waiting for the 10 seconds to elapse, it displays the word *Pending* to the right of the seconds value. After the 10 seconds,

Pending is replaced by *Executed*, and the result of calling the function is displayed. If you watch carefully, LISLab will give focus to the *Function* combo box and show that the combo box now has focus. But the Program Manager will still be receiving your keystrokes. LISLab's thread thinks that the combo box has focus, and the Program Manager's thread thinks that one of its windows has focus. However, the RIT remains "connected" to the Program Manager's thread.

One final point about windows and focus: Both the SetFocus and SetActiveWindow functions return the handle to the window that originally had focus or was active. The information for this window is displayed in the *PrevWnd* field in the LISLab dialog box. Also, just before LISLab calls SetForegroundWindow, it calls GetForeground-Window to get the handle of the window that was originally in the foreground. This information is also displayed in the *PrevWnd* field.

It's time to move on to experiments involving the mouse cursor. Whenever you move the mouse over LISLab's dialog box (but not over any of its child windows), the mouse is displayed as a vertical arrow. As mouse messages are sent to the dialog box, they are also added to the *Mouse messages received* list box. In this way, you know when the dialog box is receiving mouse messages. If you move outside the dialog box or over one of its child windows, you'll see that messages are no longer added to the list box.

Now, move the mouse to the right of the dialog box over the text *Click right mouse button to set capture*, and click and hold the right mouse button. When you do this, LISLab calls SetCapture and passes the handle of LISLab's dialog box. Notice that LISLab reflects that it has capture by updating the *Windows* group box at the top.

Without releasing the right mouse button, move the mouse over LISLab's child windows and watch the mouse messages being added to the list box. Notice that if you move the mouse outside of LISLab's dialog box, LISLab continues to be notified of mouse messages. The mouse cursor retains its vertical arrow shape no matter where you move the mouse on the screen. This is exactly how mouse capture works in 16-bit Windows.

But now we're ready to see where Windows NT behaves differently. Release the right mouse button, and watch what happens. The capture window reflected at the top of LISLab continues to show that LISLab thinks it still has mouse capture. However, if you move the mouse outside of LISLab's dialog box, the cursor no longer remains a vertical arrow and mouse messages stop going to the *Mouse messages received* list box. This is very different from the way 16-bit Windows works.

However, if you move the mouse over any of LISLab's child windows, you'll see that capture is still in effect because all the windows are using the same set of local input state variables.

When you're done experimenting with mouse capture, you can double click the right mouse button anywhere in the LISLab dialog box to have LISLab place a call to ReleaseCapture. When you do this, watch how the *Capture* field at the top changes back to reflect that no window has mouse capture.

There are only two more mouse-related experiments: One experiment involves clipping the mouse cursor's movement to a rectangle, and one experiment involves cursor visibility. When you click on the *Set to(0,0)-(200,200)* button, LISLab executes the following code:

```
RECT rc;
  .
  .
  .

SetRect(&rc, 0, 0, 200, 200);
ClipCursor(&rc);
```

This causes the mouse cursor to be confined in the upper left corner of the screen. If you use Alt+Tab to select another application's window, you'll notice that the clipping rectangle stays in effect. But if you select an application by clicking on its title or if you press Ctrl+Esc to invoke the Task Manager, the clipping rectangle is removed and the mouse is free to traverse the entire screen. You can also click on the *Remove* button in the LISLab dialog box (assuming that the button is in the clipping rectangle) to remove the clipping rectangle.

Clicking on the *Hide cursor* or *Show cursor* button causes LISLab to execute the following code:

```
ShowCursor(FALSE);
```

or

```
ShowCursor(TRUE);
```

When you hide the mouse cursor, it doesn't appear when you move the mouse over LISLab's dialog box. But the moment you move the cursor outside this dialog box, the cursor appears again. Use the *Show cursor* button to counteract the effect of the *Hide cursor* button. Note that the effects of hiding the cursor in Windows are cumulative. That is, if you press the *Hide cursor* button five times, you must press the *Show cursor* button five times to make the mouse visible.

The last experiment involves using the *Infinite loop* button. When you click on this button, LISLab executes the following code:

```
SetCursor(LoadCursor(NULL, IDC_NO));
while (TRUE)
    ;
```

The first line changes the mouse cursor into a slashed circle, and the second line starts executing an infinite loop. After pressing this button, LISLab stops responding to any input whatsoever. If you move the mouse over LISLab's dialog box, the cursor remains as the slashed circle. However, if you move the mouse outside the dialog box, the cursor changes to reflect the cursor of the window over which it is located. You can use the mouse to manipulate these other windows.

If you move back over LISLab's dialog box, the system sees that LISLab is not responding and automatically changes the cursor back to its most recent shape—the slashed circle. In 16-bit Windows, an application executing an infinite loop hangs not only the application but the whole system. As you can see, on Windows NT an infinite loop is just a minor inconvenience to the user.

Notice that if you move a window over the hung LISLab dialog box and then move it away, the system sends LISLab a WM_PAINT message. But the system also realizes that the application is not responding. The system helps out here by repainting the window for the unresponsive application. Of course, the system cannot repaint the window correctly because it doesn't know what the application was supposed to do, so the system simply erases the window's background and redraws the frame.

Now the problem is that we have a window on the screen that isn't responding to anything we do. How do we get rid of it? Well, first we must display the Task Manager. Then we simply select the application we want to terminate—Local Input State Laboratory, in this case—and then click on the *End Task* button.

The system will attempt to terminate LISLab in a nice way but will notice that the application isn't responding. The system displays the dialog box shown at the top of the following pages.

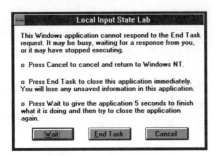

Choosing *End Task* causes the system to forcibly remove LISLab from the system. The *Wait* button delays the action; choose it if you think that an application will respond to input again within 5 seconds. We know that LISLab won't respond because its infinite loop will never end. The *Cancel* button tells the system that you changed your mind and no longer want to terminate the application. Choose *End Task* to remove LISLab from the system.

The whole point of these experiments is to demonstrate Windows NT's robustness. It's impossible for one application to place the operating system in a state that would render the other applications unusable, which is how things should be.

LISLab.ico

LISLAB.C

```
/*****************************************************************
Module name: LISLab.C
Notices: Copyright (c) 1993 Jeffrey Richter
*****************************************************************/

#include <windows.h>
#include <windowsx.h>
#include <tchar.h>
#include <string.h>
#include <stdio.h>    // For sprintf
```

Figure 6-8.   *(continued)*

The LISLab application.

Figure 6-8. *continued*

```
#include "LISLab.H"

//////////////////////////////////////////////////////////////

#define TIMER_DELAY (1 * 1000) // 1 second * 1000 milliseconds
#define ARRAY_SIZE(A) (sizeof(A) / sizeof((A)[0]))

UINT  g_uTimerId = 1;
int   g_nEventId = 0;
DWORD g_dwEventTime = 0;
HWND  g_hwndSubject = NULL;
HWND  g_hwndPM = NULL;


//////////////////////////////////////////////////////////////

void CalcWndText (HWND hwnd, LPTSTR szBuf, int nLen) {
   TCHAR szClass[50], szCaption[50], szBufT[150];

   if (hwnd == (HWND) NULL) {
      _tcscpy(szBuf, __TEXT("(no window)"));
      return;
   }

   if (!IsWindow(hwnd)) {
      _tcscpy(szBuf, __TEXT("(invalid window)"));
      return;
   }

   GetClassName(hwnd, szClass, ARRAY_SIZE(szClass));
   GetWindowText(hwnd, szCaption, ARRAY_SIZE(szCaption));

   _stprintf(szBufT, __TEXT("[%s] %s"), (LPTSTR) szClass,
      (*szCaption == 0) ? (LPTSTR) __TEXT("(no caption)") :
      (LPTSTR) szCaption);
   _tcsncpy(szBuf, szBufT, nLen - 1);
   szBuf[nLen - 1] = 0; // Force zero-terminated string.
}


//////////////////////////////////////////////////////////////

// To minimize stack use, one instance of WALKWINDOWTREEDATA
// is created as a local var in WalkWindowTree() and a
// pointer to it is passed to WalkWindowTreeRecurse.
```

(continued)

Figure 6-8. *continued*

```
// Data used by WalkWindowTreeRecurse
typedef struct {
   HWND  hwndLB;           // Handle to the output list box.
   HWND  hwndParent;       // Handle to the parent.
   int   nLevel;           // Nesting depth.
   int   nIndex;           // List box item index.
   TCHAR szBuf[100];       // Output buffer.
   int   iBuf;             // Index into szBuf.
} WALKWINDOWTREEDATA, *LPWALKWINDOWTREEDATA;

void WalkWindowTreeRecurse (LPWALKWINDOWTREEDATA pWWT) {

   const int nIndexAmount = 2;
   HWND hwndChild;

   pWWT->nLevel++;

   if (!IsWindow(pWWT->hwndParent))
      return;

   for (pWWT->iBuf = 0;
      pWWT->iBuf < pWWT->nLevel * nIndexAmount; pWWT->iBuf++)

      pWWT->szBuf[pWWT->iBuf] = __TEXT(' ');

   CalcWndText(pWWT->hwndParent, &pWWT->szBuf[pWWT->iBuf],
      ARRAY_SIZE(pWWT->szBuf) - pWWT->iBuf);
   pWWT->nIndex = ListBox_AddString(pWWT->hwndLB,
      pWWT->szBuf);
   ListBox_SetItemData(pWWT->hwndLB, pWWT->nIndex,
      pWWT->hwndParent);

   hwndChild = GetFirstChild(pWWT->hwndParent);
   while (hwndChild != NULL) {
      pWWT->hwndParent = hwndChild;
      WalkWindowTreeRecurse(pWWT);
      hwndChild = GetNextSibling(hwndChild);
   }

   pWWT->nLevel--;
}
```

(continued)

326

Figure 6-8. *continued*

```
///////////////////////////////////////////////////////////

void WalkWindowTree (HWND hwndLB, HWND hwndParent) {

   WALKWINDOWTREEDATA WWT;

   WWT.hwndLB = hwndLB;
   WWT.hwndParent = hwndParent;
   WWT.nLevel = -1;

   WalkWindowTreeRecurse(&WWT);
}


///////////////////////////////////////////////////////////

BOOL Dlg_OnInitDialog (HWND hwnd, HWND hwndFocus,
   LPARAM lParam) {

   HWND hwndT;

   // Associate an icon with the dialog box.
   SetClassLong(hwnd, GCL_HICON, (LONG)
      LoadIcon((HINSTANCE) GetWindowLong(hwnd, GWL_HINSTANCE),
      __TEXT("LisLab")));

   g_uTimerId = SetTimer(hwnd, g_uTimerId, TIMER_DELAY, NULL);

   hwndT = GetDlgItem(hwnd, ID_WNDFUNC);
   ComboBox_AddString(hwndT, __TEXT("SetFocus"));
   ComboBox_AddString(hwndT, __TEXT("SetActiveWindow"));
   ComboBox_AddString(hwndT, __TEXT("SetForegroundWnd"));
   ComboBox_AddString(hwndT, __TEXT("BringWindowToTop"));
   ComboBox_AddString(hwndT, __TEXT("SetWindowPos-TOP"));
   ComboBox_AddString(hwndT, __TEXT("SetWindowPos-BTM"));
   ComboBox_SetCurSel(hwndT, 0);

   // Fill the PMWnds list box with our window and the
   // windows of the Program Manager.

   // First, our own dialog box.
   hwndT = GetDlgItem(hwnd, ID_PMWNDS);
   ListBox_AddString(hwndT,
      __TEXT("---> This dialog box <---"));
```

(continued)

Figure 6-8. *continued*

```
    ListBox_SetItemData(hwndT, 0, hwnd);
    ListBox_SetCurSel(hwndT, 0);

    // Now, the windows of the Program Manager.
    g_hwndPM = FindWindow(__TEXT("PROGMAN"), NULL);
    WalkWindowTree(hwndT, g_hwndPM);

    return(TRUE);
}

//////////////////////////////////////////////////////////////////

void Dlg_OnDestroy (HWND hwnd) {
    if (g_uTimerId != 0)
        KillTimer(hwnd, g_uTimerId);
}

//////////////////////////////////////////////////////////////////

void Dlg_OnCommand (HWND hwnd, int id, HWND hwndCtl,
    UINT codeNotify) {

    HWND hwndT;
    RECT rc;

    switch (id) {

        case IDCANCEL:
            EndDialog(hwnd, 0);
            break;

        case ID_FUNCSTART:
            g_dwEventTime = GetTickCount() + 1000 *
                GetDlgItemInt(hwnd, ID_DELAY, NULL, FALSE);
            hwndT = GetDlgItem(hwnd, ID_PMWNDS);
            g_hwndSubject = (HWND)
                ListBox_GetItemData(hwndT,
                    ListBox_GetCurSel(hwndT));
            g_nEventId =
                ComboBox_GetCurSel(GetDlgItem(hwnd, ID_WNDFUNC));
            SetWindowText(GetDlgItem(hwnd, ID_EVENTPENDING),
                __TEXT("Pending"));
            break;
```

(continued)

Figure 6-8. *continued*

```
      case ID_THREADATTACH:
          AttachThreadInput(
              GetWindowThreadProcessId(g_hwndPM, NULL),
              GetCurrentThreadId(), TRUE);
          break;

      case ID_THREADDETACH:
          AttachThreadInput(
              GetWindowThreadProcessId(g_hwndPM, NULL),
              GetCurrentThreadId(), FALSE);
          break;

      case ID_SETCLIPRECT:
          SetRect(&rc, 0, 0, 200, 200);
          ClipCursor(&rc);
          break;

      case ID_REMOVECLIPRECT:
          ClipCursor(NULL);
          break;

      case ID_HIDECURSOR:
          ShowCursor(FALSE);
          break;

      case ID_SHOWCURSOR:
          ShowCursor(TRUE);
          break;

      case ID_INFINITELOOP:
          SetCursor(LoadCursor(NULL, IDC_NO));
          while (TRUE) ;
          break;
   }
}

///////////////////////////////////////////////////////////////

BOOL Dlg_OnSetCursor (HWND hwnd, HWND hwndCursor,
   UINT codeHitTest, UINT msg) {

   SetCursor(LoadCursor(NULL, IDC_UPARROW));
   return(TRUE);
}
```

(continued)

Figure 6-8. *continued*

```
/////////////////////////////////////////////////////////////////

void AddStr (HWND hwndLB, LPCTSTR szBuf) {
   int nIndex;

   do {
      nIndex = ListBox_AddString(hwndLB, szBuf);
      if (nIndex == LB_ERR)
         ListBox_DeleteString(hwndLB, 0);
   } while (nIndex == LB_ERR);

   ListBox_SetCurSel(hwndLB, nIndex);
}


/////////////////////////////////////////////////////////////////

int Dlg_OnRButtonDown (HWND hwnd, BOOL fDoubleClick,
   int x, int y, UINT keyFlags) {

   TCHAR szBuf[100];
   _stprintf(szBuf,
      __TEXT("Capture=%-3s, Msg=RButtonDown, ")
      __TEXT("DblClk=%-3s, x=%5d, y=%5d"),
      (GetCapture() == NULL) ? __TEXT("No") : __TEXT("Yes"),
      fDoubleClick ? __TEXT("Yes") : __TEXT("No"), x, y);

   AddStr(GetDlgItem(hwnd, ID_MOUSEMSGS), szBuf);
   if (!fDoubleClick) {
      SetCapture(hwnd);
   } else {
      ReleaseCapture();
   }
   return(0);
}


/////////////////////////////////////////////////////////////////

int Dlg_OnRButtonUp (HWND hwnd, int x, int y, UINT keyFlags) {
   TCHAR szBuf[100];
   _stprintf(szBuf,
      __TEXT("Capture=%-3s, Msg=RButtonUp,   x=%5d, y=%5d"),
      (GetCapture() == NULL) ?
         __TEXT("No") : __TEXT("Yes"), x, y);
```

(continued)

Figure 6-8. *continued*

```
        AddStr(GetDlgItem(hwnd, ID_MOUSEMSGS), szBuf);
        return(0);
}


////////////////////////////////////////////////////////////////

int Dlg_OnLButtonDown (HWND hwnd, BOOL fDoubleClick,
    int x, int y, UINT keyFlags) {

    TCHAR szBuf[100];
    _stprintf(szBuf,
        __TEXT("Capture=%-3s, Msg=LButtonDown, ")
        __TEXT("DblClk=%-3s, x=%5d, y=%5d"),
        (GetCapture() == NULL) ? __TEXT("No") : __TEXT("Yes"),
        fDoubleClick ? __TEXT("Yes") : __TEXT("No"), x, y);

    AddStr(GetDlgItem(hwnd, ID_MOUSEMSGS), szBuf);
    return(0);
}


////////////////////////////////////////////////////////////////

void Dlg_OnLButtonUp (HWND hwnd, int x, int y,
    UINT keyFlags) {
    TCHAR szBuf[100];

    _stprintf(szBuf,
        __TEXT("Capture=%-3s, Msg=LButtonUp,   x=%5d, y=%5d"),
        (GetCapture() == NULL) ?
            __TEXT("No") : __TEXT("Yes"), x, y);

    AddStr(GetDlgItem(hwnd, ID_MOUSEMSGS), szBuf);
}


////////////////////////////////////////////////////////////////

void Dlg_OnMouseMove (HWND hwnd, int x, int y,
    UINT keyFlags) {
    TCHAR szBuf[100];

    _stprintf(szBuf,
        __TEXT("Capture=%-3s, Msg=MouseMove,   x=%5d, y=%5d"),
```

(continued)

Figure 6-8. *continued*

```
        (GetCapture() == NULL)
          ? __TEXT("No") : __TEXT("Yes"), x, y);

   AddStr(GetDlgItem(hwnd, ID_MOUSEMSGS), szBuf);
}


///////////////////////////////////////////////////////////////

void Dlg_OnTimer (HWND hwnd, UINT id) {
   TCHAR szBuf[100];
   RECT rc;
   HWND hwndT;

   CalcWndText(GetFocus(), szBuf, ARRAY_SIZE(szBuf));
   SetWindowText(GetDlgItem(hwnd, ID_WNDFOCUS), szBuf);

   CalcWndText(GetCapture(), szBuf, ARRAY_SIZE(szBuf));
   SetWindowText(GetDlgItem(hwnd, ID_WNDCAPTURE), szBuf);

   CalcWndText(GetActiveWindow(), szBuf, ARRAY_SIZE(szBuf));
   SetWindowText(GetDlgItem(hwnd, ID_WNDACTIVE), szBuf);

   CalcWndText(GetForegroundWindow(), szBuf,
      ARRAY_SIZE(szBuf));
   SetWindowText(GetDlgItem(hwnd, ID_WNDFOREGROUND), szBuf);

   GetClipCursor(&rc);
   _stprintf(szBuf,
      __TEXT("left=%d, top=%d, right=%d, bottom=%d"),
      rc.left, rc.top, rc.right, rc.bottom);
   SetWindowText(GetDlgItem(hwnd, ID_CLIPCURSOR), szBuf);

   if ((g_dwEventTime == 0) ||
      (GetTickCount() < g_dwEventTime))
      return;

   switch (g_nEventId) {
      case 0:  // SetFocus
         g_hwndSubject = SetFocus(g_hwndSubject);
         break;
```

(continued)

Figure 6-8. *continued*

```
    case 1:  // SetActiveWindow
        g_hwndSubject = SetActiveWindow(g_hwndSubject);
        break;

    case 2:  // SetForegroundWindow
        hwndT = GetForegroundWindow();
        SetForegroundWindow(g_hwndSubject);
        g_hwndSubject = hwndT;
        break;

    case 3:  // BringWindowToTop
        BringWindowToTop(g_hwndSubject);
        break;

    case 4:  // SetWindowPos w/HWND_TOP
        SetWindowPos(g_hwndSubject, HWND_TOP, 0, 0, 0, 0,
            SWP_NOMOVE | SWP_NOSIZE);
        g_hwndSubject = (HWND) 1;
        break;

    case 5:  // SetWindowPos w/ HWND_BOTTOM
        SetWindowPos(g_hwndSubject, HWND_BOTTOM, 0, 0, 0, 0,
            SWP_NOMOVE | SWP_NOSIZE);
        g_hwndSubject = (HWND) 1;
        break;
    }

if (g_hwndSubject == (HWND) 1) {
    SetWindowText(GetDlgItem(hwnd, ID_PREVWND),
        __TEXT("Can't tell."));
} else {
    CalcWndText(g_hwndSubject, szBuf, ARRAY_SIZE(szBuf));
    SetWindowText(GetDlgItem(hwnd, ID_PREVWND), szBuf);
}

g_hwndSubject = NULL; g_nEventId = 0; g_dwEventTime = 0;
SetWindowText(GetDlgItem(hwnd, ID_EVENTPENDING),
    __TEXT("Executed"));
}
```

(continued)

Figure 6-8. *continued*

```
///////////////////////////////////////////////////////////////

BOOL CALLBACK Dlg_Proc (HWND hDlg, UINT uMsg,
   WPARAM wParam, LPARAM lParam) {

   BOOL fProcessed = TRUE;

   switch (uMsg) {
      HANDLE_MSG(hDlg, WM_INITDIALOG,      Dlg_OnInitDialog);
      HANDLE_MSG(hDlg, WM_DESTROY,         Dlg_OnDestroy);
      HANDLE_MSG(hDlg, WM_COMMAND,         Dlg_OnCommand);

      HANDLE_MSG(hDlg, WM_MOUSEMOVE,       Dlg_OnMouseMove);

      HANDLE_MSG(hDlg, WM_LBUTTONDOWN,     Dlg_OnLButtonDown);
      HANDLE_MSG(hDlg, WM_LBUTTONDBLCLK,   Dlg_OnLButtonDown);
      HANDLE_MSG(hDlg, WM_LBUTTONUP,       Dlg_OnLButtonUp);

      HANDLE_MSG(hDlg, WM_RBUTTONDOWN,     Dlg_OnRButtonDown);
      HANDLE_MSG(hDlg, WM_RBUTTONDBLCLK,   Dlg_OnRButtonDown);
      HANDLE_MSG(hDlg, WM_RBUTTONUP,       Dlg_OnRButtonUp);

      HANDLE_MSG(hDlg, WM_SETCURSOR,       Dlg_OnSetCursor);
      HANDLE_MSG(hDlg, WM_TIMER,           Dlg_OnTimer);

      default:
         fProcessed = FALSE;
         break;
   }
   return(fProcessed);
}


///////////////////////////////////////////////////////////////

int APIENTRY WinMain (HINSTANCE hInstance,
   HINSTANCE hPrevInstance, LPSTR lpszCmdLine, int nCmdShow) {

   DialogBox(hInstance, MAKEINTRESOURCE(DLG_LISLAB),
      NULL, Dlg_Proc);
   return(0);
}

//////////////////////// End Of File ////////////////////////
```

(continued)

Figure 6-8.   *continued*

LISLAB.H

```
/****************************************************************
Module name: LISLab.H
Notices: Copyright (c) 1993 Jeffrey Richter
****************************************************************/

// Dialog and control IDs.
#define DLG_LISLAB                    1
#define ID_WNDFOCUS                   100
#define ID_WNDACTIVE                  101
#define ID_WNDFOREGROUND              102
#define ID_WNDCAPTURE                 103
#define ID_CLIPCURSOR                 104
#define ID_WNDFUNC                    105
#define ID_FUNCSTART                  106
#define ID_DELAY                      107
#define ID_EVENTPENDING               118
#define ID_PREVWND                    119
#define ID_PMWNDS                     110
#define ID_THREADATTACH               111
#define ID_THREADDETACH               112
#define ID_MOUSEMSGS                  113
#define ID_SETCLIPRECT                114
#define ID_REMOVECLIPRECT             115
#define ID_HIDECURSOR                 116
#define ID_SHOWCURSOR                 117
#define ID_INFINITELOOP               118


/////////////////////////// End Of File ///////////////////////////
```

LISLAB.RC

```
/****************************************************************
Module name: LISLab.RC
Notices: Copyright (c) 1993 Jeffrey Richter
****************************************************************/

#include <windows.h>
#include "LISLab.h"

LISLAB  ICON  DISCARDABLE LISLab.Ico
```

(continued)

335

Figure 6-8. *continued*

```
DLG_LISLAB DIALOG DISCARDABLE  12, 38, 284, 204
STYLE WS_MINIMIZEBOX | WS_POPUP | WS_VISIBLE | WS_CAPTION |
    WS_SYSMENU
CAPTION "Local Input State Lab"
FONT 8, "MS Sans Serif"
BEGIN
    GROUPBOX          "Windows",-1,4,0,192,56
    LTEXT             "Focus:",-1,8,12,36,8
    LTEXT             "Focus window info",ID_WNDFOCUS,
                      52,12,140,8
    LTEXT             "Active:",-1,8,20,36,8
    LTEXT             "Active window info",ID_WNDACTIVE,
                      52,20,140,8
    LTEXT             "Foreground:",-1,8,28,44,8
    LTEXT             "Foreground window info",ID_WNDFOREGROUND,
                      52,28,140,8
    LTEXT             "Capture:",-1,8,36,44,8
    LTEXT             "Capture window info",ID_WNDCAPTURE,
                      52,36,140,8
    LTEXT             "Clip Cursor:",-1,8,44,44,8
    LTEXT             "Cursor clipping info",ID_CLIPCURSOR,
                      52,44,140,8
    LTEXT             "Function:",-1,200,4,30,8
    COMBOBOX          ID_WNDFUNC,200,14,82,54,CBS_DROPDOWNLIST |
                      WS_VSCROLL | WS_TABSTOP
    PUSHBUTTON        "Dela&y:",ID_FUNCSTART,200,30,26,12
    EDITTEXT          ID_DELAY,228,30,24,12,ES_AUTOHSCROLL
    LTEXT             "Executed",ID_EVENTPENDING,252,30,32,10
    LTEXT             "PrevWnd:",-1,200,46,36,8
    LTEXT             "Previous window info",ID_PREVWND,
                      208,54,76,18
    LTEXT             "&Program Manager windows and Self:",-1,
                      4,60,132,8
    LISTBOX           ID_PMWNDS,4,72,192,42,
                      WS_VSCROLL | WS_TABSTOP
    PUSHBUTTON        "&Attach to ProgMan",ID_THREADATTACH,
                      200,84,80,12
    PUSHBUTTON        "&Detach from ProgMan",ID_THREADDETACH,
                      200,100,80,12
    LTEXT             "&Mouse messages received:",-1,4,116,96,8
    LISTBOX           ID_MOUSEMSGS,4,128,192,42,
                      WS_VSCROLL | WS_TABSTOP
    LTEXT             "Click right mouse button to set capture.
```

(continued)

Figure 6-8. *continued*

```
\n\nDouble click right mouse button to release capture.",
                -1,200,128,80,42
    LTEXT           "Clipping rect:",-1,4,172,48,8
    PUSHBUTTON      "&Set to(0, 0)-(200, 200)",ID_SETCLIPRECT,
                    52,172,88,12
    PUSHBUTTON      "&Remove",ID_REMOVECLIPRECT,144,172,52,12
    PUSHBUTTON      "Hide cursor",ID_HIDECURSOR,4,188,52,12
    PUSHBUTTON      "Show cursor",ID_SHOWCURSOR,60,188,52,12
    PUSHBUTTON      "&Infinite loop",ID_INFINITELOOP,
                    200,188,80,12, WS_GROUP | NOT WS_TABSTOP
END


///////////////////////// End Of File /////////////////////////
```

Thread Queues and Message Processing

In 16-bit Windows, there's a single thread of execution. If your application sends a message to a window created by another task, your task stops running and the code to process the message starts running. After the message is processed, the system returns to your task's code so that it can continue executing. In a multithreaded environment, things are quite different.

The code in a window procedure must be executed by the thread that created the window, which might not be the same thread that sent the message. In order to let other threads process messages, some sort of cooperation must occur in which the calling thread notifies the receiving thread that it needs it to perform an action. Then the calling thread suspends itself until the receiving thread has completed the request. In this section, we'll take a look at the various methods threads can use to send and post window messages.

Posting Messages to a Thread's Message Queue

As previously mentioned, Windows NT assigns a message queue to every thread. If a single process creates 10 threads, each thread has its own message queue. Messages are placed in a message queue by calling the PostMessage function:

```
BOOL PostMessage(HWND hWnd, UINT Msg, WPARAM wParam,
    LPARAM lParam);
```

When a thread calls this function, the system determines which thread created the window identified by the *hWnd* parameter and posts the specified message to the appropriate thread's message queue.

A message can also be placed into a thread's message queue by calling PostThreadMessage:

```
BOOL PostThreadMessage(DWORD idThread, UINT Msg, WPARAM wParam,
    LPARAM lParam);
```

The desired thread is identified by the first parameter, *idThread*. When this message is placed in the queue, the *hWnd* member in the MSG structure will be set to NULL. This function is usually called when an application performs some special processing in its main message loop. The main message loop for the thread is written so that after GetMessage or PeekMessage retrieves a message, the code checks for an *hWnd* of NULL and can examine the *msg* member of the MSG structure to perform the special processing. If the thread determines that this message is not destined for a window, DispatchMessage is not called and the message loop iterates to retrieve the next message. The PostThreadMessage function replaces the 16-bit Windows function PostAppMessage. (The PM-Restore application presented in Chapter 7 demonstrates the use of the PostThreadMessage function.)

Sending Messages to a Window

A 16-bit Windows application sends a message to a window by using the SendMessage function:

```
LRESULT SendMessage(HWND hWnd, UINT Msg, WPARAM wParam,
    LPARAM lParam);
```

A call to SendMessage causes 16-bit Windows to get the address of the window procedure associated with the *hWnd* parameter and call this procedure, passing it the same values that you passed to SendMessage. If the window to which you were sending a message was created by another task, 16-bit Windows performs a task switch (meaning that 16-bit Windows switches to use the stack of the application that created the window) and allows the window procedure to perform its magic. When the window procedure returns, 16-bit Windows performs a task switch back to the task that called SendMessage in the first place and allows that task to continue executing. When a message is sent to a window created by another task, the task calling SendMessage can't continue executing code until SendMessage returns.

It is usually not a problem that SendMessage doesn't return immediately, and in fact, this is pretty much the reason why the SendMessage function exists. PostMessage sends asynchronous messages—messages that don't need to be processed in order for you to continue—and SendMessage sends synchronous messages—messages that need to be processed before you can continue.

In Windows NT, an interthread message must be executed by a thread other than the one sending the message. Windows NT must perform some additional tasks in order to temporarily suspend the sending thread when sending a window message from one thread to the window of another thread. The following paragraphs explain the steps that the system must take.

First, the sent message is appended to the receiving thread's message queue, which has the effect of setting the QS_SENDMESSAGE flag for that thread. Second, if the receiving thread is already executing code and isn't waiting on a call to GetMessage or PeekMessage, the sent message can't be processed; Windows NT won't interrupt the thread, forcing the sent message to be processed immediately. When the receiving thread does call GetMessage or PeekMessage, Windows NT first checks to see if the QS_SENDMESSAGE wake flag is set, and if it is, scans the list of messages in the message queue to find the first sent message. It is possible that several sent messages could pile up in this queue. For example, several threads could each send a message to a single window at the same time. When this happens, the system simply appends these sent messages to the end of the receiving thread's message queue.

When the receiving thread calls GetMessage, the system simply locates the first sent message in the queue and calls the appropriate window procedure to process the message. If there are no more sent messages in the message queue, the QS_SENDMESSAGE wake flag is turned off.

While the receiving thread is processing the message, the thread that called SendMessage is sitting idle. After the message has been processed, the result of the processing is returned and the thread that called SendMessage is resumed so that it can continue execution.

While a thread is waiting for SendMessage to return, it sits basically idle. It is allowed to do one thing, however: If another thread in the system sends a message to a window created by a thread that is waiting for SendMessage to return, the system will process the sent message immediately. The system doesn't have to wait for the thread to call Get-Message or PeekMessage in this case.

Because the Win32 subsystem uses this method to handle the sending of interthread messages, your thread could possibly hang. Let's say that the thread processing the sent message has a bug and enters an infinite loop. What happens to the thread that called SendMessage? Will it ever be resumed? Does this mean that a bug in one application has the ability to hang another application? The answer is yes!

Four functions allow you to defensively write code to protect yourself from this situation.

The first function is SendMessageTimeout:

```
LRESULT SendMessageTimeout(HWND hwnd, UINT uMsg, WPARAM wParam,
    LPARAM lParam, UINT fuFlags, UINT uTimeout, LPDWORD lpdwResult);
```

It allows you to specify the maximum amount of time you are willing to wait for another thread to respond to your message. The first four parameters are the same parameters that you pass to SendMessage. The *fuFlags* parameter can be any combination of SMTO_NORMAL, SMTO_ABORTIFHUNG, and SMTO_BLOCK.

You can use the SMTO_NORMAL flag, which is defined as 0 (zero) in WINUSER.H, if you don't specify either of the other two. The SMTO_ABORTIFHUNG flag tells SendMessageTimeout to check whether the receiving thread is in a hung state, and if so, to return immediately. The SMTO_BLOCK flag causes the calling thread to not process any other sent messages until SendMessageTimeout returns.

Earlier in this section I said that a thread can be interrupted while waiting for a sent message to return so that it can process another sent message. Using the SMTO_BLOCK flag stops the system from allowing this interruption. You should use this flag only if your thread could not process a sent message while waiting for its sent message to be processed. Using this flag could create a deadlock situation, for example, if you send a message to another thread and that thread needs to send a message to your thread. In this case, neither thread can continue processing, and both threads effectively hang.

The *uTimeout* parameter specifies the number of milliseconds you are willing to wait for a result. If the function returns successfully, the result of the message is copied into the buffer whose address you specify in the *lpdwResult* parameter. If the function is successful, TRUE is returned.

By the way, if you call SendMessageTimeout to send a message to a window created by the calling thread, the system simply calls the window procedure and places the return value in *lpdwResult*. Because all processing must take place with one thread, the code following the call to SendMessageTimeout cannot start executing until after the message has been processed.

The second new function that can help in sending interthread messages is:

```
BOOL SendMessageCallback(HWND hwnd, UINT uMsg, WPARAM wParam,
   LPARAM lParam, SENDASYNCPROC lpResultCallBack, DWORD dwData);
```

Again, the first four parameters are the same as those used by the SendMessage function. When a thread calls SendMessageCallback, the function sends the message off to the receiving thread and immediately returns so that your thread can continue processing. When the receiving thread has finished processing the message, the system notifies your thread by calling a function that you write using the following prototype:

```
VOID CALLBACK ResultCallBack(HWND hwnd, UINT uMsg, DWORD dwData,
   LRESULT lResult);
```

You must pass the address to this function as the *lpResultCallBack* parameter of SendMessageCallback. When this function is called, it is passed the handle of the window that finished processing the message and the message value in the first two parameters. The third parameter, *dwData*, will always be the value that you passed in the *dwData* parameter to SendMessageCallback. The system simply takes whatever you specify here and passes it directly to your ResultCallBack function. The last parameter passed to your ResultCallBack function is the result from the window procedure that processed the message.

Your thread is not really notified of the result from the processed message as soon as the receiving window procedure returns. Instead, the system keeps a queue of returned messages and can call your ResultCallBack function only while your thread is calling GetMessage, PeekMessage, or one of the SendMessage* functions.

The SendMessageCallback function has another use. Both 16-bit Windows and Win32 offer a method by which you can broadcast a message to all the existing overlapped windows in the system: You call SendMessage and pass HWND_BROADCAST (defined as –1) as the *hwnd* parameter. You'd want to use this method only to broadcast a message whose return value you weren't interested in because the function can return only a single LRESULT. But, by using the SendMessage-Callback function, you can broadcast a message to every overlapped window and see the result of each. Your ResultCallBack function will be called with the result of every window processing the message.

If you call SendMessageCallback to send a message to a window created by the calling thread, the system immediately calls the window procedure, and after the message is processed, the system calls the ResultCallBack function. After the ResultCallBack function returns, execution begins at the line following the call to SendMessageCallback.

The third new function that can help in sending interthread messages is:

```
BOOL SendNotifyMessage(HWND hwnd, UINT Msg, WPARAM wParam,
    LPARAM lParam);
```

This function places a message in the receiving thread's queue and returns to the calling thread immediately. This should sound familiar because this is exactly what the PostMessage function does. However, SendNotifyMessage differs from PostMessage in two ways:

First, if SendNotifyMessage sends a message to a window created by another thread, the sent message has higher priority than posted messages placed in the receiving thread's queue. In other words, messages the SendNotifyMessage function places in a queue are always retrieved before messages the PostMessage function posts to a queue.

Second, when you are sending a message to a window created by the calling thread, SendNotifyMessage works exactly like the Send-Message function: SendNotifyMessage doesn't return until the message has been processed.

As it turns out, most messages sent to a window are used for notification purposes. That is, the message is sent because the window needs to be aware that a state change has occurred so that it can perform some processing before you carry on with your work. For example, WM_ACTIVATE, WM_DESTROY, WM_ENABLE, WM_SIZE, WM-_SETFOCUS, and WM_MOVE, just to name a few, are all notifications that are sent to a window by the Win32 subsystem, instead of being posted. However, these messages are notifications to the window; Windows NT doesn't have to stop running so that the window can process these messages. In contrast, when Windows NT sends a WM_CREATE message to a window, the system must wait until the window has finished processing the message. If the return value is −1, the window is not created.

The fourth new function that can help in sending interthread messages is:

```
BOOL ReplyMessage(LRESULT lResult);
```

This function also exists in 16-bit Windows and is different from the three previously discussed functions. Whereas the three Send∗ functions are used by the thread sending a message to protect itself from hanging, ReplyMessage is called by the thread processing the window message. When a thread calls ReplyMessage, it tells the system that it has completed enough work to know the result of the message and that the sending thread can have this result and continue executing.

The thread calling ReplyMessage specifies the result of processing the message in the *lResult* parameter. After ReplyMessage is called, the thread that sent the message resumes, and the thread processing the message continues to process the message. Neither thread is suspended, and both can continue executing normally. When the thread processing the message returns from its window procedure, any return value that it returns is simply ignored.

The problem with ReplyMessage is that is has to be called from within the window procedure that is receiving the message and not the thread that called one of the Send∗ functions. So you are best off writing defensive code by replacing your calls to SendMessage with one of the three new Send∗ functions instead of relying on the implementor of a window procedure to make calls to ReplyMessage.

Sending Data with Messages

In Chapter 2, I explained that Windows NT does not allow two applications to share a memory block by passing the handle of the memory block from one process to another. I also said that you cannot share the block by passing the address to the data's location from one process to another. Both of these methods for sharing data work in 16-bit Windows but fail under Windows NT for the same reason: Each process has its own address space.

If you want to share memory between applications, I recommend using memory-mapped files as explained in Chapter 4. However, let's look at a situation in which one process prepares a block of data for sharing with other applications. After the data is prepared, the creating process needs to signal the other applications that the data is ready. The process can accomplish this in several ways. One way is to use event objects as discussed in Chapter 5. Another way is to send a window message to a window in the other process. In this section, we'll examine how Windows NT transfers data between processes using window messages.

Some window messages specify the address of a block of memory in their *lParam* parameter. For example, the WM_SETTEXT message uses the *lParam* parameter as a pointer to a zero-terminated string that identifies the new text for the window. Consider the following call:

```
SendMessage(FindWindow("PROGMAN", NULL), WM_SETTEXT,
    0, (LPARAM) "A Test Caption");
```

This call seems harmless enough—it determines the window handle of the Program Manager's main window and attempts to change its caption to *A Test Caption*. But let's take a closer look at what happens here.

The string of the new title is contained in your process's address space. So the address of this string in your process space will be passed as the *lParam* parameter. When the window procedure for the Program Manager's main window receives this message, it looks at the *lParam* parameter and attempts to manipulate what it thinks is a zero-terminated string in order to make it the new title.

But the address in *lParam* points to a string in your address space—not in the Program Manager's address space. This is a big problem because a memory access violation is sure to occur. But if you execute the line above, you'll see that it works successfully. How can this be?

The answer is that the system looks specifically for the WM_SETTEXT message and handles it differently from the way it handles most other messages. When you call SendMessage, the code in the function checks whether you are trying to send a WM_SETTEXT message. If you are, it packs the zero-terminated string from your address space into a block of memory that it is going to share with the other process. Then it sends the message to the thread in the other process. When the receiving thread is ready to process the WM_SETTEXT message, it determines the location, in its own address space, of the shared block of memory that contains a copy of the new window text. The *lParam* parameter is initialized to point to this address, and the WM_SETTEXT message is dispatched to the appropriate window procedure. Boy, doesn't this seem like a lot of work?

Fortunately, most messages don't require this type of processing, which takes place only when sending interprocess messages. Special processing like this has to be performed for any message whose *wParam* or *lParam* parameters represent a pointer to a data structure.

Let's look at another case that requires special handling by the system—the WM_GETTEXT message. Suppose that your application contains the following code:

```
char szBuf[200];
SendMessage(FindWindow("PROGMAN", NULL), WM_GETTEXT,
    sizeof(szBuf), (LPARAM) szBuf);
```

The WM_GETTEXT message requests that the Program Manager's main window procedure fill the buffer pointed to by *szBuf* with the title of its window. When you send this message to a window in another process, the system must actually send two messages. First, the system sends a WM_GETTEXTLEN message to the window. The window procedure responds by returning the number of characters required to hold the window's title. The system can use this count to allocate a block of memory that will end up being shared between the two processes.

Once the memory block has been allocated, the system can send the WM_GETTEXT message to fill the memory block. Then the system switches back to the process that called SendMessage in the first place, copies the data from the shared memory block into the buffer pointed to by *szBuf*, and returns from the call to SendMessage.

Well, all of this is fine and good if you are sending messages that the system is aware of, but what if you want to create your own (WM_USER + x) message that you want to send from one process to a window in another? The system will not know that you want it to allocate a shared block of memory and to update pointers when sending. If you want to do this, you can use the new WM_COPYDATA message:

```
COPYDATASTRUCT cds;
SendMessage(hwndReceiver, WM_COPYDATA,
    (WPARAM) hwndSender, (LPARAM) &cds);
```

COPYDATASTRUCT is a structure defined in WINUSER.H, and it looks like this:

```
typedef struct tagCOPYDATASTRUCT {
    DWORD dwData;
    DWORD cbData;
    PVOID lpData;
} COPYDATASTRUCT;
```

345

When you're ready to send some data to a window in another process, you must first initialize the COPYDATASTRUCT structure. The *dwData* member is reserved for your own use. You can place any 32-bit value in it. For example, you might have occasion to send different types or categories of data to the other process. You can use this value to indicate the content of the data you are sending.

The *cbData* member specifies the number of bytes that you want to transfer to the other process, and the *lpData* member points to the first byte of the data. The address pointed to by *lpData* is, of course, in the sender's address space.

When SendMessage sees that you are sending a WM_COPYDATA message, it allocates a block of memory *cbData* bytes in size and copies the data from your address space to this block. It then sends the message to the destination window. When the receiving window procedure processes this message, the *lParam* parameter points to a COPYDATASTRUCT that exists in the address space of the receiving process. The *lpData* member of this structure points to the copied block of memory, and the address has been changed to reflect where the memory exists in the receiving process's address space.

There are two important things to note about the WM_COPYDATA message. First, always send this message; never post it. You can't post a WM_COPYDATA message because the system must free the copied memory after the receiving window procedure has processed the message. If you post the message, the system doesn't know when the WM_COPYDATA is processed and therefore can't free the copied block of memory.

The second item of note is that it takes some time for the system to make a copy of the data in the other process's address space. This means that you shouldn't have another thread running in the sending application that modifies the contents of the memory block while it is still being accessed until the call to SendMessage returns.

The Copy Data Sample Application

The CopyData application (COPYDATA.EXE), listed in Figure 6-9 beginning on page 348, demonstrates how to use the WM_COPYDATA message to send a block of data from one application to another. You'll need to have at least two copies of CopyData running to see it work. Each time you start a copy of CopyData, it presents a dialog box that looks like this:

To see data copied from one application to another, first change the text in the *Data1* and *Data2* edit controls. Then click on one of the two *Send Data? to other windows* buttons. When you click on one of these buttons, the program sends the data to all the running instances of CopyData. Each instance updates the contents of its own edit box to reflect the new data.

The following describes how CopyData works. When a user clicks on one of the two buttons, CopyData performs the following:

1. Initializes the *dwData* member of COPYDATASTRUCT with 0 (zero) if the user clicked on the *Send Data1 to other windows* button or 1 if the user clicked on the *Send Data2 to other windows* button.

2. Retrieves the length of the text string (in characters) from the appropriate edit box and adds one for a zero-terminating character. This value is converted from a number of characters to a number of bytes by multiplying by sizeof(TCHAR), and the result is then placed in the *cbData* member of COPYDATA-STRUCT.

3. Calls HeapAlloc to allocate a block of memory large enough to hold the length of the string in the edit box plus its zero-terminating character. The address of this block is stored in the *lpData* member of COPYDATASTRUCT.

4. Copies the text from the edit box into this memory block.

At this point, everything is ready to be sent to the other windows. To determine which windows to send the WM_COPYDATA message to, the following is performed:

1. Get the handle of the first window that is a sibling to the instance of CopyData the user is running.

2. Get the text of CopyData's title bar.

3. Cycle through all the sibling windows, comparing each window's title bar to CopyData's title bar. If the titles match, the WM_COPYDATA message is sent to the sibling window. Because I didn't do any special checks in this loop, the instance of CopyData that is calling SendMessage will send itself a WM_COPYDATA message. This demonstrates that WM_COPYDATA messages can be sent and received from the same thread.

4. After all the windows have been checked, CopyData calls HeapFree to free the memory block that it was using to hold the edit box text.

And that's all there is to sending data from one application to another using messages.

CopyData.ico

COPYDATA.C

```
/*****************************************************************
Module name: CopyData.C
Notices: Copyright (c) 1993 Jeffrey Richter
*****************************************************************/

#include <windows.h>
#include <windowsx.h>
#include <tchar.h>
#include "CopyData.H"

#define ARRAY_SIZE(A)  (sizeof(A) / sizeof((A)[0]))


//////////////////////////////////////////////////////////////////


// Microsoft does not include message cracker macros for
// the WM_COPYDATA message in WINDOWSX.H.
// I have written them here...
```

Figure 6-9. *(continued)*
The CopyData application.

Figure 6-9. *continued*

```
/* BOOL Cls_OnCopyData(HWND hwnd, HWND hwndFrom,
      PCOPYDATASTRUCT cds) */
#define HANDLE_WM_COPYDATA(hwnd, wParam, lParam, fn) \
    ((fn)((hwnd), (HWND)(wParam), \
      (PCOPYDATASTRUCT)lParam), 0L)
#define FORWARD_WM_COPYDATA(hwnd, hwndFrom, cds, fn) \
    (BOOL)(UINT)(DWORD)(fn)((hwnd), WM_COPYDATA, \
      (WPARAM)(hwndFrom), (LPARAM)(cds))

/////////////////////////////////////////////////////////////

BOOL Dlg_OnCopyData(HWND hwnd, HWND hwndFrom,
    PCOPYDATASTRUCT cds) {

    Edit_SetText(
      GetDlgItem(hwnd, cds->dwData ? ID_DATA2 : ID_DATA1),
      cds->lpData);
    return(TRUE);
}

/////////////////////////////////////////////////////////////

BOOL Dlg_OnInitDialog (HWND hwnd, HWND hwndFocus,
    LPARAM lParam) {

    // Associate an icon with the dialog box.
    SetClassLong(hwnd, GCL_HICON, (LONG)
      LoadIcon((HINSTANCE) GetWindowLong(hwnd, GWL_HINSTANCE),
      __TEXT("CopyData")));

    // Initialize the Edit control with some test data.
    Edit_SetText(GetDlgItem(hwnd, ID_DATA1),
      __TEXT("Some test data"));
    Edit_SetText(GetDlgItem(hwnd, ID_DATA2),
      __TEXT("Some more test data"));

    return(TRUE);
}

/////////////////////////////////////////////////////////////

void Dlg_OnCommand (HWND hwnd, int id, HWND hwndCtl,
    UINT codeNotify) {
```

(continued)

Figure 6-9. *continued*

```
HWND hwndEdit, hwndSibling;
COPYDATASTRUCT cds;
TCHAR szCaption[100], szCaptionSibling[100];

switch (id) {
    case ID_COPYDATA1:
    case ID_COPYDATA2:
        if (codeNotify != BN_CLICKED)
            break;

        hwndEdit = GetDlgItem(hwnd,
            (id == ID_COPYDATA1) ? ID_DATA1 : ID_DATA2);

        // Prepare the contents of the COPYDATASTRUCT
        // 0 = ID_DATA1, 1 = ID_DATA2
        cds.dwData = (DWORD) ((id == ID_COPYDATA1) ? 0 : 1);

        // Get the length of the data block
        // that we are sending.
        cds.cbData = (Edit_GetTextLength(hwndEdit) + 1) *
            sizeof(TCHAR);

        // Allocate a block of memory to hold the string.
        cds.lpData = HeapAlloc(GetProcessHeap(),
            HEAP_ZERO_MEMORY, cds.cbData);

        // Put the Edit control's string in the data block.
        Edit_GetText(hwndEdit, cds.lpData, cds.cbData);

        // Find the first overlapped window in the list.
        hwndSibling - GetFirstSibling(hwnd);

        // Get the caption of our window.
        GetWindowText(hwnd, szCaption,
            ARRAY_SIZE(szCaption));

        while (IsWindow(hwndSibling)) {
            // Get the caption of the potential
            // window to send the data to.
            GetWindowText(hwndSibling, szCaptionSibling,
                ARRAY_SIZE(szCaptionSibling));
```

(continued)

Figure 6-9. *continued*

```
            if (_tcscmp(szCaption, szCaptionSibling) == 0) {
               // If the window's caption is the same as ours,
               // send the data. This may mean that we are
               // sending the message to ourself. This is OK;
               // it demonstrates that WM_COPYDATA can be
               // used to send data to ourself.
               FORWARD_WM_COPYDATA(hwndSibling, hwnd,
                  &cds, SendMessage);
            }

            // Get the handle of the next overlapped window.
            hwndSibling = GetNextSibling(hwndSibling);
         }

         // Free the data buffer.
         HeapFree(GetProcessHeap(), 0, cds.lpData);
         break;

      case IDCANCEL:
         EndDialog(hwnd, id);
         break;
   }
}


////////////////////////////////////////////////////////////////

BOOL CALLBACK Dlg_Proc (HWND hDlg, UINT uMsg,
   WPARAM wParam, LPARAM lParam) {

   BOOL fProcessed = TRUE;

   switch (uMsg) {
      HANDLE_MSG(hDlg, WM_INITDIALOG, Dlg_OnInitDialog);
      HANDLE_MSG(hDlg, WM_COMMAND, Dlg_OnCommand);
      HANDLE_MSG(hDlg, WM_COPYDATA, Dlg_OnCopyData);

      default:
         fProcessed = FALSE;
         break;
   }
   return(fProcessed);
}
```

(continued)

Figure 6-9. *continued*

```
//////////////////////////////////////////////////////////////

int APIENTRY WinMain (HINSTANCE hInstance,
   HINSTANCE hPrevInstance, LPSTR lpszCmdLine, int nCmdShow) {

   DialogBox(hInstance, MAKEINTRESOURCE(DLG_COPYDATA),
      NULL, Dlg_Proc);
   return(0);
}


///////////////////////// End Of File /////////////////////////
```

COPYDATA.H

```
/***************************************************************
Module name: CopyData.H
Notices: Copyright (c) 1993 Jeffrey Richter
***************************************************************/

// Dialog and control IDs.
#define DLG_COPYDATA       1
#define ID_DATA1         100
#define ID_COPYDATA1     101
#define ID_DATA2         102
#define ID_COPYDATA2     103


///////////////////////// End Of File /////////////////////////
```

COPYDATA.RC

```
/***************************************************************
Module name: CopyData.RC
Notices: Copyright (c) 1993 Jeffrey Richter
***************************************************************/

#include <windows.h>
#include "CopyData.h"

CopyData  ICON  DISCARDABLE CopyData.Ico

DLG_COPYDATA DIALOG DISCARDABLE  38, 36, 220, 42
```

(continued)

Figure 6-9. *continued*

```
STYLE WS_BORDER | WS_MINIMIZEBOX | WS_POPUP | WS_VISIBLE |
    WS_CAPTION | WS_SYSMENU
CAPTION "WM_COPYDATA Message Share Application"
BEGIN
    LTEXT           "Data&1:",-1,4,4,24,12
    EDITTEXT        ID_DATA1,28,4,76,12
    PUSHBUTTON      "&Send Data1 to other windows",
                    ID_COPYDATA1, 112,4,104,14, WS_GROUP
    LTEXT           "Data&2:",-1,4,24,24,12
    EDITTEXT        ID_DATA2,28,24,76,12
    PUSHBUTTON      "Send &Data2 to other windows",
                    ID_COPYDATA2, 112,24,104,14,WS_GROUP
END


//////////////////////// End Of File ////////////////////////
```

CHAPTER SEVEN

DYNAMIC-LINK LIBRARIES

Dynamic-link libraries (DLLs) have been the cornerstone of Windows since its very first version. All the Windows API functions are contained in DLLs. The three most important DLLs are KERNEL32.DLL, which consists of functions for managing memory; USER32.DLL, which consists of functions for performing user-interface tasks such as window creation and message sending; and GDI32.DLL, which consists of functions for drawing graphical images and displaying text.

In addition to these, Windows contains several other DLLs that contain functions for performing more specialized tasks. For example, OLECLI32.DLL is the object linking and embedding client library, COMDLG32.DLL contains the common dialogs (such as File Open and File Save), and LZ32.DLL supports file decompression.

How DLLs Have Changed from 16-Bit Windows to Windows NT

The way the system deals with DLLs has changed from 16-bit Windows to Windows NT in two big ways—how the DLL is made available to a process and how a DLL's local heap facilitates data sharing among processes. DLLs have also changed in other ways, which we'll discuss in this chapter, but let's begin by reviewing how 16-bit Windows works with DLLs and then discuss the changes in DLLs in Windows NT.

How 16-Bit Windows Makes DLLs Available to Applications

In 16-bit Windows, loading a DLL means that, in a sense, the DLL becomes part of the operating system. After the DLL is loaded, any and all applications currently running immediately have access to the DLL and the functions that the DLL contains. An application can determine whether a DLL was loaded by calling the GetModuleHandle function and passing it the name of the DLL:

```
HMODULE GetModuleHandle(LPCSTR lpszModule);
```

If GetModuleHandle returns NULL, the application knows that the DLL isn't loaded into the system yet. If the return value is not NULL, the value is a handle to the loaded DLL. This value is systemwide, meaning that any application can use the handle to manipulate the library.

An application can also load a DLL into memory by calling Load-Library:

```
HINSTANCE LoadLibrary(LPCSTR lpszLibFileName);
```

This function causes the system to search the user's hard disk for the library, loads the library into memory, and returns the handle identifying the library. Once loaded, the library acts as though it's part of the operating system—any application can access it. Calling LoadLibrary also increments a usage count associated with the library. If an application calls LoadLibrary to load a DLL that was already loaded into the system, the system simply increments the DLL's usage count and returns the handle that identifies the DLL.

Once an application has the handle of a library, it can get the memory address of a DLL function by calling GetProcAddress and passing it the handle of the library and the name of the function:

```
FARPROC GetProcAddress(HINSTANCE hinst, LPCSTR lpszProcName);
```

When an application no longer needs to access the functions in a DLL, the application calls FreeLibrary:

```
void FreeLibrary(HINSTANCE hinst);
```

This function decrements the usage count for the DLL and, if that usage count reaches 0 (zero), the DLL is removed from the system and is no longer available to any applications.

16-bit Windows has an additional function, GetModuleUsage, that returns the usage count for a loaded DLL:

```
int GetModuleUsage(HINSTANCE hinst);
```

How Windows NT Makes DLLs Available to Processes

The biggest change in DLLs from 16-bit Windows to Windows NT is how the DLL is made accessible to the different applications. In Windows

NT, DLLs don't become part of the operating system; instead, they become part of the process that loads the DLL. When a Windows NT process calls the LoadLibrary function to explicitly load a library into memory, Windows NT creates a file-mapping object for the DLL (as it does when applications are loaded) and maps the DLL into the address space of the process. It is only after the code and data have been mapped into the process's address space that the threads in the process can make calls to functions in the DLL.

If another process requires the use of the same DLL, Windows NT simply maps another view of the same DLL into the process's address space. Because each process gets its own mapped view of the DLL, it's possible that Windows NT won't map the DLL at the same address in both address spaces.

For example, the DLL function NukeDeficit could get mapped to address 0x12345678 in one process and address 0x77700066 in another process. As a result, a process would not be able to pass the function's address among processes; each process would need to call GetProcAddress individually.

If a thread within a process calls LoadLibrary to load a library that is already mapped into the process's address space, Windows NT doesn't map the library again. Instead, it simply increments a usage count associated with the library and returns the same handle to the library. However, unlike 16-bit Windows, in Windows NT this usage count is maintained on a per-process basis. That is, when a process loads a library for the first time, the usage count for that library becomes 1. If that process calls LoadLibrary to load the same DLL a second time, the usage count for the library with respect to the process becomes 2.

If another process calls LoadLibrary to load a DLL that is being used by another process, the system maps the code and data for the DLL into the calling process's address space and increments the DLL's usage count (with respect to this process) to 1.

When a process no longer needs to access the functions in a DLL, a thread in the process calls FreeLibrary. FreeLibrary decrements the usage count of the DLL and if the usage count reaches 0 (zero), the DLL is unmapped from the process's address space. Both the LoadLibrary and FreeLibrary functions affect the visibility of a DLL only with respect to the process that calls the functions. Neither of these functions can affect the visibility of a DLL with respect to other processes.

The 16-bit Windows GetModuleUsage function is no longer available in the Win32 API. Microsoft dropped this function because

GetModuleUsage could no longer report the usage count of the DLL with respect to all processes running in the system. However, I think that Microsoft should have kept the function and made it return the usage count of the DLL with respect to the process.

Sharing Data Among Processes Using a DLL's Local Heap

In 16-bit Windows, a DLL has its own data segment. This data segment houses all the static and global variables needed by the DLL as well as the DLL's own private local heap. When a DLL function allocates memory using LocalAlloc, the memory that satisfies this request is taken from the DLL's data segment. This segment, like all segments, has a maximum limit of 64 KB.

This design allows applications to easily share data among multiple processes because the DLL's local heap is available to the DLL regardless of which process called the function contained in the DLL. Here is an example of how a DLL can be used for sharing data between two applications:

```
HLOCAL g_hData = NULL;

HLOCAL SetData (LPVOID lpvData, int nSize) {
    g_hData = LocalAlloc(LMEM_MOVEABLE, nSize);
    LPVOID lpv = LocalLock(g_hData);
    memcpy(lpv, lpvData, nSize);
    LocalUnlock(g_hData);
}

void GetData (LPVOID lpvData, int nSize) {
    LPVOID lpv = LocalLock(g_hData);
    memcpy(lpvData, lpv, nSize);
    LocalUnlock(g_hData);
}
```

When SetData is called, it allocates a block of memory out of the DLL's data segment, copies the data pointed to by the *lpvData* parameter into the block, and saves the handle to the block in a global variable, *g_hData*. A totally different application can now call GetData. GetData uses the global variable identifying the local memory handle, locks the block, copies the data into the buffer identified by the *lpvData* parameter, and returns. This is an easy way to share data between two processes in 16-bit Windows.

Unfortunately, this method doesn't work at all in Windows NT for two reasons. First, DLLs in Windows NT don't receive their own local heap. When a process loads a DLL, the system maps the code and data for the DLL into the address space of the process. Any memory allocation calls made by functions in the DLL cause memory to be allocated from the process's address space—no other process has access to this allocated memory.

Second, the global and static variables allocated by a DLL are also not shared among multiple mappings of the DLL. In other words, if two processes use the same DLL, the code for the DLL is loaded into memory once but is mapped into the address space of both processes. However, each process has a separate set of the DLL's global and static variables. The system gives each mapping of a DLL its own set of variables by taking advantage of the copy-on-write mechanism (discussed in Chapter 4).

LibMain Versus DllEntryPoint Versus DllMain

Another change from 16-bit Windows to Windows NT involves the mechanics of building and initializing a DLL. When producing DLLs for 16-bit Windows, you always need to link a small assembly-language module into your DLL. This module performs some low-level initialization and calls your LibMain function, passing parameters that the system has passed to the assembly-language module in CPU registers. Fortunately, Microsoft includes the source code for this module on the SDK disks. The assembled OBJ file is also included on the SDK disks, which is helpful to those of us who don't own a macro assembler.

As mentioned earlier, Windows NT is designed as a portable operating system that's available on different hardware platforms using different CPUs. So, Microsoft needed to remove the necessity for any assembly-language modules. To create a DLL, you need only to write your code and link it as if it were an application. Most of your DLLs should port directly to Win32 with very little modification. The two areas that will require modification are the LibMain and Windows Exit Procedure (WEP) functions.

In 16-bit Windows, the system calls the library's LibMain function whenever the library is loaded into the system and calls the library's WEP function whenever the library is being removed from the system. Conceptually, the WEP function was a nice addition to Windows (it didn't exist prior to version 3.0), but Microsoft never implemented it correctly. In low-memory situations, the WEP function can actually be called before the LibMain function, and it might be called using the Kernel's very small stack. This means that using local variables in the WEP function might cause the entire system to crash. You'll be happy to know that all these problems have been solved in Windows NT.

For Win32 applications, the code in both your LibMain and WEP functions are combined into a single new DllEntryPoint function:

```
BOOL WINAPI DLLEntryPoint (HINSTANCE hinstDLL, DWORD fdwReason,
    LPVOID lpvReserved) {

    switch (fdwReason) {
    case DLL_PROCESS_ATTACH:
        // The DLL is being mapped into the process's address space.
        break;

    case DLL_THREAD_ATTACH:
        // A thread is being created.
        break;

    case DLL_THREAD_DETACH:
        // A thread is exiting cleanly.
        break;

    case DLL_PROCESS_DETACH:
        // The DLL is being unmapped from the process's address
        // space.
        break;
    }
    return(TRUE);
}
```

Windows NT calls this function whenever a DLL attaches to a process and whenever a DLL detaches from a process. The *hinstDLL* parameter contains the instance handle of the DLL. Like the *hInstance* parameter to WinMain, this value identifies the virtual address of where the view of the DLL was mapped in the process's address space. Usually, you'll save this parameter in a global variable so that you can use it in calls that load resources such as DialogBox and LoadString.

The *fdwReason* parameter indicates why Windows NT is calling DllEntryPoint. This parameter can be one of the following values:

Identifier	Meaning
DLL_PROCESS_ATTACH	The DLL is being mapped into the process's address space.
DLL_PROCESS_DETACH	The DLL is being unmapped from the process's address space.
DLL_THREAD_ATTACH	A thread is being created by the process.
DLL_THREAD_DETACH	A thread in the process is exiting cleanly.

The last parameter, *lpvReserved*, is reserved and is usually passed to you as NULL.

The return value from DllEntryPoint is ignored for all values of the *fdwReason* parameter except for one—DLL_PROCESS_ATTACH. For DLL_PROCESS_ATTACH, the return value indicates whether the DLL's initialization was successful. You should return TRUE if the initialization was successful.

Just like 16-bit Windows, Windows NT offers two ways to attach a DLL to a process—implicit attachment and explicit attachment. A DLL is loaded implicitly when the process or another DLL makes a call to a function in another DLL. This is the case when you call any of the Win32 functions from within your process. When you link a process that makes a call to CreateWindow, the linker must somehow resolve this external reference. You satisfy the linker by specifying the import library for USER32.DLL. As the linker creates your EXE file, it puts information into the file that tells the Windows NT loader that this process needs to have the USER32.DLL library attached it so that the process can call CreateWindow when necessary.

When the user invokes your application, the Windows NT loader loads (if necessary) and maps a view of the USER32.DLL library into the process's address space. When this occurs, USER32's DllEntryPoint function is called with a reason of DLL_PROCESS_ATTACH. By the time your application starts executing, the USER32.DLL library is attached and initialized. If the library's DllEntryPoint function returns FALSE (indicating unsuccessful initialization), Windows NT terminates the process with an error. None of the application's code will get a chance to execute.

You'll notice a big difference here compared to 16-bit Windows. In 16-bit Windows, a DLL's LibMain function is called only once when the DLL is loaded. If other applications are loaded and require the same DLL, 16-bit Windows doesn't call the DLL's LibMain function again. In other words, the LibMain function is called only once—when the DLL is loaded. In contrast, the DllEntryPoint function in Win32 DLLs is called with a reason of DLL_PROCESS_ATTACH every time the DLL is mapped into another process's address space. If 10 applications all require USER32.DLL, USER32's DllEntryPoint is called 10 times with a reason of DLL_PROCESS_ATTACH.

A process can also explicitly attach a DLL to itself when one of the process's threads calls LoadLibrary. This call causes Windows NT to locate the library and attach it to the process. After a view of the library is mapped into the process's address space, Windows NT calls the library's DllEntryPoint function passing a reason of DLL_PROCESS-_ATTACH. This gives the library a chance to initialize itself for this process. If the initialization is successful (TRUE is returned), the call to LoadLibrary returns and threads within the process can start making calls to functions in the library. If the library fails to initialize (returns FALSE), Windows NT unmaps the view of the library from the process's address space and does *not* call DllEntryPoint with a reason of DLL-_PROCESS_DETACH. In addition, LoadLibrary returns a library instance handle of NULL to the process, which indicates to the process that the library didn't load successfully. You should write your code expecting that you might not be able to load a library and deal with that in whichever way seems appropriate for your application.

Under 16-bit Windows, LoadLibrary indicates that an error occurs by returning a handle value less than 32. The value returned indicates the reason for the failure. In Win32, NULL is always returned if an error occurs. To determine the reason for the error, the application must call GetLastError.

Rules for Process and Thread Attachment and Detachment

DllEntryPoint is called with a reason of DLL_PROCESS_ATTACH whenever a DLL is attached to a process. At that time, the DLL performs any process-relative initialization. If the DLL is attached implicitly, DllEntryPoint is called before the process's primary thread begins executing the WinMain function.

As listed in the table on page 361, Windows NT calls DllEntryPoint with a reason of DLL_THREAD_ATTACH if a DLL is already mapped into the process's address space, and the process then creates a new thread. Windows NT doesn't call DllEntryPoint with a reason of DLL-_THREAD_ATTACH for the primary thread of the process.

If the DLL is being loaded as a result of a thread calling Load-Library, DllEntryPoint is called with a reason of DLL_PROCESS-_ATTACH before LoadLibrary returns to the application. In this case, the process could already have several threads running in the process. Because these threads are already running prior to the loading of the library, Windows NT doesn't call DllEntryPoint with DLL-_THREAD_ATTACH for any existing threads. Windows NT also doesn't call DllEntryPoint with DLL_THREAD_ATTACH for the thread that is calling LoadLibrary.

If a process calls LoadLibrary more than once to load the same library (without calling FreeLibrary in between), Windows NT doesn't call DllEntryPoint again with a reason of DLL_PROCESS_ATTACH be-cause the DLL is already attached. However, the library usage count does increment. The process will then need to call FreeLibrary twice, decrementing the usage count to 0 (zero) before the library is actually detached from the process's address space. DllEntryPoint will not be called with DLL_PROCESS_DETACH for calls to FreeLibrary unless the usage count for the library reaches 0 (zero) for the process and the view of the library is being unmapped.

Windows NT calls DllEntryPoint with DLL_THREAD_ATTACH only for new threads that are created after the DLL is mapped into the process's address space. The DLL can perform any thread-relative initialization for the newly created threads during this processing.

DllEntryPoint is called with DLL_THREAD_DETACH when a thread is exiting cleanly. Because of the rules stated above, it is possible to have the following situation occur: A process creates a thread and the thread calls LoadLibrary to load a DLL. The DLL's DllEntryPoint func-tion is called with DLL_PROCESS_ATTACH, but no call is made with DLL_THREAD_ATTACH. Now the thread that loaded the DLL exits. When this happens, the DLL's DllEntryPoint function is called with DLL_THREAD_DETACH. Notice that the DLL is being notified that the thread is detaching, but it never received a DLL_THREAD-_ATTACH notifying the library that the thread had attached. For this reason, you must be extremely careful when performing any thread-relative de-initialization. Fortunately, most programs are written so that the thread that calls LoadLibrary is the same thread that calls Free-Library. The situation described on the previous page occurs very rarely, but you should be aware of Windows NT's behavior.

Windows NT calls DllEntryPoint with a reason of DLL_PROCESS-_DETACH when a DLL is being unmapped from a process's address space. This can occur in one of two ways: explicitly—a process called FreeLibrary causing the library's usage count to become 0 (zero); or implicitly—the process is terminating. Even if the process had loaded the library explicitly by calling LoadLibrary, the library will detach if the process terminates without calling FreeLibrary. A DLL should be written to perform any of its process-relative cleanup when it receives the DLL_PROCESS_DETACH notification.

If any threads are still running when the DLL is detached, DllEntryPoint is not called with DLL_THREAD_DETACH for any of these threads. You might want to check for this in your DLL-_PROCESS_DETACH processing so that you can perform any cleanup that might be necessary.

If a process or thread is exiting by calling ExitProcess or Exit-Thread, DllEntryPoint is called with a reason of either DLL_PROCESS-_DETACH or DLL_THREAD_DETACH, respectively. However, if the process or thread is terminated with TerminateProcess or Terminate-Thread, DllEntryPoint is not notified with DLL_PROCESS_DETACH or DLL_THREAD_DETACH.

These functions should be used only when you need to terminate a process or thread if no other "clean" method exists. The system assumes that the process or thread is not responding for some reason and forces its termination. Because the process or thread is probably in a nonresponsive state when TerminateProcess or TerminateThread is called, the system doesn't call the DLL's DllEntryPoint function when the process or thread terminates. This means, of course, that the DLL cannot perform any process or thread cleanup that might be necessary, which is probably the most important reason why you should avoid making calls to TerminateProcess and TerminateThread.

DLLs and the C Runtime Library

The odds are, when you write code in a DLL, some of that code will require the use of the C Runtime Library. But before you can safely call any of the C Runtime Library functions, you must initialize the library. To do so, you call:

```
BOOL WINAPI _CRT_INIT(HINSTANCE hinstDLL, DWORD fdwReason,
   LPVOID lpReserved);
```

This function, contained in the Microsoft C Runtime Library, initializes the C Runtime Library. To properly set up your DLL to use the C Runtime Library, implement your DllEntryPoint function as follows:

```
BOOL WINAPI DllEntryPoint (HINSTANCE hinstDLL, DWORD fdwReason,
   LPVOID lpReserved) {

   BOOL fSuccess = TRUE;

   switch (fdwReason) {
      case DLL_PROCESS_ATTACH:
      case DLL_THREAD_ATTACH:
         // Initialize the C Runtime Library before calling your
         // own code.
         if (!_CRT_INIT(hinstDLL, fdwReason, lpReserved)) {
            fSuccess = FALSE;
         } else {
            fSuccess = DllMain(hinstDLL, fdwReason, lpReserved);
            if (!fSuccess) {
               // The C Runtime initialized correctly but the
               // DLL didn't -- we must de-initialize the
               // C Runtime.
               _CRT_INIT(hinstDLL,
                  (fdwReason == DLL_PROCESS_ATTACH) ?
                  DLL_PROCESS_DETACH : DLL_THREAD_DETACH,
                  lpReserved);
            }
         }
         break;

      case DLL_PROCESS_DETACH:
      case DLL_THREAD_DETACH:
         // Call your own code before terminating the C Runtime
         // Library.
         DllMain(hinstDll, fdwReason, lpReserved);
         _CRT_INIT(hinstDLL, fdwReason, lpReserved);
         break;
   }
   return(fSuccess);
}
```

When you are being notified of a process or thread attach, be sure that you call _CRT_INIT prior to calling any C Runtime Library functions.

And be sure that you de-initialize the C Runtime Library after you execute your code when the DLL is being notified of a thread or process detach.

Wouldn't it be nice if this function were already implemented by Microsoft as part of the C Runtime Library? Well, it is. The C Runtime Library includes a function called _DllMainCRTStartup that does exactly what you see on the previous page. All you need to do is change the name of your DllEntryPoint function to DllMain. Then, when you link your application, be sure that the *-entry* switch specifies _DllMainCRT-Startup like this:

```
-entry:_DllMainCRTStartup$(DLLENTRY)
```

In this way, you don't even need to think about the C Runtime initialization because it's done for you automatically. In fact, the C Runtime Library also includes a function called DllMain that looks like this:

```
BOOL WINAPI DllMain(HINSTANCE hinstDLL, DWORD fdwReason,
    LPVOID lpReserved) {

    return(TRUE);
}
```

If you don't have a function called DllMain in any of your DLL's source files, the linker automatically links this DllMain function. You don't even need to create a DllMain or a DllEntryPoint function.

Partitioning a Process's Address Space

As you know by now, every process running in Windows NT has its very own 4-GB address space. Regions of this address space are allocated for the application's executable file that identifies the program's code, any dynamic-link libraries that attach to the process, the stacks needed by each thread running in the process, the default heap (containing the local and global heap as well), and any additional heaps that are created using the HeapCreate function.

When creating an application, it is very likely that you will make calls to functions that exist in DLLs. When the compiler and linker produce the executable file, any calls to DLL functions are directed to an *image activation table*. This table is created by the linker inside the executable file. Each executable file and each DLL contain a single image activation table. When the application is invoked, the Windows NT loader must attach (map views of) any DLLs required by the application and fix up the entries in this image activation table.

For example, if an application's code contains a call to the Create-Window function, the code generated by that call is actually a call to the CreateWindow entry in the executable file's image activation table. When the loader loads the application, it first automatically maps the USER32 dynamic-link library into the process's address space. Then the loader determines the virtual address of the CreateWindow function and changes the CreateWindow entry in the application's image activation table to be a jump to this address.

In 16-bit Windows, executable files contain lookup tables to the place in the application's code where calls to DLL functions are made. Then, whenever the loader loads a code segment into memory, it uses these lookup tables to patch the code segment in memory to point to the correct address for the DLL function. In 16-bit Windows, the address of a DLL is constant for all applications using the DLL. In other words, if USER.EXE's CreateWindow function was at address 1234:2468, all processes that called CreateWindow would end up calling 1234:2468.

In Windows NT, this is not true. A DLL can be mapped into a different address space depending on the process that maps it. If Microsoft had continued to use the 16-bit Windows scheme for fixing up dynamic links, Windows NT would require additional memory and would run much slower. So, to help make the system more responsive and to use less memory, Microsoft included this image activation table in each 32-bit executable. Needing only to update the image activation table makes the system perform faster because the loader has only one location in memory to which it can update an address.

In 16-bit Windows, if a single code segment has 10 separate calls to CreateWindow, the loader needs to fix up 10 different locations whenever the segment is loaded into memory. In Windows NT, this is not the case. The loader must fix up only one address in the image activation table. All the calls to CreateWindow in the program's code call this single address in the image activation table. The drawback of this method is that each call to a DLL function requires a call to an entry in the image activation table, which in turn jumps to the actual function. This additional jump makes running the program slower but loading the program faster.

Here is another way the image activation table uses memory more efficiently. In 16-bit Windows, the CreateWindow function is at the same address regardless of the process calling it. In Windows NT, this is not necessarily true. If the Windows NT loader behaved like the 16-bit Windows loader and modified the address of the function as it appeared in the code, multiple instances of the same application would be unable to share the same physical pages of code. This is because the address of the DLL functions differs for each process. If Windows NT attempted to alter the address of the DLL function, it would detect a write to a page containing code. This would cause Windows NT to perform its copy-on-write logic, and as a result, allocate a new physical page of memory, copy the contents of the original page, and then change the address in this newly allocated page to point to the DLL function.

Because calls to DLL functions are frequently sprinkled throughout an application's code, this could require an enormous amount of memory. The image activation table helps to alleviate this problem. By placing all the DLL function fixups into a contiguous section in the executable, only this section will need to be copied for each instance of a process. The bulk of the application's code will go unmodified and can therefore be easily shared among all instances.

You can see how the image activation table is used to help conserve memory, but now you can also see that programs run a little slower by making all their DLL function calls via the table.

A DLL's Base Address

In this section, we'll look at another technique that Windows NT uses to increase the speed of loading an application. This technique also reduces the amount of memory required by multiple instances of an application.

To help reduce the load time of an application, Windows NT makes some assumptions about how an address space is partitioned. First, Windows NT reserves the first 64 KB of a process's address space. If a process attempts to read or write to any memory with a virtual address between 0x0000000 and 0x0000FFFF, an access violation occurs. Microsoft built the system in this way so that application developers can quickly find any references to memory using NULL pointers. Windows NT also reserves the 64 KB just below the process's 2-GB boundary (between 0x7FFF0000 and 0x7FFFFFFF). Because Windows NT uses virtual memory, reserving these two memory ranges doesn't cause an actual loss of physical memory. The system also reserves the top 2 GB of the process's address space. Any access from 0x80000000 to 0xFFFFFFFF also causes an access violation.

All the system DLLs are usually loaded at the same virtual address regardless of the process. The DLLs load in this way by specifying the /BASE:address switch to the linker or by using the *BASE* switch in the LIBRARY statement in the module's definition file. The two tables in Figures 7-1 and 7-2 show most of the more common system DLLs and their base addresses. The first table is sorted by DLL name, and the second table is the identical information sorted by address:

DLL	Address	DLL	Address
AB32	03800000	HTUI	6B300000
ACLEDIT	76000000	IFSUTIL	09D40000
ADVAPI32	60300000	IMPEXP32	07800000
ALRSVC	6AE00000	IOLOGMSG	09700000
BASESRV	60800000	KBDUS	73700000
BDE	79000000	KERNEL32	60600000
BOWSVC	6B700000	LMUICMN0	77000000
CARDS	1D000000	LMUICMN1	78000000
CFG3270	1C000000	LOCALMON	6AA00000
COMCTL32	000D0000	LOCALSPL	6A200000
COMDLG32	44000000	LSASRV	6B400000
CRTDLL	10010000	LZ32	1C000000
CSRRTL	60400000	MAILM32	04000000
CSRSRV	60500000	MAPI32	07000000
CUFAT	09E50000	MCIAVI32	1C000000
CUHPFS	09F60000	MCICDA	68300000
DEMIL32	02000000	MCIOLE32	70E00000
DLC3270	1C000000	MCISEQ	6A800000
DLCAPI	6A000000	MCIWAVE	67F00000
FMIFS	0A070000	MF3216	20000000
FRAME32	02800000	MMDRV	69F00000
FTENG32	1C000000	MMSNDSRV	6B500000
FTUI32	1D000000	MORICONS	01020000
GDI32	64000000	MPR	76100000
HAL	80400000	MPRUI	76500000
HEAPTAGS	7E100000	MSAUDITE	6AB00000

Figure 7-1.
System DLLs and their base addresses, sorted by DLL name.

(continued)

Figure 7-1. *continued*

DLL	Address	DLL	Address
MSNCDET	79100000	RASMSG	09700000
MSOBJS	6AC00000	RASMXS	30000000
MSPRIVS	63600000	RASRES	01000000
MSSCHD32	08000000	RASSAUTH	66000000
MSSFS32	05000000	RASSER	30000000
MSV1_0	63500000	RESOLVER	75400000
MSVFW32	1C100000	RPCLTC1	68100000
MSVIDC32	1C200000	RPCLTC3	6B200000
MVAPI32	1E000000	RPCLTC5	6A400000
NDDEAPI	79000000	RPCLTS1	68000000
NETAPI32	61800000	RPCLTS3	6B100000
NETBIOS	79000000	RPCLTS5	6A300000
NETDTECT	79000000	RPCNS4	10000000
NETEVENT	09700000	RPCRT4	67B00000
NETH	09680000	SAMLIB	635A0000
NETLOGON	6A500000	SAMSRV	69D00000
NETMSG	09600000	SCHMSG32	08800000
NETRAP	63700000	SENDFL32	0B800000
NTDLL	60100000	SETUPDLL	01000000
NTLANMAN	76200000	SHELL32	1C500000
NTVDM	01000000	SNA3270	1C000000
OLECLI32	68E00000	SOCKUTIL	75300000
OLESVR32	68D00000	SPOOLSS	6BA00000
PABNSP32	04800000	SRVSVC	6AF00000
PERFCTRS	07500000	STORE32	06000000
PSXDLL	63200000	TCPIPSVC	75700000
RASADMIN	66000000	TRC3270	1C000000
RASAPI32	7E000000	TRNSCH32	09000000
RASCAUTH	66000000	UFAT	09B20000
RASCFG	01000000	UHPFS	09A10000
RASFIL32	7D000000	ULIB	09800000
RASGTWY	66000000	UNTFS	09C30000
RASMAN	56000000	UREG	0A290000

(continued)

Figure 7-1. *continued*

DLL	Address	DLL	Address
USER32	60A00000	WINMM	67D00000
VDMDBG	7A000000	WINSPOOL	62600000
VDMREDIR	03000000	WINSRV	60C00000
VERSION	44000000	WINSTRM	75200000
VFORM32	03000000	WKSSVC	6B000000
VGA	62200000	WOW32	02000000
VGA256	62200000	WSHTCPIP	75A00000
WGPOMG32	06800000	WSOCK32	75000000
WIN32SPL	6A100000	XACTSRV	69B00000

Address	DLL	Address	DLL
000D0000	COMCTL32	08000000	MSSCHD32
01000000	NTVDM	08800000	SCHMSG32
01000000	RASCFG	09000000	TRNSCH32
01000000	RASRES	09600000	NETMSG
01000000	SETUPDLL	09680000	NETH
01020000	MORICONS	09700000	IOLOGMSG
02000000	DEMIL32	09700000	NETEVENT
02000000	WOW32	09700000	RASMSG
02800000	FRAME32	09800000	ULIB
03000000	VDMREDIR	09A10000	UHPFS
03000000	VFORM32	09B20000	UFAT
03800000	AB32	09C30000	UNTFS
04000000	MAILM32	09D40000	IFSUTIL
04800000	PABNSP32	09E50000	CUFAT
05000000	MSSFS32	09F60000	CUHPFS
06000000	STORE32	0A070000	FMIFS
06800000	WGPOMG32	0A290000	UREG
07000000	MAPI32	0B800000	SENDFL32
07500000	PERFCTRS	10000000	RPCNS4
07800000	IMPEXP32	10010000	CRTDLL

Figure 7-2. *(continued)*

System DLLs and their base addresses, sorted by address.

Figure 7-2. *continued*

Address	DLL	Address	DLL
1C000000	CFG3270	635A0000	SAMLIB
1C000000	DLC3270	63600000	MSPRIVS
1C000000	FTENG32	63700000	NETRAP
1C000000	LZ32	64000000	GDI32
1C000000	MCIAVI32	66000000	RASADMIN
1C000000	SNA3270	66000000	RASCAUTH
1C000000	TRC3270	66000000	RASGTWY
1C100000	MSVFW32	66000000	RASSAUTH
1C200000	MSVIDC32	67B00000	RPCRT4
1C500000	SHELL32	67D00000	WINMM
1D000000	CARDS	67F00000	MCIWAVE
1D000000	FTUI32	68000000	RPCLTS1
1E000000	MVAPI32	68100000	RPCLTC1
20000000	MF3216	68300000	MCICDA
30000000	RASMXS	68D00000	OLESVR32
30000000	RASSER	68E00000	OLECLI32
44000000	COMDLG32	69B00000	XACTSRV
44000000	VERSION	69D00000	SAMSRV
56000000	RASMAN	69F00000	MMDRV
60100000	NTDLL	6A000000	DLCAPI
60300000	ADVAPI32	6A100000	WIN32SPL
60400000	CSRRTL	6A200000	LOCALSPL
60500000	CSRSRV	6A300000	RPCLTS5
60600000	KERNEL32	6A400000	RPCLTC5
60800000	BASESRV	6A500000	NETLOGON
60A00000	USER32	6A800000	MCISEQ
60C00000	WINSRV	6AA00000	LOCALMON
61800000	NETAPI32	6AB00000	MSAUDITE
62200000	VGA	6AC00000	MSOBJS
62200000	VGA256	6AE00000	ALRSVC
62600000	WINSPOOL	6AF00000	SRVSVC
63200000	PSXDLL	6B000000	WKSSVC
63500000	MSV1_0	6B100000	RPCLTS3

(continued)

Figure 7-2. *continued*

Address	DLL	Address	DLL
6B200000	RPCLTC3	76100000	MPR
6B300000	HTUI	76200000	NTLANMAN
6B400000	LSASRV	76500000	MPRUI
6B500000	MMSNDSRV	77000000	LMUICMN0
6B700000	BOWSVC	78000000	LMUICMN1
6BA00000	SPOOLSS	79000000	BDE
70E00000	MCIOLE32	79000000	NDDEAPI
73700000	KBDUS	79000000	NETBIOS
75000000	WSOCK32	79000000	NETDTECT
75200000	WINSTRM	79100000	MSNCDET
75300000	SOCKUTIL	7A000000	VDMDBG
75400000	RESOLVER	7D000000	RASFIL32
75700000	TCPIPSVC	7E000000	RASAPI32
75A00000	WSHTCPIP	7E100000	HEAPTAGS
76000000	ACLEDIT	80400000	HAL

You can obtain the base address of a DLL (or EXE) by executing the following line at the command prompt:

```
C:\>LINK32 -dump -headers USER32.DLL
```

This line displays all kinds of information. Only the beginning of the output is shown here. The base address of the DLL can be found in the **OPTIONAL HEADER VALUES** section.

```
Dump of file user32.dll

PE signature found

FILE HEADER VALUES
     14C machine (i386)
       9 number of sections
2B951787 time date stamp Wed Mar 03 12:39:35 1993
    3C2C0 file pointer to symbol table
    1321 number of symbols
      E0 size of optional header
    A18E characteristics
            Executable
            Line numbers stripped
```

(continued)

373

```
                    Local symbols stripped
                    Bytes reversed
                    32 bit word machine
                    DLL

        OPTIONAL HEADER VALUES
             10B magic #
            2.29 linker version
           2D200 size of code
           44200 size of initialized data
             400 size of uninitialized data
            D5BC address of entry point
            1000 base of code
           2F000 base of data
                 ----- new -----
        60A00000 image base          <-- Look over here!
            1000 section alignment
             200 file alignment
               2 subsystem (Windows GUI)
             0.B operating system version
             0.0 image version
             3.A subsystem version
           78000 size of image
             400 size of headers
               0 checksum
          100000 size of stack reserve
            1000 size of stack commit
          100000 size of heap reserve
            1000 size of heap commit
           31000 [    3a80] address [size] of Export Directory
           39000 [      50] address [size] of Import Directory
           35000 [     3a0] address [size] of Resource Directory
               0 [       0] address [size] of Exception Directory
               0 [       0] address [size] of Security Directory
           3B000 [    1444] address [size] of Base Relocation Directory
           30020 [      54] address [size] of Debug Directory
               0 [       0] address [size] of Description Directory
               0 [       0] address [size] of Special Directory
               0 [       0] address [size] of Thread
            Local Storage Directory
               0 [       0] address [size] of NTDLL Configuration Directory
               0 [       0] address [size] of Application
            Specific Directory
               0 [       0] address [size] of Application
            Specific Directory
```

(continued)

```
    0 [        0] address [size] of Application
       Specific Directory
    0 [        0] address [size] of Application
       Specific Directory
    0 [        0] address [size] of Application
       Specific Directory

SECTION HEADER #1
   .text name
       0 physical address
    1000 virtual address
   2D200 size of raw data
     400 file pointer to raw data
       0 file pointer to relocation table
       0 file pointer to line numbers
       0 number of relocations
       0 number of line numbers
60000020 flags
         Code
         Execute Read

SECTION HEADER #2
   .bss name
       0 physical address
   2F000 virtual address
     400 size of raw data
       0 file pointer to raw data
       0 file pointer to relocation table
       0 file pointer to line numbers
       0 number of relocations
       0 number of line numbers
C0000080 flags
         Uninitialized Data
         Read Write
       .
       .
       .
```

Most of the processes running make most of their calls to the system DLLs, which can save both memory and time. All the entries in the image activation table are grouped together by DLL. That is, all the calls to functions in USER32 are grouped together and all the calls to functions in GDI32 are grouped together. Because of the *BASE* switch, it is very likely that a DLL will be mapped to the same virtual address regardless of the instance of the application. When the Windows NT loader detects a DLL loading at an address other than its preferred address, the loader must fix the contents of the process's image activation table. As the loader is modifying the process's image activation table, the system detects that the loader is writing to the image activation table, which involves the system's copy-on-write logic, and a new image activation table is created for the process.

If you are designing your own DLLs, you can use the *BASE* switch yourself to help reduce memory usage and to make your application load quicker. If the loader cannot map the DLL into the requested virtual address, the DLL will be mapped elsewhere and the loader will fix up the references in the image activation table. The following table shows how the process's address space is partitioned.

Virtual Address	Contents
2 GB to 4 GB	Reserved for operating system use.
64 KB to (2 GB – 64 KB)	System DLLs (that is, NT.DLL, KERNEL32.DLL, USER32.DLL, GDI32.DLL, etc.). For efficiency, should be mapped to same address for multiple processes.
64 KB to (2 GB – 64 KB)	Application DLLs. For efficiency, should be mapped to same address for multiple processes.
64 KB to (2 GB – 64 KB)	Heaps and thread stacks. Allocated anywhere in the process's address space.
64 KB to (2 GB – 64 KB)	The executable's file image. This includes debugger information, image activation table, data, code, and header.
0 – 64 KB	Reserved.

The Sections of an EXE or a DLL

Every EXE or DLL file is composed of a collection of sections. In Win32 programs, each section name begins with a period. For example, when you compile your program, the compiler places all the code in a section called *.text*. All the uninitialized data is placed in a *.bss* section, and all the initialized data is placed in a *.data* section.

You can assign one or more of the following attributes to each section:

Attribute	Meaning
READ	The bytes in the section can be read from.
WRITE	The bytes in the section can be written to.
SHARED	The bytes in the section are shared across multiple instances.
EXECUTE	The bytes in the section can be executed.

By running the LINK32 utility, you can see the number and name of sections in an executable or DLL. The following program listing shows the result of running LINK32 on both the PMREST.EXE and PMRSTSUB.DLL files, the sample programs presented later in this chapter:

```
LINK32 -DUMP -SUMMARY PMREST.EXE
Dump of file pmrest.exe

    Summary
      .text    1600
       .bss     600
     .rdata     200
      .rsrc     400
      .data     600
       .CRT     200
     .idata     400
     .reloc    1400
     .debug    5600

LINK32 -DUMP -SUMMARY PMRSTSUB.DLL
Dump of file pmrstsub.dll

    Summary
      .text    1E00
       .bss     600
     .sdata     200
     .edata     200
      .data    1000
      .rsrc     600
       .CRT     200
     .idata     600
     .reloc    1400
```

In addition to the summary list of sections above, you can get a more detailed list of each section by specifying the *-HEADERS* switch to

LINK32. For example, you'll notice that when I ran *LINK32 -HEADERS* on USER32.DLL earlier (see pages 373 through 375), it displayed more detailed information about each section. Although I didn't reproduce the entire listing, we can see that the .text section can be executed and read from and that the .bss section can be read from and written to.

The table below shows the names of some of the more common sections and what each contains:

Section Name	Contains
.text	Application's or DLL's code
.bss	Uninitialized data
.rdata	Read-only runtime data
.rsrc	Resources
.edata	Exported names table
.data	Initialized data
.xdata	Exception handling table
.idata	Image activation table
.CRT	Read-only C Runtime data
.reloc	Fix-up table information
.debug	Debugging information
.sdata	Shared data
.tls	Thread-local storage

Notice how the PMRSTSUB.DLL has an additional section—called .sdata—that does not exist in the application's file. I created this section myself. You can easily create sections when compiling an application or DLL by using the following directive when you compile:

```
#pragma data_seg("segname")
```

So, for example, the PMRSTSUB.C file contains these lines:

```
#pragma data_seg(".sdata")

DWORD g_dwThreadIdPMRestore = 0;
HWND  g_hWndPM = NULL;

#pragma data_seg()
```

When the compiler compiles this code, it creates a new section—.sdata—and places all the initialized data variables that it sees after this pragma into this new section. In the example above, the two variables—

g_dwThreadIdPMRestore and *g_hWndPM*—are both placed into the .sdata section. Following the two variables, the *#pragma dataseg()* line tells the compiler to stop putting variables into the .sdata section and to start putting them back into the default data section. It is extremely important to note that the compiler will store only initialized variables in the new section. The compiler always places uninitialized variables in the .bss section. So, for example, if I had removed the initializations from the previous code fragment as follows, the compiler would end up putting all of these variables in the .bss section and none of them in the .sdata section:

```
#pragma data_seg(".sdata")

DWORD g_dwThreadIdPMRestore;
HWND  g_hWndPM;

#pragma data_seg()
```

Probably the most common reason to put variables in their own section is to share them among multiple mappings of an application or a DLL. By default, each mapping of an application or a DLL gets its very own set of variables. However, you can group into their own section any variables that you want to share among all mappings of an application or a DLL. When you group variables, the system doesn't create new instances of the variables for every mapping of the application or DLL. A section containing variables that you want to share is normally called .sdata; although you can give it any name you choose.

Just telling the compiler to place certain variables in their own section is not enough to share those variables. You must also tell the linker that the variables in a particular section are to be shared. You can do this in one of two ways. The first way is to use the *-SECTION* switch on the linker's command line. Following the colon, place the name of the section for which you want to alter attributes:

```
-SECTION:name, attributes
```

For PMRstSub.DLL, we want to change the attributes of the .sdata section. Don't forget to specify the period before the section name if you also use a period to name the section in the pragma directive. Following the comma, you must specify the attributes of the section. Use an *R* for READ, a *W* for WRITE, an *S* for SHARED, and an *E* for EXECUTE. So, to make the .sdata section readable, writable, and shared, the switch must look like this:

```
-SECTION:.sdata,RWS
```

If you want to change the attributes of more than one section, you must specify the *-SECTION* switch multiple times—once for each section for which you want to change attributes.

The second way to change the attributes of a section is to modify the DEF file, if you have one. The linker recognizes a SECTIONS section in the DEF file. The section must look like this:

```
SECTIONS
    .sdata      READ WRITE SHARED
    .
    .
    .
```

The SECTIONS line tells the linker that attributes for different sections follow. Each line in the SECTIONS section specifies the name of the section followed by the attributes that it should have. Again, the example above shows that the .sdata section will be readable, writable, and shared.

Although it is possible to create shared sections, sharing sections is greatly discouraged for two reasons: First, sharing memory in this way violates b-level security policy; second, sharing variables means that an error in one application can affect the operation of another application because there is no way to protect a block of data from being randomly written to by an application.

Pretend that you have written two applications that each require the user to enter a password. However, you decide to add a feature to your applications that makes things a little easier on the user: If the user is already running one of the applications when the second is started, the second application examines the contents of shared memory in order to get the password. In this way, the user doesn't need to enter the password a second time if one of the programs is already being used.

This sounds innocent enough. After all, no other applications but your own load the DLL and know where to find the password contained within the shared section. However, hackers lurk about, and if they want to get your password, all they need to do is write a small program of their own to load your company's DLL and monitor the shared memory blocks. Now, when the user enters a password, this program can learn the user's password and send it to you in a mail message.

An industrious program like the hacker's might also try to repeatedly guess at passwords and write them to the shared memory. Once the program guesses the correct password, it can send all kinds of commands to one of the two applications.

Perhaps this problem could be solved if there were a way to grant access to only certain applications for loading a particular DLL, but this is not the case. Any program can call LoadLibrary to explicitly load a DLL.

Simulating the GetModuleUsage Function: The ModUse Sample Application

Earlier in this chapter, I said that Win32 does not support the Get-ModuleUsage function offered by 16-bit Windows. But by using shared memory you can implement this feature yourself. The MODUSE.EXE and MODULE.DLL files demonstrate how to do this. Figure 7-3 shows MODULE.DLL, which we'll look at first.

```
MODULE.C
/************************************************************
Module name: Module.C
Notices: Copyright (c) 1993 Jeffrey Richter
************************************************************/

#include <windows.h>
#include "Module.H"


///////////////////////////////////////////////////////////

// Data shared between all mappings of this DLL.
#pragma data_seg(".sdata")

DWORD g_dwModuleUsage = 0;

#pragma data_seg()

// Per-mapping instance data for this DLL.
HMODULE g_hMod = NULL;

// 'g_uMsgModCountChange' could be shared but I chose not to.
UINT g_uMsgModCntChange = 0;

///////////////////////////////////////////////////////////

BOOL WINAPI DllMain (HMODULE hMod, DWORD fdwReason,
    LPVOID lpvReserved) {
```

Figure 7-3. *(continued)*
The Module dynamic-link library.

Figure 7-3. *continued*

```
switch (fdwReason) {

case DLL_PROCESS_ATTACH:
    // DLL is attaching to the address
    // space of the current process.
    g_hMod = hMod;

    // Increment this module's usage count when it is
    // attached to a process.
    InterlockedIncrement(&g_dwModuleUsage);

    // Reserve a systemwide window message for ourselves.
    // This message is used to notify all of the top-level
    // windows that this module's usage count has changed.
    g_uMsgModCntChange =
        RegisterWindowMessage(__TEXT("MsgModUsgCntChange"));

    // Notify all the top-level windows that this
    // module's usage count has changed.
    PostMessage(HWND_BROADCAST, g_uMsgModCntChange, 0, 0);
    break;

case DLL_THREAD_ATTACH:
    // A new thread is being created in the current process.
    break;

case DLL_THREAD_DETACH:
    // A thread is exiting cleanly.
    break;

case DLL_PROCESS_DETACH:
    // The calling process is detaching
    // the DLL from its address space.

    // Decrement this module's usage count when it
    // gets detached from a process.
    InterlockedDecrement(&g_dwModuleUsage);

    // Notify all the top-level windows that this
    // module's usage count has changed.
    PostMessage(HWND_BROADCAST, g_uMsgModCntChange, 0, 0);

    break;
}
```

(continued)

Figure 7-3. *continued*

```
    return(TRUE);
}

//////////////////////////////////////////////////////////////

DWORD GetModuleUsage (void) {
    return(g_dwModuleUsage);
}

///////////////////////// End Of File /////////////////////////
```

MODULE.H

```
/************************************************************
Module name: Module.H
Notices: Copyright (c) 1993 Jeffrey Richter
************************************************************/

// Function to return the module's usage count.
DWORD GetModuleUsage (void);

///////////////////////// End Of File /////////////////////////
```

MODULE.DEF

```
;************************************************************
;Module name: Module.Def
;Notices: Copyright (c) 1993 Jeffrey Richter
;************************************************************

EXPORTS
;   EntryName [=InternalName] [@Ordinal [ NONAME]] [CONSTANT]
    GetModuleUsage    @2   NONAME

;IMPORTS
;   [InternalName=] ModuleName.Entry
```

The most important thing to note in MODULE.C is that I have created a global variable, *g_ lModuleUsage,* in its very own section and have specified that this section be SHARED by specifying the *-SECTION* switch to the linker. I have also initialized *g_lModuleUsage* to be –1. Now whenever MODULE.DLL is mapped into a process's address space, DllMain is called with a reason of DLL_PROCESS_ATTACH. The DLL processes this call by calling:

```
InterlockedIncrement(&g_lModuleUsage);
```

This call increments the *g_lModuleUsage* variable. You might wonder why I increment this long by calling InterlockedIncrement instead of just using:

```
g_lModuleUsage++;
```

I admit that it is a subtle difference and that most of the time you would never notice the difference and everything would work just fine. If I use only the C postfix increment operator, a potential problem can occur. If two processes were to call LoadLibrary to load MODULE.DLL into memory at the same time, the value of *g_lModuleUsage* can become corrupted. Actually, this would probably never happen on a single-CPU machine because the CPU can preempt a thread only in between machine instructions. But on a multiprocessor machine, several CPUs can access the same memory location simultaneously. By using Interlocked-Increment, the system guarantees that no more than one CPU can access the 4 bytes of memory at any one time.

The next step in maintaining MODULE.DLL's usage count is to decrement the usage count whenever DllMain is called with a reason of DLL_PROCESS_DETACH. When this happens, *g_lUsageCount* is decremented by making a call to InterlockedDecrement. See Chapter 5 for more information on the InterlockedIncrement and Interlocked-Decrement functions.

The only other function in this DLL is GetModuleUsage:

```
DWORD GetModuleUsage(void);
```

This function accepts no parameters and simply returns the value in the *g_lUsageCount* variable. An application can now call this function to determine the number of processes that have mapped MODULE.DLL into their own address spaces.

To make this demonstration a little more exciting, I also created the ModUse (MODUSE.EXE) sample application, listed in Figure 7-4 beginning on page 386. This is a very simple program that displays a dialog box. After the dialog box is displayed, its dialog box procedure simply sits around and waits for the registered window message[1], MsgModCntChange. This message is registered by MODULE.DLL when its DllMain function is called with a reason of DLL_PROCESS- _ATTACH. This same message is registered by MODUSE.EXE first when its WinMain function is called. The value for the message is saved in the global *g_uMsgModCntChange* variable.

Whenever the DLL is attached or detached from a process, it calls

```
PostMessage(HWND_BROADCAST, g_uMsgCntChange, 0, 0);
```

This causes the value of the registered window message to be broadcast to all the overlapped windows in the system. The only window that will recognize this systemwide window message is the dialog box created by any instances of the ModUse application that happen to be running. MODUSE.C's dialog box procedure contains an explicit check for this registered window message:

```
if (uMsg == g_uMsgModCntChange) {
    SetDlgItemInt(hDlg, IDC_MODCNT, GetModuleUsage(), FALSE);
}
```

When this message is received, the DLL's GetModuleUsage function is called to get the current module usage. This value is then placed in a static window control that is a child of the dialog box.

When you run the ModUse program, the MODULE.DLL file is implicitly mapped into the process's address space. The attachment of this DLL to the process causes the registered message to be posted to all the overlapped windows in the system. The windows will ignore this message except for the dialog box displayed by ModUse. When the dialog box receives the message, it calls the GetModuleUsage function in the DLL to obtain MODULE.DLL's usage count, which is 1. This value is then placed in the dialog box:

Now if you ran a second instance of ModUse, the same thing would occur. This time, MODULE.DLL's usage count is 2, and two dialog

---

1. For more information about using registered window messages, see the Register-WindowMessage function in the SDK documentation.

boxes that can process the registered window message are displayed. Both dialog box procedures call GetModuleUsage, see that the count is 2, and then update their static controls appropriately:

This technique of sharing data in a section across multiple file mappings is not limited to DLLs alone—applications can also use it. For an application, the data would be shared among all running instances of the application.

ModUse.ico

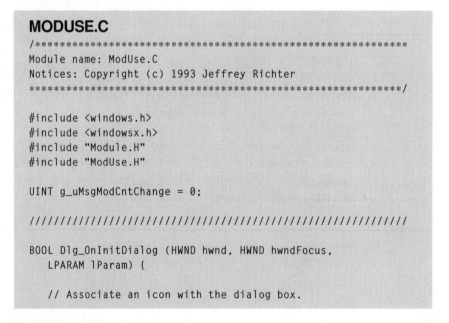

```
MODUSE.C
/*****************************************************************
Module name: ModUse.C
Notices: Copyright (c) 1993 Jeffrey Richter
*****************************************************************/

#include <windows.h>
#include <windowsx.h>
#include "Module.H"
#include "ModUse.H"

UINT g_uMsgModCntChange = 0;


//////////////////////////////////////////////////////////////

BOOL Dlg_OnInitDialog (HWND hwnd, HWND hwndFocus,
    LPARAM lParam) {

    // Associate an icon with the dialog box.
```

Figure 7-4.   *(continued)*
The ModUse application.

Figure 7-4. *continued*

```
   SetClassLong(hwnd, GCL_HICON, (LONG)
      LoadIcon((HINSTANCE) GetWindowLong(hwnd, GWL_HINSTANCE),
      __TEXT("ModUse")));

   // Force the static control to be initialized correctly.
   PostMessage(hwnd, g_uMsgModCntChange, 0, 0);
   return(TRUE);
}


///////////////////////////////////////////////////////////////

void Dlg_OnCommand (HWND hwnd, int id, HWND hwndCtl,
   UINT codeNotify) {

   switch (id) {
      case IDCANCEL:
         EndDialog(hwnd, id);
         break;
   }
}


///////////////////////////////////////////////////////////////

BOOL CALLBACK Dlg_Proc (HWND hDlg, UINT uMsg,
   WPARAM wParam, LPARAM lParam) {

   BOOL fProcessed = TRUE;

   if (uMsg == g_uMsgModCntChange) {
      SetDlgItemInt(hDlg, ID_USAGECOUNT,
         GetModuleUsage(), FALSE);
   }

   switch (uMsg) {
      HANDLE_MSG(hDlg, WM_INITDIALOG, Dlg_OnInitDialog);
      HANDLE_MSG(hDlg, WM_COMMAND, Dlg_OnCommand);

      default:
         fProcessed = FALSE;
         break;
   }
   return(fProcessed);
}
```

(continued)

Figure 7-4. *continued*

```
//////////////////////////////////////////////////////////////

int APIENTRY WinMain (HINSTANCE hInstance,
   HINSTANCE hPrevInstance, LPSTR lpszCmdLine, int nCmdShow) {

   // Get the numeric value of the systemwide window message
   // used by the module to notify all top-level windows when
   // its usage count has changed.
   g_uMsgModCntChange =
      RegisterWindowMessage(__TEXT("MsgModUsgCntChange"));

   DialogBox(hInstance, MAKEINTRESOURCE(DLG_MODUSE),
      NULL, Dlg_Proc);
   return(0);
}


//////////////////////// End Of File //////////////////////////
```

MODUSE.H

```
/************************************************************
Module name: ModUse.H
Notices: Copyright (c) 1993 Jeffrey Richter
************************************************************/

// Dialog and control IDs.
#define DLG_MODUSE        1
#define ID_USAGECOUNT   100


//////////////////////// End Of File //////////////////////////
```

MODUSE.RC

```
/************************************************************
Module name: ModUse.RC
Notices: Copyright (c) 1993 Jeffrey Richter
************************************************************/

#include <windows.h>
#include "ModUse.h"
```

(continued)

Figure 7-4. *continued*

```
ModUse ICON "moduse.ico"

DLG_MODUSE DIALOG DISCARDABLE  0, 0, 76, 20
STYLE WS_BORDER | WS_POPUP | WS_VISIBLE | WS_CAPTION |
   WS_SYSMENU | WS_MINIMIZEBOX
CAPTION "Module Usage"
BEGIN
   CONTROL "Module usage:", -1, "STATIC",
      SS_NOPREFIX | WS_CHILD | WS_VISIBLE | WS_GROUP,
      4, 4, 52, 12
   CONTROL "#", ID_USAGECOUNT, "STATIC",
      SS_RIGHT | SS_NOPREFIX | WS_CHILD | WS_VISIBLE |
      WS_GROUP, 56, 4, 16, 12
END

///////////////////////// End Of File /////////////////////////
```

Prohibiting Multiple Instances of an Application from Running: The MultInst Sample Application

In 16-bit Windows, many programmers used the value of *hPrevInstance*, which Windows passed to WinMain to determine whether an instance of an application was already running. Applications that allowed only one instance of themselves to run at a time would check the value of *hPrevInstance*, and, if its value wasn't NULL, they would terminate. Under Windows NT, the value of *hPrevInstance* passed to WinMain is always NULL. Because of this, an application cannot easily determine whether another instance of itself is running.

One way for an application to know how many instances of itself are running is to use the shared data section technique just discussed. The MultInst (MULTINST.EXE) sample application, listed in Figure 7-5 beginning on the following page, demonstrates how to allow only one instance of an application to run.

MultInst.ico

MULTINST.C

```
/*****************************************************************
Module name: MultInst.C
Notices: Copyright (c) 1993 Jeffrey Richter
*****************************************************************/

#include <windows.h>
#include "MultInst.H"


///////////////////////////////////////////////////////////////

// Data shared between all mappings of this executable.
#pragma data_seg(".sdata")

LONG g_lUsageCount = -1;

#pragma data_seg()


///////////////////////////////////////////////////////////////

int APIENTRY WinMain (HINSTANCE hInstance,
   HINSTANCE hPrevInstance, LPSTR lpszCmdLine, int nCmdShow) {

   // An instance is running; increment the counter.
   BOOL fFirstInstance =
      (InterlockedIncrement(&g_lUsageCount) == 0);

   // If more than one instance is running, tell
   // the user and terminate the program.
   if (!fFirstInstance) {
      MessageBox(NULL,
         __TEXT("Application is already running - ")
         __TEXT("Terminating this instance."),
         __TEXT("Mult Instance"), MB_OK | MB_ICONINFORMATION);
   } else {

      // We are the only instance running;
      // wait for the user to terminate us.
      MessageBox(NULL,
         __TEXT("Running first instance of application.\n")
         __TEXT("Select OK to terminate."),
         __TEXT("Multiple Instance"),
         MB_OK | MB_ICONINFORMATION);
   }
```

Figure 7-5. *(continued)*

The MultInst application.

Figure 7-5. *continued*

```
    // We are no longer running; decrement the usage counter.
    InterlockedDecrement(&g_lUsageCount);
    return(0);
}


////////////////////////// End Of File //////////////////////////
```

MULTINST.H

```
/**************************************************************
Module name: MultInst.H
Notices: Copyright (c) 1993 Jeffrey Richter
**************************************************************/

// Dialog and control IDs.

////////////////////////// End Of File //////////////////////////
```

MULTINST.RC

```
/**************************************************************
Module name: MultInst.RC
Notices: Copyright (c) 1993 Jeffrey Richter
**************************************************************/

MultInst  ICON    DISCARDABLE    MultInst.Ico

////////////////////////// End Of File //////////////////////////
```

Exporting Functions from a DLL

Most DLLs would be pretty useless if there were no way for an application to call the functions contained inside them. For an application to call functions contained inside a DLL, you need to export them.

In 16-bit Windows, you can export functions by specifying them in the library's module definitions file. For Win32, the format of the lines in the EXPORT section of the DEF file is almost identical to the format used by 16-bit Windows, as shown at the top of the following page.

```
EXPORTS
;   EntryName [=InternalName] [@Ordinal [ NONAME]] [CONSTANT]
    GetTwoPlusTwo = GetFour
    GetFour
```

The name of the function that an external application or a DLL can call appears first. This name doesn't have to be the name of the function in the DLL, although it usually is. For example, you might have a function in the DLL called GetFour. But you may want to export this function by two different names: GetTwoPlusTwo and GetFour (as shown above).

Here we have exported a function, GetTwoPlusTwo, that other applications and DLLs can call. When they call this function, the DLL's internal function, GetFour, will actually be called. The last line above says that we also want to export a function called GetFour. Because there is no internal name specified on this line, the linker assumes that the internal name is identical to the external name.

After including a function name, you have the option of including an ordinal number, as shown in the line below:

```
EXPORTS
    SubclassProgManFrame      @2 NONAME
```

This number provides a shorthand method for getting the address of the function using GetProcAddress:

```
FARPROC GetProcAddress(HINSTANCE hinstDll, LPCTSTR lpszProc);
```

This function retrieves the address of a function in a DLL. The *hinstDll* parameter specifies the handle to the DLL. The return value from LoadLibrary identifies this handle value. The *lpszProc* parameter can take one of two forms. First, it can be the address to a zero-terminated string containing the name of the function whose address we want:

```
lpfn = GetProcAddress(hinstDll, "SubclassProgManFrame");
```

Second, the *lpszProc* parameter can indicate the ordinal number of the function whose address we want:

```
lpfn = GetProcAddress(hinstDll, MAKEINTRESOURCE(2));
```

This usage assumes that we know that the SubclassProgManFrame function was assigned the ordinal value of 2 by the creator of the DLL.

The result of either method is the same: the address to the SubclassProgManFrame function contained inside the DLL. If the function cannot be found, GetProcAddress returns NULL. There are some subtle disadvantages in using either method. The first method works more slowly than the second because the system must perform string comparisons and searches on the function name string passed in. In the second method, if you pass in an ordinal number that hasn't been assigned to any of the exported functions, GetProcAddress might return a non-NULL value (this is true for 16-bit Windows as well). This return value will trick your application into thinking that you have a valid address when in fact you don't. Attempting to call this address will almost certainly cause the thread to generate an access violation. Early in my Windows programming career, I didn't fully understand this behavior and was burned by it several times—watch out.

The new NONAME flag indicates that you don't want the function's name to be exported—only the ordinal value. When you link a DLL, the linker places all of the function names in a table. Then, when you call GetProcAddress and pass in a pointer to a string, the system looks in this table for a match and returns the address of the desired function. If you add the NONAME flag, the linker won't add the function's name to this table inside the DLL. This means that applications won't be able to call GetProcAddress passing in the name of a function.

However, the linker can also produce an import library for a DLL. This import library is usually the means by which an application gains access to the functions contained inside a DLL. When building the application, the name of the DLL's import library is specified to the linker. The linker then looks up the names of the functions that you call in your application and attempts to match the names with names in the import library. When a match is found, the linker writes some information into the application's EXE file.

Specifying the NONAME flag doesn't cause the names of the DLL's functions to be removed from the import library. If it did, an application would not be able to link to a DLL using function names.

This NONAME flag is useful for several reasons. First, whenever you export functions by name, the names of the functions must be placed somewhere in the DLL file. The names must be placed so that GetProcAddress can locate the function by name. Putting all of these string names into the DLL can take up quite a bit of space, however, especially if your DLL exports several functions. The USER32.DLL exports nearly 550 functions.

A second reason to use this flag is for security. If you're shipping a DLL that you expect other people to use, you might have some internal functions that you want to export but that you don't want your customers to use. By specifying the NONAME flag, the names of the functions are omitted from the DLL file, making it much harder for people to look into your DLL and determine its undocumented capabilities.

Exporting Data from a DLL

The CONSTANT flag is an interesting flag that adds new capabilities to DLLs that weren't easily available under 16-bit Windows. A DLL designed for Windows NT has the ability to export global data as well as functions. The following line exports the global variable *g_hHook*:

```
EXPORTS
    g_hHook         @3 NONAME CONSTANT
```

Actually, the system exports the address of a variable, not the variable itself. So the line above says that we want to export the address of the variable *g_hHook*. If the application were now going to reference this variable, it would need to precede every occurrence with an asterisk. So, if an application wants to check whether this variable is NULL, its code would look like this:

```
extern HHOOK *g_hHook;
.
.
.
if (*g_hHook == NULL) {
// g_hHook is NULL
} else {
// g_hHook is not NULL
}
```

Using Hungarian notation, the code above looks a little odd because in the application *g_hHook* is really an address to the variable, not the variable itself. The code would be clearer if written as follows:

```
extern HHOOK *lpg_hHook;
.
.
.
if (*lpg_hHook == NULL) {
// g_hHook is NULL
} else {
// g_hHook is not NULL
}
```

All I did was change the first line to read *lpg_ hHook* instead of *g_ hHook*. Adding the *lp* prefix makes it immediately obvious that we are working with a pointer to the variable and not the variable itself. But if we wrote the code like this, it wouldn't link because the DLL doesn't export *lpg_ hHook*—it exports *g_ hHook*. This problem can be solved easily by changing the line in the EXPORTS section of the DEF file to the following:

```
EXPORTS
    lpg_hHook = g_hHook        @3 NONAME CONSTANT
```

Here we're saying that, inside the DLL, the variable we're exporting is called *g_ hHook*. But outside the DLL, other applications and DLLs want to refer to this variable's address as *lpg_ hHook*. Having made the change to the DEF file, we can implement our code using the second, clearer, method.

I mentioned earlier that the NONAME flag can be used to add a level of security to your DLL by hiding the names of exported functions. The method described below provides another way to restrict access to internal functions.

As we all know by now, DLLs are mapped into the address space of the process that loads the DLL. This means that if you could somehow get the address to a function in the DLL, you can simply call the function. It is as if the function in the DLL were part of the application's code. Here is a sample:

```
// This typedef goes in your internal header file
// which is NOT distributed with the DLL.
typedef struct {
    BOOL (*lpFuncToSaveLotsOfWork)(void);
    long (*lpFuncToSaveTonsOfWork)(LPCTSTR, int);
} INTERNALFUNCS;

const INTERNALFUNCS *GetInternalFuncs (void);
```

Then, in the DLL, insert the following functions:

```
// Internal function that does lots of great stuff.
BOOL FuncToSaveLotsOfWork (void) {
    .
    .
    .
}
```

(continued)

```
// Internal function that does tons of great stuff.
long FuncToSaveTonsOfWork (LPCTSTR sz, int n) {
    .
    .
    .
}

// Create and initialize global structure containing
// pointers to internal functions.
const INTERNALFUNCS g_InternalFunctions = {
    FuncToSaveLotsOfWork,
    FuncToSaveTonsOfWork
};


// Internal function to return the address of a structure
// where the members point to the other internal functions.
const INTERNALFUNCS *GetInternalFuncs (void) {
    return(&g_InternalFuncs);
}
```

With everything set up in this way, you need only to export one function, GetInternalFuncs, in the DEF file. It would be pretty near impossible for anyone to figure out what parameters this function expects or what it returns. And, if someone did figure out what it returns, he or she would have a difficult time determining what parameters all the internal functions take as well as what they return.

The main point of what I am saying is that, unlike 16-bit Windows, you don't need to export functions in the DEF file simply because they are going to be called. You need to export functions in the DEF file only if you want someone to access those functions by using either implicit linking (linking with an import library) or explicit linking (calling GetProcAddress).

Dynamic-Link Libraries and Hooks

Windows offers a mechanism whereby processes can be notified of events occurring in the system even when the event is occurring in another process. This mechanism is called a hook.[2] The following table briefly describes the 12 different types of hooks you can install. Once a hook is installed, Windows notifies the installed hook filter function when specific events have occurred.

---

2. A full explanation of hooks is beyond the scope of this book.

Hook	Description
Call window procedure WH_CALLWNDPROC	Windows notifies the process that a window message is being sent.
Get message WH_GETMESSAGE	Windows notifies the process that a window message was retrieved from GetMessage or PeekMessage.
Keyboard WH_KEYBOARD	Windows notifies the process that a keyboard message was retrieved from GetMessage or PeekMessage.
Mouse WH_MOUSE	Windows notifies the process that a mouse message was retrieved from GetMessage or PeekMessage.
Hardware WH_HARDWARE	Windows notifies the process that a hardware message, other than a keyboard or mouse message, was retrieved from GetMessage or PeekMessage.
System message filter WH_SYSMSGFILTER	Windows notifies the process that a dialog box, a menu, or a scroll bar is about to process a message.
Message filter WH_MSGFILTER	Windows notifies the process that a dialog box, a menu, or a scroll bar is about to process a message.
Journal record WH_JOURNALRECORD	Windows notifies the process that a hardware event has been retrieved from the input queue.
Journal playback WH_JOURNALPLAYBACK	Windows notifies the process that a hardware event is being requested from the input queue.
Computer-based training WH_CBT	Windows notifies the process that a window is being created, destroyed, activated, minimized, maximized, moved, sized, etc.
Shell WH_SHELL	Windows notifies the process that an overlapped window has been created or destroyed.
Debug WH_DEBUG	Windows notifies the process that a hook function is about to be called.

Most of the hooks listed above can be installed as either thread-specific hooks or system-global hooks. Three of the hooks—journal record, journal playback, and system message filter—must be installed as system-global hooks. Installing a hook requires a call to:

```
HHOOK SetWindowsHookEx(int idHook, HOOKPROC hkprc,
    HINSTANCE hinst, DWORD dwThreadID);
```

The *idHook* parameter identifies one of the identifiers listed in the table on the previous page. The *hkprc* parameter is the address of the function that Windows should call when it needs to notify you of the event; *hinst* is the instance handle of the application or DLL that contains the notification function. The *dwThreadID* parameter identifies the thread whose events you want to watch. The call to SetWindows-HookEx can be contained in one thread, but you might want to be notified of events that are occurring to a different thread identified by *dwThreadID*. If you are installing a system-global hook, you must pass NULL as *dwThreadID*.

The following examines what happens when Windows NT attempts to call a system-global hook function.

Your application starts running and calls SetWindowsHookEx to install a WH_GETMESSAGE hook function. You pass NULL for the *dwThreadId* parameter so that Windows NT notifies your function when any thread running in the system retrieves a message by calling Get-Message or PeekMessage.[3] Now when an application calls GetMessage, Windows NT must call your hook function. But there is a problem here: The process that called GetMessage is the current process, and it doesn't have the DLL that contains the hook function code attached to the process. Windows NT could attempt to call a hook function at the address specified by the *hkprc* parameter of SetWindowsHookEx. But, because the DLL containing the function is not mapped into the process's address space, this call would surely cause the process to crash.

So, how can Windows NT make system-global hooks work? The answer is that Windows NT must map the DLL containing the hook function into the address space of the process for which the hook notification occurred. Windows NT can do this because the call to Set-WindowsHookEx also contains the handle to the DLL in the *hinst* parameter. From this parameter, SetWindowsHookEx is able to note which DLL contains the hook filter function code. Before Windows NT calls the hook function, it checks to see whether the DLL containing the code is already attached into the current process's address space.

If the DLL isn't attached, Windows NT implicitly calls LoadLibrary to attach the DLL. Once the DLL has been attached, Windows NT must determine the address of the hook function. Because DLLs can be mapped into one address for one process and a different address for

---

3. This is how Microsoft's SPY.EXE works, by the way. It watches as messages are pulled from the thread's message queues and displays the parameters of the message in its list box.

another process, the address of the hook function might be different from one process to another. Windows NT is able to determine the address of the hook function in the newly attached DLL by performing calculations using the *hkprc* and *hinst* parameters that were passed to SetWindowsHookEx. First, it can determine the base address where the DLL identified by *hinst* was loaded. Then it can subtract this base address from the *hkprc* address. The resulting value indicates the number of bytes into the DLL at which the hook function is located. Because the system knows the base address where it mapped the newly attached DLL, it needs only to add the relative offset to get the address of the hook function with respect to the current process. Windows NT can now call the hook function.

This is a very interesting technique that has a lot of potential. Using this technique, you can actually *inject* code into the address space of another process. The Program Manager Restore sample application, shown later, demonstrates the use of this technique.

You should be aware of two things here. First, setting a system-global hook will eventually cause the DLL containing the hook function to be mapped into the address space of every process in the system. To detach the DLL from all of the processes, you must unhook the hook by using UnhookWindowsHookEx:

```
BOOL UnhookWindowsHookEx(HHOOK hhook);
```

When this function is called, Windows NT cycles through all the processes and detaches the DLL containing the hook function from each process's address space. It's possible that a thread could be executing code contained inside a hook filter function at the time you call UnhookWindowsHookEx. In this case, the system does not unmap the view of the DLL immediately. Instead, it watches for the thread to leave the hook filter function and then unmaps the view of the DLL. If the system unmapped the view of the DLL immediately, the thread would start executing memory in an address space that was no longer committed or reserved, which would cause an access violation.

The second thing to be aware of is that each time a DLL is mapped into a process's address space, the DLL gets its own set of global and static variables. So, if your hook function is called in the context of one process and the function changes a global integer to 5, all of the other mappings of the DLL won't see the changed value—the 5; they will see their own value of the integer. This can be solved by using the shared data techniques described earlier in this chapter.

Subclassing Windows Created by Other Processes

Window subclassing is a very powerful feature. The idea is that a window class exists that performs the type of behavior you need—almost. For example, you might have need for an Edit control that accepts only numbers or a list box that supports drag and drop capabilities. One way to produce windows with this type of behavior is to create them yourself. But this usually isn't the most ideal way because many of these controls are quite complex and you could end up spending several months (at least) trying to accomplish what has already been accomplished. Window subclassing allows you to *steal* the desired behavior from a control and allows you to alter or add other behaviors as you see fit.

For the most part, Windows NT supports window subclassing just as 16-bit Windows does. However, Windows NT does not allow window subclassing to take place in a couple of unusual situations—well, at least not without making you jump through some hoops first.

Let's discuss the easy case first. Most applications subclass only windows that were created by themselves—by far the most common usage of window subclassing. Windows NT allows this type of subclassing without any problems. If your 16-bit Windows code subclasses only windows that it creates itself, you should have no trouble porting your code.

A few applications attempt to subclass windows that were created by other applications. When you subclass a window, you give Windows NT the new address for the window's window procedure. Then, when a message is about to be dispatched to the window, Windows NT reroutes the message to the new address. If you are specifying an address that is in another process, Windows NT has no idea that you meant to say that the address of the new window procedure was relative to a different process. When the message is dispatched, the address you specify is called and whatever happens to be located at the address in the process that created the window you subclass is called. This will almost definitely cause the process that created the (now subclassed) window to crash.

So, the question is: How can you subclass a window created from another process? The code for the new subclass window procedure must somehow get into the address space of the process that created the window. You can easily place the code for the subclass window procedure in a DLL and have the process that created the window somehow load the DLL into its address space.

The problem here is that it's not easy to get a process to call LoadLibrary when it doesn't know anything about the DLL. However, you can use hooks. Remember from the previous section that when a hook filter function needs to be called from the context of a process that doesn't have the DLL mapped into its address space, Windows NT automatically maps the DLL into the process's address space.

Now you have all the pieces you need to subclass a window in another process. First, you must install a hook filter function that gets called when an event occurs in the process containing the window you want to subclass. Second, you must force an event to occur so that the hook filter function does get called. When the hook filter function is called, Windows NT maps the DLL containing the hook filter function into the address space of the other process. During the processing of the hook filter function, you can call SetWindowLong to subclass the desired window. The only restrictions on this method are

1. The code for the subclass window procedure must be contained in the same DLL as the code for the hook filter function.

2. You must not unhook the hook until you unsubclass the window. If you were to unhook the hook with the window still subclassed, Windows NT would unmap the DLL. Then, the next time the system needed to dispatch a message to the window, it would call the address of a window procedure that no longer existed, which would cause an access violation.

The Program Manager Restore Sample Application

When I first got Windows 3.0, I liked it right away. Even the new Program Manager shell was much better than the old MS-DOS Executive. But I just didn't like one "feature" of the Program Manager: If the Program Manager is minimized and I close my last running application, the Program Manager stays minimized. At this point, there's nothing I can do except move the mouse all the way down to the bottom of my screen and double click on the Program Manager so that I can execute another program.

Well, laziness being the mother of invention, I created (fanfare, please) PMRest. PMRest consists of a small executable program and a small DLL. The program (in conjunction with the DLL) subclasses the Windows Program Manager. Whenever the Program Manager is running minimized and the user closes the last running application, the subclass procedure detects this and forces the Program Manager to automatically restore itself. This saves the user wear and tear on their mouse ball by not forcing him or her to move the mouse over the Program Manager and double click on its icon.

When you run PMRest (PMREST.EXE), listed in Figure 7-6 beginning on page 405, it subclasses the Program Manager's main window. It calls the SubclassProgManFrame function contained in the PMRST-SUB.DLL, passing it the thread ID of PMRest's primary thread. You'll see why this is needed later.

If SubclassProgManFrame can subclass the Program Manager's main window successfully, SubclassProgManFrame returns TRUE. At this point, PMRest enters into a GetMessage loop:

```
while (GetMessage(&msg, NULL, 0, 0))
   ;
```

This loop simply causes PMRest to wait for a WM_QUIT message. PMRest doesn't create any windows itself, so there is no call to TranslateMessage or DispatchMessage. When a WM_QUIT message is finally received, PMRest unhooks the hook that was set by the previous call to SubclassProgManFrame and terminates. Unhooking the hook causes Windows NT to unmap PMRSTSUB.DLL from the Program Manager's address space.

So, as you can see, all the hard work is actually performed by the PMRSTSUB.DLL, listed in Figure 7-7 beginning on page 407. Let's take a look at what it does now.

SubclassProgManFrame first obtains the window handle of the Program Manager's main window by calling FindWindow:

```
g_hWndPM = FindWindow("PROGMAN", NULL);
```

This window handle is then saved in a global variable, *g_ hWndPM*. This variable is also shared between all views of this PMRSTSUB.DLL. If the Program Manager's window can't be found for some reason, SubclassProgManFrame returns FALSE to PMRest so that it can exit cleanly.

Now we're ready to subclass the Program Manager's window. PMRSTSUB.DLL does this by installing a WH_GETMESSAGE hook:

```
g_hHook = SetWindowsHookEx(WH_GETMESSAGE, GetMsgProc,
   g_hinstDll, GetWindowThreadProcessId(g_hWndPM, NULL));
```

The address of the hook filter function is identified by GetMsgProc, the handle of the module containing the function is identified by *g_ hinstDll*, and the ID of the thread that we want to watch for events is the thread that created the Program Manager's main window. This thread ID is obtained by calling GetWindowThreadProcessId. SetWindowsHookEx returns the hook handle that identifies the installed hook. This handle is saved in the global *g_ hHook* variable.

If the hook was installed successfully, we now force a benign window message to be posted to the Program Manager's main window:

```
PostMessage(g_hWndPM, WM_NULL, 0, 0);
```

When the thread that handles messages for the Program Manager calls GetMessage to retrieve the WM_NULL message, Windows NT automatically maps PMRSTSUB.DLL into the address space of the Program Manager and calls the GetMsgProc filter function. The filter function checks that the message being processed is, in fact, a WM_NULL message that was destined for the Program Manager's main window. If not, GetMsgProc does nothing interesting and simply passes the hook notification on to the next installed WH_GETMESSAGE filter function.

If, on the other hand, a WM_NULL message is pulled from the thread's message queue and is destined for the Program Manager's main window, GetMsgProc calls the SubclassWindow macro (which is defined in WINDOWSX.H) to subclass the window. At this point, the PMRSTSUB.DLL is mapped into the Program Manager's address space, and the Program Manager's window is subclassed. From now on, any messages destined for the Program Manager's main window will be rerouted to our own subclass window procedure, PMSubclass.

We'll get to what the subclass procedure does in a minute. For now, let's get back to discussing PMRest's own thread. Assuming that the hook was installed successfully and that the WM_NULL message was posted to the Program Manager's main window, PMRSTSUB.DLL next adds two new top-level menu items to the Program Manager's menu bar:

```
hMenu = GetMenu(g_hWndPM);

AppendMenu(hMenu, MF_ENABLED | MF_STRING,
   IDM_PMRESTOREABOUT, "A&bout PM Restore...");
AppendMenu(hMenu, MF_ENABLED | MF_STRING,
   IDM_PMRESTOREREMOVE, "&Remove PM Restore");

DrawMenuBar(g_hWndPM);      // Update the new menu bar
```

Finally, just before SubclassProgManFrame returns, it saves the ID of PMRest's primary thread into a global shared variable, *g_dw-ThreadIdPMRestore*.

Here's a summary of what has happened so far: The WH_GET-MESSAGE hook is still installed, and any messages destined for the Program Manager's main window are being routed to the PMSubclass function. Also, the PMRest program is waiting for a WM_QUIT message at its GetMessage loop.

The PMSubclass function is designed to process only two different window messages—WM_ACTIVATEAPP and WM_COMMAND. For any other window message, PMSubclass simply calls CallWindowProc so that the message gets processed in its normal fashion.

If PMSubclass receives a WM_ACTIVATEAPP message, it calls the PM_OnActivateApp function to determine whether other windows belonging to other applications are running. If other applications are displaying windows, PMSubclass does nothing and passes the WM-_ACTIVATEAPP message on to the original window procedure. However, if PM_OnActivateApp determines that other processes aren't displaying windows, PM_OnActivateApp calls ShowWindow, forcing the Program Manager to be restored from its minimized state.

PMSubclass processes the WM_COMMAND message so that it can perform the necessary actions when one of the two new menu options has been selected by the user. When the user selects the *About PM Restore* option, the subclassing procedure displays PMRest's *About* dialog box. If the user selects the *Remove PM Restore* menu option, PMRSTSUB.DLL performs the following:

1. Restores the Program Manager main window's original window procedure.

2. Removes the two menu items that it added to the Program Manager's menu bar.

3. Posts a WM_QUIT message to PMRest's thread by calling PostThreadMessage and passing the ID of PMRest's thread. PMRest's thread ID was saved earlier in the global shared variable *g_dwThreadIdPMRestore*. This variable must be shared so that the Program Manager's mapping of PMRSTSUB.DLL can share this variable, which was initialized by PMREST.EXE's mapping of PMRSTSUB.DLL.

When I first wrote PMRest, I attempted to use a WH_CALL-WNDPROC hook instead of a WH_GETMESSAGE hook and *sent* a WM_NULL message instead of *posting* it. My method didn't work.

As it turns out, the system calls WH_CALLWNDPROC hook filter functions in the context of the process *sending* the message, not *receiving* the message. This meant that the hook filter function was called when PMRest called SendMessage, not when the Program Manager's window received the message. Because WH_CALLWNDPROC hooks work in this way, a view of the PMRSTSUB.DLL never got mapped into the Program Manager's address space.

PMRest.ico

PMREST.C

```
/***********************************************************
Module name: PMRest.C
Notices: Copyright (c) 1993 Jeffrey Richter
***********************************************************/


#include <windows.h>
#include <stdio.h>
#include "PMRstSub.H"


///////////////////////////////////////////////////////////

int APIENTRY WinMain (HINSTANCE hInstance,
    HINSTANCE hPrevInstance, LPSTR lpszCmdLine, int nCmdShow) {

    MSG msg;

    // Find the Program Manager and modify its menu.
    if (!SubclassProgManFrame(GetCurrentThreadId()))
        return(1);
```

Figure 7-6.   *(continued)*

The PMRest application.

Figure 7-6. *continued*

```
    // Begin message loop so that our application
    // doesn't terminate.  If we terminated, our subclass
    // function would be removed from memory.  When Windows
    // tried to call it, it would jump to garbage and cause
    // an access violation.
    while (GetMessage(&msg, NULL, 0, 0))
        ;

    // Uninstall the WH_GETMESSAGE hook.
    // This causes the DLL to be unmapped
    // from the Program Manager.
    if (!UnhookWindowsHookEx(*lpg_hHook)) {
        MessageBox(NULL, __TEXT("Error unhooking"),
            __TEXT("PM Restore"), MB_OK);
    }

    return(0);
}

//////////////////////// End Of File ////////////////////////
```

PMREST.H

```
/************************************************************
Module name: PMRest.H
Notices: Copyright (c) 1993 Jeffrey Richter
************************************************************/

// Dialog and control IDs.

//////////////////////// End Of File ////////////////////////
```

PMREST.RC

```
/************************************************************
Module name: PMRest.RC
Notices: Copyright (c) 1993 Jeffrey Richter
************************************************************/

PMRest   ICON  DISCARDABLE PMRest.Ico

//////////////////////// End Of File ////////////////////////
```

PMRSTSUB.C

```
/************************************************************
Module name: PMRstSub.C
Notices: Copyright (c) 1993 Jeffrey Richter
************************************************************/

#include <windows.h>
#include <windowsx.h>
#include "PMRstSub.H"

///////////////////////////////////////////////////////////////

// Forward references.
LRESULT CALLBACK GetMsgProc (int nCode, WPARAM wParam,
   LPARAM lParam);

LRESULT CALLBACK PMSubclass (HWND hWnd, UINT uMsg,
   WPARAM wParam, LPARAM lParam);
BOOL CALLBACK AnyAppsRunning (HWND, LPARAM);

// Shared memory variables must be initialized.
#pragma data_seg(".sdata")

DWORD g_dwThreadIdPMRestore = 0;
HWND  g_hWndPM = NULL;

#pragma data_seg()

// Nonshared variables.
HHOOK     g_hHook = NULL;
WNDPROC   g_wpOrigPMProc = NULL;
HINSTANCE g_hinstDll = NULL;

///////////////////////////////////////////////////////////////

BOOL WINAPI DllMain (HINSTANCE hinstDll, DWORD fdwReason,
   LPVOID lpvReserved) {

   switch (fdwReason) {
```

Figure 7-7. *(continued)*
The PMRSTSUB.DLL file.

Figure 7-7. *continued*

```
    case DLL_PROCESS_ATTACH:
        // DLL is attaching to the address space
        // of the current process.
        g_hinstDll = hinstDll;
        break;

    case DLL_THREAD_ATTACH:
        // A new thread is being created in the current process.
        break;

    case DLL_THREAD_DETACH:
        // A thread is exiting cleanly.
        break;

    case DLL_PROCESS_DETACH:
        // The calling process is detaching the
        // DLL from its address space.
        break;
    }
    return(TRUE);
}


//////////////////////////////////////////////////////////////////


// Menu IDs from Program Manager's menu.
#define IDM_PMRESTOREABOUT      (4444)
#define IDM_PMRESTOREREMOVE     (4445)

BOOL SubclassProgManFrame (DWORD dwThreadIdPMRestore) {
    HMENU hMenu;

    // Find window handle of Program Manager.  Do not specify a
    // caption because the Program Manager's caption changes
    // depending on whether a group is maximized.
    g_hWndPM = FindWindow(__TEXT("PROGMAN"), NULL);

    if (!IsWindow(g_hWndPM)) {
        // If the Program Manager cannot be found,
        // we must terminate.
        MessageBox(NULL, __TEXT("Cannot find Program Manager."),
            NULL, MB_OK);
        return(FALSE);
    }
```

(continued)

Figure 7-7. *continued*

```
    // First we must install a systemwide WH_GETMESSAGE hook.
    g_hHook = SetWindowsHookEx(WH_GETMESSAGE, GetMsgProc,
        g_hinstDll, GetWindowThreadProcessId(g_hWndPM, NULL));

    // The hook cannot be installed (maybe there is greater
    // security in this environment).
    if (g_hHook == NULL)
        return(FALSE);

    // The hook was installed successfully; force a
    // benign message to the window so that the hook
    // function gets called.
    PostMessage(g_hWndPM, WM_NULL, 0, 0);


    // Get Menu handle to Program Manager's "Options" menu.
    hMenu = GetMenu(g_hWndPM);

    AppendMenu(hMenu, MF_ENABLED | MF_STRING,
        IDM_PMRESTOREABOUT, __TEXT("A&bout PM Restore..."));
    AppendMenu(hMenu, MF_ENABLED | MF_STRING,
        IDM_PMRESTOREREMOVE, __TEXT("&Remove PM Restore"));

    DrawMenuBar(g_hWndPM);          // Update the new menu bar.

    // The window in the other process is subclassed.
    g_dwThreadIdPMRestore = dwThreadIdPMRestore;
    return(TRUE);
}

///////////////////////////////////////////////////////////////

LRESULT CALLBACK GetMsgProc (int nCode, WPARAM wParam,
    LPARAM lParam) {

    static BOOL fPMSubclassed = FALSE;

    if (!fPMSubclassed && (nCode == HC_ACTION)  &&
        (wParam == PM_REMOVE) &&
        (((MSG *) lParam)->hwnd == g_hWndPM) &&
        (((MSG *) lParam)->message == WM_NULL)) {
        // If we have not yet subclassed the Program Manager
        // and it is retrieving a message and
```

(continued)

Figure 7-7. *continued*

```
      // the window handle identifies the Program Manager and
      // the message is a WM_NULL.

      // This DLL is now mapped into the Program Manager's
      // address space.  Time to subclass the Program Manager.
      g_wpOrigPMProc = SubclassWindow(g_hWndPM, PMSubclass);

      // Remind ourselves that we have subclassed the
      // Program Manager so that we don't do it again if we
      // ever get another WM_NULL message.
      fPMSubclassed = TRUE;
   }

   return(CallNextHookEx(g_hHook, nCode, wParam, lParam));
}


///////////////////////////////////////////////////////////////////

int PM_OnActivateApp(HWND hwnd, BOOL fActivate,
   DWORD dwThreadId) {

   BOOL fAnyWindowsUp;

   // The Program Manager is being either activated
   // or deactivated.
   if (!fActivate)
      return(0);      // PROGMAN being deactivated.

   if (!IsIconic(hwnd))
      return(0);      // PROGMAN isn't an icon.

   // Program Manager is being made active and is an icon.
   // Check whether any other applications are running.
   fAnyWindowsUp = (EnumWindows(AnyAppsRunning, 0) == 0);

   // If the enumeration was stopped prematurely, there must
   // be at least one other application running.
   if (fAnyWindowsUp)
      return(0);

   // No other apps running; restore PROGMAN to "open" state.
   ShowWindow(hwnd, SW_RESTORE);
   return(0);
}
```

(continued)

Figure 7-7. *continued*

```
/////////////////////////////////////////////////////////////////

// Function to process About box.
BOOL CALLBACK AboutProc (HWND hDlg, UINT uMsg,
   WPARAM wParam, LPARAM lParam) {

   BOOL fProcessed = TRUE;

   switch (uMsg) {
      case WM_INITDIALOG:
         break;

      case WM_COMMAND:
         switch (GET_WM_COMMAND_ID(wParam, lParam)) {
            case IDOK:
            case IDCANCEL:
               if (GET_WM_COMMAND_CMD(wParam, lParam) ==
                  BN_CLICKED)
                  EndDialog(hDlg,
                     GET_WM_COMMAND_ID(wParam, lParam));
               break;

            default:
               break;
         }
         break;

      default:
         fProcessed = FALSE;
         break;
   }
   return(fProcessed);
}


/////////////////////////////////////////////////////////////////

void PM_OnCommand (HWND hwnd, int id, HWND hwndCtl,
   UINT codeNotify) {

   HMENU hMenu;

   switch (id) {
```

(continued)

411

Figure 7-7. *continued*

```
        case IDM_PMRESTOREABOUT:
            // Our added menu option to display
            // "About PM Restore..." was chosen.
            DialogBox(g_hinstDll, MAKEINTRESOURCE(DLG_ABOUT),
                hwnd, AboutProc);
            break;

        case IDM_PMRESTOREREMOVE:
            // Stop window subclassing by putting back the
            // address of the original window procedure.
            (void) SubclassWindow(hwnd, g_wpOrigPMProc);

            // Get menu handle to the Program Manager's
            // "Options" menu.
            hMenu = GetMenu(hwnd);
            RemoveMenu(hMenu, IDM_PMRESTOREABOUT, MF_BYCOMMAND);
            RemoveMenu(hMenu, IDM_PMRESTOREREMOVE, MF_BYCOMMAND);
            DrawMenuBar(hwnd);          // Update the new menu bar.

            // Post WM_QUIT to our task to remove it from memory.
            PostThreadMessage(g_dwThreadIdPMRestore, WM_QUIT,
                0, 0);
            break;

        default: // Pass other WM_COMMANDs to original WndProc.
            break;
    }
}


//////////////////////////////////////////////////////////////

// Subclass function for the Program Manager. Any message for
// the Program Manager window comes here before reaching the
// original window function.
LRESULT CALLBACK PMSubclass (HWND hWnd, UINT uMsg,
    WPARAM wParam, LPARAM lParam) {

    switch (uMsg) {
        case WM_ACTIVATEAPP:
            HANDLE_WM_ACTIVATEAPP(hWnd, wParam,
                lParam, PM_OnActivateApp);
            break;
```

(continued)

Figure 7-7. *continued*

```
        case WM_COMMAND:
            HANDLE_WM_COMMAND(hWnd, wParam, lParam,
                PM_OnCommand);
            break;

        default: // Pass other messages to original procedure.
            break;
    }

    // Call original window procedure and return the result to
    // whoever sent this message to the Program Manager.
    return(CallWindowProc(g_wpOrigPMProc, hWnd,
        uMsg, wParam, lParam));
}


///////////////////////////////////////////////////////////////////

// Window's callback function to determine whether any
// windows exist that should stop us from restoring
// the Program Manager.
BOOL CALLBACK AnyAppsRunning (HWND hWnd, LPARAM lParam) {

    // If window is the Windows desktop, continue enumeration.
    if (hWnd == GetDesktopWindow())
        return(1);

    // If the window is invisible (hidden), continue
    // enumeration.
    if (!IsWindowVisible(hWnd))
        return(1);

    // If window was created by PROGMAN, continue enumeration.
    if (GetWindowThreadProcessId(g_hWndPM, NULL) ==
        GetWindowThreadProcessId(hWnd, NULL))
        return(1);

    // Any other type of window, stop enumeration.
    return(0);
}

///////////////////////// End Of File /////////////////////////
```

(continued)

Figure 7-7. *continued*

PMRSTSUB.H

```
/********************************************************************
Module name: PMRstSub.H
Notices: Copyright (c) 1993 Jeffrey Richter
********************************************************************/

// External function and variable prototypes.
BOOL SubclassProgManFrame (DWORD ThreadIdPMRestore);

// The handle of the WH_GETMESSAGE hook.
// This data member is shared between the DLL and the
// application.
extern HHOOK *lpg_hHook;

// Dialog and control IDs.
#define DLG_ABOUT      1

//////////////////////// End Of File ////////////////////////
```

PMRSTSUB.RC

```
/********************************************************************
Module name: PMRstSub.RC
Notices: Copyright (c) 1993 Jeffrey Richter
********************************************************************/

#include <windows.h>
#include "PMRstSub.h"

PMRest   ICON   DISCARDABLE PMRest.Ico

DLG_ABOUT DIALOG 16, 20, 126, 59
CAPTION "About Program Manager Restore"
STYLE WS_CAPTION | WS_DLGFRAME
   | WS_SYSMENU | WS_VISIBLE | WS_POPUP
BEGIN
   CONTROL "PMRest", -1, "static", SS_ICON
      | WS_CHILD, 4, 16, 16, 16
   CONTROL "Program Manager Restore", -1, "static",
      SS_CENTER | WS_CHILD, 22, 8, 100, 12
   CONTROL "Copyright (c) 1993 by:", -1, "static",
      SS_CENTER | WS_CHILD, 22, 20, 100, 12
```

(continued)

Figure 7-7. *continued*

```
    CONTROL "Jeffrey Richter", -1, "static",
        SS_CENTER | WS_CHILD, 22, 32, 100, 12
    CONTROL "&OK", IDOK, "button",
        BS_DEFPUSHBUTTON | WS_TABSTOP | WS_CHILD,
        40, 44, 44, 12
END


/////////////////////// End Of File ///////////////////////
```

PMRSTSUB.DEF
```
;************************************************************
;Module name: PMRstSub.Def
;Notices: Copyright (c) 1993 Jeffrey Richter
;************************************************************

EXPORTS
;   EntryName [=InternalName] [@Ordinal [ NONAME]] [CONSTANT]
    SubclassProgManFrame   @2 NONAME

    ;Internally, g_hHook is used. Externally, a pointer to the
    ;data variable is used. So, externally, we will refer to
    ;the object as lpg_hHook.
    lpg_hHook = g_hHook    @3 NONAME CONSTANT

;IMPORTS
;   [InternalName=] ModuleName.Entry
```

The 16-Bit Windows GlobalNotify Function

16-bit Windows supports a function called GlobalNotify:

```
void GlobalNotify(GNOTIFYPROC lpNotifyProc);
```

This function tells 16-bit Windows to call the function specified by the *lpNotifyProc* parameter whenever Windows is about to discard a block of memory. Because 16-bit Windows can discard a block of memory owned by one task while trying to satisfy a memory allocation for another task, the notify procedure must be implemented within a DLL. In this way, 16-bit Windows can call the notify procedure and tell it that a block is being discarded without having to perform a context switch.

Because Windows NT's memory management is so different compared to 16-bit Windows and because there is no way Windows NT can have one process notify another process of a memory block discard, this function has been removed from the API set. Fortunately, this function was very rarely used by developers.

The GMEM_SHARE and GMEM_DDESHARE Flags

In 16-bit Windows, when a DLL calls GlobalAlloc, the memory block allocated is owned by the task that calls the DLL function, which in turn calls GlobalAlloc. This means that, if the DLL is removed from the system (by a call to FreeLibrary), the memory block is not destroyed. It remains until the task that owns the block is destroyed. Also, it's possible that a task can terminate but the DLL can stay in memory. This happens if the DLL is being used by several tasks at once. In this case, the memory block allocated by the DLL on behalf of the task is destroyed when the task is destroyed. If another task places a call to a function in the DLL to retrieve the contents of the memory block, that block is destroyed and the program will probably crash.

The GMEM_SHARE flag tells 16-bit Windows to make the DLL the owner of the memory block instead of the task. If the GMEM-_SHARE flag is used when a task calls GlobalAlloc, the memory block isn't destroyed until all instances of the task are terminated. By making the DLL an owner of the memory block, the block is destroyed only when the DLL is removed from memory.

Because, in Windows NT, DLLs attach themselves to processes, memory can be owned only by an individual process. DLLs are not entities by themselves anymore. For this reason, the GMEM_SHARE flag is ignored in Windows NT.

In 16-bit Windows, the GMEM_SHARE and GMEM_DDESHARE flags had exactly the same meaning. In fact, both identifiers were defined to be the same value—0x2000.

CHAPTER EIGHT

THREAD-LOCAL STORAGE

Sometimes it's convenient to associate data with an instance of an object. For example, window extra bytes (SetClassWord, SetClassLong) associate data with a specific window by using the SetWindowWord and SetWindowLong functions. Thread-local storage (TLS) allows you to associate data with a specific thread of execution. For example, you might want to associate the creation time of a thread with a thread. Then, when the thread terminates, you can determine how long the thread has been executing. You can use this information for profiling your application to help determine the location of bottlenecks.

The C Runtime Library uses TLS. Because the library was designed before multithreaded applications were common, most functions in the library are intended for use with single-threaded applications. The *strtok* function is an excellent example. The first time an application calls *strtok*, the function passes the address to a string and saves the address of the string in its own static variable. Then, when you make future calls to *strtok* passing NULL, the function refers to the saved string address.

In a multithreaded environment, it's possible that one thread could call *strtok*, and before it can make another call, another thread could also call *strtok*. In this case, the second thread causes *strtok* to overwrite its static variable with a new address, which happens unbeknownst to the first thread. And the first thread's future calls to *strtok* use the second thread's string, which can lead to all kinds of difficult-to-find-and-fix bugs.

To fix this problem, the C Runtime uses TLS. In this case, each thread is assigned its very own string pointer that is reserved for use by the *strtok* function. Other C Runtime functions that require the same treatment include *asctime* and *gmtime*.

TLS can be a lifesaver if your application relies heavily on global or static variables. Fortunately, software developers tend to minimize the use of such variables and rely much more on automatic (stack-based) variables and data passing via function parameters. This is good because stack-based variables are always associated with a particular thread.

It is both fortunate and unfortunate that the Standard C Library has existed for so many years. It has been implemented and reimplemented by various compiler vendors; no C compiler would be worth buying if it didn't include the Standard C Library. Programmers have used it for years and will continue to do so, which means that the prototype and behavior of functions such as *strtok* must remain exactly as the Standard C Library describes them. If the C Runtime Library were to be redesigned today, it would be designed for environments that support multithreaded applications, and extreme measures would be taken to avoid the use of global and static variables.

In my own software projects, I avoid global variables as much as possible. If your application uses global and static variables, I strongly suggest that you examine each variable and check the possibilities for changing it to be a stack-based variable. This effort can save you an enormous amount of time if you decide to add additional threads to your application, and even single-threaded applications can benefit.

Although the two TLS techniques discussed in this chapter can be used in both applications and DLLs, you will more frequently find them useful when creating DLLs because DLLs often don't know the structure of the application to which they are linked. If you're writing an application (versus a DLL), you typically know how many threads will be created and how those threads will be used. The application developer can then create makeshift methods, or better yet, use stack-based methods (local variables) for associating data with each created thread.

A DLL implementor typically doesn't know how the application to which it is linked creates and uses threads. TLS was created with the intent of helping the DLL developer. However, the information discussed in this chapter can be used just as easily by an applications developer.

Dynamic Thread-Local Storage

An application takes advantage of dynamic, thread-local storage by calling a set of four functions. Although these functions can be used by an application or a DLL, they are most often used by DLLs.

Figure 8-1 shows the internal data structures that Windows NT uses for managing TLS.

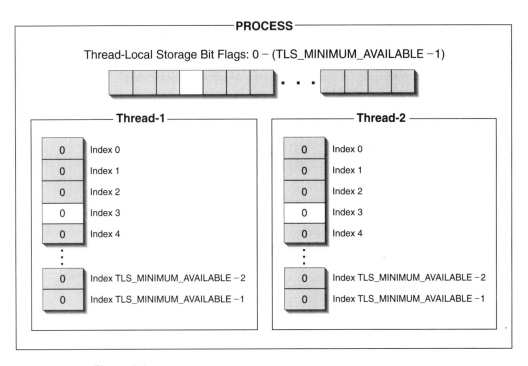

Figure 8-1.
Internal data structures that manage thread-local storage.

The figure shows a single set of in-use flags for each process running in the system. Each flag is either FREE or INUSE, indicating whether the TLS slot is in use. Microsoft guarantees that at least TLS-_MINIMUM_AVAILABLE bit flags will be available no matter which CPU platform Windows NT is ported to. By the way, TLS_MINIMUM-_AVAILABLE is defined as 64 in WINNT.H. On some platforms, the system might actually expand this flag array to accommodate the needs of the application or the DLL.

To use dynamic TLS, a call must first be made to TlsAlloc:

```
DWORD TlsAlloc(VOID);
```

This function instructs Windows NT to scan the bit flags in the process and locate a FREE flag. The system then changes the flag from FREE to INUSE, and TlsAlloc returns the index of the flag in the bit array. A DLL (or an application) usually saves the index in a global variable.[1]

---

1. This is one of those times in which a global variable is actually the best choice because the value is used on a per-process basis rather than a per-thread basis.

If TlsAlloc cannot find a FREE flag in the list, it returns TLS_OUT-_OF_INDEXES (defined as 0xFFFFFFFF in WINBASE.H).

The first time TlsAlloc is called, Windows NT recognizes that the first flag is FREE and changes the flag to INUSE, and TlsAlloc returns 0 (zero). That's 99 percent of what TlsAlloc does. I'll get to the other 1 percent later.

When a thread is created, an array of TLS_MINIMUM_AVAILABLE 32-bit values (LPVOIDs) is allocated, initialized to 0 (zero), and associated with the thread by the system. As Figure 8-1 shows, each thread gets its own array, and each LPVOID in the array can store any 32-bit value.

Before you can store information in a thread's LPVOID array, you must know which index in the array is available for use. This is what the earlier call to TlsAlloc is for; conceptually, TlsAlloc is reserving an index for you. If TlsAlloc returns index 3, it is effectively saying that index 3 is reserved for you in every thread currently executing in the process as well as in any threads that might be created in the future.

To place a value in a thread's array, you call the TlsSetValue function:

```
BOOL TlsSetValue(DWORD dwTlsIndex, LPVOID lpvTlsValue);
```

This function puts an LPVOID value or any other 32-bit value, identified by the *lpvTlsValue* parameter, into the thread's array at the index identified by the *dwTlsIndex* parameter. The value of *lpvTlsValue* is associated with the thread making the call to TlsSetValue. If the call is successful, TRUE is returned.

A thread changes its own array when it calls TlsSetValue. But a thread cannot set a thread local storage value for another thread. Personally, I wish there were another *Tls* function that allowed one thread to store data in another thread's array, but no such function exists. Currently, the only way to pass initialization data from one thread to another is by passing a single 32-bit value to CreateThread. CreateThread then passes this value to the thread function as its only parameter.

When calling TlsSetValue, be extremely careful that you always pass an index returned from an earlier call to TlsAlloc. Microsoft implemented these functions to be as fast as possible, and in so doing, gave up error checking. If you pass an index that was never allocated by a call to TlsAlloc, the system stores the 32-bit value in the thread's array anyway—no check is performed.

To retrieve a value from a thread's array, you call TlsGetValue:

```
LPVOID TlsGetValue(DWORD dwTlsIndex);
```

This function returns the value that was associated with the TLS slot at index *dwTlsIndex*. Like TlsSetValue, TlsGetValue looks only at the array that belongs to the calling thread. And again like TlsSetValue, no test is made to check the validity of the passed index.

When you come to a point in your process where you no longer need to reserve a TLS slot among all threads, you should call TlsFree:

```
BOOL TlsFree(DWORD dwTlsIndex);
```

This function simply tells the system that this slot no longer needs to be reserved. The INUSE flag managed by the process's bit flags array is set to FREE again and might be allocated in the future if a thread later calls TlsAlloc. TlsFree returns TRUE if the function is successful. Attempting to free a slot that was not allocated results in an error.

Using Dynamic Thread-Local Storage

Usually, if a DLL uses TLS, it calls TlsAlloc when its DllMain function is called with DLL_PROCESS_ATTACH, and it calls TlsFree when Dll-Main is called with DLL_PROCESS_DETACH. The calls to TlsSetValue and TlsGetValue are most likely made during calls to functions contained within the DLL.

One method for adding TLS to an application is to add it when you need it. For example, you might have a function in a DLL that works similarly to *strtok*. The first time your function is called, the thread passes a pointer to a 40-byte structure. You need to save this structure so that future calls can reference it. So you might code your function like this:

```
DWORD g_dwTlsIndex;    // Assume that this is initialized
                       // with the result of a call to TlsAlloc.
.
.
.
void MyFunction (LPSOMESTRUCT lpSomeStruct) {
   if (lpSomeStruct != NULL) {
      // The caller is priming this function.

      // See if we already allocated space to save the data.
      if (TlsGetValue(g_dwTlsIndex) == NULL) {
         // Space was never allocated. This is the first
         // time this function has ever been called.
```

```
        TlsSetValue(g_dwTlsIndex,
           HeapAlloc(GetProcessHeap(), 0,
              sizeof(*LPSOMESTRUCT)));
     }

     // Memory already exists for the data; save the newly
     // passed values.
     memcpy(TlsGetValue(g_dwTlsIndex), lpSomeStruct,
        sizeof(*LPSOMESTRUCT));

  } else {

     // The caller already primed the function. Now it
     // wants to do something with the saved data.

     // Get the address of the saved data.
     lpSomeStruct = (LPSOMESTRUCT) TlsGetValue(g_dwTlsIndex);

     // The saved data is pointed to by lpSomeStruct; use it.
     .
     .
     .

  }
```

If the application's thread never calls MyFunction, a memory block is never allocated for the thread.

It might seem that 64 (at least) TLS locations are more than you will ever need. However, keep in mind that an application can dynamically link to several DLLs. One DLL can allocate 10 TLS indexes, a second DLL can allocate 5 indexes, and so on. So it is always best to reduce the number of TLS indexes you need. The best way to do this is to use the same method used by MyFunction above. Sure, I can save all 40 bytes across 10 TLS indexes, but doing so is not only wasteful, it makes working with the data difficult. Instead, allocate a memory block for the data and simply save the pointer in a single TLS index just like MyFunction does.

When I discussed the TlsAlloc function earlier, I described only 99 percent of what it did. To understand the remaining 1 percent, look at this code fragment:

```
DWORD dwTlsIndex;
LPVOID lpvSomeValue;
  .
  .
  .
```

```
dwTlsIndex = TlsAlloc();
TlsSetValue(dwTlsIndex, (LPVOID) 12345);
TlsFree(dwTlsIndex);

// Assume that the dwTlsIndex value returned from
// this call to TlsAlloc is identical to the index
// returned by the earlier call to TlsAlloc.
dwTlsIndex = TlsAlloc();

lpvSomeValue = TlsGetValue(dwTlsIndex);
```

What do you think *lpvSomeValue* contains after the code above executes? 12345? The answer is 0 (zero). TlsAlloc, before returning, cycles through every thread existing in the process and places a 0 (zero) in each thread's array at the newly allocated index. This is very fortunate.

It's possible that an application will call LoadLibrary to load a DLL. And the DLL might call TlsAlloc to allocate an index. Then the thread might call FreeLibrary to remove the DLL. The DLL should free its index with a call to TlsFree, but who knows which values the DLL code placed in any of the thread's arrays? Next, a thread calls LoadLibrary to load a different DLL into memory. This DLL also calls TlsAlloc when it starts and gets the same index used by the previous DLL.

This new DLL might want to check whether memory for a thread has ever been allocated by calling TlsGetValue, as in the code fragment shown above. If TlsAlloc doesn't clear out the array entry for every thread, the old data from the first DLL is still available. If a thread calls MyFunction, MyFunction thinks that a memory block has already been allocated and calls *memcpy* to copy the new data into what MyFunction thinks is a memory block. This could have disastrous results. Fortunately, TlsAlloc initializes the array elements so that the disaster can never happen.

The Dynamic Thread-Local Storage Sample Application

The TLSDyn (TLSDYN.EXE) application, listed in Figure 8-2 at the end of this section, demonstrates how to take advantage of dynamic TLS. The program implicitly links to a dynamic-link library called SOME-LIB.DLL, listed in Figure 8-3. This dynamic-link library allocates a single TLS index when it receives its DLL_PROCESS_ATTACH notification and frees this TLS index when it receives a DLL_PROCESS-_DETACH notification.

SOMELIB.DLL contains a function called LoadResString. When this function is called, it first checks whether the calling thread previously called LoadResString. LoadResString determines this by calling TlsGetValue and checking whether the return value is NULL. A NULL value indicates a first-time call to LoadResString. In this case, LoadResString allocates a block of memory from the process's heap and stores the address of the block in the calling thread's TLS slot.

Whether or not this is the first time this thread is calling LoadResString, we have an address to a block of memory in the heap allocated for this thread. LoadResString now calls LoadString to load a string from the DLL's string table into this block of memory. This string is now associated with the calling thread.

Finally, LoadResString increments an internal counter (stored in the static variable *nStringId*) and returns the address of the loaded string resource. Every time a thread calls LoadResString, a different string is retrieved from the DLL's string table.

Now let's look at how the TLSDyn application works. When you invoke it, the following message box appears:

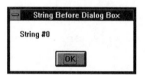

When WinMain begins executing, it makes a call to the LoadResString function, which in turn loads *String#0* from the DLL's string table and associates the string with the process's primary thread. The primary thread then makes a call to MessageBox in order to show you that it was successful.

After you click on the OK button, the primary thread creates a dialog box and five threads. Each of these threads makes its own initial call to LoadResString so that each will have its own associated string. Then each thread iterates through a loop four times. With each iteration, the thread creates a string containing the thread number and its associated string. The string is then added to the list box. After all five threads have completed their loops, the dialog box appears as shown at the top of the next page.

The order of the strings might be different on your machine. Simply note that the LoadResString function assigns every thread its own string. Also note that if no thread in the program ever makes a call to

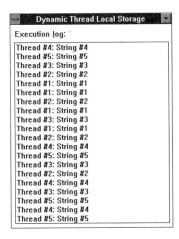

LoadResString, memory isn't allocated from the heap for this thread. We could allocate the memory in the DllMain function whenever the program receives either a DLL_PROCESS_ATTACH or a DLL_PROCESS_DETACH notification, but doing that allocates memory from the heap for all threads created by the process even if they never called LoadResString. The method used by SOMELIB.DLL is much more efficient.

After the program runs you can terminate it, which causes another message box to appear:

This message box appears as a result of WinMain making another call to LoadResString. LoadResString associates a new string with the primary thread, overwriting the original string, *String #0.*

Notice how the DllMain function in SOMELIB.C cleans up after itself when it receives either a DLL_THREAD_DETACH or a DLL_PROCESS_DETACH. In both cases, the DLL checks whether memory from the heap was allocated for the thread, and if so, frees that memory block. Although the memory would be freed automatically when TLSDyn terminates, it's best to clean up yourself. Always check that memory is, in fact, allocated before attempting to free it (just like DllMain does). Also, notice how TLSFree is called when DllMain is notified that the library is being detached from the process.

425

Now suppose that an application is already running when one of its threads calls LoadLibrary to attach to SOMELIB.DLL. SOMELIB's DllMain allocates a TLS index that is guaranteed to be unique for all existing threads and new threads for this process. Let's say that some threads call LoadResString, which results in memory allocation, and a thread calls FreeLibrary to detach SOMELIB.DLL. DllMain receives a DLL_PROCESS_DETACH message and frees any memory block associated with the calling thread. But what about other threads in the process that might have called LoadResString? These threads will have allocated memory that will never be freed—we have a pretty bad memory leak here.

Unfortunately, this problem has no good solutions. Your DLL needs to track its allocations in an array, and when it receives a DLL_PROCESS_DETACH notification, it needs to traverse through all the pointers in the array and call HeapFree for each one.

TLSDyn.ico

TLSDYN.C

```
/****************************************************************
Module name: TLSDyn.C
Notices: Copyright (c) 1993 Jeffrey Richter
****************************************************************/

#include <windows.h>
#include <windowsx.h>
#include <tchar.h>
#include <stdio.h>          // for sprintf
#include "SomeLib.H"
#include "TLSDyn.H"


HWND g_hwndLog = NULL;


//////////////////////////////////////////////////////////////////////
```

Figure 8-2.   *(continued)*
The TLSDyn application.

Figure 8-2. *continued*

```
DWORD WINAPI ThreadFunc (LPVOID lpvThreadParm) {
    int nThreadNum = (int) lpvThreadParm;
    int nNumCycles = 4;
    TCHAR szBuf[100];
    LPCTSTR szString = LoadResString();

    while (nNumCycles--) {
        _stprintf(szBuf, __TEXT("Thread #%d: %s"),
            nThreadNum, szString);

        ListBox_AddString(g_hwndLog, szBuf);

        Sleep(nThreadNum * 50);
    }
    return(0);
}
//////////////////////////////////////////////////////////////

BOOL Dlg_OnInitDialog (HWND hwnd, HWND hwndFocus,
    LPARAM lParam) {

    int nThreadNum;

    // Associate an icon with the dialog box.
    SetClassLong(hwnd, GCL_HICON, (LONG)
        LoadIcon((HINSTANCE) GetWindowLong(hwnd, GWL_HINSTANCE),
        __TEXT("TLSDyn")));

    g_hwndLog = GetDlgItem(hwnd, ID_LOG);

    for (nThreadNum = 1; nThreadNum <= 5; nThreadNum++) {
        HANDLE hThread;
        DWORD dwIDThread;

        hThread = CreateThread(NULL, 0, ThreadFunc,
            (LPVOID) nThreadNum, 0, &dwIDThread);

        CloseHandle(hThread);
    }

    return(TRUE);
}

//////////////////////////////////////////////////////////////
```

(continued)

Figure 8-2.   *continued*

```
void Dlg_OnCommand (HWND hwnd, int id, HWND hwndCtl,
   UINT codeNotify) {

   switch (id) {
      case IDCANCEL:
         EndDialog(hwnd, id);
         break;
   }
}

//////////////////////////////////////////////////////////////////

BOOL CALLBACK Dlg_Proc (HWND hDlg, UINT uMsg,
   WPARAM wParam, LPARAM lParam) {

   BOOL fProcessed = TRUE;

   switch (uMsg) {
      HANDLE_MSG(hDlg, WM_INITDIALOG, Dlg_OnInitDialog);
      HANDLE_MSG(hDlg, WM_COMMAND, Dlg_OnCommand);

      default:
         fProcessed = FALSE;
         break;
   }
   return(fProcessed);
}

//////////////////////////////////////////////////////////////////

int APIENTRY WinMain (HINSTANCE hInstance,
   HINSTANCE hPrevInstance, LPSTR lpszCmdLine, int nCmdShow) {

   MessageBox(NULL, LoadResString(),
      __TEXT("String Before Dialog Box"), MB_OK);

   DialogBox(hInstance, MAKEINTRESOURCE(DLG_TLSDYN),
      NULL, Dlg_Proc);

   MessageBox(NULL, LoadResString(),
      __TEXT("String After Dialog Box"), MB_OK);

   return(0);
}

//////////////////////// End Of File ////////////////////////////
```

(continued)

Figure 8-2. *continued*

TLSDYN.H

```
/************************************************************
Module name: TLSDyn.H
Notices: Copyright (c) 1993 Jeffrey Richter
************************************************************/

// Dialog and control IDs.
#define DLG_TLSDYN         1
#define ID_LOG           100


/////////////////////////// End Of File ///////////////////////////
```

TLSDYN.RC

```
/************************************************************
Module name: TLSDyn.RC
Notices: Copyright (c) 1993 Jeffrey Richter
************************************************************/

#include <windows.h>
#include "TLSDyn.h"


TLSDyn   ICON  DISCARDABLE TLSDyn.Ico

DLG_TLSDYN DIALOG 25, 21, 147, 180
STYLE WS_OVERLAPPED | WS_VISIBLE | WS_CAPTION | WS_SYSMENU |
    WS_MINIMIZEBOX
CAPTION "Dynamic Thread Local Storage"
BEGIN
    CONTROL "Execution &log:", -1, "STATIC",
        WS_CHILD | WS_VISIBLE | WS_GROUP, 4, 4, 52, 8
    CONTROL "", ID_LOG, "LISTBOX", LBS_NOINTEGRALHEIGHT |
        WS_CHILD | WS_VISIBLE | WS_BORDER | WS_VSCROLL,
        4, 16, 140, 160
END


/////////////////////////// End Of File ///////////////////////////
```

SOMELIB.C

```
/**************************************************************
Module name: SomeLib.C
Notices: Copyright (c) 1993 Jeffrey Richter
**************************************************************/

#include <windows.h>
#include "SomeLib.H"

///////////////////////////////////////////////////////////////

DWORD g_dwTlsIndex = TLS_OUT_OF_INDEXES;

// Per mapping instance data for this DLL.
HMODULE g_hMod = NULL;

///////////////////////////////////////////////////////////////

BOOL WINAPI DllMain (HMODULE hMod, DWORD fdwReason,
   LPVOID lpvReserved) {

   LPTSTR lpszStr;

   switch (fdwReason) {

      case DLL_PROCESS_ATTACH:
         // DLL is attaching to the address space
         // of the current process.
         g_hMod = hMod;

         // Allocate a thread-local storage index.
         g_dwTlsIndex = TlsAlloc();

         if (g_dwTlsIndex == TLS_OUT_OF_INDEXES) {
            // The TLS index couldn't be allocated -- have the
            // DLL return that initialization was
            // NOT successful.
            return(FALSE);
         }

         break;
```

Figure 8-3.
The SOMELIB.DLL file.

(continued)

Figure 8-3. *continued*

```
case DLL_THREAD_ATTACH:
   // A new thread is being created in the process.
   break;

case DLL_THREAD_DETACH:
   // A thread is exiting cleanly.

   // Ensure that the TLS index was
   // allocated successfully.
   if (g_dwTlsIndex != TLS_OUT_OF_INDEXES) {

      // Get the pointer to the allocated memory.
      lpszStr = TlsGetValue(g_dwTlsIndex);

      // Test whether memory was ever allocated
      // for this thread.
      if (lpszStr != NULL) {
         HeapFree(GetProcessHeap(), 0, lpszStr);
      }
   }
   break;

case DLL_PROCESS_DETACH:
   // The calling process is detaching the DLL
   // from its address space.

   // Ensure that the TLS index was
   // allocated successfully.
   if (g_dwTlsIndex != TLS_OUT_OF_INDEXES) {

      // Get the pointer to the allocated memory.
      lpszStr = TlsGetValue(g_dwTlsIndex);

      // Test whether memory was ever allocated
      // for this thread.
      if (lpszStr != NULL) {
         HeapFree(GetProcessHeap(), 0, lpszStr);
      }
```

(continued)

Figure 8-3. *continued*

```
         // Free the TLS index.
         TlsFree(g_dwTlsIndex);
      }
      break;
   }
   return(TRUE);
}


//////////////////////////////////////////////////////////////////
#define RESSTR_SIZE      (1000 * sizeof(TCHAR))

LPCTSTR LoadResString (void) {
   static int nStringId = 0;

   LPTSTR lpszStr = TlsGetValue(g_dwTlsIndex);

   if (lpszStr == NULL) {
      lpszStr = HeapAlloc(GetProcessHeap(), 0, RESSTR_SIZE);
      TlsSetValue(g_dwTlsIndex, lpszStr);
   }

   LoadString(g_hMod, IDS_STRINGFIRST + nStringId,
      lpszStr, RESSTR_SIZE);

   nStringId = (nStringId + 1) % IDS_STRINGNUM;

   return(lpszStr);
}


//////////////////////// End Of File ////////////////////////
```

SOMELIB.H

```
/*****************************************************************
Module name: SomeLib.H
Notices: Copyright (c) 1993 Jeffrey Richter
*****************************************************************/

// IDs for use by the string table resource.
#define IDS_STRINGFIRST  1000
#define IDS_STRINGLAST   (IDS_STRINGFIRST + 9)
#define IDS_STRINGNUM    (IDS_STRINGLAST - \
                          IDS_STRINGFIRST + 1)
```

(continued)

Figure 8-3. *continued*

```
// Function to return the address of a string in memory.
LPCTSTR LoadResString (void);

/////////////////////// End Of File ///////////////////////
```

SOMELIB.RC

```
/***************************************************************
Module name: SomeLib.RC
Notices: Copyright (c) 1993 Jeffrey Richter
***************************************************************/

#include "SomeLib.h"

STRINGTABLE
BEGIN
   IDS_STRINGFIRST,     "String #0"
   IDS_STRINGFIRST + 1, "String #1"
   IDS_STRINGFIRST + 2, "String #2"
   IDS_STRINGFIRST + 3, "String #3"
   IDS_STRINGFIRST + 4, "String #4"
   IDS_STRINGFIRST + 5, "String #5"
   IDS_STRINGFIRST + 6, "String #6"
   IDS_STRINGFIRST + 7, "String #7"
   IDS_STRINGFIRST + 8, "String #8"
   IDS_STRINGFIRST + 9, "String #9"
END

/////////////////////// End Of File ///////////////////////
```

SOMELIB.DEF

```
;***************************************************************
;Module name: SomeLib.Def
;Notices: Copyright (c) 1993 Jeffrey Richter
;***************************************************************

EXPORTS
;  EntryName [=InternalName] [@Ordinal [ NONAME]] [CONSTANT]
   LoadResString     @2   NONAME

;IMPORTS
;  [InternalName=] ModuleName.Entry
```

Static Thread-Local Storage

Static thread-local storage uses the same concept as dynamic TLS—it associates data with a thread. And static TLS is much easier to use in your code. To take advantage of static TLS, you don't need to call any functions.

Let's say that you want to associate a start time with every thread created by your application. All you need to do is declare the start-time variable as follows:

```
__declspec(thread) DWORD gt_dwStartTime = 0;
```

The *__declspec(thread)* prefix in the line above is a new modifier that Microsoft added for version 8.0 of its 32-bit C/C++ compiler. It tells the compiler that the corresponding variable should be placed in its own section inside the EXE or DLL file. The variable following *__declspec-(thread)* must be declared as either a global variable or a static variable inside (or outside) a function. You cannot declare a local variable to be of type *__declspec(thread)*. This shouldn't be a problem because local variables are always associated with a specific thread anyway. I use the *gt_* prefix for global TLS variables and *st_* for static TLS variables.

When the compiler compiles your program, it puts all the TLS variables into their own section named, unsurprisingly enough, *.tls*. The linker combines all the *.tls* sections together from all the object modules to produce one big *.tls* section in the resulting EXE or DLL file.

To actually make static TLS work, the operating system needs to get involved. When your application is loaded into memory, the system looks for the *.tls* section in your EXE file and dynamically allocates a block of memory large enough to hold all the static TLS variables. Every time the code in your application refers to one of these variables, the reference resolves to a memory location contained in the allocated block of memory. As a result, the compiler must generate additional code in order to reference the static TLS variables, which makes your application both larger in size and slower to execute. On an Intel CPU, three additional machine instructions are generated for every reference to a static TLS variable.

If another thread is created in your process, the system traps it and automatically allocates another block of memory to contain the new thread's static TLS variables. The new thread has access only to its own static TLS variables and isn't able to access the TLS variables belonging to any other thread.

That's basically how static TLS works. Now let's add DLLs to the story. It's likely that your application will use static TLS variables and that you will link to a DLL that also wants to use static TLS variables. When Windows NT loads your application, it first determines the size of your application's *.tls* section and adds the value to the size of any *.tls* sections contained in any DLLs to which your application links. When threads are created in your process, the system automatically allocates a block of memory large enough to hold all the TLS variables required by your application and all the implicitly linked DLLs. This is pretty cool.

But let's look at what happens when your application calls LoadLibrary to link to a DLL that also contains static TLS variables. The system needs to look at all the threads that already exist in the process and enlarge their TLS memory blocks to accommodate the additional memory requirements of the new DLL. Also, if FreeLibrary is called to free a DLL containing static TLS variables, the memory block associated with each thread in the process should be compacted.

Alas, this is too much for Windows NT to manage. The system allows libraries containing static TLS variables to be explicitly loaded at runtime; however, the TLS data isn't properly initialized, and any attempt to access it may result in an access violation. This is the only disadvantage of using static TLS; this problem doesn't occur when using dynamic TLS. Libraries that use dynamic TLS can be loaded at runtime and freed at runtime with no problems at all.

The Static Thread-Local Storage Sample Application

The TLSStat (TLSSTAT.EXE) application, listed in Figure 8-4 at the end of this section, demonstrates the use of static TLS. When you first invoke TLSStat, the following dialog box appears:

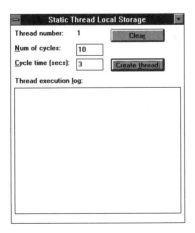

This dialog box allows you to dynamically create new threads and monitor their execution.

The following line is included toward the top of TLSSTAT.C:

```
__declspec(thread) DWORD gt_dwStartTime = 0;
```

This line declares a static TLS variable called *gt_dwStartTime*. The system creates a new instance of this variable every time a new thread is created in the process. Whenever any thread refers to *gt_dwStartTime*, that thread is always referring to its own copy of this variable.

Clicking on the *Create thread* button dynamically creates a new thread by allocating a data structure from the heap and filling the members of the structure with information that needs to be passed to the newly created thread. This information includes the thread number, the number of cycles that the thread should execute, and the duration of each cycle. The pointer to this data structure is then passed to CreateThread, which passes the pointer to the thread function. The thread function is responsible for freeing this memory block when it no longer needs it.[2]

When each new thread starts, it records the system time (in *gt_dwStartTime*) and begins executing a loop. As each iteration of the loop begins, the thread displays the total amount of time that the thread has been in existence in the *Thread execution log* list box.

You should notice that in this example I could have done away with the *gt_dwStartTime* variable by creating a local (stack-based) variable called *dwStartTime* and placing it inside ThreadFunc. In fact, this would have been a better way to write the application because it would have avoided the additional size and speed overhead incurred when using static TLS. However, if I had done this, the demonstration program would no longer have demonstrated static TLS.

The real point I'm trying to make is that an application "understands" the nature of the program, whereas a DLL most likely doesn't. This is why TLS was really designed for DLLs, although it can be used in applications.

Before creating a thread, you can set the number of iterations in the loop and the duration of each iteration by adjusting the contents of the *Num of cycles* and *Cycle time (secs)* edit boxes. Because a new thread can take several seconds to execute, you can create additional threads

---

2. While I was writing this section of code, I thought it would be useful to have a new Win32 function that offered some way for one thread to alter the thread-local storage variables used by another thread. If this function existed, I probably could have avoided using the heap altogether by simply assigning values to the new thread.

before the first thread finishes executing by adjusting the *Num of cycles* and *Cycle time (secs)* edit boxes and clicking on the *Create thread* button again. The screen shot below was taken while three threads were executing simultaneously:

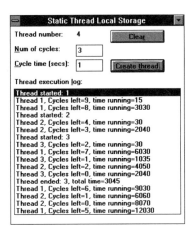

The three threads were created using the following settings:

Thread Number	Num of Cycles	Cycle Time
1	10	3
2	5	2
3	3	1

Every time a new thread is created, the *Thread number* value is incremented. You can reset the application by clicking on the *Clear* button, which causes the *Thread number* value to reset to 1 and the contents of the list box to be cleared.

One last thing to note: When you terminate TLSStat, it displays the following message box:

The box displays the total amount of time that the application (or primary thread) has been executing by referencing its own *gt_dwStartTime* TLS variable.

TLSStat.ico

TLSSTAT.C

```
/*************************************************************
Module name: TLSStat.C
Notices: Copyright (c) 1993 Jeffrey Richter
*************************************************************/

#include <windows.h>
#include <windowsx.h>
#include <tchar.h>
#include <stdlib.h>      // for rand
#include <stdio.h>       // for sprintf
#include "TLSStat.H"


///////////////////////////////////////////////////////////

// Structure used to pass data from one thread to another.
typedef struct {
   int nThreadNum;        // The number used for recordkeeping.
   int nNumCycles;        // Number of iterations in the loop.
   DWORD dwCycleTime;     // Time spent in each loop iteration.
} THREADDATA, *LPTHREADDATA;

// Global handle to list box window used for
// logging execution.
HWND g_hwndLogLB = NULL;


// Our global static TLS variable
// to hold each thread's start time.
// The system will automatically allocate one of these
// for every thread created in this process.
#ifdef __BORLANDC__
DWORD __thread gt_dwStartTime = 0;
#else
__declspec(thread) DWORD gt_dwStartTime = 0;
#endif


///////////////////////////////////////////////////////////
```

Figure 8-4.   *(continued)*

The TLSStat application.

Figure 8-4. *continued*

```
DWORD WINAPI ThreadFunc (LPVOID lpvThreadParm) {
   // The parameter passed to us is a pointer to a THREADDATA
   // structure.  Let's save it in a local variable.
   LPTHREADDATA lpThreadData = (LPTHREADDATA) lpvThreadParm;

   TCHAR szBuf[100];

   // Store the thread's start time in its very
   // own static TLS variable.
   gt_dwStartTime = GetTickCount();

   // Write a log entry stating that we're starting.
   _stprintf(szBuf, __TEXT("Thread started: %d"),
      lpThreadData->nThreadNum);
   ListBox_AddString(g_hwndLogLB, szBuf);
   ListBox_SetCurSel(g_hwndLogLB, 0);

   // Start doing some work...
   while (lpThreadData->nNumCycles--) {
      // Write to the log how many cycles this thread
      // has left before it dies and how long this thread
      // has been running.
      _stprintf(szBuf,
         __TEXT("Thread %d, Cycles left=%d, time running=%d"),
         lpThreadData->nThreadNum, lpThreadData->nNumCycles,
         GetTickCount() - gt_dwStartTime);

      ListBox_AddString(g_hwndLogLB, szBuf);

      // Sleep for a while and let other threads run.
      Sleep(lpThreadData->dwCycleTime);
   }

   // This thread is done executing; write a log entry
   // that says so and displays the total execution time
   // of the thread.
   _stprintf(szBuf, __TEXT("Thread ended: %d, total time=%d"),
      lpThreadData->nThreadNum,
      GetTickCount() - gt_dwStartTime);
   ListBox_AddString(g_hwndLogLB, szBuf);

   // The thread is responsible for deleting the THREADDATA
   // structure that was allocated by the primary thread.
   HeapFree(GetProcessHeap(), 0, lpvThreadParm);
```

(continued)

439

Figure 8-4. *continued*

```
    return(0);
}

/////////////////////////////////////////////////////////////

BOOL Dlg_OnInitDialog (HWND hwnd, HWND hwndFocus,
    LPARAM lParam) {

    // Associate an icon with the dialog box.
    SetClassLong(hwnd, GCL_HICON, (LONG)
        LoadIcon((HINSTANCE) GetWindowLong(hwnd, GWL_HINSTANCE),
        __TEXT("TLSStat")));

    // Default the thread number to 1.
    SetDlgItemInt(hwnd, ID_THREADNUM, 1, FALSE);

    // Default the number of cycles to 10.
    SetDlgItemInt(hwnd, ID_NUMCYCLES, 10, FALSE);

    // Default the maximum cycle time to 3 seconds.
    SetDlgItemInt(hwnd, ID_CYCLETIME, 3, FALSE);

    // Save the handle of the dialog box in a global
    // variable so that it can be accessed easily from
    // the thread function.
    g_hwndLogLB = GetDlgItem(hwnd, ID_LOG);

    // Let's start with the "Create thread"
    // button having focus.
    SetFocus(GetDlgItem(hwnd, IDOK));

    // I set focus, so the Dialog Manager shouldn't.
    return(FALSE);
}

/////////////////////////////////////////////////////////////

void Dlg_OnCommand (HWND hwnd, int id, HWND hwndCtl,
    UINT codeNotify) {

    DWORD       dwIDThread;
    HANDLE      hThread;
    LPTHREADDATA lpThreadData;

    switch (id) {
```

(continued)

Figure 8-4. *continued*

```
case ID_CLEAR:
    // Reset the application.
    SetDlgItemInt(hwnd, ID_THREADNUM, 1, FALSE);
    ListBox_ResetContent(g_hwndLogLB);
    break;

case IDOK:
    // Allocate a block of memory that can be used to
    // give data from this thread to the new thread we
    // are about to create.
    lpThreadData = (LPTHREADDATA)
        HeapAlloc(GetProcessHeap(), 0,
        sizeof(THREADDATA));

    if (lpThreadData == NULL) {
        // Memory could not be allocated; display message
        // box and break.
        MessageBox(hwnd,
            __TEXT("Error creating ThreadData"),
            __TEXT("TLS Static"), MB_OK);
        break;
    }

    // Fill the memory block with the data from
    // the dialog box.
    lpThreadData->nThreadNum =
        GetDlgItemInt(hwnd, ID_THREADNUM, NULL, FALSE);
    lpThreadData->nNumCycles =
        GetDlgItemInt(hwnd, ID_NUMCYCLES, NULL, FALSE);

    // Multiply the cycle time by 1000
    // to convert to seconds.
    lpThreadData->dwCycleTime = (DWORD)
        (1000 * GetDlgItemInt(hwnd,
        ID_CYCLETIME, NULL, FALSE));

    // Increment the thread number for the next thread.
    SetDlgItemInt(hwnd, ID_THREADNUM,
        lpThreadData->nThreadNum + 1, FALSE);

    // Create the new thread and pass it the address of
    // our allocated memory block containing the
    // attributes that the thread should use.  The
    // thread is responsible for freeing the memory
    // block when it no longer needs it.
```

(continued)

Figure 8-4. *continued*

```
        hThread = CreateThread(NULL, 0, ThreadFunc,
           (LPVOID) lpThreadData, 0, &dwIDThread);

        if (hThread != NULL) {
            // If the thread was created successfully, close
            // the handle because this thread never needs to
            // refer to the new thread again.
            CloseHandle(hThread);

        } else {

            // The thread could not be created;
            // display message box and break.
            MessageBox(hwnd,
                __TEXT("Error creating the new thread"),
                __TEXT("TLS Static"), MB_OK);
            HeapFree(GetProcessHeap(), 0,
                (LPVOID) lpThreadData);
        }
        break;

    case IDCANCEL:
        EndDialog(hwnd, id);
        break;
    }
}


//////////////////////////////////////////////////////////////

BOOL CALLBACK Dlg_Proc (HWND hDlg, UINT uMsg,
    WPARAM wParam, LPARAM lParam) {

    BOOL fProcessed = TRUE;

    switch (uMsg) {
        HANDLE_MSG(hDlg, WM_INITDIALOG, Dlg_OnInitDialog);
        HANDLE_MSG(hDlg, WM_COMMAND, Dlg_OnCommand);

        default:
            fProcessed = FALSE;
            break;
    }
    return(fProcessed);
}
```

(continued)

Figure 8-4. *continued*

```
////////////////////////////////////////////////////////////////

int APIENTRY WinMain (HINSTANCE hInstance,
   HINSTANCE hPrevInstance, LPSTR lpszCmdLine, int nCmdShow) {

   TCHAR szBuf[100];

   // The primary thread also gets its own TLS copy
   // of the gt_dwStartTime variable.  Let's initialize it to
   // the time when the application started executing.
   gt_dwStartTime = GetTickCount();

   DialogBox(hInstance, MAKEINTRESOURCE(DLG_TLSSTAT),
      NULL, Dlg_Proc);

   // The user has terminated the dialog box; let's show
   // how long the whole application has been running.
   _stprintf(szBuf,
      __TEXT("Total time running application=%d."),
      GetTickCount() - gt_dwStartTime);
   MessageBox(NULL, szBuf, __TEXT("TLS Static"), MB_OK);

   return(0);
}


//////////////////////// End Of File ////////////////////////
```

TLSSTAT.H

```
/***************************************************************
Module name: TLSStat.H
Notices: Copyright (c) 1993 Jeffrey Richter
***************************************************************/

// Dialog and control IDs.
#define DLG_TLSSTAT        1
#define ID_CLEAR         100
#define ID_THREADNUM     101
#define ID_NUMCYCLES     102
#define ID_CYCLETIME     103
#define ID_LOG           104


//////////////////////// End Of File ////////////////////////
```

(continued)

Figure 8-4. *continued*

TLSSTAT.RC

```
/*****************************************************************
Module name: TLSStat.RC
Notices: Copyright (c) 1993 Jeffrey Richter
*****************************************************************/

#include <windows.h>
#include "TLSStat.h"

TLSStat  ICON  DISCARDABLE TLSStat.Ico

DLG_TLSSTAT DIALOG DISCARDABLE  18, 18, 180, 215
STYLE WS_BORDER | WS_OVERLAPPED | WS_MINIMIZEBOX |
   WS_VISIBLE | WS_CAPTION | WS_SYSMENU
CAPTION "Static Thread Local Storage"
FONT 8, "Helv"
BEGIN
    LTEXT           "Thread number:",-1,4,4,56,8
    RTEXT           "1",ID_THREADNUM,60,4,13,8
    PUSHBUTTON      "Clea&r",ID_CLEAR,104,4,56,14
    LTEXT           "&Num of cycles:",-1,4,20,60,12
    EDITTEXT        ID_NUMCYCLES,68,20,28,13
    LTEXT           "&Cycle time (secs):",-1,4,36,60,12
    EDITTEXT        ID_CYCLETIME,68,36,28,13
    DEFPUSHBUTTON   "Create &thread",IDOK,104,36,56,14,
                    WS_GROUP
    LTEXT           "Thread execution &log:",-1,4,56,88,8
    LISTBOX         ID_LOG,4,68,172,144,NOT LBS_NOTIFY |
                    WS_VSCROLL | WS_GROUP | WS_TABSTOP

END

/////////////////////// End Of File ///////////////////////
```

FILE SYSTEMS AND FILE I/O

One important aspect of any operating system is the way in which it manages files. In good old MS-DOS, managing files is about all the operating system did, especially when 16-bit Windows was running on top of it. Windows pretty much took care of everything but did leave the manipulation of files on hard disks and floppy disks up to MS-DOS. (As time went on, though, 16-bit Windows took on more of even this responsibility by adding direct 32-bit access support and going right to the disk controller to manipulate the system's paging file.)

As MS-DOS was, Windows NT is responsible for managing the user's files and drives, but Windows NT is capable of supporting multiple file systems—all of them simultaneously. In the first version of Windows NT, four different file systems are supported:

The File Allocation Table (FAT) file system is the familiar file system currently used by all versions of MS-DOS and will therefore probably be the most common file system used with Windows NT—at least in the initial release of Windows NT. For users who will occasionally need to boot MS-DOS instead of Windows NT, the FAT file system will certainly be the file system of choice. Note too that the FAT file system is the only file system Windows NT supports for floppy disks.

The High Performance File System (HPFS), originally designed for use with the OS/2 operating system, was created to overcome many of the limitations of the FAT file system. However, it didn't deal with data corruption problems very well at all. In the event of a system crash, it was possible that some important file-related information wouldn't be written back to the disk. The next time that OS/2 would be booted, a CHKDSK that could take several hours to reconstruct the important file-related data would have to be performed. Windows NT supports the HPFS file system for backward compatibility with the files of users who are upgrading from OS/2 to Windows NT and don't want to reformat their hard disks just yet.

The New Technology File System (NTFS) is, as its name implies, brand new for Windows NT. It's the next-generation file system after HPFS, fixing all the problems with HPFS and adding several new features. The most important of the new features is a file system recovery scheme that makes for quick restoration of disk-based data after a system failure.

Other features of NTFS include the ability to manipulate extremely large storage media and to have filenames up to 255 characters in length. Several security features, such as execute-only files (that make it far more difficult to have a virus attach itself to an application), have been added. NTFS stores all filenames and directory names by means of the international Unicode. This means among other things that files will retain their names when they're copied to systems that use different languages. For POSIX compatibility, NTFS supports file system features such as hard links, case-sensitive filenames, and the ability to retain information about when a file was last opened.

NTFS was designed to be extended. Features that will be supported include transaction-based operations to support fault tolerant applications, user-controlled version numbers for files, multiple data streams per file, flexible options for file naming and file attributes, and support for the popular file servers. For security-minded installations, the NTFS file system will certainly become the standard, and it should eventually replace the FAT file system standard.

The CD-ROM File System (CDFS) is used specifically for a CD-ROM drive, once considered a high-ticket peripheral for a personal computer. Today a CD-ROM drive is becoming more a necessity than a luxury. More and more software is becoming available on CD-ROM, and Windows NT itself is available on CD-ROM. In the future more software will use CD-ROMs as its distribution medium because they offer several advantages:

- CD-ROMs are less expensive to mass produce when compared to the sheer number of floppy disks involved in so much of software distribution. This should lower the cost of retail software products.

- Because the average end-user doesn't have CD-ROM duplication equipment, it's much harder for end-users to pirate copies of software distributed on CD-ROM. People who want to use the software will have to buy it. This should also help lower the cost of retail software products.

- CD-ROMs are more reliable than floppies because CD-ROMs aren't magnetic and therefore aren't subject to magnetic disturbances as floppies are.

- Data can be accessed directly from a CD-ROM without having to be installed on your hard drive. This can save enormous amounts of precious hard disk space.

- Applications are much easier to install from a CD-ROM because you don't have to baby-sit the computer, switching floppies on demand.

Microsoft's having built CD-ROM support directly into Windows NT will certainly help to promote the use and wide acceptance of CD-ROMs in the marketplace.

The best aspect of Windows NT support for all of these file systems is that it's simultaneous. You could easily have one partition on your hard disk formatted for HPFS and another formatted for NTFS. Once you are using Windows NT, you could easily copy files from either of these partitions to a floppy disk formatted for the FAT file system. The first time Windows NT accesses a disk partition (volume), it determines which file system that partition has been formatted for.

Of course, some of the file systems contain features that aren't supported by other file systems. For example, the NTFS file system saves the date and time a file was first created regardless of updates, but this information is not saved in the FAT file system. If you copy a file from an NTFS partition to a FAT partition, this additional information is lost.

Windows NT Filename Conventions

So that Windows NT can support several different file systems, all the file systems must observe some ground rules. The most important rule is that each file system must organize files into a hierarchical directory tree just as the MS-DOS FAT file system does. Directory names and filenames in the pathname must be separated by the backslash (\) character. In addition to the rules for constructing pathnames, there are rules for constructing directory names and filenames.

- All pathnames must be zero-terminated.

- Directory names and filenames must not contain the backslash separator character (\), a numeric character in the range 0 through 31, or any character explicitly disallowed by any of the file systems.

447

- For the Win32 subsystem, directory names and filenames can be created in mixed case, but users must anticipate that searches for directories and files will always be performed by means of case-insensitive comparisons. If a file called ReadMe-.Txt already exists and you try to name a file README.TXT, the naming of the second file will fail. The POSIX subsystem, on the other hand, does support filenames constructed of mixed-case characters by performing case-sensitive searches.

- When used to specify a directory name, the period (.) identifies the current directory. For example, the pathname .\READ-ME.TXT indicates that the file is in the current directory.

- When used to specify a directory name, two periods (..) identify the parent directory of the current directory. For example, the pathname ..\README.TXT indicates that the file is in the current directory's parent directory.

- When used as part of a directory name or filename, a period (.) separates individual components of the name. For example, in the file README.TXT, the period separates the file's name (in the smaller sense) from the file's extension.

- Directory names and filenames must not contain some special characters: less-than (<), greater-than (>), colon (:), double quotation marks (""), and the pipe (|).

All file systems supported by Windows NT must follow these ground rules. The differences among the file systems have to do with how each file system interprets the ground rules and with the additional features or information a file system adds that distinguishes it from others. For example, the FAT file system allows directory names and filenames to be only eight characters long with a three-character extension for filenames while both the HPFS and NTFS file systems allow directory names and filenames to be as many as 255 characters long.

System and Volume Operations

Let's look at the Windows NT file system at the highest level first and work our way down to the nitty-gritty stuff. At the highest level, your application might need to know what logical drives exist in the user's environment. The most primitive call you can make to determine this is:

```
DWORD GetLogicalDrives(void);
```

This function simply returns a 32-bit value in which each bit represents whether a logical drive exists. For example, if the system has a drive A, bit 0 (zero) will be set, and if the system has a drive Z, bit 25 will be set.

You can determine whether a particular drive letter was assigned to a logical drive on the system by executing this function:

```
BOOL DoesDriveExist(char cDriveLetter) {
    cDriveLetter = (char) CharUpper(cDriveLetter);
    return(GetLogicalDrives() & (1 << (cDriveLetter - 'A')));
}
```

The result from GetLogicalDrives can also be used to count the number of logical drives in the system:

```
UINT GetNumDrivesInSys (void) {
    DWORD dw = GetLogicalDrives();
    UINT uDrivesInSys = 0;

    // Repeat until there are no more drives.
    while (dw != 0) {

        if (dw & 1) {
            // If low-bit is set, drive exists.
            uDrivesInSys++;
        }

        // Shift all the drive information down 1 bit.
        dw >>= 1;
    }

    // Return number of logical drives.
    return(uDrivesInSys);
}
```

The GetLogicalDrives function is very fast but doesn't return a lot of useful information. The GetLogicalDriveStrings function doesn't require all the bit manipulations and returns more complete information:

```
DWORD GetLogicalDriveStrings(DWORD cchBuffer, LPTSTR lpszBuffer);
```

This function fills the buffer pointed to by *lpszBuffer* with the root directory information associated with every logical drive on the system. The *cchBuffer* parameter tells the function the maximum size of the buffer. The function returns the number of bytes required to hold all the data. When calling this function, you should always compare the return value with the value passed in the *cchBuffer* parameter. If the return value is smaller, the buffer was large enough to hold all of the data. If the return value is larger, there was more data than could fit into the buffer.

449

The best way to use this function is to call it once, passing in 0 (zero) as the *cchBuffer* parameter. Then use the return value to dynamically allocate a block of memory the size returned by the call to Get-LogicalDriveStrings. Then call the function again, this time passing in the address of the newly allocated buffer:

```
DWORD dw = GetLogicalDriveStrings(0, NULL);
LPSTR lpDriveStrings = HeapAlloc(GetProcessHeap(), 0, dw);
GetLogicalDriveStrings(dw, lpDriveStrings);
```

The contents of the returned buffer have the same format as an environment string buffer: items separated by a zero character with an extra, terminating zero character at the end. For example, on my machine the buffer comes back looking like this:

```
A:\<null>
B:\<null>
C:\<null>
D:\<null>
E:\<null>
F:\<null>
G:\<null>
<null>
```

Now that you have the root directories for every logical drive on the system, you might want to determine exactly what type of drive each is on. You can use GetDriveType:

```
UINT GetDriveType(LPTSTR lpszRootPathName);
```

The GetDriveType function returns the type of drive identified by the *lpszRootPathName* parameter. Here are the possible return values:

Identifier	Meaning
0	Drive type can't be determined.
1	Root directory doesn't exist.
DRIVE_REMOVEABLE	Disk can be removed from the drive. This value is returned for floppy drives.
DRIVE_FIXED	Disk can't be removed from the drive. This value is returned for hard drives.
DRIVE_REMOTE	Drive is a remote drive. This value is returned for network drives.
DRIVE_CDROM	Drive is a CD-ROM drive.
DRIVE_RAMDISK	Drive is a RAM disk.

You may be familiar with the 16-bit Windows version of the Get-DriveType function:

```
UINT GetDriveType(int nDriveNumber);
```

You'll want to take note of some differences in the Win32 version. First, Win32's version of this function takes a pointer to a zero-terminated string as its parameter, whereas the 16-bit Windows version accepts an integer identifying the drive to be tested (A=0, B=1, and so on).

Using an integer instead of a string has always been a problem for 16-bit Windows programmers. Using MS-DOS's JOIN command, you can logically connect a drive to another drive as a subdirectory of that drive's root directory. For example, if you execute:

```
JOIN A: C:\DRIVE-A
```

MS-DOS creates a new logical directory called DRIVE-A as a subdirectory of drive C's root directory. If you were to issue the following command:

```
DIR C:\DRIVE-A
```

the contents of the floppy disk in drive A would be displayed. Using the 16-bit Windows GetDriveType function, you can pass only a drive letter to the function. In this case, we would have to pass the value of 2 (for drive C) and GetDriveType would return DRIVE_FIXED. Using the Win32 version of GetDriveType, you can pass C:\DRIVE-A as the parameter. In this case, the Win32 version will return DRIVE_REMOVE-ABLE, which is the correct value.

As it turns out, Microsoft made so many improvements to the file systems in Windows NT that the JOIN command is no longer necessary and is not supported under Windows NT. In MS-DOS, the SUBST command is the complement of the JOIN command. Whereas the JOIN command attaches the root directory of a drive as a subdirectory to another drive, the SUBST command creates a new drive letter for a subdirectory on another drive. The SUBST command is not as useful under Windows NT as it was under MS-DOS, and Microsoft discouraged its use for 16-bit Windows, but unlike JOIN, it is still supported under Windows NT and there are no problems with using SUBST under Windows NT.

Another big limitation of the 16-bit Windows version of GetDrive-Type is that it doesn't always return as much information as you'd like. If you query the type of a CD-ROM drive, DRIVE_REMOVEABLE is returned, and if you query the type of RAM disk, DRIVE_FIXED is returned. Frequently, applications that really need to make use of this information are required to make additional tests to determine whether a drive is really a CD-ROM or RAM disk.

451

Getting Volume Specific Information

When developing an application for Windows NT, you should always keep in mind that the user might be using any combination of the present four file systems (FAT, HPFS, NTFS, and CDFS) and that new file systems will emerge in the future.[1] Any new file systems will need to follow the ground rules, so with a little extra work, you can write an application so that it runs correctly regardless of which file system or systems the user is using. If your application needs some specific information about a particular file system, it can call GetVolumeInformation:

```
BOOL GetVolumeInformation(LPTSTR lpRootPathName,
   LPTSTR lpVolumeNameBuffer, DWORD nVolumeNameSize,
   LPDWORD lpVolumeSerialNumber, LPDWORD lpMaximumComponentLength,
   LPDWORD lpFileSystemFlags, LPTSTR lpFileSystemNameBuffer,
   DWORD nFileSystemNameSize);
```

The GetVolumeInformation function returns file system specific information associated with the directory path specified in the *lpRootPathName* parameter. Most of the remaining parameters are pointers to buffers or DWORDs that the function will fill.

GetVolumeInformation returns the name of the volume in *lpVolumeNameBuffer*. For the FAT file system, this is the label of the floppy disk drive or hard drive. The *nVolumeNameSize* parameter indicates the maximum size of the buffer. The DWORD pointed to by the *lpVolumeSerialNumber* parameter gets filled with the serial number of the volume. If you are not interested in this information, NULL can be passed as the *lpVolumeSerialNumber* parameter.

The serial number is most useful when another disk has been inserted in the drive. Starting with MS-DOS 4.0, the FORMAT command puts serial number information on a disk. This way, even if two disks have the same volume label, each has its own unique serial number. If the user removes one disk and inserts the other, the volume labels could be the same but the serial numbers would be different. An application can check to determine whether the user has swapped disks.

The DWORD pointed to by the *lpMaximumComponentLength* parameter gets filled with the maximum number of characters supported for directory names and filenames. For a FAT file system, the value is 12 and for both HPFS and NTFS, the value is 255. Many applications

---

1. Even as you read this, Microsoft is hard at work on a new file system called OFS (Object File System), which will help realize Bill Gates's vision of "Information at Your Fingertips."

hardcode lengths in their source code for pathname and filename buffers. This is a Big No, No! For many applications, everything may seem OK as such an application manipulates files and paths on a FAT system, but when the application runs on an NTFS partition you'll get stack overwrites, invalid memory accesses, and other assorted problems.

When you are developing an application, create an NTFS partition on your hard disk and use it—create some looong filenames and some huuuuge pathnames and bury some of your application's data files deep down in the bowels of the directory hierarchy to see how your application performs. It's much better for you to catch file system problems during development rather than after you ship.

Another easy to forget consideration is Unicode. If you are using Unicode in your application, your buffers need to be twice as big. Windows NT knows whether your application is Unicode and knows whether the file system you are fiddling with is Unicode. When you request paths and filenames, the system will perform any and all conversions for you, but you must ensure that your buffers will be big enough to hold the results of these conversions.

The DWORD pointed to by the *lpFileSystemFlags* parameter is filled with flags about the file system. Here are the possible values:

Flag Identifier	Meaning
FS_CASE_IS_PRESERVED	The case of a filename is preserved when the name is put on disk.
FS_CASE_SENSITIVE	The file system supports case-sensitive filename lookup.
FS_UNICODE_STORED_ON_DISK	The file system supports Unicode in filenames as they appear on disk.

The *lpFileSystemNameBuffer* parameter points to a buffer that Get-VolumeInformation will fill with the name of the file system (FAT, HPFS, NTFS, or CDFS). The last parameter, *nFileSystemNameSize*, is the maximum size of the *lpFileSystemNameBuffer* buffer.

Most of the information returned by GetVolumeInformation is determined when the user's disk is formatted and can't be changed unless the user's disk is reformatted. The one piece of information that you can change without reformatting is the disk's volume label. You can change it by calling:

```
BOOL SetVolumeLabel(LPTSTR lpRootPathName, LPTSTR lpVolumeName);
```

453

The first parameter of SetVolumeLabel is the root directory of the file system whose volume label you want to change. If you specify NULL here, the system changes the volume label for the process's current disk. The *lpVolumeName* parameter indicates the new name you want the volume to have. Specifying NULL here causes SetVolumeLabel to remove any volume label from the disk.

Another function you can call to get disk volume information is the GetDiskFreeSpace function:

```
BOOL GetDiskFreeSpace(LPTSTR lpszRootPathName,
    LPDWORD lpSectorsPerCluster, LPDWORD lpBytesPerSector,
    LPDWORD lpFreeClusters, LPDWORD lpClusters);
```

The GetDiskFreeSpace function returns space availability statistics about the volume identified by the *lpszRootPathName* parameter. All the bytes available on floppy disks and hard drives are packaged together into sectors—usually 512 bytes per sector. Sectors are then grouped together to form clusters. In the FAT file system, the number of sectors per cluster can vary dramatically, as this table indicates:

Disk Type	Sectors Per Cluster
360-KB floppy disk	2
1.2-MB floppy disk	4
200-MB hard disk	8
400-MB hard disk	32

When parts of a disk are allocated to a file, the minimum amount of memory that can be allocated to a file is a single cluster. For example, a 10-byte file would occupy 2 sectors or 1 KB (2×512 bytes) on a 360-KB floppy, but the same file would occupy 8 sectors or 4 KB (8×512 bytes) on a 200-MB hard disk.

Let's say that we have two 1-KB files on a floppy disk and try to copy both files to a 200-MB hard drive that has only 4 KB of free space. The first file will be copied successfully, but there will be insufficient disk space on the hard drive for the second file. We've tried to copy 2 KB of data into a 4-KB space and failed. On very large media, this cluster overhead can become a serious problem.

While I was writing this book, I upgraded my 250-MB hard drive to a 1-GB hard drive. I also decided to partition the new drive into two 512-MB partitions. Each partition used 32 sectors per cluster. This meant that a 1-byte file required a minimum of 16 KB. After I'd finished installing about 200 MB of file data, the amount of wasted space was about 100 MB. That 100 MB of wasted space was almost half my original hard drive's total capacity. I was impressed by the extent of the clustering overhead. I quickly repartitioned my new hard drive into several partitions, each about 250 MB because clusters for a 250-MB drive contain only 8 sectors each.

From the values returned by the GetDiskFreeSpace function, you can calculate the total disk space, the amount of free disk space, and the amount of used disk space:

```
DWORD dwSectorsPerCluster, dwBytesPerSector;
DWORD dwFreeClusters, dwClusters;
DWORD dwTotalDiskSpace, dwFreeDiskSpace, dwUsedDiskSpace;

GetDiskFreeSpace("C:\\", &dwSectorsPerCluster,
    &dwBytesPerSector, &dwFreeClusters, &dwClusters);

dwTotalDiskSpace =
    dwSectorsPerCluster * dwBytesPerSector * dwClusters;

dwFreeDiskSpace =
    dwSectorsPerCluster * dwBytesPerSector * dwFreeClusters;

dwUsedDiskSpace =
    dwSectorsPerCluster * dwBytesPerSector *
        (dwClusters - dwFreeClusters);
.
.
.
```

One other function you can use to manipulate a disk's volume is the DeviceIoControl function:

```
BOOL DeviceIoControl(HANDLE hDevice, DWORD dwIoControlCode,
    LPVOID lpvInBuffer, DWORD cbInBuffer,
    LPVOID lpvOutBuffer, DWORD cbOutBuffer,
    LPDWORD lpcbBytesReturned, LPOVERLAPPED lpOverlapped);
```

The DeviceIoControl function is used to send commands to or to request information directly from a disk's device driver. The *hDevice* parameter specifies a handle to a disk device. This handle is obtained by placing a call to the CreateFile function. If you want to get a device handle to a floppy drive or to a single partition on a hard drive, call CreateFile as shown at the top of the next page.

```
hDevice = CreateFile("\\\\.\\X:",
    0, FILE_SHARE_WRITE, NULL, OPEN_EXISTING, 0, NULL);
```

The X in the string parameter represents the drive letter for the device. To obtain a device handle to drive C, for example, make this call:

```
hDevice = CreateFile("\\\\.\\C:",
    0, FILE_SHARE_WRITE, NULL, OPEN_EXISTING, 0, NULL);
```

You can get a device handle to a physical hard disk by calling CreateFile like this:

```
hDevice = CreateFile("\\\\.\\PhysicalDriveN",
    0, FILE_SHARE_WRITE, NULL, OPEN_EXISTING, 0, NULL);
```

The N in the first parameter represents a hard drive on the user's system. The first hard drive on the system would be drive 0 (zero). You can get the device handle to a physical disk only if you have administrative privileges; otherwise, the call will fail.

Once you have a valid device handle, you can pass the handle as the first parameter of the DeviceIoControl function. The second parameter of DeviceIoControl specifies the command you want to send to the device. Here is a list of the possible values:

Command Identifier	Meaning
IOCTL_DISK_CHECK_VERIFY	Checks for a change in a removable media device.
IOCTL_DISK_EJECT_MEDIA	Ejects medium from a SCSI device.
IOCTL_DISK_FORMAT_TRACKS	Formats a contiguous set of disk tracks.
IOCTL_DISK_GET_DRIVE_GEOMETRY	Obtains information on the physical disk's geometry.
IOCTL_DISK_GET_DRIVE_LAYOUT	Provides information about each partition on a disk.
IOCTL_DISK_GET_MEDIA_TYPES	Obtains information about media support.
IOCTL_DISK_GET_PARTITION_INFO	Obtains disk partition information.
IOCTL_DISK_LOAD_MEDIA	Loads medium into a device.
IOCTL_DISK_MEDIA_REMOVAL	Enables or disables the media eject mechanism.
IOCTL_DISK_PERFORMANCE	Provides disk performance information.
IOCTL_DISK_REASSIGN_BLOCKS	Maps disk blocks to the spare-block pool.
IOCTL_DISK_SET_DRIVE_LAYOUT	Partitions a disk.

(continued)

Command Identifier	Meaning
IOCTL_DISK_SET_PARTITION_INFO	Sets the disk partition type.
IOCTL_DISK_VERIFY	Performs a logical format of a disk extent.
IOCTL_SERIAL_LSRMST_INSERT	Enables or disables the placement of line and modem status data into the data stream.

The meanings of the remaining DeviceIoControl parameters depend on the operation you passed in the *dwIoControlCode* parameter. For example, if you want to format tracks, you must allocate and initialize a FORMAT_PARAMETERS structure:

```
typedef struct _FORMAT_PARAMETERS {
    MEDIA_TYPE MediaType;
    DWORD StartCylinderNumber;
    DWORD EndCylinderNumber;
    DWORD StartHeadNumber;
    DWORD EndHeadNumber;
} FORMAT_PARAMETERS;
```

and pass the address to this structure in DeviceIoControl's *lpvInBuffer* parameter. You must also pass the length of this structure, in bytes, in the *cbInBuffer* parameter. When you're formatting tracks, the DeviceIo-Control function doesn't return any special information to you—only the news that the function succeeded (TRUE) or failed (FALSE).

If you are requesting a disk's geometry information, you must allocate a DISK_GEOMETRY structure:

```
typedef struct _DISK_GEOMETRY {
    MEDIA_TYPE  MediaType;
    LARGE_INTEGER  Cylinders;
    DWORD  TracksPerCylinder;
    DWORD  SectorsPerTrack;
    DWORD  BytesPerSector;
} DISK_GEOMETRY;
```

and pass the address and the length of this structure (in bytes) as the *lpvOutBuffer* and *cbOutBuffer* parameters, respectively. You will also want to pass the address of a DWORD variable in as the *lpcbBytesReturned* parameter. Just before DeviceIoControl returns, it fills this structure with the disk device's geometry and fills the DWORD pointed to by *lpcb-BytesReturned* with the number of bytes copied into the buffer.

Because requesting a disk's geometry doesn't require that you pass any information into DeviceIoControl, you can pass NULL and 0 (zero) as the *lpvInBuffer* and *cbInBuffer* parameters. Similarly, because formatting tracks doesn't cause DeviceIoControl to return information, you can pass NULL and 0 (zero) for the *lpvOutBuffer* and *cbOutBuffer* parameters.

For some operations, such as disk formatting, DeviceIoControl can format the disk asynchronously. If DeviceIoControl is to perform an operation asynchronously, the device must be opened by a specification of the FILE_FLAG_OVERLAPPED flag when CreateFile is called, and you must pass the address of an OVERLAPPED structure in as the *lpOverlapped* parameter of DeviceIoControl. The *hEvent* member of this structure must also contain the handle of a manual-reset event. The other members of the OVERLAPPED structure are ignored by the DeviceIoControl function.

If DeviceIoControl completes the operation before returning, DeviceIoControl returns TRUE. If the operation hasn't been completed by the time DeviceIoControl returns, FALSE is returned. When the operation is complete, the manual-reset event gets signaled. You should call GetOverlappedResult (discussed later in the asynchronous file I/O section of this chapter) when the thread needs to sleep until the operation has been completed.

When you have finished calling DeviceIoControl, you must close the device handle by calling CloseHandle. More information on using the DeviceIoControl function can be found in the *Win32 Programmer's Reference*.

The Disk Information Viewer Sample Application

The DiskInfo (DISKINFO.EXE) application, listed in Figure 9-1 beginning on page 460, demonstrates the use of most of the functions we've just surveyed. When you execute DiskInfo, the Disk Volume Information Viewer dialog box appears, as shown at the top of the next page.

The combo box at the top of the dialog box shows all the logical drives connected to the system. This information is obtained by a call to GetLogicalDriveStrings. When you select a logical drive, the remaining fields in the dialog box change to show information about the newly selected drive. The *Drive type* field is updated by a call to GetDriveType, the *Volume Information* fields are updated by a call to GetVolumeInformation, and the *Disk free space* fields are updated by a call to GetDiskFreeSpace.

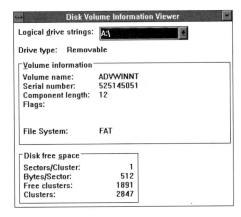

The following are the results after I selected various logical drives on my system:

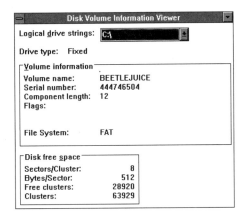

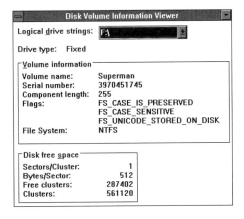

DiskInfo.ico

DISKINFO.C

```
/***************************************************************
Module name: DiskInfo.C
Notices: Copyright (c) 1993 Jeffrey Richter
***************************************************************/

#include <windows.h>
#include <windowsx.h>
#include <tchar.h>
#include <stdio.h>        // for sprintf
#include <string.h>       // for strchr
#include "DiskInfo.H"

#define ARRAY_SIZE(A)  (sizeof(A) / sizeof((A)[0]))


///////////////////////////////////////////////////////////////

void Dlg_FillDriveInfo (HWND hwnd, LPTSTR lpszRootPathName) {
   // Variables for processing the drive type information.
   int nDriveType;
   LPCTSTR p;
```

Figure 9-1.   *(continued)*

The DiskInfo application.

Figure 9-1. *continued*

```
// Variables for processing the volume information.
TCHAR szBuf[200];
TCHAR lpVolumeNameBuffer[200];
DWORD dwVolumeSerialNumber, dwMaximumComponentLength;
DWORD dwFileSystemFlags;
TCHAR lpFileSystemNameBuffer[50];

// Variables for processing the disk space information.
DWORD dwSectorsPerCluster, dwBytesPerSector;
DWORD dwFreeClusters, dwClusters;

// Get the drive type information.
nDriveType = GetDriveType(lpszRootPathName);
switch (nDriveType) {
    case 0:
        p = __TEXT("Cannot be determined.");
        break;

    case 1:
        p = __TEXT("Path does not exist.");
        break;

    case DRIVE_REMOVABLE:
        p = __TEXT("Removable");
        break;

    case DRIVE_FIXED:
        p = __TEXT("Fixed");
        break;

    case DRIVE_REMOTE:
        p = __TEXT("Remote");
        break;

    case DRIVE_CDROM:
        p = __TEXT("CD-ROM");
        break;

    case DRIVE_RAMDISK:
        p = __TEXT("RAM disk");
        break;
```

(continued)

461

Figure 9-1. *continued*

```
    default:
        p = __TEXT("Unknown");
        break;
}

SetWindowText(GetDlgItem(hwnd, ID_DRIVETYPE), p);


// Get the volume information.
if (GetVolumeInformation(lpszRootPathName,
    lpVolumeNameBuffer,
    ARRAY_SIZE(lpVolumeNameBuffer), &dwVolumeSerialNumber,
    &dwMaximumComponentLength, &dwFileSystemFlags,
    lpFileSystemNameBuffer,
    ARRAY_SIZE(lpFileSystemNameBuffer))) {

    _stprintf(szBuf, __TEXT("%s\n%u\n%u\n"),
        lpVolumeNameBuffer, dwVolumeSerialNumber,
        dwMaximumComponentLength);

    if (dwFileSystemFlags & FS_CASE_IS_PRESERVED)
        _tcscat(szBuf, __TEXT("FS_CASE_IS_PRESERVED"));
    _tcscat(szBuf, __TEXT("\n"));

    if (dwFileSystemFlags & FS_CASE_SENSITIVE)
        _tcscat(szBuf, __TEXT("FS_CASE_SENSITIVE"));
    _tcscat(szBuf, __TEXT("\n"));

    if (dwFileSystemFlags & FS_UNICODE_STORED_ON_DISK)
        _tcscat(szBuf, __TEXT("FS_UNICODE_STORED_ON_DISK"));
    _tcscat(szBuf, __TEXT("\n"));

    _tcscat(szBuf, lpFileSystemNameBuffer);
} else {
    _tcscpy(szBuf, __TEXT("NO VOLUME INFO"));
}
SetWindowText(GetDlgItem(hwnd, ID_VOLINFO), szBuf);


// Get the disk space information.
if (GetDiskFreeSpace(lpszRootPathName,
    &dwSectorsPerCluster, &dwBytesPerSector,
    &dwFreeClusters, &dwClusters)) {
```

(continued)

Figure 9-1. *continued*

```
      _stprintf(szBuf, __TEXT("%u\n%u\n%u\n%u"),
         dwSectorsPerCluster, dwBytesPerSector,
         dwFreeClusters, dwClusters);
   } else {
      _tcscpy(szBuf, __TEXT("NO\nDISK\nSPACE\nINFO"));
   }
   SetWindowText(GetDlgItem(hwnd, ID_DISKINFO), szBuf);
}


////////////////////////////////////////////////////////////////

BOOL Dlg_OnInitDialog (HWND hwnd, HWND hwndFocus,
   LPARAM lParam) {

   DWORD  dwNumBytesForDriveStrings;
   HANDLE hHeap;
   LPTSTR lp;
   TCHAR  szLogDrive[100];
   HWND   hwndCtl = GetDlgItem(hwnd, ID_LOGDRIVES);
   int    nNumDrives = 0, nDriveNum;

   // Associate an icon with the dialog box.
   SetClassLong(hwnd, GCL_HICON, (LONG)
      LoadIcon((HINSTANCE) GetWindowLong(hwnd, GWL_HINSTANCE),
      __TEXT("DiskInfo")));

   // Get the number of bytes needed to hold all
   // the logical drive strings.
   dwNumBytesForDriveStrings =
      GetLogicalDriveStrings(0, NULL) * sizeof(TCHAR);

   // Allocate memory from the heap for the drive
   // string names.
   hHeap = GetProcessHeap();
   lp = (LPTSTR) HeapAlloc(hHeap, HEAP_ZERO_MEMORY,
      dwNumBytesForDriveStrings);

   // Get the drives string names in our buffer.
   GetLogicalDriveStrings(HeapSize(hHeap, 0, lp), lp);

   // Parse the memory block, and fill the combo box.
   while (*lp != 0) {
```

(continued)

Figure 9-1. *continued*

```
        ComboBox_AddString(hwndCtl, lp);
        nNumDrives++;
        lp = _tcschr(lp, 0) + 1;    // Point to next string.
    }

    HeapFree(hHeap, 0, lp);

    // Initialize the volume information for the first FIXED
    // drive so that we don't try to read volume
    // information from a drive that doesn't contain a
    // disk.
    for (nDriveNum = 0; nDriveNum < nNumDrives; nDriveNum++) {
        ComboBox_GetLBText(hwndCtl, nDriveNum, szLogDrive);
        if (GetDriveType(szLogDrive) == DRIVE_FIXED)
            break;
    }

    if (nDriveNum == nNumDrives) {
        // There are no FIXED drives -- just use the
        // first drive.
        ComboBox_GetLBText(hwndCtl, nDriveNum = 0, szLogDrive);
    }

    // Select the first FIXED drive, or select the first
    // drive if no FIXED drives exist.
    ComboBox_SetCurSel(hwndCtl, nDriveNum);

    Dlg_FillDriveInfo(hwnd, szLogDrive);

    return(TRUE);
}

///////////////////////////////////////////////////////////////

void Dlg_OnCommand (HWND hwnd, int id, HWND hwndCtl,
    UINT codeNotify) {

    TCHAR szLogDrive[100];

    switch (id) {
        case ID_LOGDRIVES:
            if (codeNotify != CBN_SELCHANGE)
                break;
```

Figure 9-1. *continued*

```
        ComboBox_GetText(hwndCtl, szLogDrive,
            ARRAY_SIZE(szLogDrive));
        Dlg_FillDriveInfo(hwnd, szLogDrive);
        break;

    case IDCANCEL:
        EndDialog(hwnd, id);
        break;
    }
}


///////////////////////////////////////////////////////////////

BOOL CALLBACK Dlg_Proc (HWND hDlg, UINT uMsg,
    WPARAM wParam, LPARAM lParam) {

    BOOL fProcessed = TRUE;

    switch (uMsg) {
        HANDLE_MSG(hDlg, WM_INITDIALOG, Dlg_OnInitDialog);
        HANDLE_MSG(hDlg, WM_COMMAND, Dlg_OnCommand);

        default:
            fProcessed = FALSE;
            break;
    }
    return(fProcessed);
}


///////////////////////////////////////////////////////////////

int APIENTRY WinMain (HINSTANCE hInstance,
    HINSTANCE hPrevInstance, LPSTR lpszCmdLine, int nCmdShow) {

    DialogBox(hInstance, MAKEINTRESOURCE(DLG_DISKINFO),
        NULL, Dlg_Proc);
    return(0);
}


//////////////////////// End Of File //////////////////////////
```

(continued)

465

Figure 9-1. *continued*

DISKINFO.H

```
/****************************************************************
Module name: DiskInfo.H
Notices: Copyright (c) 1993 Jeffrey Richter
****************************************************************/

// Dialog and control IDs.
#define DLG_DISKINFO       1
#define ID_LOGDRIVES     100
#define ID_DRIVETYPE     101
#define ID_VOLINFO       102
#define ID_DISKINFO      103


/////////////////////// End Of File ///////////////////////////
```

DISKINFO.RC

```
/****************************************************************
Module name: DiskInfo.RC
Notices: Copyright (c) 1993 Jeffrey Richter
****************************************************************/

#include <windows.h>
#include "DiskInfo.h"

DiskInfo  ICON  DISCARDABLE DiskInfo.Ico

DLG_DISKINFO DIALOG 15, 24, 198, 163
STYLE WS_BORDER | DS_NOIDLEMSG |
   WS_POPUP | WS_VISIBLE | WS_CAPTION |
   WS_SYSMENU | WS_MINIMIZEBOX
CAPTION "Disk Volume Information Viewer"
BEGIN
   LTEXT "Logical &drive strings:", -1,
      4, 4, 72, 8, WS_CHILD | WS_VISIBLE | WS_GROUP
   CONTROL "", ID_LOGDRIVES, "COMBOBOX",
      CBS_DROPDOWNLIST | WS_CHILD | WS_VISIBLE | WS_GROUP |
      WS_TABSTOP, 78, 4, 80, 76
   CONTROL "&Volume information", -1, "button",
      BS_GROUPBOX | WS_CHILD | WS_VISIBLE | WS_GROUP |
      WS_TABSTOP, 4, 32, 192, 76
```

(continued)

Figure 9-1.   *continued*

```
    CONTROL "Disk free &space", -1, "button",
        BS_GROUPBOX | WS_CHILD | WS_VISIBLE | WS_GROUP |
        WS_TABSTOP, 4, 112, 108, 48
    LTEXT "Volume name:\nSerial number:\nComponent
length:\nFlags:\n\n\nFile System:",
        -1, 8, 44, 64, 56, WS_CHILD | WS_VISIBLE | WS_GROUP
    CONTROL "Label\n12345678\n10\nFS_CASE_IS_PRESERVED\nFS_
CASE_SENSITIVE\nFS_UNICODE_STORED_ON_DISK\nNTFS",
        ID_VOLINFO, "STATIC",
        SS_LEFT | SS_NOPREFIX | WS_CHILD | WS_VISIBLE |
        WS_GROUP, 77, 44, 116, 60
    LTEXT
"Sectors/Cluster:\nBytes/Sector:\nFree clusters:\nClusters:",
        -1, 8, 124, 52, 32, WS_CHILD | WS_VISIBLE | WS_GROUP
    CONTROL "8\n512\n300\n400", ID_DISKINFO, "STATIC",
        SS_RIGHT | SS_NOPREFIX | WS_CHILD | WS_VISIBLE |
        WS_GROUP, 64, 124, 44, 32
    LTEXT "Drive type:", -1, 4, 20, 40, 8
    LTEXT "Text", ID_DRIVETYPE, 48, 20, 96, 8,
        WS_CHILD | WS_VISIBLE | WS_GROUP
END

/////////////////////// End Of File ///////////////////////
```

Directory Operations

Every process has a directory associated with it called the current directory. By default, file operations are performed inside the process's current directory. When a process is first created, it inherits the current directory used by its parent process.

Getting the Current Directory

A process determines its current directory by calling:

```
DWORD GetCurrentDirectory(DWORD cchCurDir, LPTSTR lpszCurDir);
```

The GetCurrentDirectory function fills the buffer pointed to by *lpszCurDir* with the process's current path. The *cchCurDir* parameter indicates the maximum size of the buffer in characters. If the function fails, 0 (zero) is returned; otherwise, the function returns the number of characters copied to the buffer, not including the terminating zero. If the buffer isn't large enough to hold the current path, the return value indicates the number of characters required to hold the path. To ensure that GetCurrentDirectory succeeded, you need to write code similar to this:

```
TCHAR szCurDir[MAX_PATH];

DWORD dwResult = GetCurrentDirectory(
    sizeof(szCurDir) / sizeof(TCHAR), szCurDir);

if (dwResult == 0) {
    // Total function failure.
} else {
    if (dwResult < (sizeof(szCurDir) / sizeof(TCHAR))) {
        // Buffer was big enough for the full path.
    } else {
        // Buffer was too small.
    }
}
```

Notice the use of MAX_PATH in this routine. The MAX_PATH value is defined in WINDEF.H as 260. For MS-DOS development, some C compilers define a macro called _MAX_PATH as only 80. The big difference in this value is attributable to the new file systems Windows NT supports. It's difficult to stress enough the significance of Windows NT support for several different file systems—and more file systems are on the way. I've seen too many programs that create buffers for filenames along these lines:

```
char szFileName[13];   // "Filename" + '.' + "ext" + zero byte
```

These buffers will be far too small for HPFS and NTFS filenames. It's likely that a function in the application will overwrite a buffer because the application made the assumption that filenames will never be more than 13 characters.

One way to handle the longer filenames is to make your buffers much larger. Using MAX_PATH as we've just seen is an example of this approach. Unfortunately, the Windows NT header files don't define a macro called MAX_FILE, but you could define MAX_FILE to be 260 as well. The value 260 would accommodate the HPFS and NTFS filenames of as many as 255 characters.

This approach would work for NTFS, but a new file system in the future might allow filenames as long as 512 characters. So the best way to allocate buffers for file system components is dynamically, by first calling GetVolumeInformation and checking the value returned in the buffer pointed to by the *lpMaximumComponentLength* parameter.

Changing the Current Directory

A process can change its current directory by calling:

```
BOOL SetCurrentDirectory(LPTSTR lpszCurDir);
```

Changing the current directory alters the current directory of only the process making the call; the change of directory doesn't affect any other running processes. However, if the process making the call spawns a new process after changing its current directory, the new process will inherit the current directory of the parent, which will now be the directory that was specified in the last call to SetCurrentDirectory.

Getting the System Directory

In addition to getting its own current directory, an application can determine the system directory by calling:

```
UINT GetSystemDirectory(LPTSTR lpszSysPath, UINT cchSysPath);
```

The GetSystemDirectory function fills the buffer pointed to by *lpszSysPath* with the system directory name. Usually, this directory will be something like:

```
C:\WINNT\SYSTEM32
```

The return values for GetSystemDirectory should be interpreted just as they were for the GetCurrentDirectory function. Applications typically don't use the system directory for anything. In fact, on shared versions of Windows, the system directory is protected so that files can't be created or written to on the system directory. A benefit of this protection is that viruses won't be able to attach themselves to any of the files contained in the system directory.

Getting the Directory Path

If a process wants to create or write to a file that is to be shared by multiple processes, the process can use the Windows directory. The path of the Windows directory can be obtained by calling:

```
UINT GetWindowsDirectory(LPTSTR lpszWinPath, UINT cchWinPath);
```

The GetWindowsDirectory function fills the buffer pointed to by *lpszWinPath* with the Windows directory. Usually, this directory will be something like:

```
C:\WINNT
```

When running a shared version of Windows, the system creates a Windows directory private to each user. This is the only directory guaranteed to be private for an individual user. If a user wants to keep certain files hidden from all other users, the files must be created either in the Windows directory or in a subdirectory of the Windows directory.

Creating and Removing Directories

Finally, there are two additional functions for manipulating directories:

```
BOOL CreateDirectory(LPTSTR lpszPath, LPSECURITY_ATTRIBUTES lpsa);
```

and

```
BOOL RemoveDirectory(LPTSTR lpszDir);
```

As their names imply, these functions allow a process to create and remove a directory, respectively. When creating a directory, a process can specify a SECURITY_ATTRIBUTES structure in order to assign special privileges to the directory. For example, an application could create the directory so that another user couldn't go into the directory or remove the directory.

Both these functions return TRUE when they're successful and FALSE when they fail. RemoveDirectory will fail if the directory contains files or other subdirectories or if the process doesn't have delete access for removing the directory.

Copying, Deleting, Moving, and Renaming Files

16-bit Windows and MS-DOS have always lacked a function for copying files from one place to another. Applications have typically implemented this important functionality by opening a source file for reading and creating a destination file for writing. Then, using a buffer, the application would read part of the source file into memory and write the buffer back out to the destination file. After the source file had been read and written, the application would close both files. And the time stamp of the destination file would reflect the time of the copy—not the time of the source file's last update. This problem would usually have to be fixed by the addition of a few more function calls.

Copying a File

With Windows NT, we finally have an operating system call available to us for copying files:

```
BOOL CopyFile(LPTSTR lpszExistingFile, LPTSTR lpszNewFile,
    BOOL fFailIfExists);
```

CopyFile is a simple function that copies the file identified by the *lpsz-ExistingFile* parameter to a new file whose pathname is specified by the *lpszNewFile* parameter. The last parameter, *fFailIfExists*, specifies whether you want the function to fail if a file already exists that matches the name pointed to by the *lpszNewFile* parameter. If a file with the same name does exist and *fFailIfExists* is TRUE, the function fails; otherwise, the function destroys the existing file and creates the new file. CopyFile returns TRUE if it is successful. Only closed files or files that are open with read-access only can be copied. The function fails if any process has the existing file open with write-access.

Deleting a File

Deleting a file by means of the DeleteFile function is even easier than copying a file:

```
BOOL DeleteFile(LPTSTR lpszFileName);
```

This function deletes the file identified by the *lpszFileName* parameter and returns TRUE if successful. The function fails if the specified file doesn't exist or if the file is open. If any process has the file open, the file can't be deleted.

Moving a File

Two functions allow you to move a file from one directory to another directory:

```
BOOL MoveFile(LPTSTR lpszExisting, LPTSTR lpszNew);
```

and

```
BOOL MoveFileEx(LPTSTR lpszExisting, LPTSTR lpszNew,
    DWORD fdwFlags);
```

Both functions move the existing file, identified by the *lpszExisting* parameter, to the new location identified by the *lpszNew* parameter. The *lpszNew* parameter must include the name of the file. For example, this

471

instruction won't move the CLOCK.EXE file from the WINNT directory on drive C to the root directory of drive C:

```
MoveFile("C:\\WINNT\\CLOCK.EXE", "C:\\");
```

This instruction will:

```
MoveFile("C:\\WINNT\\CLOCK.EXE", "C:\\CLOCK.EXE");
```

Moving a file is not always identical to copying the file to another location and then deleting the original file. If you are moving a file from one directory on a drive to another directory on the same drive, MoveFile and MoveFileEx don't move any of the data in the file at all. Both functions simply remove the file's entry in the first directory and add a new entry to the second directory the file is supposedly copied to. Simply adjusting the directory entries copies a file significantly faster because no data is moved around. Less disk space is needed during the move too. When a file is moved from one drive to another, Windows NT must actually create a duplicate file before it deletes the original. At the moment after the copy and before the deletion of the original, there are two whole copies of the file in existence. If the file is huge, this can take up a serious amount of disk space.

If Windows NT had to copy and delete a file it was moving from one directory to another on the same drive, the function might fail because of insufficient disk space. If the file were 1 MB long and only 512 KB of disk space were available, Windows NT wouldn't be able to copy the file before deleting the original. But since only directory entries are altered, no additional disk space is required and the move is much more likely to succeed.

If the move does succeed, both MoveFile and MoveFileEx return TRUE. The move can fail if insufficient disk space is available for interdrive moves or if a filename matching the name specified in *lpszNew* already exists.

You wouldn't be able to guess it from their names, but both MoveFile and MoveFileEx can also be used to change the name of a subdirectory. For example, to change the name of the subdirectory UTILITY to TOOLS, use this statement:

```
MoveFile("C:\\UTILITY", "C:\\TOOLS");
```

It would certainly be useful if MoveFile(Ex) could move an entire subdirectory tree elsewhere in the drive's directory hierarchy, but these functions are not capable of this sweeping kind of operation. To move a subdirectory tree to another location on the same drive, you would have to use the FindFirstFile, FindNextFile, and FindClose functions discussed later in this chapter to walk down the directory hierarchy three different times. The first time you'd need to call CreateDirectory to create a similar directory structure in the new location. The second time you'd need to call MoveFile to move each individual file in the directory structure. The last time you'd need to call RemoveDirectory to remove the old directory hierarchy.

The Differences Between MoveFile and MoveFileEx

By offering one more parameter, *fdwFlags*, MoveFileEx gives you more control over moving a file or renaming a subdirectory than the MoveFile function does.

MoveFileEx comes into its own when moving a file fails because a filename matching the name specified in *lpszNew* already exists. To destroy the existing file and give the moved file the same name anyway, you can specify the MOVEFILE_REPLACE_EXISTING flag when you call MoveFileEx. This flag has no effect when you're renaming a subdirectory.

By default, MoveFileEx will not move a file from one drive to another drive. If you want to allow this behavior, you must specify the MOVEFILE_COPY_ALLOWED flag. Internally, the MoveFile function calls the MoveFileEx function, specifying the MOVEFILE_COPY-_ALLOWED flag, so you don't have to worry about this if you use the MoveFile function instead of the MoveFileEx function. Like the MOVE-FILE_REPLACE_EXISTING flag, this flag has no effect when you're renaming a subdirectory.

The last flag, MOVEFILE_DELAY_UNTIL_REBOOT, provokes some interesting behavior. If this flag is specified, Windows NT doesn't move the file or rename the directory at the time the call is placed. Instead, it keeps a list in the registry of all the files that have been moved with this flag specified. Then, the next time the operating system is booted, the system examines the registry and moves or renames all the files in the list. The files are moved or renamed just after the drives are checked and before any paging files are created.

The MOVEFILE_DELAY_UNTIL_REBOOT flag is customarily used by installation programs. Let's say that you recently received a new device driver for your video card. When you try to install the new driver, Windows NT can't delete or overwrite the old video driver because the file is still in use by the system. In this case, the Setup program will copy

473

the new driver into another directory, leaving the original driver file. Setup will then issue a call to MoveFileEx, specifying the current path of the new file in the *lpszExisting* parameter and the location where the file should be in the *lpszNew* parameter. Setup will also pass the MOVE-FILE_DELAY_UNTIL_REBOOT flag to MoveFileEx. Windows NT will add the new path to its list in the registry and simply return to Setup. When the system is rebooted, Windows NT will replace the old video driver with the new driver before the system is fully started. Once the system is up, the new device driver will be used instead of the old one.

One other way in which MoveFileEx differs from MoveFile is that it provides a novel way of deleting a file. You can delete a file with Move-FileEx by passing NULL as the *lpszNew* parameter. In a sense, you are telling the system you want to move the existing file (*lpszExisting*) to nowhere, which has the effect of deleting the file.

Renaming a File

There is no RenameFile function. Renaming a file is accomplished by calling MoveFile or MoveFileEx. To rename a file, all you do is move the file from its directory to the same directory. To rename CLOCK.EXE to WATCH.EXE, for example, you'd use this statement:

```
MoveFile("C:\\WINNT\\CLOCK.EXE", "C:\\WINNT\\WATCH.EXE");
```

Because we are not moving the file from one drive to another drive or from one directory to another directory, Windows NT simply removes WINNT's directory entry for CLOCK.EXE and adds a new directory entry for WATCH.EXE—the file is effectively renamed.

The Setup program could have copied the new video device driver file to the system directory, giving it a different name. Then the Setup program would issue a call to MoveFileEx, still specifying the MOVE-FILE_DELAY_UNTIL_REBOOT flag. This time, since the file would already be in the correct directory, rebooting Windows NT would have the effect of renaming the file instead of actually copying it.

I'd like to see Microsoft enhance these file functions by adding wildcard support. Wouldn't it be nice to be able to issue a command like this one:

```
DeleteFile("*.BAK");
```

and have the system delete all of the BAK files in the current directory? If you want to do a mass deletion in the current version of Windows NT, you must create a list of all the BAK files in the current directory first and then call DeleteFile for each file. To create a list of the BAK files, you would use the FindFirstFile, FindNextFile, and FindClose functions we'll get to in detail later in this chapter.

Creating, Opening, and Closing Files

In 16-bit Windows, files could be created and opened by means of the OpenFile, _lcreat, and _lopen functions. For backward compatibility, these functions were carried over into Win32, but they're considered to be obsolete and you should avoid using them. For Win32 applications, files should be created or opened by means of the much more powerful CreateFile function:

```
HANDLE CreateFile(LPCTSTR lpszName, DWORD fdwAccess,
    DWORD fdwShareMode, LPSECURITY_ATTRIBUTES lpsa,
    DWORD fdwCreate, DWORD fdwAttrsAndFlags, HANDLE hTemplateFile);
```

When you call this function, the *lpszName* parameter identifies the name of the file you want to create or open. The *fdwAccess* parameter specifies how you want to access the data in the file. You can specify GENERIC_READ if you are going to read from the file, GENERIC_WRITE if you are going to write to the file, or GENERIC_READ | GENERIC_WRITE if you are going to both read from and write to the file.

The *fdwShareMode* parameter specifies file sharing privileges. In Windows NT more so than in 16-bit Windows, it's likely that a single file can and will be accessed by several computers at the same time (in a networking environment) or by several processes at the same time (in a multithreaded environment). The potential for file sharing means that you must give some thought to whether you should and how you will restrict other computers or processes from accessing the data in the file. The *fdwShareMode* flag can be set to 0 (zero), FILE_SHARE_READ, and FILE_SHARE_WRITE. Specifying 0 (zero) means that, after you open the file, the file cannot be opened again until you close it.

Probably the most common flag to use here is FILE_SHARE_READ. This flag tells Windows NT that other computers and processes may open the file as long as they intend only to read from the file. Any attempts from another computer or process to open the file for writing will fail as long as you have the file open. The last flag, FILE_SHARE_WRITE, is rarely used. It tells Windows NT that other computers and processes may open the file as long as they intend only to write to the file. If you specify FILE_SHARE_READ | FILE_SHARE_WRITE, you tell Windows NT that the file may be opened by others, allowing them to both read from and write to the file at will.

Of course, a strange situation can come up. Let's say that a process has opened a file for reading and has specified the FILE_SHARE_READ flag. Now another process comes along and tries to open the file, passing in 0 for the *fdwShareMode* parameter. This means that the second process wants to open the file but doesn't want to allow anybody else to open the file for reading or writing. But another process already has the file open for reading. In such a case, Windows NT won't allow the second open to succeed since it can't guarantee that the first process will stop accessing the file while the second process has the file open.

The fourth parameter of CreateFile is *lpsa*. As always, this parameter points to a SECURITY_ATTRIBUTES structure that allows you to specify special access writes to a file. The parameter can be NULL if you don't want any special security for the file. For the file to be secure, it must be created on a file system that supports security. As of this writing, the NTFS file system is the only file system among the four supported by Windows NT that offers this capability.

The *fdwCreate* parameter specifies flags that allow you to fine-tune the behavior of CreateFile. You can specify several of these flags by *OR*ing them together:

Identifier	Meaning
CREATE_NEW	Tells CreateFile to create a new file and to fail if the file already exists.
CREATE_ALWAYS	Tells CreateFile to create a file regardless of whether it already exists. If the file already exists, CreateFile overwrites the existing file.
OPEN_EXISTING	Tells CreateFile to open an existing file and to fail if the file doesn't already exist.
OPEN_ALWAYS	Tells CreateFile to open a file if it exists and to create the file if it doesn't exist.
TRUNCATE_EXISTING	Tells CreateFile to open an existing file and truncate its size to 0 bytes and to fail if the file doesn't already exist. The GENERIC_WRITE flag must be used with this flag.

CreateFile's *fdwAttrsAndFlags* parameter has two purposes: It assigns special attributes to the file if the file is being created, and it alters the method Windows NT uses to read from and write to a file. If CreateFile is opening an existing file, the attribute information in *fdwAttrsAndFlags* is ignored but the flag information is used.

Let's look at the file attributes first and then at the file flags. Most of the attributes will already be familiar to you because they originated with the MS-DOS FAT file system:

Identifier	Meaning
FILE_ATTRIBUTE_ARCHIVE	The file is an archive file. Applications use this flag to mark files for backup or removal. When CreateFile creates a new file, this flag is automatically set.
FILE_ATTRIBUTE_HIDDEN	The file is hidden. It won't be included in an ordinary directory listing.
FILE_ATTRIBUTE_NORMAL	The file has no other attributes set. This attribute is valid only if it's used alone.
FILE_ATTRIBUTE_READONLY	The file is read-only. Applications can read the file but can't write to it or delete it.
FILE_ATTRIBUTE_SYSTEM	The file is part of the operating system or is used exclusively by the operating system.

In addition to those familiar attributes, Windows NT offers two more file attributes. Use FILE_ATTRIBUTE_TEMPORARY if you are creating a temporary file. When CreateFile creates a file with the temporary attribute, it tries to keep the file's data in memory instead of on the disk. This makes accessing the file's contents much faster. If you keep writing to the file and Windows NT can no longer keep the data in RAM, the operating system will be forced to start writing the data to the hard disk.

FILE_ATTRIBUTE_ATOMIC_WRITE causes Windows NT to flush buffered file data to the disk more often. Normally, Windows NT buffers all file reads and writes in memory blocks. If you write to a file, Windows NT updates a memory block with the new information. The information is not immediately flushed to the disk because this would slow system performance. When the system is idle, or the file is closed, or Windows NT is running low on available RAM, the buffered file data is automatically flushed to the disk. The problem with this scheme is that, in the case of a power failure or some other unforeseen disaster, data can be lost.

To minimize the impact of lost data, you can open a file with the FILE_ATTRIBUTE_ATOMIC_WRITE attribute. When you specify this flag, you are telling Windows NT that the data contained in the file is extremely important. You are also telling the system that any data you write isn't useful unless all previous writes are guaranteed to have been written as well.

For example, your application might keep track of a person's finances—one record in a file for each transaction the user makes to a checking account. If the user enters two transactions—a deposit followed by a withdrawal—this causes the application to call WriteFile twice. Windows NT might, because of its caching techniques, actually write the second transaction (the withdrawal) out to the file before the first (the deposit). If a power failure occurs after the second transaction has been written but before the first transaction has been written, the user's data has been corrupted. The next time the user starts the application, the second transaction but not the first will be recorded.

The user might not notice that the first transaction never got written until he or she looks down at the total amount of money in the account and sees a disconcerting negative balance. If the FILE_AT-TRIBUTE_ATOMIC_WRITE flag is set, the system guarantees that all writes will be flushed to disk as they happen—there will be no delayed writing. The system also guarantees that any file system structures still contained only in RAM will also be flushed to disk.

Now let's turn our attention to the file flags. Most of these flags are signals that tell Windows NT how you intend to use a file. Windows NT can then optimize its caching algorithms to help your application work more efficiently with the file.

Let's start with the case in which you don't want Windows NT to help you with file buffering at all. If you don't want the system to perform any buffering on a file, use the FILE_FLAG_NO_BUFFERING flag. When you use this flag, you must read from or write to the file on sector boundaries. Use the GetDiskFreeSpace function to determine the sector size the file system is using.

The next two flags, FILE_FLAG_RANDOM_ACCESS and FILE-_FLAG_SEQUENTIAL_SCAN, are used to tell Windows NT whether you intend to access a file randomly or sequentially, respectively. Setting one or the other of these flags is simply a hint to the system so that it can optimize its caching. You can access the file any way you want to after using one of these flags, but access may not be as fast as possible if you access the file opposite the way you've told the system you would.

When you've set the FILE_FLAG_SEQUENTIAL_SCAN flag, Windows NT expects the file to be accessed from the beginning through to the end. If you perform any direct seeks on the file, you are violating the system's expectation and it won't be able to use the optimum caching it's set to do for sequential access.

The last cache-related flag is FILE_FLAG_WRITE_THROUGH. The FILE_FLAG_WRITE_THROUGH flag disables intermediate caching in order to reduce the potential for data loss. When you specify this flag, Windows NT immediately flushes any modified file data to disk. The data is still cached in memory to make read operations perform quickly.

That's it for the buffer-related flags. The remaining CreateFile *fdwAttrsAndFlags* flags don't seem to fall into a category.

Use the FILE_FLAG_DELETE_ON_CLOSE flag to have Windows NT delete the file after the file is closed. This flag is most frequently used with the FILE_ATTRIBUTE_TEMPORARY attribute. When these two flags are used together, your application can create a temporary file, write to it, read from it, and close it. When the file is closed, Windows NT automatically deletes the file—what a convenience! If your process closes its handle to the file and the same file is opened by somebody else, Windows NT won't immediately close the file. The system will wait until all open handles to the file are closed before deleting it.

Use the FILE_FLAG_BACKUP_SEMANTICS flag in backup and restore software. Before opening or creating any files, Windows NT normally performs security checks to be sure that the process trying to open or create a file has the requisite access privileges. However, backup and restore software is special in that it can override certain file security checks. When you specify the FILE_FLAG_BACKUP_SEMANTICS flag, Windows NT checks to be sure that a process has the access rights, and if it does, allows opening the file for backup or restore purposes only.

Use the FILE_FLAG_POSIX_SEMANTICS flag to tell Windows NT to use POSIX rules for accessing a file. File systems used by POSIX allow case-sensitive file names. This means that the files JEFFREY.DOC, Jeffrey.Doc, and jeffrey.doc are all different files. MS-DOS, 16-bit Windows, Win32, and OS/2 were designed to expect that filenames would be case-insensitive. Use the FILE_FLAG_POSIX_SEMANTICS flag with extreme caution. If you use this flag when you create a file, that file might not be accessible to MS-DOS, 16-bit Windows, Win32, or OS/2 applications.

The last flag, FILE_FLAG_OVERLAPPED, tells Windows NT that you want to access a file asynchronously. In MS-DOS and 16-bit Windows, files must be accessed synchronously; that is, when you make a call to read from a file, your program is suspended, waiting for the information to be read. Once the information has been read, your program regains control and continues executing.

File I/O is slow when compared with most other operations. If a user wants to save a document and print it, the user must wait for the file to be saved before starting to print the document. Wouldn't it be nice if, when the user told the application to save the document, the application told Windows NT to write the data without the application's having to wait until the file write operation is complete? The system could use another thread to write the file data while the application's main thread continued to respond to requests, such as a request to print, from the user.

In Windows NT, you can do this asynchronous file I/O. You can tell Windows NT to write or read the file in the background while you continue processing. When Windows NT has finished the background process, it will notify you. If you can't continue processing until all the data has been read or written, you can suspend your thread until the file I/O is complete. This method of working with files is discussed in detail later in this chapter.

CreateFile's last parameter, *hTemplateFile*, either identifies the handle of an open file or is NULL. If *hTemplateFile* identifies a file handle, CreateFile ignores the *fdwAttrsAndFlags* parameter completely and uses the attributes and flags associated with the file identified by *hTemplateFile*. The file identified by *hTemplateFile* must have been opened with the GENERIC_READ flag for this to work. If CreateFile is opening an existing file (as opposed to creating a new file), the *hTemplateFile* parameter is ignored.

If CreateFile succeeds in creating or opening a file, the handle of the file is returned. If CreateFile fails, INVALID_HANDLE_VALUE is returned. Take special note here that, for most of the Win32 functions, an invalid handle is returned as NULL. For CreateFile, INVALID-_HANDLE_VALUE is returned, and this identifier is defined as –1. I have often seen code like this:

```
HANDLE hFile = CreateFile(...);
if (hFile == NULL) {
   // File not created.
} else {
   // File created OK.
}
```

.
.
.

The code is incorrect because for backward compatibility with MS-DOS and 16-bit Windows the system will return valid file handles with a value of 0 (zero). Here's the correct way to check for an invalid file handle:

```
HANDLE hFile = CreateFile(...);
if (hFile == INVALID_HANDLE_VALUE) {
    // File not created.
} else {
    // File created OK.
}
```

.
.
.

Now you know all the possibilities available to you for creating and opening a file. The next two sections discuss how to read from and write to an open file synchronously and asynchronously. For now, just imagine that we've finished using the file. We tell Windows NT that we no longer need to access the file by closing it using the ever-popular:

```
BOOL CloseHandle(HANDLE hObject);
```

where *hObject* identifies the handle of the file that was returned by the earlier call to CreateFile.

Reading and Writing Files Synchronously

This section discusses the Win32 functions for reading and writing files. These functions and methods are based on procedures that should be familiar to anyone who has ever performed file I/O on any operating system. Windows NT offers these familiar functions, but I recommend that anyone interested in doing 32-bit file I/O consider using Windows NT's memory-mapped files' capabilities. Memory-mapped files offer more convenient access. More information about memory-mapped files and how to use them appears in the discussion of memory-mapped files in Chapter 4.

Without a doubt, the easiest and most-used method of reading from and writing to files is to use these two functions:

```
BOOL ReadFile(HANDLE hFile, LPVOID lpBuffer,
    DWORD nNumberOfBytesToRead, LPDWORD lpNumberOfBytesRead,
    LPOVERLAPPED lpOverlapped);
```

and

```
BOOL WriteFile(HANDLE hFile, CONST VOID *lpBuffer,
    DWORD nNumberOfBytesToWrite, LPDWORD lpNumberOfBytesWritten,
    LPOVERLAPPED lpOverlapped);
```

The ReadFile and WriteFile functions are similar to 16-bit Windows' _lread and _lwrite functions, which are included in the Win32 API for backward compatibility only. The *hFile* parameter identifies the handle of the file you want to access. The *lpBuffer* parameter points to the buffer to which the file's data should be read or to the buffer containing the data that should be written out to the file. The *nNumberOf-BytesToRead* and *nNumberOfBytesToWrite* parameters tell ReadFile and WriteFile how many bytes to read from the file and how many bytes to write to the file, respectively.

The 16-bit Windows functions _lread and _lwrite return the number of bytes actually read from or written to the file. For ReadFile and WriteFile, you need to pass the address of a DWORD, *lpNumberOfBytesRead* or *lpNumberOfBytesWritten*, that the functions will fill with this information.

Use the last parameter, *lpOverlapped*, if you want to read from or write to the file asynchronously. If you're doing synchronous file I/O, simply pass NULL for the *lpOverlapped* parameter. We'll look into this parameter in more detail in the next section, on asynchronous file I/O.

Both functions return TRUE if successful. By the way, ReadFile can be called only for files that were created or opened with the GENERIC_READ flag. Likewise, WriteFile can be called only if the file was created or opened with the GENERIC_WRITE flag.

When CreateFile returns a handle to a file, the system associates a file pointer with the handle. Initially, this file pointer is set to 0 (zero); so if you call ReadFile immediately after a call to CreateFile, you will start reading from offset 0 (zero) in the file. If you read 100 bytes into memory, the system updates the pointer associated with the file handle so that the next call to ReadFile starts reading at the 101st byte in the file. Remember that a file pointer is associated with a file handle and not with file operations or the file itself. For example, look at this code:

```
HFILE hFile = CreateFile(...);
ReadFile(hFile, lpBuffer, 100, &dwBytesRead, NULL);
WriteFile(hFile, lpBuffer, 100, &dwBytesWritten, NULL);
```

In the code fragment above, the first 100 bytes from the file are read into the buffer and these same 100 bytes are written to the file. The bytes are written from offset 100 in the file to offset 199. If there is another file operation after the call to WriteFile, it will start at offset 200 in the file.

It's also possible to open the same file two or more times. Every time the file is opened, a new file handle is returned. Because a file pointer is associated with each file handle, file manipulations using one file handle don't affect the pointer associated with other file handles, even if all handles refer to the same file. Look at the code below:

```
HFILE hFile1 = CreateFile("MYFILE.DAT", ...);
HFILE hFile2 = CreateFile("MYFILE.DAT", ...);
ReadFile(hFile1 lpBuffer, 100, &dwBytesRead, NULL);
WriteFile(hFile2, lpBuffer, 100, &dwBytesWritten, NULL);
```

In this code, the first 100 bytes from MYFILE.DAT are read into a buffer. After this read, the pointer associated with *hFile1* points to the 101st byte in the file. Now the code writes 100 bytes back to the same file. In this case, the pointer associated with *hFile2* is still initialized to 0 (zero), causing the first 100 bytes in MYFILE.DAT to be overwritten with the same data that was originally read from the file. The net result is that there is no change to the contents of the file. But after the calls to ReadFile and WriteFile have been completed, both handle file pointers point to the 101st byte in the file.

Positioning a File Pointer

If you need to access a file randomly, you will need to alter the file pointer associated with the file's handle. You do this by calling SetFile-Pointer:

```
DWORD SetFilePointer(HANDLE hFile, LONG lDistanceToMove,
   PLONG lpDistanceToMoveHigh, DWORD dwMoveMethod);
```

The *hFile* parameter identifies the file handle the pointer is associated with. The *lDistanceToMove* parameter tells the system by how many bytes you want to move the pointer. The number you specify is added to the current value of the file's pointer, so a negative number has the effect of stepping backward in the file. For most files, being able to move the pointer forward or backward by a 32-bit value is good enough. But for those really big files, you might need a 64-bit value.

This is exactly what the *lpDistanceToMoveHigh* parameter is for. If you are moving the pointer within plus or minus 2 gigabytes of its current position, pass NULL in for the *lpDistanceToMoveHigh* parameter. If you want to move the pointer somewhere within 18 billion gigabytes of its current position, you need to pass the high 32-bit part of this value in the *lpDistanceToMoveHigh* parameter. Actually, you can't pass the high 32-bit part of the value indirectly; you must store the value in a variable and pass the address of this variable in as the parameter.

The reason for this indirection is that SetFilePointer returns the previous location of the file pointer. If all you are interested in is the low 32 bits of this pointer, the function returns that value directly. If you are also interested in the high 32 bits of the pointer, the SetFilePointer function fills the variable pointed to by *lpDistanceToMoveHigh* before it returns.

The last parameter, *dwMoveMethod*, tells SetFilePointer how to interpret the two parameters *lDistanceToMove* and *lpDistanceToMoveHigh*. Here are the three possible values you can pass into *dwMoveMethod* to specify the starting point for the move:

Identifier	Meaning
FILE_BEGIN	The file's pointer becomes the unsigned value specified by the two *DistanceToMove* parameters.
FILE_CURRENT	The file's pointer is added to the signed value specified by the two *DistanceToMove* parameters.
FILE_END	The file's pointer becomes the number of bytes in the file added to the signed value specified by the two *DistanceToMove* parameters. The *DistanceToMove* parameters should identify a negative number in this case.

If SetFilePointer fails to alter the file's pointer, it returns 0xFFFFFFFF and the contents of the *lpDistanceToMoveHigh* buffer will contain NULL.

Setting the End of a File

Usually, the system takes care of setting the end of a file when the file is closed. However, you might sometimes want to make a file smaller or larger. On those occasions, call:

```
BOOL SetEndOfFile(HANDLE hFile);
```

This SetEndOfFile function changes the length of a file such that the value indicated by the file pointer becomes the length of the file. For example, if you wanted to force a file to be 1024 bytes long, you'd use SetEndOfFile this way:

```
HFILE hFile = CreateFile(...);
SetFilePointer(hFile, 1024, NULL, FILE_BEGIN);
SetEndOfFile(hFile);
CloseHandle(hFile);
```

If you use the File Manager to examine the directory containing this file, you'll see that the file is exactly 1024 bytes long.

Forcing Cached Data to Be Written to Disk

You'll remember from our look at the CreateFile function that there were quite a few flags you could pass to alter the way in which Windows NT cached file data. Windows NT also offers a function you can use to force all unwritten file data to be flushed to disk:

```
BOOL FlushFileBuffers(HANDLE hFile);
```

The FlushFileBuffers function forces all the buffered data that is associated with a file identified by the *hFile* parameter to be flushed to disk. The file must have been created or opened with the GENERIC_WRITE flag. If the function is successful, TRUE is returned. Usually, you won't need to call this function. Windows NT will guarantee that all of the buffered data will be flushed to disk when the file is closed.

Locking and Unlocking Regions of a File

The FILE_SHARE_READ and FILE_SHARE_WRITE flags let you tell the system whether a file can be opened by others and how. But think of a company that has a large customer database that contains 1 million records. Such a database is probably opened by almost everyone in the company. If everybody is performing searches only, that would be fine—the file could just always be opened with the FILE_SHARE-_READ flag specified.

But what if a group in the company needed to enter additional names and addresses in the customer database? These employees would need to open the database for writing. And somehow write access would need to be coordinated so that when one employee was appending a record to the database, another employee would not be able to append a record at the same time. If both employees could write to the database at the same time, the integrity of the database would be compromised. File locking is a solution to this problem.

File locking is similar to using the FILE_SHARE_* flags, but the FILE_SHARE_* flags affect an entire file whereas file locking affects small sections of a file. For example, if a customer moves to a new address, you'll need to update the customer's record. Before you write out the new information, you'll want to be sure that no one else can access the customer's data record while you do it. You'll want to lock that part of the database by calling:

```
BOOL LockFile(HANDLE hFile, DWORD dwFileOffsetLow,
    DWORD dwFileOffsetHigh, DWORD cbLockLow, DWORD cbLockHigh);
```

The first parameter, *hFile*, identifies the handle to the file you want to lock a subsection of. The next two parameters, *dwFileOffsetLow* and *dwFileOffsetHigh*, specify the 64-bit offset into the file where you want to begin the file lock. The last two parameters, *cbLockLow* and *cbLockHigh*, specify the number of bytes you want to lock. If you were going to update the 100th customer in the database, you would use LockFile this way:

```
LockFile(hFile, sizeof(CUSTOMER_RECORD) * (100 - 1), 0,
    sizeof(CUSTOMER_RECORD), 0);
```

If LockFile is successful, TRUE is returned. While a region of a file is locked, all other processes that try to read from or write to the locked region will fail. This is why it's crucial to check the number of bytes read or written when ReadFile and WriteFile return—in case some other process has already locked regions of the file. You must design your program to handle such a case gracefully, perhaps allowing the user to close other applications and try to read or write the data again.

It's perfectly legal to lock a region that falls beyond the current end of the file. You'd want to do that when you were adding customer records to the end of the file. You'd lock the region of the file just beyond the end of the file and write the new customer record to this region.

Note that you can't lock a region that includes an already locked region. The second call to LockFile below, for example, will fail:

```
LockFile(hFile, sizeof(CUSTOMER_RECORD) * (100 - 1), 0,
    sizeof(CUSTOMER_RECORD), 0);

LockFile(hFile, sizeof(CUSTOMER_RECORD) * (100 - 2), 0,
    2 * sizeof(CUSTOMER_RECORD), 0);
```

In the first call to LockFile, we have locked the 100th customer record. In the second call, we're trying to lock the 99th through 100th customer records. Since the 100th record has already been locked, this second call fails.

Naturally, when you have finished with a locked region of a file, you'll need to unlock it:

```
BOOL UnlockFile(HANDLE hFile, DWORD dwFileOffsetLow,
   DWORD dwFileOffsetHigh, DWORD cbUnlockLow, DWORD cbUnlockHigh);
```

The UnlockFile parameters correspond to the LockFile parameters, and the return value is the same. When you unlock a region, you must unlock it in the same way that it was locked. For example, these calls won't work together correctly:

```
LockFile(hFile, sizeof(CUSTOMER_RECORD) * (100 - 1), 0,
   sizeof(CUSTOMER_RECORD), 0);

LockFile(hFile, sizeof(CUSTOMER_RECORD) * (100 - 2), 0,
   sizeof(CUSTOMER_RECORD), 0);

UnlockFile(hFile, sizeof(CUSTOMER_RECORD) * (100 - 2), 0,
   2 * sizeof(CUSTOMER_RECORD), 0);
```

The first two calls to LockFile lock the 100th and 99th records of the database, respectively. Then the call to UnlockFile tries to unlock both records with one call. This call to UnlockFile will fail. If two separate calls are made to LockFile, two separate and similar calls must be made to UnlockFile.

W A R N I N G: Remember to unlock all locked regions of a file before you close the file or terminate the process.

There are two other functions you can call to lock and unlock a region of a file:

```
BOOL LockFileEx(HANDLE hFile, DWORD dwFlags, DWORD dwReserved,
   DWORD nNumberOfBytesToLockLow, DWORD nNumberOfBytesToLockHigh,
   LPOVERLAPPED lpOverlapped);
```

and

```
BOOL UnlockFileEx(HANDLE hFile, DWORD dwReserved,
   DWORD nNumberOfBytesToUnlockLow,
   DWORD nNumberOfBytesToUnlockHigh,
   LPOVERLAPPED lpOverlapped);
```

The LockFileEx and UnlockFileEx functions offer a superset of the LockFile and UnlockFile file capabilities. In fact, the LockFile and

UnlockFile functions are implemented internally as calls to the LockFileEx and UnlockFileEx functions.

LockFileEx adds two capabilities to LockFile. You can use LockFileEx to lock a region of a file so that no other process can write to the locked region, as with LockFile, but also so that other processes can still read from the locked region. By default, the LockFileEx function requests such a shared lock; you can request an exclusive lock by *OR*ing with the LOCKFILE_EXCLUSIVE_LOCK flag in the *dwFlags* parameter. (LockFile uses the LOCKFILE_EXCLUSIVE_LOCK flag when it calls LockFileEx.)

The other capability LockFileEx adds to LockFile is that you can tell LockFileEx to wait until a lock is granted if a thread in your process asks to lock a region of a file that is already locked by another process. In such a case, the LockFile function would return immediately, indicating that the call had failed. If your thread couldn't continue processing unless it could lock the region of the file, you would have to call LockFile repeatedly until it was able to lock the region and return TRUE. To simplify your program, you can call LockFileEx, which by default won't return until it has been able to lock the region of the file you've asked it to. If you want the function to return immediately, regardless of whether it can lock the region, *OR* the LOCKFILE_FAIL_IMMEDIATELY flag into the *dwFlags* parameter.

Most of the other LockFileEx parameters—*hFile*, *nNumberOfBytesToLockLow*, and *nNumberOfBytesToLockHigh*—are self-explanatory. The *dwReserved* parameter is reserved for Microsoft's future use, so it should always be 0 (zero). The last parameter, *lpOverlapped*, must point to an OVERLAPPED structure:

```
typedef struct _OVERLAPPED {
    DWORD  Internal;
    DWORD  InternalHigh;
    DWORD  Offset;
    DWORD  OffsetHigh;
    HANDLE hEvent;
} OVERLAPPED;
```

The only members of the OVERLAPPED structure that LockFileEx uses are the *Offset* and *OffsetHigh* members; LockFileEx ignores all the other members. Before calling LockFileEx, you must initialize the *Offset* and *OffsetHigh* members so that they indicate the starting byte of the region of the file you want to lock.

When you're ready to unlock the locked region of the file, you can call either UnlockFile or UnlockFileEx. The UnlockFileEx function will someday offer enhancements of UnlockFile. It currently offers no capabilities in addition to the regular UnlockFile function's.

Reading and Writing Files Asynchronously

Compared to most other operations carried out by a computer, file I/O is one of the slowest. The CPU is much faster at performing arithmetic operations and even painting the screen than it is at reading data from or writing data to a file. And depending on the type of medium—CD-ROM, hard disk, or floppy disk—file I/O can take an excruciatingly long time. For MS-DOS and 16-bit Windows, the time it took an application to read data from or write data out to a file was precious time wasted during which the user couldn't continue working with the application.

By taking advantage of Windows NT's multithreaded architecture, you can perform asynchronous file I/O. That is, you can tell the system to read from or write to the disk file while the rest of the code in your application continues to execute in parallel. Suppose you were developing a simple database application. When the user opened a database, you'd have to have your application read the contents of the database into memory as well as into an index file. After the user selected the OK button in the File Open dialog box, your application would display an hourglass cursor while the database file was opened and read. After reading the database records into memory, the application would have to open the index file and read the index as well. While all this work goes on, the hourglass cursor would be displayed and the user wouldn't be able to start manipulating the records in the database—not until all the files had been read.

By taking advantage of asynchronous file I/O, you can cut this file opening time down substantially. If the user will run the database application on a machine with several CPUs, one CPU could be assigned responsibility for opening and reading the database records and another CPU could be assigned responsibility for opening and reading the index file. Since each of these tasks would be assigned to its very own CPU, the two tasks could execute at the same time. This would reduce the time it would take to open the database, and the user would be able to start manipulating records much sooner.

Of course, the file containing the index for the database would probably be much smaller than the file containing the records themselves. The index file would probably be loaded into memory before the database records were loaded. The application couldn't allow the user access until both files had been completely read into memory, though. So that the application would know when both files had been completely read, you'd have to use some form of thread synchronization.

To access a data file asynchronously, you must first create or open the file by calling CreateFile, specifying the FILE_FLAG_OVER-LAPPED flag in the *fdwAttrsAndFlags* parameter. This flag notifies the system that you intend to access the file asynchronously.

Once the file is opened, you can read from and write to it by using the ReadFile and WriteFile functions we've already seen in the discussion of synchronous file I/O:

```
BOOL ReadFile(HANDLE hFile, LPVOID lpBuffer,
   DWORD nNumberOfBytesToRead, LPDWORD lpNumberOfBytesRead,
   LPOVERLAPPED lpOverlapped);
```

and

```
BOOL WriteFile(HANDLE hFile, CONST VOID *lpBuffer,
   DWORD nNumberOfBytesToWrite, LPDWORD lpNumberOfBytesWritten,
   LPOVERLAPPED lpOverlapped);
```

However, when you use the ReadFile and WriteFile functions to perform asynchronous file I/O, you must pass the address to an initialized OVERLAPPED structure as the *lpOverlapped* parameter. Win32 uses the word *overlapped* in this context to indicate that the time spent performing the file operation overlaps the time your application spends doing other things. Here's the form of an OVERLAPPED structure again:

```
typedef struct _OVERLAPPED {
   DWORD    Internal;
   DWORD    InternalHigh;
   DWORD    Offset;
   DWORD    OffsetHigh;
   HANDLE   hEvent;
} OVERLAPPED;
typedef OVERLAPPED *LPOVERLAPPED;
```

When you call either ReadFile or WriteFile, you must allocate an OVER-LAPPED structure (usually on your function's stack as a local variable) and initialize the *Offset, OffsetHigh*, and *hEvent* members of the structure.

The *Offset* and *OffsetHigh* members indicate the byte position within the file at which you want the file operation to begin. For example, if you want to read 100 bytes from the file starting at byte position 345, write:

```
// Open file for asynchronous file I/O.
HANDLE hFile = CreateFile(..., FILE_FLAG_OVERLAPPED, ...);

// Create a buffer to hold the data.
BYTE bBuffer[100];

// Boolean value to indicate whether read started successfully.
BOOL fReadStarted;

// Initialize an OVERLAPPED structure to tell
// the system where to start reading the data.
OVERLAPPED Overlapped;
Overlapped.Offset = 345;
Overlapped.OffsetHigh = 0;

Overlapped.hEvent = NULL;    // Explained later.

// Start reading the data asynchronously.
fReadStarted = ReadFile(hFile, bBuffer, sizeof(bBuffer),
    NULL, &Overlapped);

// Code below ReadFile executes while the system
// reads the file's data into the buffer.
 .
 .
 .
```

Note several things as you perform asynchronous file I/O. In synchronous file I/O, each file handle has a file pointer associated with it. When another request to read from or write to the file is made, the system knows to start accessing the file at the location identified by the file pointer. After the operation is complete, the system updates the file pointer automatically so that the next operation can pick up where the last operation left off.

Things work quite differently in asynchronous file I/O. Imagine what would happen if you didn't have to use an OVERLAPPED structure. If your code placed a call to ReadFile immediately followed by another call to ReadFile (for the same file handle), the system wouldn't know where to start reading the file for the second call to ReadFile. You probably wouldn't want to start reading the file at the same location used by the first call to ReadFile. You might want to start the second read at the byte in the file following the last byte read by the first call to Read-File. To avoid confusion, Microsoft designed ReadFile and WriteFile so that for every asynchronous I/O operation the starting byte in the file must be specified in the OVERLAPPED structure.

The next thing to notice is that in the code above the call to Read-File has NULL passed in the *lpNumberofBytesRead* parameter. Since you are performing asynchronous file I/O, it's unlikely that the call to Read-File will actually return before all the data has been read into the buffer. Because all the data won't have been read from the file when ReadFile returns, ReadFile can't possibly fill the buffer pointed to by the *lpNumberOfBytesRead* parameter with a meaningful value. That's why NULL is passed. This concept extends to asynchronous file writes. When you call WriteFile to initiate an asynchronous file write, you should pass NULL for the *lpNumberOfBytesWritten* parameter.

The last thing to notice is the return value from ReadFile. For synchronous file I/O, ReadFile returns regardless of whether the data was read successfully. For asynchronous file I/O, ReadFile returns before all the data has been read and can therefore return only whether the data has started to be read. Similarly, for asynchronous file I/O, WriteFile's return value indicates only whether the write operation has been started. ReadFile and WriteFile both return FALSE if an error occurred in the call. For example, both of these functions return FALSE if the *hFile* parameter is an invalid file handle.

Once the asynchronous file operation has started, your thread can continue initializing or do any other processing it sees fit to do. Eventually, you will need to synchronize your thread with the file I/O operation. In other words, you'll hit a point in your thread's code at which the thread can't continue to execute unless the data from the file is fully loaded into the buffer.

Windows NT considers a file handle to be a synchronization object—that is, that it can be in either a signaled or a not-signaled state. When you call ReadFile or WriteFile, one of the first things these functions do is reset the file handle to its not-signaled state. Then, when all the data has been read from or written to the file, the system sets the file handle to the signaled state. By calling the WaitForSingleObject or Wait-ForMultipleObjects function, your thread can determine when the asynchronous file operation has completed—that is, when the file handle has been set to the signaled state. Here is an extension of the code we've been looking at:

```
// Open file for asynchronous file I/O.
HANDLE hFile = CreateFile(..., FILE_FLAG_OVERLAPPED, ...);

// Create a buffer to hold the data.
BYTE bBuffer[100];

// Boolean value to indicate whether read started successfully.
BOOL fReadStarted;

// Initialize an OVERLAPPED structure to tell
// the system where to start reading the data.
OVERLAPPED Overlapped;
Overlapped.Offset = 345;
Overlapped.OffsetHigh = 0;

Overlapped.hEvent = NULL;    // Explained later.

// Start reading the data asynchronously.
fReadStarted = ReadFile(hFile, bBuffer, sizeof(bBuffer),
    NULL, &Overlapped);

// Code below ReadFile executes while the system
// reads the file's data into the buffer.
    .
    .
    .
// The application can't continue until we know that all
// the requested data has been read into our buffer.
WaitForSingleObject(hFile, INFINITE);

// Initialization complete and file data read,
// so the application can continue.
    .
    .
    .
```

Something important is missing from this code. We should be checking to be sure that the file operation has completed successfully before we allow the application to continue running. We can get the result of an asynchronous file operation by calling:

```
BOOL GetOverlappedResult(HANDLE hFile, LPOVERLAPPED lpOverlapped,
    LPDWORD lpcbTransfer, BOOL fWait);
```

When we call the GetOverlappedResult function, the *hFile* and *lpOverlapped* parameters must indicate the same file handle and OVERLAPPED structure that were used in the call to ReadFile or WriteFile.

The *lpcbTransfer* parameter points to a DWORD that will be filled with the number of bytes that were successfully transferred to or from the buffer during the write or read operation. If you aren't interested in this information, you must pass a valid address here to avoid an access violation.

The last parameter, *fWait*, is a boolean value that tells GetOverlappedResult whether it should wait until the overlapped file operation is complete before returning. If *fWait* is FALSE, GetOverlappedResult doesn't wait and returns immediately to the application. An application can call GetOverlappedResult passing TRUE for the *fWait* parameter to suspend the thread while an operation continues execution instead of calling WaitForSingleObject as in the code we just looked at.

GetOverlappedResult returns TRUE if the function is successful. If you pass FALSE for the *fWait* parameter and the file operation has not yet been completed, GetOverlappedResult will return FALSE. You can determine whether the call failed or whether the file operation is still proceeding by following the call to GetOverlappedResult with a call to GetLastError. If GetLastError returns ERROR_IO_INCOMPLETE, the call was good but the file operation is still in progress.

Note that you can't reuse the OVERLAPPED structure in your application until the file operation has been completed. The example shown below is totally incorrect:

```
void Func1 (void) {

    // Open file for asynchronous file I/O.
    HANDLE hFile = CreateFile(..., FILE_FLAG_OVERLAPPED, ...);

    // Create a buffer to hold the data.
    BYTE bBuffer[100];

    Func2(hFile, bBuffer, sizeof(bBuffer));
    .
    .
    .
}


void Func2 (HANDLE hFile, LPVOID bBuffer, DWORD dwBufSize) {

    // Initialize an OVERLAPPED structure to tell
    // the system where to start reading the data.
    OVERLAPPED Overlapped;
    memset(&Overlapped, 0, sizeof(Overlapped));
```

```
    // Start reading the data asynchronously.
    fReadStarted = ReadFile(hFile, bBuffer,
        dwBufSize, NULL, &Overlapped);
}
```

This code fragment is incorrect because the locally defined OVER-LAPPED structure in Func2 will go out of scope when Func2 returns. Windows NT remembers the address of the OVERLAPPED structure when you call ReadFile or WriteFile. When the file operation is complete, Windows NT needs to reference the *Internal, InternalHigh,* and *hEvent* members of the structure. If the structure goes out of scope, Windows NT will manipulate whatever garbage happens to be on the stack—and this could introduce difficult to find bugs into your application!

The *Internal* and *InternalHigh* members of the OVERLAPPED structure, which Windows NT must update when the file operation is complete, were reserved for internal use during very early betas of Windows NT. As time went on, it became clear to Microsoft that the information contained in these members would be useful to all of us. They left the names of the members *Internal* and *InternalHigh* so that any code already relying on these names wouldn't have to be changed. If the file operation is completed because of an error, the *Internal* member contains a system-dependent status. The *InternalHigh* member is updated with the number of bytes that have been transferred. This is the same value that is put into the buffer pointed to by the *lpcbTransfer* parameter of GetOverlappedResult.

There is one more thing to watch out for when you try to perform asynchronous file I/O. Suppose you were trying to carry out multiple asynchronous operations on the same file at the same time. Say that you wanted to read a sequence of bytes from the beginning of the file and simultaneously write another sequence of bytes to the end of the file. In this situation, you can't synchronize your thread by waiting for the file handle to become signaled.

The handle becomes signaled as soon as either of the file operations completes, so if you call WaitForSingleObject passing it the file handle, you will be unsure when WaitForSingleObject returns and whether it returned because the read operation was completed or because the write operation was completed. Clearly, there needs to be a better way to perform asynchronous file I/O so that we don't run into this predicament—fortunately, there is.

The last member of the OVERLAPPED structure, *hEvent*, identifies a Windows NT event synchronization object you must create by calling CreateEvent. When Windows NT completes an asynchronous file I/O operation, it checks to see whether the *hEvent* member of the OVERLAPPED structure is NULL. If *hEvent* is not NULL, Windows NT signals the event by calling SetEvent using *hEvent* as the event handle. Windows NT also sets the file handle to signaled state just as it did before. However, if you are using events to determine when a file operation has been completed, you shouldn't wait for the file handle object to become signaled—wait for the event instead.

Performing Multiple Asynchronous File I/O Operations Simultaneously

If you want to perform multiple asynchronous file I/O operations simultaneously, you should create an event for each of the operations, initialize the *hEvent* member in the respective file operation's OVERLAPPED structure, and then call ReadFile or WriteFile. When you reach the point in your code at which you need to synchronize with the completion of the file operation, simply call WaitForSingleObject. But instead of passing the file's handle, pass the handle to the event that you stored in the OVERLAPPED structure. With this scheme, you can easily and reliably perform multiple asynchronous file I/O operations simultaneously using the same file handle.

You can use the GetOverlappedResult function to synchronize your application with its impending file I/O. If you pass TRUE in as the *fWait* parameter for GetOverlappedResult, the function internally calls WaitForSingleObject and passes the *hEvent* member of the OVERLAPPED structure.

The potential problem here is that, if you are using an auto-reset event instead of a manual-reset event to signal the end of a file operation, you might permanently suspend your thread. If you use an auto-reset event and call WaitForSingleObject from your own code to wait for the file operation to be completed, the event will be reset automatically to the not-signaled state when WaitForSingleObject returns. If you then call GetOverlappedResult to determine the number of bytes that were successfully transferred and pass TRUE for *fWait*, you will cause GetOverlappedResult to make its own call to WaitForSingleObject. When GetOverlappedResult does this, the call to WaitForSingleObject will never return because the file operation already completed will have caused the event to become signaled. The event won't be signaled again. GetOverlappedResult will never return to your thread's code, and the thread will be hung!

Alertable Asynchronous File I/O

Windows NT offers another set of file I/O functions that allow you to perform asynchronous file I/O:

```
BOOL ReadFileEx(HANDLE hFile, LPVOID lpBuffer,
    DWORD nNumberOfBytesToRead, LPOVERLAPPED lpOverlapped,
    LPOVERLAPPED_COMPLETION_ROUTINE lpCompletionRoutine);
```

and

```
BOOL WriteFileEx(HANDLE hFile, CONST VOID *lpBuffer,
    DWORD nNumberOfBytesToWrite, LPOVERLAPPED lpOverlapped,
    LPOVERLAPPED_COMPLETION_ROUTINE lpCompletionRoutine);
```

The ReadFileEx and WriteFileEx functions allow you to start a file I/O operation just as the asynchronous functions ReadFile and WriteFile do. The difference is that, with the ReadFileEx and WriteFileEx alertable functions, you must also pass the address to a callback function, called a completion routine. This routine must have the following prototype:

```
VOID FileIOCompletionRoutine(DWORD fdwError, DWORD cbTransferred,
    LPOVERLAPPED lpo);
```

I'll get back to this completion routine function shortly. First let's look at how the system handles the asynchronous file I/O operation.

When you call ReadFileEx or WriteFileEx, the system queues your file request into a system buffer. The system periodically (and asynchronously) examines the buffer of queued requests and performs the specified operations. As the file operations are completed, the system creates a list of the completed events and associates this list with the thread that originally called ReadFileEx or WriteFileEx. For example, the following code queues three different asynchronous file operations:

```
hFile = CreateFile(...);

// Perform 1st ReadFileEx.
ReadFileEx(hFile, ...);

// Perform 1st WriteFileEx.
WriteFileEx(hFile, ...);
```

```
// Perform 2nd ReadFileEx.
ReadFileEx(hFile, ...);

SomeFunc();
```

If the call to SomeFunc takes some time to execute, the system will complete the three file operations before SomeFunc returns. While the thread is executing the SomeFunc function, the system is creating a list of file I/O completion records for the thread. The list might look something like this:

```
1st WriteFileEx completed
2nd ReadFileEx completed
1st ReadFileEx completed
```

This list of events is maintained in internal data structures—you have no access to the list. You'll also notice from the list that the system can execute your queued file operations in any order and that file operations you invoke last may be completed first and vice versa.

The completed file operations are just queued—the system doesn't call the FileIOCompletionRoutine function as soon as each file operation is completed. If you want to suspend your thread and allow the system to call the FileIOCompletionRoutine function for each of the file operations as it's completed, you must call one of three alertable functions:

```
DWORD SleepEx(DWORD dwTimeout, BOOL fAlertable);
```

or

```
DWORD WaitForSingleObjectEx(HANDLE hObject, DWORD dwTimeout,
    BOOL fAlertable);
```

or

```
DWORD WaitForMultipleObjectsEx(DWORD cObjects,
    LPHANDLE lphObjects, BOOL fWaitAll, DWORD dwTimeout,
    BOOL fAlertable);
```

All three extended functions work exactly as their nonalertable counterparts (Sleep, WaitForSingleObject, and WaitForMultipleObjects) except that they have that additional parameter, *fAlertable*. If you pass FALSE for the *fAlertable* value, you are saying that the function is not alertable, which makes the function operate just as the nonalertable versions described in Chapter 5, the thread synchronization chapter. In fact, the Sleep, WaitForSingleObject, and WaitForMultipleObjects functions are implemented internally as calls to the alertable versions of the functions with FALSE passed for the *fAlertable* parameter.

If you pass TRUE for *fAlertable*, the system puts your thread to sleep while it waits for file I/O operations to be completed. While your thread is asleep, the system checks the list of completed file I/O operations. If the system finds one, it wakes up your thread and calls the FileIOCompletionRoutine function. When the FileIOCompletionRoutine function returns, the system removes the entry from the list and checks again to see whether there are any more. If there are, the system again wakes your thread and calls the FileIOCompletionRoutine function.

N O T E: The thread that calls an extended wait function must be the same thread that called the file I/O function.

When the list of completed file operations is empty, the system wakes up your thread again and returns from the call to SleepEx, WaitForSingleObjectEx, or WaitForMultipleObjectsEx. The return value from any of these three functions will be WAIT_IO_COMPLETION if the return is because the FileIOCompletionRoutine was executed one or more times.

If you call one of the extended wait functions and there are no completed file operations to be processed, the functions work just as though you had called them and passed FALSE for the *fAlertable* parameter. If, while the system waits, a single file operation or several file operations are completed, your thread wakes, the system calls the FileIOCompletionRoutine using your thread for all the finished operations, and then these functions return WAIT_IO_COMPLETION.

These alertable functions in their extended form are most useful in a client-server situation. You might have a server application that guards a database of information. You might also have a client application that periodically needs to request data from the server application. The server and client applications would communicate with each other using named pipes.

The server application would start by calling ReadFileEx and then pass the handle to a named pipe instead of a handle to a file. When a client application sent information to the server through the named pipe, the asynchronous call would read the client's request and call the FileIOCompletionRoutine function. The FileIOCompletionRoutine function would interpret the client's request and locate the requested information in the database. The server would do this by initiating its own call to ReadFileEx. When the database information had been read, another FileIOCompletionRoutine call would be executed and the retrieved data would be transferred back through the named pipe to the client application.

The Alertable I/O Sample Application

The AlertIO (ALERTIO.EXE) application, listed in Figure 9-2 beginning on page 502, demonstrates the use of alertable file I/O. The program simply copies a file the user specifies to a new file called ALERTIO.CPY. When the user executes Alertio, the Alertable I/O File Copy dialog box appears:

The user presses the *Browse...* button to select the file to be copied. To best see the effects of using the alertable I/O functions, it's a good idea to select a large file (the Win32 API help file, API32WH.HLP, for instance). After a file to be copied has been selected, the *Source file* and *File size* fields are updated.

When the user presses the *Copy* button, the program opens the source file, creates the destination file (saving both file handles in the global *g_hFileSrc* and *g_hFileDst* variables), and begins copying the file. After the file has been copied, the file handles are closed.

The file is copied by means of four internal buffers. Each buffer is a different size, as shown below:

Buffer Number	Size in Bytes
0	32768
1	16384
2	10922
3	8192

The entire file will be copied, piece by piece, using these buffers. First, four chunks of the file, one chunk per buffer, will be read. These file read operations are initiated by calls to the ReadFileEx function. The address of the InputCompletion function is specified in the call to Read-FileEx, causing InputCompletion to be called automatically when the file read operation for an individual buffer has been completed. Because the buffers are different sizes, the reads might not be finished in the order they were requested.

After the four initial reads have been initiated, the program enters a loop that executes until the destination file has been written or until a file copy error occurs.

```
while ((g_CopyStatus != csError) &&
       (g_CopyStatus != csDoneWriting)) {

   // Put this thread to sleep until it is awakened by
   // an alertable file I/O completion.
   SleepEx(INFINITE, TRUE);
}
```

Inside the loop, the thread calls SleepEx, the alertable version of the Sleep function. If the system is still performing the asynchronous file read operations, the call to SleepEx causes the thread to be suspended. However, as soon as the asynchronous buffer reads have been completed, the thread is in an alertable state and executes the Input-Completion function—once for each of the completed buffer reads.

The code inside the InputCompletion function first verifies that the part of the file has been read into the buffer successfully. Then it calls WriteFileEx so that the contents of the buffer are written to the destination file. The call to WriteFileEx writes the contents of the buffer to the same byte offset in the destination as the offset that was used when the source data was read from the source file. The call to WriteFileEx also specifies the address of the OutputCompletion function so that the system will automatically call the OutputCompletion function after all file write operations have been completed and the thread is in an alertable state.

During the file copy, the Alertable I/O File Copy dialog box, shown at the top of the next page, indicates whether information is being read from the source file into a buffer or whether data is being written from a buffer to the destination file.

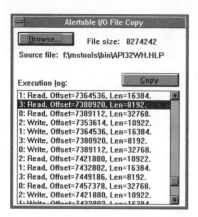

From left to right, each line shows a buffer number, whether the data is being read into or written out from the buffer, the location in the source or destination file at which the data is being read from or written to, and the number of bytes in the buffer that will be read or written.

Most of the time, the number of bytes written will be the number of bytes that were read. However, when the last part of the source file is read into a buffer, it often doesn't completely fill the buffer. Therefore, when the information in this buffer is written to the destination file, only the actual number of bytes that were read is written, not the size in bytes of the whole buffer. If the whole buffer were written, the destination file would end up larger than the source file.

AlertIO.ico

ALERTIO.C
```
/*****************************************************************
Module name: AlertIO.C
Written by: Jim Harkins and Jeffrey Richter
Notices: Copyright (c) 1993 Jeffrey Richter
*****************************************************************/

#include <windows.h>
#include <windowsx.h>
```

Figure 9-2.
The AlertIO application.

(continued)

Figure 9-2. *continued*

```c
#include <tchar.h>
#include <stdio.h>
#include <stdlib.h>
#include "AlertIO.h"

#define BUFFSIZE (32 * 1024)
#define BUFFNUM  4

#define ARRAY_SIZE(A)  (sizeof(A) / sizeof((A)[0]))

#define DSTFILENAME       __TEXT("AlertIO.CPY")

// Status of the copy.

typedef enum {
   csCopying,
   csDoneReading,
   csDoneWriting,
   csError,
} COPYSTATUS;

HWND g_hwndLB = NULL;

// Data used by copy.
HANDLE g_hFileSrc, g_hFileDst;

// hEvent contains the buffer number.
OVERLAPPED g_Overlapped[BUFFNUM];

// Pointer to file copy buffers.
BYTE g_bBuffers[BUFFSIZE * BUFFNUM];

// Offset in source file where next read begins.
DWORD  g_dwNextReadOffset = 0;

// Status of the file copy.
COPYSTATUS g_CopyStatus = csCopying;

DWORD g_dwLastError = NO_ERROR;

int g_nReadsInProgress    = 0;
int g_nMaxReadsInProgress = 0;
int g_nCompletedReads     = 0;
```

(continued)

Figure 9-2. *continued*

```
int g_nWritesInProgress    = 0;
int g_nMaxWritesInProgress = 0;
int g_nCompletedWrites     = 0;

VOID WINAPI InputCompletion (DWORD fdwError,
   DWORD cbTransferred, LPOVERLAPPED lpo);

VOID WINAPI OutputCompletion (DWORD fdwError,
   DWORD cbTransferred, LPOVERLAPPED lpo);


///////////////////////////////////////////////////////////////

// This function constructs a string using the format string
// passed and the variable number of arguments and adds the
// string to the shopper events list box identified from the
// global g_hwndLB variable.
void AddStr (LPCTSTR szFmt, ...) {
   TCHAR szBuf[150];
   int nIndex;
   va_list va_params;

   // Make va_params point to the first argument after szFmt.
   va_start(va_params, szFmt);

   // Build the string to be displayed.
   _vstprintf(szBuf, szFmt, va_params);

   do {
      // Add the string to the end of the list box.
      nIndex = ListBox_AddString(g_hwndLB, szBuf);

      // If the list box is full, delete the first item in it.
      if (nIndex == LB_ERR)
         ListBox_DeleteString(g_hwndLB, 0);

   } while (nIndex == LB_ERR);

   // Select the newly added item.
   ListBox_SetCurSel(g_hwndLB, nIndex);

   // Indicate that we're done referencing
   // the variable arguments.
   va_end(va_params);
}
```

(continued)

Figure 9-2. *continued*

```
//////////////////////////////////////////////////////////////

void ReadNext (LPOVERLAPPED lpOverlapped) {
   BOOL  fReadOk;
   DWORD dwLastError;
   int nBufSize = BUFFSIZE / ((int) lpOverlapped->hEvent + 1);

   if (csCopying != g_CopyStatus) {
      // Either an error has occurred or we have read past
      // the end of the file.  In either case,
      // let's not start to read a new block from the file.
      return;
   }

   // The file is still being copied.

   // Figure out where to start
   // reading the next portion of the file.
   lpOverlapped->Offset = g_dwNextReadOffset;
   lpOverlapped->OffsetHigh = 0;

   // Set the global file offset variable so that it knows
   // where it should begin reading the next time.
   g_dwNextReadOffset += nBufSize;


   AddStr(__TEXT("%d: Read, Offset=%d, Len=%d."),
      (int) lpOverlapped->hEvent, lpOverlapped->Offset,
      nBufSize);
   // Initiate the alertable read from the
   // file into the appropriate buffer.
   fReadOk = ReadFileEx(g_hFileSrc,
      g_bBuffers + (int) lpOverlapped->hEvent * BUFFSIZE,
      nBufSize, lpOverlapped, InputCompletion);

   if (fReadOk) {
      // The read is successful; update the counters.
      g_nReadsInProgress++;
      g_nMaxReadsInProgress =
         max(g_nMaxReadsInProgress, g_nReadsInProgress);
   } else {
      // The read is unsuccessful.
      // Get the reason for the failure.
      dwLastError = GetLastError();
```

(continued)

Figure 9-2. *continued*

```
        if (ERROR_HANDLE_EOF == dwLastError) {
            // Read failed because of an attempt to read past the
            // end of the file; set global status indicator.
            g_CopyStatus = csDoneReading;
            AddStr(__TEXT("%d: Read past End-of-File."),
                (int) lpOverlapped->hEvent);
        } else {
            // Read failed because of another error;
            // set global status indicator and global error.
            g_CopyStatus = csError;
            g_dwLastError = dwLastError;

            AddStr(__TEXT("%d: Read caused an error (%d)."),
                (int) lpOverlapped->hEvent, g_dwLastError);
        }
    }
}


///////////////////////////////////////////////////////////////////

VOID WINAPI InputCompletion (DWORD fdwError,
    DWORD cbTransferred, LPOVERLAPPED lpOverlapped) {

    BOOL fWriteOk;
    // Signal that a read has been completed.
    g_nReadsInProgress--;

    switch (fdwError) {
        case 0:
            // The read has been completed successfully.
            g_nCompletedReads++;

            AddStr(__TEXT("%d: Write, Offset=%d, Len=%d."),
                (int) lpOverlapped->hEvent, lpOverlapped->Offset,
                cbTransferred);

            // Write this buffer to the destination file.
            // The overlapped structure contains the offset
            // the buffer was read from.  This is the same offset
            // the buffer should be written to.
            fWriteOk = WriteFileEx(g_hFileDst,
                g_bBuffers + (int) lpOverlapped->hEvent * BUFFSIZE,
                cbTransferred, lpOverlapped, OutputCompletion);
```

(continued)

Figure 9-2. *continued*

```
        if (fWriteOk) {
            // The write is successful; update the counters.
            g_nWritesInProgress++;
            g_nMaxWritesInProgress = max(
                g_nMaxWritesInProgress, g_nWritesInProgress);
        } else {
            // The write is unsuccessful.
            // Get the reason for the failure, and set global
            // status indicator and global error.
            g_CopyStatus = csError;
            g_dwLastError = GetLastError();

            AddStr(__TEXT("%d: Write caused an error (%d)."),
                (int) lpOverlapped->hEvent, g_dwLastError);
        }
        break;

    case ERROR_HANDLE_EOF:
        // Read past the end of the file.
        // Update the global status indicator.
        g_CopyStatus = csDoneReading;
        AddStr(__TEXT("%d: Done reading source file."),
            (int) lpOverlapped->hEvent);
        break;
    }
}


//////////////////////////////////////////////////////////////

VOID WINAPI OutputCompletion (DWORD fdwError,
    DWORD cbTransferred, LPOVERLAPPED lpOverlapped) {

    // Signal that a write has been completed.
    g_nWritesInProgress--;

    if (fdwError == 0) {
        // The write has been completed successfully.
        g_nCompletedWrites++;

        // Start reading the next chunk of the file if we're not
        // done reading the file yet.
        if (csCopying == g_CopyStatus) {
            ReadNext(lpOverlapped);
        }
```

(continued)

Figure 9-2. *continued*

```
        // Test to see if this was the last write, and if so,
        // update the global status indicator so that the main
        // copy loop will know the file has been copied.
        if ((g_CopyStatus == csDoneReading) &&
            (g_nWritesInProgress == 0)) {
          g_CopyStatus = csDoneWriting;
          AddStr(__TEXT("%d: Done writing destination file."),
            (int) lpOverlapped->hEvent);
        }
      }
    }
  }


//////////////////////////////////////////////////////////////////

BOOL FileCopy (LPCTSTR pszFileSrc, LPCTSTR pszFileDst) {
  int nBuffer;

  // Open the existing source file for input.
  g_hFileSrc = CreateFile(pszFileSrc, GENERIC_READ,
    FILE_SHARE_READ, NULL, OPEN_EXISTING,
    FILE_ATTRIBUTE_NORMAL | FILE_FLAG_OVERLAPPED |
    FILE_FLAG_SEQUENTIAL_SCAN, NULL);

  if (g_hFileSrc == INVALID_HANDLE_VALUE) {
    g_dwLastError = GetLastError();
    return(FALSE);
  }

  // Create the new destination file for output.
  g_hFileDst = CreateFile(pszFileDst, GENERIC_WRITE,
    0, NULL, CREATE_ALWAYS,
    FILE_ATTRIBUTE_NORMAL | FILE_FLAG_OVERLAPPED |
    FILE_FLAG_SEQUENTIAL_SCAN, NULL);

  if (g_hFileDst == INVALID_HANDLE_VALUE) {
    CloseHandle(g_hFileSrc);
    g_dwLastError = GetLastError();
    return(FALSE);
  }

  // Get ready to start copying the file.
  g_CopyStatus = csCopying;
  g_dwNextReadOffset    = 0;
```

(continued)

Figure 9-2. *continued*

```
g_nReadsInProgress      = 0;
g_nMaxReadsInProgress   = 0;
g_nCompletedReads       = 0;
g_nWritesInProgress     = 0;
g_nMaxWritesInProgress  = 0;
g_nCompletedWrites      = 0;

// Start the copy engine by allowing the buffers to begin
// reading data from the file.
for (nBuffer = 0; nBuffer < BUFFNUM; nBuffer++) {
   g_Overlapped[nBuffer].hEvent = (HANDLE) nBuffer;
   ReadNext(&g_Overlapped[nBuffer]);
}

// Loop until an error has occurred or until the
// destination file has been written.
while ((g_CopyStatus != csError) &&
       (g_CopyStatus != csDoneWriting)) {

   // Put this thread to sleep until it's awakened by
   // an alertable file I/O completion.
   SleepEx(INFINITE, TRUE);
}

CloseHandle(g_hFileDst);
CloseHandle(g_hFileSrc);

if (g_CopyStatus == csError) {
   SetLastError(g_dwLastError);
   AddStr(__TEXT("File copy error %d."), g_dwLastError);
} else {
   AddStr(__TEXT("File copied successfully."));
}

// Put some statistical information in the list box.
AddStr(__TEXT("Max reads in progress=%d."),
   g_nMaxReadsInProgress);
AddStr(__TEXT("Completed reads=%d."), g_nCompletedReads);
AddStr(__TEXT("Max writes in progress=%d."),
   g_nMaxWritesInProgress);
AddStr(__TEXT("Completed writes=%d."), g_nCompletedWrites);

return(g_CopyStatus != csError);
}
```

(continued)

Figure 9-2. *continued*

```
//////////////////////////////////////////////////////////////

BOOL Dlg_OnInitDialog (HWND hwnd, HWND hwndFocus,
   LPARAM lParam) {

   // Save the handle of the dialog's list box in a global
   // so that the threads can easily gain access to it.
   g_hwndLB = GetDlgItem(hwnd, ID_LOG);

   // Associate an icon with the dialog box.
   SetClassLong(hwnd, GCL_HICON, (LONG)
      LoadIcon((HINSTANCE) GetWindowLong(hwnd, GWL_HINSTANCE),
      __TEXT("AlertIO")));

   // Disable the "Copy" button because no file
   // has been selected yet.
   EnableWindow(GetDlgItem(hwnd, IDOK), FALSE);

   return(TRUE);
}


//////////////////////////////////////////////////////////////

void Dlg_OnCommand (HWND hwnd, int id,
   HWND hwndCtl, UINT codeNotify) {

   TCHAR szPathname[_MAX_DIR];
   BOOL fOk;
   OPENFILENAME ofn;

   switch (id) {
      case IDOK:
         // Copy the source file to the destination file.
         ListBox_ResetContent(g_hwndLB);
         Static_GetText(GetDlgItem(hwnd, ID_SRCFILE),
            szPathname, sizeof(szPathname));
         SetCursor(LoadCursor(NULL, IDC_WAIT));
         FileCopy(szPathname, DSTFILENAME);
         break;

      case ID_BROWSE:
         memset(&ofn, 0, sizeof(ofn));
         ofn.lStructSize = sizeof(ofn);
         ofn.hwndOwner = hwnd;
         ofn.lpstrFilter = __TEXT("*.*\0");
```

(continued)

Figure 9-2. *continued*

```
            _tcscpy(szPathname, __TEXT("*.*"));
            ofn.lpstrFile = szPathname;
            ofn.nMaxFile = sizeof(szPathname);
            ofn.Flags = OFN_FILEMUSTEXIST;
            fOk = GetOpenFileName(&ofn);

            if (fOk) {
               HANDLE hFile;
               Static_SetText(GetDlgItem(hwnd, ID_SRCFILE),
                  szPathname);
               hFile = CreateFile(szPathname, GENERIC_READ,
                  0, NULL, OPEN_EXISTING, 0, NULL);

               SetDlgItemInt(hwnd, ID_SRCFILESIZE,
                  GetFileSize(hFile, NULL), FALSE);
               CloseHandle(hFile);
            }

            // Enable the "Copy" button if the user selected
            // a valid pathname.
            GetWindowText(GetDlgItem(hwnd, ID_SRCFILE),
               szPathname, sizeof(szPathname));
            EnableWindow(GetDlgItem(hwnd, IDOK),
               szPathname[0] != __TEXT('('));

            if (fOk) {
               // If the user pressed the OK button in the file
               // dialog box, change focus to the "Copy" button.
               FORWARD_WM_NEXTDLGCTL(hwnd, GetDlgItem(hwnd, IDOK),
                  TRUE, SendMessage);
            }
            break;

         case IDCANCEL:
            EndDialog(hwnd, id);
            break;
      }
   }
}

///////////////////////////////////////////////////////////

BOOL CALLBACK Dlg_Proc (HWND hDlg, UINT uMsg,
   WPARAM wParam, LPARAM lParam) {
```

(continued)

Figure 9-2. *continued*

```
   BOOL fProcessed = TRUE;

   switch (uMsg) {
      HANDLE_MSG(hDlg, WM_INITDIALOG, Dlg_OnInitDialog);
      HANDLE_MSG(hDlg, WM_COMMAND, Dlg_OnCommand);

      default:
         fProcessed = FALSE;
         break;
   }

   return(fProcessed);
}

///////////////////////////////////////////////////////////////

int APIENTRY WinMain (HINSTANCE hInstance,
   HINSTANCE hPrevInstance, LPSTR lpszCmdLine, int nCmdShow) {

   DialogBox(hInstance, MAKEINTRESOURCE(DLG_ALERTIO),
      NULL, Dlg_Proc);

   return(0);
}

///////////////////////// End Of File /////////////////////////
```

ALERTIO.H

```
/**************************************************************
Module name: AlertIO.H
Notices: Copyright (c) 1993 Jeffrey Richter
**************************************************************/

// Dialog and control IDs.
#define DLG_ALERTIO       1
#define ID_BROWSE         100
#define ID_SRCFILE        101
#define ID_SRCFILESIZE    102
#define ID_LOG            103


///////////////////////// End Of File /////////////////////////
```

(continued)

Figure 9-2. *continued*

ALERTIO.RC

```
/*****************************************************************
Module name: AlertIO.RC
Notices: Copyright (c) 1993 Jeffrey Richter
*****************************************************************/

#include <windows.h>
#include "AlertIO.h"

AlertIO  ICON  AlertIO.Ico

DLG_ALERTIO DIALOG 18, 18, 158, 158
STYLE WS_BORDER | WS_POPUP | WS_CAPTION | WS_SYSMENU
CAPTION "Alertable I/O File Copy"
BEGIN
    PUSHBUTTON "&Browse...", ID_BROWSE, 4,
        4, 52, 12, WS_CHILD | WS_VISIBLE | WS_TABSTOP
    LTEXT "Source file:", -1, 5, 20, 40, 8
    CONTROL "(use Browse to select a file)", ID_SRCFILE,
        "STATIC", SS_LEFT | SS_NOPREFIX | WS_CHILD |
        WS_VISIBLE | WS_GROUP, 46, 20, 108, 8
    LTEXT "File size:", -1, 68, 8, 36, 8
    LTEXT "0", ID_SRCFILESIZE, 104, 8, 36, 8
        WS_CHILD | WS_VISIBLE | WS_GROUP
    DEFPUSHBUTTON "&Copy", IDOK, 100, 40, 52, 12,
        WS_CHILD | WS_VISIBLE | WS_TABSTOP
    LTEXT "Execution &log:", -1, 4, 45, 48, 8
    CONTROL "", ID_LOG, "LISTBOX", LBS_NOINTEGRALHEIGHT |
        WS_TABSTOP | WS_CHILD | WS_VISIBLE |
        WS_BORDER | WS_VSCROLL, 4, 56, 148, 100
END

/////////////////////////// End Of File ///////////////////////////
```

Manipulating File Attributes

A set of attributes is associated with every file. Many of the file attributes are initialized when the file is created, some are altered when a file is accessed, and some can be altered specifically under program control. Often, you might not have any interest in altering the values but just want to see what the current attributes are for a file. Most file attributes have to do with flag settings, file size, and time stamps.

File Flags

A file's attributes are initially set when the file is created with the CreateFile function. When CreateFile is called, the *fdwAttrsAndFlags* parameter specifies the attributes the file should have when it is created. To see what these attributes are later, an application can call:

```
DWORD GetFileAttributes(LPTSTR lpszFileName);
```

The GetFileAttributes function retrieves the attributes associated with the file identified by the *lpszFileName* parameter. When the function returns, you can *AND* the return value with any of these identifiers we saw in the discussion of CreateFile's *fdwAttrsAndFlags* parameter earlier in this chapter:

```
FILE_ATTRIBUTE_ARCHIVE
FILE_ATTRIBUTE_DIRECTORY
FILE_ATTRIBUTE_HIDDEN
FILE_ATTRIBUTE_NORMAL
FILE_ATTRIBUTE_READONLY
FILE_ATTRIBUTE_SYSTEM
```

Although it's not frequently done, you can alter any of these file attributes by calling SetFileAttributes:

```
BOOL SetFileAttributes(LPTSTR lpFileName, DWORD dwFileAttributes);
```

SetFileAttributes returns TRUE if it successfully alters the file's attributes. The code below, for example, turns off the archive flag for CLOCK.EXE:

```
DWORD dwFileAttributes = GetFileAttributes("CLOCK.EXE");
dwFileAttributes &= ~FILE_ATTRIBUTE_ARCHIVE;
SetFileAttributes("CLOCK.EXE", dwFileAttributes);
```

File Size

You might also want to query a file's size by calling GetFileSize:

```
DWORD GetFileSize(HANDLE hFile, LPDWORD lpdwFileSizeHigh);
```

You'll immediately notice that the GetFileSize function requires that the file be open and that the handle to the file be passed as the *hFile* parameter. GetFileSize returns the low 32-bit value representing the file's size directly. If you are interested in the file's high 32-bit part of the size, you need to pass an address to a DWORD that GetFileSize will fill with this information.

There is no direct way to alter a file's size. A file's size can be altered only by writing to the file or by calling SetEndOfFile.

File Time Stamp

In MS-DOS and more specifically, in FAT file systems, a file has only one time stamp associated with it—the last time the file was written to. But in the HPFS and NTFS, a file can have three time stamps associated with it: the date and time the file was created, the date and time the file was last accessed, and the date and time the file was last written to. To retrieve the time stamp information for a file, call:

```
BOOL GetFileTime(HANDLE hFile, LPFILETIME lpftCreation,
    LPFILETIME lpftLastAccess, LPFILETIME lpftLastWrite);
```

For files stored on a FAT file system, the creation time and the last access time will be 0 (zero). As with GetFileSize, the file must be opened before the call to GetFileTime is made so that we can pass its file handle as the *hFile* parameter. The next three parameters are all pointers to FILETIME structures:

```
typedef struct _FILETIME {
    DWORD dwLowDateTime;
    DWORD dwHighDateTime;
} FILETIME, *PFILETIME, *LPFILETIME;
```

If you aren't interested in when the file was created, you can pass NULL in as the *lpftCreation* parameter. The same is true for either of the other two time stamp parameters.

The 64-bit value composed of the *dwLowDateTime* and *dwHighDateTime* members in the FILETIME structure represent the number of 100-nanosecond intervals since January 1, 1601. I'll grant you that this isn't very useful, but the date does, after all, mark the start of a new quadricentury. Still not too impressed? I guess Microsoft didn't think you'd be too impressed either, so they wrote some additional functions to help you realize the usefulness of file times.

Perhaps all you need to do is check to see which of two files is older. That's easy:

```
LONG CompareFileTime(LPFILETIME lpft1, LPFILETIME lpft2);
```

CompareFileTime returns one of these long values:

Result of CompareFileTime	Meaning
−1	*lpft1* is less than (older than) *lpft2*
0	*lpft1* is same (age) as *lpft2*
+1	*lpft1* is greater than (younger than) *lpft2*

Using CompareFileTime, you could also check to see whether the last time a file was accessed it was also written to:

```
lResult = CompareFileTime(&ftLastAccess, &ftLastWrite);
if (lResult == 0) {
   // Last access was a write.
} else {
   // Last access was not a write.
}
```

You may want to show the user one of the file's time stamps. In this case, you will need to convert FILETIME structures to the SYSTEM-TIME structures or vice versa using:

```
BOOL FileTimeToSystemTime(LPFILETIME lpft, LPSYSTEMTIME lpst);
```

and

```
BOOL SystemTimeToFileTime(LPSYSTEMTIME lpst, LPFILETIME lpft);
```

These functions convert the time stamp easily between the FILETIME and SYSTEMTIME structures. A SYSTEMTIME structure looks like this:

```
typedef struct  SYSTEMTIME {
   WORD wYear;
   WORD wMonth;
   WORD wDayOfWeek;
   WORD wDay;
   WORD wHour;
   WORD wMinute;
   WORD wSecond;
   WORD wMilliseconds;
} SYSTEMTIME;
typedef SYSTEMTIME *PSYSTEMTIME, *LPSYSTEMTIME;
```

With this information, it's easy to construct a string that will be meaningful to an end-user. Note that when you convert from SYSTEM-TIME to FILETIME, the *wDayOfWeek* member in the SYSTEMTIME structure is ignored.

You can convert a file's time to local time and back again by using these functions:

```
BOOL FileTimeToLocalFileTime(LPFILETIME lpft,
    LPFILETIME lpftLocal);
```

and

```
BOOL LocalFileTimeToFileTime(LPFILETIME lpftLocal,
    LPFILETIME lpft);
```

Both these functions take two pointers to FILETIME structures. When you use these functions, be careful not to pass the same address as both parameters—the functions won't work correctly.

And if you're an MS-DOS and FAT diehard who doesn't want to port the existing file time stamp code in your applications over to the new way of doing things just yet, you can use these two functions to convert a FILETIME structure to the time format used by MS-DOS and vice versa:

```
BOOL FileTimeToDosDateTime(LPFILETIME lpft,
    LPWORD lpwDOSDate, LPWORD lpwDOSTime);
```

and

```
BOOL DosDateTimeToFileTime(WORD wDOSDate, WORD wDOSTime,
    LPFILETIME lpft);
```

The FileTimeToDosDateTime function takes the address of the FILETIME structure containing the file's time and converts it to two WORD values that MS-DOS uses—one WORD for the date and the other WORD for the time.

After you have manipulated and converted the time values all you want, you can change the time associated with a file by calling Get-FileTime's complementary function:

```
BOOL SetFileTime(HANDLE hFile, LPFILETIME lpftCreation,
    LPFILETIME lpftLastAccess, LPFILETIME lpftLastWrite);
```

If you don't want to change the creation time stamp of the file, you can pass NULL in for the *lpftCreation* parameter. The FAT file system doesn't store a creation and last access time stamp with a file, so parameters for these times are ignored if the file resides on a FAT file system.

The other way to get the attribute information associated with a file is to call the GetFileInformationByHandle function:

```
BOOL GetFileInformationByHandle(HANDLE hFile,
    LPBY_HANDLE_FILE_INFORMATION lpFileInformation);
```

This function requires the handle of an open file identified by the *hFile* parameter and the address of a BY_HANDLE_FILE_INFORMATION structure, which the function fills with information about the file:

```
typedef struct _BY_HANDLE_FILE_INFORMATION {
    DWORD dwFileAttributes;
    FILETIME ftCreationTime;
    FILETIME ftLastAccessTime;
    FILETIME ftLastWriteTime;
    DWORD dwVolumeSerialNumber;
    DWORD nFileSizeHigh;
    DWORD nFileSizeLow;
    DWORD nNumberOfLinks;
    DWORD nFileIndexHigh;
    DWORD nFileIndexLow;
} BY_HANDLE_FILE_INFORMATION,
    *PBY_HANDLE_FILE_INFORMATION, *LPBY_HANDLE_FILE_INFORMATION;
```

The GetFileInformationByHandle function gathers all of the attribute information available for the file. In addition to the file's attributes contained in the *dwFileAttributes* member and the three time stamps contained in the *ftCreationTime, ftLastAccessTime,* and *ftLastWriteTime* members, the function gets the serial number of the disk volume on which the file resides in the *dwVolumeSerialNumber* member, and the file's size in the *nFileSizeHigh* and *nFileSizeLow* members. It finds the number of links (used by the POSIX subsystem) in the *nNumberOfLinks* member.

The system assigns every file, each time it's opened, a unique ID contained in the *nFileIndexHigh* and *nFileIndexLow* members. The ID might not be constant across openings of the file and will almost definitely be different if the file is opened during a different Windows NT session. However, if one application opens a file and another application opens the same file, the ID will be the same. An application can use the ID in conjunction with the volume's serial number to determine whether two (or more) different file handles actually reference the same file.

Searching for Files

Almost all applications use files. Because an application can create many files and because applications are often designed to read files created by other applications (Microsoft Excel reading Lotus 1-2-3 files, for example), file searching has become a common task—so common, in fact, that Microsoft has created a set of common dialog boxes that help users search their drives for particular files. For some applications, though, the File Open and File Save As dialog boxes aren't enough. Some applications might need to search for files or allow access to files by means of methods not accommodated by the standard file dialog boxes.

One common operation is to convert a simple filename or a file with a relative path to its full pathname. In 16-bit Windows, a call to OpenFile using the OF_PARSE flag accomplished the conversion. In Win32, the call is to:

```
DWORD GetFullPathName(LPCTSTR lpszFile, DWORD cchPath,
    LPTSTR lpszPath, LPTSTR *ppszFilePart);
```

The GetFullPathName function accepts a filename (and optional path information) in the *lpszFile* parameter. The function then uses the current drive and current directory information associated with the process, calculates the full pathname for the file, and fills the buffer pointed to by *lpszPath*. The *cchPath* parameter indicates the maximum size of the buffer for the drive and path in characters. In the *ppszFilePart* parameter you must pass the address of an LPTSTR variable. GetFullPathName will fill the variable with the address within *lpszPath* at which the filename resides. Applications can use this information when they construct their caption text.

For example, if I am using Notepad and open a file called HIMOM.TXT, Notepad's caption becomes

```
Notepad - HIMOM.TXT
```

This last parameter, **ppszFilePart*, is simply a convenience. You could get the address of the filename by calling

```
szFilePart = strrchr(szPath, '\\') + 1;
```

GetFullPathName doesn't really search for a file on the system. It just converts a filename to its full pathname. In fact, GetFullPathName doesn't examine anything on the disk at all. If you want to actually scan the user's disks for a file, you can use:

```
DWORD SearchPath(LPCTSTR lpszPath, LPCTSTR lpszFile,
    LPCSTR lpszExtension, DWORD cchReturnBuffer,
    LPTSTR lpszReturnBuffer, LPTSTR *plpszFilePart);
```

The SearchPath function looks for a file in a list of directories you specify. You pass the list of paths to be scanned in the *lpszPath* parameter. If this parameter is NULL, the file is searched for in the paths listed at the top of the next page.

1. The directory from which the application was loaded

2. The current directory

3. The Windows system directory

4. The Windows directory

5. The directories listed in the PATH environment variable

You specify the file you want to search for in the *lpszFile* parameter. If the *lpszFile* parameter includes an extension, you should pass NULL in for the *lpszExtension* parameter; otherwise, you can pass an extension in the *lpszExtension* parameter that must begin with a period. The extension is appended to the filename only if the filename doesn't have an extension already. The last three parameters have the same meanings as the last three parameters of the GetFullPathName function.

Another method of looking for files allows you to find a file by traversing the user's entire hard disk looking at every directory and file in existence if you wish. You tell Windows NT what directory to start in and the filename to search for by calling FindFirstFile:

```
HANDLE FindFirstFile(LPTSTR lpszSearchFile,
  LPWIN32_FIND_DATA lpffd);
```

The FindFirstFile function tells Windows NT you want to search for a file. The first parameter, *lpszSearchFile*, points to a zero-terminated string containing a filename. The filename can include wildcard characters (* and ?), and you can preface the filename with a starting path. The *lpffd* parameter is the address to a WIN32_FIND_DATA structure:

```
typedef struct _WIN32_FIND_DATA {
    DWORD dwFileAttributes;
    FILETIME ftCreationTime;
    FILETIME ftLastAccessTime;
    FILETIME ftLastWriteTime;
    DWORD nFileSizeHigh;
    DWORD nFileSizeLow;
    DWORD dwReserved0;
    DWORD dwReserved1;
    CHAR cFileName[ MAX_PATH ];
    CHAR cAlternateFileName[ 14 ];
} WIN32_FIND_DATA, *PWI32_FIND_DATA, *LPWIN32_FIND_DATA;
```

If FindFirstFile succeeds in locating a file matching the filespec in the specified directory, it fills in the members of the WIN32_FIND-

_DATA structure and returns a handle. If FindFirstFile fails to find a file that matches the filespec, it returns INVALID_HANDLE_VALUE, and the structure isn't changed.

The WIN32_FIND_DATA structure contains information about the matching file—its attributes, its time stamps, and its size. At the end of the structure are two names for the file. The *cFileName* member is the real name of the file. This is the member you should use most often. The *cAlternateFileName* is a synthesized name for the file.

Let's say you are using a program designed for 16-bit Windows. When you select the application's File Open dialog box, you see a list of the files in the current directory. If the current directory is on an NTFS file system and the names of the files in that directory average 50 characters, what gets displayed?

Under OS/2, a program that wasn't designed to recognize HPFS filenames couldn't see HPFS files at all. For Windows NT, Microsoft decided (correctly) that such files should be made accessible to the user. Well, since the 16-bit Windows application isn't prepared to work with long filenames, Windows NT must convert the long filenames to fit an 8.3 system. This converted, or alternate, filename is what you'll find in the *cAlternateFileName* member of the WIN32_FIND_DATA structure.

For FAT file systems, of course, the contents of the *cFileName* and *cAlternateFileName* members will be identical, and for the HPFS and NTFS file systems, the *cFileName* member will contain the real name and the *cAlternateFileName* member will contain the synthesized name. For example, the filename "Hello Mom and Dad" can have a truncated, or alternate, name "HELLOM~1."

If FindFirstFile has successfully found a matching file, you can call FindNextFile to search for the next file matching the file specification originally passed to FindFirstFile:

```
BOOL FindNextFile(HANDLE hFindFile, LPWIN32_FIND_DATA lpffd);
```

The *hFindFile* parameter is the handle that was returned by the earlier call to FindFirstFile, and the *lpffd* parameter is, again, the address to a WIN32_FIND_DATA structure—not necessarily the same structure you used in the earlier call to FindFirstFile, although it can be if you'd like.

If FindNextFile is successful, it returns TRUE and fills the WIN32_FIND_DATA structure. If the function can't find a match, it returns FALSE.

When you have finished finding files, you must close the handle returned by FindFirstFile by calling FindClose:

```
BOOL FindClose(HANDLE hFindFile);
```

This is one of the very few times in Win32 that you don't call CloseHandle to close a handle. You must call FindClose instead so that some additional bookkeeping information maintained by the system will also be freed.

The FindFirstFile and FindNextFile functions just cycle through all the files (and subdirectories) within a single directory you've specified. If you want to walk up and down the entire directory hierarchy, you will need to write a recursive function.

The Directory Walker Sample Application

The DirWalk (DIRWALK.EXE) application, listed in Figure 9-3 beginning on page 525, demonstrates use of the FindFirstFile, FindNextFile, FindClose, GetCurrentDirectory, and SetCurrentDirectory functions to walk the entire directory tree of a disk volume. When the user executes DIRWALK.EXE, it starts at the root directory of the current drive, walks the whole tree, and displays a dialog box containing a list box that shows the entire drive's directory tree. Here is what the Directory Walker dialog box looks like when DirWalk is run on my machines:

When the dialog box receives its WM_INITDIALOG message, it performs some simple initialization and calls the DirWalk function located in DIRWALK.C:

```
void DirWalk (HWND hwndTreeLB, LPCTSTR pszRootPath);
```

The *hwndTreeLB* parameter is the handle of the list box window that the function should fill, and the *pszRootPath* is the starting directory. The call to DirWalk passes ''\\'' in the *pszRootPath* parameter so that the directory walk starts at the root of the current drive. It would certainly be possible to specify a different directory here so that the tree would be walked from the specified directory downward.

When the DirWalk function is called, it performs some initialization before calling the DirWalkRecurse function. This recursive function will be called by itself over and over as different levels of the drive's directory tree are walked. Before the directory tree can be walked, DirWalk performs some initialization by saving the current directory in a temporary variable and then setting the current directory to the path specified in the *pszRootPath* parameter.

Then the thread is ready to start walking by calling DirWalkRecurse. This function starts by adding the current directory to the list box. Then it calls FindFirstFile to get the name of the first file in the current directory. If a file is found, its name is displayed and FindNextFile is called in order to get the next file in the directory.

After all the files have been displayed, DirWalkRecurse tests the *fRecurse* member of the DIRWALKDATA structure to see if it should recurse into subdirectories. In the DirWalk sample application, this member will always be TRUE. I added the *fRecurse* member because these functions are used in the FILECHNG.EXE application presented in the next section.

When DirWalkRecurse needs to go into a subdirectory, it calls FindFirstChildDir. This little function that also appears in DIRWALK.C is a simple wrapper around the FindFirstFile function. FindFirstChildDir filters out all the filenames in a directory and returns only subdirectory names. The helper function FindNextChildDir is just a wrapper around the FindNextFile function that also filters out filenames.

As each subdirectory is found, DirWalkRecurse moves into the new subdirectory and calls itself so that the new subtree can be walked. After the subtree is walked, DirWalkRecurse calls:

```
SetCurrentDirectory("..");
```

so that the current directory is restored to what it was before making the recursive call to DirWalkRecurse.

Before any tree walking can start, DirWalk creates a local DIR-WALKDATA structure, called *DW*, on the stack. This structure contains information used by DirWalkRecurse.

When I first wrote this program, I had all the members inside the DIRWALKDATA structure as local variables declared inside DirWalk-Recurse. Then each time DirWalkRecurse called itself, another set of these variables would be created on the stack. As I soon discovered, this could eat up quite a bit of stack space if a directory tree goes down pretty deep, so I looked for a more efficient method of storing these variables.

The next method I tried was to create the DIRWALKDATA members as static variables. That way, I thought, there would be only one set of them and they wouldn't be allocated on the stack at all. This sounded pretty good to me except that it meant that the DirWalk and Dir-WalkRecurse functions were no longer multithread safe. If two threads wanted to walk the tree simultaneously, they would be sharing the same static local variables—with undesirable effects. This realization led me to modify the program again.

I made all of the variables static thread-local storage variables by putting __*declspec(thread)* in front of each one. This, I thought, would force a new set of the static variables for every thread, created in the process. The only thing I didn't like about this approach was that a set of these variables would be created for every thread, even for those threads that never called DirWalk or DirWalkRecurse.

This problem could be fixed by using dynamic thread-local storage. This way, I reasoned, I'd be allocating only a TLS index, which isn't a memory allocation anyway. Then when DirWalk was called, it would call HeapAlloc to allocate a DIRWALKDATA structure and store the address of this structure using TlsSetValue. This dynamic approach solved the problem of allocating additional memory for threads that never called DirWalk, and as a bonus, the memory containing the data structure would be around only while the DirWalk function was called. Just before DirWalk returned, it would free the buffer.

After I got to this point, the best solution finally hit me: Create a data structure on the stack for the thread and provide just the pointer to the structure with each recursive call. This solution is what you see in the sample program's code. This method creates the variables on the stack, memory is allocated for them only when it is needed, and only a 4-byte pointer is passed on the stack with each recursive call. This seems to me to be the best compromise among all of the possibilities.

In spite of all this effort, it turns out that DirWalk and Dir-WalkRecurse are still not multithread safe. Can you guess why? Because of the calls to SetCurrentDirectory. You should think of the current directory as being stored in a global variable for a process. If you change the current directory in one thread, you are changing it for all threads in the process. To make DirWalk and DirWalkRecurse multithread safe, you would have to get rid of the calls to SetCurrentDirectory. You could get rid of the calls to SetCurrentDirectory by managing the walked path in a string variable and by calling FindFirstDir using a full path instead of using paths relative to the current directory. Since I also wanted to demonstrate the use of the GetCurrentDirectory and SetCurrentDirectory functions, I leave this last modification of the program as an exercise for you.

DirWalk.ico

DIRWALK.C
```
/*****************************************************************
Module name: DirWalk.C
Notices: Copyright (c) 1993 Jeffrey Richter
*****************************************************************/

#include <windows.h>
#include <windowsx.h>
#include <tchar.h>
#include <stdlib.h>
#include <stdio.h>      // for sprintf
#include <string.h>
#include "DirWalk.H"

#define ARRAY_SIZE(A)  (sizeof(A) / sizeof((A)[0]))

void DirWalk (HWND hwndTreeLB, LPCTSTR pszRootPath,
    BOOL fRecurse);

/////////////////////////////////////////////////////////////////
```

Figure 9-3.   *(continued)*

The DirWalk application.

Figure 9-3. *continued*

```
BOOL Dlg_OnInitDialog (HWND hwnd, HWND hwndFocus,
  LPARAM lParam) {

  RECT rc;

  // Associate an icon with the dialog box.
  SetClassLong(hwnd, GCL_HICON, (LONG)
    LoadIcon((HINSTANCE) GetWindowLong(hwnd, GWL_HINSTANCE),
    __TEXT("DirWalk")));

  DirWalk(GetDlgItem(hwnd, ID_TREE), __TEXT("\\"), TRUE);

  GetClientRect(hwnd, &rc);
  SetWindowPos(GetDlgItem(hwnd, ID_TREE), NULL,
    0, 0, rc.right, rc.bottom, SWP_NOZORDER);

  return(TRUE);
}


//////////////////////////////////////////////////////////////


void Dlg_OnSize (HWND hwnd, UINT state, int cx, int cy) {
  SetWindowPos(GetDlgItem(hwnd, ID_TREE), NULL, 0, 0,
    cx, cy, SWP_NOZORDER);
}


//////////////////////////////////////////////////////////////


void Dlg_OnCommand (HWND hwnd, int id, HWND hwndCtl,
  UINT codeNotify) {

  switch (id) {
    case IDCANCEL:
      EndDialog(hwnd, id);
      break;

    case IDOK:
      // Call the recursive routine to walk the tree.
      DirWalk(GetDlgItem(hwnd, ID_TREE), __TEXT("\\"),
        TRUE);
      break;
  }
}
```

(continued)

Figure 9-3. *continued*

```
/////////////////////////////////////////////////////////////////

BOOL IsChildDir (WIN32_FIND_DATA *lpFindData) {

   return(
      (lpFindData->dwFileAttributes &
      FILE_ATTRIBUTE_DIRECTORY) &&
      (lpFindData->cFileName[0] != __TEXT('.')));
}


/////////////////////////////////////////////////////////////////

BOOL FindNextChildDir (HANDLE hFindFile,
   WIN32_FIND_DATA *lpFindData) {

   BOOL fFound = FALSE;

   do {
      fFound = FindNextFile(hFindFile, lpFindData);
   } while (fFound && !IsChildDir(lpFindData));

   return(fFound);
}


/////////////////////////////////////////////////////////////////

HANDLE FindFirstChildDir (LPTSTR szPath,
   WIN32_FIND_DATA *lpFindData) {

   BOOL fFound;
   HANDLE hFindFile = FindFirstFile(szPath, lpFindData);

   if (hFindFile != INVALID_HANDLE_VALUE) {
      fFound = IsChildDir(lpFindData);

      if (!fFound)
         fFound = FindNextChildDir(hFindFile, lpFindData);

      if (!fFound) {
         FindClose(hFindFile);
         hFindFile = INVALID_HANDLE_VALUE;
      }
```

(continued)

Figure 9-3.   *continued*

```
    }
    return(hFindFile);
}


/////////////////////////////////////////////////////////////////////

// To minimize stack use, one instance of the DIRWALKDATA
// structure is created as a local var in DirWalk() and a
// pointer to it is passed to DirWalkRecurse.

// Data used by DirWalkRecurse
typedef struct {
    HWND    hwndTreeLB;    // Handle to the output list box.
    int     nDepth;        // Nesting depth.
    BOOL    fRecurse;      // Set to TRUE to list subdirectories.
    TCHAR   szBuf[500];    // Output formatting buffer.
    int     nIndent;       // Indentation character count.
    BOOL    fOk;           // Loop control flag.
    BOOL    fIsDir;        // Loop control flag.
    WIN32_FIND_DATA FindData; // File information.
} DIRWALKDATA, *LPDIRWALKDATA;

// Walk the directory structure and fill a list box with
// filenames. If pDW->fRecurse is set, list any child
// directories by recursively calling DirWalkRecurse.
void DirWalkRecurse (LPDIRWALKDATA pDW) {
    HANDLE hFind;

    pDW->nDepth++;

    pDW->nIndent = 3 * pDW->nDepth;
    _stprintf(pDW->szBuf, __TEXT("%*s"), pDW->nIndent,
      __TEXT(""));
    }
    pDW->szBuf[pDW->iBuf] = 0;

    GetCurrentDirectory(ARRAY_SIZE(pDW->szBuf) - pDW->nIndent,
      &pDW->szBuf[pDW->nIndent]);
    ListBox_AddString(pDW->hwndTreeLB, pDW->szBuf);

    hFind = FindFirstFile(__TEXT("*.*"), &pDW->FindData);
    pDW->fOk = (hFind != INVALID_HANDLE_VALUE);
```

(continued)

Figure 9-3. *continued*

```
while (pDW->fOk) {
   pDW->fIsDir = pDW->FindData.dwFileAttributes &
      FILE_ATTRIBUTE_DIRECTORY;
   if (!pDW->fIsDir ||
      (!pDW->fRecurse && IsChildDir(&pDW->FindData))) {

      _stprintf(pDW->szBuf,
         pDW->fIsDir ? __TEXT("%*s[%s]") : __TEXT("%*s%s"),
         pDW->nIndent, __TEXT(""),
         pDW->FindData.cFileName);

      ListBox_AddString(pDW->hwndTreeLB, pDW->szBuf);
   }
   pDW->fOk = FindNextFile(hFind, &pDW->FindData);
}
if (hFind != INVALID_HANDLE_VALUE)
   FindClose(hFind);

if (pDW->fRecurse) {
   // Get the first child directory.
   hFind = FindFirstChildDir(
      __TEXT("*.*"), &pDW->FindData);
   pDW->fOk = (hFind != INVALID_HANDLE_VALUE);
   while (pDW->fOk) {
      // Change into the child directory.
      SetCurrentDirectory(pDW->FindData.cFileName);

      // Perform the recursive walk into the
      // child directory.
      // Remember that some members of pWD will be
      // overwritten by this call.

      DirWalkRecurse(pDW);

      // Change back to the child's parent directory.
      SetCurrentDirectory(__TEXT(".."));

      pDW->fOk = FindNextChildDir(hFind, &pDW->FindData);
   }

   if (hFind != INVALID_HANDLE_VALUE)
      FindClose(hFind);
}

pDW->nDepth--;
}
```

(continued)

Figure 9-3. *continued*

```
//////////////////////////////////////////////////////////////

// Walk the directory structure and fill a list box with
// filenames. This function sets up a call to
// DirWalkRecurse, which does the real work.

void DirWalk (HWND hwndTreeLB, LPCTSTR pszRootPath,
   BOOL fRecurse) {

   TCHAR szCurrDir[_MAX_DIR];
   DIRWALKDATA DW;

   // Clear out the list box.
   ListBox_ResetContent(hwndTreeLB);

   // Save the current dir so that it can be restored later.
   GetCurrentDirectory(ARRAY_SIZE(szCurrDir), szCurrDir);

   // Set the current dir to where we want to start walking.
   SetCurrentDirectory(pszRootPath);

   // nDepth is used to control indenting. -1 will cause
   // the first level to display flush left.
   DW.nDepth = -1;

   DW.hwndTreeLB = hwndTreeLB;
   DW.fRecurse = fRecurse;

   // Call the recursive function to walk the subdir.
   DirWalkRecurse(&DW);

   // Restore the current directory to what it was before the
   // function was called.
   SetCurrentDirectory(szCurrDir);
}

//////////////////////////////////////////////////////////////

BOOL CALLBACK Dlg_Proc (HWND hDlg, UINT uMsg,
   WPARAM wParam, LPARAM lParam) {

   BOOL fProcessed = TRUE;

   switch (uMsg) {
      HANDLE_MSG(hDlg, WM_INITDIALOG, Dlg_OnInitDialog);
      HANDLE_MSG(hDlg, WM_SIZE,       Dlg_OnSize);
      HANDLE_MSG(hDlg, WM_COMMAND,    Dlg_OnCommand);
```

(continued)

Figure 9-3. *continued*

```
    default:
        fProcessed = FALSE;
        break;
    }
    return(fProcessed);
}


///////////////////////////////////////////////////////////////

int APIENTRY WinMain (HINSTANCE hInstance,
    HINSTANCE hPrevInstance, LPSTR lpszCmdLine, int nCmdShow) {

    DialogBox(hInstance, MAKEINTRESOURCE(DLG_DIRWALK),
        NULL, Dlg_Proc);
    return(0);
}


///////////////////////// End Of File /////////////////////////
```

DIRWALK.H

```
/*************************************************************
Module name: DirWalk.H
Notices: Copyright (c) 1993 Jeffrey Richter
*************************************************************/

// Dialog and control IDs.
#define DLG_DIRWALK      1
#define ID_TREE          100


///////////////////////// End Of File /////////////////////////
```

DIRWALK.RC

```
/*************************************************************
Module name: DirWalk.RC
Notices: Copyright (c) 1993 Jeffrey Richter
*************************************************************/

#include <windows.h>
#include "DirWalk.h"
```

(continued)

Figure 9-3. *continued*

```
DirWalk  ICON  DISCARDABLE DirWalk.Ico

DLG_DIRWALK DIALOG 10, 18, 250, 250
STYLE WS_THICKFRAME | WS_POPUP | WS_VISIBLE | WS_CAPTION |
   WS_SYSMENU | WS_MAXIMIZEBOX | WS_MINIMIZEBOX
CAPTION "Directory Walker"
BEGIN
   CONTROL "", ID_TREE, "LISTBOX", LBS_NOINTEGRALHEIGHT |
      WS_CHILD | WS_VISIBLE | WS_HSCROLL | WS_VSCROLL |
      WS_GROUP | WS_TABSTOP, 0, 0, 0, 0
END


////////////////////// End Of File //////////////////////////
```

File System Change Notifications

There are so many applications that would like to be notified when something in the file system has been altered. Wouldn't it be nice if the File Manager updated its windows automatically to reflect any changes made to the file system? Let's say, for example, that you are looking at the contents of C:\ in one of the File Manager's windows and that from the command prompt, you copy a file from a floppy to C:\. It would be nice if the File Manager would then instantly refresh its window.

This has been a feature long wished for in 16-bit Windows, and actually, 16-bit Windows does have a function, FileCDR, that an application can call in order to be notified of changes in the file system. The problems with FileCDR, though, are that it is an undocumented function and that it allows only one application at a time to get file system notifications. If another application calls the FileCDR function, the first application will stop getting notifications.

The ability to have an application be notified of file system changes dynamically was requested by so many people that Microsoft built direct support for this capability right into Windows NT. Here is how it works:

First, your application must tell the system that it's interested in being notified of file system changes by calling FindFirstChangeNotification:

```
HANDLE FindFirstChangeNotification(LPTSTR lpszPath,
   BOOL fWatchSubTree, DWORD fdwFilter);
```

The *lpszPath* parameter specifies the root of the directory tree that you want to monitor. You can specify the root directory of a drive or any subdirectory. If you specify a subdirectory, you won't be notified of events occurring in directories above the specified subdirectory. If you want to monitor directory trees on different drives, you must make multiple calls to FindFirstChangeNotification—one for each drive that you want to monitor.

The second parameter, *fWatchSubTree*, tells the system whether you want to watch events that occur in directories beneath the *lpszPath* directory. If you pass FALSE, you will be notified only of events that occur in the single directory you've specified.

In the *fdwFilter* parameter you tell the system what type of file changes you're interested in. You can combine the *fdwFilter* flags by *OR*ing them. Here's the list of valid flags and their meanings:

Flag	Meaning
FILE_NOTIFY_CHANGE_FILE_NAME	A file has been created, renamed, or deleted.
FILE_NOTIFY_CHANGE_DIR_NAME	A directory has been created, renamed, or deleted.
FILE_NOTIFY_CHANGE_ATTRIBUTES	A file's attribute has changed.
FILE_NOTIFY_CHANGE_SIZE	A file's size has changed.
FILE_NOTIFY_CHANGE_LAST_WRITE	A file's last write time has changed.
FILE_NOTIFY_CHANGE_SECURITY	A security-descriptor for a directory or file has been changed.

Note that the system frequently buffers file changes. A file's size doesn't change, for example, until buffered information is flushed to the disk. You will be notified of the change in the file size only when the system flushes the data to disk, not when an application actually changes the data.

If FindFirstChangeNotification is successful, it returns a handle your thread can use with the various synchronization functions such as WaitForSingleObject and WaitForMultipleObjects. If you pass an invalid parameter, such as a nonexistent path, INVALID_HANDLE_VALUE is returned.

Personally, I think it would have made more sense to call the Find-FirstChangeNotification function something like CreateFileChange-Notification since the function doesn't really find a file change at all; it simply creates a file change notification object and returns its handle.

Once you have the notification object's handle, you can use it in calls to the WaitForSingleObject and WaitForMultipleObjects functions. Whenever a change occurs in the file system that meets the criteria you specified in the call to FindFirstChangeNotification, the object will become signaled. You can think of a file change notification object as a manual-reset event with some additional logic built into it—when a change occurs in the file system, the event is signaled. When your call to WaitForSingleObject or WaitForMultipleObjects returns, you know that you need to walk the drive's directory tree (starting from *lpszPath*) so that you can refresh the directory and file information in your application.

Note that the system accumulates many file changes and notifies you of them all at once. For example, if the user entered this command on the command line:

```
rmdir . /s
```

to erase all of the files in the current directory and all its subdirectories, the command shell's thread might delete several files before the system signaled the file change notification object allowing your thread to resume execution. The handle won't be signaled once for every single file change. This improves performance greatly.

When the file change notification object is signaled, your thread wakes up and you can perform whatever operations you want to. When you have finished, you must call FindNextChangeNotification:

```
BOOL FindNextChangeNotification(HANDLE hChange);
```

The FindNextChangeNotification function resets the file change notification object to its not-signaled state—similar to calling ResetEvent. However, this is where file change notification objects differ from manual-reset events. While your thread was walking the drive's directory tree, the command shell's thread might have preempted your thread and been able to continue deleting more files and directories. The call to FindNextChangeNotification checks to see whether this has happened, and if more file change events have occurred since the object became signaled, the object is not reset to the not-signaled state and remains signaled.

That way, if your thread waits for the object again, the wait will be satisfied immediately and you will again walk the drive's directory tree. You should always wait for a file change notification object after every call to FindNextChangeNotification. Without this wait, your thread might miss a file change event.

As usual, when you no longer want file change notifications, you must close the object. However, you don't call the familiar CloseHandle function to close the notification object. Instead, you must call:

```
BOOL FindCloseChangeNotification(HANDLE hChange);
```

The FindCloseChangeNotification function differs from CloseHandle in that it also has the system delete any record of file changes that have been made since the file change notification object was last signaled.

The File Change Sample Application

The FileChng (FILECHNG.EXE) application, listed in Figure 9-4 beginning on page 537, demonstrates use of the three change notification functions to monitor changes made to a drive's directory tree. When the user executes FileChng, the FileChangeNotification dialog box appears:

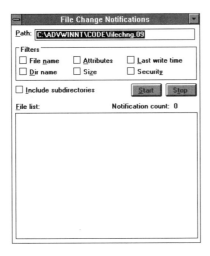

Before the program starts monitoring file changes, you must tell it what you are interested in monitoring by setting all of the parameters in the *Filters* group box. When you press the *Start* button, the program retrieves all of the parameters from the dialog box controls and calls FindFirstChangeNotification so that the system will start to notify the program of any file system changes. The program also resets the *Notification count* value to 0 (zero) and performs an initial directory tree walk starting at the path you've specified, filling the list box with a list of the directories and files in the tree.

The program then sits idle waiting for the system to signal the file change notification object. When a change occurs in the file system that matches your filter criteria, the system signals the notification object causing FileChng's thread to wake up, increment the *Notification count* value, and rewalk the directory tree. After each walk, the thread calls FindNextChangeNotification and waits for the object again. You can stop monitoring changes to the file system by pressing the *Stop* button or by changing some of the notification criteria values.

The program code is pretty self-explanatory, but I do want to draw your attention to the WinMain function. I've structured this function pretty differently from WinMain in the other sample programs in this book. I wanted to write the FileChange program so that it had only a single thread of execution. To do this, I needed some method whereby my thread could suspend itself until either a window message entered the thread's queues or the file change notification object became signaled. I racked my brain for a while and then remembered the MsgWaitFor-MultipleObjects function.

This function was just what the doctor ordered. It's just like WaitFor-MultipleObjects except that it also checks for window messages. Using this function also meant that I could no longer create a modal dialog box for this program, though, because modal dialog boxes call GetMessage for their message processing and there would be no way for me to wait for the file change notification object. Since I had to get more involved with the message loop for the program, I had to use CreateDialog instead of DialogBox in order to create a modeless dialog box. Then I had to code the message loop myself.

Here's a little more detail on what the program does. First it calls CreateDialog to create a modeless dialog box that will be the user interface for the program. Next the thread starts executing the message loop, which repeatedly checks the *fQuit* variable to find out when it should terminate. The *fQuit* variable is initialized to FALSE when the program starts and is set to TRUE when a WM_QUIT message is pulled from the thread's queue.

Once in the message loop, the thread checks whether the handle to the file change notification object is valid and stores the result in the *fWait4FileChanges* variable. The handle won't be valid if the user hasn't pressed the *Start* button yet. Then the program makes this call:

```
dwResult = MsgWaitForMultipleObjects(
    (fWait4FileChanges) ? 1 : 0,
    &s_hChange, FALSE, INFINITE, QS_ALLEVENTS);
```

If there is a valid handle to a file change notification object, the call to MsgWaitForMultipleObjects tells the system to wait for either this object to become signaled or for a message to enter one of the thread's message queues. If the handle is invalid, the thread will just wait until a message is available.

When the system awakens the thread, the thread checks to see what the reason is. If it has been awakened because of a file change, the *Notification count* value is incremented, the directory tree is rewalked, and FindNextChangeNotification is called. The thread then loops around to the top of the message loop and makes another call to MsgWaitFor-MultipleObjects.

If the thread has been awakened because of a window message, the message must now be retrieved from the queue by a call to PeekMessage specifying the PM_REMOVE flag. Next IsDialogMessage is called, passing the retrieved message. This call allows the user to navigate through the controls in the modeless dialog box by means of the keyboard. If the message isn't a navigational keyboard message, there is a check to see whether it is a WM_QUIT message. If it is, the *fQuit* variable is set to TRUE, causing the message loop to terminate before it begins its next iteration.

If the message isn't a navigational keyboard message and is also not a WM_QUIT message, TranslateMessage is called, followed by Dispatch-Message, just as they would be called in any normal message loop.

You'll notice that I call PeekMessage in a loop here—in order to give the user interface a higher priority than the processing for file change notifications.

FileChng.ico

FILECHNG.C
```
/****************************************************************
Module name: FileChng.C
Written by: Jim Harkins and Jeffrey Richter
Notices: Copyright (c) 1993 Jeffrey Richter
****************************************************************/
```

Figure 9-4.
(continued)
The FileChng application.

Figure 9-4. *continued*

```
#include <windows.h>
#include <windowsx.h>
#include <tchar.h>
#include <stdio.h>
#include <stdlib.h>
#include <string.h>
#include "FileChng.H"

#define ARRAY_SIZE(A)  (sizeof(A) / sizeof((A)[0]))

void DirWalk (HWND hwndTreeLB, LPCTSTR pszRootPath,
   BOOL fRecurse);

HANDLE g_hChange = INVALID_HANDLE_VALUE;
int    g_nCount = 0;

///////////////////////////////////////////////////////////////

void Dlg_ErrorBox (LPCTSTR pszSource) {
   TCHAR szBuf[100];   // Output formatting buffer.

   _stprintf(szBuf, __TEXT("%s reported error %lu"),
      pszSource, GetLastError());

   MessageBox(NULL, szBuf, __TEXT("File Change"), MB_OK);
}

///////////////////////////////////////////////////////////////

DWORD Dlg_GetFilter (HWND hwnd) {
   DWORD fdwFilter = 0;

   if (IsDlgButtonChecked(hwnd, ID_FILENAME))
      fdwFilter |= FILE_NOTIFY_CHANGE_FILE_NAME;

   if (IsDlgButtonChecked(hwnd, ID_DIRNAME))
      fdwFilter |= FILE_NOTIFY_CHANGE_DIR_NAME;

   if (IsDlgButtonChecked(hwnd, ID_ATTRIBS))
      fdwFilter |= FILE_NOTIFY_CHANGE_ATTRIBUTES;

   if (IsDlgButtonChecked(hwnd, ID_SIZE))
      fdwFilter |= FILE_NOTIFY_CHANGE_SIZE;
```

(continued)

Figure 9-4.   *continued*

```
    if (IsDlgButtonChecked(hwnd, ID_LASTWRITE))
        fdwFilter |= FILE_NOTIFY_CHANGE_LAST_WRITE;

    if (IsDlgButtonChecked(hwnd, ID_SECURITY))
        fdwFilter |= FILE_NOTIFY_CHANGE_SECURITY;

    return(fdwFilter);
}

///////////////////////////////////////////////////////////////

// Validate the dialog box controls and configure a
// valid call to FindFirstChangeNotification:
// At least one filter flag must be set, and
// the path must be valid.
BOOL Dlg_Validate (HWND hwnd) {
    BOOL  fValid = FALSE;
    TCHAR szPath[_MAX_DIR];

    // Test whether at least one flag is set.
    if (0 != Dlg_GetFilter(hwnd)) {

        // Verify that the path exists.
        GetDlgItemText(hwnd, ID_PATH, szPath,
            ARRAY_SIZE(szPath));
        fValid = SetCurrentDirectory(szPath);
    }
    return(fValid);
}

///////////////////////////////////////////////////////////////

// Stop close change notification.
void Dlg_CloseChange (HWND hwnd) {
    BOOL fDisableFocus =
        (GetFocus() == GetDlgItem(hwnd, ID_STOP));

    EnableWindow(GetDlgItem(hwnd, ID_STOP), FALSE);

    if (Dlg_Validate(hwnd)) {
        EnableWindow(GetDlgItem(hwnd, ID_START), TRUE);
        if (fDisableFocus) {
            SetFocus(GetDlgItem(hwnd, ID_START));
        }
```

(continued)

Figure 9-4. *continued*

```
  } else {
    fDisableFocus = fDisableFocus ||
      (GetFocus() == GetDlgItem(hwnd, ID_START));

    EnableWindow(GetDlgItem(hwnd, ID_START), FALSE);
    if (fDisableFocus) {
      SetFocus(GetDlgItem(hwnd, ID_INCSUBDIRS));
    }
  }
}

if (INVALID_HANDLE_VALUE != g_hChange) {
  if (!FindCloseChangeNotification(g_hChange)) {
    Dlg_ErrorBox(__TEXT("FindCloseChangeNotification"));
  }
  g_hChange = INVALID_HANDLE_VALUE;
}
}

///////////////////////////////////////////////////////////////

// Start close change notification.
void Dlg_OpenChange (HWND hwnd) {
  TCHAR szPath[_MAX_DIR];
  BOOL fDisableFocus =
    (GetFocus() == GetDlgItem(hwnd, ID_START));

  Dlg_CloseChange(hwnd);

  g_nCount = 0;
  SetDlgItemInt(hwnd, ID_NCOUNT, g_nCount, FALSE);

  GetDlgItemText(hwnd, ID_PATH, szPath, ARRAY_SIZE(szPath));

  g_hChange = FindFirstChangeNotification(szPath,
    IsDlgButtonChecked(hwnd, ID_INCSUBDIRS),
    Dlg_GetFilter(hwnd));

  if (INVALID_HANDLE_VALUE == g_hChange) {
    Dlg_ErrorBox(__TEXT("FindFirstChangeNotification"));
    g_hChange = INVALID_HANDLE_VALUE;
  } else {
    EnableWindow(GetDlgItem(hwnd, ID_START), FALSE);
    EnableWindow(GetDlgItem(hwnd, ID_STOP), TRUE);
```

(continued)

Figure 9-4. *continued*

```
      if (fDisableFocus) {
         SetFocus(GetDlgItem(hwnd, ID_STOP));
      }
      DirWalk(GetDlgItem(hwnd, ID_TREE), szPath,
         IsDlgButtonChecked(hwnd, ID_INCSUBDIRS));
   }
}

///////////////////////////////////////////////////////////////

BOOL Dlg_OnInitDialog (HWND hwnd, HWND hwndFocus,
   LPARAM lParam) {
   TCHAR szPath[_MAX_DIR];

   // Associate an icon with the dialog box.
   SetClassLong(hwnd, GCL_HICON, (LONG)
      LoadIcon((HINSTANCE) GetWindowLong(hwnd, GWL_HINSTANCE),
      __TEXT("FileChng")));

   // Path defaults to the current path.
   GetCurrentDirectory(ARRAY_SIZE(szPath), szPath);
   SetDlgItemText(hwnd, ID_PATH, szPath);

   Dlg_CloseChange(hwnd);

   return(TRUE);
}

///////////////////////////////////////////////////////////////

void Dlg_OnCommand (HWND hwnd, int id, HWND hwndCtl,
   UINT codeNotify) {

   switch (id) {
      case ID_PATH:
         // If change notification is started and
         // the user updates the path,
         // stop notifications.
         if (EN_CHANGE == codeNotify) {
            Dlg_CloseChange(hwnd);
         }
         break;
```

(continued)

Figure 9-4. *continued*

```
        case ID_INCSUBDIRS:
        case ID_FILENAME:
        case ID_DIRNAME:
        case ID_ATTRIBS:
        case ID_SIZE:
        case ID_LASTWRITE:
        case ID_SECURITY:
        case ID_STOP:
            Dlg_CloseChange(hwnd);
            break;

        case ID_START:
            Dlg_OpenChange(hwnd);
            break;

        case IDCANCEL:
            Dlg_CloseChange(hwnd);
            PostQuitMessage(0);
            break;
    }
}


///////////////////////////////////////////////////////////////

BOOL CALLBACK Dlg_Proc (HWND hDlg, UINT uMsg, WPARAM wParam,
    LPARAM lParam) {

    BOOL fProcessed = TRUE;

    switch (uMsg) {
        HANDLE_MSG(hDlg, WM_INITDIALOG, Dlg_OnInitDialog);
        HANDLE_MSG(hDlg, WM_COMMAND, Dlg_OnCommand);

        default:
            fProcessed = FALSE;
            break;
    }
    return(fProcessed);
}

///////////////////////////////////////////////////////////////
```

(continued)

Figure 9-4. *continued*

```
int APIENTRY WinMain (HINSTANCE hInstance,
   HINSTANCE hPrevInstance, LPSTR lpszCmdLine, int nCmdShow) {

   HWND  hwnd;
   MSG   msg;
   DWORD dwResult;
   BOOL  fQuit = FALSE, fWait4FileChanges;
   TCHAR szPath[_MAX_DIR];

   // Create a modeless dialog box instead of a modal
   // dialog box because we need to have more control of
   // the message loop processing.
   hwnd = CreateDialog(hInstance,
      MAKEINTRESOURCE(DLG_FILECHNG), NULL, Dlg_Proc);

   // Continue to loop until a WM_QUIT
   // message comes out of the queue.
   while (!fQuit) {

      // Do we have a valid file change notification handle?
      fWait4FileChanges = (INVALID_HANDLE_VALUE != g_hChange);

      // If we do, wait until a file change occurs OR until
      // a message shows up in our queue,
      dwResult = MsgWaitForMultipleObjects(
         (fWait4FileChanges) ? 1 : 0,
         &g_hChange, FALSE, INFINITE, QS_ALLEVENTS);

      if (fWait4FileChanges && (WAIT_OBJECT_0 == dwResult)) {
         // We awoke because of a file change notification.
         // Let's update the list box.

         // Increment the counter indicating the number
         // of notifications we have received.
         SetDlgItemInt(hwnd, ID_NCOUNT, ++g_nCount, FALSE);

         // Get the root path and fill the list box with the
         // list of files in the path and the root
         // directory's subdirectories
         // if the subdirectories check box is checked.
         GetDlgItemText(hwnd, ID_PATH, szPath,
            ARRAY_SIZE(szPath));
         DirWalk(GetDlgItem(hwnd, ID_TREE), szPath,
            IsDlgButtonChecked(hwnd, ID_INCSUBDIRS));
```

(continued)

Figure 9-4. *continued*

```
            // Tell the system that we processed the
            // notification.
            FindNextChangeNotification(g_hChange);
        } else {

            // We awoke because there is at least one message in
            // the queue. Let's dispatch all the queued messages.
            while (PeekMessage(&msg, NULL, 0, 0, PM_REMOVE)) {

                // Call IsDialogMessage so that the keyboard can
                // be used to control focus in the dialog box.
                if (!IsDialogMessage(hwnd, &msg) ) {
                    if (msg.message == WM_QUIT) {
                        // If we have a WM_QUIT message,
                        // set the flag so that the
                        // loop terminates.
                        fQuit = TRUE;
                    } else {
                        // Not a WM_QUIT message. Translate it
                        // and dispatch it.
                        TranslateMessage(&msg);
                        DispatchMessage(&msg);
                    }
                } // if (!IsDialogMessage())
            } // while messages are still in the queue
        } // if file change notification OR message
    } // while (!fQuit)

    // The application is terminating.
    // Close the file notification object.
    Dlg_CloseChange(hwnd);

    // Destroy the modeless dialog box.
    DestroyWindow(hwnd);

    return(0);
}

///////////////////////////////////////////////////////////////

// The following functions are taken directly from DIRWALK.C.

BOOL IsChildDir (WIN32_FIND_DATA *lpFindData) {
```

(continued)

Figure 9-4.   *continued*

```
    return(
        (lpFindData->dwFileAttributes &
        FILE_ATTRIBUTE_DIRECTORY) &&
        (lpFindData->cFileName[0] != __TEXT('.')));
}


//////////////////////////////////////////////////////////////////

BOOL FindNextChildDir (HANDLE hFindFile,
    WIN32_FIND_DATA *lpFindData) {

    BOOL fFound = FALSE;

    do {
        fFound = FindNextFile(hFindFile, lpFindData);
    } while (fFound && !IsChildDir(lpFindData));

    return(fFound);
}

//////////////////////////////////////////////////////////////////

HANDLE FindFirstChildDir (LPTSTR szPath,
    WIN32_FIND_DATA *lpFindData) {

    BOOL fFound;
    HANDLE hFindFile = FindFirstFile(szPath, lpFindData);

    if (hFindFile != INVALID_HANDLE_VALUE) {
        fFound = IsChildDir(lpFindData);

        if (!fFound)
            fFound = FindNextChildDir(hFindFile, lpFindData);

        if (!fFound) {
            FindClose(hFindFile);
            hFindFile = INVALID_HANDLE_VALUE;
        }
    }
    return(hFindFile);
}

//////////////////////////////////////////////////////////////////
```

(continued)

545

Figure 9-4. *continued*

```
// To minimize stack use, one instance of the DIRWALKDATA
// structure is created as a local var in DirWalk() and a
// pointer to it is passed to DirWalkRecurse.

// Data used by DirWalkRecurse
typedef struct {
    HWND    hwndTreeLB;    // Handle to the output list box.
    int     nDepth;        // Nesting depth.
    BOOL    fRecurse;      // Set to TRUE to list subdirectories.
    TCHAR   szBuf[500];    // Output formatting buffer.
    int     nIndent;       // Indentation character count.
    BOOL    fOk;           // Loop control flag.
    BOOL    fIsDir;        // Loop control flag.
    WIN32_FIND_DATA FindData; // File information.
} DIRWALKDATA, *LPDIRWALKDATA;

// Walk the directory structure, and fill a list box with
// filenames. If pDW->fRecurse is set, list any child
// directories by recursively calling DirWalkRecurse.
void DirWalkRecurse (LPDIRWALKDATA pDW) {
    HANDLE hFind;

    pDW->nDepth++;

    pDW->nIndent = 3 * pDW->nDepth;
    _stprintf(pDW->szBuf, __TEXT("%*s"), pDW->nIndent,
        __TEXT(""));

    GetCurrentDirectory(ARRAY_SIZE(pDW->szBuf) - pDW->nIndent,
        &pDW->szBuf[pDW->nIndent]);
    ListBox_AddString(pDW->hwndTreeLB, pDW->szBuf);

    hFind = FindFirstFile(__TEXT("*.*"), &pDW->FindData);
    pDW->fOk = (hFind != INVALID_HANDLE_VALUE);
    while (pDW->fOk) {
        pDW->fIsDir = pDW->FindData.dwFileAttributes &
            FILE_ATTRIBUTE_DIRECTORY;
        if (!pDW->fIsDir ||
            (!pDW->fRecurse && IsChildDir(&pDW->FindData))) {

            _stprintf(pDW->szBuf,
                pDW->fIsDir ? __TEXT("%*s[%s]") : __TEXT("%*s%s"),
                pDW->nIndent, __TEXT(""),
                pDW->FindData.cFileName);
```

(continued)

Figure 9-4. *continued*

```
            ListBox_AddString(pDW->hwndTreeLB, pDW->szBuf);
        }
        pDW->fOk = FindNextFile(hFind, &pDW->FindData);
    }
    if (hFind != INVALID_HANDLE_VALUE)
        FindClose(hFind);

    if (pDW->fRecurse) {
        // Get the first child directory.
        hFind = FindFirstChildDir(
            __TEXT("*.*"), &pDW->FindData);
        pDW->fOk = (hFind != INVALID_HANDLE_VALUE);
        while (pDW->fOk) {
            // Change into the child directory.
            SetCurrentDirectory(pDW->FindData.cFileName);

            // Perform the recursive walk into the child
            // directory. Remember that some members of pWD
            // will be overwritten by this call.

            DirWalkRecurse(pDW);

            // Change back to the child's parent directory.
            SetCurrentDirectory(__TEXT(".."));

            pDW->fOk = FindNextChildDir(hFind, &pDW->FindData);
        }

        if (hFind != INVALID_HANDLE_VALUE)
            FindClose(hFind);
    }

    pDW->nDepth--;
}

////////////////////////////////////////////////////////////////

// Walk the directory structure, and fill a list box with
// filenames. This function sets up a call to
// DirWalkRecurse, which does the real work.

void DirWalk (HWND hwndTreeLB, LPCTSTR pszRootPath,
    BOOL fRecurse) {
```

(continued)

Figure 9-4. *continued*

```
    TCHAR szCurrDir[_MAX_DIR];
    DIRWALKDATA DW;

    // Clear out the list box.
    ListBox_ResetContent(hwndTreeLB);

    // Save the current directory so that it can be
    // restored later.
    GetCurrentDirectory(ARRAY_SIZE(szCurrDir), szCurrDir);

    // Set the current directory to where we want to
    // start walking.
    SetCurrentDirectory(pszRootPath);

    // nDepth is used to control indenting. -1 will cause
    // the first level to display flush left.
    DW.nDepth = -1;

    DW.hwndTreeLB = hwndTreeLB;
    DW.fRecurse = fRecurse;

    // Call the recursive function to walk the subdirectories.
    DirWalkRecurse(&DW);

    // Restore the current directory to what it was before the
    // function was called.
    SetCurrentDirectory(szCurrDir);
}

//////////////////////// End Of File ////////////////////////
```

FILECHNG.H

```
/**********************************************************
Module name: FileChng.H by Jim Harkins
Notices: Copyright (c) 1993 Jeffrey Richter
**********************************************************/

// Dialog and control IDs.
#define DLG_FILECHNG              1

#define ID_PATH                 100
#define ID_INCSUBDIRS           101
#define ID_NCOUNT               102
```

(continued)

Figure 9-4. *continued*

```
#define ID_FILENAME              103
#define ID_DIRNAME               104
#define ID_ATTRIBS               105
#define ID_SIZE                  106
#define ID_LASTWRITE             107
#define ID_SECURITY              108
#define ID_START                 109
#define ID_STOP                  110
#define ID_TREE                  111
#define ID_COPY                  112


///////////////////////// End Of File /////////////////////////
```

FILECHNG.RC

```
/************************************************************
Module name: FileChng.RC
Notices: Copyright (c) 1993 Jeffrey Richter
************************************************************/

#include <windows.h>
#include "FileChng.h"


FileChng  ICON  DISCARDABLE FileChng.Ico

DLG_FILECHNG DIALOG 6, 18, 195, 237
STYLE WS_OVERLAPPED | WS_VISIBLE | WS_CAPTION |
   WS_SYSMENU | WS_MINIMIZEBOX
CAPTION "File Change Notifications"
FONT 8, "Helv"
BEGIN
    LTEXT "&Path:", -1, 4, 4, 20, 12, WS_CHILD |
        WS_VISIBLE | WS_GROUP
    CONTROL "", ID_PATH, "EDIT", ES_LEFT |
        ES_AUTOHSCROLL | WS_CHILD | WS_VISIBLE |
        WS_BORDER | WS_TABSTOP, 24, 4, 166, 12
    CONTROL "&Include subdirectories", ID_INCSUBDIRS,
        "BUTTON", BS_AUTOCHECKBOX | WS_CHILD |
        WS_VISIBLE | WS_TABSTOP, 4, 64, 100, 12
    LTEXT "Notification count:", -1, 104, 84, 62, 9,
        SS_LEFT | SS_NOPREFIX | WS_CHILD | WS_VISIBLE | WS_GROUP
```

(continued)

Figure 9-4. *continued*

```
    LTEXT "0", ID_NCOUNT, 168, 84, 24, 8, SS_LEFT |
        SS_NOPREFIX | WS_CHILD | WS_VISIBLE | WS_GROUP
    CONTROL "Filters", -1, "button", BS_GROUPBOX |
        WS_CHILD | WS_VISIBLE, 4, 20, 188, 40
    CONTROL "File &name", ID_FILENAME, "BUTTON",
        BS_AUTOCHECKBOX | WS_CHILD | WS_VISIBLE |
        WS_TABSTOP, 8, 32, 48, 12
    CONTROL "&Dir name", ID_DIRNAME, "BUTTON",
        BS_AUTOCHECKBOX | WS_CHILD | WS_VISIBLE |
        WS_TABSTOP, 8, 44, 44, 12
    CONTROL "&Attributes", ID_ATTRIBS, "BUTTON",
        BS_AUTOCHECKBOX | WS_CHILD | WS_VISIBLE |
        WS_TABSTOP, 64, 32, 48, 12
    CONTROL "Si&ze", ID_SIZE, "BUTTON",
        BS_AUTOCHECKBOX | WS_CHILD | WS_VISIBLE |
        WS_TABSTOP, 64, 44, 32, 12
    CONTROL "&Last write time", ID_LASTWRITE, "BUTTON",
        BS_AUTOCHECKBOX | WS_CHILD | WS_VISIBLE |
        WS_TABSTOP, 120, 32, 64, 12
    CONTROL "Securit&y", ID_SECURITY, "BUTTON",
        BS_AUTOCHECKBOX | WS_CHILD | WS_VISIBLE |
        WS_TABSTOP, 120, 44, 40, 12
    DEFPUSHBUTTON "&Start", ID_START, 124, 64, 32, 14,
        WS_CHILD | WS_VISIBLE | WS_TABSTOP
    PUSHBUTTON "S&top", ID_STOP, 160, 64, 32, 14, WS_CHILD |
        WS_VISIBLE | WS_TABSTOP
    CONTROL "&File list:", -1, "STATIC", WS_CHILD |
        WS_VISIBLE | WS_GROUP, 4, 84, 32, 8
    CONTROL "", ID_TREE, "LISTBOX", LBS_NOINTEGRALHEIGHT |
        WS_CHILD | WS_VISIBLE | WS_BORDER |
        WS_VSCROLL | WS_HSCROLL | WS_TABSTOP, 4, 96, 188, 136
END

//////////////////////////// End Of File ////////////////////////
```

C H A P T E R   T E N

STRUCTURED EXCEPTION HANDLING

Close your eyes for a moment and imagine writing your application as if your code could never fail. That's right—there's always enough memory, no one ever passes you an invalid pointer, and files you count on always exist. Wouldn't it be a pleasure to write your code if you could make these assumptions? Your code would be so much easier to write, to read, and to understand. No more fussing with *if* statements here and *gotos* there—in each function, you'd just write your code top to bottom.

If this kind of straightforward programming environment seems like a dream to you, you'll love structured exception handling (SEH). The virtue of structured exception handling is that as you write your code, you can focus on getting your task done. If something goes wrong at runtime, the system catches it and notifies you of the problem.

With SEH you can't totally ignore the possibility of an error in your code, but SEH does allow you to separate the main job from the error handling chores. This division makes it easy to concentrate on the problem at hand and focus on the possible errors later.

One of Microsoft's main motivations for implementing structured exception handling in Windows NT was to ease the development of the operating system itself and make Windows NT more robust. The developers of the Windows NT operating system and its various subsystems used SEH to make the system more robust. And having the ability to use SEH in our own applications can make our own applications more robust. In fact, structured exception handling is so useful and powerful that Microsoft has seen fit to make it one of the few Windows NT features they've ported backward to Win32s.

The burden of making SEH work falls more on the compiler than on Windows NT. Your C compiler must generate special code when exception blocks are entered into and exited from. The compiler must produce tables of support data structures to handle SEH and must supply callback functions that the operating system can call so that exception blocks can be traversed. The compiler is also responsible for preparing stack frames and other internal information that is used and referenced by the operating system. Adding SEH support to a compiler is not an easy task, and you shouldn't be surprised if your favorite compiler vendor delays shipment of its Windows NT compiler because of SEH implementation problems.

Nor should it surprise you that different compiler vendors implement structured exception handling in different ways. Fortunately, we can ignore compiler implementation details and just use the compiler's SEH capabilities.

Differences among compiler implementation of SEH could make it difficult to discuss in specific ways with specific code examples how you can take advantage of SEH. However, most compiler vendors follow Microsoft's suggested syntax. The syntax and keywords I use in the examples may differ from another compiler's but the main SEH concepts are the same. I'll use Microsoft's syntax throughout this chapter.

Structured exception handling really consists of two main capabilities: termination handling and exception handling. We'll turn our attention to termination handlers first.

NOTE: Don't confuse structured exception handling with C++ exception handling. C++ exception handling is a different form of exception handling, one that makes use of the new C++ keywords *catch* and *throw*. Microsoft has promised to add C++ exception handling to a future version of its compiler and that it will be implemented by taking advantage of the structured exception handling capabilities already present in the compiler.

Termination Handlers

A termination handler guarantees that a block of code (the termination handler) will be called and executed regardless of how another section of code (the guarded body) is exited. The syntax (using the Microsoft C/C++ compiler) for a termination handler is as follows:

```
__try {
   // Guarded body
   .
   .
   .
}
__finally {
   // Termination handler
   .
   .
   .
}
```

The new _ _ *try* and _ _*finally* keywords delineate the two sections of the termination handler. In the code above, the operating system and the compiler work together to guarantee that the _ _*finally* block code in the termination handler will be executed no matter how the guarded body is exited. Regardless of whether you put a *return*, a *goto*, or even a call to *longjump* in the guarded body, the termination handler will be called. Here's the flow of code execution:

```
// 1. Code before the try block executes.

__try {
   // 2. Code inside the try block executes.
}
__finally {
   // 3. Code inside the finally block executes.
}

// 4. Code after the finally block executes.
```

To appreciate the ramifications of using termination handlers, let's examine a more concrete coding example:

```
DWORD Funcenstein1 (void) {
   DWORD dwTemp;

   // 1. Do any processing here.
   .
   .
   .

   __try {
      // 2. Request permission to access
      //    protected data, and then use it.
      WaitForSingleObject(g_hSem, INFINITE);
```

(continued)

553

```
      g_dwProtectedData = 5;
      dwTemp = g_dwProtectedData;
   }
   __finally {
      // 3. Allow others to use protected data.
      ReleaseSemaphore(g_hSem, 1, NULL);
   }

   // 4. Continue processing.
   return(dwTemp);
}
```

In Funcenstein1, using the *try-finally* blocks really isn't doing very much for you. The code will wait for a semaphore, alter the contents of the protected data, save the new value in the local variable *dwTemp*, release the semaphore, and return the new value to the caller.

Now, let's modify the function a little and see what happens:

```
DWORD Funcenstein2 (void) {
   DWORD dwTemp;

   // 1. Do any processing here.
   .
   .
   .

   __try {
      // 2. Request permission to access
      //    protected data, and then use it.
      WaitForSingleObject(g_hSem, INFINITE);

      g_dwProtectedData = 5;
      dwTemp = g_dwProtectedData;

      // Return the new value.
      return(dwTemp);
   }
   __finally {
      // 3. Allow others to use protected data.
      ReleaseSemaphore(g_hSem, 1, NULL);
   }

   // Continue processing -- this code
   // will never execute in this version.
   dwTemp = 9;
   return(dwTemp);
}
```

In Funcenstein2, a *return* statement has been added to the end of the *try* block. This *return* statement tells the compiler that you want to exit the function and return the contents of the *dwTemp* variable, which now contains the value 5. However, if this *return* statement executed, the semaphore would not have been released by the thread—and no other thread would ever be able to gain control of the semaphore. As you can imagine, this kind of sequence can become a really big problem because threads waiting for the semaphore might never be able to resume execution.

However, by using the termination handler, you have avoided the premature execution of the *return* statement. When the *return* statement tries to exit the *try* block, the compiler makes sure that the code in the *finally* block executes first. The code inside the *finally* block is guaranteed to execute before the *return* statement in the *try* block is allowed to exit. In Funcenstein2, putting the semaphore-release code into a termination handler block ensures that the semaphore will always be released—there is no chance for the semaphore to accidentally continue to be owned by the thread, which would cause all other threads waiting for the semaphore to remain suspended.

After the code in the *finally* block executes, the function does, in fact, return. Any code appearing below the *finally* block doesn't execute because the function returns in the *try* block. Therefore, this function returns the value 5 and not the value 9.

You might be asking yourself how the compiler guarantees that the *finally* block executes before the *try* block can be exited. When the compiler examines your source code, it sees that you have coded a *return* statement inside a *try* block. Having seen this, the compiler generates code to save the return value (5 in our example) in a temporary variable created by the compiler. The compiler then generates code to execute the instructions contained inside the *finally* block—this is called a "local unwind." More specifically, a local unwind occurs when the system executes the contents of a *finally* block because of the premature exit of code in a *try* block. After the instructions inside the *finally* block execute, the value in the compiler's temporary variable is retrieved and returned from the function.

As you can see, the compiler must generate additional code and the system must perform additional work to pull this whole thing off. On different CPUs, the steps necessary to make termination handling work vary. The MIPS processor, for example, must execute several hundreds or even thousands of instructions in order to capture the *try* block's premature return and call the *finally* block. You should avoid writing code that causes premature exits from the *try* block of a termination handler because the performance of your application could be adversely impacted. Later in this section, I'll discuss the _ _*leave* keyword, which can help you avoid writing code that forces local unwinds.

Exception handling is designed to capture exceptions (in our example, the premature *return*)—the exceptions to the rule or the things you expect to happen infrequently. If a situation is the norm, it's much more efficient to check for the situation explicitly rather than rely on the structured exception handling capabilities of Windows NT and your compiler to trap common occurrences.

Note that when the flow of control naturally leaves the *try* block and enters the *finally* block (as shown in Funcenstein1), the overhead of entering the *finally* block is minimal. On the Intel CPU using the Microsoft compiler, a single machine instruction is executed as execution leaves the *try* block to enter the *finally* block—I doubt that you will even notice this overhead at all in your application. When the compiler has to generate additional code and the system has to perform additional work, as in Funcenstein2, the overhead is much more noticeable.

Now, let's modify the function again and take a look at what happens:

```
DWORD Funcenstein3 (void) {
    DWORD dwTemp;

    // 1. Do any processing here.
    .
    .
    .

    __try {
        // 2. Request permission to access
        //     protected data, and then use it.
        WaitForSingleObject(g_hSem, INFINITE);

        g_dwProtectedData = 5;
        dwTemp = g_dwProtectedData;

        // Try to jump over the finally block.
        goto ReturnValue;
    }
```

(continued)

```
   __finally {
      // 3. Allow others to use protected data.
      ReleaseSemaphore(g_hSem, 1, NULL);
   }

   dwTemp = 9;
   // 4. Continue processing.
   ReturnValue:
   return(dwTemp);
}
```

In Funcenstein3, when the compiler sees the *goto* statement in the *try* block, it generates a local unwind to execute the contents of the *finally* block first. However, this time, after the code in the *finally* block executes, the code after the ReturnValue label is executed because no return occurs in either the *try* or the *finally* block. This code causes a 5 to be returned from the function. Again, because you have interrupted the natural flow of control from the *try* block into the *finally* block, you may incur a high performance penalty depending on the CPU your application is running on.

Now let's look at another scenario in which termination handling really proves its value. Look at this function:

```
DWORD Funcfurter1 (void) {
   DWORD dwTemp;

   // 1. Do any processing here.
   .
   .
   .

   __try {
      // 2. Request permission to access
      //     protected data, and then use it.
      WaitForSingleObject(g_hSem, INFINITE);

      dwTemp = Funcinator(g_dwProtectedData);
   }
   __finally {
      // 3. Allow others to use protected data.
      ReleaseSemaphore(g_hSem, 1, NULL);
   }

   // 4. Continue processing.
   return(dwTemp);
}
```

Now imagine that the Funcinator function, called in the *try* block, contains a bug that causes an invalid memory access. In 16-bit Windows, this would present the user with the ever-popular Application Error dialog box. When the user dismissed the error dialog box, the application would be terminated. If the code were running under Windows NT with no *try-finally* block and the application were terminated because Funcinator generated an invalid memory access, the semaphore would still be owned and would never be released—any threads in other processes that were waiting for this semaphore would be suspended forever.

But placing the call to ReleaseSemaphore in a *finally* block guarantees that the semaphore gets released even if some other function causes a memory access violation.

If termination handlers are powerful enough to capture an application terminating because of an invalid memory access, we should have no trouble believing that they will also capture *setjump-longjump* combinations and, of course, simple statements such as *break* or *continue*.

Now for a test. Can you guess what the function below returns?

```
DWORD FuncaDoodleDoo (void) {
   DWORD dwTemp = 0;

   while (dwTemp < 10) {

      __try {
         if (dwTemp == 2)
            continue;

         if (dwTemp == 3)
            break;
      }
      __finally {
         dwTemp++;
      }

      dwTemp++;
   }

   dwTemp += 10;
   return(dwTemp);
}
```

Let's analyze what the function does step by step. First, *dwTemp* is set to 0 (zero). The code in the *try* block executes, but neither of the *if* statements evaluates to TRUE. Execution moves naturally to the code in the *finally* block, which increments *dwTemp* to 1. Then, the instruction after the *finally* block increments *dwTemp* again, making it 2.

When the loop iterates, *dwTemp* is 2 and the *continue* statement in the *try* block will execute. Without a termination handler to force execution of the *finally* block before exit from the *try* block, this would cause an immediate jump back up to the *while* loop, *dwTemp* would not be changed, and we would have started up an infinite loop. With a termination handler, the system notes that the *continue* statement causes the flow of control to exit the *try* block prematurely and moves execution to the *finally* block. In the *finally* block, *dwTemp* is incremented to 3. However, the code after the *finally* block doesn't execute because the flow of control moves back to *continue* and thus to the top of the loop.

Now, we are processing the loop's third iteration. This time, the first *if* statement evaluates to FALSE but the second *if* statement to TRUE. The system again catches our attempt to break out of the *try* block and executes the code in the *finally* block first. Now *dwTemp* is incremented to 4. Because a *break* statement was executed, control resumes after the loop. Thus, the code after the *finally* block and still inside the loop doesn't execute. The code below the loop adds 10 to *dwTemp* for a grand total of 14—the result of calling this function. It should go without saying that you should never actually write code like Funca-DoodleDoo. I placed the *continue* and *break* statements in the middle of the code only to demonstrate the operation of the termination handler.

Although a termination handler will catch most situations in which the *try* block would otherwise be exited prematurely, it can't cause the code in a *finally* block to be executed if the thread or process is terminated. A call to ExitThread or ExitProcess will immediately terminate the thread or process without executing any of the code in a *finally* block. Also, if your thread or process should die because some application called TerminateThread or TerminateProcess, the code in a *finally* block again won't execute. Some C Runtime functions, such as *abort*, which in turn call ExitProcess, again preclude the execution of *finally* blocks. You can't do anything to prevent another application from terminating one of your threads or processes, but you can prevent your own premature calls to ExitThread and ExitProcess.

Let's take a look at one more termination handling scenario.

```
DWORD Funcenstein4 (void) {
    DWORD dwTemp;
    // 1. Do any processing here.
        .
        .
        .

    __try {
        // 2. Request permission to access
        //    protected data, and then use it.
        WaitForSingleObject(g_hSem, INFINITE);

        g_dwProtectedData = 5;
        dwTemp = g_dwProtectedData;

        // Return the new value.
        return(dwTemp);
    }
    __finally {
        // 3. Allow others to use protected data.
        ReleaseSemaphore(g_hSem, 1, NULL);
        return(103);
    }

    // Continue processing -- this code will never execute.
    dwTemp = 9;
    return(dwTemp);
}
```

In Funcenstein4, the *try* block will execute and try to return the value of *dwTemp* (5) back to Funcenstein4's caller. As we noted in the discussion of Funcenstein2, trying to return prematurely from a *try* block causes the generation of code that puts the return value into a temporary variable created by the compiler. Then, the code inside the *finally* block is executed. Notice that in this variation on Funcenstein2 I have added a *return* statement to the *finally* block. Will Funcenstein4 return 5 to the caller, or 103? The answer is that 103 will be returned because the *return* statement in the *finally* block causes the value 103 to be stored in the same temporary variable in which the value 5 had been stored, overwriting the 5. When the *finally* block completes execution, the value now in the temporary variable (103) is returned from Funcenstein4 to its caller.

We've seen termination handlers do an effective job of rescuing execution from a premature exit of the *try* block and termination handlers produce an unwanted result as they prevented a premature exit of the *try* block. A good rule of thumb is to avoid any statements that would cause a premature exit of the *try* block part of a termination handler. In fact, it is always best to remove all *returns, continues, breaks, gotos,* and so on from inside both the *try* and the *finally* blocks of a termination handler and to put these statements outside the handler. Such a practice will cause the compiler to generate smaller code because it won't have to catch premature exits from the *try* block and faster code because it will have fewer instructions to execute in order to perform the local unwind. In addition, your code will be much easier to read and maintain.

We have pretty much covered the basic syntax and semantics of termination handlers. Now, let's look at how a termination handler could be used to simplify a more complicated programming problem. Let's look at a function that doesn't take advantage of termination handlers at all.

```
BOOL Funcarama1 (void) {
   HANDLE hFile = INVALID_HANDLE_VALUE;
   LPVOID lpBuf = NULL;
   DWORD dwNumBytesRead;
   BOOL fOk;

   hFile = CreateFile("SOMEDATA.DAT", GENERIC_READ,
      FILE_SHARE_READ, NULL, OPEN_EXISTING,
      0, NULL);
   if (hFile == INVALID_HANDLE_VALUE) {
      return(FALSE);
   }

   lpBuf = VirtualAlloc(NULL, 1024, MEM_COMMIT,
      PAGE_READWRITE);
   if (lpBuf == NULL) {
      CloseHandle(hFile);
      return(FALSE);
   }

   fOk = ReadFile(hFile, lpBuf, 1024,
      &dwNumBytesRead, NULL);
   if (!fOk || (dwNumBytesRead == 0)) {
      VirtualFree(lpBuf, MEM_RELEASE | MEM_DECOMMIT);
      CloseHandle(hFile);
      return(FALSE);
   }
```

(continued)

561

```
    // Do some calculation on the data.
    .
    .
    .

    // Clean up all the resources.
    VirtualFree(lpBuf, MEM_RELEASE | MEM_DECOMMIT);
    CloseHandle(hFile);
    return(TRUE);
}
```

All the error checking in Funcaramal makes the function difficult to read, which also makes the function difficult to understand, maintain, and modify. Of course, it's possible to rewrite Funcaramal so that it is a little cleaner and easier to understand:

```
BOOL Funcarama2 (void) {
    HANDLE hFile = INVALID_HANDLE_VALUE;
    LPVOID lpBuf = NULL;
    DWORD dwNumBytesRead;
    BOOL fOk, fSuccess = FALSE;

    hFile = CreateFile("SOMEDATA.DAT", GENERIC_READ,
        FILE_SHARE_READ, NULL, OPEN_EXISTING,
        0, NULL);

    if (hFile != INVALID_HANDLE_VALUE) {

        lpBuf = VirtualAlloc(NULL, 1024, MEM_COMMIT,
            PAGE_READWRITE);

        if (lpBuf != NULL) {

            fOk = ReadFile(hFile, lpBuf, 1024,
                &dwNumBytesRead, NULL);

            if (fOk && (dwNumBytesRead != 0)) {
                // Do some calculation on the data.
                .
                .
                .
                fSuccess = TRUE;
            }

        }

        VirtualFree(lpBuf, MEM_RELEASE | MEM_DECOMMIT);
```

(continued)

```
    }

    CloseHandle(hFile);
    return(fSuccess);
}
```

Funcarama2 is easier to understand, but it is still difficult to modify and maintain. Also, the indentation level gets to be pretty extreme as more conditional statements are added, and soon, with such a rewrite, you end up writing code on the far right of your screen and wrapping statements after every five characters! Let's rewrite the first version, Funcarama1, to take advantage of an SEH termination handler:

```
DWORD Funcarama3 (void) {
    HANDLE hFile = INVALID_HANDLE_VALUE;
    LPVOID lpBuf = NULL;

    __try {
        DWORD dwNumBytesRead;
        BOOL fOk;

        hFile = CreateFile("SOMEDATA.DAT", GENERIC_READ,
            FILE_SHARE_READ, NULL, OPEN_EXISTING,
            0, NULL);
        if (hFile == INVALID_HANDLE_VALUE) {
            return(FALSE);
        }

        lpBuf = VirtualAlloc(NULL, 1024, MEM_COMMIT,
            PAGE_READWRITE);
        if (lpBuf == NULL) {
            return(FALSE);
        }

        fOk = ReadFile(hFile, lpBuf, 1024,
            &dwNumBytesRead, NULL);
        if (!fOk || (dwNumBytesRead != 1024)) {
            return(FALSE);
        }

        // Do some calculation on the data.
        .
        .
        .
    }
```

(continued)

563

```
   __finally {
      // Clean up all the resources.
      if (lpBuf != NULL)
         VirtualFree(lpBuf, MEM_RELEASE | MEM_DECOMMIT);
      if (hFile != INVALID_HANDLE_VALUE)
         CloseHandle(hFile);
   }
   // Continue processing.
   return(TRUE);
}
```

The real virtue of the Funcarama3 version is that all of the function's clean-up code is localized in one place and one place only—the *finally* block. If we ever need to add some additional code to this function, we can simply add a single clean-up line in the *finally* block—we won't have to go back to every possible location of failure and add our clean-up line to each failure location.

The real problem with the Funcarama3 version is the overhead. As we noted after the discussion of Funcenstein4, we really should avoid putting *return* statements into *try* blocks as much as possible.

To help make such avoidance easier, Microsoft introduced the _ _*leave* keyword in its C/C++ compiler. Here is the Funcarama4 version, which takes advantage of the new _ _*leave* keyword:

```
DWORD Funcarama4 (void) {
   HANDLE hFile = INVALID_HANDLE_VALUE;
   LPVOID lpBuf = NULL;

   // Assume that the function will not execute successfully.
   BOOL fFunctionOk = FALSE;

   __try {
      DWORD dwNumBytesRead;
      BOOL fOk;

      hFile = CreateFile("SOMEDATA.DAT", GENERIC_READ,
         FILE_SHARE_READ, NULL, OPEN_EXISTING,
         0, NULL);
      if (hFile == INVALID_HANDLE_VALUE) {
         __leave;
      }

      lpBuf = VirtualAlloc(NULL, 1024, MEM_COMMIT,
         PAGE_READWRITE);
```

(continued)

```
      if (lpBuf == NULL) {
         __leave;
      }

      fOk = ReadFile(hFile, lpBuf, 1024,
         &dwNumBytesRead, NULL);
      if (!fOk || (dwNumBytesRead == 0)) {
         __leave;
      }

      // Do some calculation on the data.
      .
      .
      .

      // Indicate that the entire function executed successfully.
      fFunctionOk = TRUE;
   }
   __finally {
      // Clean up all the resources.
      if (lpBuf != NULL)
         VirtualFree(lpBuf, MEM_RELEASE | MEM_DECOMMIT);
      if (hFile != INVALID_HANDLE_VALUE)
         CloseHandle(hFile);
   }
   // Continue processing.
   return(fFunctionOk);
}
```

The use of the _ _ *leave* keyword in the *try* block causes a jump to the end of the *try* block. You can think of it as jumping to the *try* block's closing brace. Because the flow of control will exit naturally from the *try* block and enter the *finally* block, no overhead is incurred. However, it was necessary to introduce a new boolean variable to indicate the success or failure of the function—a relatively small price to pay.

When designing your functions to take advantage of termination handlers in this way, remember to initialize all of your resource handles to invalid values before entering your *try* block. Then, in the *finally* block, you can check to see which resources have been allocated successfully so that you'll know which ones to free. Another popular method for tracking which resources will need to be freed is to set a flag when a resource allocation is successful. Then the code in the *finally* block can examine the state of the flag to determine whether the resource needs freeing.

So far, we have explicitly identified two scenarios that force the *finally* block to be executed:

- Normal flow of control from the *try* block into the *finally* block

- Local unwind: premature exit from the *try* block (*goto, long-jump, continue, break, return*, and so on) forcing control to the *finally* block

A third scenario, a global unwind, occurred without explicit identification as such in the Funcfurter1 function we saw earlier (page 557). Inside the *try* block of this function was a call to the Funcinator function. If the Funcinator function caused a memory access violation, a global unwind caused Funcfurter1's *finally* block to execute. We'll look at global unwinding in greater detail when we get to the exception filters and exception handlers section of this chapter.

Code in a *finally* block always starts executing as a result of one of these three situations. To determine which of the three caused the *finally* block to execute, you can call the intrinsic function[1] Abnormal-Termination:

```
BOOL AbnormalTermination(VOID);
```

This intrinsic function can be called only from inside a *finally* block and returns a boolean value indicating whether the *try* block associated with the *finally* block was exited prematurely. In other words, if the flow of control leaves the *try* block and naturally enters the *finally* block, AbnormalTermination will return FALSE. If the flow of control exits the *try* block abnormally—usually because a local unwind has been caused by a *goto, return, break*, or *continue* statement or because a global unwind has been caused by a memory access violation—a call to Abnormal-Termination will return TRUE. If AbnormalTermination returns TRUE, it doesn't indicate whether a local unwind or a global unwind caused the *finally* block to execute. It is impossible to determine whether a *finally* block is executing because of a global or a local unwind.

---

1. An intrinsic function is a special function recognized by the compiler. The compiler generates the code for the function inline rather than generating code to call the function. For example, *memcpy* is an intrinsic function (if the */Oi* compiler switch is specified). When the compiler sees a call to *memcpy*, it puts the *memcpy* code directly into the function that called *memcpy* instead of generating a call to the *memcpy* function. This usually has the effect of making your code run faster at the expense of code size.

   The intrinsic AbnormalTermination function is different from the intrinsic *memcpy* function in that it exists only in an intrinsic form. No C Runtime Library contains the AbnormalTermination function.

Here is Funcfurter2, which demonstrates use of the Abnormal-Termination intrinsic function:

```
DWORD Funcfurter2 (void) {
   DWORD dwTemp;

   // 1. Do any processing here.
   .
   .
   .

   __try {
      // 2. Request permission to access
      //    protected data, and then use it.
      WaitForSingleObject(g_hSem, INFINITE);

      dwTemp = Funcinator(g_dwProtectedData);
   }
   __finally {
      // 3. Allow others to use protected data.
      ReleaseSemaphore(g_hSem, 1, NULL);

      if (!AbnormalTermination()) {
         // No errors occurred in the try block, and
         // control flowed naturally from try into finally
         .
         .
         .

      } else {

         // Something caused an exception, and
         // since there is no code in the try block
         // that would cause a premature exit, we must
         // be executing in the finally block
         // because of a global unwind.

         // If there were a goto in the try block,
         // we wouldn't know how we got here.
         .
         .
         .

      }
   }

   // 4. Continue processing.
   return(dwTemp);
}
```

Now that you know how to write termination handlers, you'll see that termination handlers can be even more useful and important when we look at exception filters and exception handlers in the next section. Before we move on, let's review the reasons for using termination handlers. Termination handlers

- Simplify error processing because all cleanup is in one location and is guaranteed to execute
- Improve program readability
- Ease code maintainability
- Have minimal speed and size overhead if used appropriately

The SEH Termination Sample Application

The SEHTerm (SEHTERM.EXE) application, listed in Figure 10-1 beginning on page 572, demonstrates the use of termination handlers by simulating the execution of a function that counts the number of words in a file. Here are the steps that the program's Dlg_CountWordsInFile function performs:

1. Open the file.
2. Get the size of the file.
3. Allocate a memory block using the result of step 2.
4. Read the contents of the file into the allocated memory block.
5. Calculate the number of words in the file in the memory block.

After the calculation, the function must clean up everything it has done and return the number of words counted:

6. Free the memory block.
7. Close the file.
8. Return the number of words in the file. If an error occurred, return −1.

During the initialization for this function, any of steps 1 through 4 could fail. If this happens, the function needs to clean up any allocations it's already made before returning –1 to the caller. Termination handlers ensure that everything is cleaned up properly.

When you first invoke SEHTerm, this dialog box appears:

In the *Results of execution* section at the top of the dialog box, you get to specify which of the four initialization operations are to succeed and which ones are to fail. Remember, this program only simulates the work to be done; it doesn't actually open a file, read the file's contents, and count the number of words in the file. In a sense, you get to play Operating System here—you can tell the simulation which operations you want to succeed and which operations you want to fail.

After you have set the four check boxes the way you want them, click on the *Execute* button. The simulation will now try to perform steps 1 through 4 in the list of steps that the Dlg_CountWordsInFile performs. All these steps are performed from within a single *try* block. If any of the steps fail, a _ _ *leave* statement in the *try* block is executed and processing moves immediately into the *finally* block, skipping the remainder of the code in the *try* block.

The code in the *finally* block examines the state of the initialization by checking the *hFile* and *lpvFileData* variables, and then it executes the appropriate cleanup routines. The result of each step of the Dlg-_CountWordsInFile function's execution is shown in the *Execution log* list box at the bottom of the SEH Termination Handler Test dialog box.

In our first experiment, we'll allow all of the four operations to succeed. To simulate this success, we must be sure that all four check boxes are checked before we press the *Execute* button. After the code executes, we can see the results in the *Execution log*:

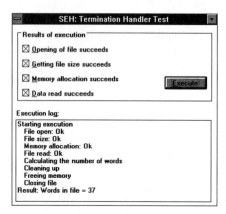

The *Execution log* tells us that everything was successfully initialized, the number of words was calculated, and everything was cleaned up OK. We even see a simulated result of the calculation: 37 words. (I just chose this number arbitrarily.)

Now let's pretend that the memory allocation failed when the Dlg-_CountWordsInFile function attempted it. Here is the result:

The function opened the file, obtained its size, and tried to allocate a block of memory. When we forced this allocation to fail, execution jumped over the remainder of the *try* block code to an immediate execution of the *finally* block's code. The code in the *finally* block can see that the file was opened successfully by checking the *hFile* variable. It calls CloseHandle to close the file.

The *finally* block code also checks the *lpvFileData* variable to see whether the memory allocation has been successful. Since *lpvFileData* is NULL, the code doesn't try to free the memory block. That's why *Freeing memory* doesn't appear in the *Execution log* this time.

The function will also return −1, indicating that an error has occurred. This causes the *Error occurred in function* line to appear in the *Execution log*.

Let's do just one more experiment. You can try others on your own machine. Here is another simulation:

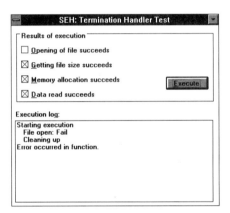

In this experiment, we force the opening of the file to fail and everything else to succeed. However, the code in the *try* block stops executing as soon as it can't open the file. In this case, the remainder of the initialization doesn't execute and the code in the *finally* block starts executing. The cleanup code sees that the file was never opened and that the memory block was never allocated and therefore does nothing.

You can experiment yourself by checking and un-checking the various options and pressing the *Execute* button. Notice how the *Execution log* changes with each test. As you experiment, it's a good idea to have the SEHTerm source code (see pages 572 through 578) beside you to help you understand how termination handlers work.

SEHTerm.ico

SEHTERM.C

```
/**************************************************************
Module name: SEHTerm.C
Notices: Copyright (c) 1993 Jeffrey Richter
**************************************************************/

#include <windows.h>
#include <windowsx.h>
#include <tchar.h>
#include <stdio.h>
#include "SEHTerm.H"


// The SIMULATION define should always be defined.
// It exists so that you can easily separate the simulation
// aspects of this program from the actual code that you would
// use to perform the various operations.
#define SIMULATION


///////////////////////////////////////////////////////////////

BOOL Dlg_OnInitDialog (HWND hwnd, HWND hwndFocus,
   LPARAM lParam) {

   // Associate an icon with the dialog box.
   SetClassLong(hwnd, GCL_HICON, (LONG)
      LoadIcon((HINSTANCE) GetWindowLong(hwnd, GWL_HINSTANCE),
      __TEXT("SEHTerm")));

   Button_SetCheck(GetDlgItem(hwnd, ID_OPENSUCCEEDS), TRUE);
   Button_SetCheck(GetDlgItem(hwnd, ID_SIZESUCCEEDS), TRUE);
   Button_SetCheck(GetDlgItem(hwnd, ID_MEMSUCCEEDS),  TRUE);
   Button_SetCheck(GetDlgItem(hwnd, ID_READSUCCEEDS), TRUE);
   return(TRUE);
}
```

Figure 10-1.   *(continued)*
The SEHTerm application.

Figure 10-1. *continued*

```
////////////////////////////////////////////////////////////////

LONG Dlg_CountWordsInFile (HWND hwndLog,
    BOOL fOpenSucceeds, BOOL fFileSizeSucceeds,
    BOOL fMemSucceeds, BOOL fReadSucceeds) {

    HANDLE hFile = INVALID_HANDLE_VALUE;
    DWORD  dwFileSize = 0;
    LPVOID lpvFileData = NULL;
    BOOL   fFileReadOk = FALSE;
    LONG   lNumWords = -1;
    DWORD  dwLastError;

    __try {
        // Clear the "Execution log" list box.
        ListBox_ResetContent(hwndLog);
        ListBox_AddString(hwndLog,
            __TEXT("Starting execution"));

        // Open the file.
#ifdef SIMULATION
        hFile = (fOpenSucceeds ?
            !(INVALID_HANDLE_VALUE) :
            INVALID_HANDLE_VALUE);
#else
        hFile = CreateFile(...);
#endif
        if (hFile == INVALID_HANDLE_VALUE) {
            // The file could not be opened.
            ListBox_AddString(hwndLog,
                __TEXT("   File open: Fail"));
            __leave;
        } else {
            ListBox_AddString(hwndLog,
                __TEXT("   File open: Ok"));
        }

        // Determine the size of the file.
#ifdef SIMULATION
        dwLastError = fFileSizeSucceeds ? NO_ERROR : !NO_ERROR;
#else
        dwFileSize = GetFileSize(hFile);
        dwLastError = GetLastError();
#endif
```

(continued)

Figure 10-1. *continued*

```
        if (dwLastError != NO_ERROR) {
            // The file size could not be obtained.
            ListBox_AddString(hwndLog,
                __TEXT("   File size: Fail"));
            __leave;
        } else {
            ListBox_AddString(hwndLog,
                __TEXT("   File size: Ok"));
        }


        // Allocate a block of memory to store the entire file.
#ifdef SIMULATION
        lpvFileData = fMemSucceeds ? !NULL : NULL;
#else
        lpvFileData = HeapAlloc(GetProcessHeap(), dwFileSize);
#endif
        if (lpvFileData == NULL) {
            // Allocation failed.
            ListBox_AddString(hwndLog,
                __TEXT("   Memory allocation: Fail"));
            __leave;
        } else {
            ListBox_AddString(hwndLog,
                __TEXT("   Memory allocation: Ok"));
        }


        // Read the file into the buffer.
#ifdef SIMULATION
        fReadSucceeds = fReadSucceeds;
#else
        ReadFile(hFile, lpvFileData, dwFileSize, NULL, NULL);
        fReadSucceeds = (GetLastError() == NO_ERROR);
#endif
        if (!fReadSucceeds) {
            // The file's data could not be loaded into memory.
            ListBox_AddString(hwndLog,
                __TEXT("   File read: Fail"));
            __leave;
        } else {
            ListBox_AddString(hwndLog,
                __TEXT("   File read: Ok"));
            fFileReadOk = TRUE;
        }
```

(continued)

Figure 10-1. *continued*

```
        // Calculate the number of words in the file.
        // The algorithm to calculate the number of words in the
        // file would go here. For simulation purposes, I'll
        // just set lNumWords to 37.
        ListBox_AddString(hwndLog,
            __TEXT("   Calculating the number of words"));
        lNumWords = 37;

    }  // try

    __finally {
        // Display a notification that we are cleaning up.
        ListBox_AddString(hwndLog, __TEXT("   Cleaning up"));

        // Guarantee that the memory is freed.
        if (lpvFileData != NULL) {
            ListBox_AddString(hwndLog,
                __TEXT("   Freeing memory"));
#ifndef SIMULATION
            HeapFree(GetProcessHeap(), lpvFileData);
#endif
        }

        // Guarantee that the file is closed.
        if (hFile != INVALID_HANDLE_VALUE) {
            ListBox_AddString(hwndLog,
                __TEXT("   Closing file"));
#ifndef SIMULATION
            CloseHandle(hFile);
#endif
        }

    }  // finally

    return(lNumWords);
}

//////////////////////////////////////////////////////////////

void Dlg_OnCommand (HWND hwnd, int id, HWND hwndCtl,
    UINT codeNotify) {

    TCHAR szBuf[100];
    LONG  lNumWords;
```

(continued)

Figure 10-1. *continued*

```
        switch (id) {
           case IDOK:
              lNumWords = Dlg_CountWordsInFile(
                 GetDlgItem(hwnd, ID_LOG),
                 Button_GetCheck(GetDlgItem(hwnd,
                    ID_OPENSUCCEEDS)),
                 Button_GetCheck(GetDlgItem(hwnd,
                    ID_SIZESUCCEEDS)),
                 Button_GetCheck(GetDlgItem(hwnd, ID_MEMSUCCEEDS)),
                 Button_GetCheck(GetDlgItem(hwnd, ID_READSUCCEEDS))
                 );

              if (lNumWords == -1) {
                 ListBox_AddString(GetDlgItem(hwnd, ID_LOG),
                    __TEXT("Error occurred in function."));
              } else {
                 _stprintf(szBuf,
                    __TEXT("Result: Words in file = %d"),
                    lNumWords);
                 ListBox_AddString(GetDlgItem(hwnd,
                    ID_LOG), szBuf);
              }

              break;

           case IDCANCEL:
              EndDialog(hwnd, id);
              break;
        }
}

//////////////////////////////////////////////////////////////////

BOOL CALLBACK DlgProc (HWND hDlg, UINT uMsg,
   WPARAM wParam, LPARAM lParam) {

   BOOL fProcessed = TRUE;

   switch (uMsg) {
      HANDLE_MSG(hDlg, WM_INITDIALOG, Dlg_OnInitDialog);
      HANDLE_MSG(hDlg, WM_COMMAND, Dlg_OnCommand);
```

(continued)

Figure 10-1.   *continued*

```
        default:
            fProcessed = FALSE;
            break;
    }
    return(fProcessed);
}


////////////////////////////////////////////////////////////////

int APIENTRY WinMain (HINSTANCE hInstance,
    HINSTANCE hPrevInstance, LPSTR lpszCmdLine, int nCmdShow) {

    DialogBox(hInstance, MAKEINTRESOURCE(DLG_SEHTERM),
        NULL, DlgProc);
    return(0);
}


///////////////////////// End Of File /////////////////////////
```

SEHTERM.H

```
/*************************************************************
Module name: SEHTerm.H
Notices: Copyright (c) 1993 Jeffrey Richter
*************************************************************/

// Dialog and control IDs.
#define DLG_SEHTERM          1
#define ID_OPENSUCCEEDS      100
#define ID_SIZESUCCEEDS      101
#define ID_MEMSUCCEEDS       102
#define ID_READSUCCEEDS      103
#define ID_LOG               104


///////////////////////// End Of File /////////////////////////
```

(continued)

Figure 10-1. *continued*

SEHTERM.RC

```
/************************************************************
Module name: SEHTerm.RC
Notices: Copyright (c) 1993 Jeffrey Richter
************************************************************/

#include <windows.h>
#include "SEHTerm.h"


SEHTerm  ICON  DISCARDABLE SEHTerm.Ico

DLG_SEHTERM DIALOG 18, 18, 214, 196
STYLE WS_BORDER | WS_OVERLAPPED | WS_VISIBLE | WS_CAPTION |
  WS_SYSMENU | WS_MINIMIZEBOX
CAPTION "SEH: Termination Handler Test"
FONT 8, "Helv"
BEGIN
   GROUPBOX "Results of execution", -1, 5, 5, 204, 78,
      WS_CHILD | WS_VISIBLE | WS_GROUP
   CONTROL "&Opening of file succeeds", ID_OPENSUCCEEDS,
      "BUTTON", BS_AUTOCHECKBOX | WS_CHILD | WS_VISIBLE |
      WS_GROUP | WS_TABSTOP, 10, 20, 112, 12
   CONTROL "&Getting file size succeeds", ID_SIZESUCCEEDS,
      "BUTTON", BS_AUTOCHECKBOX | WS_CHILD | WS_VISIBLE |
      WS_GROUP | WS_TABSTOP, 10, 36, 104, 12
   CONTROL "&Memory allocation succeeds", ID_MEMSUCCEEDS,
      "BUTTON", BS_AUTOCHECKBOX | WS_CHILD | WS_VISIBLE |
      WS_GROUP | WS_TABSTOP, 10, 52, 136, 12
   CONTROL "&Data read succeeds", ID_READSUCCEEDS, "BUTTON",
      BS_AUTOCHECKBOX | WS_CHILD | WS_VISIBLE | WS_GROUP |
      WS_TABSTOP, 10, 68, 136, 12
   CONTROL "&Execute", IDOK, "BUTTON",
      BS_PUSHBUTTON | WS_CHILD | WS_VISIBLE | WS_GROUP |
      WS_TABSTOP, 160, 56, 44, 14
   CONTROL "Execution lo&g:", -1, "STATIC",
      SS_LEFT | WS_CHILD | WS_VISIBLE | WS_GROUP, 4, 92, 56, 8
   CONTROL "", ID_LOG, "LISTBOX", WS_CHILD | WS_VISIBLE |
      WS_BORDER | WS_VSCROLL | WS_GROUP | WS_TABSTOP,
      4, 104, 204, 88
END

///////////////////// End Of File /////////////////////////
```

Exception Filters and Exception Handlers

An exception is an event you don't expect. In a well-written application, you don't expect attempts to access an invalid memory address or to divide a value by 0 (zero). Nevertheless, such errors do occur. The CPU is responsible for catching invalid memory accesses and divides by zero and will generate an exception in response to these errors. When the CPU generates an exception, it's known as a hardware exception. We'll see later that the operating system and your applications can generate their own exceptions—software exceptions.

When a hardware or software exception is generated, the operating system offers your application the opportunity to see what type of exception was generated and allows the application to handle the exception itself. Here is the syntax for an exception handler:

```
__try {
   // Guarded body
   .
   .
   .
}
__except (exception filter) {
   // Exception handler
   .
   .
   .
}
```

The new keyword is _ _ *except*. Whenever you create a *try* block, it must be followed by either a *finally* block or an *except* block. A *try* block can't have both a *finally* block and an *except* block, and a *try* block can't have multiple *finally* or *except* blocks. However, it is possible to nest *try-finally* blocks inside *try-except* blocks and vice versa. Here's a more concrete coding example of a *try-except* block:

```
DWORD Funcmeister1 (void) {
   DWORD dwTemp;

   // 1. Do any processing here.
   .
   .
   .
```

(continued)

```
    __try {
        // 2. Perform some operation.
        dwTemp = 0;
    }
    __except (EXCEPTION_EXECUTE_HANDLER) {
        // Handle an exception -- this never executes.
        .
        .
        .
    }

    // 3. Continue processing.
    return(dwTemp);
}
```

In the Funcmeister1 *try* block, we simply move a 0 (zero) into the *dwTemp* variable. This operation will never cause an exception to be generated, so the code inside the *except* block will never execute. Note this difference from *try-finally* behavior. After *dwTemp* is set to 0, the next instruction to execute is the *return* statement.

Although *return, goto, continue,* and *break* statements are strongly discouraged in the *try* block of a termination handler, no speed or code-size penalty is associated with using these statements inside the *try* block of an exception handler. Such a statement in the *try* block associated with an *except* block won't incur the overhead of a local unwind.

Let's modify the function and see what happens:

```
DWORD Funcmeister2 (void) {
    DWORD dwTemp = 0;

    // 1. Do any processing here.
    .
    .
    .

    __try {
        // 2. Perform some operation(s).
        dwTemp = 5 / dwTemp; // Generates an exception
        dwTemp += 10;        // Never executes
    }
    __except ( /* 3. Evaluate filter. */
    EXCEPTION_EXECUTE_HANDLER) {
        // 4. Handle an exception.
```

(continued)

```
        MessageBeep(0);
          .
          .
          .
    }

    // 5. Continue processing.
    return(dwTemp);
}
```

In Funcmeister2 an instruction inside the *try* block calls for the attempt to divide 5 by 0 (zero). The CPU will catch this event and generate a hardware exception. When this exception is generated, the system will locate the beginning of the *except* block and evaluate the exception filter expression, an expression that must evaluate to one of the following three identifiers as defined in the Win32 EXCPT.H file:

Identifier	#defined as
EXCEPTION_EXECUTE_HANDLER	1
EXCEPTION_CONTINUE_SEARCH	0
EXCEPTION_CONTINUE_EXECUTION	−1

EXCEPTION_EXECUTE_HANDLER

In Funcmeister2, the exception filter expression evaluates to EXCEPTION_EXECUTE_HANDLER. This value basically says to the system: "I recognize the exception; that is, I had a feeling that this exception might occur sometime, and I've written some code to deal with it that I'd like to execute now." Execution immediately jumps to the code inside the *except* block (the exception handler code). After the code in the *except* block has executed, the system considers the exception to be handled and allows your application to continue executing.

This is pretty different from 16-bit Windows, where a divide by zero causes a System Error box to appear that allows the user only one option: closing the application right then and there. In Win32 (and Win32s), you can trap the error, handle it in your own way, and allow your application to continue running without the user's ever knowing that the error happened.

But where does execution resume from? With a little bit of thought, it's easy to imagine several possibilities.

The first possibility would be for execution to resume after the CPU instruction that generates the exception. In Funcmeister2, execution would resume with the instruction that adds 10 to *dwTemp*. This may seem like a reasonable thing to do but, in reality, most programs are written so that they cannot continue executing successfully if one of the earlier instructions fails to execute.

In Funcmeister2, the code can continue to execute normally; however, Funcmeister2 is not the normal situation. Most likely, your code will be structured so that the CPU instructions following the instruction that generates the exception expect a valid return value. For example, you might have a function that allocates memory, in which case a whole series of instructions will be executed to manipulate that memory. If the memory cannot be allocated, all the lines will fail, making the program generate exceptions repeatedly.

Here is another example of why execution cannot continue after the failed CPU instruction. What if we replace the C statement that generated the exception in Funcmeister2 with the following line:

```
malloc(5 / dwTemp);
```

For the line above, the compiler generates CPU instructions to perform the division, pushes the result on the stack, and calls the *malloc* function. If the division fails, the code can't continue executing properly. The system would have to push something on the stack; if it doesn't, the stack would get corrupted.

Fortunately, Microsoft has not made it possible for us to have the system resume execution on the instruction following the instruction that generates the exception. This decision saves us from potential problems like these.

The second possibility would be for execution to resume with the instruction that generated the exception. This is an interesting possibility. What if inside the *except* block you had this statement:

```
dwTemp = 2;
```

With this assignment in the *except* block, you could resume execution with the instruction that generated the exception. This time, you would be dividing 5 by 2, and execution would continue just fine without generating another exception. You can alter something and have the system retry the instruction that generated the exception. However, you should be aware that this technique can result in some subtle behaviors. We'll discuss this technique in the following section.

The third and last possibility would be for execution to pick up with the first instruction following the *except* block. This is actually what happens when the exception filter expression evaluates to EXCEPTION_EXECUTE_HANDLER. After the code inside the *except* block finishes executing, control resumes at the first instruction after the *except* block.

EXCEPTION_CONTINUE_EXECUTION

Let's take a closer look at the exception filter to see how it evaluates to one of the three exception identifiers defined in EXCPT.H. In Funcmeister2, the EXCEPTION_EXECUTE_HANDLER identifier is hard-coded directly into the filter for simplicity's sake, but you can make the filter call a function that will determine which of the three identifiers should be returned. Let's look at another code example:

```
char g_szBuffer[100];

void FunclinRoosevelt1 (void) {
    int x = 0;
    char *lpBuffer = NULL;

    __try {
        *lpBuffer = 'J';
        x = 5 / x;
    }
    __except (MyFilter1(&lpBuffer)) {
        MessageBox(NULL, "An exception occurred", NULL, MB_OK);
    }
    MessageBox(NULL, "Function completed", NULL, MB_OK);
}

LONG MyFilter1 (char **lplpBuffer) {
    if (*lplpBuffer == NULL) {
        *lplpBuffer = g_szBuffer;
        return(EXCEPTION_CONTINUE_EXECUTION);
    }
    return(EXCEPTION_EXECUTE_HANDLER);
}
```

We first run into a problem when we try to put a *'J'* into the buffer pointed to by *lpBuffer*. Unfortunately, we didn't initialize *lpBuffer* to point to our global buffer *g_szBuffer*, and *lpBuffer* points to NULL. The CPU will generate an exception and evaluate the exception filter in the *except* block associated with the *try* block in which the exception occurred. In the *except* block, the MyFilter1 function is passed the address of the *lpBuffer* variable.

When MyFilter1 gets control, it checks to see whether **lplpBuffer* is NULL, and if it is, sets it to point to the global buffer *g_szBuffer*. The filter then returns EXCEPTION_CONTINUE_EXECUTION. When the system sees that the filter evaluated to EXCEPTION_CONTINUE_EXECUTION, it jumps back to the instruction that generated the exception and tries to execute it again. This time, the instruction will succeed, and *'J'* will be put into the first byte of the *g_szBuffer* buffer.

As the code continues to execute, we run up against the divide by zero problem in the *try* block. Again, the system evaluates the exception filter. This time, MyFilter1 sees that **lplpBuffer* is not NULL and returns EXCEPTION_EXECUTE_HANDLER, which tells the system to execute the *except* block code. This causes a message box to appear displaying the text *An exception occurred.*

As you can see, you can do an awful lot of work inside an exception filter. Of course, the filter must return one of the three exception identifiers, but the filter can also perform any other tasks you want it to.

Use EXCEPTION_CONTINUE_EXECUTION with Caution

As it turns out, trying to correct the situation shown in the function on the previous page and having the system continue execution might or might not work—it depends on the target CPU for your application, on how your compiler generates instructions for C statements, and on your compiler options.

A compiler might generate two machine instructions to perform the statement:

```
*lpBuffer = 'J';
```

The first instruction would load the contents of *lpBuffer* into a register, and the second instruction would try to copy a *'J'* into the address. It is this second instruction that would generate the exception. The exception filter would catch the exception, correct the value in *lpBuffer*, and tell the system to reexecute the second instruction. The problem is that the contents of the register wouldn't be changed to reflect the new value loaded into *lpBuffer* and reexecuting the instruction would therefore generate another exception. We'd have an infinite loop!

And continuing execution could be fine if the compiler optimizes the code but might fail if the compiler doesn't optimize the code. This can be an incredibly difficult bug to fix, and you will have to examine the assembly language generated for your source code in order to determine what has gone wrong in your application. The moral of this story is to be very, very careful when returning EXCEPTION_CONTINUE-_EXECUTION from an exception filter.

EXCEPTION_CONTINUE_SEARCH

The examples have been pretty tame so far. Let's shake things up a bit by adding a function call:

```
void FunclinRoosevelt2 (void) {
    char *lpBuffer = NULL;

    __try {
        FuncSinatra2(lpBuffer);
    }
    __except (MyFilter2(&lpBuffer)) {
        MessageBox(NULL, ...);
    }
}

void FuncSinatra2 (char *sz) {
    *sz = 0;
}

LONG MyFilter2 (char **lplpBuffer) {
    if (*lplpBuffer == NULL) {
        *lplpBuffer = g_szBuffer;
        return(EXCEPTION_CONTINUE_EXECUTION);
    }
    return(EXCEPTION_EXECUTE_HANDLER);
}
```

When FunclinRoosevelt2 executes, it calls FuncSinatra2, passing it NULL. When FuncSinatra2 executes, an exception is generated. Just as before, the system evaluates the exception filter associated with the most-recently executing *try* block. In this example, the *try* block inside FunclinRoosevelt2 is the most-recently executing *try* block, so the system calls the MyFilter2 function to evaluate the exception filter—even though the exception was generated inside the FuncSinatra2 function.

Now let's shake things up a little more by adding another *try-except* block.

```
void FunclinRoosevelt3 (void) {

    char *lpBuffer = NULL;

    __try {
        FuncSinatra3(lpBuffer);
    }
    __except (MyFilter3(&lpBuffer)) {
        MessageBox(NULL, ...);
    }
}

void FuncSinatra3 (char *sz) {
    __try {
        *sz = 0;
    }
    __except (EXCEPTION_CONTINUE_SEARCH) {
        // This never executes.

          .

          .

          .

    }
}

LONG MyFilter3 (char **lplpBuffer) {
    if (*lplpBuffer == NULL) {
        *lplpBuffer = g_szBuffer;
        return(EXCEPTION_CONTINUE_EXECUTION);
    }
    return(EXCEPTION_EXECUTE_HANDLER);
}
```

Now when FuncSinatra3 tries to fill address NULL with 0 (zero), an exception is still generated but FuncSinatra3's exception filter will get executed. FuncSinatra3's exception filter is very simple and evaluates to EXCEPTION_CONTINUE_SEARCH. This identifier tells the system to walk up to the previous *try* block that's matched with an *except* block and call this previous *try* block's exception filter.

Because FuncSinatra3's filter evaluates to EXCEPTION_CONTINUE_SEARCH, the system will walk up to the previous *try* block (in FunclinRoosevelt3) and evaluate its exception filter, MyFilter3. MyFilter3 will see that *lpBuffer* is NULL, will set *lpBuffer* to point to the global buffer, and will then tell the system to resume execution on the instruction that generated the exception. This will allow the code inside FuncSinatra3's *try* block to execute but, unfortunately, FuncSinatra3's local *sz* variable will not have been changed and resuming execution on the failed instruction will simply cause another exception to be generated. What we have here is another infinite loop!

You'll notice I said that the system walks up to the most-recently executing *try* block that's matched with an *except* block and evaluates its filters. This means that any *try* blocks that are matched with *finally* blocks instead of *except* blocks are skipped by the system while it walks up the chain. This expectation should be pretty obvious since *finally* blocks don't have exception filters and therefore give the system nothing to evaluate. If FuncSinatra3 in the last example contained a *finally* block instead of its *except* block, the system would have started evaluating exception filters beginning with FunclinRoosevelt3's MyFilter3.

Figure 10-2, on page 589, shows a flowchart describing the actions taken by the system when an exception is generated.

Global Unwinds

Exception handling involves a global unwind. When an exception filter evaluates to EXCEPTION_EXECUTE_HANDLER, the system must perform a global unwind. The global unwind causes all of the outstanding *try-finally* blocks that started executing below the *try-except* block that is handling the exception to execute. These two functions are an example:

```
void FuncOStimpy1 (void) {

   // 1. Do any processing here.
   .
   .
   .


   __try {
      // 2. Call another function.
      FuncORen1();

      // Code here never executes.
   }

   __except (/* 6. Evaluate filter */
      EXCEPTION_EXECUTE_HANDLER) {
      // 8. After the unwind, the exception handler executes.
      MessageBox(NULL, ...);
   }
```

(continued)

```
    // 9. Exception handled -- continue execution.
    .
    .
    .

}
void FuncORen1 (void) {
    DWORD dwTemp = 0;

    // 3. Do any processing here.
    .
    .
    .

    __try {
        // 4. Request permission to access protected data.
        WaitForSingleObject(g_hSem, INFINITE);

        // 5. Modify the data.
        //     An exception is generated here.
        g_dwProtectedData = 5 / dwTemp;
    }
    __finally {
        // 7. Global unwind occurs because filter evaluated
        //     to EXCEPTION_EXECUTE_HANDLER.

        // Allow others to use protected data.
        ReleaseSemaphore(g_hSem, 1, NULL);
    }

    // Continue processing -- never executes.
    .
    .
    .

}
```

FuncOStimpy1 and FuncORen1 together illustrate the most confusing aspects of structured exception handling. The numbers at the beginnings of the comments show the order of execution, but let's hold hands and go through it together.

FuncOStimpy1 begins execution by entering its *try* block and calling FuncORen1. FuncORen1 starts by entering its own *try* block and waiting to obtain a semaphore. Once it has the semaphore, FuncORen1 tries to alter the global data variable, *g_dwProtectedData*. However, the division by zero causes an exception to be generated. The system grabs control now and searches for a *try* block matched with an *except* block. Since the *try* block in FuncORen1 is matched by a *finally* block, the

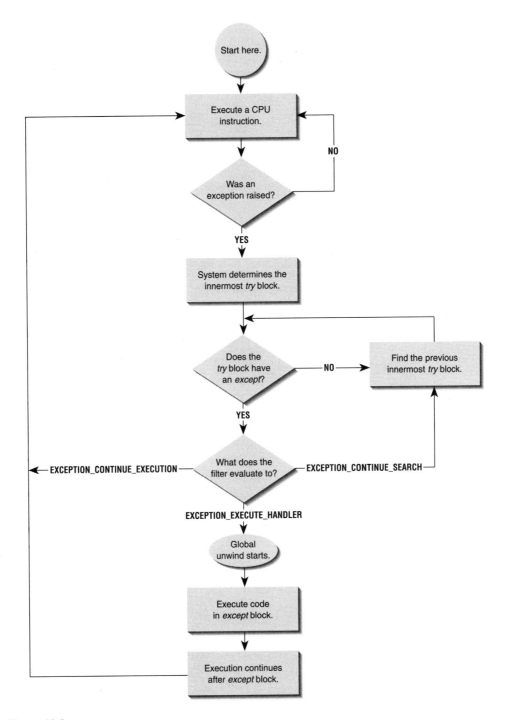

Figure 10-2.
How the system processes an exception.

589

system searches upward for another *try* block. This time, it finds the *try* block in FuncOStimpy1, and it sees that FuncOStimpy1's *try* block is matched by an *except* block.

The system now evaluates the exception filter that's associated with FuncOStimpy1's *except* block and waits for the return value. When the system sees that EXCEPTION_EXECUTE_HANDLER is returned, the system begins a global unwind in FuncORen1's *finally* block. Note that the unwind takes place *before* the system begins execution of the code in FuncOStimpy1's *except* block. For a global unwind, the system starts back at the bottom of all outstanding *try* blocks and searches this time for *try* blocks matched by *finally* blocks. The *finally* block that the system finds here is the one contained inside FuncORen1.

When the system executes the code in FuncORen1's *finally* block, you can really see the power of structured exception handling. Because FuncORen1's *finally* block is executed, the semaphore is released, allowing other threads to resume execution. If the call to ReleaseSemaphore were not contained inside the *finally* block, the semaphore would never be released.

After the code contained in the *finally* block has executed, the system continues to walk upward looking for outstanding *finally* blocks that need to be executed. In this example there are none. The system stops walking upward when it reaches the *try-except* block that decided to handle the exception. At this point, the global unwind is complete and the system can execute the code contained inside the *except* block.

Figure 10-3 shows a flowchart that describes how the system performs a global unwind.

That's how structured exception handling works. SEH can be difficult to understand because the system really gets involved with the execution of your code. No longer does the code flow from top to bottom; the system gets involved and makes sections of code execute according to its notions of order. This order of execution is complex but predictable, and by following the two flowcharts in this chapter, you should be able to use SEH with confidence.

More About Exception Filters

Often, an exception filter must analyze the situation before it can determine what value to return. For example, your handler might know what to do if a divide by zero exception occurs, but it might not know how to handle a memory access exception. The exception filter has the responsibility for examining the situation and returning the appropriate value.

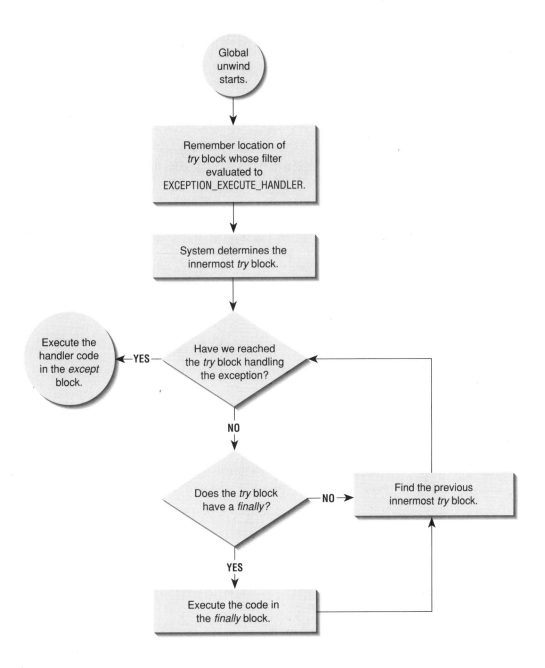

Figure 10-3.
How the system performs a global unwind.

This code demonstrates a method for identifying the kind of exception that has occurred:

```
__try {
   x = 0;
   y = 4 / x;
}

__except ((GetExceptionCode() == EXCEPTION_INT_DIVIDE_BY_ZERO) ?
   EXCEPTION_EXECUTE_HANDLER : EXCEPTION_CONTINUE_SEARCH) {
   // Handle divide by zero exception.
}
```

The GetExceptionCode intrinsic function returns a value identifying the kind of exception that has occurred:

```
DWORD GetExceptionCode(VOID);
```

The following list of all predefined exceptions and their meanings is adapted from the Windows NT SDK documentation. The exception identifiers can be found in the Win32 EXCPT.H header file.

EXCEPTION_ACCESS_VIOLATION   The thread tried to read from or write to a virtual address for which it doesn't have the appropriate access.

EXCEPTION_BREAKPOINT   A breakpoint was encountered.

EXCEPTION_DATATYPE_MISALIGNMENT   The thread tried to read or write data that is misaligned on hardware that doesn't provide alignment. For example, 16-bit values must be aligned on 2-byte boundaries; 32-bit values on 4-byte boundaries, and so on.

EXCEPTION_SINGLE_STEP   A trace trap or other single-instruction mechanism signaled that one instruction has been executed.

EXCEPTION_ARRAY_BOUNDS_EXCEEDED   The thread tried to access an array element that is out of bounds, and the underlying hardware supports bounds checking.

EXCEPTION_FLT_DENORMAL_OPERAND   One of the operands in a floating-point operation is denormal. A denormal value is one that is too small to represent a standard floating-point value.

EXCEPTION_FLT_DIVIDE_BY_ZERO   The thread tried to divide a floating-point value by a floating-point divisor of zero.

EXCEPTION_FLT_INEXACT_RESULT The result of a floating-point operation can't be represented exactly as a decimal fraction.

EXCEPTION_FLT_INVALID_OPERATION This exception represents any floating-point exception not included in this list.

EXCEPTION_FLT_OVERFLOW The exponent of a floating-point operation is greater than the magnitude allowed by the corresponding type.

EXCEPTION_FLT_STACK_CHECK The stack overflowed or underflowed as the result of a floating-point operation.

EXCEPTION_FLT_UNDERFLOW The exponent of a floating-point operation is less than the magnitude allowed by the type.

EXCEPTION_INT_DIVIDE_BY_ZERO The thread tried to divide an integer value by an integer divisor of zero.

EXCEPTION_INT_OVERFLOW The result of an integer operation caused a carry out of the most significant bit of the result.

EXCEPTION_PRIV_INSTRUCTION The thread tried to execute an instruction whose operation is not allowed in the current machine mode.

EXCEPTION_NONCONTINUABLE_EXCEPTION The thread tried to continue execution after a noncontinuable exception occurred.

The GetExceptionCode intrinsic function can be called only in an exception filter (between the parentheses following _ _*except*) or inside an exception handler. The following code is legal:

```
__try {
   y = 0;
   x = 4 / y;
}

__except (
   ((GetExceptionCode() == EXCEPTION_ACCESS_VIOLATION) ||
    (GetExceptionCode() == EXCEPTION_INT_DIVIDE_BY_ZERO)) ?
   EXCEPTION_EXECUTE_HANDLER : EXCEPTION_CONTINUE_SEARCH) {
```

(continued)

593

```
    switch (GetExceptionCode()) {
       case EXCEPTION_ACCESS_VIOLATION:
          // Handle the access violation.
          .
          .
          .
          break;

    case EXCEPTION_INT_DIVIDE_BY_ZERO:
       // Handle the integer divide by zero.
       .
       .
       .
       break;
    }
}
```

However, you cannot call GetExceptionCode from inside an exception filter function. To help you catch such errors, the compiler will produce a compilation error if you try to compile the following code:

```
__try {
   y = 0;
   x = 4 / y;
}

__except (CoffeeFilter()) {

   // Handle the exception.
   .
   .
   .
}

LONG CoffeeFilter (void) {
   // Compilation error: illegal call to GetExceptionCode.
   return((GetExceptionCode() == EXCEPTION_ACCESS_VIOLATION) ?
      EXCEPTION_EXECUTE_HANDLER : EXCEPTION_CONTINUE_SEARCH);
}
```

You can get this effect by rewriting the code this way:

```
__try {
   y = 0;
   x = 4 / y;
}
```

```
__except (CoffeeFilter(GetExceptionCode())) {

    // Handle the exception.
    .
    .
    .
}

LONG CoffeeFilter (DWORD dwExceptionCode) {
    return((dwExceptionCode == EXCEPTION_ACCESS_VIOLATION) ?
        EXCEPTION_EXECUTE_HANDLER : EXCEPTION_CONTINUE_SEARCH);
}
```

Exception codes follow the rules for error codes in Windows NT as defined inside the Win32 WINERROR.H file. Each DWORD is divided as shown in this table:

Bits:	31–30	29–28	27–16	15–0
Contents:	Severity	Flags	Facility code	Exception code
Meaning:	0 = Success	Bit 29	Programmer defined	Programmer defined
	1 = Informational	0 = Microsoft		
	2 = Warning	1 = Customer		
	3 = Error	Bit 28 is reserved (must be zero)		

The table below shows the meaning of all the system-defined exception codes:

Exception Codes	Code	Severity
EXCEPTION_ACCESS_VIOLATION	0xC0000005	Error
EXCEPTION_BREAKPOINT	0x80000003	Warning
EXCEPTION_DATATYPE_MISALIGNMENT	0x80000002	Warning
EXCEPTION_SINGLE_STEP	0x80000004	Warning
EXCEPTION_ARRAY_BOUNDS_EXCEEDED	0xC000008C	Error
EXCEPTION_FLT_DENORMAL_OPERAND	0xC000008D	Error
EXCEPTION_FLT_DIVIDE_BY_ZERO	0xC000008E	Error
EXCEPTION_FLT_INEXACT_RESULT	0xC000008F	Error
EXCEPTION_FLT_INVALID_OPERATION	0xC0000030	Error
EXCEPTION_FLT_OVERFLOW	0xC0000091	Error

(continued)

595

Exception Codes	Code	Severity
EXCEPTION_FLT_STACK_CHECK	0xC0000032	Error
EXCEPTION_FLT_UNDERFLOW	0xC0000033	Error
EXCEPTION_INT_DIVIDE_BY_ZERO	0xC0000094	Error
EXCEPTION_INT_OVERFLOW	0xC0000035	Error
EXCEPTION_PRIV_INSTRUCTION	0xC0000096	Error
EXCEPTION_NONCONTINUABLE_EXCEPTION	0xC0000025	Error

GetExceptionInformation is another intrinsic function you can use to retrieve information about an exception that has been generated:

```
LPEXCEPTION_POINTERS GetExceptionInformation(VOID);
```

The most important thing to remember about the GetExceptionInformation function is that it can be called only in an exception filter—never inside an exception handler and never inside an exception filter function. This intrinsic function returns a pointer to an EXCEPTION-_POINTERS structure:

```
typedef struct _EXCEPTION_POINTERS {
    PEXCEPTION_RECORD ExceptionRecord;
    PCONTEXT ContextRecord;
} EXCEPTION_POINTERS;
```

When an exception occurs, the operating system pushes the EXCEP-TION_POINTERS structure onto the stack of the thread that generated the exception. The structure on the stack is valid only during the exception filter processing. Once control has transferred to the exception handler, the data on the stack is destroyed, which is why the function can be called only during evaluation of the exception filter.

If you have a need to get to the information from inside your exception handler, you must save the data pointed to by the EXCEPTION-_POINTERS structure in a variable that you create. The code below demonstrates how to save the data structure:

```
void FuncSkunk (void) {
    // Declare a variable that we can use to save the
    // exception record if an exception should occur.
    EXCEPTION_RECORD SavedExceptRec;

    .
    .
    .
```

```
__try {
   .
   .
   .
}

__except (SavedExceptRec =
   *(GetExceptionInformation())->ExceptionRecord,
   EXCEPTION_EXECUTE_HANDLER) {
   switch (SavedExceptRec.ExceptionCode) {
      .
      .
      .
   }
}

   .
   .
   .
}
```

Notice the use of the C language's comma (,) operator in the exception
filter. Many programmers aren't used to seeing this operator. It tells the
compiler to execute the comma-separated expressions from left to right.
When all of the expressions have been evaluated, the result of the last
(or rightmost) expression is returned.

In FuncSkunk, the left expression will execute, which causes the
EXCEPTION_RECORD on the stack to be stored in the *SavedExceptRec*
local variable. The result of this expression is the value of *SavedExceptRec*.
However, this result is discarded and the next expression to the right
is evaluated. This is a very simple expression that evaluates to
EXCEPTION_EXECUTE_HANDLER. It is the result of this rightmost
expression that is the result of the entire comma-separated expression.

Since the exception filter evaluated to EXCEPTION_EXECUTE-
_HANDLER, the code inside the *except* block executes. At this point,
the *SavedExceptRec* variable has been initialized and can be used inside
the *except* block. Note that it is important that the *SavedExceptRec* variable be declared outside the *try* block.

As you've probably guessed, the *ExceptionRecord* member of the
EXCEPTION_POINTERS structure points to an EXCEPTION_RE-
CORD structure:

```
typedef struct _EXCEPTION_RECORD {
   DWORD ExceptionCode;
   DWORD ExceptionFlags;
   struct _EXCEPTION_RECORD *ExceptionRecord;
```

(continued)

597

```
        PVOID ExceptionAddress;
        DWORD NumberParameters;
        DWORD ExceptionInformation[EXCEPTION_MAXIMUM_PARAMETERS];
} EXCEPTION_RECORD;
```

The EXCEPTION_RECORD structure contains detailed, platform-independent information about the exception that has most recently occurred:

ExceptionCode contains the code of the exception. This is the same information that is returned from the GetExceptionCode intrinsic function.

ExceptionFlags contains flags about the exception. Currently, the only two values are 0 (which indicates a continuable exception) and EXCEPTION_NONCONTINUABLE (which indicates a noncontinuable exception). Any attempt to continue execution after a noncontinuable exception causes the EXCEPTION_NONCONTINUABLE_EXCEPTION exception.

ExceptionRecord points to an associated EXCEPTION_RECORD structure. Exception records can be chained to provide additional information when nested exceptions occur. A nested exception occurs if an exception is generated during the processing of an exception filter.

ExceptionAddress specifies the address of the instruction in your code at which the exception occurred.

NumberParameters specifies the number of parameters associated with the exception. This is the number of defined elements in the *ExceptionInformation* array.

ExceptionInformation specifies an array of additional 32-bit arguments that describe the exception. For some exception codes, the array elements are undefined.

The last two members of the EXCEPTION_RECORD structure, *NumberParameters* and *ExceptionInformation*, offer the exception filter some additional information about the exception. Currently, only one type of exception involves additional information: EXCEPTION_ACCESS_VIOLATION. All of the other possible exceptions will have the *NumberParameters* member set to 0 (zero). When you look at the additional information about a generated exception, you can examine the *NumberParameters* member to see how many DWORDs of information are available.

For an EXCEPTION_ACCESS_VIOLATION exception, *ExceptionInformation[0]* contains a read-write flag that indicates the type of operation that caused the access violation. If this value is 0, the thread tried to read the inaccessible data. If this value is 1, the thread tried to write to an inaccessible address. *ExceptionInformation[1]* specifies the virtual address of the inaccessible data.

By using these members, you can produce exception filters that offer you a significant amount of information about your application. For example, you might write an exception filter like this one:

```
__try {
    .
    .
    .
}
__except (ExpFltr(GetExceptionInformation())) {
    .
    .
    .
}

LONG ExpFltr (LPEXCEPTION_POINTERS lpEP) {
    char szBuf[300], *p;
    DWORD dwExceptionCode = lpEP->ExceptionRecord->ExceptionCode;

    sprintf(szBuf, "Code = %x, Address = %x",
        dwExceptionCode,
        lpEP->ExceptionRecord->ExceptionAddress);

    // Find the end of the string.
    p = strchr(szBuf, 0);

    // I used a switch statement in case Microsoft adds
    // information for other exception codes in the future.
    switch (dwExceptionCode) {
    case EXCEPTION_ACCESS_VIOLATION:
        wsprintf(p, "Attempt to %s data at address %x",
            lpEP->ExceptionRecord->ExceptionInformation[0] ?
                "read" : "write",
            lpEP->ExceptionRecord->ExceptionInformation[1]);
        break;

    default:
        break;
    }

    MessageBox(NULL, szBuf, "Exception",
        MB_OK | MB_ICONEXCLAMATION);

    return(EXCEPTION_CONTINUE_SEARCH);
}
```

The *ContextRecord* member of the EXCEPTION_POINTERS structure points to a CONTEXT structure. This structure is platform dependent; that is, the contents of this structure will differ from one CPU platform to another. Here is the CONTEXT structure for an *x*86 CPU:

```
typedef struct _CONTEXT {

    // Flags describing contents of CONTEXT record
    DWORD ContextFlags;

    // Debug registers
    DWORD    Dr0;
    DWORD    Dr1;
    DWORD    Dr2;
    DWORD    Dr3;
    DWORD    Dr6;
    DWORD    Dr7;

    // Floating point registers
    FLOATING_SAVE_AREA FloatSave;

    // Segment registers
    DWORD    SegGs;
    DWORD    SegFs;
    DWORD    SegEs;
    DWORD    SegDs;

    // Integer registers
    DWORD    Edi;
    DWORD    Esi;
    DWORD    Ebx;
    DWORD    Edx;
    DWORD    Ecx;
    DWORD    Eax;

    // Control registers
    DWORD    Ebp;
    DWORD    Eip;
    DWORD    SegCs;
    DWORD    EFlags;
    DWORD    Esp;
    DWORD    SegSs;

} CONTEXT;
```

Basically, this structure contains one member for each of the registers available on the CPU. When an exception is generated, you can find out even more information by examining the members of this structure. Unfortunately, realizing the benefit of such a possibility requires you to write platform-dependent code that recognizes the machine it's running on and uses the appropriate CONTEXT structure. The best way to handle this is to put *#ifdef*s into your code. The CONTEXT structures for the *x*86, MIPS, and Alpha CPUs are in the WINNT.H header file.

You can change some or all of the members in the CONTEXT structure in an exception filter and have the filter return EXCEP-TION_CONTINUE_EXECUTION. Just before the system tries to restart the instruction at which the exception occurred, it would reload all of the CPU registers for the thread with the modified values in the CONTEXT structure. You could use this to your advantage. For example, if you know that an exception occurred because the Eax register was 0 (zero), you could change the Eax register to some other value in the exception filter. Needless to say, this down-and-dirty technique is not for the squeamish. Of course, any code you write to manipulate CPU registers is platform specific and you'll have to change it if you want to port your code to another CPU platform.

The SEH Exceptions Sample Application

The SEHExcpt (SEHEXCPT.EXE) sample application, listed in Figure 10-4 beginning on page 605, demonstrates the use of exception filters and handlers. When you invoke SEHExcpt, this dialog box appears:

When you click on the *Execute* button, the program calls VirtualAlloc to reserve a region of memory in the process's address space big enough to contain an array of 50 elements, each 4 KB in size. Notice that I said the address space is reserved—not committed.

After reserving the address space, the program tries to write to randomly selected elements in the array. You get to specify the number of accesses the program will try by entering a number in the *Number of writes to perform* field.

For the first randomly selected element, an access violation exception will occur because memory has only been reserved—not committed. At this point, the exception filter, identified by the ExpFilter function in SEHEXCPT.C, gets called by the operating system.

This filter is responsible for calling VirtualAlloc again, but this time, it passes MEM_COMMIT to VirtualAlloc in order to actually commit memory to the reserved address space. But, before the filter can do this, it must determine that the exception that it is filtering occurred because of an invalid memory access in the reserved address space.

It's important that the program not accidentally absorb exceptions. When you implement an exception filter, be sure to perform whatever tests are necessary in order to ensure that you are actually handling the exception for which you designed the filter. If any other exception occurs, an exception that the filter can't handle, the filter must return EXCEPTION_CONTINUE_SEARCH.

The ExpFilter function determines whether the occurring exception comes from an invalid array access by performing the following tests:

1. Is the exception code EXCEPTION_ACCESS_VIOLATION?

2. Had memory for the array been reserved when the exception occurred? An exception might have occurred before memory for the array had even been reserved.

3. Is the address of the invalid memory access within the memory region reserved for the array?

If any of the three tests fails, the filter was not written to handle the occurring exception and the filter returns EXCEPTION-_CONTINUE_SEARCH. If all three tests succeed, the filter assumes that the invalid access was in the array and calls CommitMemory. CommitMemory determines whether the invalid memory access was an attempt to read from or to write to the array and creates a string to be displayed in the *Execution log* list box. For this sample program, the memory access will always be an attempt to write to the memory. Finally, CommitMemory calls VirtualAlloc to commit memory to the region of the array memory occupied by the individual array element that was accessed.

When CommitMemory returns to the exception filter, the filter returns EXCEPTION_CONTINUE_EXECUTION. This causes the machine instruction that generated the exception to execute again. This time, the memory access will succeed because memory will have been committed.

Earlier in this chapter I said that you must be careful when returning EXCEPTION_CONTINUE_EXECUTION from a filter. I said that there could be a problem if your compiler generates multiple machine instructions for a single C/C++ statement. In this case, there would be no problem. This example is guaranteed to work on any CPU platform using any programming language or compiler because we are not trying to change any variables that the compiler might decide to load into registers.

As the program executes, it keeps a record of the amount of time required to run the whole access loop. The program also keeps track of the time that was spent in the exception filter. I didn't go to great lengths to get an accurate count. I just wanted to get an idea of how much overhead was involved in processing the exception filter. At the end of the *Execution log*, the program displays these two time values as well as the percentage of the total time that was spent in the exception filter.

OK, let's look at a sample run of the program:

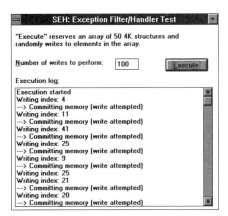

The log shows the results of performing 100 randomly selected write accesses to the array. In the beginning, no memory had been committed, causing the exception filter to be invoked for array indexes 4, 11, 41, 25, and 9. But then index 25 was written to again. This time, no access violation occurred, and the exception filter didn't get called.

Now, let's scroll to the bottom of the *Execution log*:

At the end of the 100 accesses, we have very few exceptions occurring because most of the array indexes have already been selected and memory for these indexes has been committed.

We can also see that the entire access loop ran in 105 milliseconds and that 15 milliseconds of that time was spent in the exception filter. This gives us a grand total (drum roll, please) of 14 percent of the total execution time being used by the exception filter.

For comparison's sake, I'll execute the program again, but this time, I'll perform 1000 accesses. Here is what the bottom of the *Execution log* looks like:

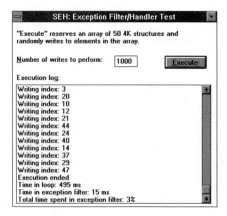

This time, the loop required 495 milliseconds to run with the exception filter requiring 15 milliseconds, which tells us that the exception filter used only 3 percent of the loop's total execution time.

You'll notice that I put a *try-finally* block inside the ExpFilter function. I did this as a demonstration that it's perfectly legal and useful to use structured exception handling inside an exception filter. It's also possible to put *try-finally* or *try-except* blocks inside *finally* blocks or *except* blocks, and it's even possible to nest *try-finally* and *try-except* blocks inside one another. Nesting of exception handlers inside an exception filter will be demonstrated in the SEHSoft sample application coming up a little later.

As with the SEHTerm program we looked at earlier, you can experiment with SEHExcpt yourself by changing the number of array accesses and seeing how this number affects the amount of time used by the exception filter.

SEHExcpt.ico

SEHEXCPT.C

```
/******************************************************************
Module name: SEHExcpt.C
Notices: Copyright (c) 1993 Jeffrey Richter
******************************************************************/

#include <windows.h>
#include <windowsx.h>
#include <tchar.h>
#include <stdio.h>      // for sprintf
#include <stdlib.h>     // for rand
#include "SEHExcpt.H"


////////////////////////////////////////////////////////////////

// This variable is used to calculate the amount of time that
// the application spends executing code in the exception
// filter.
```

Figure 10-4. *(continued)*

The SEHExcpt application.

Figure 10-4. *continued*

```
DWORD g_dwTimeInExceptionFilter = 0;

#define NUMELEMENTS    (50)

// Declare each array element to be 4KB.
typedef struct {
   BYTE bReserved[4 * 1024];
} ELEMENT, *LPELEMENT;

/////////////////////////////////////////////////////////////////

void CommitMemory(HWND hwndLog, LPEXCEPTION_POINTERS lpEP,
   LPBYTE lpAttemptedAddr) {

   BOOL fAttemptedWrite;
   TCHAR szBuf[100];

   // Find out whether a memory access was tried.
   fAttemptedWrite = (BOOL)
      lpEP->ExceptionRecord->ExceptionInformation[0];

   // Add an entry to the "Execution log" list box.
   _stprintf(szBuf,
      __TEXT("---> Committing memory (%s attempted)"),
      fAttemptedWrite ? __TEXT("write") : __TEXT("read"));
   ListBox_AddString(hwndLog, szBuf);

   // The attempted memory access did occur while the program
   // was accessing an element in our array. Let's try to
   // commit memory to an individual element of the reserved
   // array's address space.
   VirtualAlloc(lpAttemptedAddr, sizeof(ELEMENT), MEM_COMMIT,
      PAGE_READWRITE);
}

/////////////////////////////////////////////////////////////////

int ExpFilter (LPEXCEPTION_POINTERS lpEP, LPBYTE lpArray,
   LONG lNumBytesInArray, HWND hwndLog) {

   // Save the time at which the function began executing.
   DWORD  dwStartTimeInFilter = GetTickCount();
```

(continued)

Figure 10-4. *continued*

```
// Get the exception code explaining
// why the filter is executing.
DWORD  dwExceptionCode =
   lpEP->ExceptionRecord->ExceptionCode;

// Assume that this filter will NOT handle the
// exception and will let the system continue
// scanning for other filters.
int    nFilterResult = EXCEPTION_CONTINUE_SEARCH;

LPBYTE lpAttemptedAddr;

__try {
   // We must first determine whether the exception is
   // occurring because of a memory access to our array of
   // elements. This filter and handler does not process
   // any other types of exceptions.

   if (dwExceptionCode != EXCEPTION_ACCESS_VIOLATION) {
      // If the exception is not a memory access violation,
      // the exception doesn't come from an array element
      // access. The system should continue its search for
      // another exception filter.
      nFilterResult = EXCEPTION_CONTINUE_SEARCH;
      __leave;
   }

   if (lpArray == NULL) {
      // The exception occurred before the
      // program tried to reserve the address
      // space, or the array's address
      // space was unsuccessfully reserved.
      nFilterResult = EXCEPTION_CONTINUE_SEARCH;
      __leave;
   }

   // Get the address of the attempted memory access.
   lpAttemptedAddr = (LPBYTE)
      lpEP->ExceptionRecord->ExceptionInformation[1];

   if ((lpAttemptedAddr < lpArray) ||
      ((lpArray + lNumBytesInArray) < lpAttemptedAddr)) {
```

(continued)

Figure 10-4. *continued*

```
            // Address attempted is BELOW the beginning of the
            // array's reserved space or is ABOVE the end of the
            // array's reserved space. We'll let some other
            // filter handle this exception.
            nFilterResult = EXCEPTION_CONTINUE_SEARCH;
            __leave;
        }

        // *** This filter will handle the exception.

        CommitMemory(hwndLog, lpEP, lpAttemptedAddr);

        // Memory is committed now. Let's restart the
        // instruction that caused the exception in the first
        // place. This time, the instruction will succeed
        // and not cause another exception.
        nFilterResult = EXCEPTION_CONTINUE_EXECUTION;
    }

    __finally {
        // Add the amount of time spent in the filter
        // to our global counter. With this code in the
        // finally block, it is guaranteed to execute.
        g_dwTimeInExceptionFilter +=
            GetTickCount() - dwStartTimeInFilter;
    }

    // Now that memory is committed, we can continue execution
    // at the instruction that generated the exception in
    // the first place.
    return(nFilterResult);
}

//////////////////////////////////////////////////////////////////

void Dlg_ReserveArrayAndAccessIt (HWND hwndLog,
    int nNumAccesses) {

    LPELEMENT lpArray = NULL;
    ELEMENT Element;
    TCHAR szBuf[100];
    int nElementNum;
```

(continued)

608

Figure 10-4. *continued*

```
const LONG lNumBytesInArray = sizeof(ELEMENT) *
   NUMELEMENTS;

// Get the time at which this function started executing.
DWORD dwTimeInAccessLoop = GetTickCount();

// Zero the amount of time that has
// been spent in the exception filter.
g_dwTimeInExceptionFilter = 0;

// Clear the "Execution Log" list box.
ListBox_ResetContent(hwndLog);
ListBox_AddString(hwndLog, __TEXT("Execution started"));

__try {
   // Reserve an address space large enough to
   // hold NUMELEMENTS number of ELEMENTs.
   lpArray = VirtualAlloc(NULL, lNumBytesInArray,
      MEM_RESERVE, PAGE_NOACCESS);

   while (nNumAccesses--) {
      // Get the index of a random element to access.
      nElementNum = rand() % NUMELEMENTS;

      // Try a write access.
      _stprintf(szBuf,
         __TEXT("Writing index: %d"), nElementNum);
      ListBox_AddString(hwndLog, szBuf);

      // The exception will occur at this line.
      lpArray[nElementNum] = Element;

   } // while

   // We have finished the execution.
   ListBox_AddString(hwndLog, __TEXT("Execution ended"));

   // Calculate the total time
   // spent in the array access loop.
   dwTimeInAccessLoop = GetTickCount() -
      dwTimeInAccessLoop;

   // Display the number of milliseconds
   // the whole loop took.
```

(continued)

Figure 10-4. *continued*

```
        _stprintf(szBuf, __TEXT("Time in loop: %d ms"),
            dwTimeInAccessLoop);
        ListBox_AddString(hwndLog, szBuf);

        // Display the number of milliseconds
        // the exception filter took.
        _stprintf(szBuf,
            __TEXT("Time in exception filter: %d ms"),
            g_dwTimeInExceptionFilter);
        ListBox_AddString(hwndLog, szBuf);

        // Display the percentage of the total
        // time used by the exception filter.
        _stprintf(szBuf,
            __TEXT("Total time spent in exception filter: %d%%"),
            (100 * g_dwTimeInExceptionFilter) /
            dwTimeInAccessLoop);
        ListBox_AddString(hwndLog, szBuf);

        // Free all the memory.
        VirtualFree(lpArray, 0, MEM_RELEASE);
    }  // __try

    __except (
        ExpFilter(GetExceptionInformation(), (LPBYTE) lpArray,
            lNumBytesInArray, hwndLog)) {

        // Since the filter never returns
        // EXCEPTION_EXECUTE_HANDLER, there is nothing
        // to do in the except block.

    }  // __except
}

////////////////////////////////////////////////////////////////

BOOL Dlg_OnInitDialog (HWND hwnd, HWND hwndFocus,
    LPARAM lParam) {

    // Associate an icon with the dialog box.
    SetClassLong(hwnd, GCL_HICON, (LONG)
        LoadIcon((HINSTANCE) GetWindowLong(hwnd, GWL_HINSTANCE),
        __TEXT("SEHExcpt")));
```

(continued)

Figure 10-4. *continued*

```
    // Default the number of accesses to 100.
    SetDlgItemInt(hwnd, ID_NUMACCESSES, 100, FALSE);
    return(TRUE);
}


///////////////////////////////////////////////////////////

void Dlg_OnCommand (HWND hwnd, int id, HWND hwndCtl,
    UINT codeNotify) {

    int  nNumAccesses;
    BOOL fTranslated;

    switch (id) {
        case IDOK:
            nNumAccesses = GetDlgItemInt(hwnd, ID_NUMACCESSES,
                &fTranslated, FALSE);

            if (fTranslated) {
                Dlg_ReserveArrayAndAccessIt(
                    GetDlgItem(hwnd, ID_LOG), nNumAccesses);
            } else {
                MessageBox(hwnd,
                    __TEXT("Invalid number of accesses."),
                    __TEXT("SEHExcpt"), MB_OK);
            }
            break;

        case IDCANCEL:
            EndDialog(hwnd, id);
            break;
    }
}

///////////////////////////////////////////////////////////

BOOL CALLBACK Dlg_Proc (HWND hDlg, UINT uMsg,
    WPARAM wParam, LPARAM lParam) {

    BOOL fProcessed = TRUE;

    switch (uMsg) {
        HANDLE_MSG(hDlg, WM_INITDIALOG, Dlg_OnInitDialog);
        HANDLE_MSG(hDlg, WM_COMMAND, Dlg_OnCommand);
```

(continued)

Figure 10-4. *continued*

```
    default:
        fProcessed = FALSE;
        break;
    }
    return(fProcessed);
}


///////////////////////////////////////////////////////////////

int APIENTRY WinMain (HINSTANCE hInstance,
    HINSTANCE hPrevInstance, LPSTR lpszCmdLine, int nCmdShow) {

    DialogBox(hInstance, MAKEINTRESOURCE(DLG_SEHEXCPT),
        NULL, Dlg_Proc);
    return(0);
}


//////////////////////// End Of File ////////////////////////
```

SEHEXCPT.H

```
/**************************************************************
Module name: SEHExcpt.H
Notices: Copyright (c) 1993 Jeffrey Richter
**************************************************************/

// Dialog and control IDs.
#define DLG_SEHEXCPT        1
#define ID_NUMACCESSES      100
#define ID_LOG              101


//////////////////////// End Of File ////////////////////////
```

SEHEXCPT.RC

```
/**************************************************************
Module name: SEHExcpt.RC
Notices: Copyright (c) 1993 Jeffrey Richter
**************************************************************/

#include "windows.h"
#include "SEHExcpt.h"
```

(continued)

Figure 10-4. *continued*

```
SEHExcpt  ICON  DISCARDABLE SEHExcpt.Ico

DLG_SEHEXCPT DIALOG 18, 18, 214, 200
STYLE WS_BORDER | WS_OVERLAPPED | WS_VISIBLE | WS_CAPTION |
    WS_SYSMENU | WS_MINIMIZEBOX
CAPTION "SEH: Exception Filter/Handler Test"
FONT 8, "Helv"
BEGIN
    LTEXT """Execute""" reserves an array of 50 4K
structures and randomly writes to elements in the array.",
        -1, 4, 8, 188, 24
    CONTROL "&Number of writes to perform:", -1, "STATIC",
        WS_CHILD | WS_VISIBLE | WS_GROUP, 4, 36, 124, 8
    EDITTEXT ID_NUMACCESSES, 108, 36, 24, 12,
        ES_LEFT | WS_CHILD | WS_VISIBLE | WS_BORDER | WS_TABSTOP
    CONTROL "&Execute", IDOK, "BUTTON",
        BS_PUSHBUTTON | WS_CHILD | WS_VISIBLE | WS_GROUP |
        WS_TABSTOP, 160, 36, 44, 14
    LTEXT "Execution lo&g:", -1, 4, 56, 56, 8
    CONTROL "", ID_LOG, "LISTBOX", WS_CHILD | WS_VISIBLE |
        WS_BORDER | WS_VSCROLL | WS_GROUP | WS_TABSTOP,
        4, 68, 204, 128
END

//////////////////////// End Of File ////////////////////////
```

Software Exceptions

So far, we have been looking at handling hardware exceptions in which the CPU catches an event and generates an exception. Often, it's useful to generate software exceptions, in which the operating system or your application generates its own exceptions. The HeapAlloc function provides a good occasion for software exception use. When you call the HeapAlloc function, you can specify the HEAP_GENERATE_EXCEPTIONS flag. Then if HeapAlloc is unable to satisfy the memory request, HeapAlloc generates a STATUS_NO_MEMORY software exception.

If you want to take advantage of this exception, you can code your *try* block as though the memory allocation will always succeed and then, if the allocation fails, you can either handle the exception by using an *except* block or have your function clean up by matching the *try* block with a *finally* block.

Your application doesn't need to know whether it is processing a hardware exception or a software exception, and you implement your *try-finally* and *try-except* blocks identically. However, you can have portions of your code generate software exceptions themselves just as HeapAlloc does. To generate a software exception in your code, call the RaiseException function:

```
VOID RaiseException(DWORD dwExceptionCode, DWORD dwExceptionFlags,
    DWORD cArguments, LPDWORD lpArguments);
```

The first parameter, *dwExceptionCode*, must be a value that identifies the generated exception. The HeapAlloc function passes STATUS_NO-_MEMORY for this parameter. If you generate your own exception identifiers, you should follow the same format the standard Windows NT error codes as defined in WINERROR.H follow. You'll recall that each DWORD is divided as shown in this table:

Bits:	31–30	29–28	27–16	15–0
Contents:	Severity	Flags	Facility code	Exception code
Meaning:	0 = Success	Bit 29	Programmer defined	Programmer defined
	1 = Informational	0 = Microsoft		
	2 = Warning	1 = Customer		
	3 = Error	Bit 28 is reserved (must be zero)		

If you create your own exception code, fill out all four fields of the DWORD: Bits 30 and 31 should contain the severity, bit 29 should be 1 (0 is reserved for Microsoft-created exceptions, such as HeapAlloc's STATUS_NO_MEMORY), bit 28 should be 0, bits 16 through 27 and bits 0 through 15 should be any arbitrary values you choose to identify the section of your application that generated the exception.

RaiseException's second parameter, *dwExceptionFlags*, must be either 0 or EXCEPTION_NONCONTINUABLE. Specifying the EX-CEPTION_NONCONTINUABLE flag tells the system that the type of exception you are generating can't be continued. The EXCEPTION-_NONCONTINUABLE flag is used internally in Windows NT to signal fatal (nonrecoverable) errors.

When HeapAlloc raises the STATUS_NO_MEMORY exception, it uses the EXCEPTION_NONCONTINUABLE flag to tell the system that this exception cannot be continued and that it is illegal for an exception filter to evaluate to EXCEPTION_CONTINUE_EXECUTION. If this type of exception is generated and an exception filter does evaluate to EXCEPTION_CONTINUE_EXECUTION, the system generates a new exception: EXCEPTION_NONCONTINUABLE_EXCEPTION.

That's right—I haven't mentioned the possibility before, but it is possible for an exception to be generated while the application is trying to process another exception. This of course makes sense. While we're at it, let's note that it's also possible for an invalid memory access to occur inside a *finally* block, an exception filter, or an exception handler. When this happens, the system stacks exceptions. Remember the GetExceptionInformation function? This function returns the address of an EXCEPTION_POINTERS structure. The *ExceptionRecord* member of the EXCEPTION_POINTERS structure points to an EXCEPTION_RECORD structure that contains another *ExceptionRecord* member. This member is a pointer to another EXCEPTION_RECORD, which contains information about the previously generated exception.

Usually, the system is processing only one exception at a time and the *ExceptionRecord* member is NULL. However, if during the processing of one exception another exception is generated, the first EXCEPTION_RECORD structure contains information about the most-recently generated exception and the *ExceptionRecord* member of this first EXCEPTION_RECORD structure points to the EXCEPTION_RECORD structure for the previously generated exception. If additional exceptions have not been completely processed, you can continue to walk this linked list of EXCEPTION_RECORD structures to determine how to handle the exception.

RaiseException's third and fourth parameters, *cArguments* and *lpArguments*, are used to pass additional information about the generated exception. If you don't need additional arguments, you can pass NULL to *lpArguments*, in which case RaiseException ignores the *cArguments* parameter. If you do wish to pass additional arguments, the *cArguments* parameter must indicate the number of elements in the DWORD array pointed to by the *lpArguments* parameter. This parameter cannot exceed EXCEPTION_MAXIMUM_PARAMETERS, which is defined in WINNT.H as 15.

During the processing of this exception, you can have an exception filter refer to the *NumberParameters* and the *ExceptionInformation* members of the EXCEPTION_RECORD structure to examine the information in the *cArguments* and *lpArguments* parameters.

You might want to generate your own software exceptions in your application for any of several reasons. You might want to send informational messages to the system's event log. Whenever a function in your application sensed some sort of problem, you could call RaiseException and have some exception handler further up the call tree look for certain exceptions and add them to the event log or pop up a message box. You might also want to create software exceptions to signal internal fatal errors in your application. This device would be much easier than trying to return error values all the way up the call tree.

Software Exceptions in C++ Constructors

One of my favorite uses for software exceptions is in C++ code. I often design classes that have their own constructors. Many of these class constructors need to allocate additional memory or resources before an instance of the class can be considered "created." The problem with C++ is that the constructor is a special type of function that is not allowed to return a value. A value would be useful so that your application would know whether the required resources were allocated and whether the instance of the class was successfully created. A great way to get this information as the class's constructor executes is to call RaiseException in the constructor if the required resources couldn't be allocated.

The function creating the class instances could surround the declaration of the class objects with a *try-except* block. If the constructor raised an exception, the calling function's exception filter would get evaluated. The filter would then call GetExceptionCode to determine why the exception was raised and handle the exception in any way that it sees fit. When generating exceptions for ill-constructed C++ class objects, you might need to be careful when dealing with the destructor for the class as well. It's possible that the destructor will get called for an ill-constructed object.

For example, you might design a C++ class that contains a pointer to an array of integers. Memory is allocated for the integer array in the constructor of the class. In the constructor, you should initialize the pointer to be NULL first and then attempt to allocate the memory block for the array. If the array allocation fails, you could generate a software exception. If you didn't initialize the pointer to NULL first, the pointer would contain whatever garbage just happened to be in the memory at the same location as the new object. Now, in the destructor, be sure that you free the memory block only if the pointer is not NULL.

The SEH Software Exceptions Sample Application

The SEHSoft (SEHSOFT.EXE) application, listed in Figure 10-5 beginning on page 620, demonstrates how to create and use your own software exceptions. The program is based on the earlier SEHExcpt sample program. When you invoke SEHSoft, this dialog box appears:

This box is similar to SEHExcpt's dialog box, but this program will try to read from as well as write to the array of elements.

In the Dlg_ReserveArrayAndAccessIt function, the access loop gets the index of a random element to access and then has been modified to select another random number. This second number is used to determine whether the program should try to write the element to the array or read the element from the array.

You might be asking yourself what it means to read an element from the array if the array has never been initialized. You'd be quite correct. I have enhanced the program to automatically zero the contents of an array element when memory is commited because the program has tried to read an array element. I did this by generating a software exception.

617

Inside the ExpFilter function, instead of just calling Commit-Memory as I did in SEHEXCPT.C, I put the call to CommitMemory into a *try* block. The filter expression for the *except* block associated with this *try* block checks whether the call to CommitMemory has generated an exception and whether that exception code is SE_ZERO_ELEM.

SE_ZERO_ELEM is a define that identifies a software exception code I have created at the top of SEHSOFT.C:

```
// Useful macro for creating our own software exception codes.
#define MAKESOFTWAREEXCEPTION(Severity, Facility, Exception) \
   ((DWORD) ( \
   /* Severity code */      (Severity << 30) |    \
   /* MS(0) or Cust(1) */   (1         << 29) |    \
   /* Reserved(0) */        (0         << 28) |    \
   /* Facility code */      (Facility << 16) |    \
   /* Exception code */     (Exception << 0)))

// Our very own software exception. This exception is raised when
// an element of the array needs to be initialized to all zeroes.
#define SE_ZERO_ELEM   MAKESOFTWAREEXCEPTION(3, 0, 1)
```

The exception filter expression looks like this:

```
__except ((GetExceptionCode() == SE_ZERO_ELEM) ?
   (lpEP2 = GetExceptionInformation(),
     EXCEPTION_EXECUTE_HANDLER) :
     EXCEPTION_CONTINUE_SEARCH) {

   .
   .
   .

}
```

The exception handler is prepared to handle only SE_ZERO_ELEM exceptions. If GetExceptionCode returns any other exception, EX-CEPTION_CONTINUE_SEARCH is returned. If the exception code is SE_ZERO_ELEM, EXCEPTION_EXECUTE_HANDLER should be returned so that the code inside the *except* block will be executed. But the code inside the *except* block will need access to the exception infor-mation, so a call to GetExceptionInformation is made before the return. EXCEPTION_EXECUTE_HANDLER and the pointer to the excep-tion information are stored in the local *lpEP2* variable.

Now that the code inside the *except* block is executing, it gets the address of the array element that needs to be zeroed by looking into the exception information structures and calls *memset* to zero this one array element.

The only thing that I've left out is how the exception is generated. The code appears at the bottom of the CommitMemory function:

```
if (!fAttemptedWrite) {
   // The program is trying to read an array ELEMENT
   // that has never been created. We'll raise our very own
   // software exception so that this array element will be
   // zeroed before it is accessed.
   RaiseException(SE_ZERO_ELEM, 0, 1, (LPDWORD) &lpAttemptedAddr);
}
```

If the attempted access is a read, the program calls RaiseException passing it a SE_ZERO_ELEM software exception code and a 0 flag. We can also pass, using the third and fourth arguments, a maximum of EX-CEPTION_MAXIMUM_PARAMETERS (15) parameters to the exception filter. In this example, I want to pass just one parameter to the filter: the address to the array element that needs to be zeroed. To do this, I send 1 as the third argument to RaiseException and the address to that parameter as the fourth argument.

Here is an example of what SEHSoft looks like when it's executed:

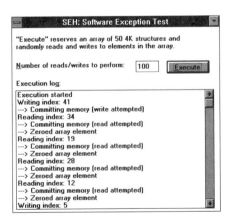

Every time the software exception is raised, the exception handler adds an entry to the *Execution log* showing that it zeroed the array element.

SEHSoft.ico

SEHSOFT.C

```c
/***************************************************************
Module name: SEHSoft.C
Notices: Copyright (c) 1993 Jeffrey Richter
***************************************************************/

#include <windows.h>
#include <windowsx.h>
#include <tchar.h>
#include <stdio.h>        // for sprintf
#include <stdlib.h>       // for rand
#include "SEHSoft.H"


//////////////////////////////////////////////////////////////////


// This variable is used to calculate the amount of time
// that the application spends executing code in the
// exception filter.
DWORD g_dwTimeInExceptionFilter = 0;

#define NUMELEMENTS       (50)

// Declare each array element to be 4KB.
typedef struct {
   BYTE bReserved[4 * 1024];
} ELEMENT, *LPELEMENT;

// Useful macro for creating our own software exception codes.
#define MAKESOFTWAREEXCEPTION(Severity, Facility, Exception) \
   ((DWORD) ( \
   /* Severity code */      (Severity  << 30) |      \
   /* MS(0) or Cust(1) */   (1         << 29) |      \
   /* Reserved(0) */        (0         << 28) |      \
   /* Facility code */      (Facility  << 16) |      \
   /* Exception code */     (Exception <<  0)))
```

Figure 10-5.
The SEHSoft application.

(continued)

Figure 10-5. *continued*

```
// Our very own software exception. This exception is raised
// when an element of the array needs to be initialized
// to all zeroes.
#define SE_ZERO_ELEM   MAKESOFTWAREEXCEPTION(3, 0, 1)


//////////////////////////////////////////////////////////////

void CommitMemory(HWND hwndLog, LPEXCEPTION_POINTERS lpEP,
   LPBYTE lpAttemptedAddr) {

   BOOL fAttemptedWrite;
   TCHAR szBuf[100];

   // Find out whether a memory read or write was tried.
   fAttemptedWrite = (BOOL)
      lpEP->ExceptionRecord->ExceptionInformation[0];

   // Add an entry to the "Execution log" list box.
   _stprintf(szBuf,
      __TEXT("---> Committing memory (%s attempted)"),
      fAttemptedWrite ? __TEXT("write") : __TEXT("read"));
   ListBox_AddString(hwndLog, szBuf);

   // The attempted memory access did occur while the
   // program was accessing an element in our array.
   // Let's try to commit memory to an individual element of
   // the reserved array's address space.
   VirtualAlloc(lpAttemptedAddr, sizeof(ELEMENT), MEM_COMMIT,
      PAGE_READWRITE);

   if (!fAttemptedWrite) {
      // The program is trying to read an array element
      // that has never been created. We'll raise our very
      // own software exception so that this array element
      // will be zeroed before it is accessed.
      RaiseException(SE_ZERO_ELEM, 0, 1,
         (LPDWORD) &lpAttemptedAddr);
   }
}


//////////////////////////////////////////////////////////////

int ExpFilter (LPEXCEPTION_POINTERS lpEP, LPBYTE lpArray,
   LONG lNumBytesInArray, HWND hwndLog) {
```

(continued)

Figure 10-5. *continued*

```
// Save the time when the function began executing.
DWORD  dwStartTimeInFilter = GetTickCount();

// Get the exception code explaining
// why the filter is executing.
DWORD  dwExceptionCode =
  lpEP->ExceptionRecord->ExceptionCode;

// Assume that this filter will NOT handle the exception
// and will let the system continue scanning
// for other filters.
int    nFilterResult = EXCEPTION_CONTINUE_SEARCH;

LPBYTE lpAttemptedAddr;

__try {
  // Declare an EXCEPTION_RECORD
  // structure that is local to this __try frame. This
  // variable is used in the __except block below.
  EXCEPTION_RECORD SavedExceptRec;

  // We must first determine if the exception is
  // occurring because of a memory access to zero the
  // array of elements. This filter and handler does not
  // process any other types of exceptions.

  if (dwExceptionCode != EXCEPTION_ACCESS_VIOLATION) {
      // If the exception is not a memory access violation,
      // the exception is not due to an array element
      // access. The system should continue its search for
      // another exception filter.
      nFilterResult = EXCEPTION_CONTINUE_SEARCH;
      __leave;
  }

  if (lpArray == NULL) {
      // The exception occurred before attempting to
      // reserve the address space or the array's address
      // space was unsuccessfully reserved.
      nFilterResult = EXCEPTION_CONTINUE_SEARCH;
      __leave;
  }
```

(continued)

622

Figure 10-5. *continued*

```
    // Get the address of the attempted memory access.
    lpAttemptedAddr = (LPBYTE)
        lpEP->ExceptionRecord->ExceptionInformation[1];

    if ((lpAttemptedAddr < lpArray) ||
        ((lpArray + lNumBytesInArray) < lpAttemptedAddr)) {
        // Address attempted is BELOW the beginning of the
        // array's reserved space or is ABOVE the end of the
        // array's reserved space. We'll let some other
        // filter handle this exception.
        nFilterResult = EXCEPTION_CONTINUE_SEARCH;
        __leave;
    }

    // *** The exception is to be handled by this filter.

    __try {
        // Call the function that commits memory to the
        // accessed array element. This function will raise
        // a software exception if read-access was attempted.
        // In this case, we want to zero the contents of the
        // array element before the read continues.
        CommitMemory(hwndLog, lpEP, lpAttemptedAddr);
    }

    // We only want to handle the exception if it is our
    // very own software exception telling us to zero the
    // contents of the array element. If this happens, we
    // need to save the additional information given to us
    // with the SE_ZERO_ELEM exception code so that the
    // handler knows which array element to zero.
    __except ((GetExceptionCode() == SE_ZERO_ELEM) ?
        (SavedExceptRec =
        *((GetExceptionInformation())->ExceptionRecord),
            EXCEPTION_EXECUTE_HANDLER) :
            EXCEPTION_CONTINUE_SEARCH) {

        // Get the address of the array element to zero.
        LPELEMENT lpArrayElementToZero = (LPELEMENT)
            SavedExceptRec.ExceptionInformation[0];

        // Zero the array element before reading from it.
        memset((LPVOID) lpArrayElementToZero, 0,
            sizeof(ELEMENT));
```

(continued)

Figure 10-5. *continued*

```
        ListBox_AddString(hwndLog,
            __TEXT("---> Zeroed array element"));
    }

    // Memory is committed now, let's restart the
    // instruction that caused the exception in the first
    // place. This time, it will succeed and not cause
    // another exception.
    nFilterResult = EXCEPTION_CONTINUE_EXECUTION;
}

__finally {
    // Add the amount of time in the filter to our global
    // counter. With this code in the finally block, it is
    // guaranteed to execute.
    g_dwTimeInExceptionFilter += GetTickCount() -
        dwStartTimeInFilter;
}

// Now that memory is committed, we can continue execution
// on the instruction that generated the exception in
// the first place.
return(nFilterResult);
}


//////////////////////////////////////////////////////////////

void Dlg_ReserveArrayAndAccessIt (HWND hwndLog,
    int nNumAccesses) {

    LPELEMENT lpArray = NULL;
    ELEMENT Element;
    TCHAR szBuf[100];
    int nElementNum;
    const LONG lNumBytesInArray = sizeof(ELEMENT) *
        NUMELEMENTS;

    // Get the time when this function started executing.
    DWORD dwTimeInAccessLoop = GetTickCount();

    // Zero the amount of time that has been
    // spent in the exception filter.
    g_dwTimeInExceptionFilter = 0;
```

(continued)

Figure 10-5.   *continued*

```
// Clear the "Execution log" list box.
ListBox_ResetContent(hwndLog);
ListBox_AddString(hwndLog, __TEXT("Execution started"));

__try {
   // Reserve an address space large enough to
   // hold NUMELEMENTS number of ELEMENTs.
   lpArray = VirtualAlloc(NULL, lNumBytesInArray,
      MEM_RESERVE, PAGE_NOACCESS);

   while (nNumAccesses--) {
      // Get the index of a random element to access.
      nElementNum = rand() % NUMELEMENTS;

      // Give us a 50% chance of reading and a
      // 50% chance of writing.
      if ((rand() % 2) == 0) {
         // Attempt a read access.
         _stprintf(szBuf, __TEXT("Reading index: %d"),
            nElementNum);
         ListBox_AddString(hwndLog, szBuf);

         // The exception will occur on this line.
         Element = lpArray[nElementNum];

      } else {

         // Attempt a write access.
         _stprintf(szBuf, __TEXT("Writing index: %d"),
            nElementNum);
         ListBox_AddString(hwndLog, szBuf);

         // The exception will occur on this line.
         lpArray[nElementNum] = Element;
      }

   }  // while

   // We are done with the execution.
   ListBox_AddString(hwndLog, __TEXT("Execution ended"));

   // Calculate the total time spent
   // in the array access loop.
```

(continued)

Figure 10-5. *continued*

```
        dwTimeInAccessLoop = GetTickCount() -
            dwTimeInAccessLoop;

        // Display the number of milliseconds
        // the whole thing took.
        _stprintf(szBuf, __TEXT("Time in loop: %d ms"),
            dwTimeInAccessLoop);
        ListBox_AddString(hwndLog, szBuf);

        // Display the number of milliseconds
        // that the exception filter took.
        _stprintf(szBuf,
            __TEXT("Time in exception filter: %d ms"),
            g_dwTimeInExceptionFilter);
        ListBox_AddString(hwndLog, szBuf);

        // Display the percentage of the total
        // time used by exception filter.
        _stprintf(szBuf,
            __TEXT("Total time spent in exception filter: %d%%"),
            (100 * g_dwTimeInExceptionFilter) /
            dwTimeInAccessLoop);
        ListBox_AddString(hwndLog, szBuf);

        // Decommit and free the array of ELEMENTs.
        VirtualFree(lpArray, 0, MEM_RELEASE);
    } // __try

    __except (
        ExpFilter(GetExceptionInformation(), (LPBYTE) lpArray,
            lNumBytesInArray, hwndLog)) {

        // Since the filter never returns
        // EXCEPTION_EXECUTE_HANDLER, there is nothing
        // to do here.

    } // __except
}


//////////////////////////////////////////////////////////////////


BOOL Dlg_OnInitDialog (HWND hwnd, HWND hwndFocus,
    LPARAM lParam) {
```

(continued)

Figure 10-5. *continued*

```
    // Associate an icon with the dialog box.
    SetClassLong(hwnd, GCL_HICON, (LONG)
        LoadIcon((HINSTANCE) GetWindowLong(hwnd, GWL_HINSTANCE),
        __TEXT("SEHSoft")));

    // Default the number of accesses to 100.
    SetDlgItemInt(hwnd, ID_NUMACCESSES, 100, FALSE);
    return(TRUE);
}


///////////////////////////////////////////////////////////////

void Dlg_OnCommand (HWND hwnd, int id,
    HWND hwndCtl, UINT codeNotify) {

    int  nNumAccesses;
    BOOL fTranslated;

    switch (id) {
        case IDOK:
            nNumAccesses =
                GetDlgItemInt(hwnd, ID_NUMACCESSES,
                    &fTranslated, FALSE);

            if (fTranslated) {
                Dlg_ReserveArrayAndAccessIt(
                    GetDlgItem(hwnd, ID_LOG), nNumAccesses);
            } else {
                MessageBox(hwnd,
                    __TEXT("Invalid number of accesses."),
                    __TEXT("SEHSoft"), MB_OK);
            }
            break;

        case IDCANCEL:
            EndDialog(hwnd, id);
            break;
    }
}


///////////////////////////////////////////////////////////////
```

(continued)

Figure 10-5. *continued*

```
BOOL CALLBACK Dlg_Proc (HWND hDlg, UINT uMsg,
   WPARAM wParam, LPARAM lParam) {

   BOOL fProcessed = TRUE;

   switch (uMsg) {
      HANDLE_MSG(hDlg, WM_INITDIALOG, Dlg_OnInitDialog);
      HANDLE_MSG(hDlg, WM_COMMAND, Dlg_OnCommand);

      default:
         fProcessed = FALSE;
         break;
   }
   return(fProcessed);
}


//////////////////////////////////////////////////////////////////


int APIENTRY WinMain (HINSTANCE hInstance,
   HINSTANCE hPrevInstance, LPSTR lpszCmdLine, int nCmdShow) {

   DialogBox(hInstance, MAKEINTRESOURCE(DLG_SEHSOFT),
      NULL, Dlg_Proc);
   return(0);
}


///////////////////////// End Of File /////////////////////////
```

SEHSOFT.H

```
/************************************************************
Module name: SEHSoft.H
Notices: Copyright (c) 1993 Jeffrey Richter
************************************************************/

// Dialog and control IDs.
#define DLG_SEHSOFT          1
#define ID_NUMACCESSES       100
#define ID_LOG               101


///////////////////////// End Of File /////////////////////////
```

(continued)

Figure 10-5. *continued*

SEHSOFT.RC

```
/*****************************************************************
Module name: SEHSoft.RC
Notices: Copyright (c) 1993 Jeffrey Richter
*****************************************************************/

#include "windows.h"
#include "SEHSoft.h"

SEHSoft  ICON  DISCARDABLE SEHSoft.Ico

DLG_SEHSOFT DIALOG 18, 18, 214, 200
STYLE WS_BORDER | WS_OVERLAPPED | WS_VISIBLE | WS_CAPTION |
    WS_SYSMENU | WS_MINIMIZEBOX
CAPTION "SEH: Software Exception Test"
FONT 8, "Helv"
BEGIN
    LTEXT
        """Execute""" reserves an array of 50 4K structures and
randomly reads and writes to elements in the array.",
    -1, 4, 8, 188, 24
    CONTROL "&Number of reads/writes to perform:",
        -1, "STATIC",
        WS_CHILD | WS_VISIBLE | WS_GROUP, 4, 36, 124, 8
    EDITTEXT ID_NUMACCESSES, 128, 36, 24, 12,
        ES_LEFT | WS_CHILD | WS_VISIBLE | WS_BORDER | WS_TABSTOP
    CONTROL "&Execute", IDOK, "BUTTON",
        BS_PUSHBUTTON | WS_CHILD | WS_VISIBLE | WS_GROUP |
        WS_TABSTOP, 160, 36, 44, 14
    LTEXT "Execution lo&g:", -1, 4, 56, 56, 8
    CONTROL "", ID_LOG, "LISTBOX", WS_CHILD | WS_VISIBLE |
        WS_BORDER | WS_VSCROLL | WS_GROUP | WS_TABSTOP,
        4, 68, 204, 128
END

//////////////////////// End Of File ////////////////////////
```

Halting Global Unwinds

It's possible to stop the system from completing a global unwind by
putting a *return* statement inside a *finally* block. Let's look at the code on
the following page.

```
void FuncMonkey (void) {
   __try {
      FuncFish(;)
   }
   __except (EXCEPTION_EXECUTE_HANDLER) {
      MessageBeep(0);
   }
   MessageBox(...);
}

void FuncFish (void) {
   FuncPheasant();
   MessageBox(...);
}

void FuncPheasant (void) {

   __try {
      strcpy(NULL, NULL);
   }

   __finally {
      return;
   }
}
```

When the *strcpy* function is called in FuncPheasant's *try* block, a memory access violation exception will be generated. When this happens, the system will start scanning to see whether any exception filters exist that can handle the exception. The system will find that the exception filter in FuncMonkey wants to handle the exception, and the system will start a global unwind.

The global unwind starts by executing the code inside FuncPheasant's *finally* block. However, this block of code contains a *return* statement. The *return* statement causes the system to stop unwinding, and FuncPheasant will actually end up returning to FuncFish. FuncFish will continue executing and will display a message box on the screen. Function FuncFish will then return to FuncMonkey. The code in FuncMonkey continues executing by calling MessageBox.

Notice that the code inside FuncMonkey's exception block never executes the call to MessageBeep. The *return* statement in FuncPheasant's *finally* block causes the system to stop unwinding altogether, and execution continues as though nothing ever happened.

Microsoft has designed SEH to work this way on purpose. You might occasionally want to stop unwinding and allow execution to continue, and this method allows you to do this. Usually, though, this isn't the sort of thing you want to do. As a rule, be careful to avoid putting *return* statements inside *finally* blocks.

Unhandled Exceptions

All through this chapter I've been pointing out that, when an exception occurs, the system tries to locate an exception filter that is willing to handle the exception. This is true, but it's actually not the first thing the system does when an exception occurs. When an exception is generated, the system first checks to see whether the process is attached to a debugger. If the process isn't attached to a debugger, then the system scans for exception filters.

If the process is being debugged, the system sends a debugging event to the debugger and fills out this EXCEPTION_DEBUG_INFO structure:

```
typedef struct _EXCEPTION_DEBUG_INFO {
    EXCEPTION_RECORD ExceptionRecord;
    DWORD dwFirstChance;
} EXCEPTION_DEBUG_INFO;
```

The EXCEPTION_DEBUG_INFO structure tells the debugger that an exception has occurred. The *ExceptionRecord* member contains the same information you would get by calling the Get-ExceptionInformation function. The debugger can use this information to determine how it wants to handle the exception. The *dwFirstChance* member will be set to nonzero. Typically, a debugger will be written to process breakpoint and single-step exceptions and can thus stop these exceptions from percolating up through your application.

If a debugger is monitoring the process and handles the exception, the process is allowed to continue processing. The debugger can also decide to freeze the process and allow you to inspect the reason for the generated exception.

If the debugger doesn't handle the exception, the system scans your application in search of an exception filter that returns either EXCEPTION_EXECUTE_HANDLER or EXCEPTION_CONTINUE-_EXECUTION. As soon as an exception filter returns one of these identifiers, execution continues as described for each identifier earlier in this chapter.

If the system reaches the top of the application without locating an exception filter to handle the exception, the system notifies the debugger again. This time, the *dwFirstChance* member in the EXCEPTION-_DEBUG_INFO structure will be *0*. The debugger can tell from this value that an unhandled exception occurred in the application and will display a message box notifying you of this unhandled exception and allow you to start debugging the application.

Unhandled Exceptions Without a Debugger Attached

But let's look at what happens if every exception filter returns EXCEP-TION_CONTINUE_SEARCH when your application is not being debugged. In this case, the system traverses all the way to the top of the application and can't find an exception filter willing to handle the exception. When this happens, the system calls a built-in exception filter function called UnhandledExceptionFilter:

```
LONG UnhandledExceptionFilter(
   LPEXCEPTION_POINTERS lpexpExceptionInfo);
```

The first thing that this function does is check whether the process is being debugged; if so, UnhandledExceptionFilter returns EXCEP-TION_CONTINUE_SEARCH, which causes the debugger to be notified of the exception.

If the process is not being debugged, the function displays a message box notifying the user that an exception occurred in the process. This message box looks similar to the following:

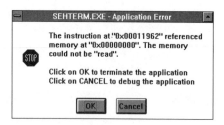

The first paragraph of the text indicates which exception occurred and the address of the instruction in the process's address space that generated the exception. It just so happens that a memory access violation caused this message box to appear, so the system can report the invalid memory address that was accessed and specify that the attempted access was for reading. The UnhandledExceptionFilter function gets this additional information by referencing the *Exception-Information* member of the *ExceptionRecord* structure generated for this exception.

Following the description of the exception, the message box indicates the user's two choices. The first is to click on the *OK* button, which causes UnhandledExceptionFilter to return EXCEPTION_EXECUTE-_HANDLER. This causes the system to execute a built-in exception handler that terminates the process by calling:

```
ExitProcess(GetExceptionCode());
```

The second choice, clicking on the *Cancel* button, is a developer's dream come true. When you click on the *Cancel* button, UnhandledExceptionFilter attempts to automatically load a debugger and attach the debugger to the process. With the debugger attached to the process, you can examine the state of variables, set breakpoints, restart the process, and do anything else you would normally do as you debug a process.

The real boon is that you can handle the failure of your application when it occurs. For most other operating systems, you must invoke your application through the debugger in order to debug it. If an exception occurred in a process for these other operating systems, you would have to terminate the process, start a debugger, and invoke the application again using the debugger. The problem is that you would have to try to reproduce the bug before you could fix it. And who knows what the values of the different variables were when the problem originally occurred? It's much harder to resolve a bug this way. The ability to dynamically attach a debugger to the process as it's running is one of Windows NT's best features.

UnhandledExceptionFilter invokes the debugger by looking into the registry. Specifically, the key contains the command line that UnhandledExceptionFilter executes:

```
HKEY_LOCAL_MACHINE\SOFTWARE\Microsoft\
    Windows NT\CurrentVersion\AeDebug\Debugger
```

When you install the Microsoft Windows NT SDK, the value of this key is set to:

```
F:\MSTOOLS\bin\windbg -p %ld -e %ld
```

This line tells the system which program to run (WINDBG.EXE) and where to find it (in F:\MSTOOLS\bin on my machine). UnhandledExceptionFilter also passes two parameters on the command line to WINDBG.EXE. The first parameter is the ID of the process that is to be debugged. The second parameter identifies an inheritable manual-reset event that was created in the not-signaled state by the UnhandledExceptionFilter function. WINDBG recognizes the -*p* and -*e* switches as identifying the process ID and the event handle.

After the process ID and event handle are parsed into the string, UnhandledExceptionFilter executes the debugger by calling CreateProcess and waits for the manual-reset event to become signaled. The debugger can then attach itself to the process by calling DebugActiveProcess and passing it the ID of the process to be debugged:

```
BOOL DebugActiveProcess(DWORD idProcess);
```

When the debugger attaches to the process, the system sends debug events back to the debugger so that the debugger is aware of the process's state. For example, the system sends information about active threads in the process and about dynamic-link libraries mapped into the process's address space.

While the system is bringing the debugger up-to-date, the debuggee is suspended, still waiting for the manual-reset event to become signaled. When the debugger is ready to let you debug the process, it calls the SetEvent function passing the handle of the manual-reset event. The debugger can use the event's handle value directly because the event was created so that it could be inherited by any child processes of the debuggee. And because the UnhandledExceptionFilter function in the process called CreateProcess to invoke the debugger, the debugger is a child of the process.

When the debuggee sees that the manual-reset event has become signaled, it wakes up, and UnhandledExceptionFilter returns EXCEPTION_CONTINUE_SEARCH. Returning EXCEPTION_CONTINUE_SEARCH causes the unhandled exception to be filtered up again. This time, the process is being debugged and the debugger will be notified of the exception.

Turning Off the Exception Message Box

There may be times when you don't want the exception message box to be displayed if an exception occurs. For example, you might not want the message box to appear in the shipping version of your product. If it did appear, it could easily lead an end-user to accidentally start debugging your application. An end-user needs only to click on the *Cancel* button in the message box to enter unfamiliar, scary territory—the debugger. There are several methods you can use to prevent this message box from appearing.

To prevent UnhandledExceptionFilter from displaying the exception message box, you can call the SetErrorMode function,

```
UINT SetErrorMode(UINT fuErrorMode);
```

passing it the SEM_NOGPFAULTERRORBOX identifier. Then, when UnhandledExceptionFilter is called to handle the exception, it simply terminates your application. The user is given no warning; the application just goes away.

Another method you can use to disable the message box is to place a *try-except* block around the entire contents of your WinMain function. Make sure that the exception filter always evaluates to EXCEPTION-_EXECUTE_HANDLER so that the exception is handled, preventing the system from calling the UnhandledExceptionFilter function. In WinMain's exception handler, you can display a dialog box with some diagnostic information. The user can copy the information and report it to your customer service lines to help you track the source of problems in your application. You should create the dialog box so that the user can only terminate the application and not invoke the debugger.

The problem with this method is that it catches only exceptions that occur in your process's primary thread. If any other threads are running, and an unhandled exception occurs in one of these threads, the system calls the built-in UnhandledExceptionFilter function. To fix this, you would need to include *try-except* blocks before all the thread functions in your code and in the WinMain function.

Because it is so easy to forget this when writing new code, Microsoft added another Win32 function, SetUnhandledExceptionFilter, to help you:

```
LPTOP_LEVEL_EXCEPTION_FILTER SetUnhandledExceptionFilter(
   LPTOP_LEVEL_EXCEPTION_FILTER lpTopLevelExceptionFilter);
```

After calling this function, an unhandled exception occurring in any of your process's threads causes your own exception filter to be called. You need to pass the address of this filter as the only parameter to SetUnhandledExceptionFilter. The prototype of this function looks like this:

```
LONG UnhandledExceptionFilter(
    LPEXCEPTION_POINTERS lpexpExceptionInfo);
```

You'll notice that this function is identical in form to the Unhandled-ExceptionFilter function. You can perform any processing you desire in your exception filter as long as you return one of the three EXCEP-TION_* identifiers. The table below shows what happens when each identifier is returned:

Identifier	What Happens
EXCEPTION_EXECUTE_HANDLER	The process simply terminates because the system doesn't perform any action in its exception handler block.
EXCEPTION_CONTINUE_EXECUTION	Execution continues at the instruction that raised the exception. You can modify the exception information referenced by the LPEXCEPTION-_POINTERS parameter.
EXCEPTION_CONTINUE_SEARCH	The normal Win32 Unhandled-ExceptionFilter function is called.

To make the UnhandledExceptionFilter function the default filter again, you can simply call SetUnhandledExceptionFilter and pass it NULL. Also, whenever you set a new unhandled exception filter, Set-UnhandledExceptionFilter returns the address of the previously installed exception filter. This address will be NULL if Unhandled-ExceptionFilter was the currently installed filter.

The last method for turning off UnhandledExceptionFilter's message box is really designed for the software developer and not for the end-user. Another subkey in the registry affects the UnhandledExceptionFilter function:

```
HKEY_LOCAL_MACHINE\SOFTWARE\Microsoft\
    Windows NT\CurrentVersion\AeDebug\Auto
```

This key can be set to either 0 (zero) or 1. If set to 1, UnhandledExceptionFilter does not display a message box showing the user the exception and immediately invokes the debugger. If Auto is set to 0 (zero), UnhandledExceptionFilter displays the exception message box first and operates as described in the previous section.

Calling UnhandledExceptionFilter Yourself

The UnhandledExceptionFilter function is a Win32 function that you can call directly from within your own code. Here is an example of how you can use it:

```
void Funcadelic (void) {
  __try {
    .
    .
    .
  }
  __except (ExpFltr(GetExceptionInformation())) {
    .
    .
    .
  }
}

LONG ExpFltr (LPEXCEPTION_POINTERS lpEP) {
  DWORD dwExceptionCode = lpEP->ExceptionRecord->ExceptionCode;

  if (dwExceptionCode == EXCEPTION_ACCESS_VIOLATION) {
    // Do some work here...
    return(EXCEPTION_CONTINUE_EXECUTION);
  }

  return(UnhandledExceptionFilter(lpEP));
}
```

In the Funcadelic function, an exception in the *try* block causes the ExpFltr function to be called. The ExpFilter function is passed the return value from GetExceptionInformation. Inside the exception filter, the exception code is determined and compared with EXCEPTION-_ACCESS_VIOLATION. If an access violation has occurred, the exception filter corrects the situation and returns EXCEPTION-_CONTINUE_EXECUTION from the filter. The return value causes the system to continue execution at the instruction that originally caused the exception in the first place.

If any other exception has occurred, ExpFltr calls Unhandled-ExceptionFilter, passing it the address of the EXCEPTION_POINTERS structure. UnhandledExceptionFilter then displays a message box that allows you to terminate the application or to begin debugging the application. The return value from UnhandledExceptionFilter is returned from ExpFltr.

Unhandled Kernel-Mode Exceptions

So far in this chapter, we have looked at what happens when a user-mode thread generates an exception, but a kernel-mode thread might also generate an exception. Exceptions in kernel mode are handled exactly like exceptions in user mode. If a low-level virtual memory function generates an exception, the system checks whether any kernel-mode exception filters are prepared to handle the exception. If the system is unable to find an exception filter to handle the exception, the exception is unhandled. This time, the unhandled exception is in the operating system and not in an application. Such an exception would be a serious bug in the operating system!

It isn't safe for the system to continue running if an unhandled exception occurs in kernel mode, so Windows NT doesn't call UnhandledExceptionFilter in such a case but instead switches the video mode back to text mode, displays some debugging information on the screen, and halts the system. You should jot down the debugging information and send it to Microsoft so they can use it to correct the code in future versions of the operating system. Then you'll need to reboot your machine before you can do anything else. Any unsaved work is lost.

CHAPTER ELEVEN

UNICODE

With Microsoft Windows becoming more and more popular around the world, it is becoming increasingly important that we, as developers, target the various international markets. Previously, it was common for U.S. versions of software to ship as much as six months prior to the shipping of international versions. But with Windows NT, Microsoft is closing that gap, and international versions of Windows NT will be available at the same time as the U.S. versions.

But what about your own applications? How important is localization to you? Maybe you're designing a small in-house application that doesn't require any localization. Or, on the other hand, you might be designing an application that you expect to sell commercially.

Windows has always offered support to help with the localization of applications. An application can get country-specific information from various functions and can examine Control Panel settings to determine the user's preferences. Windows even supports different fonts for our applications.

Character Sets

The real problem with localization has always been manipulating different character sets. For many years, most of us have been coding text strings as a series of single-byte characters with a zero at the end. This is second nature to us. When we call *strlen*, it returns the number of characters in a zero-terminated array of single-byte characters.

The problem is that some languages (Kanji always being the classic example) have so many symbols in their character sets that a single byte, offering no more than 256 different symbols at best, is just not enough.

So DBCSs (double-byte character sets) were created to support these languages.

Single-Byte and Double-Byte Character Sets

In a double-byte character set, each character in a string consists of either 1 or 2 bytes. For Kanji, if the first character is between 0x81 and 0x9F or between 0xE0 and 0xFC, you must look at the next byte to determine the full character in the string. Working with double-byte character sets is a programmer's nightmare because some characters are 1 byte wide and some are 2 bytes wide.

Simply placing a call to *strlen* doesn't really tell you how many characters are in the string—it tells you the number of bytes before you hit a terminating zero. None of the C Runtime functions that manipulate strings, with the possible exception of *strcpy*, can be used to manipulate these character strings. And even *strcpy* won't work on the double-byte character 0xE0 followed by 0x00; it will only copy the characters in the string up to this zero byte and stop. The copied string will not even be valid because it won't have a terminating zero byte.

To help manipulate these DBCS strings, 16-bit Windows offers a set of helper functions, listed below:

Function	Description
`LPSTR AnsiNext(LPCSTR lpchCurrentChar);`	Returns the address of the next character in a string.
`LPSTR AnsiPrev(LPCSTR lpchStart, LPCSTR lpchCurrentChar);`	Returns the address of the previous character in a string.
`BOOL IsDBCSLeadByte(BYTE bTestChar);`	Returns TRUE if the byte is the first character of a DBCS string.

The two functions AnsiNext and AnsiPrev allow you to traverse through a DBCS string one character forward or backward at a time. And the third function, IsDBCSLeadByte, returns TRUE if the byte passed to it is the first byte of a 2-byte character.

When porting the first two functions to the Win32 API, someone realized that the functions don't process ANSI strings at all and that the functions should undergo name-change surgery. So the AnsiNext and AnsiPrev functions have been renamed and added to the Win32 API as:

```
LPTSTR CharNext(LPCTSTR lpszCurrentChar);
```

and

```
LPTSTR CharPrev(LPCTSTR lpszStart, LPCTSTR lpszCurrentChar);
```

In the new WINUSER.H file, AnsiNext and AnsiPrev are macros that call CharNext and CharPrev, respectively.

Although these functions make manipulating DBCS strings a little easier, a better approach is definitely needed. Enter Unicode.

Unicode: The Wide-Byte Character Set

Unicode is a standard that was originally founded by Apple and Xerox in 1988. In 1991, a consortium was created to develop and promote Unicode. The consortium consists of Adobe, Aldus, Apple, Borland, Digital, Go, IBM, Lotus, Metaphor, Microsoft, NeXT, Novell, the Research Libraries Group, Sun, WordPerfect, and Xerox. This group of companies is responsible for maintaining the Unicode standard. The full description of Unicode can be found in *The Unicode Standard: Worldwide Character Encoding, Version 1.0,* from Addison-Wesley.

Unicode offers a simple and consistent way of representing strings. All characters in a Unicode string are 16-bit values (2 bytes). There are no special bytes that indicate whether the next byte is part of the same character or a new character. This means that you can traverse the characters in a string by simply incrementing or decrementing a pointer. Calls to functions such as CharNext, CharPrev, and IsDBCSLeadByte are no longer necessary.

Because Unicode represents each character with a 16-bit value, more than 65,000 characters are available, making it possible to encode all the characters that make up written languages throughout the world. This is a far cry from the 256 characters available with a single-byte character set.

Currently, Unicode code points[1] are defined for the Japanese kana, Latin (English), Cyrillic (Russian), Greek, Hebrew, Arabic, Korean hangul, and Chinese bopomofo alphabets, as well as for others. A large number of punctuation marks, mathematical symbols, technical symbols, arrows, dingbats, diacritics, and other characters are also included in the character sets. When you add all these alphabets and symbols together, they total about 29,000 different code points, which leaves

---

1. A code point is the position of a symbol in a character set.

about half the 65,000 total code points available for future expansion.

These 65,536 characters are divided into regions. The table below shows some of the regions and the characters that are assigned to them:

16-Bit Code	Characters
0000 - 007F	ASCII
0080 - 00FF	Latin1 Characters
0100 - 017F	European Latin
0180 - 01FF	Extended Latin
0250 - 02AF	Standard Phonetic
02B0 - 02FF	Modified Letters
0300 - 036F	Generic Diacritical Marks
0370 - 03FF	Greek
0400 - 04FF	Cyrillic
0530 - 058F	Armenian
0590 - 05FF	Hebrew
0600 - 06FF	Arabic
0900 - 097F	Devanagari

Approximately 30,000 code points remain currently unassigned but reserved for future use. And approximately 6000 code points are reserved for your own personal use.

Why You Should Use Unicode

When developing an application, you should definitely consider taking advantage of Unicode. Even if you're not planning to localize your application today, developing with Unicode in mind will certainly simplify conversion in the future. In addition, Unicode

- Enables easy data exchange between languages

- Allows you to distribute a single binary EXE or DLL file that supports all languages

- Improves the efficiency of your application (discussed in more detail later)

How to Write Unicode Source Code

Microsoft designed an application programming interface for Unicode so that it would have as little impact on your code as possible. In fact, it is possible to write a single source code file so that it can be compiled with or without using Unicode—you only need to define two macros to make the change, and then recompile.

Microsoft also designed the system so that a Unicode application can easily talk to a non-Unicode application and vice versa. Windows NT automatically performs any necessary conversions on the strings, which also simplifies the porting of applications from 16-bit Windows to Win32.

However, conversions are performed not only between applications. Windows NT uses Unicode internally for everything. If your application doesn't use Unicode, the system must perform conversions for you. For example, if you call CreateWindowEx and pass non-Unicode strings for the class name and window caption text, CreateWindowEx must allocate blocks of memory (in your process's default heap), convert the non-Unicode strings to Unicode strings and store the result in the allocated memory blocks, and make a function call to the Unicode version of CreateWindowEx.

For functions that fill buffers with strings, the system must convert from Unicode to non-Unicode equivalents before your application can process the string. Because the system must perform all these conversions, your application requires more memory and runs slower. You can make your application perform more efficiently by developing your application using Unicode from the start.

Unicode Support in the C Runtime Library

To take advantage of Unicode character strings, some new data types have been defined. The standard C header file, STRING.H, has been modified to define a new data type called *wchar_t*, which is the data type of a Unicode character:

```
typedef unsigned short wchar_t;
```

For example, if you want to create a buffer to hold a Unicode string of up to 99 characters and a terminating zero character, you can use the following statement:

```
wchar_t szBuffer[100];
```

This statement creates an array of 100 16-bit values. Of course, the standard C Runtime string functions, such as *strcpy*, *strchr*, and *strcat*, operate on ANSI strings only; they don't process Unicode strings correctly. So a new, complementary set of functions was created. Figure 11-1 shows the standard C ANSI string functions followed by their equivalent Unicode functions.

```
char * strcat(char *, const char *);
wchar_t * wcscat(wchar_t *, const wchar_t *);

char * strchr(const char *, int);
wchar_t * wcschr(const wchar_t *, wchar_t);

int strcmp(const char *, const char *);
int wcscmp(const wchar_t *, const wchar_t *);

int _stricmp(const char *, const char *);
int _wcsicmp(const wchar_t *, const wchar_t *);

int strcoll(const char *, const char *);
int wcscoll(const wchar_t *, const wchar_t *);

int _stricoll(const char *, const char *);
int _wcsicoll(const wchar_t *, const wchar_t *);

char * strcpy(char *, const char *);
wchar_t * wcscpy(wchar_t *, const wchar_t *);

size_t strcspn(const char *, const char *);
size_t wcscspn(const wchar_t *, const wchar_t *);

char * _strdup(const char *);
wchar_t * _wcsdup(const wchar_t *);

size_t strlen(const char *);
size_t wcslen(const wchar_t *);

char * _strlwr(char *);
wchar_t * _wcslwr(wchar_t *);

char * strncat(char *, const char *, size_t);
wchar_t * wcsncat(wchar_t *, const wchar_t *, size_t);
```

Figure 11-1. *(continued)*
Standard C ANSI string functions and their Unicode equivalents.

Figure 11-1.   *continued*

```
int strncmp(const char *, const char *, size_t);
int wcsncmp(const wchar_t *, const wchar_t *, size_t);

int _strnicmp(const char *, const char *, size_t);
int _wcsnicmp(const wchar_t *, const wchar_t *, size_t);

char * strncpy(char *, const char *, size_t);
wchar_t * wcsncpy(wchar_t *, const wchar_t *, size_t);

char * _strnset(char *, int, size_t);
wchar_t * _wcsnset(wchar_t *, wchar_t, size_t);

char * strpbrk(const char *, const char *);
wchar_t * wcspbrk(const wchar_t *, const wchar_t *);

char * strrchr(const char *, int);
wchar_t * wcsrchr(const wchar_t *, wchar_t);

char * _strrev(char *);
wchar_t * _wcsrev(wchar_t *);

char * _strset(char *, int);
wchar_t * _wcsset(wchar_t *, wchar_t);

size_t strspn(const char *, const char *);
size_t wcsspn(const wchar_t *, const wchar_t *);

char * strstr(const char *, const char *);
wchar_t * wcsstr(const wchar_t *, const wchar_t *);

char * strtok(char *, const char *);
wchar_t * wcstok(wchar_t *, const wchar_t *);

char * _strupr(char *);
wchar_t * _wcsupr(wchar_t *);

size_t strxfrm (char *, const char *, size_t);
size_t wcsxfrm(wchar_t *, const wchar_t *, size_t);
```

Notice that all the new functions begin with *wcs*, which stands for *wide character set*. You simply replace the *str* prefix of any string function with the new *wcs* prefix in order to call the Unicode function.

Code that includes explicit calls to either the *str* functions or the *wcs* functions cannot be compiled easily for both ANSI and Unicode. Earlier in this chapter, I said it's possible to make a single source code file that can be compiled for both. To set up the dual capability, you include the new TCHAR.H file in addition to including STRING.H.

TCHAR.H exists for the sole purpose of helping you create ANSI/ Unicode generic source code files. It consists of a set of macros that you should use in your source code instead of making direct calls to either the *str* or *wcs* functions. If you define _UNICODE when you compile your source code, the macros reference the *wcs* set of functions. If you don't define _UNICODE, the macros reference the *str* set of functions. Figure 11-2 lists the macros in TCHAR.H and what they reference depending on whether _UNICODE is defined:

TCHAR.H Macro	_UNICODE Defined	_UNICODE Not Defined
_tprintf	wprintf	printf
_ftprintf	fwprintf	fprintf
_stprintf	swprintf	sprintf
_sntprintf	_snwprintf	_snprintf
_vtprintf	vwprintf	vprintf
_vftprintf	vfwprintf	vfprintf
_vstprintf	vswprintf	vsprintf
_vsntprintf	_vsnwprintf	_vsnprintf
_tscanf	wscanf	scanf
_ftscanf	fwscanf	fscanf
_stscanf	swscanf	sscanf
_fgettc	fgetwc	fgetc
_fgettchar	fgetwchar	fgetchar
_fgetts	fgetws	fgets
_fputtc	fputwc	fputc
_fputtchar	fputwchar	fputchar
_fputts	fputws	fputs
_gettc	getwc	getc

Figure 11-2. *(continued)*
Macros in TCHAR.H and their references.

646

Figure 11-2. *continued*

TCHAR.H Macro	_UNICODE Defined	_UNICODE Not Defined
_getts	getws	gets
_puttc	putwc	putc
_putts	putws	puts
_ungettc	ungetwc	ungetc
_tcstod	wcstod	strtod
_tcstol	wcstol	strtol
_tcstoul	wcstoul	strtoul
_tcscat	wcscat	strcat
_tcschr	wcschr	strchr
_tcscmp	wcscmp	strcmp
_tcscpy	wcscpy	strcpy
_tcscspn	wcspn	strcspn
_tcslen	wcslen	strlen
_tcsncat	wcsncat	strncat
_tcsncmp	wcsncmp	strncmp
_tcsncpy	wcsncpy	strncpy
_tcspbrk	wcspbrk	strpbrk
_tcsrchr	wcsrchr	strrchr
_tcsspn	wcsspn	strspn
_tcsstr	wcsstr	strstr
_tcstok	wcstok	strtok
_tcsdup	_wcsdup	strdup
_tcsicmp	_wcsicmp	stricmp
_tcsnicmp	_wcsnicmp	_strnicmp
_tcsnset	_wcsnset	_strnset
_tcsrev	_wcsrev	_strrev
_tcsset	_wcsset	_strset
_tcslwr	_wcslwr	_strlwr
_tcsupr	_wcsupr	_strupr
_tcsxfrm	wcsxfrm	strxfrm
_tcscoll	wcscoll	strcoll

(continued)

Figure 11-2. *continued*

TCHAR.H Macro	_UNICODE Defined	_UNICODE Not Defined
_tcsicoll	_wcsicoll	_stricoll
_istalpha	iswalpha	isalpha
_istupper	iswupper	isupper
_istlower	iswlower	islower
_istdigit	iswdigit	isdigit
_istxdigit	iswxdigit	isxdigit
_istspace	iswspace	isspace
_istpunct	iswpunct	ispunct
_istalnum	iswalnum	isalnum
_istprint	iswprint	isprint
_istgraph	iswgraph	isgraph
_istcntrl	iswcntrl	iscntrl
_istascii	iswascii	isascii
_totupper	towupper	toupper
_totlower	towlower	tolower

By using the identifiers in the leftmost column, you can write your source code so that it can be compiled using either Unicode or ANSI. This isn't quite the whole story, however. TCHAR.H includes some additional macros.

To define an array of string characters that is ANSI/Unicode generic, use the following new TCHAR data type. If _UNICODE is defined, TCHAR is declared as follows:

```
typedef wchat_t TCHAR;
```

If _UNICODE is not defined, TCHAR is declared as:

```
typedef char TCHAR;
```

Using this data type, you can allocate a string of characters as follows:

```
TCHAR szString[100];
```

You can also create pointers to strings:

```
TCHAR *szError = "Error";
```

However, there is a problem with the previous line. By default, the C compiler compiles all strings as though they were ANSI strings, not Unicode strings. So the compiler will compile this line correctly if _UNICODE is not defined but will generate an error if _UNICODE is defined. To generate a Unicode string instead of an ANSI string, you would have to rewrite the line as follows:

```
TCHAR *szError = L"Error";
```

An uppercase _L_ before a literal string informs the compiler that the string should be compiled as a Unicode string. When the compiler places the string in the program's data section, it intersperses zero bytes between every character. The problem with this change is that now the program will compile successfully only if _UNICODE is defined. We need another macro that selectively adds the uppercase _L_ before a literal string. This is the job of the _ _TEXT macro, also defined in TCHAR.H. If _UNICODE is defined, _ _TEXT is defined as:

```
#define _TEXT(x)    L ## x
```

and if _UNICODE is not defined, _ _TEXT is defined as:

```
#define _TEXT(x)    x
```

Using this macro, we can rewrite the line above so that it compiles correctly whether or not the _UNICODE macro is defined:

```
TCHAR *szError = __TEXT("Error");
```

The _ _TEXT macro can also be used for literal characters. For example, to check whether the first character of a string is an uppercase _J_, execute the following:

```
if (szError[0] == __TEXT('J')) {
   // First character is a "J."
   .
   .
   .
} else {
   // First character is not a "J."
   .
   .
   .
}
```

Unicode Data Types Defined by Win32

The Win32 header files define the data types listed below:

Data Type	Description
WCHAR	A Unicode character.
LPWSTR	A pointer to a Unicode string.
LPCWSTR	A pointer to a constant Unicode string.

These data types always refer to Unicode characters and strings. The Win32 header files also define the ANSI/Unicode generic data types LPTSTR and LPCTSTR. These data types point to either an ANSI string or a Unicode string depending on whether the UNICODE macro is defined when you compile the module.

Notice that this time the UNICODE macro is not preceded by an underscore. The _UNICODE macro is used for the C Runtime header files, and the UNICODE macro is used for the Win32 header files. You usually need to define both macros when compiling a source module.

Unicode and ANSI Functions in Win32

Earlier I implied that there are two functions called CreateWindowEx: One CreateWindowEx accepts Unicode strings, and another Create-WindowEx accepts ANSI strings. This is true, but the two functions are actually prototyped as follows:

```
HWND WINAPI CreateWindowExW(DWORD dwExStyle, LPCWSTR lpClassName,
    LPCWSTR lpWindowName, DWORD dwStyle, int X, int Y,
    int nWidth, int nHeight, HWND hWndParent, HMENU hMenu,
    HINSTANCE hInstance, LPVOID lpParam);
```

and

```
HWND WINAPI CreateWindowExA(DWORD dwExStyle, LPCSTR lpClassName,
    LPCSTR lpWindowName, DWORD dwStyle, int X, int Y,
    int nWidth, int nHeight, HWND hWndParent, HMENU hMenu,
    HINSTANCE hInstance, LPVOID lpParam);
```

CreateWindowExW is the version that accepts Unicode strings. The uppercase *W* at the end of the function name stands for *wide*. Unicode characters are 16 bits each, so they are frequently referred to as wide characters. CreateWindowExA has an uppercase *A* at the end, which indicates that it accepts ANSI character strings.

But we usually just include a call to CreateWindowEx in our code and don't directly call either CreateWindowExW or CreateWindowExA. In WINUSER.H, CreateWindowEx is actually a macro defined as:

```
#ifdef UNICODE
#define CreateWindowEx   CreateWindowExW
#else
#define CreateWindowEx   CreateWindowExA
#endif // !UNICODE
```

Whether UNICODE is defined when you compile your source code module determines which version of CreateWindowEx is called. When you port a 16-bit Windows application to Win32, you probably won't define UNICODE when you compile. Any calls you make to CreateWindowEx evaluate to calls to CreateWindowExA—the ANSI version of CreateWindowEx. Because 16-bit Windows offers only an ANSI version of CreateWindowEx, your porting will go much easier.

Microsoft's source code for CreateWindowExA is simply a thunking, or translation, layer that allocates memory to convert ANSI strings to Unicode strings and then calls CreateWindowExW passing the converted strings. When CreateWindowExW returns, CreateWindowExA frees its memory buffers and returns the window handle to you.

If you're creating dynamic-link libraries that other software developers will use, consider using this technique: Supply two entry points in the DLL—an ANSI version and a Unicode version. In the ANSI version, simply allocate memory, perform the necessary string conversions, and call the Unicode version of the function. (This process is demonstrated later in this chapter.)

Certain functions in the Win32 API, such as WinExec and Open-File, exist solely for backward compatibility for 16-bit Windows programs and should be avoided. You should replace any calls to WinExec and OpenFile with calls to the new CreateProcess and CreateFile functions. Internally, the old functions call the new functions anyway.

The big problem with the old functions is that they don't accept Unicode strings. When you call these functions, you must pass ANSI strings. All the new and nonobsolete functions, on the other hand, do have both ANSI and Unicode versions.

WinMain is a special, nonobsolete function that exists only in an ANSI version:

```
int WinMain(HINSTANCE hInstance, HINSTANCE hPrevInstance,
    LPSTR lpszCmdLine, int nCmdShow);
```

The string pointed to by the *lpszCmdLine* parameter is always an ANSI string, which is indicated by its type—LPSTR. If the type were LPTSTR, we might have guessed that the function existed in both ANSI and Unicode forms. But this function cannot exist in both forms because it's called by the C Runtime Library's startup code. Because you didn't compile this code yourself, Microsoft had to choose either ANSI or Unicode. For backward compatibility reasons, the string had to be ANSI.

This leads us to a new question: What do we do if we need to parse the command line as a Unicode string? The answer lies in the Get-CommandLine function. This function returns a pointer to the application's command line. As with most Win32 functions, it exists in both ANSI and Unicode versions:

```
#ifdef UNICODE
#define GetCommandLine   GetCommandLineW
#else
#define GetCommandLine   GetCommandLineA
#endif // !UNICODE
```

The difference between the buffer pointed to by the *lpszCmdLine* parameter and the buffer pointed to by GetCommandLine is that *lpszCmdLine's* buffer doesn't contain the program's pathname, only the program's command-line arguments. The buffer returned by Get-CommandLine includes the name of the executable program as well, which means that you'll need to skip this token in the buffer in order to retrieve the actual arguments.

Converting Your Application to Be ANSI and Unicode Aware

It's a good idea to start converting your application to be Unicode aware even if you don't plan to use Unicode right away. Here are the basic steps you should follow:

1. Start thinking of text strings as arrays of characters, not as arrays of *chars* or arrays of bytes.

2. Use generic data types (such as TCHAR and LPTSTR) for text characters and strings.

3. Use explicit data types (such as BYTE and LPBYTE) for bytes, byte pointers, and data buffers.

4. Use the _ _TEXT() macro for literal characters and strings.

5. Perform global replaces. (For example, replace LPSTR with LPTSTR.)

6. Modify string arithmetic problems. (For example, convert *sizeof(szBuffer)* to *(sizeof(szBuffer) / sizeof(TCHAR))*.)

When I was developing the sample programs for this book, I originally wrote them all so that they compiled natively as ANSI only. Then, when I began to write this chapter, I knew that I wanted to encourage the use of Unicode and was going to create sample programs to demonstrate how easy it is to create programs that can be compiled both in Unicode and ANSI. I decided that the best course of action was to convert all of the sample programs in the book to be compilable as both Unicode and ANSI.

I converted all the programs in about four hours, which isn't bad considering that I didn't have any prior conversion experience.

String Functions in Win32

The Win32 API also offers a set of functions for manipulating Unicode strings, as described below:

Function	Description
lstrcat	Concatenates one string onto the end of another.
lstrcmp	Performs case-sensitive comparison of two strings.
lstrcmpi	Performs case-insensitive comparison of two strings.
lstrcpy	Copies one string to another location in memory.
lstrlen	Returns the length of a string in characters.

These functions are implemented as macros that call either the Unicode version of the function or the ANSI version of the function depending on whether UNICODE is defined when the source module is compiled. For example, if UNICODE is not defined, lstrcat will expand to lstrcatA, and if UNICODE is defined, lstrcat will expand to lstrcatW.

Calling lstrcatA is really no different from calling the C Runtime function *strcat,* and calling lstrcatW is identical to calling *wcscat.* In fact, the Win32 versions of these functions are implemented internally by making direct calls to the C Runtime Library's *strcat* and *wcscat* functions, respectively. Really, the lstrlen, lstrcpy, and lstrcat functions exist for backward compatibility and should be avoided in favor of the C Runtime functions.

The remaining two Win32 string functions, lstrcmp and lstrcmpi, do behave differently from their equivalent C Runtime functions. The C Runtime functions *strcmp*, *strcmpi*, *wcscmp*, and *wcscmpi* simply compare the values of the code points in the strings. That is, the functions ignore the meaning of the actual characters and simply check the numeric value of each character in the first string with the numeric value of the character in the second string. The Win32 functions lstrcmpA, lstrcmpiA, lstrcmpW, and lstrcmpiW, on the other hand, are implemented as calls to the new Win32 function CompareStringW:

```
int CompareStringW(LCID lcid, DWORD fdwStyle,
    LPCWSTR lpString1, int cch1, LPCWSTR lpString2, int cch2);
```

This function compares two Unicode strings. A call to either lstrcmpA or lstrcmpiA converts the ANSI string parameters to their Unicode equivalents before calling CompareStringW. The first parameter to CompareStringW specifies a locale ID (LCID), a 32-bit value that identifies a particular language. CompareStringW uses this LCID to compare the two strings by checking the meaning of the characters as they apply to a particular language. This action is much more meaningful than the simple number comparison performed by the C Runtime functions.

When any of the lstrcmp family of functions calls CompareStringW, it passes the result of calling the Win32 GetThreadLocale function as the first parameter:

```
LCID GetThreadLocale(VOID);
```

Every time a thread is created, it is assigned a locale. This function returns the current locale setting for the thread.

The second parameter of CompareStringW identifies flags that modify the method used by the function to compare the two strings. The table below shows the possible flags:

Flag	Description
NORM_IGNORECASE	Ignore case differences.
NORM_IGNORENONSPACE	Ignore nonspacing characters.
NORM_IGNORESYMBOLS	Ignore symbols.
SORT_STRINGSORT	Treat punctuation the same as symbols.

When lstrcmpA and lstrcmpW call CompareStringW, they pass 0 (zero) for the *fdwStyle* parameter. But when lstrcmpiA and lstrcmpiW call the function, they pass NORM_IGNORECASE. The remaining four parameters of CompareStringW specify the two strings and their respective lengths. If you pass −1 in for the *cch1* parameter, the function assumes that the *lpString1* string is zero-terminated and calculates the length of the string. This also is true for the *cch2* parameter with respect to the *lpString2* string.

Other C Runtime functions don't offer good support for manipulating Unicode strings. For example, the *tolower* and *toupper* functions don't properly convert characters with accent marks. To compensate for these deficiencies in the C Runtime Library, you'll need to call the Win32 functions listed below to convert the case of a Unicode string. These functions also work correctly for ANSI strings.

The first two functions,

```
LPTSTR CharLower(LPTSTR lpszString);
```

and

```
LPTSTR CharUpper(LPTSTR lpszString);
```

convert either a single character or an entire zero-terminated string. To convert an entire string, simply pass the address of the string. To convert a single character, you must pass the individual character as follows:

```
TCHAR cLowerCaseChar = CharLower((LPTSTR) szString[0]);
```

Casting the single character to an LPTSTR causes the high 16 bits of the pointer to be 0 (zero) and the low 16 bits to contain the character. When the function sees that the high 16 bits are 0 (zero), the function knows that you want to convert a single character versus a whole string. The value returned will be a 32-bit value with the converted character in the low 16 bits.

The next two functions are similar to the previous two except that they convert the characters contained inside a buffer (which does not need to be zero-terminated):

```
DWORD CharLowerBuff(LPTSTR lpszString, DWORD cchString);
```

and

```
DWORD CharUpperBuff(LPTSTR lpszString, DWORD cchString);
```

Other C Runtime functions, such as *isalpha*, *islower*, and *isupper* return a value that indicates whether a given character is alphabetic, lowercase, or uppercase. The Win32 API offers functions that return this information as well, but the Win32 functions also consider the language indicated by the user in the Control Panel:

```
BOOL IsCharAlpha(TCHAR ch);

BOOL IsCharAlphaNumeric(TCHAR ch);

BOOL IsCharLower(TCHAR ch);

BOOL IsCharUpper(TCHAR ch);
```

The *printf* family of functions are the last C Runtime functions we'll discuss. If you compile your source module with _UNICODE defined, the *printf* family of functions expect that all the character and string parameters represent Unicode characters and strings. However, if you compile without defining _UNICODE, the *printf* family expects that all the characters and strings passed to it are ANSI.

The Win32 function wsprintf is an enhanced version of the C Runtime's *sprintf* function. It offers some additional field types that allow you to state explicitly whether a character or string is ANSI or Unicode. Using these extended field types, you can mix ANSI and Unicode characters and strings in a single call to wsprintf.

Resources

When the resource compiler compiles all your resources, the output file is a binary representation of the resources. Any string values in your resources (string tables, dialog box templates, menus, and so on) are always written as Unicode strings. The system performs internal conversions if your application doesn't define the UNICODE macro. For example, if UNICODE is not defined when you compile your source module, a call to LoadString will actually call the LoadStringA function. LoadStringA will read the string from your resources and convert the string to ANSI. The ANSI representation of the string will be returned from the function to your application.

Translating Strings Between Unicode and ANSI

The Win32 API function MultiByteToWideChar converts multibyte-character strings to wide-character strings:

```
int MultiByteToWideChar(UINT uCodePage, DWORD dwFlags,
    LPCSTR lpMultiByteStr, int cchMultiByte,
    LPWSTR lpWideCharStr, int cchWideChar);
```

The *uCodePage* parameter identifies a code-page number that is associated with the multibyte string. The *dwFlags* parameter allows you to specify additional control that affects characters with diacritical marks, such as accents. Usually, the flags aren't used and 0 (zero) is passed in the *dwFlags* parameter. The *lpMultByteStr* parameter specifies the string to be converted, and the *cchMultiByte* parameter indicates the length (in bytes) of the string. The function determines the length of the source string if you pass −1 for the *cchMultiByte* parameter.

The Unicode version of the string resulting from the conversion is written to the buffer located in memory at the address specified by the *lpWideCharStr* parameter. You must specify the maximum size of this buffer (in characters) in the *cchWideChar* parameter. If you call Multi-ByteToWideChar passing 0 (zero) for the *cchWideChar* parameter, the function doesn't perform the conversion and, instead, returns the size of the buffer required for the conversion to succeed. Typically, you'll convert a multibyte character string to its Unicode equivalent by performing the following steps:

1. Call MultiByteToWideChar passing NULL for the *lpWideCharStr* parameter and 0 (zero) for the *cchWideChar* parameter.

2. Allocate a block of memory large enough to hold the converted Unicode string. This size is returned by the previous call to MultiByteToWideChar.

3. Call MultiByteToWideChar again, this time passing the address of the buffer as the *lpWideCharStr* parameter and the size returned by the first call to MultiByteToWideChar as the *cchWideChar* parameter.

4. Use the converted string.

5. Free the memory block occupying the Unicode string.

The Win32 API function WideCharToMultiByte converts a wide-character string to its multibyte string equivalent, as shown on the following page.

```
int WideCharToMultiByte(UINT uCodePage, DWORD dwFlags,
   LPCWSTR lpWideCharStr, int cchWideChar,
   LPSTR lpMultiByteStr, int cchMultiByte,
   LPCSTR lpDefaultChar, LPBOOL lpfUsedDefaultChar);
```

This function is very similar to the MultiByteToWideChar function. Again, the *uCodePage* parameter identifies the code page to be associated with the newly converted string. The *dwFlags* parameter allows you to specify additional control over the conversion. The flags affect characters with diacritical marks and characters that the system is unable to convert. Most often, you won't need this degree of control over the conversion, and you'll pass 0 (zero) for the *dwFlags* parameter.

The *lpWideCharStr* parameter specifies the address in memory of the string to be converted, and the *cchWideChar* parameter indicates the length (in characters) of this string. The function determines the length of the source string if you pass –1 for the *cchWideChar* parameter.

The multibyte version of the string resulting from the conversion is written to the buffer indicated by the *lpMultiByteStr* parameter. You must specify the maximum size of this buffer (in bytes) in the *cchMultiByte* parameter. Passing 0 (zero) as the *cchMultiByte* parameter of the WideCharToMultiByte function causes the function to return the size required by the destination buffer. You'll typically convert a wide-byte character string to a multibyte character string using a sequence of events similar to those discussed when converting a multibyte string to a wide-byte string.

You'll notice that the WideCharToMultiByte function accepts two parameters more than the MultiByteToWideChar function: *lpDefaultChar* and *lpfUsedDefaultChar*. These parameters are used by the WideCharToMultiByte function only if it comes across a wide character that doesn't have a representation in the code page identified by the *uCodePage* parameter. If the wide character cannot be converted, the function uses the character pointed to by the *lpDefaultChar* parameter. If this parameter is NULL, which is most common, the function uses a system default character. This default character is usually a question mark.

The *lpfUsedDefaultChar* parameter points to a boolean variable that the function sets to TRUE if at least one character in the wide-character string could not be converted to its multibyte equivalent. The function sets the variable to FALSE if all of the characters convert successfully.

You can test this variable after the function returns to check whether the wide-character string was converted successfully. Again, you usually pass NULL for this parameter.

For a more complete description of how to use these functions, please refer to the *Win32 Programmer's Reference*.

You could use these two functions to easily create both Unicode and ANSI versions of functions. For example, you might have a dynamic-link library that contains a function that reverses all the characters in a string. You could write the Unicode version of the function as follows:

```
BOOL StringReverseW (LPWSTR lpWideCharStr) {

   // Get a pointer to the last character in the string.
   LPWSTR lpEndOfStr = lpWideCharStr + wcslen(lpWideCharStr) - 1;
   wchar_t cCharT;

   // Repeat until we reach the center character in the string.
   while (lpWideCharStr < lpEndOfStr) {
      // Save a character in a temporary variable.
      cCharT = *lpWideCharStr;

      // Put the last character in the first character.
      *lpWideCharStr = *lpEndOfStr;

      // Put the temporary character in the last character.
      *lpEndOfStr = cCharT;

      // Move in one character from the left.
      lpWideCharStr++;

      // Move in one character from the right.
      lpEndOfStr--;
   }

   // The string is reversed; return success.
   return(TRUE);
}
```

And you could write the ANSI version of the function so that it doesn't perform the actual work of reversing the string at all. Instead, you could write the ANSI version so that it converts the ANSI string to Unicode, passes the Unicode string to the StringReverseW function, and then converts the reversed string back to ANSI. The function would look like this:

```
BOOL StringReverseA (LPSTR lpMultiByteStr) {
    LPWSTR lpWideCharStr;
    int nLenOfWideCharStr;
    BOOL fOk = FALSE;

    // Calculate the number of bytes needed to hold
    // the wide-character version of the string.
    nLenOfWideCharStr = MultiByteToWideChar(CP_ACP, 0,
        lpMultiByteStr, -1, NULL, 0);

    // Allocate memory from the process's default heap to
    // accommodate the size of the wide-character string.
    lpWideCharStr = HeapAlloc(GetProcessHeap(), 0,
        nLenOfWideCharStr);

    if (lpWideCharStr == NULL)
        return(fOk);

    // Convert the multibyte string to a wide-character string.
    MultiByteToWideChar(CP_ACP, 0, lpMultiByteStr, -1,
        lpWideCharStr, nLenOfWideCharStr);

    // Call the wide-character version of this
    // function to do the actual work.
    fOk = StringReverseW(lpWideCharStr);

    if (fOk) {
        // Convert the wide-character string back
        // to a multibyte string.
        WideCharToMultiByte(CP_ACP, 0, lpWideCharStr, -1,
            lpMultiByteStr, strlen(lpMultiByteStr), NULL, NULL);
    }

    // Free the memory containing the wide-character string.
    HeapFree(GetProcessHeap(), 0, lpWideCharStr);

    return(fOk);
}
```

Finally, in the header file that you distribute with the dynamic-link library, you would prototype the two functions as follows:

```
BOOL StringReverseW (LPWSTR lpWideCharStr);
BOOL StringReverseA (LPSTR lpMultiByteStr);

#ifdef UNICODE
#define StringReverse   StringReverseW
#else
#define StringReverse   StringReverseA
#endif // !UNICODE
```

Window Classes and Procedures

When you register a new window class, you must tell the system the address of the window procedure responsible for processing messages for this class. For certain messages (such as WM_SETTEXT), the *lParam* parameter for the message is a pointer to a string. The system needs to know whether the window procedure requires that the string be in ANSI or Unicode before dispatching the message so that the message will be processed correctly.

You tell the system whether a window procedure expects ANSI strings or Unicode strings depending on which function you use to register the window class. If you construct the WNDCLASS structure and call RegisterClassA, the system thinks that the window procedure expects all strings and characters to be ANSI. Registering the window class with RegisterClassW causes the system to dispatch only Unicode strings and characters to the window procedure. Of course, the macro RegisterClass expands to either RegisterClassA or RegisterClassW depending on whether UNICODE is defined when you compile the source module.

If you have a handle to a window, you can determine what type of characters and strings the window procedure expects by calling:

```
BOOL IsWindowUnicode(HWND hwnd);
```

If the window procedure for the specified window expects Unicode, the function returns TRUE; otherwise, FALSE is returned.

If you create an ANSI string and send a WM_SETTEXT message to a window whose window procedure expects Unicode strings, the system will automatically convert the string for you before sending the message. It is very rare that you'll ever need to call the IsWindowUnicode function.

The system will also perform automatic translations if you subclass a window procedure. Let's say that the window procedure for an Edit control expects its characters and strings to be in Unicode. Then somewhere in your program you create an Edit control and subclass the window's procedure by calling

```
LONG SetWindowLongA(HWND hwnd, int nIndex, LONG lNewLong);
```

or

```
LONG SetWindowLongW(HWND hwnd, int nIndex, LONG lNewLong);
```

and passing GWL_WNDPROC as the *nIndex* parameter and the address to your subclass procedure as the *lNewLong* parameter. But what happens if your subclass procedure expects ANSI characters and strings? This could potentially create a big problem. The system determines how to convert the strings and characters depending on which of the two functions you use above to perform the subclassing. If you call Set-WindowLongA, you're telling the system that the new window procedure (your subclass procedure) is to receive ANSI characters and strings. In fact, if you were to call IsWindowUnicode after calling Set-WindowLongA, you would see that it would return FALSE, indicating that the subclassed Edit window procedure no longer expects Unicode characters and strings.

But now we have a new problem: How do we ensure that the original window procedure gets the correct type of characters and strings? The system needs to have two pieces of information to correctly convert the characters and strings. The first is the form that the characters and strings are currently in. We inform the system by calling either Call-WindowProcA or CallWindowProcW:

```
LRESULT CallWindowProcA(WNDPROC wndprcPrev, HWND hwnd,
    UINT uMsg, WPARAM wParam, LPARAM lParam);
```

and

```
LRESULT CallWindowProcW(WNDPROC wndprcPrev, HWND hwnd,
    UINT uMsg, WPARAM wParam, LPARAM lParam);
```

If the subclass procedure has ANSI strings that it wants to pass to the original window procedure, the subclass procedure must call Call-WindowProcA. If the subclass procedure has Unicode strings that it wants to pass to the original window procedure, the subclass procedure must call CallWindowProcW.

The second piece of information that the system needs is the type of characters and strings that the original window procedure expects. The system gets this information from the address of the original window procedure. When you call the SetWindowLongA or SetWindow-LongW function, the system checks whether you are subclassing a Unicode window procedure with an ANSI subclass procedure or vice versa. If you're not changing the type of strings expected, SetWindowLong simply returns the address of the original window procedure. If you're changing the types of characters and strings that the window procedure expects, SetWindowLong doesn't return the actual address of the original window procedure; instead, it returns a handle to an internal Win32 subsystem data structure.

This structure contains the actual address of the original window procedure and a value that indicates whether that procedure expects Unicode or ANSI strings. When you call CallWindowProc, the system checks whether you are passing a handle of one of the internal data structures or the actual address of a window procedure. If you're passing the address of a window procedure, the original window procedure is called and no character and string conversions need to be performed.

If, on the other hand, you're passing the handle of an internal data structure, the system converts the characters and strings to the appropriate type (Unicode or ANSI) and then calls the original window procedure.

A P P E N D I X

MESSAGE CRACKERS

When Windows was introduced, there were only two programming languages that could be used for developing Windows-based applications: C and assembly language. And the only C compiler that could produce executable files for Windows was Microsoft's; no other compiler on the market supported the development of applications for Windows. Well, things have changed significantly over the past few years. Now you can develop Windows-based applications using Ada, assembly language, C, C++, COBOL, dBASE, FORTRAN, LISP, Modula-2, Pascal, REXX, and Smalltalk/V. And let's not forget Basic. There are even languages that have been invented to make programming for Windows easier: Actor and ToolBook, to name just two.

But even with all these languages that support Windows coming out of the woodwork, C is still the language used most often, with C++ slowly gaining popularity. When it came time to choose a language for presenting the sample code in this book, I narrowed down the choices to these four:

1. Straight C

2. C with message crackers

3. Straight C++

4. C++ using the Microsoft Foundation Classes

It was a tough decision.

Because I wanted the book to appeal to the broadest possible audience, I decided to rule out option 4. Since several companies produce C++ class libraries for Windows development, I didn't want to require one particular class library. Also, some class libraries do more for you

665

than just put a wrapper around the Windows APIs, and I didn't want to introduce extraneous code or procedures into the code samples. I will say, however, that I personally love the Microsoft Foundation Classes and use them when I develop large applications of my own.

Option 3 didn't seem to offer much. Even without a class library, developing Windows-based applications in C++ can be easier than using straight C, but since the programs in this book are relatively small, using C++ wouldn't offer many advantages. Another big reason for not choosing option 3 or 4 is that most people are still doing development for Windows in C and haven't yet switched to C++.

Option 1 would have been a good choice because there would be almost no learning curve for people trying to understand my programs, but I chose to go with option 2. When I go to conferences, I frequently ask people if they are using the message crackers, and usually I get a "no" response. When I probe further, I discover that they don't even know what the message crackers are and what they do. By using C with message crackers to present the sample code in this book, I get to introduce these little-known but useful macros to many people who may not know about them.

The message crackers are contained in the WINDOWSX.H file supplied with the Windows and Windows NT SDKs. You usually include this file immediately after the WINDOWS.H file. The WINDOWSX.H file is nothing more than a bunch of *#define* statements that create a set of macros for you to use. Microsoft designed the macros to provide the following advantages:

1. The macros reduce the amount of casting necessary in an application and make the casting that is required error free. One of the big problems with programming for Windows in C has been the amount of casting required. You hardly ever see a call to a Windows API function that doesn't require some sort of cast. Casts should be avoided because they prevent the compiler from catching potential errors in your code. A cast tells the compiler, "I know I'm passing the wrong type here, but that's OK; I know what I'm doing." When you do so much casting, it's easy to make a mistake. The compiler should be doing as much work to help you as it possibly can. If you use these macros, you'll have much less casting to perform.

2. The macros make your code more readable.

3. They simplify porting between the 16-bit Windows API and the Win32 API.

4. They're easy to understand—they're just macros, after all.

5. They're easy to incorporate into existing code. You can leave old code alone and immediately start using the macros in new code. You don't have to retrofit an entire application.

6. They can be used in C and C++ code, although they're not necessary if you're using a class library.

7. If you need some feature that the macros don't support, you can easily write your own macros by following the model used in the header file.

8. If you use the macros, you don't need to reference or remember obscure Windows constructs. For example, many functions in Windows expect a long parameter where the value in the long's high-word means one thing and the value in its low-word means something else. Before calling these functions, you must construct a long value out of the two individual values. This is usually done by using the MAKELONG macro from WINDOWS.H. But I can't tell you how many times I've accidentally reversed the two values, causing an incorrect value to be passed to a function. The macros in WINDOWSX.H come to the rescue.

The macros contained in WINDOWSX.H are actually divided into three groups: message crackers, child control macros, and API macros.

Message Crackers

The message crackers make it easier to write window procedures. Typically, window procedures are implemented as one huge *switch* statement. In my travels, I have seen window procedure *switch* statements that contained well over 500 lines of code. We all know that implementing window procedures this way is a bad practice, but we do it anyway. I have been known to do it myself on occasion. Message crackers force you to break up your *switch* statements into smaller functions—one function per message. This makes your code much more manageable.

Another problem with window procedures is that every message has *wParam* and *lParam* parameters, and depending on the message, these parameters have different meanings. Sometimes, such as for a WM_COMMAND message, *wParam* contains two different values. The high-word of the *wParam* parameter is the notification code, and the low-word is the ID of the control. Or is it the other way around? I always forget. Even worse, in 16-bit Windows the *lParam* parameter for a WM_ COMMAND message contains the window handle and the notification code. If you use the message crackers, you don't have to remember or look up any of this: These macros are called message crackers because they crack apart the parameters for any given message. If you want to process the WM_COMMAND message, you simply write a function that looks like this:

```
void Cls_OnCommand(HWND hwnd, int id, HWND hwndCtl,
    UINT codeNotify) {

    switch (id) {

        case ID_SOMELISTBOX:
            if (codeNotify != LBN_SELCHANGE)
                break;

            // Do LBN_SELCHANGE processing.
            break;

        case ID_SOMEBUTTON:
            break;

        .
        .
        .

    }
}
```

Look at how easy it is! The crackers look at a message's *wParam* and *lParam* parameters, break the parameters apart, and call your function. There is a WINDOWSX.H file for Win32 and a WINDOWSX.H file for 16-bit Windows. The WM_COMMAND cracker for 16-bit Windows cracks *wParam* and *lParam* differently from the Win32 version. No matter how the parameters are cracked, you still write just one function. Instantly you have code that will compile and work correctly for both 16-bit Windows and Win32!

To use the message crackers, you need to make some changes to your window procedure's *switch* statement. Take a look at this window procedure:

```
LRESULT WndProc (HWND hwnd, UINT uMsg,
   WPARAM wParam, LPARAM lParam) {

   switch (uMsg) {
      HANDLE_MSG(hwnd, WM_COMMAND, Cls_OnCommand);
      HANDLE_MSG(hwnd, WM_PAINT, Cls_OnPaint);
      HANDLE_MSG(hwnd, WM_DESTROY, Cls_OnDestroy);
      default:
         return(DefWindowProc(hwnd, uMsg, wParam, lParam));
}
```

In both the 16-bit Windows and the Win32 versions of WINDOWSX.H, the HANDLE_MSG macro is defined as follows:

```
#define HANDLE_MSG(hwnd, message, fn)     \
   case (message): \
      return HANDLE_##message((hwnd), (wParam), (lParam), (fn))
```

For a WM_COMMAND message, the preprocessor expands this macro to read as follows:

```
case (WM_COMMAND):
   return HANDLE_WM_COMMAND((hwnd), (wParam), (lParam),
      (Cls_OnCommand));
```

The HANDLE_WM_* macros are also defined in WINDOWSX.H. These macros are actually the message crackers. They crack the contents of the *wParam* and *lParam* parameters, perform all the necessary casting, and call the appropriate message function, such as the Cls_OnCommand function shown earlier. The macro for the 16-bit Windows version of HANDLE_WM_COMMAND is:

```
#define HANDLE_WM_COMMAND(hwnd, wParam, lParam, fn) \
   ((fn)((hwnd), (int)(wParam), (HWND)LOWORD(lParam),
      (UINT) HIWORD(lParam)), 0L)
```

The macro for the Win32 version is:

```
#define HANDLE_WM_COMMAND(hwnd, wParam, lParam, fn) \
   ( (fn) ((hwnd), (int) (LOWORD(wParam)), (HWND)(lParam),
      (UINT) HIWORD(wParam)), 0L)
```

When the preprocessor expands this macro, the result is a call to the Cls_OnCommand function with the contents of the *wParam* and *lParam* parameters broken down into their respective parts and cast appropriately.

When you are going to use the message cracker macros to process a message, you should open the WINDOWSX.H file and search for the message you want to process. For example, if you search for WM_COM-MAND, you see the part of the file that contains these lines:

```
/* void Cls_OnCommand(HWND hwnd, int id, HWND hwndCtl,
    UINT codeNotify); */
#define HANDLE_WM_COMMAND(hwnd, wParam, lParam, fn) \
    ((fn)((hwnd), (int)(LOWORD(wParam)), (HWND)(lParam), \
    (UINT)HIWORD(wParam)), 0L)
#define FORWARD_WM_COMMAND(hwnd, id, hwndCtl, codeNotify, fn) \
    (void)(fn)((hwnd), WM_COMMAND, \
    MAKEWPARAM((UINT)(id),(UINT)(codeNotify)), \
    (LPARAM)(HWND)(hwndCtl))
```

The first line is a comment that shows you the prototype of the function you have to write. This prototype is the same whether you are looking at the 16-bit Windows version or the Win32 version of the WIN-DOWSX.H file. The next line is the HANDLE_WM_* macro, which we have already discussed. The last line is a message forwarder. Let's say that during your processing of the WM_COMMAND message you want to call the default window procedure to have it do some work for you. This function would look like this:

```
void Cls_OnCommand (HWND hwnd, int id, HWND hwndCtl,
    UINT codeNotify) {

    // Do some normal processing.

    // Do default processing.
    FORWARD_WM_COMMAND(hwnd, id, hwndCtl, codeNotify,
        DefWindowProc);
}
```

The FORWARD_WM_* macro takes the cracked message parameters and reconstructs them to their *wParam* and *lParam* equivalents. The macro then calls a function that you supply. In the example above, the macro calls the DefWindowProc function, but you could just as easily have used SendMessage or PostMessage. In fact, if you want to send (or post) a message to any window in the system, you can use a FORWARD-_WM_* macro to help combine the individual parameters. Like the HANDLE_WM_* macros, the FORWARD_WM_* macros are defined differently depending on whether you are compiling for 16-bit Windows or for Win32.

Child Control Macros

The child control macros make it easier to send messages to child controls. They are very similar to the FORWARD_WM_* macros. Each of the macros starts with the type of control you are sending the message to, followed by an underscore and the name of the message. For example, to send an LB_GETCOUNT message to a list box, you would use the following macro from WINDOWSX.H:

```
#define ListBox_GetCount(hwndCtl) \
    ((int)(DWORD)SendMessage((hwndCtl), LB_GETCOUNT, 0, 0L))
```

Let me point out a couple of things about this macro. First, it takes only one parameter, *hwndCtl*, which is the window handle of the list box. Since the LB_GETCOUNT message ignores the *wParam* and *lParam* parameters, you don't need to be bothered with them at all. The macro will pass zeros in, as you can see above.

Second, when SendMessage returns, the result is cast to an *int* to remove the necessity for you to supply your own cast. Normally you would write code like this:

```
int n = (int) SendMessage(hwndCtl, LB_GETCOUNT, 0, 0);
```

When this line is compiled for 16-bit Windows, the compiler warns you that you might lose significant digits. The reason is that you are attempting to put a DWORD value (returned from SendMessage) into an integer. It's much simpler to write:

```
int n = ListBox_GetCount(hwndCtl);
```

Also, I'm sure you'll agree that the line above is a little easier to read than the SendMessage line.

The one thing I don't like about the child control macros is that they all take the handle of the control window. Most of the time the controls you need to send messages to are children of a dialog box. So you end up having to call GetDlgItem all the time, producing code like this:

```
int n = ListBox_GetCount(GetDlgItem(hDlg, ID_ListBox));
```

This code doesn't run any slower than if you had used SendDlgItemMessage, but your application does contain some extra code because of the additional call to GetDlgItem. If you need to send several messages to the same control, you may want to call GetDlgItem once, save the child window's handle, and then call all the macros you need, as shown in the following code.

```
HWND hwndCtl = GetDlgItem(hDlg, ID_LISTBOX);
int n = ListBox_GetCount(hwndCtl);
ListBox_AddString(hwndCtl, "Another string");
    .
    .
    .
```

If you design your code this way, your application runs faster because it doesn't repeatedly call GetDlgItem. GetDlgItem can be a slow function if your dialog box has many controls and the control you are looking for is toward the end of the z-order.

API Macros

The API macros make some common operations a little simpler. For example, one common operation is to create a new font, select the font into a device context, and save the handle of the original font. The code looks something like this:

```
HFONT hFontOrig = (HFONT) SelectObject(hDC, (HGDIOBJ) hFontNew);
```

This one line requires two casts to get a warning-free compilation. One of the macros in WINDOWSX.H was designed for exactly this purpose:

```
#define SelectFont(hdc, hfont) \
    ((HFONT)SelectObject( (hdc), (HGDIOBJ) (HFONT) (hfont)))
```

If you use this macro, the line of code in your program becomes:

```
HFONT hFontOrig = SelectFont(hDC, hFontNew);
```

This code is easier to read and is far less subject to error.

Several more API macros are defined in WINDOWSX.H to help with commonly performed Windows tasks. I urge you to examine them and to use them.

INDEX

Italic page-number references indicate figures, listings, and tables.

About the Author

Jeffrey Richter is the author of *Windows 3.1: A Developer's Guide* (M & T Books) and is a contributing editor of *Microsoft Systems Journal*. He also developed DeMystifiers, a suite of 16-bit Windows developers' tools. A consultant and in-house trainer, Jeff is a frequent speaker at developers' conferences.

About This book

The manuscript for this book was prepared and submitted to Microsoft Press in electronic form. Text files were prepared using Microsoft Word 2.0 for Windows. Pages were composed by Microsoft Press using the Magna Composition System, with text in New Baskerville and display type in Helvetica Bold. Composed pages were delivered to the printer as electronic prepress files.

Cover Designer
Hornall Anderson Design

Principal Illustrator
Peggy Herman

Cover Color Separator
Color Service, Inc.

Principal Typographer
Lisa Iversen

Interior Graphic Designer
Kim Eggleston

Principal Editorial Compositor
Barb Runyan

Indexer
Foxon-Maddocks Associates

Printed on recycled paper stock.

Solid Programming Advice

Microsoft® Windows NT™ Resource Kit

Microsoft Corporation

This exclusive three-volume Microsoft collection is a comprehensive source of technical information and tools necessary for self-support of installations of Windows NT. The *Microsoft Windows NT Resource Kit* includes *Windows NT Resource Guide* (with four 3.5-inch disks), *Windows NT Messages* (with three 3.5-inch disks), and *Optimizing Windows NT* (with one 3.5-inch disk). These volumes are available separately.

Three-volume set boxed with eight 3.5-inch disks and one CD-ROM
$109.95 ($148.95 Canada)
ISBN 1-55615-602-2

BONUS! The three-volume set also includes a compact disk containing all the disk-based utilities PLUS tools and utilities for RISC-based computers.

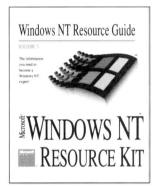  

Microsoft® Windows NT™ Resource Kit *Volume 1: Windows NT Resource Guide*	**Microsoft® Windows NT™ Resource Kit** *Volume 2: Windows NT Messages*	**Microsoft® Windows NT™ Resource Kit** *Volume 3: Optimizing Windows NT*

Microsoft® Windows NT™
Resource Kit
Volume 1: Windows NT
Resource Guide

A complete technical guide to Windows NT. Includes information about installing, configuring, customizing, and troubleshooting Windows NT. It also includes information on applications compatibility and migration from Windows 3.1, MS-DOS, OS/2, and LAN Manager, and using database services with Windows NT. The four disks include a number of tools, utilities, and value-added software, including tools to manage users and groups of servers, a computer profile setup to easily set up large groups of workstations, an adapter card Help file, and an online registry database.

950 pages, with four 3.5-inch disks
$49.95 ($67.95 Canada)
ISBN 1-55615-598-0

Microsoft® Windows NT™
Resource Kit
Volume 2: Windows NT Messages

An alphabetic reference and online database that provides in-depth, accessible discussions about Windows NT and Windows NT Advanced Server messages. The messages were loaded into a Microsoft Access database with a simple user interface, which enables the user to search the database, add personal notes under a message, back up the database, and print a selected group of messages. The three disks contain a runtime version of Microsoft Access and the Messages database.

624 pages with three 3.5-inch disks
$39.95 ($53.95 Canada)
ISBN 1-55615-600-6

Microsoft® Windows NT™
Resource Kit
Volume 3: Optimizing
Windows NT

The complete guide to bottleneck detection and capacity planning of Windows NT for the desktop and network. Also includes information on designing and tuning your Windows NT applications for high performance. Included with the book is one disk full of software accessories and utilities for troubleshooting, fine-tuning, and optimizing PC performance.

488 pages with one 3.5-inch disk
$34.95 ($46.95 Canada)
ISBN 1-55615-619-7

Register Today!

Return the
Advanced Windows NT™
registration card for:

✔ a Microsoft Press catalog

✔ exclusive offers on specially priced books

Fill in information below and mail postage free. Please mail the bottom half of this page only.

NAME

COMPANY

ADDRESS

CITY   STATE   ZIP

Your feedback is important to us.

Include your daytime telephone number and we may call to find out how you use *Advanced Windows NT* and what we can do to make future editions even more useful. If we call you, we'll send you a **FREE GIFT** for your time!

(   )

DAYTIME TELEPHONE NUMBER

Information... Straight from the Source

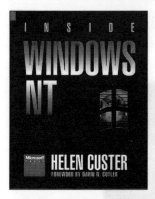
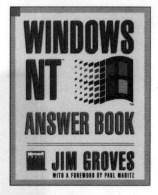